5th CANADIAN EDITION

FUNDAMENTALS OF SOCIAL RESEARCH

EARL BABBIE
Chapman University

JASON D. EDGERTON
University of Manitoba

LANCE W. ROBERTS
University of Manitoba

NELSON

NELSON

Fundamentals of Social Research, Fifth Canadian Edition
by Earl Babbie, Lance W. Roberts, and Jason D. Edgerton

VP, Product Solutions, K–20:
Claudine O'Donnell

Director, Qualitative Publishing:
Jackie Wood

Senior Publisher:
Leanna MacLean

Marketing Manager:
Sydney Pope

Content Manager:
Toni Chahley

Photo and Permissions Researcher:
Jessie Coffey

Production Project Manager:
Shannon Martin

Production Service:
SPi Global

Copy Editor:
Linda Jenkins

Proofreader:
SPi Global

Indexer:
SPi Global

Design Director:
Ken Phipps

Post-secondary Design PM:
Pamela Johnston

Interior Design:
Sharon Lucas

Cover Design:
Sharon Lucas

Cover Image:
Sharon Lucas

Compositor:
SPi Global

Printed and bound in Canada
1 2 3 4 23 22 21 20

For more information contact
Nelson Education Ltd., 1120 Birchmount Road, Toronto, Ontario, M1K 5G4. Or you can visit our Internet site at nelson.com

Library and Archives Canada Cataloguing in Publication

Title: Fundamentals of social research / Earl Babbie, Chapman University, Jason D. Edgerton, University of Manitoba, Lance W. Roberts.

Names: Babbie, Earl R., author. | Edgerton, Jason, 1970- author. | Roberts, Lance W., 1950-2019, author.

Description: 5th Canadian edition. | Includes bibliographical references and index.

Identifiers: Canadiana 20190224029 | ISBN 9780176895952 (paperback)

Subjects: LCSH: Social sciences—Research—Textbooks. | LCSH: Social sciences—Methodology—Textbooks. | LCGFT: Textbooks.

Classification: LCC H62 .B32 2020 | DDC 300.72—dc23

ISBN-13: 978-0-17-689595-2
ISBN-10: 0-17-689595-7

Suzanne Babbie—E.B.

Henry and Charlie Lask, two delightful little men—L.W.R.

Tate and Jordan, for always reminding me what is most important—J.D.E.

In memory of Lance Roberts—scientist, teacher, friend, and mentor. He touched the lives of many students and colleagues; we are all better for having known him.

ABOUT THE AUTHORS

EARL BABBIE

Suzanne Babbie

Writing is my joy, sociology my passion. I delight in putting words together in a way that makes people learn or laugh or both. Sociology is one way I can do just that. It represents our last, best hope for planet-training our race and finding ways for us to live together. I feel a special excitement at being present when sociology, at last, comes into focus as an idea whose time has come.

I grew up in small-town Vermont and New Hampshire. When I announced I wanted to be an auto-body mechanic like my dad, my teacher told me I should go to college instead. When Malcolm X announced he wanted to be a lawyer, his teacher told him a coloured boy should be something more like a carpenter. The difference in our experiences says something powerful about the idea of a level playing field. The inequalities among ethnic groups run deep.

I ventured out into the outer world by way of Harvard, the USMC, U.C. Berkeley, and 12 years teaching at the University of Hawaii. Along the way, I married Sheila two months after our first date, and we created Aaron three years after that: two of my wisest acts.

I resigned from teaching in 1980 and wrote full-time for seven years, until the call of the classroom became too loud to ignore. For me, teaching is like playing jazz. Even if you perform the same number over and over, it never comes out the same twice, and you don't know exactly what it'll sound like until you hear it. Teaching is like writing with your voice.

At last, I have matured enough to rediscover and appreciate my roots in Vermont each summer. Rather than a return to the past, it feels more like the next turn in a widening spiral. I can't wait to see what's around the next bend.

LANCE W. ROBERTS

Source: Courtesy of Lance Roberts

I grew up in a restricted, working-class world, where discipline and conformity were touted as the keys to success. Surrounding social realities were to be respected, even revered.

Some excellent teachers in public schools produced cracks in this rigid world view, allowing breathing room for individuality. My liberal arts undergraduate education widened the degrees of freedom and my graduate studies in sociology helped clarify my path toward optimizing autonomy within existing realities.

In short, like many before and after me, education provided an escape route from one form of social reality to another. I am truly grateful to the teachers, authors, and public education system that made this possible.

Two keys to growth through education come in the form of good teaching and good books. I have spent my academic career trying to contribute on both accounts.

JASON EDGERTON

Courtesy of Jason Edgerton

I was the first person in my working-class family to graduate from university. I wavered back and forth between potential career paths, changing majors several times over the course of my educational journey. Given my innate love of reading, writing, and learning, and my tendency to stand back and analyze my surroundings, academia seemed an enticing possibility. But my blue collar practicality prevailed and I chose to enter the work world after completing my MEd.

I spent nearly a decade doing frontline work with marginalized youth who had fallen through the cracks, having left or been expelled from school. My job was to help equip them to re-enter into the mainstream (e.g., remedial classes, life skills and vocational skills classes). Although each youth was unique, I noticed consistently that they had been failed in similar ways by a system that had deep flaws and structural inequalities. Eventually I knew that rather than working on a case-by-case basis as I had been, I wanted to study the larger systems that had tilted the tables against so many of these young people.

So I once again changed career paths, this time to sociology. As a sociologist and an educator, my efforts are aimed at helping students come away from my classes—and this text—with increased critical awareness and capacity for analytical thought that will serve them constructively not only in the workplace, but also as future citizens/parents/leaders in their communities. My teaching practice is guided by this desire to illustrate, and excite awareness of, the everyday relevance of sociological thought and methods to students' lives. It is not just playing Ivory Tower word games, not just jumping through hoops to get your ticket punched; we are helping students equip themselves for life.

CONTENTS IN BRIEF

CONTENTS

PART TWO
The Structuring of Inquiry 77

BOXED FEATURES

APPLYING CONCEPTS IN EVERDAY LIFE

HOW TO DO IT

SPOTLIGHT ON MIXED METHODS

PREFACE

Sociological investigation can help uncover the larger, seemingly invisible, social forces that shape our lives, including how our actions affect and are affected by these forces. It is an orientation to questioning the social world we live in, to recognizing the contested and contingent nature of social arrangements; it offers a conceptual and methodological toolbox for diagnosing, highlighting, and hopefully ameliorating important social problems.

Accordingly, the main objective of this text is to provide students with a general understanding of the principles of social scientific research methods such that they are better prepared to undertake their own research projects and/or be critical consumers of published research. Ultimately, students should come away with increased readiness and capacity to effectively use these vital tools to understand and affect their world—whether at home, at work, in the local community, or on a larger scale still.

Fundamentals of Social Research, like all good works, has been improved over various editions through incremental revisions. The previous four Canadian editions have made many useful changes to increase the Canadian flavour of the text, and this fifth edition continues these updates and refinements.

Professors' and students' experiences with the structure and content of the text have provided many useful suggestions for improvement. So have the many reviewers who have given their thoughtful feedback on the text. In addition to these sources, we have drawn on our many years of experience teaching research methods and social statistics to students.

We hope students will find the ideas and techniques covered in this book challenging. Serious learning involves change and change is always challenging. With sustained effort, however, everyone can fully master the book's contents. My efforts (Edgerton) in spearheading the fifth Canadian edition were guided by a strong belief that understanding how scientific knowledge is generated and how it differs from other types of knowledge is vital to the education of social science students. By further honing students' facility for critical thought, it contributes to their personal intellectual development and to the skill set they take into the future, whether that be as academics, public servants, activists, business people, or simply responsible, engaged citizens in a democratic society.

CHANGES IN THE FIFTH CANADIAN EDITION

The new edition of *Fundamentals of Social Research* has been revised in close consultation with instructors across Canada who teach research methods. The goal was to create a new edition that would reflect changes and cutting-edge developments in social research, including the growing migration of social life to the online realm and the technical and ethical opportunities and challenges this presents for researchers. These and other changes are animated with interesting and relevant examples intended to spark students' interest and facilitate the practical application of research methods with engaging boxes and activities. To meet this goal, the new edition boasts the following enhancements:

- Greatly expanded and enhanced coverage of mixed methods, including a general introduction in Chapter 1, and new Spotlight on Mixed Methods boxes, found throughout the book

- New coverage of ethics issues related to Internet-mediated research
- Expanded coverage of web-based experiments
- New coverage of network analysis
- New discussion of big data
- Updated examples of studies using focus group and oral history methods
- Enhanced discussion of key aspects of qualitative data analysis, including narrative analysis and discourse analysis, and a new section on deductive qualitative coding

There are numerous updates and additions throughout the text. Some material has been deleted and new sections have been added. More recent examples have been included and the number of examples increased, including numerous new Canadian research examples. Here are some further, specific changes to this edition presented by chapter:

Chapter 1

- New section on mixed methods research.
- New figure to help distinguish inductive from deductive thinking.

Chapter 2

- Enhanced and revised explanation of how concepts are interrelated by propositions that refers to the concepts used in the chapter.
- Section on operationalization linked to the relationship between social inequality of health and how we might operationalize these factors.

Chapter 3

- New section on ethical complexities of Internet-mediated research, with examples.
- Updated material on the Tri-Council Policy statement to reflect the 2018 revisions to TCPS 2.

Chapter 4

- Streamlined chapter by moving material on how to design a research project and elements of a research proposal to Chapter 17.

Chapter 5

- Added a brief discussion of indexes and scales.
- New example of the Problem Gambling Severity Index.
- Streamlined material on conceptualization.
- New Spotlight on Mixed Methods box: Incorporating Qualitative Evidence into the Validation of Quantitative Instruments.

Chapter 6

- New discussion of why polls were wrong about the 2016 U.S. presidential election.
- New online appendix containing detailed examples of complex sampling designs.
- New box on software for randomly generating numbers.
- New Spotlight on Mixed Methods box: A Multisite Case Study Sampling Design.

Chapter 7

- Enhanced discussion of random assignment.
- Added new examples of Web-based experiments and elaborated on the pros, cons, and ethical issues related to Web-based experiments.
- New Spotlight on Mixed Methods box: Mixing Laboratory and Field Experiments within the Same Study.

Chapter 8

- Expanded discussion distinguishing between CAPI and CATI, as well as CAWI.
- Included new Canadian survey research examples.
- New Spotlight on Mixed Methods box: Mixing Self-Administered Surveys and In-Depth Interviews.

Chapter 9

- New section on unobtrusive online research (big data, data mining, social network analysis) with examples.
- New Spotlight on Mixed Methods box: Using Unobtrusive Observational Data to Assess Nonresponse Bias in Surveys.

Chapter 10

- Streamlined discussion of Grounded theory.
- New discussion of types of field notes.
- New Spotlight on Mixed Methods box: Mixing Online and Offline Ethnography.

Chapter 11

- New discussion on transcription software.
- New section on online interviews and focus groups.
- New examples of in-depth interview research.
- Updated examples of focus group research.

- Updated Canadian examples of oral history research.
- New Spotlight on Mixed Methods box: Mixing Methods Online: Combining Quantitative Data with Participant Observation and In-Depth Interviews.

Chapter 13

- New online appendix containing extended examples of computer-assisted qualitative data analysis.
- Expanded section on Grounded theory.
- New section on narrative analysis.
- New section on discourse analysis.
- New example of coding from prisoner interview data.
- New section on deductive qualitative coding.

Chapter 14

- Enhanced discussion about when to report proportions.

Chapter 17

- New section on reading, designing, and writing social research.

FEATURES IN THE FIFTH CANADIAN EDITION

NEW **Spotlight on Mixed Methods** boxes expose students to research that combines qualitative and qualitative methods. By profiling studies ranging from Indigenous Canadians and HIV to social capital in multiplayer online (MMO) games, these boxes provide students with practical examples of mixed methods research in action

SPOTLIGHT ON MIXED METHODS RESEARCH

Mixed Methods Online: Combining Quantitative Data with Participant Observation and In-Depth Interviews

Putnam (2000) argued that social capital had been diminishing across the closing decades of the 20th century, as people were increasingly drawn away from engagement in vibrant community life into their own isolated worlds of media consumption. Williams et al. (2006) wondered if this trend was affected by the advent of new interactive and more socially engaging online media spaces like massively multiplayer online (MMO) games. They suggested such effects could occur via increased *bridging social capital*, "the loose connections between relative strangers that lead to diverse networks and information streams" or via increased *bonding social capital*, "which is traditional social, emotional, and substantive support" (p. 339).

To investigate this possibility, they decided to study the social dynamics of players within the MMO game World of Warcraft (WoW). More specifically, they focused "on player behavior, attitudes, and opinions, [to] explore the meanings they make, the social capital they derive, and the networks they form" (p. 339). Their study combined in-depth ethnographic methods with survey-based quantitative data collection, and unfolded in three stages:

1. *Participant observation*: To learn and understand the social context of play, research team members immersed themselves in WoW, playing the game and joining guilds. (Time spent playing by team members ranged between 15 and 1,351 hours over 16 months.)
2. *Quantitative data collection*: They used bot or automated characters that log into the system to collect data on player behaviour around the clock; this allowed them to have an ongoing census of how many players there where, when they were online, and what guilds they belonged to. It also allowed them to map and analyze social networks.
3. *In-depth interviews*: These were conducted with players randomly selected from the sampling frame (generated in stage 2). The interviews were conducted within WoW using direct text chat and guided by 13 base questions, but Williams and colleagues also allowed for spontaneous or off-script exchanges.

Their findings indicate that many players used the game to maintain and reinforce offline relationships, while others used it to meet new people and form new relationships. For most it was a form of affiliation akin to playing on a sports team or hanging out in traditional "third places" (e.g., coffee shops, pubs, clubs, churches) that Putnam holds as integral to vibrant civic life. Thus the authors conclude, although far from a panacea, such socially interactive online third places may be a space "... where such revitalization is possible for some players and in a new way" (p. 357).

How to Do It boxes offer practical guidance on applying concepts, such as framing a hypothesis, identifying the unit of analysis, conducting an online survey, and reading and evaluating documents.

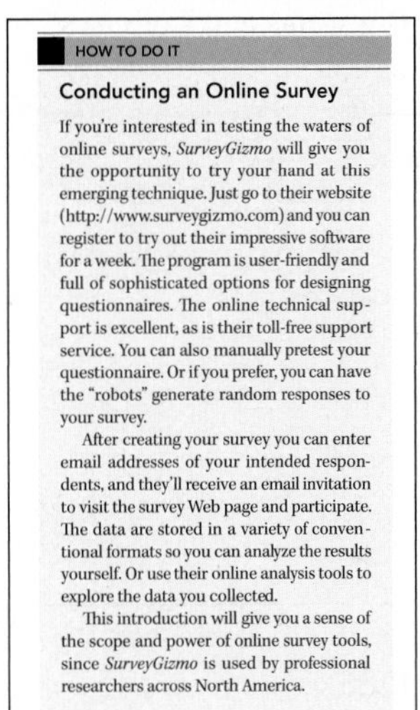

HOW TO DO IT

Conducting an Online Survey

If you're interested in testing the waters of online surveys, *SurveyGizmo* will give you the opportunity to try your hand at this emerging technique. Just go to their website (http://www.surveygizmo.com) and you can register to try out their impressive software for a week. The program is user-friendly and full of sophisticated options for designing questionnaires. The online technical support is excellent, as is their toll-free support service. You can also manually pretest your questionnaire. Or if you prefer, you can have the "robots" generate random responses to your survey.

After creating your survey you can enter email addresses of your intended respondents, and they'll receive an email invitation to visit the survey Web page and participate. The data are stored in a variety of conventional formats so you can analyze the results yourself. Or use their online analysis tools to explore the data you collected.

This introduction will give you a sense of the scope and power of online survey tools, since *SurveyGizmo* is used by professional researchers across North America.

Applying Concepts in Everyday Life boxes help students see how the ideas they're reading about actually apply to real research projects—as well as their own lives.

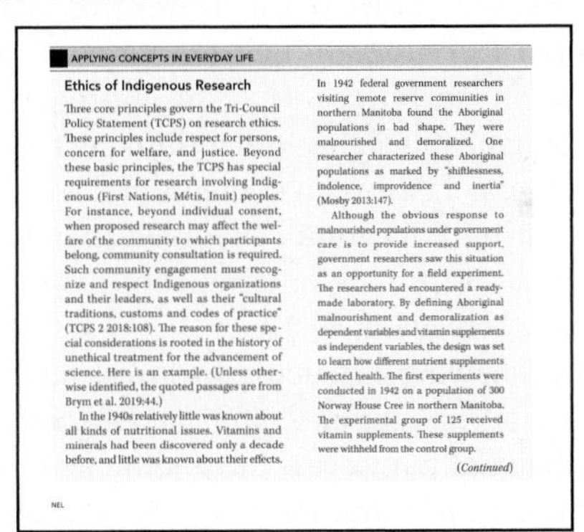

APPLYING CONCEPTS IN EVERYDAY LIFE

Ethics of Indigenous Research

Three core principles govern the Tri-Council Policy Statement (TCPS) on research ethics. These principles include respect for persons, concern for welfare, and justice. Beyond these basic principles, the TCPS has special requirements for research involving Indigenous (First Nations, Métis, Inuit) peoples. For instance, beyond individual consent, when proposed research may affect the welfare of the community to which participants belong, community consultation is required. Such community engagement must recognize and respect Indigenous organizations and their leaders, as well as their "cultural traditions, customs and codes of practice" (TCPS 2 2018:108). The reason for these special considerations is rooted in the history of unethical treatment for the advancement of science. Here is an example. (Unless otherwise identified, the quoted passages are from Brym et al. 2019:44.)

In the 1940s relatively little was known about all kinds of nutritional issues. Vitamins and minerals had been discovered only a decade before, and little was known about their effects. In 1942 federal government researchers visiting remote reserve communities in northern Manitoba found the Aboriginal populations in bad shape. They were malnourished and demoralized. One researcher characterized these Aboriginal populations as marked by "shiftlessness, indolence, improvidence and inertia" (Mosby 2013:147).

Although the obvious response to malnourished populations under government care is to provide increased support, government researchers saw this situation as an opportunity for a field experiment. The researchers had encountered a ready-made laboratory. By defining Aboriginal malnourishment and demoralization as dependent variables and vitamin supplements as independent variables, the design was set to learn how different nutrient supplements affected health. The first experiments were conducted in 1942 on a population of 300 Norway House Cree in northern Manitoba. The experimental group of 125 received vitamin supplements. These supplements were withheld from the control group.

(Continued)

NEL

Continuity Projects at the end of each chapter move students from thinking about selected topics in each chapter to applying them. These exercises put methods, concepts, principles, and techniques to work.

CONTINUITY PROJECT

■ THINKING ABOUT INEQUALITY

Theories are narratives, composed of ideas systematically linked together. Three concepts are prevalent in the research literature:

- inequality
- social cohesion
- violence

Review Figure 2-2 and create a model relating these three concepts. Write out the three

Key Terms bolded in the text, defined in the margin, and compiled in a **Glossary** at the end of the book.

- A summary of the **Main Points** found in each chapter.
- **Review Questions and Exercises**

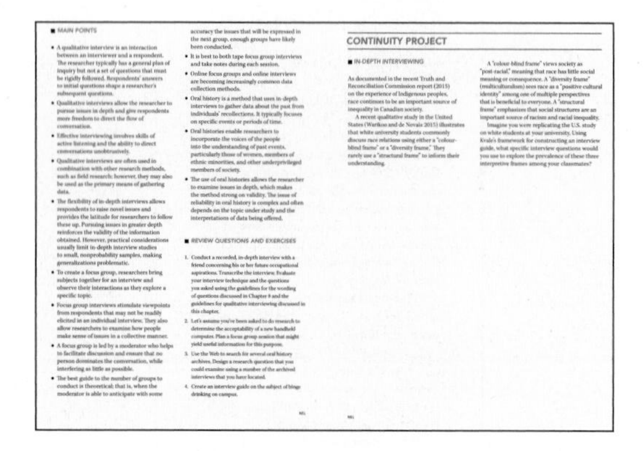

MAIN POINTS

- A qualitative interview is an interaction between an interviewer and a respondent. The researcher typically has a general plan of inquiry but not a set of questions that must be rigidly followed. Respondents' answers to initial questions shape a researcher's subsequent questions.
- Qualitative interviews allow the researcher to pursue issues in depth and give respondents more freedom to direct the flow of conversation.
- Effective interviewing involves skills of active listening and the ability to direct conversations unobtrusively.
- Qualitative interviews are often used in combination with other research methods, such as field research; however, they may also be used as the primary means of gathering data.
- The flexibility of in-depth interviews allows respondents to raise novel issues and provides the latitude for researchers to follow these up. Pursuing issues in greater depth reinforces the validity of the information obtained. However, practical considerations usually limit in-depth interview studies to small, nonprobability samples, making generalizations problematic.
- To create a focus group, researchers bring subjects together for an interview and observe their interactions as they explore a specific topic.
- Focus group interviews stimulate viewpoints from respondents that may not be readily elicited in an individual interview. They also allow researchers to examine how people make sense of issues in a collective manner.
- A focus group is led by a moderator who helps to facilitate discussion and ensure that no person dominates the conversation, while interfering as little as possible.
- The best guide to the number of groups to conduct is theoretical; that is, when the moderator is able to anticipate with some accuracy the issues that will be expressed in the next group, enough groups have likely been conducted.
- It is best to both tape focus group interviews and take notes during each session.
- Online focus groups and online interviews are becoming increasingly common data collection methods.
- Oral history is a method that uses in-depth interviews to gather data about the past from individuals' recollections. It typically focuses on specific events or periods of time.
- Oral histories enable researchers to incorporate the voices of the people into the understanding of past events, particularly those of women, members of ethnic minorities, and other underprivileged members of society.
- The use of oral histories allows the researcher to examine issues in depth, which makes the method strong on validity. The issue of reliability in oral history is complex and often depends on the topic under study and the interpretations of data being offered.

REVIEW QUESTIONS AND EXERCISES

1. Conduct a recorded, in-depth interview with a friend concerning his or her future occupational aspirations. Transcribe the interview. Evaluate your interview technique and the questions you asked using the guidelines for the wording of questions discussed in Chapter 8 and the guidelines for qualitative interviewing discussed in this chapter.
2. Let's assume you've been asked to do research to determine the acceptability of a new handheld computer. Plan a focus group session that might yield useful information for this purpose.
3. Use the Web to search for several oral history archives. Design a research question that you could examine using a number of the archived interviews that you have located.
4. Create an interview guide on the subject of binge drinking on campus.

CONTINUITY PROJECT

IN-DEPTH INTERVIEWING

As documented in the recent Truth and Reconciliation Commission report (2015) on the experience of Indigenous peoples, race continues to be an important source of inequality in Canadian society.

A recent qualitative study in the United States (Warikoo and de Novais 2015) illustrates that white university students commonly discuss race relations using either a "colour-blind frame" or a "diversity frame." They rarely use a "structural frame" to inform their understanding.

A "colour-blind frame" views society as "post-racial," meaning that race has little social meaning or consequence. A "diversity frame" (multiculturalism) sees race as a "positive cultural identity" among one of multiple perspectives that is beneficial to everyone. A "structural frame" emphasizes that social structures are an important source of racism and racial inequality.

Imagine you were replicating the U.S. study on white students at your university. Using Kvale's framework for constructing an interview guide, what specific interview questions would you use to explore the prevalence of these three interpretive frames among your classmates?

ANCILLARIES

Instructor Resources

The **Nelson Education Teaching Advantage (NETA)** program delivers research-based instructor resources that promote student engagement and higher-order thinking to enable the success of Canadian students and educators. Visit Nelson Education's **Inspired Instruction** website at http://www.nelson.com/inspired/ to find out more about NETA.

The following instructor resources have been created for *Fundamentals of Social Research*, Fifth Canadian Edition. Access these ultimate tools for customizing lectures and presentations at www.nelson.com/instructor.

NETA Test Bank This resource was written by Karen Kampen of the University of Manitoba. It includes over 600 multiple-choice questions written according to NETA guidelines for effective construction and development of higher-order questions. Also included are more than 100 true/false questions and over 200 essay questions.

The NETA Test Bank is available in a new, cloud-based platform. **Nelson Testing Powered by Cognero**® is a secure online testing system that allows instructors to author, edit, and manage test bank content from anywhere Internet access is available. No special installations or downloads are needed, and the desktop-inspired interface, with its drop-down menus and familiar, intuitive tools, allows instructors to create and manage tests with ease. Multiple test versions can be created in an instant, and content can be imported or exported into other systems. Tests can be delivered from a learning management system, the classroom, or wherever an instructor chooses. Nelson Testing Powered by Cognero for *Fundamentals of Social Research* can be accessed through www.nelson.com/instructor.

NETA PowerPoint Microsoft® PowerPoint® lecture slides for every chapter have been created by Maria Majerski of University of Toronto. There is an average of 40 slides per chapter, many featuring key figures, tables, and photographs from *Fundamentals of Social Research*, Fifth Canadian Edition. Other features include chapter summaries, suggested in-class and online activities, and lists of additional resources including videos, Internet sites, and readings. NETA principles of clear design and engaging content have been incorporated throughout, making it simple for instructors to customize the deck for their courses.

Image Library This resource consists of digital copies of figures, short tables, and photographs used in the book. Instructors may use these jpegs to customize the NETA PowerPoint or create their own PowerPoint presentations. An Image Library Key describes the images and lists the codes under which the jpegs are saved. Codes normally reflect the chapter number (e.g., C01 for Chapter 1), the figure or photo number (e.g., F15 for Figure 15), and the page in the textbook. C01-F15-pg26 corresponds to Figure 1-15 on page 26.

NETA Instructor Guide This resource was written by Markus Shafer of the University of Toronto. It is organized according to the textbook chapters and addresses key educational concerns, such as typical stumbling blocks student face and how to address them. Other features include chapter summaries, suggested in-class and online activities, and lists of additional resources including videos, Internet sites, and readings.

MindTap Offering personalized paths of dynamic assignments and applications, **MindTap** is a digital learning solution that turns cookie-cutter into cutting-edge, apathy into engagement, and memorizers into higher-level thinkers. MindTap enables students to analyze and apply chapter concepts within relevant assignments and allows instructors to measure skills and promote better outcomes with ease. A fully online learning solution, MindTap combines all student learning tools—readings, multimedia, activities, and assessments—into a single Learning Path that guides the student through the curriculum. Instructors personalize the experience by customizing the presentation of these learning tools to their students, even seamlessly introducing their own content into the Learning Path.

STUDENT ANCILLARIES

MindTap Stay organized and efficient with **MindTap**—a single destination with all the course material and study aids you need to succeed. Built-in apps leverage social media and the latest learning technology. For example:

- ReadSpeaker will read the text to you.
- Flashcards are pre-populated to provide you with a jump start for review—or you can create your own.
- You can highlight text and make notes in your MindTap Reader. Your notes will flow into Evernote, the electronic notebook app that you can access anywhere when it's time to study for the exam.
- Self-quizzing allows you to assess your understanding.

ACKNOWLEDGMENTS

This newest Canadian edition of *Fundamentals of Social Research* stands on the work of Earl Babbie. His scholarship, skillful writing, and enthusiasm for sociology have provided a solid foundation from which all subsequent co-authors have benefited.

The development and evolution of this edition owes a great deal to the many reviewers whose time, energy, and careful consideration have been instrumental in shaping its contents. They are

Shyon Baumann, University of Toronto, Mississauga
Lisa Kaida, McMaster University
Stephen Lin, Western University
Maria Majerski, Bishops University
Oral Robinson, University of British Columbia
Nathalie Viau, Vanier College

The text continues to benefit from the many thoughtful and detailed suggestions offered by reviewers of the four previous editions:

Zelda Abramson, York University
Bruce Arai, Wilfrid Laurier University
Hans I. Bakker, University of Guelph
Patricia Churchryk, University of Lethbridge
Colleen Anne Dell, Carleton University
Lawrence Felt, Memorial University
Eric Fong, University of Toronto
Paul Gingrich, University of Regina
Paul Glavin, McMaster University
Shelley Goldenberg, University of Calgary
Wendi Hadd, John Abbott College
Tim Haney, Mount Royal University
John Irwin, University of Guelph-Humber
Clifford Jansen, York University
Karen Kampen, University of Manitoba
Fiona Kay, Queen's University
Catherine Krull, Queen's University
Bill Marshall, Western University
Kevin McQuillan, University of Calgary
Andrea Perella, Wilfrid Laurier University
Tracy Peressini, University of Toronto
B. Gail Perry, University of Western Ontario
Steven Prus, Carleton University
James Richardson, University of New Brunswick
Wendy Roth, University of British Columbia
Vincent Sacco, Queen's University
Bryan Sluggett, University of Alberta
Nicholas Spence, Western University
Donald Swenson, Mount Royal University
James Teevan, University of Western Ontario
Russell Westhaver, Simon Fraser University
Li Zong, University of Saskatchewan

This project has also benefited greatly from the publishing professionals employed by Nelson. They are a wonderful team who work backstage to make works like this one possible. The following list acknowledges their contribution, bringing them frontstage to take a well-deserved bow:

Leanna MacLean, Senior Publisher
Toni Chahley, Content Development Manager
Shannon Martin, Production Project Manager
Daniela Glass, Project Manager, Rights Acquisition and Policy
R.S. Praveenkumar, Senior Project Manager (SPi-Global)
Linda Jenkins, Copy Editor

FINAL WORD

One key to growth is acknowledging there is always room for improvement. This edition of the text is the latest in a series of iterations, each new edition building on the previous one in an ongoing process of incremental refinement. Thus, I encourage all users of this book to send me your feedback, especially constructive suggestions for continued improvement. I am at J.Edgerton@umanitoba.ca and look forward to hearing from you.

Jason D. Edgerton

PART 1

AN INTRODUCTION TO INQUIRY

Science is a familiar word used by everyone. Yet people's understandings of science differ greatly. For some, science is mathematics; for others, it's white coats and laboratories. It's often confused with technology or equated with tough high school or university courses.

Science is, of course, none of these things per se. It's difficult, however, to specify exactly what science is. Scientists themselves disagree on the proper definition. For the purposes of this book, we'll look at science as a method of inquiry—a way of learning and knowing things about the world around us. Contrasted with other ways of learning and knowing about the world, science has some special characteristics. It is a conscious, deliberate, and rigorous undertaking. We'll examine these and other traits in this opening set of chapters. Before you've read very far, it will become clear to you that you already know a great deal about the practice of scientific social research. In fact, you've been using basic features of scientific research all your life. From that perspective, the purpose of this book is to help you sharpen skills you already have and perhaps to show you some tricks that may not have occurred to you.

Part 1 of this book lays the groundwork for the rest of the book by examining the fundamental characteristics and issues that make science different from other ways of knowing things. In Chapter 1, we'll begin with a look at native human inquiry, the sort of thing you've been doing all your life. In the course of that examination, we'll see some of the ways people go astray in trying to understand the world around them, and we'll summarize the primary characteristics of scientific inquiry that guard against those errors.

Chapter 2 deals with social theories and the links between theory and research. We'll look at some of the theoretical paradigms that shape the nature of inquiry and largely determine what scientists look for and how they interpret what they see.

Chapter 3 introduces some of the ethical considerations that social researchers deal with, and guidelines they should follow, when designing and implementing social research. Although much of this book concerns the scientific aspects of social research, the ethical dimension of social research is an important and integral part of the process of conducting research studies.

The overall purpose of Part 1 is to construct a backdrop against which to view the specifics of research design and execution. After completing Part 1, you'll be ready to look at some of the more concrete aspects of social research.

Timothy Harding/Shutterstock.com

HUMAN INQUIRY AND SCIENCE

All of us try to understand and predict the social world. Science—and social research in particular—are designed to avoid the common pitfalls of ordinary human inquiry.

IN THIS CHAPTER ...

INTRODUCTION

This book is about knowing things—not so much *what* we know as *how* we know it. Let's start by examining a few things you probably know already. You know the world is round. You may also know it's cold on the dark side of the Moon, and that people speak Swahili in Uganda. You probably know that vitamin C helps prevent colds and that unprotected sex can result in AIDS.

How do you know? Unless you've been to the dark side of the Moon lately or done experimental research on the virtues of vitamin C, you know these things because somebody told them to you, and you believed what you were told. You may have read in *National Geographic* that people speak Swahili in Uganda, and that made sense to you, so you didn't question it. Perhaps your physics or astronomy instructor told you it was cold on the dark side of the Moon, or maybe you read it in a magazine.

Some of the things you know seem absolutely obvious to you. If you were asked how you know the world is round, you'd probably say, "Everybody knows that." There are a lot of things everybody knows. Of course, at one time, everyone "knew" the world was flat.

Most of what you know is a matter of agreement and belief. Little of it is based on personal experience and discovery. A big part of growing up in any society, in fact, is the process of learning to accept what everybody around you "knows" is so. If you don't know those same things, you can't really be a part of the group. If you were to question seriously whether the world is really round, you'd quickly find yourself set apart from other people. You might be sent to live in a hospital with other people who question things like that.

Although it's important to realize that most of what we know is a matter of believing what we've been told, there's nothing wrong with us in that respect. It's simply the way human societies are structured. The basis of knowledge is agreement. Because we can't learn all we need to know through personal experience and discovery alone, things are set up so we can simply believe what others tell us. We know some things through tradition, some things from "experts."

There are other ways of knowing things, however. In contrast to knowing things through agreement, we can know them through direct experience—through observation. If you dive into a glacial stream flowing through the Canadian Rockies, you don't need anyone to tell you it's cold. You notice it all by yourself. The first time you stepped on a thorn, you knew it hurt before anyone told you.

When our experience conflicts with what everyone else knows, though, there's a good chance we'll surrender our experience in favour of the agreement.

For example, imagine you've come to a party at one of our homes. It's a high-class affair, and the drinks and food are excellent. In particular, you're taken by one of the appetizers brought around on a tray: a breaded, deep-fried tidbit that's especially zesty. You have a couple—they're so delicious! You have more. Soon you find yourself subtly moving around the room so that you'll be wherever the person next arrives with a tray of these nibbles.

Finally, you can't contain yourself any more. "What are they?" you ask. "How can I get the recipe?" And you are let in on the secret: "You've been eating breaded, deep-fried worms!" Your response is dramatic: your stomach rebels, and you promptly throw up all over the living room rug. Awful! What a terrible thing to serve guests!

The point of the story is that both of your feelings about the appetizer would be quite real. Your initial liking for them, based on your own experience, was certainly real. But so was the feeling of disgust you had when you found out that you'd been eating worms. It should be evident, however, that this feeling of disgust was strictly a product of the agreement you have with those around you that worms aren't fit to eat. That's an agreement you entered into the first time your parents found you sitting in a pile of dirt with half of a wriggling worm dangling from your lips. You learned that worms are not acceptable food in our society when they pried your mouth open and reached down your throat for the other half of the worm.

Aside from these agreements, what's wrong with worms? They're probably high in protein and low in calories. Bite-sized and easily packaged, they're a distributor's dream. They are also a delicacy for some people who live in societies that lack our agreement that worms are disgusting. Some people might love the worms but be turned off by the deep-fried breading.

Here's a question you might consider: "Are worms *really* good or *really* bad to eat?" And here's a more interesting question: "*How could you know* which was really so?" This book is about answering the second kind of question.

The rest of this chapter looks at how we know what is real. We'll begin by examining inquiry as a natural human activity, something we all have engaged in every day of our lives. We'll look at the source of everyday knowledge and at some kinds of errors we make in normal inquiry. We'll then examine what makes science—in particular, social science—different. After considering some of the underlying ideas of social research, we'll conclude with an initial consideration of issues in social research.

LOOKING FOR REALITY

Reality is a tricky business. You probably already suspect that some of the things you "know" may not be true, but how can you really know what's real? People have grappled with this question for thousands of years.

One answer that has arisen out of that grappling is **science**, which offers an approach to both **agreement reality** and **experiential reality**.

Scientists have certain criteria that must be met before they'll accept the reality of something they haven't personally experienced. In general, a scientific assertion must have both **logical** and **empirical** support: it must make sense, and it must be supported by actual observation. Why do earthbound scientists accept the assertion that it's cold on the dark side of the Moon? First, it makes sense, because the Moon's surface heat comes from the Sun's rays, and the dark side of the Moon is dark because it's turned away from the Sun. Second, the scientific measurements made on the Moon's dark side confirm this logical expectation. So, scientists accept the reality of things they don't personally experience—they accept an agreement reality—but they have special standards for doing so.

More to the point of this book, however, science offers a special approach to the discovery of reality through personal experience. In other words, it offers a special approach to the business of inquiry. That special approach is called **methodology**. Methodology is the set of practices and techniques used to collect, process, and interpret information aimed at enhancing our understanding of reality. Methodology illuminates procedures for scientific investigation. This book is an examination and presentation of social science methodology, or how social scientists find out about human social life.

Why do we need social science to discover the reality of social life? To find out, let's first consider what happens in ordinary, nonscientific inquiry.

ORDINARY HUMAN INQUIRY

Practically all people, and many other animals as well, exhibit a desire to predict their future circumstances. Humans seem predisposed to undertake this task using *causal* and *probabilistic* reasoning. **Causal reasoning** recognizes that future circumstances are somehow rooted in or conditioned by present ones. We learn that getting an education will affect how much money we earn later in life and that swimming beyond the reef may bring an unhappy encounter with a shark. As students, we learn that studying hard will result in better examination grades.

---

science A body of knowledge about reality as well as a set of systematic methods for generating this knowledge.

agreement reality What we "know" as part and parcel of the culture we share with those around us.

experiential reality What we "know" from personal experience and discovery.

logical The criterion for assessing the validity of arguments.

empirical The criterion requiring sensory experience as evidence.

methodology A set of practices and techniques used to collect, process, and interpret information aimed at enhancing our understanding of reality.

causal reasoning The recognition that future circumstances are rooted in or conditioned by present ones.

We also learn that such patterns of cause and effect are *probabilistic* in nature. **Probabilistic reasoning** argues that effects occur more often when the causes occur than when the causes are absent—but not always. Thus, students learn that studying hard produces good grades in most instances, but not every time. We recognize the danger of swimming beyond the reef without believing that every such swim will be fatal. As we'll see throughout the book, science makes these concepts of causality and probability more explicit and provides techniques for dealing with them more rigorously than does casual human inquiry. It sharpens the skills we already have by making us more conscious, rigorous, and explicit in our inquiries.

As we suggested earlier in the chapter, our attempts to learn about the world are only partly linked to direct personal inquiry or experience. Another, much larger, part comes from the agreed-upon knowledge that others give us, those things "everyone knows." This agreement reality both assists and hinders our attempts to find out for ourselves. To see how, consider two important sources of our secondhand knowledge—tradition and authority.

TRADITION

Each of us inherits a culture made up, in part, of firmly accepted knowledge about the workings of the world. We may learn from others that eating too much candy will decay our teeth, that the circumference of a circle is approximately 22 sevenths of its diameter, that masturbation will blind us, or even that great fortunes are primarily the result of hard work. We may test a few of these "truths" on our own, but we simply accept the great majority of them. These are things that "everybody knows."

Tradition, in this sense of the term, offers some clear advantages to human inquiry. By accepting what everybody knows, we are spared the overwhelming task of starting from scratch in our search for regularities and understanding. Knowledge is cumulative, and an inherited body of information and understanding is the jumping-off point for the development of more knowledge. We often speak of "standing on the shoulders of giants"—that is, of previous generations.

At the same time, tradition may hinder human inquiry. If we seek a fresh understanding of something everybody already understands and has always understood, we may be marked as fools for our efforts. More to the point, however, it rarely occurs to most of us to seek a different understanding of something we all "know" to be true.

AUTHORITY

Despite the power of tradition, new knowledge appears every day. Quite aside from our own personal inquiries, we benefit throughout our lives from new discoveries and understandings produced by others. Often, acceptance of these new acquisitions depends on the status of the discoverer. You're more likely to believe the medical researcher who declares that the common cold can be transmitted through kissing, for example, than to believe your Uncle Pete.

Like tradition, authority can both assist and hinder human inquiry. We do well to trust in the judgment of the person who has special training, expertise, and credentials in a given matter, especially in the face of controversy. At the same time, inquiry can be greatly hindered by the legitimate authorities that err within their own province. Biologists, after all, make mistakes in the field of biology. Moreover, biological knowledge changes over time.

Inquiry is also hindered when we depend on the authority of experts speaking outside their realm of expertise. For example, consider the political or religious leader with no medical or biochemical expertise who declares that marijuana can fry your brain. The advertising industry plays heavily on this misuse of authority by, for example, having popular athletes discuss the nutritional value of breakfast cereals or having movie actors evaluate the performance of automobiles.

Both tradition and authority, then, are double-edged swords in the search for knowledge about the world. Simply put, they provide us with a starting point for our own inquiry, but they can

probabilistic reasoning The recognition that effects occur more often, but not always, when specific causes are present.

lead us to start at the wrong point and push us off in the wrong direction.

ERRORS IN INQUIRY AND SOME SOLUTIONS

Quite aside from the potential dangers of tradition and authority, we often stumble and fall when we set out to learn for ourselves. Let's look at some of the common errors we make in our casual inquiries and look at the ways science guards against those errors.

Inaccurate Observations Frequently, we make mistakes in our observations. For example, what was your methodology instructor wearing on the first day of class? If you have to guess, it's because most of our daily observations are casual and semiconscious. That's why we often disagree about what really happened.

In contrast to casual human inquiry, scientific observation is a conscious activity. Simply making observation more deliberate helps reduce error. In trying to recall what your instructor was wearing on the first day of class, you'd probably make a mistake. However, if you had gone to the first class with a conscious plan to observe and record what your instructor was wearing, you'd be far more likely to be accurate.

In many cases, both simple and complex measurement devices help guard against inaccurate observations. Moreover, they add a degree of precision well beyond the capacity of the unassisted human senses. Suppose, for example, that you had taken colour photographs of your instructor that day.

Overgeneralization When we look for patterns among the specific things we observe around us, we often assume that a few similar events are evidence of a general pattern. That is, we overgeneralize on the basis of limited observations. Probably the tendency to overgeneralize is greatest when the pressure to arrive at a general understanding is high. Yet it also occurs without such pressure. Whenever overgeneralization does occur, it can misdirect or impede inquiry.

Imagine you are a reporter covering an animal rights demonstration. You have orders to turn in your story in just two hours, and you need to know why people are demonstrating. Rushing to the scene, you start interviewing them, asking for their reasons. If the first three demonstrators you interview give you essentially the same reason, you may simply assume that the other 3,000 are also there for that reason. Unfortunately, when your story appears, your editor gets scores of letters from protesters who were there for an entirely different reason.

Scientists guard against overgeneralization by committing themselves in advance to a sufficiently large and representative sample of observations. The **replication** of inquiry provides another safeguard. Basically, replication means repeating a study and checking to see whether the same results are produced each time. Then, as a further test, the study may be repeated again under slightly varied conditions.

Selective Observation One danger of overgeneralization is that it may lead to selective observation. Once we have concluded that a particular pattern exists and have developed a general understanding of why it exists, we tend to focus on future events and situations that fit the pattern and ignore those that don't. Racial and ethnic prejudices depend heavily on selective observation for their persistence.

Listen to any bigot calling in to a radio talk show and you will hear selective observation at work. The pattern of argument is predictable. The caller complains about the conduct of the group that is the target of their hostility. They recite well-worn stereotypes of the racial, ethnic, religious, or other category under consideration. When asked for evidence of their views, they emphatically recite an illustrative example as though that is the end of the story.

Selective observation is a part of **confirmation bias**, the tendency to seek out, recall, or interpret information that supports one's existing views. To guard against selective observation, research

replication Repetition of a research study in order to either confirm the findings of a previous study or bring them into question.

confirmation bias The tendency to seek out, recall, or interpret information that supports one's existing views.

designs often specify in advance the number and kind of observations to be made as a basis for reaching a conclusion. If we wanted to learn whether women were more likely than men to support freedom to choose an abortion, we'd commit ourselves to making a specified number of observations on that question in a research project. We might select 1,000 carefully chosen people to be interviewed on the issue. Alternately, when making direct observations of an event, such as attending the animal rights demonstration, social scientists make a special effort to find "deviant cases"—precisely those who do not fit into the general pattern.

Illogical Reasoning There are other ways in which we often deal with observations that contradict our understanding of the way things are in daily life. One example is the often-heard idea that "the exception proves the rule." This idea makes no sense at all. An exception can draw attention to a rule or to a supposed rule, but in no system of logic can it prove the rule it contradicts. Yet we often use this pithy saying to brush away contradictions with a simple stroke of illogic.

What statisticians call the **gambler's fallacy** is an illustration of illogic in day-to-day reasoning. Often we assume that a consistent run of either good or bad luck foreshadows its opposite. An evening of bad luck at poker may kindle the belief that a winning hand is just around the corner. Many a poker player has stayed in a game much too long because of that mistaken belief. Conversely, an extended period of good weather may lead you to worry that it is certain to rain on the weekend picnic.

Although all of us sometimes fall into embarrassingly illogical reasoning, scientists try to avoid this pitfall by using systems of logic consciously and explicitly. Chapter 2 will examine the logic of science in more depth. For now, just note that logical reasoning is a conscious activity for scientists and that other scientists are always around to keep them honest.

Science, then, attempts to protect its inquiries from the common pitfalls in ordinary inquiry. Accurately observing and understanding reality is not an obvious or trivial matter, as we'll see throughout this book.

WHAT'S REALLY REAL?

Philosophers sometimes use the term "naive realism" to describe the way most of us operate in our daily lives. When you sit at a table to write, you probably don't spend a lot of time thinking about whether the table is really made up of atoms, which in turn are mostly empty space. When you step into the street and see a city bus hurtling toward you, it's not the best time to reflect on methods for testing whether the bus really exists. We all live with a view that what's real is pretty obvious—and that view usually gets us through the day.

We don't want this book to interfere with your ability to deal with everyday life. We hope, however, that the preceding discussions have demonstrated that the nature of "reality" is perhaps more complex than we tend to assume in our everyday functioning. Since the subject of this book (research methods) centres on obtaining a better understanding of social reality, we need to enlarge our view beyond naive realism. The following description of terms and their relationships aims to expand your understanding. The model is based on the idea that there are different levels of experience and that reality is socially constructed (Brym et al. 2016; Roberts et al. 2015).

Two Levels of Experience The slogan on a student's t-shirt declared: *La vie est simple.* It is doubtful whether many university students juggling academic studies, employment, family, and romantic, recreational, and other obligations would agree. Your life experience is more likely complex and confusing, and occurring at many levels.

For current purposes it is useful to distinguish three levels of experience, the first of which is concrete. **Concrete experience** is empirical; it is composed of sensations. Concrete experience includes touching, tasting, smelling, hearing, and seeing. The components of concrete experience are called **percepts**, which come together to form

---

gambler's fallacy The mistaken belief that random events will "balance out" over time.

concrete experience The empirical experience of sensation, including touch, taste, sight, smell, and hearing.

percepts Components of concrete experience.

patterns. For example, a single dot on this page is a visual percept, while a collection of dots forms a pattern (letter, word, paragraph, etc.).

Two features of concrete experience are worth noting. First, we share this form of experience with other living creatures. Like you, a goldfish and a gorilla experience the world concretely. Second, by itself, concrete experience is meaningless. Think of a newborn infant, thrust into a world of light, sounds, and smells of which she has no understanding.

Fortunately, your experience is not restricted to concrete meaninglessness. You also have abstract experiences. **Abstract experience** occurs in your mind; it is imaginary. Abstract experience is composed of **concepts** that, when related, form **propositions**. Concepts are abstract terms for organizing sensory experience. Take three pens and examine them carefully. You will notice that they are concretely different objects. They are different sizes, colours, shapes, and the like. But in your mind, these very different concrete objects are organized in *the same* abstract category. You label each of them by the same term, "pen."

When you express a relationship between different concepts you are stating a proposition. In everyday language, propositions are called ideas. The proposition "The pen is on the table" states an understanding of how two concepts (pen and table) are related (one is "on" the other).

Abstract experience is important because through it you give meaning to your life. One wonder of childhood is the acquisition of language. Through it, children learn the shared concepts of their cultural community and, in doing so, add meaning to their lives. This imaginative understanding expands dramatically when they begin to link concepts together in the form of ideas. What parent does not melt when their little one says, "Mommy, I love you."

patterns Aggregations of percepts.

abstract experience Imaginary experience occurring in the mind.

concepts Abstract terms for organizing sensory experience.

propositions Statements (ideas) expressing the relationship between concepts.

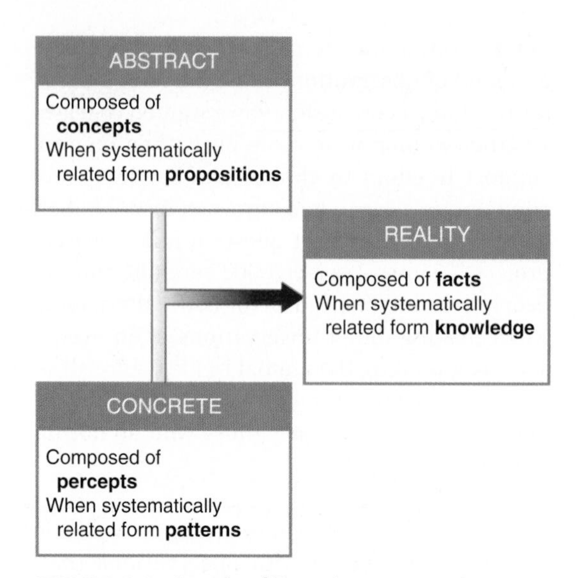

FIGURE 1-1 Levels of Experience. Here are two examples that illustrate the social construction of reality.

Social Construction of Reality It is possible to have experiences that are mostly concrete (e.g., noise) or largely abstract (e.g., fantasies). However, most of the time people report living in the "real" world, which is a third level of experience. Sociologists have a long tradition of referring to the social construction of reality (Berger and Luckmann 1966; Elder-Vass 2013), and here is one way of understanding what they are talking about: *Reality appears through a merger of concrete and abstract experience.* Figure 1-1 illustrates the merger.

Example 1: Is the Big Dipper Real? If you grew up in the northern hemisphere and spent time away from the glare of city lights, you probably have a childhood memory of looking at the night sky and being amazed at the mass of twinkling light. At that time in your early childhood, if someone asked you about the "Big Dipper" you probably had no idea what they were talking about. They might as well have been using a concept from a completely foreign language. In short, at that stage in your life, although you were fully capable of the concrete experience of seeing twinkling light in the sky, the Big Dipper was not real. But today the Big Dipper is probably very real to you. How did that transformation occur?

KEE PIL CHO/Alamy Stock Photo

FIGURE 1-2 **The Big Dipper.**

It occurred through a merger of abstract and concrete experience that probably happened by a process something like the following. First, somebody explained to you what the anachronistic term "dipper" means and talked until you got the abstract idea in mind of a cup with a long handle. Then you were taken outside and carefully shown the image of a dipper in the night sky. This probably took several trials, since at the outset the concrete experience of the stars was a random collage of light. But slowly and surely, over many repetitions, the pattern of seven stars comprising the Big Dipper came into focus (see Figure 1-2). It became "real." And it is probably now so "real" that, when you look into the night sky, you cannot imagine how you could not have seen it!

Example 2: Was the Crime Suspect Really Resisting Arrest? In the summer of 2014, Eric Garner was confronted by New York City police officers for selling illegal cigarettes (Goldstein and Santora 2014). This was not his first encounter with the law for this offence. Video footage of the interaction shows that, in short order, Garner found himself face down on the cement with a police officer on top holding his head against the sidewalk and four others surrounding him. His left hand is secured behind his back while his right arm is extended, palm up. While the police repeatedly tell him to put his right hand behind his back, Garner desperately repeats, "I can't breathe." Police ignore his plea and, shortly afterward, Garner dies.

You can find footage of this sad encounter on YouTube. For now, let's focus on the following replay. More than a year after Eric Garner's highly publicized experience, a reporter sat down with a New York police officer (not involved in the case) and reviewed the video footage of what occurred. With regard to the precise situation in which Garner is pinned face down on the sidewalk, left arm behind his back, right arm extended, held by five men, the interviewer's assessment of the reality and that of the police officer are opposite. From a transcript of the discussion (Glass 2015):

> We watched it over and over. She [the police officer] only saw it as him [Garner] not complying, basically, wrestling and refusing to be arrested. And I [the interviewer] can only ever see it, I mean, as the opposite. I can only ever see it as, like, a person who seems thoroughly detained. Like, I'm thinking at this point, it's under control.

Here we have competing constructions of reality in operation. Both individuals are viewing exactly the same concrete experience, but because they apply different conceptualizations, alternative versions of reality are constructed. And in this case, these opposing versions of what is real had life-or-death consequences. For the police officer, the reality was that Garner was resisting arrest and the fact he is "clearly not under control" meant that "there is more force to be applied" (Glass 2015).

These examples of reality construction illustrate the process that goes on in all cultures all the time. People continuously try to "make sense" of their concrete experiences and, in doing so, construct "reality." Before moving on to how this model of reality construction assists us in understanding research methods, it is worth emphasizing one other point—one that concerns the "social" nature of reality construction.

Sociologists speak of the social construction of reality. From our discussion, you might conclude that it is possible to construct a private reality. In a very limited sense, this is a possibility. The possibility is very limited because almost nobody invents their own concepts. Most abstract terms used by our imaginations come from our shared (social) culture. Alternatively, it is possible to link

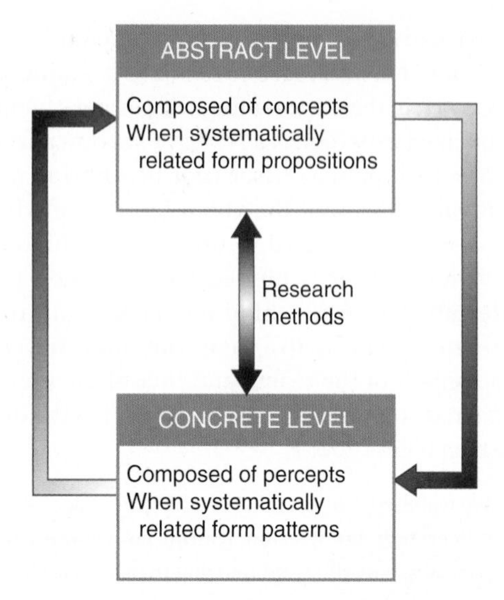

FIGURE 1-3 **Focus of Research Methods.**

concrete experience with abstract terms in idiosyncratic ways and, in doing so, create a unique reality. But such unique realities are very difficult to sustain. How often could you request the salt shaker by asking your family to "Please pass the zebra" before you succumb to social pressure? How about if you expressed your affection to someone you love by saying, "I banana split you"?

The point is that stable realities are supported through shared agreements of how concrete experiences should be labelled—how abstract and concrete experiences should be merged. To do otherwise is to risk being labelled mentally ill, as powerfully illustrated in Rokeach's (1964) classic study of three men who believed they were really Jesus Christ.

Research Methods and Reality Construction

With this model of different levels of experience in mind, we can situate what the focus of this text, research methods, is about. The specific issues in research methods are in one way or another related to forging links between the abstract and concrete levels of experience. Figure 1-3 diagrams the linkage. As we shall see, topics related to research methods are sometimes about clarifying our abstract imaginings, sometimes about focusing on concrete details, sometimes about deciding how to move from concrete to abstract, and sometimes vice versa. But however mired we become in the details of specific research methods topics, it is useful to remember that the goal of research methods is to construct a defensible version of reality. The methods of social science are essentially a set of rules, tools, and techniques for constructing social reality by merging abstract and concrete levels of experience.

theory A set of interrelated propositions providing a logical explanation of empirical regularities.

THE FOUNDATIONS OF SOCIAL SCIENCE

The twin pillars of science are logic and observation. That is, a scientific understanding of the world must (1) provide an understanding of reality that makes sense and (2) correspond to what we empirically observe. Both elements are essential to science and relate to three major aspects of the social scientific enterprise: *theory*, *data collection*, and *data analysis*.

To oversimplify just a bit, data collection focuses on accurately observing empirical patterns, data analysis with interpreting empirical evidence, and scientific **theory** on producing a logical explanation of realities produced through data collection and interpretation. Although this book is primarily about data collection and data analysis—that is, how to conduct social research—the rest of Part 1 is devoted to the theoretical context of research. Parts 2 and 3 then focus on data collection, and Part 4 offers an introduction to the analysis of data.

Underlying the concepts presented in the rest of the book are some fundamental ideas that distinguish social science—theory, data collection, and analysis—from other ways of looking at social phenomena. Let's consider these ideas.

THEORY, NOT PHILOSOPHY OR BELIEF

Today, social theory concerns itself with what is, not with what should be. For many centuries, however, social theory didn't distinguish between these two orientations. Social philosophers liberally mixed their observations of what happened around them, their speculations about why, and their ideas about how things ought to be. Although modern social scientists may do the same from time to time, as scientists they focus on how things actually are and why.

This means that scientific theory—and, more broadly, science itself—cannot settle debates about **values**. Science cannot determine whether capitalism is better or worse than socialism. What it can do is determine how these systems perform in terms of some set of agreed-upon criteria. For example, we could determine scientifically whether capitalism or socialism most supports human dignity and freedom only if we first agreed on some measurable definitions of dignity and freedom. Our conclusions would then be limited to the meanings specified in our definitions. They would have no general meaning beyond that.

By the same token, if we could agree that, say, suicide rates or giving to charity were good measures of the quality of a religion, then we could determine scientifically whether Buddhism or Christianity is the more effective religion. Again, our conclusion would be inextricably tied to our chosen criterion. As a practical matter, people seldom agree on precise criteria for determining issues of value, so science is seldom useful in settling such debates. In fact, questions like these are so much a matter of opinion and belief that scientific inquiry is often viewed as a threat to what is "already known."

We'll consider this issue in more detail in Chapter 12, when we look at evaluation research. As you'll see, researchers have become increasingly involved in studying programs that reflect ideological points of view, such as needle exchange or welfare reform. One of the biggest problems they face is getting people to agree on criteria of success and failure. Yet such criteria are essential if social research is to tell us anything useful about matters of value. By analogy, a stopwatch can't tell us if one sprinter is better than another unless we first agree that speed is the critical criterion.

Social science, then, can help us know only what is and why. We can use it to determine what ought to be only when people agree on the criteria for deciding what outcomes are better than others—an agreement that seldom occurs.

As we indicated earlier, even knowing "what is and why" is no simple task. Let's turn now to some of the fundamental ideas that underlie social science's efforts to describe and understand social reality.

SOCIAL REGULARITIES

In large part, social research aims to find patterns of regularity in social life. Although that aim is shared by all science, it is sometimes a barrier for people when they first approach social science.

Certainly at first glance the subject matter of the physical sciences seems to be more governed by regularities than does that of the social sciences. A heavy object falls to earth every time we drop it, but a person may vote for a particular candidate in one election and against that same candidate in the next. Similarly, ice always melts when heated enough, but habitually honest people sometimes steal. Despite such examples, however, social affairs do exhibit a high degree of regularity that can be revealed by research and explained by theory.

It is no accident that social life contains regularities. There are good evolutionary, cultural, and structural reasons for this state of affairs (Turner 2010). But, for now, all you need do is look around and you will see that the norm is organization, not chaos, and pattern, not idiosyncrasy. Shared cultural scripts guide human conduct virtually everywhere, from bedrooms to boardrooms, from sporting contests to political campaigns. Data collection methods are designed to detect these social regularities, while data analysis techniques are used to interpret these patterns and theory to explain them.

WHAT ABOUT EXCEPTIONS?

The objection that there are always exceptions to any social regularity does not mean that the regularity itself is unreal or unimportant. A particular woman may earn more money than most

values Statements of what is ultimately preferable or desirable.

men, but that will be a small consolation to the majority of women, who earn less. The pattern of gender inequality still exists. Social regularities, in other words, are probabilistic patterns, and they are no less real simply because some cases don't fit the general pattern.

This point applies in physical science as well as social science. In genetics, for example, the mating of a blue-eyed person with a brown-eyed person will *probably* result in a brown-eyed offspring. The birth of a blue-eyed child does not destroy the observed regularity, because the geneticist states only that the brown-eyed offspring is more likely and, further, that brown-eyed offspring will be born in a certain percentage of the cases. The social scientist makes a similar, probabilistic prediction—that women overall are likely to earn less than men. Once a pattern like this is observed, the social scientist has grounds for asking why it exists.

AGGREGATES, NOT INDIVIDUALS

Although social scientists often study motivations that affect individuals, the individual as such is seldom the subject of social science. Instead, social scientists create theories about the aggregate behaviour of many individuals. Similarly, the objects of their research are typically aggregates, or collections, rather than individuals.

Sometimes the collective regularities are amazing. Consider the birthrate, for example. People have babies for any number of personal reasons. Some do it because their own parents want grandchildren. Some feel it's a way of completing their womanhood or manhood. Others want to hold their marriages together, enjoy the experience of raising a child, or perpetuate their family name. Still others have babies by accident.

If you are a parent, you could probably tell a much more detailed, idiosyncratic story. Why did you have the baby when you did, rather than a year earlier or later? Maybe you lost your job and had to delay a year before you could afford to have the baby. Maybe you felt that being a family person would demonstrate maturity.

Everyone who had a baby last year had her or his own reasons for doing so. Yet, despite this vast diversity, and despite the idiosyncrasy of each individual's reasons, the overall birthrate in a society (the number of live births per 1,000 population) is remarkably consistent from year to year. Table 1-1 presents recent birthrates for Canada.

TABLE 1-1 Birthrates, Canada (per 1,000 population)

Year	Birthrate
2001	10.7
2002	10.5
2003	10.6
2004	10.5
2005	10.6
2006	10.9
2007	11.2
2008	11.3
2009	11.3
2010	11.1
2011	11.0
2012	11.0
2013	10.8
2014	10.8
2015	10.7
2016	10.6
2017	10.3

Source: Statistics Canada Table 13-10-0418-01 Crude birth rate, age-specific fertility rates and total fertility rate (live births), https://www150.statcan.gc.ca/t1/tbl1/en/cv.action?pid=1310041801#timeframe. Accessed February 19, 2019. Reproduced and distributed on an "as is" basis with the permission of Statistics Canada.

If the Canadian birthrate were 16.2, 36.5, 8.8, 24.2, and 15.9 in five successive years, demographers who study such issues would begin dropping like flies. As you can see, however, social life is far more orderly than that. Moreover, this regularity occurs without society-wide regulation. No one plans how many babies will be born or determines who will have them. You don't need a permit to have a baby; in fact, many babies are conceived unexpectedly, and some are borne unwillingly.

A VARIABLE LANGUAGE

Our most natural attempts at understanding usually take place at the level of the concrete and idiosyncratic. That's just the way we think.

Imagine that someone says to you, "Women ought to get back into the kitchen where they belong." You are likely to hear that comment in

APPLYING CONCEPTS IN EVERYDAY LIFE

Birthrate Implications

Take a minute to reflect on the practical implications of the data presented in Table 1-1. Imagine you were in the baby food or baby diaper business. How does the evidence affect your business?

What other sectors might benefit from the social pattern evident in the evidence? What about healthcare and education? Can you think of others?

What if we organized birthrates by province, or by ethnicity, or by income level, and so forth? How might these birthrate data become even more useful?

Social scientific theories, then, typically deal with aggregated, not individual, behaviour. Their purpose is to explain why aggregate patterns of behaviour are so regular even when the individuals participating in them may change over time. It could be said that social scientists don't even seek to explain *people.* They try to understand the *systems* in which people operate, the systems that explain why people do what they do. The features of systems that shape individual conduct can be characterized in different ways. One way is to look at variables.

the context of what you know about the speaker. If it's your old Uncle Harry who, you recall, is also strongly opposed to daylight saving time, postal codes, and personal computers, you are likely to think his latest pronouncement simply fits into his rather dated point of view about things in general.

If, on the other hand, the same statement was made by a politician trailing a female challenger, who has also taken to making statements about women being emotionally unfit for public office, his comments would probably be interpreted in the context of his political challenge.

In both examples, you're trying to understand the behaviour of a particular individual. In social science, researchers aim to go beyond this level of understanding and seek insights into classes or types of individuals. In other words, they try to place the specific individual in a set of similar individuals. They do this by applying concepts. Remember, concepts are abstract (mental) categories for organizing sensory experience. Just as in the earlier example where three concretely different writing objects could be labelled by the same concept ("pen"), the verbal utterances of old Uncle Harry and the politician can be both labelled with the concept of "bigot."

By examining an individual in this way and by placing them in a similar class, social scientists can make sense of more than one person. In probing what makes the bigoted politician think the way he does, researchers also learn about other people who are "like him." Their efforts in this regard are aided by thinking in terms of variables.

Variables are properties of objects that can change. Variables change across a set of scores called **attributes**. Let's apply this approach to Uncle Harry and the politician. Both men are different objects (individuals). One way of characterizing any object (including an individual) is to consider it as a unique combination of attributes, which are scores on specific variables. In other words, both men are a unique combination of attributes on variables like sex, blood type, social class, height, ethnicity, IQ, and level of bigotry (see Figure 1-4).

By focusing on a variable (in this case, bigotry) our attention shifts from a specific, unique individual to the general case. We are no longer exclusively interested in Uncle Harry or the ambitious politician but in their shared property—the variable bigotry. Thus, the question under consideration shifts from "Why is Person X a bigot?" to "What are the roots of bigotry?"

This shift in perspective has several implications. To begin, look at the profiles of the individuals in Figure 1-4. With respect to the variable "level of bigotry," both Uncle Harry and the ambitious politician score high. This illustrates the difference between a variable (a property that

variables Properties of objects that can change.

attributes The different scores that comprise a variable.

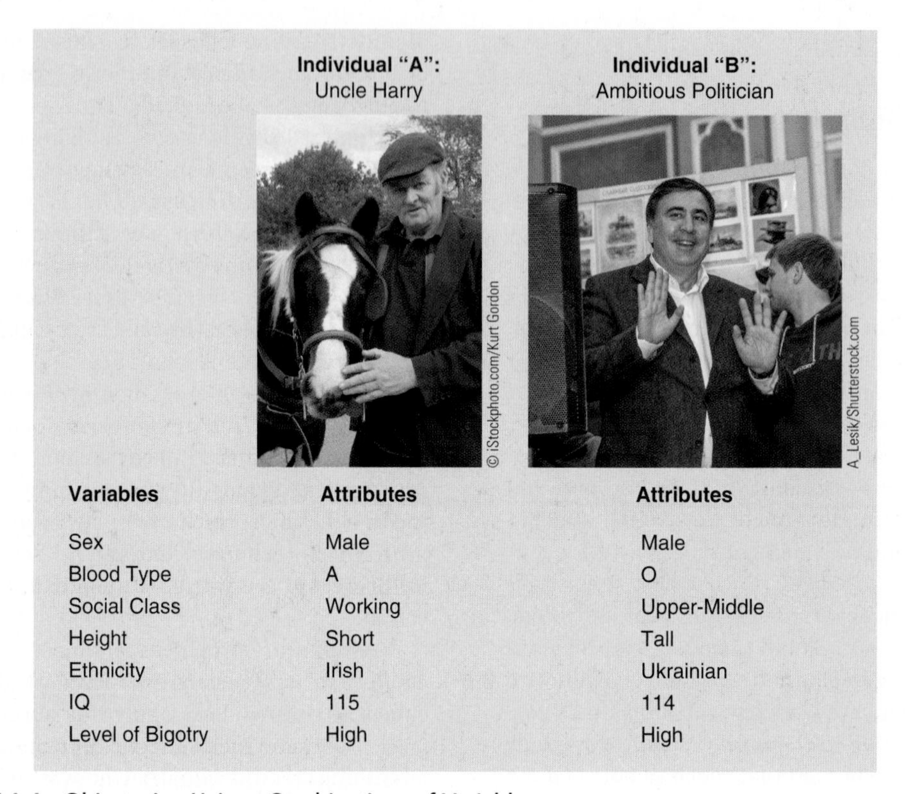

Variables	Attributes	Attributes
Sex	Male	Male
Blood Type	A	O
Social Class	Working	Upper-Middle
Height	Short	Tall
Ethnicity	Irish	Ukrainian
IQ	115	114
Level of Bigotry	High	High

FIGURE 1-4 **Objects Are Unique Combinations of Variables.**

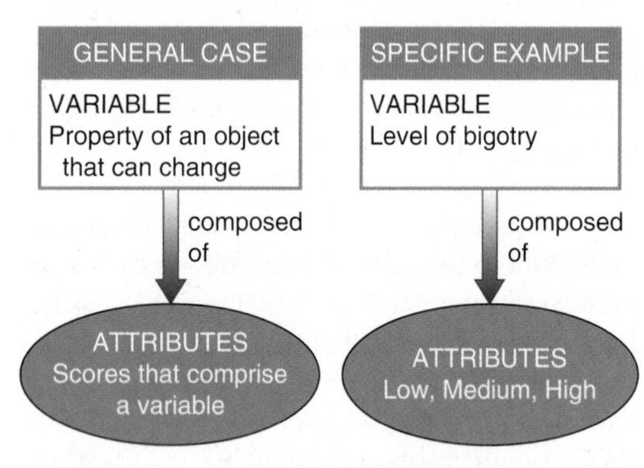

FIGURE 1-5 **Variables and Attributes.**

can change) and it components (attributes). Figure 1-5 elaborates on this distinction.

Figure 1-5 illustrates how, in general, a variable is composed of, and changes across, its component attributes. The figure also applies this understanding to the specific case of "level of bigotry." In the specific example, level of bigotry is a personal characteristic that differs between individuals (which qualifies it as a *variable*) that ranges across different attributes (low, medium, and high).

Commonly, variables are used for two kinds of descriptive purposes, both of which are illustrated in Figure 1-4. One descriptive use of variables is to *characterize a single object.* Take an orange from your fridge and place it on your desk. If you were asked to describe the orange, what would you say? Probably you would say something like "It is orange, round, and quite smooth." Notice that your response reports the attributes of several variables (colour, shape, and texture). In Figure 1-4, Uncle Harry is likewise characterized by attributes of several variables (sex, blood type, social class, height, etc.). So, from the perspective of variables, we can think of any object as a unique combination of specific attributes (scores) on some collection of variables.

A second descriptive use of variables is to *compare different objects.* Such comparisons are done by comparing the *different objects* on the *same variable*. An apple differs from an orange with respect to colour. They also differ with respect to shape. Look at Figure 1-4 and you can observe the differences between Uncle Harry and the ambitious politician with respect to several variables. Notice that with respect to level of bigotry both the uncle and the politician are similar; they are both highly bigoted individuals. But on other variables they are different. It is their distinctive combinations of attributes on different variables that give them their unique character.

The characterization and comparison of objects using variables is not restricted to individuals: the same principles can be used to compare aggregates of individuals. For example, you could describe a city in terms of its attributes (scores) on several variables, such as population size, ethnic diversity, and crime rate. Or you could compare two cities with respect to their scores on these variables. This same application can occur to aggregates of any size. You can describe a family, a sports team, a religious organization, or a nation using the same principles. Likewise, you could compare two or more families, sports teams, religious organizations, or nations the same way. Look again at Table 1-1 and you will see that Canada, a nation including tens of millions of individuals, is described with respect to the variable birthrate in any specific year (e.g., 2003) which, in turn, can be compared to Canada in other years (e.g., 2012).

In summary, variables provide a powerful tool for describing and comparing any kind of objects. For this reason, variables play a central role in scientific understanding of reality. But, as the next section explains, variables have another important purpose in scientific work. This purpose relates to explanation.

EXPLAINING DIFFERENCES

Imagine two people reporting on what they did Saturday night. Person X's report is short: they had dinner, watched the television news, went to bed, and fell asleep by 9:00 p.m. Person Y's report is extended and includes vivid details of how they partied heavily in a bar, hooked up with a person 15 years older, and spent the night performing spectacular sex acts. Whose story is more interesting? Which one will gain the attention of an audience?

It is a fact of life that we are more interested in change and difference than we are in constancy and similarity. Person X's Saturday night was boring because there was very little action. Action, change, and difference capture our attention and interest. How often would you listen to a friend's report about how they successfully drove to the 7-11 and purchased a Slurpee? Compare that to how much attention you would give to their report of having been in a serious car accident or held up at gunpoint at the 7-11. How often do people comment on your old hairstyle compared to a bold new one?

Everyday human interest in change and difference can be translated into the language of variables. In the language of science, we are more interested in variables than constants. **Constants** are features of objects that are fixed, that do not change. They are the opposite of variables, which are properties of objects that can change.

Our interest in variables is evident in the attention we give to accounting for the changes we observe. Are your friends more likely to gossip about somebody's continuing romantic relationship or about their terrible breakup? Is a criminologist more likely to be invited to comment on the television news when dramatic changes occur in the crime rate or when there are none? In short, not only does change get our attention, but we like to explain why the changes occurred. Again, this interest applies not only to individuals but to aggregates at all levels. Attention perks up when hockey teams go on losing streaks, businesses fail, nations go to war, or Martians invade.

Our interests, then, are not limited to description; we are also interested in explanation. **Explanation** focuses on accounting for events that have occurred in the past. Explanation is a historical activity. Something happens that we can describe; then we try to develop an explanation that helps us understand why the event

constants Properties that do not change across objects or over time.

explanation Accounting for events that have occurred in the past.

occurred. When we ask "what" occurred, we are focusing on description. When we ask "why" events occurred, we shift from description to explanation.

In science, we are commonly interested in explaining differences we observe in variables. Some groups are rich and some are poor, and we want to know why. Some students pass and some fail, and we are interested in an explanation. During some historical periods there are many suicide bombings, and in other periods there are few. What accounts for these differences? Whenever we observe changes of consequence, it is likely that calls for explanation will come into play.

Explaining differences or changes in variables relies on the following key principle: *You cannot explain a variable with a constant.* In other words, you cannot explain differences by pointing to something that is fixed. If your study habits remain the same yet your grades from one test to another change from high to low, it is not your study habits that explain your grade variations.

Well then. If constants do not explain variables, what does? The answer is other variables.

VARIABLES, RELATIONSHIPS, AND EXPLANATIONS

Before moving on, let's review. People are complex; so are aggregates of persons like marriages, teams, businesses, and nations. This complexity makes it impossible for any one study, investigation, or report to account for an entire person or organization. Instead, research focuses on specific components of individuals or aggregates. The components of interest are commonly expressed as variables, which can change across a range of scores called attributes.

One important use of variables is for description. In description, we report on what attribute (score) an object (or objects) has on a variable (or set of variables). Your grade on your last test provides a narrow description of you as an individual. The grade distribution for your class's last test tells us something about this group. If we could add your or your class's attributes on other variables (such as gender and happiness) we would have more complete descriptions (see Figure 1-6).

A second important use of variables is for purposes of explanation. Explanation provides an account of why some event occurred. In science, the event being questioned is often expressed as a variable. For example, why do some students get better test results than others? Or, why are some students happier than others? Explanations begin with a description of some change or differences of interest. To account for the changes in the variable of interest, explanations point to some other variable or variables.

As later chapters will show, explanatory accounts can become quite complicated. But for now, let's look at a simple example involving two variables—*education* and *prejudice*. For the sake of simplicity, let's assume that the variable *education* has only two attributes: educated and uneducated. Similarly, let's give the variable *prejudice* two attributes: prejudiced and unprejudiced.

Now let's suppose that we have 20 people—10 are educated and 10 are uneducated. Let's also suppose that 90 percent of the uneducated are prejudiced, and the other 10 percent are unprejudiced, and that 30 percent of the educated people are prejudiced, and the other 70 percent are unprejudiced. This is illustrated graphically in Figure 1-7A.

Figure 1-7A illustrates a relationship or association between the variables *education* and *prejudice*. This relationship can be seen in the pairings of attributes on the two variables. There are two predominant pairings: (1) those who are educated and unprejudiced and (2) those who are uneducated and prejudiced.

Here are two other useful ways of viewing that relationship. First, let's suppose that we play a game in which we bet on your ability to guess whether a person is prejudiced or unprejudiced. We'll pick the people one at a time (not telling you which ones we've picked), and you have to guess whether each person is prejudiced. We'll do it for all 20 people in Figure 1-7A. Your best strategy in this case would be to guess prejudiced each time, since 12 out of the 20 are categorized that way. Thus, you'll get 12 right and 8 wrong, for a net success of 4.

Now let's suppose that when we pick a person from the figure, we have to tell you whether the person is educated or uneducated. Your best

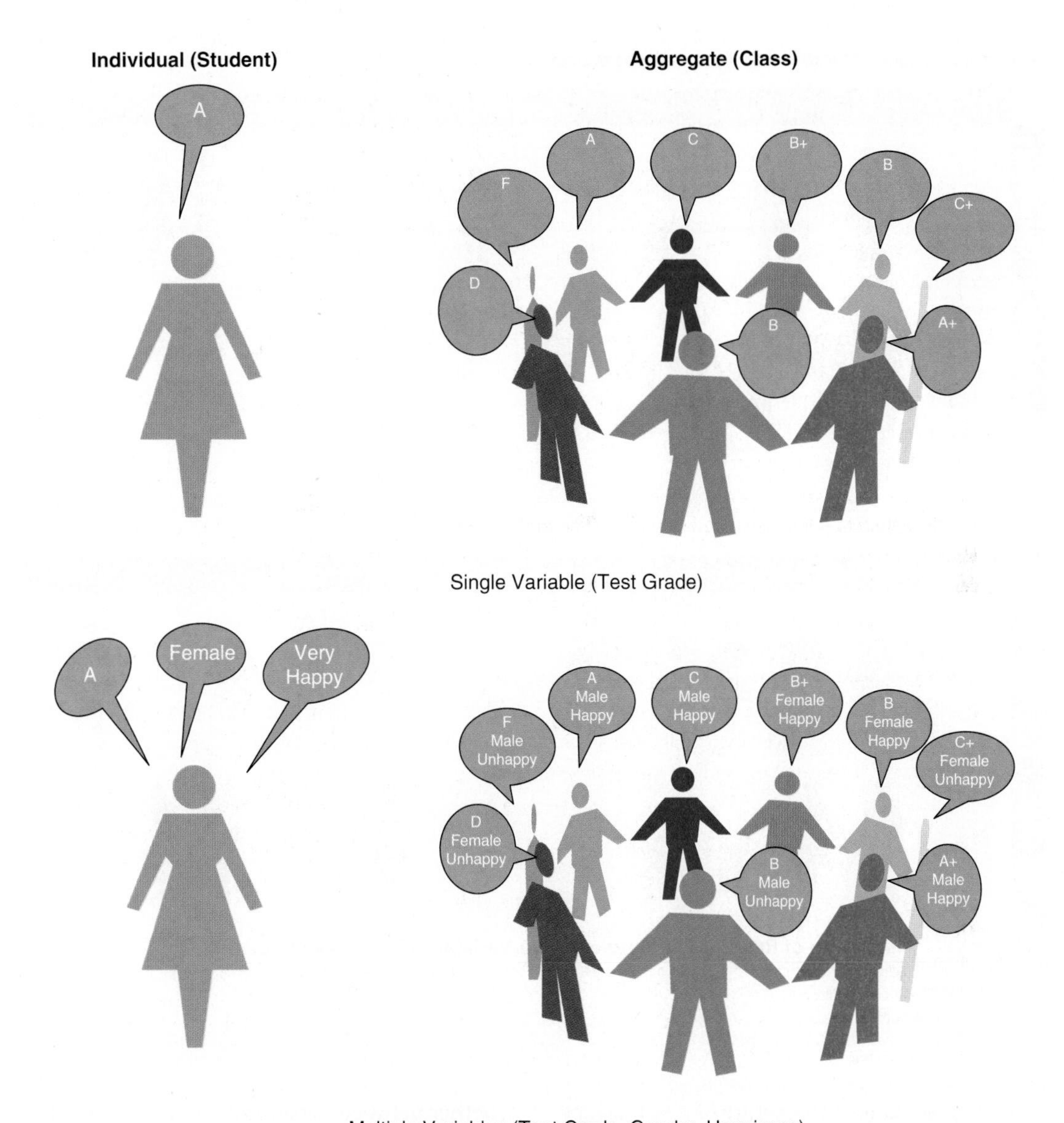

FIGURE 1-6 **Using Variables for Description.**

strategy now would be to guess prejudiced for each uneducated person and unprejudiced for each educated person. If you followed that strategy, you'd get 16 right and 4 wrong. Your improvement in guessing prejudice by knowing education is an illustration of what it means to say that variables are related.

Second, by contrast, let's consider how the 20 people would be distributed if education and prejudice were unrelated to each other. This is illustrated in Figure 1-7B. Recall that half the people are educated, and half are uneducated. Also notice that 12 of the 20 (60 percent) are prejudiced. If 6 of the 10 people in each group were prejudiced, we would conclude that the two variables were unrelated to each other. Knowing a person's education would not be of any value to you in guessing whether that person was prejudiced. Those who are educated are equally as prejudiced as those who are uneducated.

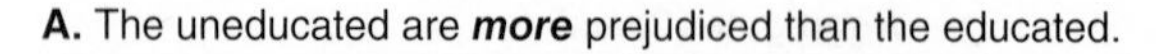
A. The uneducated are ***more*** prejudiced than the educated.

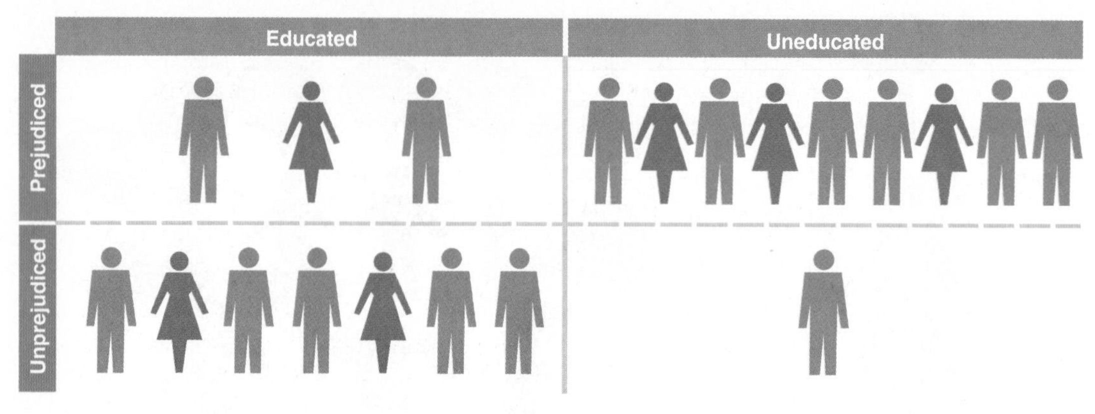

B. There is ***no*** apparent relationship between education and prejudice.

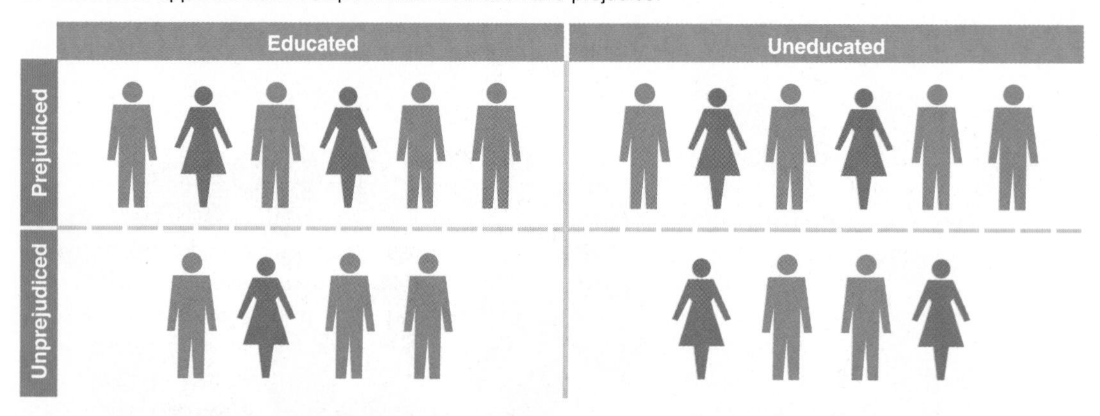

FIGURE 1-7 **Illustration of Relationship between Two Variables (Two Possibilities).**
Variables such as *education* and *prejudice* and their attributes (*educated/uneducated, prejudiced/unprejudiced*) are the foundation for the examination of causal relationships in social research.
Source: © Cengage Learning

We'll be looking at the nature of relationships between variables in some depth in Part 4. In particular, we'll explore some of the ways relationships can be discovered and interpreted in research analysis. For now, though, a general understanding of relationships is important so you can appreciate the logic of social scientific theories.

Relationships express connections. In everyday experience, relationships express connections between people. In science, relationships about the connection between variables are used for explanation. Evidence of a relationship, whether between persons or variables, is the following: *A* **relationship** *exists when a change in one thing (person, variable) is associated with a systematic change in the other.* For now, two things about this understanding are worth emphasizing. First, relationships exist between things that change (like people and variables). For example, a sure sign that your relationship with a former romantic partner is over occurs when your calling, texting, sending flowers, begging, and pleading make no difference (change) to the former lover's attitude. No change, no difference, no relationship. Second, for a relationship to exist it is not sufficient that two things change; they must change *systematically*. Right now there is

relationship A connection identified by a change in one thing being associated with a systematic change in another.

TABLE 1-2 Education and Attitudes toward Indigenous Peoples

	Attitudes toward Indigenous Peoples		
	Less Than High School	High School, Technical or Community College	University Degree
Dislike	39.3%	26.9%	19.0%
Like	60.7%	73.1%	81.%

Source: Canadian Elections Survey, 2011. Author's calculations.

somebody who is alive and well and enjoying his life in some remote region of a South American rainforest. You do not have a relationship with this person. Why? Because the changes in your life make no systematic difference to his life. This is what it means to be strangers—no relationship exists.

You can apply this same understanding to the evidence in Figure 1-7. In panel A, where a relationship exists, changes in education level are systematically connected to changes in levels of prejudice. In panel B, where no relationship is evident, changes in education make no systematic difference to prejudice levels.

Theories describe the relationships we might logically expect among variables. Often, the expectation involves the idea of causation. That is, a person's attributes on one variable are expected to cause, predispose, or encourage a particular attribute on another variable. In the example illustrated earlier, we might theorize that a person's being educated or uneducated causes a lesser or greater likelihood of that person being prejudiced.

As we'll discuss in more detail later in the book, *education* and *prejudice* in this example would be regarded as **independent** and **dependent variables**, respectively. These two concepts are implicit in causal, or deterministic, models. In this example, we assume that the likelihood of being prejudiced is determined or caused by something. In other words, *prejudice* depends on something else, and so it is called the dependent variable. What the dependent variable depends on is an independent variable, in this case *education.* For the purposes of this study, *education* is an "independent" variable because it is independent of *prejudice* (i.e., people's level of education is not caused by whether or not they are prejudiced).

Of course, variations in levels of education can, in turn, be found to depend on something else. People whose parents have a lot of education, for example, are more likely to get a lot of education than are people whose parents have little education. In this relationship, the subject's education is the dependent variable, and the parents' education is the independent variable. We can say the independent variable is the producer, and the dependent variable is the effect.

Returning to our example in Figure 1-7, we looked at the distribution of the 20 people in terms of the two variables. In constructing a social scientific theory, we would derive an expectation regarding the relationship between the two variables based on what we know about each. We know, for example, that education exposes people to a wide range of cultural variation and to diverse points of view—in short, it broadens their perspectives. Prejudice, on the other hand, represents a narrower perspective. Logically, then, we might expect education and prejudice to be somewhat incompatible. We might therefore arrive at an expectation that increasing education would reduce the occurrence of prejudice, an expectation that would be supported by the observations.

Since Figure 1-7 illustrates two possibilities—that education reduces the likelihood of prejudice or that it has no effect—you might be interested in seeing some real data. Table 1-2 contains Canadian evidence about the relationship between respondents' level of education and their attitudes toward Indigenous peoples. Differences in level of education (the independent variable)

independent variable A variable believed to produce changes in a dependent variable.

dependent variable A variable whose changes we are interested in explaining.

included three attributes: Less than high school, High school or technical/community college, and University degree. Differences in attitudes toward Indigenous peoples (the dependent variable) were categorized by the attributes "like" or "dislike." Let's look at Table 1-2 and see what relationship exists between these variables.

In Table 1-2 you see clear evidence that among Canadian adults, level of education is systematically related to levels of prejudice regarding Indigenous peoples. As education level increases, there is a systematic increase in the percentages of respondents who "like" Indigenous peoples.

SOME DIALECTICS OF SOCIAL RESEARCH

There is no one way to do social research. (If there were, this would be a much shorter book.) In fact, much of the power and potential of social research lies in the many valid approaches it comprises.

Four broad and interrelated distinctions, however, underlie the variety of research approaches. Although these distinctions can be seen as competing choices, a good social researcher learns each of these orientations. What we mean by the "dialectics" of social research, therefore, is that there is a fruitful tension between the complementary concepts we are about to describe.

IDIOGRAPHIC AND NOMOTHETIC EXPLANATION

All of us go through life explaining things. We do it every day. You explain why you did poorly or well on an exam, why your favourite team is winning or losing, why you may be having trouble getting dates you enjoy. In our everyday explanations, we engage in two distinct forms of accounting, though we do not ordinarily distinguish them.

Sometimes we attempt to explain a single situation exhaustively. Thus, for example, you may have done poorly on an exam because (1) you had forgotten there was an exam that day, (2) it was in your worst subject, (3) a traffic jam made you late for class, (4) your roommate had kept you up the night before the exam with loud music, (5) the police kept you until dawn demanding to know what you had done with your roommate's stereo—and what you had done with your roommate, for that matter, and (6) a wild band of coyotes ate your textbook. Given all these circumstances, it's no wonder that you did poorly.

This type of accounting is called an **idiographic explanation**. *Idio* in this context means unique, separate, peculiar, or distinct, as in the word "idiosyncrasy." When we have completed an idiographic explanation, we feel that we fully understand the causes of what happened in this particular instance. At the same time, the scope of our explanation is limited to the single case at hand. While parts of the idiographic explanation might apply to other situations, our intention is to explain one case fully.

Now consider a different kind of explanation, illustrated in the following examples. Every time you study with a group, you do better on the exam than if you study alone. Your favourite sports team does better when playing at home than on the road. Adolescent males spend more time gaming than adolescent females. Notice that the type of explanation in these examples is more general, covering a wider range of experience or observation. It speaks implicitly of the relationship between variables. For example, in the first illustration, whether or not someone studies in a group is being connected to exam performance. This type of explanation—labelled **nomothetic**—seeks to explain a class of situations or events rather than a single one. Moreover, it seeks to explain "economically," using only one or just a few explanatory factors. Finally, it settles for a partial rather than a full explanation.

In each of these nomothetic examples, you might qualify your causal statements with such words or phrases as "on the whole," "usually," or "all else being equal." Thus, you usually do better on exams when you've studied in a group, but not always. Similarly, your team has won some games on the road and lost some at home. And some adolescent girls spend a lot of time gaming, while not

idiographic explanation An accounting that aims to understand or make sense of the multiple causes of a specific event.

nomothetic explanation An accounting that identifies a few common causes of a broad category of events.

all boys are gamers. Such exceptions are accepted in the trade-off for a broader range of overall explanation. As we noted earlier, patterns are real and important even when they are not perfect.

Both the idiographic and the nomothetic approaches to understanding can be useful to you in your daily life. The nomothetic patterns you discover might offer a good guide for planning your study habits, for example, while the idiographic explanation might be more convincing to your parole officer. By the same token, both idiographic and nomothetic reasoning are powerful tools for social research. Here is a pair of contrasting examples related to environmental activism.

For many Canadians, the state of the environment is a pressing social concern. Think global warming, air pollution, water contamination. Confronting environmental concerns presents real issues, since the actions any individual can take make very little difference. To make a real impact, collective action is required. The question becomes this: What factors need to be taken into account in order to mobilize a collective, community response to environmental concerns?

The case of British Columbia illustrates the difference between idiographic and nomothetic responses to this question. Beyond basic demographic, economic, and political considerations, here is a list of specific factors that need to be taken into account in mobilizing an effective response in British Columbia (from Tindall 2014:397):

- "the relatively later industrial development of the province (at least by European colonialists)"
- "the related fact that there is relatively more nature left to contest"
- "the fact that the Aboriginal Land Question (the question of who owns the land) is largely unresolved"
- "the infusion of draft dodgers from the United States in the 1960s and 1970s who apparently became involved in the environmental movement"

These are the kinds of context-specific considerations that underwrite idiographic understanding. Compare this idiographic list of specific factors to a more general nomothetic approach to the same mobilization issue. A nomothetic approach focuses on one general consideration: "network centrality is positively associated with level of environmental movement participation" (Tindall 2002; 2014). In other words, people who are centres of attention and subject to more communication, information, and social pressure are more likely candidates for mobilized responses to social issues. This is the kind of core idea used in nomothetic explanations. In this case, the idea is so generally applicable that it is thought, with slight modification, to "apply to participation in the women's movement in Italy" (Tindall 2014:397).

So here you see a clear contrast in approaches. An idiographic approach points toward taking Indigenous land claims and American draft dodgers into account, while a nomothetic one indicates that one core principle can be used to understanding mobilization in both British Columbia and Italy. Different approaches yield very different insights. Just as physicists treat light sometimes as a particle and other times as a wave, so social scientists can search for broad patterns of relationships today and probe the narrowly particular tomorrow. Both are good science, both are rewarding, and both can be fun.

INDUCTIVE AND DEDUCTIVE APPROACHES

Like the idiographic and nomothetic forms of explanation, inductive and deductive thinking both play a role in our daily lives. They, too, represent an important variation in social research.

There are two routes to the conclusion that you do better on exams if you study with others. On the one hand, you might find yourself puzzling, halfway through your university career, why you do so well on exams sometimes but poorly at other times. You might list all the exams you've taken, noting how well you did on each. Then you might try to recall any circumstances shared by all the good exams and by all the poor ones. Did you do better on multiple-choice exams or essay exams? Morning exams or afternoon exams? Exams in the natural sciences, the humanities, or the social sciences? Times when you studied alone or ... SHAZAM! It occurs to you that you have almost always done best on exams when you studied with others. This mode of inquiry is known as *induction*.

Inductive reasoning, or **induction**, moves from the particular to the general, from a set of specific observations to the discovery of a pattern that represents some degree of order among all the given events. Notice, incidentally, that your discovery doesn't necessarily tell you *why* the pattern exists—just that it does.

On the other hand, you might arrive at the same conclusion about studying for exams in a very different way. Imagine approaching your first set of exams in university. You wonder about the best ways to study—how much you should review the readings, how much to focus on class notes. You learn that some students prepare by reorganizing their notes in an orderly fashion. Then you consider whether to study at a measured pace or pull an all-nighter just before the exam. Among these kinds of musings, you might ask whether you should get together with other students in the class or just study on your own. You could evaluate the pros and cons of both options.

Studying with others might not be as efficient, because a lot of time might be spent on things you already understand. On the other hand, you can understand something even better when you've explained it to someone else. And other students might understand parts of the course you haven't gotten yet. Several minds can reveal perspectives that might have escaped you. Also, your commitment to study with others makes it more likely that you'll study rather than decide to scroll through photos on Instagram.

In this fashion, you might add up the pros and cons and conclude, logically, that you'd benefit from studying with others. It seems reasonable to you, the way it seems reasonable that you'll do better if you study rather than not. Sometimes, we say things like this are true "in theory." To complete the process, we test whether they're true in practice. For a complete test, you might study alone for half your exams and study with others for the other exams. This procedure would test your logical reasoning.

induction A form of reasoning that moves from specific cases to the general case.

deduction A form of reasoning that moves from the general principles to a specific case.

This second mode of inquiry, known as deductive reasoning or **deduction**, moves from the general (abstract/conceptual) to the specific (concrete/empirical observations). It moves from (1) a pattern that might be logically or theoretically expected to (2) observations that test whether the expected pattern actually occurs. Notice that deduction begins with "why" and moves to "whether," while induction moves in the opposite direction.

As you'll see later in this book, these two very different approaches are both valid avenues for science. Moreover, as illustrated in Figure 1-8, induction and deduction often work together to provide ever more powerful and complete understandings.

Notice, by the way, that the distinction between deductive and inductive reasoning is not necessarily linked to the distinction between nomothetic and idiographic modes of explanation. These four characterizations represent four possibilities, in everyday life as much as in social research.

For example, idiographically and deductively, you might prepare for a particular date by taking into account everything you know about the person you're dating, trying to anticipate logically how you can prepare—what kinds of clothing, behaviour, hairstyle, oral hygiene, and so forth are likely to produce a successful date. Or, idiographically and inductively, you might try to figure out what it was exactly that caused your date to call 911.

A nomothetic, deductive approach arises when you coach others on your "rules of dating," when you wisely explain why their dates will be impressed to hear them expound on the dangers of satanic messages concealed in music lyrics. When you later review your life and wonder why you didn't date more musicians, you might engage in nomothetic induction.

We'll return to induction and deduction in Chapter 2. Let's turn now to a third broad distinction that generates rich variations in social research.

QUANTITATIVE AND QUALITATIVE DATA

The distinction between quantitative and qualitative data in social research is essentially the

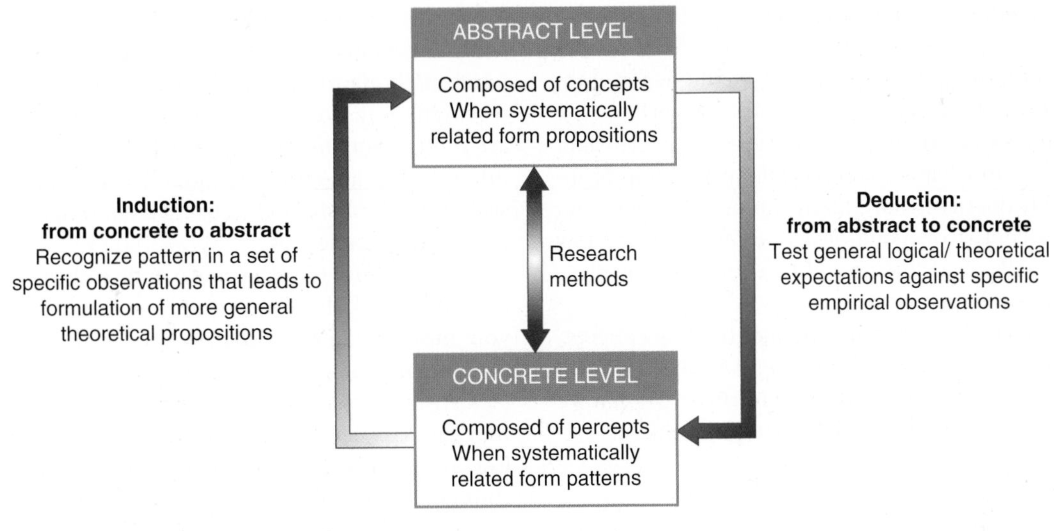

FIGURE 1-8 **Induction and Deduction.**

distinction between numerical and nonnumerical evidence. When we say someone is attractive, we've made a qualitative assertion. When we say he or she is a 9 on a scale from 1 to 10, we are attempting to quantify that qualitative assessment. Similarly, when a figure skater's performance is evaluated as a 9 on a scale of 10, the judge is attempting to quantify her or his qualitative assessment of the excellent performance.

Every observation is qualitative at the outset, whether it is our experience of someone's attractiveness, our assessment of someone's artistic or athletic ability, the location of a pointer on a measuring scale, or a check mark entered in a questionnaire. None of these things is inherently numerical or quantitative, but sometimes it is useful to convert them to a numerical form.

Quantification often makes our observations more explicit. It can also make it easier to aggregate, compare, and summarize data. Further, it opens up the possibility of statistical analyses, ranging from simple averages to complex formulas and mathematical models.

Quantitative data, then, offer the advantages that numbers have over words as measures of some quality. On the other hand, they also have the disadvantages that numbers have, including a potential loss of richness of meaning. For example, a social researcher might want to know whether university students aged 18 to 22 tend to date people older or younger than themselves. A quantitative answer to this question seems easily attained. The researcher asks a number of university students how old each of their dates has been, calculates an average, and compares it with the age of the subject. Case closed.

Or is it? While "age" here represents the number of years people have been alive, sometimes people use the term differently; perhaps for some, "age" really means "maturity." Though your dates may tend to be younger than you, you may date people who act more maturely and thus represent the same "age." Or someone might see "age" as how young or old your dates look, or maybe the degree of variation in their life experiences and worldliness. These latter meanings would be lost in the quantitative calculation of average age. In short, qualitative data can be richer in meaning than quantified data. This is implicit in the cliché "He is older than his years." The poetic meaning of this expression would be lost in attempts to specify *how much* older.

On the other hand, qualitative data can have the disadvantages of purely verbal descriptions. For example, the richness of meaning we just mentioned is partly a function of ambiguity. If the expression "older than his years" meant something to you when you read it, that meaning arises from your own experiences, from people you have known who might fit the description of being "older than their years," or perhaps the times you have heard others use that expression. Two things are certain: (1) the expression probably doesn't mean exactly the same thing to you as it does to someone else, and (2) you don't know exactly what someone else means by the expression and vice versa.

It might be possible to quantify this concept, however. For example, we might establish a list of life experiences that would contribute to what we mean by worldliness. These might include

- getting married
- getting divorced
- losing a parent to a fatal illness
- seeing a murder committed
- being arrested
- being exiled
- being fired from a job
- becoming homeless

We might quantify people's worldliness as the number of such experiences they've had: the more such experiences, the more worldly we'd say they were. If we thought of some experiences as more powerful than others, we could give those experiences more points. Once we had made our list and point system, scoring people and comparing their worldliness on a numerical scale would be straightforward. We would have no difficulty agreeing on who had more points than whom.

To quantify a nonnumerical concept like worldliness, then, we need to be explicit about what the concept means. By focusing specifically on what we'll include in our measurement of the concept, however, we also exclude any other meanings. Inevitably, then, we face a trade-off: any explicated, quantitative measure will be less rich in meaning than the corresponding qualitative description.

What a dilemma! Which approach should we choose? Which is better? Which is more appropriate to social research?

pure research Investigations driven by curiosity and satisfied by understanding something previously unknown.

The good news is that we don't need to choose. In fact, we shouldn't. Both qualitative and quantitative methods are useful and legitimate in social research. Some research situations and topics are more amenable to qualitative examination, others more amenable to quantification, and still others best studied to using a combination of both approaches.

Yet you'll find that these two approaches call for different skills and procedures. As a result, you may feel more comfortable with—and become more adept in—one or the other. You'll be a stronger researcher, however, to the extent that you can effectively use both approaches. Certainly, all researchers, whatever their personal inclinations, should recognize the legitimacy of both.

You may have noticed that the qualitative approach seems more aligned with idiographic explanations, while nomothetic explanations are more easily achieved through quantification. Although this is true, these relationships are not absolute. Moreover, both approaches present considerable grey area. Recognizing the distinction between qualitative and quantitative research doesn't mean that you must identify your research activities with one to the exclusion of the other. A complete understanding of a topic often requires both techniques. In fact, the realization that multiple techniques, both quantitative and qualitative, have a place in a social scientist's toolkit has led to the growing importance and formalization of mixed methods approaches to research (discussed in the last section of this chapter).

PURE AND APPLIED RESEARCH

The research of social scientists is driven by two distinct motivations: understanding and application. On the one hand, researchers are fascinated by the nature of human social life and are driven to explain it, to make sense out of apparent chaos. **Pure research** in all scientific fields finds justification in "knowledge for knowledge's sake." In this regard, satisfying our curiosity about some topic of interest is its own reward.

At the same time, perhaps inspired by their subject matter, social scientists are committed to having what they learn make a difference—to seeing their knowledge of society put into action. Sometimes they focus on making things better. In **applied research** the motivation is to find ways of living more efficiently or effectively. Applied social scientists aim to put their research into practice in many immediate and direct ways. Experiments and surveys, for example, can be used in marketing products. In-depth interviewing techniques can be especially useful in social work encounters. Chapter 12 deals with evaluation research, by which social scientists determine the effectiveness of social interventions.

As with each of the other dialectics just discussed, some social scientists are more inclined toward pure research, others toward application. Ultimately, both orientations are valid and vital elements in social research as a whole.

A BRIEF INTRODUCTION TO MIXED METHODS RESEARCH

Many of us have heard some version of the *blind men and the elephant* parable. A group of blind men encountering an elephant for the very first time attempt to make sense of it. The first man, patting its side, says, "It is like a wall." The second, touching its massive leg, declares, "It is like a tree." The third, grasping its tail, claims, "It is like a rope." The fourth, holding a tusk, offers, "It is like a spear." The fifth man, feeling its twisting trunk, is sure "It is like a snake." The sixth, feeling an ear, concludes "It is like a fan."

Just as there are slightly different versions of this parable, there are various lessons drawn from it. Most relate to some notion of complexity—that you cannot properly understand the fullness of some phenomenon from a single standpoint, since every approach is limited and partial. Enhanced understanding requires incorporating information from multiple viewpoints. This reasoning underlies the importance of mixed methods social science research. Generally defined, **mixed methods research (MMR)** is research that combines quantitative and qualitative research methods in order to increase breadth and depth of understanding (Johnson et al. 2007).

Creswell and Plano Clark[1] (2011:5) offer a more detailed identification of mixed methods research characteristics. When conducting MMR, a researcher

- collects and analyzes persuasively and rigorously qualitative and quantitative data (based on research questions);
- mixes (or integrates or links) the two forms of data concurrently by combining (or merging) them sequentially by having one build on the other, or embedding one within the other;
- gives priority to one or both forms of data (in terms of what the research emphasizes);
- uses these procedures in a single study or in multiple phases of a program of study;
- frames these procedures within philosophical worldviews and theoretical lenses;
- combines the procedures into specific research designs that direct the plan for conducting the study.

WHY USE MMR?

There are a host of reasons justifying MMR (for overviews, see Creswell and Plano Clark 2011; Plano Clark and Ivankova 2016). However, four prominent—and somewhat overlapping—reasons are key.

Triangulation: This term was borrowed from navigation and surveying, where it refers to determining the precise location of a point in space by measuring its angle from two known points. In the social sciences, triangulation emphasizes the advantage of using different methods, observers, or data sources to get multiple views of some phenomenon. The idea is to compare the different viewpoints and detect

1 Republished with permission of SAGE Publications, from John W. Creswell and and Vicki I. Plano Clark. (2011). Designing and Conducting Mixed Methods Research, 2nd Edition; permission conveyed through Copyright Clearance Center, Inc.

applied research Investigations directed toward insights that allow us to live more efficiently or effectively.

mixed methods research (MMR) Research that combines quantitative and qualitative approaches to increase the breadth and depth of understanding of research problems.

what they have in common, When different viewpoints yield similar results, confidence in the validity of our understanding increases. For example, we could evaluate participants' satisfaction with a time management seminar using both qualitative interviews (Chapter 11) and structured survey questionnaires (Chapter 8). If the observations using the different methods are similar (convergence), this helps corroborate and reinforce our conclusions. If different viewpoints of the same phenomenon yield different results (divergence), then examining the nature and source of discrepancies can enrich our understanding by helping us refine our methods and theories.

Offsetting Strengths and Weaknesses: All methods are imperfect. Therefore, the differing strengths and weaknesses of different methods can be combined to take advantage of and/or compensate for these differences (Bryman 2006; Plano Clark and Ivankova 2016; Greene et al. 1989). Typically this advantage comes from combining qualitative and quantitative methods. For example, laboratory experiments are good at helping us identify theorized connections between causes (independent variables) and effects (dependent variables). But, due to their highly controlled nature (see Chapter 7), experiments may not capture the contextual complexity of the real world. This shortcoming might be offset by field study methods (Chapter 10), which allow researchers to observe people in their actual social environment and to see how the laboratory findings translate into a real-world setting.

Complementarity: This advantage of MMR holds that different methods can provide different pieces of the puzzle. Using different quantitative and qualitative methods can generate understanding of different aspects of a phenomenon. These findings can then be combined to generate more comprehensive conclusions. Although the difference between triangulation and complementarity may not seem clear at first, the defining difference is that triangulation emphasizes the benefits of checking qualitative and quantitative results against each other to strengthen the validity of conclusions, whereas complementarity seeks to increase the meaningfulness and completeness of conclusions "by using the two methods to get results that enhance coverage and clarify and/or supplement each other to address the complexity of a topic" (Plano Clark and Ivankova 2016:85). For example, you might combine quantitative data that indicate outcomes (e.g., how many job training participants obtained employment post-program) with qualitative data that provides information about process (interview data where participants discuss their actual job-seeking experiences) to create a fuller account of whether the program is effective and, if so, how.

Development: This advantage focuses on how the findings of one method can be used sequentially to shape or inform the findings of another method in order to strengthen and enrich results (Greene et al. 1989; Plano Clark and Ivankova 2016). There are a number of aspects to development. For example, one method could be used to inform the sampling plan for a method used later. We could use a structured quantitative survey to screen for problem gamblers, in order to identify candidates for in-depth qualitative interviews about their gambling experiences (see the Spotlight on Mixed Methods Box in Chapter 6 for an in-depth example of mixed methods sampling). Another example can be seen in the construction and validation of a measurement instrument. We might first use a small number of in-depth qualitative interviews to develop a structured survey questionnaire that can then be pilot tested with another small sample, revised according to participant feedback, and then administered to a larger sample for quantitative validation (see the Spotlight on Mixed Methods Box in Chapter 5 for an in-depth example of using mixed methods to validate a questionnaire).

MMR NOTATIONAL SYSTEM

The conventional shorthand for representing various MMR designs is based on a few key distinctions, including the following (Morse 2003):

1. The primary method is written in upper case (QUAL or QUAN). The secondary method is written in lower case (qual or quan).

2. A plus sign (+) indicates a concurrent/parallel design in which both approaches are employed simultaneously. An arrow (➠) indicates a sequential design in which one approach follows the other.
3. If an approach is embedded in another, it is placed in parentheses: QUAN (qual) or QUAL (quan).
4. If both methods are given equal priority, then they are both upper case (QUAN + QUAL, QUAL ➠ QUAN, etc.)

TYPES OF MMR DESIGN

Various typologies have been proposed to summarize the diversity of MMR designs (see Teddlie and Tashakkori 2009). We will briefly highlight the typology developed by Creswell and Plano Clark (2011), which proposes four basic types (with variants) of MMR design; these are summarized in Table 1-3.

1. In *convergent parallel* designs, qualitative and quantitative data are collected and

TABLE 1-3 Types of MMR Design

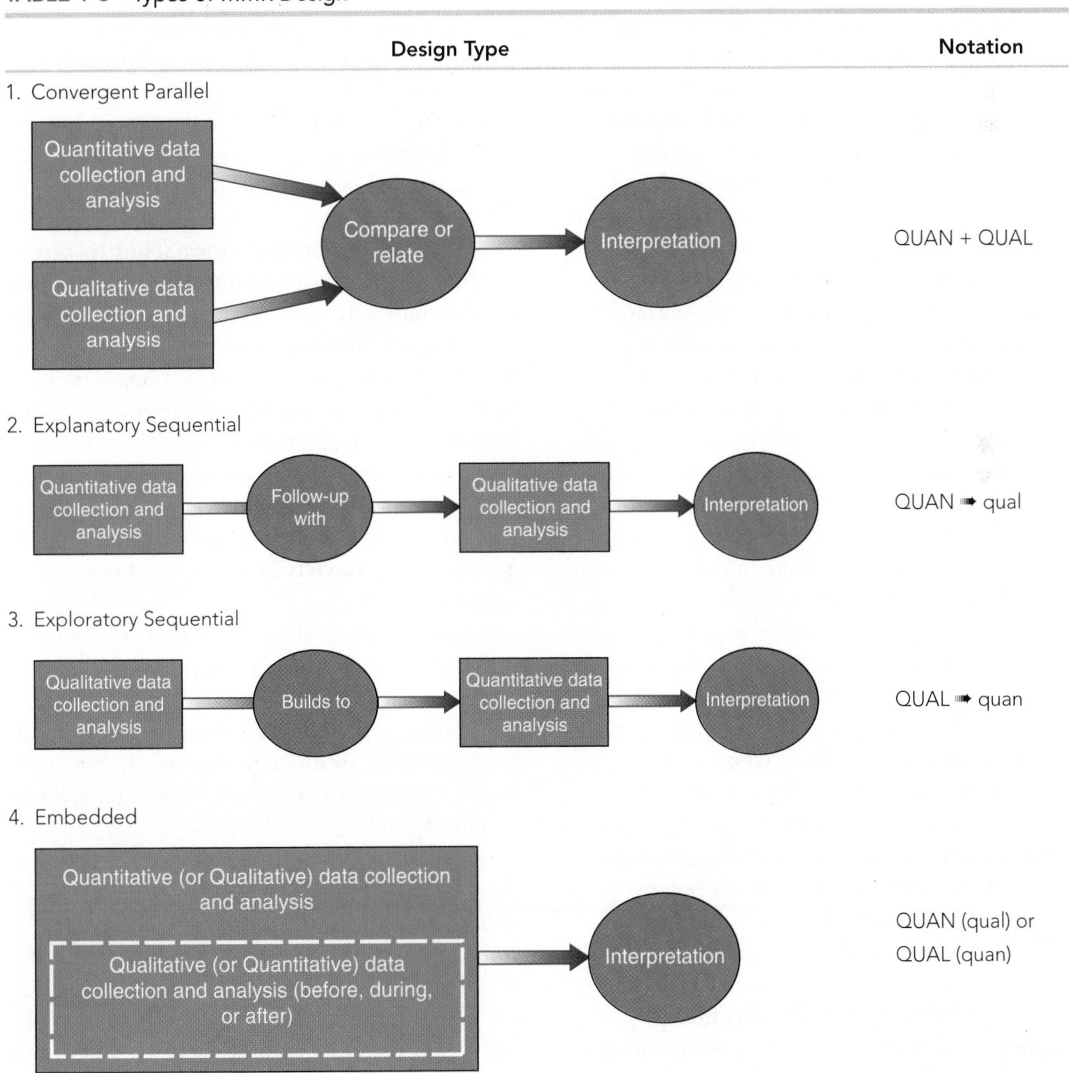

Table adapted from Teddlie and Tashakkori (2009) and Creswell and Plano Clark (2011).

analyzed in the same phase, and then the results are combined to generate an overall interpretation. If we are interested in student attitudes toward cannabis use, we could ask students to fill out a survey and participate in focus groups. Then we would analyze the survey results quantitatively and the focus group results qualitatively. Our interpretation would then be informed by how the two sets of results converge and diverge.

2. *Explanatory sequential* designs have two distinct phases. The first phase involves quantitative data collection and analysis. This is followed by a qualitative phase, the data from which may enhance understanding of the initial quantitative results. For example, if the first research phase found an unexpected association between cannabis use and social media consumption, the second phase could follow this up with qualitative interviews of cannabis users in an effort to explain this novel finding.
3. *Exploratory sequential* designs also have two phases. The initial phase generates exploratory (initial) qualitative results. Quantitative methods are then used to test or generalize the initial results. Then, the researcher interprets how the quantitative findings add to the initial qualitative findings. For example, imagine you have been hired by the public transit authority to find ways to increase student ridership. Initial focus group findings may highlight a number of features of public transit that students find appealing and others they find off-putting. But before recommending changes to increase ridership based on these exploratory qualitative focus group data, you would be wise to follow up with a quantitative phase, such as a survey with a larger representative sample of students, to see whether these opinions generalize to the broader student body.
4. *Embedded designs* involve combining the collection and analysis of quantitative *and* qualitative data in a traditional quantitative or qualitative design. The secondary method is embedded in the primary design, and the collection and analysis of the secondary data may occur before, during, or after the collection and analysis of the primary data set. Common variants of this design include *embedded experimental designs* in which the researcher embeds qualitative data collection within an experimental trial. Here the primary method is quantitative experimental, but the quantitative outcomes are supplemented with qualitative data (e.g., from interviews or focus groups). Similarly, in an *embedded instrument development and validation design*, the researcher might collect qualitative data (e.g., field notes or responses to open-ended questions) while pilot testing a new quantitative instrument (e.g., an "attitudes toward social diversity" scale) to provide further evidence that the instrument is indeed measuring what it is intended to.

The literature on and approaches to mixed methods are too vast and diverse for us to cover comprehensively. To help illustrate the impressive variety of designs and approaches that use MMR, various chapters of this book include boxes ("Spotlight on Mixed Methods") highlighting published MMR studies that incorporate one or more of the methods covered in that chapter. This assortment of examples shows how widespread MMR has become, moving in recent decades from novelty to staple in the world of social research.

The dialectics discussed in this chapter provide a sense of how wide-ranging scientific research can be: pure or applied, quantitative or qualitative, inductive or deductive, nomothetic or idiographic, or any combination in between. Social science encompasses many approaches and many tools.

This completes our overview of the foundations of social science. We hope you have a sense of how exciting and vibrant research can be. All you need is an open mind, a sense of adventure, and a good grounding in the basic tools of the trade. The following chapters provide these tools, beginning with an elaboration of the place and importance of theory.

MAIN POINTS

- This book's subject is how we find out about social reality.
- Inquiry is a natural human activity. Much of ordinary human inquiry seeks to explain events and predict future events.
- Much of what we know, we know by agreement rather than by experience. Two important sources of agreed-upon knowledge are tradition and authority. However, these useful sources of knowledge can lead us astray.
- When we understand through direct experience, we make observations and seek patterns of regularities in what we observe.
- Science seeks to protect against mistakes we make in day-to-day inquiry.
- Although we often observe inaccurately, researchers seek to avoid such errors by making observation a careful and deliberate activity.
- Sometimes we jump to general conclusions on the basis of only a few observations, so scientists try to avoid overgeneralization by using a sufficient number of observations and by replicating studies.
- In everyday life, we sometimes reason illogically. Researchers seek to avoid illogical reasoning by being as careful and deliberate in their reasoning as in their observations. Moreover, the public nature of science means that others are always there to challenge faulty reasoning.
- Reality is constructed through mergers of concrete and abstract levels of experience. The tools and techniques of research methods focus on systematically connecting these levels.
- Social theory tries to discuss and explain what is, not what should be. Theory should not be confused with philosophy or belief.
- Social science looks for regularities in social life.
- Social scientists are interested in explaining human aggregates, not individuals.
- Theories are written in the language of variables. A variable is a logical set of attributes. An attribute is a characteristic, such as male, female, or non-binary. Gender, for example, is a variable made up of these attributes.
- In causal explanation, the presumed cause is the independent variable; the affected variable is the dependent variable.
- Idiographic explanations seek to understand specific cases fully, whereas nomothetic explanations seek a generalized understanding of many cases.
- Inductive theories reason from specific observations to general patterns.
- Deductive theories start from general statements and predict specific observations.
- Quantitative data are numerical; qualitative data are not. Both types of data are useful for different research purposes, and they are often combined into MMR.
- Both pure and applied research are valid and vital parts of the social scientific enterprise.

REVIEW QUESTIONS AND EXERCISES

1. Review the common errors of human inquiry discussed in this chapter. Find a magazine, newspaper, or online article that illustrates one of these errors. Discuss how a scientist would have avoided it.
2. List five social variables and the attributes they comprise.
3. Go to one of the following websites and find examples of both qualitative and quantitative data.
    a. Library and Archives of Canada/Bibliothèque et Archives Canada; http://www.bac-lac.gc.ca/eng/Pages/home.aspx
    b. UN High Commissioner for Refugees; http://www.unhcr.org/cgi-bin/texis/vtx/home
    c. National Library of Australia; http://www.nla.gov.au/app/eresources
    d. Inter-university Consortium for Political and Social Research (ICPSR); http://www.icpsr.umich.edu/icpsrweb/landing.jsp

4. Think of some research problems that might be best addressed using a mix of quantitative and qualitative methods. For these problems, why would a combination of both approaches be better than either approach by itself?

CONTINUITY PROJECT

■ REALIZING INEQUALITY

Like all sciences, sociology uses a specialized jargon to describe topics of interest. One of these concepts is "inequality."

Look up the definition of inequality in a dictionary of sociology. This gives you an abstract understanding of what sociologists have in mind what they use the concept.

Given this sociological understanding, what concrete indicators could a macrolevel, quantitative researcher use to confirm the reality of inequality in Canadian society?

What concrete indicators could a microlevel, qualitative researcher use to confirm the reality of unequal treatment in a university classroom?

Thomas La Mela/Shutterstock.com

PARADIGMS, THEORY, AND RESEARCH

Social scientific theory is an interplay of theory and research, logic and observation, induction and deduction—and the fundamental frames of reference known as paradigms.

IN THIS CHAPTER ...

INTRODUCTION

"Research findings" based only on the observation of patterns are insufficient. Unless we can offer logical explanations for such patterns, the regularities we've observed may be mere flukes, chance occurrences. If you flip coins long enough, you'll get 10 heads in a row. Scientists might adapt a street expression to describe this situation: "Patterns happen."

Theories seek to provide logical explanations of these patterns. Theories function three ways in research. First, they prevent our being taken in by flukes. If we can't explain why certain polls are successful in predicting elections, we run the risk of supporting a fluke. If we know why it has happened, we can anticipate whether it will be successful in the future.

Second, theories make sense of observed patterns in ways that can suggest other possibilities. If we understand the reasons why "tight" societies, characterized by strong norms and little tolerance for deviance, use different political institutions than "loose" societies, opportunities for global understanding and security are enhanced (Gelfand et al. 2011).

Third, theories can shape and direct research efforts, pointing toward likely discoveries through empirical observation. If you were looking for your lost keys on a dark street, you could whip your flashlight around randomly, hoping to chance upon the errant keys—or you could use your memory of where you had been to limit your search to more likely areas. Theories, by analogy, direct researchers' flashlights where they are most likely to observe interesting patterns of social life.

While theories try to provide logical explanations, as noted in Chapter 1, not all social science research seeks to explain. Some research is conducted to describe—for example, what social life is like in an Inuit community—or to determine whether a social program is effective. Still other research may be conducted to find out the general public's opinion on an issue. Therefore, not all research is tightly linked to theory. Nonetheless, many researchers do seek to explain—they want to know why. Theory directly relates to "why" questions.

This chapter explores some specific ways theory and research work hand in hand during the adventure of inquiry into social life. We'll begin by looking at some fundamental frames of reference, called *paradigms*, that underlie social theories and inquiry. Theories seek to explain; paradigms provide ways of looking.

SOME SOCIAL SCIENCE PARADIGMS

There is usually more than one way to make sense of things. Different points of view usually yield different explanations. In daily life, for example, liberals and conservatives often explain the same phenomenon—the existence of homeless people, for example—quite differently. So might atheists and Christians. But, underlying these different explanations, or theories, are **paradigms**—the fundamental models or frames of reference we use to organize our observations and reasoning.

Paradigms are often hard to recognize as such because they are so implicit, assumed, taken for granted. They seem more like "the way things are" than like one possible point of view among many. Here's an illustration of what we mean.

Where do you stand on the issue of human rights? Do you believe that the individual human being is sacred? Are there some things that no government should do to its citizens? More concretely, how do you feel about using civilians as human shields in wartime to protect military targets or organized programs of rape and murder in support of "ethnic cleansing"?

Those of us who are horrified and incensed by such practices will probably find it hard to see our individualistic paradigm as only one of many possible viewpoints. Yet many cultures view the Western commitment to the sanctity of the individual as bizarre. Historically, it is decidedly a minority viewpoint. There are those who believe that the "rights" of families and society at large, for example, should be held in higher regard than those of individuals. As some world leaders point out, adhering to a belief in the sanctity of individuals has its costs in their view—for instance,

paradigm A theoretical perspective including a set of assumptions about reality that guide research questions.

the high crime rates and social disorganization that Western societies experience.

We are not trying to change your viewpoint on individual human dignity. It's useful, however, to recognize that our views and feelings on this matter are the result of the paradigm in which we have been socialized; they are not an objective fact of nature. All of us operate within many such paradigms.

There are benefits in recognizing that we are operating within a paradigm. First, we are better able to understand the seemingly bizarre views and actions of others who are operating from a different paradigm. Second, we can sometimes profit from stepping outside our paradigm. It opens our eyes to new ways of seeing and explaining things. That's not possible if we mistake our paradigm for reality.

Paradigms play a fundamental role in science, just as they do in daily life. Thomas Kuhn (1970) drew attention to the role of paradigms in the history of the natural sciences. Major scientific paradigms have included such fundamental viewpoints as Newtonian mechanics, Einstein's relativity, Darwin's theory of evolution, and Copernicus's conception of Earth moving around the Sun (instead of the reverse). Which scientific theories "make sense" depends on which paradigm scientists are maintaining.

Sometimes we think of science as developing gradually over time, marked by important discoveries and inventions. Kuhn, however, says scientific paradigms typically become entrenched, resisting any substantial change. Thus, theories and research take a certain fundamental direction. Eventually, however, as the shortcomings of a particular paradigm become obvious, a new one emerges and supplants the old one. The seemingly natural view that the rest of the universe revolves around Earth, for example, compelled astronomers to devise ever more elaborate ways to account for the motions of heavenly bodies that they actually observed. This paradigm was eventually supplanted by the view that Earth and other planets revolve around the Sun. This was nothing less than a revolutionary change in perspective that fundamentally altered the direction of theory and research. Kuhn's classic book on this subject is titled, appropriately enough, *The Structure of Scientific Revolutions.*

Social scientists have developed several paradigms for understanding social behaviour. The fate of supplanted paradigms in the social sciences, however, has differed from what Kuhn has observed in the natural sciences. Natural scientists generally believe that the succession from one paradigm to another represents progress from a false view to a true one. For example, no modern astronomer believes that the Sun revolves around Earth.

In the social sciences, on the other hand, theoretical paradigms may gain or lose popularity, but they're seldom discarded completely. Social science paradigms represent a variety of views, each of which offers insights the others lack and ignores aspects of social life that the others reveal.

The next section offers a brief overview of some major macro and micro paradigms used in sociology. This is not the place to discuss these paradigms in detail. Our point is simply to let you see that different paradigms offer very different perspectives on social life and thereby shape the formulation of research questions. As you will see, paradigms are not true or false; they are simply ways of looking that are more or less useful. Each can open up new understandings, suggest different kinds of theories, and inspire different kinds of research.

MACRO AND MICRO PERSPECTIVES

Let's begin with a distinction concerning a focus on macrotheory versus microtheory that stretches across research paradigms. Some social theorists focus their attention on society at large, or at least on large portions of it. Topics of study for such macrotheory include the struggle among economic classes in a society, international relations, or the interrelations among major institutions in society, such as government, religion, and family. **Macrotheory** deals with large, aggregate entities of society or even whole societies.

macrotheory Theoretical perspectives aimed at understanding the "big picture" of institutions, whole societies, and the interactions among societies.

TABLE 2-1 Four Sociological Paradigms

Theoretical Tradition	Main Level of Analysis	Main Focus	Main Question	Image of Ideal Society
Functionalism	Macro	Values	How do the institutions of society contribute to social stability?	A state of equilibrium
Conflict theory	Macro	Class inequality	How do privileged groups seek to maintain their advantages and subordinate groups seek to increase theirs, often causing social change in the process?	The elimination of privilege, especially class privilege
Symbolic interactionism	Micro	Meaning	How do individuals communicate so as to make their social settings meaningful?	Respect for the validity of minority views
Feminist theory	Micro and macro	Patriarchy	Which social structures and interaction processes maintain male dominance and female subordination?	The elimination of gender inequality

Source: From Brym/Roberts/Strohschein/Lie. *Sociology: Your Compass for a New World*, 5E. © 2016 Nelson Education Ltd. Reproduced by permission. www.cengage.com/permissions.

Some scholars have taken a more intimate view of social life. **Microtheory** deals with issues of social life at the level of individuals and small groups. Dating behaviour, jury deliberations, and student–faculty interactions are apt subjects for a microtheoretical perspective. Such studies often come close to the realm of psychology, but whereas psychologists typically focus on what goes on inside humans, social scientists study what goes on *between* them.

The distinction between macrotheory and microtheory cuts across the paradigms used in sociology. Table 2-1 provides a brief comparison of four major sociological paradigms—including functionalism, conflict theory, symbolic interactionism, and feminist perspectives—which is probably similar to one you saw in the textbook of your introductory course. Table 2-1 also provides the foundational ideas for the detailed study of sociological theory you may take in courses devoted to theory.

Begin by noting that different paradigms focus on different levels of analysis. Functionalism and conflict theory generally focus on macro considerations, symbolic interactionism uses a micro orientation, and feminist perspectives use both macro and micro. Notice also that these different paradigms focus on different things. Functionalism keys on values, the conflict perspective on inequality, interactionism on meaning, and feminism on patriarchy. These key considerations follow from the very different images of how society operates. Functionalism is rooted in a conservative view of society idealizing cooperation and equilibrium. By contrast, conflict perspectives see society as shaped by struggle and power dynamics. Interactionists, emphasizing the social construction of meaning, are concerned with understanding this dynamic and its consequences. Feminism stresses the place and importance of embedded gender inequalities and privilege.

Given these very different starting points, it is not surprising that these different paradigms generate very different kinds of theories and associated research agendas. For example, asking how the institutions of society contribute to social stability is bound to lead to very different avenues of inquiry compared to those interested in how privileged groups seek to maintain their advantages. Out of these roots come the wonderful theoretical and research traditions that comprise sociology's past and present. Functionalism sweeps from Durkheim's classic

microtheory Theoretical perspectives aimed at understanding social life at the intimate level of individuals and their interactions.

work to Alexander's studies. Conflict approaches range from Marx's classics to Foucault's poststructuralism. Interactionism ranges from Mead to Becker, and feminist perspectives from Martineau to Collins.

The different, and often contrasting, views set forth by social scientists indicate how paradigms influence research. These fundamental viewpoints shape the kinds of methods researchers are likely to use, the sorts of facts they seek to discover, and the conclusions they draw from those facts. Paradigms also help determine which concepts and concerns are important. Despite the different orientations paradigms provide, researchers within these traditions seek to be rational, reasonable, and objective. Let's next clarify what these qualities entail.

RATIONALITY, REASONABLENESS, AND OBJECTIVITY RECONSIDERED

As a way of knowing, science is generally held in high esteem. And rightly so. In recent centuries, researchers using a scientific approach have a wonderful record of achievement. A moment's comparison of life in the Middle Ages to yours today gives you a sense of what a profound difference science has made.

Still, given the place and importance of science, many people have odd views of what science and scientists are like. These stereotypes are probably related to the fact that only a small proportion of the public are engaged in science and have little direct experience. Therefore, they rely on stereotypes. Stereotypes of scientists have remained quite stable since Margaret Mead introduced her "draw a scientist" test almost 60 years ago (Mead and Métraux 1957). Think male, old, lab coat, frizzy hair, test tubes, and you get the picture (Highfield 2011). You can also add to the list qualities of character like rational, emotionless, value-free, and objective. Think Mr. Spock in *Star Trek*.

Given the stereotypes, it is little wonder serious challenges exist in recruiting talented young people like you to do scientific research. After all, you probably take your values seriously, are full of emotion, and are a mixture of rationality and irrationality. You are not at all like the stereotypical profile, so how can you imagine conducting scientific research? Fortunately, like many stereotypes, those of scientists are largely inaccurate. For current purposes, let's clarify what science means by the terms *rationality*, *reasonableness*, and *objectivity*. Such clarification should help you see that an ordinary person like you is capable of doing scientific work.

Chapter 1 emphasized that a scientific approach relies on the use of logic and empirical evidence. Let's begin by linking these features to an understanding of rationality and reasonableness. Both rationality and reasonableness are qualities of mind; however, they are very different qualities. Rationality refers to a quality of thinking; specifically, **rationality** refers to logical consistency, to a lack of contradiction in linking thoughts together. So, when a friend reports you are thinking "irrationally," they mean that the conclusions you are drawing do not follow from your argument. You will see rationality applied to theoretical thinking in the next section.

Being rational is different from being reasonable. **Reasonableness** refers to a quality of mind that is open to new ideas and evidence. Reasonable people are willing to reconsider their beliefs based on new arguments or findings. Reasonable people are willing to change their minds with respect to an issue; unreasonable ones are not. If no conceivable argument or evidence will lead a person to change her mind, she is unreasonable.

While being rational and being reasonable are both desirable qualities, they are not necessarily linked. Importantly, it is very possible for a person to be rational but unreasonable with respect to something they believe. In other words, an individual can have an internally consistent set of views that they stubbornly cling to no matter what. We call such people dogmatic; they have no doubts about their beliefs. This pairing of rationality and unreasonableness is common among the political, the religious, and those with ideological commitments. It is even found among

rationality The criterion for assessing thinking in terms of its logical consistency.

reasonableness A quality of mind that is open to new ideas and evidence.

paranoids, who have compelling arguments for their understanding based on faulty premises.

As a method of knowing, science values both rationality and reasonableness. As you will see in the next section, science uses rationality as a key criterion for assessing its theoretical narratives. Where thinking is faulty, theories are revised to remove the contradictions. Likewise, science values reasonableness. The success of science as a way of knowing rests on its willingness to continuously challenge existing beliefs with new ideas and empirical evidence. Through this process older understandings are replaced with newer ones, and through successive approximation we get a better understanding of reality.

Given the high value science places on being rational and reasonable, perhaps you consider yourself an unlikely candidate for participation in this way of knowing. After all, you are probably stubbornly dogmatic with respect to all kinds of things and, in addition, have shown serious displays of irrationality. You clearly do not fit the scientific stereotype of a cool, detached, rational being. But the fact that you are human should not deter you from thinking you can participate in science. It turns out that scientists are humans too! So how does science proceed if scientists are not special kinds of humans?

The key is to understand that the criteria of rationality and reasonableness are specifically emphasized with respect to product and process. The cartoon in Figure 2-1 illustrates the point. Here we have the scientist trying to work out some theory in mathematical form. He is making every effort to logically link the ideas together. As you can see, he comes up a little short!

This cartoon scientist is doing what all scientists do in their practice—the best they can. Scientists try to be rational; they try to be reasonable. They do the best they can in using the scientific *process*. They try to get their thinking straight; they try to gather and interpret empirical evidence fairly to test their ideas. But, as in the cartoon, their efforts often come up short. Whether a work meets the criteria of science is judged primarily on the *product*. Importantly, judgments of a product of science are in part based on judgments of the process that led to (i.e., produced) it. And, as in the cartoon, the

FIGURE 2-1 **Working toward a Rational Theory.**
Source: ScienceCartoonsPlus.com.

product assessment is done by others. Scientific advancement is a community enterprise. Individual researchers or teams do the best they can. Then they communicate, as transparently as possible, to the scientific community (via scientific publications, conferences, and the like) what they found (the product) and how (the process). Then others judge whether their thinking is rational and/or their conclusions reasonable.

In short, even with all your human faults, you are fully capable of participating in the scientific enterprise. With respect to rationality and reasonableness, all you need do is commit to trying to put these values into action in your work—to do the best you can. After that, others in the scientific community will be only too happy to point out your deficiencies and let you know whether you have successfully met the criteria.

In a related way, much confusion exists about the criterion of *objectivity* in scientific work. Here again we run up against the stereotype that claims scientists are supposedly "value-free" (or at least value-neutral), cool and detached from their work. How does this square with scientists being human? How is it even possible to be "free" of your values, objective rather than subjective?

Scientists—just like every human—are hopelessly subjective. They do their work using their eyes to look through a telescope, their hands to assess levels of stress in the neck, their nose to detect olfactory sensations, and their mind to determine if discrimination has occurred. And their minds, noses, hands, and eyes (indeed, all their senses) are imperfect. Some of these imperfections are rooted in biology (e.g., poor eyesight), others in socialization (e.g., racist attitudes). No matter what the cause, scientists are deformed, as everyone is. They experience the world the only way anyone can—as a subject.

There is no way out of this condition. We can only see through our own eyes, and anything peculiar to our eyes will shape what we see. We can only hear things the way our particular ears and brain transmit and interpret sound waves. Each of us has our own experiences.

So what do scientists mean when they talk about objectivity? **Objectivity** exists where multiple observations produce high intersubjective reliability. Unpacking this definition lets you see how an ordinary person like you can participate in scientific objectivity. The process begins with some subjective report (the only kind any person can provide). Let's say a student reports "My professor is a fool." This is merely a subjective statement, an opinion. Now imagine another student in the same class giving the same assessment of the professor, and then another, and another. Each of these reports is, by itself, subjective. But if we look between the reports (i.e., look intersubjectively), a pattern is present. And this pattern is reliable; it is consistent. This is what science means by objectivity. Science transforms subjective reports into objective ones by comparing reports and looking for consistency.

Despite the inescapable subjectivity of our experience, we humans seem to be wired to seek an agreement on what is *really real*—what is objectively so. Objectivity is a conceptual attempt to get beyond our individual views. It is ultimately a matter of communication, as we attempt to find a common ground in our subjective experiences. Whenever we succeed in our search, we say we are dealing with objective reality. This is the *agreement reality* discussed in Chapter 1.

While our subjectivity is individual, our search for objectivity is social. This is true in all aspects of life, not just in science. Although each of us may prefer different foods, we must agree to some extent on what is fit to eat and what is not, or else there could be no restaurants or grocery stores. The same argument could be made regarding every other form of consumption. Without agreement reality there could be no movies or television, and no sports.

Social scientists have also found benefits in the concept of a socially agreed-upon objective reality. As people try to impose order on their experience of life, they find it useful to pursue this goal as a collective venture. What are the causes of and cures for prejudice? Working together, social researchers have uncovered some answers that hold up to *intersubjective* scrutiny. Whatever your subjective experience of things, for example, you can discover for yourself that as education increases, prejudice generally tends to decrease. Since each of us can discover this independently, we say that it is objectively true.

The understanding that reality is a social construction is a comparatively recent appreciation. From the 17th century through the middle of the 20th century, the belief in an objective reality that was independent of individual perceptions predominated in science. This view rested on the belief in an independent reality waiting to be discovered, if only scientists could put aside their biases and see it objectively. For the most part, this view was not simply held as a useful paradigm but as The Truth. The term **positivism** has generally represented the belief in a logically ordered, objective reality that we can come to know better and better through science.

The positivistic view that an independent reality exists outside of human experience is largely discredited (Outhwaite 2006). In social science, many positivistic "truths" were actually agreements primarily among white, middle-class

objectivity A series of observations with high intersubjective reliability.

positivism The belief in an objective reality independent of human experience.

European men. Equally real experiences common to women, to ethnic minorities, to non-Western cultures, or to the poor were not necessarily represented in that reality.

Perhaps the following example will solidify your understanding of the important difference between discovering and creating reality. In the 1500s Michelangelo produced the incredibly beautiful statue called *Moses*. When asked about the production of his work, Michelangelo reported that all he did was chip the excess marble away to reveal the Moses that was locked inside the block (Bredemeier 1998). The idea that all Michelangelo did was "discover" the pre-existing Moses is, of course, only poetic. In fact, the sculpture began in Michelangelo's imagination. The sculptor's image of Moses was then transmitted into the marble block through dexterous hands endlessly chipping and polishing away. Michelangelo constructed *Moses* by creatively merging the concrete and the abstract. Moses wasn't there waiting to be discovered like some treat in a Kinder Surprise.

As always, reality depends on what you bring to experience. In science, the imaginations we bring to the construction of reality are rooted in the paradigms and theories. Let's now turn our attention to the latter.

ELEMENTS OF SOCIAL THEORY

As we have seen, paradigms are general theoretical frameworks or viewpoints—literally "points from which to view." They provide ways of looking at life and are grounded in sets of assumptions about the nature of reality.

Theories, by contrast, are systematic sets of interrelated statements intended to explain some aspect of social life. Thus, theories flesh out and specify paradigms. However, a paradigm offers a way of looking, whereas a theory aims at explaining what we see. More formally, a theory is a set of interrelated propositions used for understanding observed realities. The elements of this definition of theory can be tied to our discussion in Chapter 1 at several points, including the following.

theory A set of interrelated propositions used for understanding observed realities.

First, note that the components of a theory are propositions, which are statements expressing relationships between concepts. The building blocks of a theory are propositions or, in everyday language, ideas. The proposition "As the level of social inequality in a society grows, the health of its citizens declines" qualifies as a potential building block of a theory. Note that this proposition contains two concepts (social inequality and public health) and one relationship (the more of one, the less of the other).

Also notice that the concepts being connected in the example proposition are, like all concepts, imaginary. "Social inequality," like "public health," is an abstract term for organizing some set of concrete experiences. Social inequality is not the experience of a full stomach compared to an empty one, or the contrast between treated with respect and treated like a nobody. But the concept of social inequality certainly refers to, organizes, and helps us clearly categorize such experiences.

This understanding leads us to appreciate a second feature of theories: they are abstract. Theories are composed of propositions which, in turn, are generated from concepts. Since the concepts are abstract and the propositions are abstract, it follows that a theory using these pieces is abstract. Theories are generated in someone's mind. And when theorists share their theories they are effectively sharing what is in their mind.

Consider this set of abstract propositions:

- As the level of social inequality in a society grows, the health of its citizens declines.
- The more a student practises a musical instrument, the more competent she becomes.
- As group integration increases, individual happiness increases.

As you read these ideas, you probably don't get a sense that they compose a theory. Why not?

The problem is that these ideas are not coherent; they are not linked to one another. Taken together, they are irrational. This point leads us to a third feature of theories: the propositions (ideas) in a theory are interrelated. *Interrelated* means that the ideas are connected or knit together. And here we have another connection to what you learned in the last chapter. You may recall that the two fundamental features of science are that it tries to account for changes in real things (i.e., it is empirical) and that it is logical. The coherence of a theory, the interrelationships between its propositions, comes from logic. Logic is what knits together theoretical ideas. When a set of ideas have a logical connection the narrative is rational.

Here is another pair of theoretical propositions for you to consider (from Roberts et al. 2015):

Proposition 1: People living in societies with greater social inequality experience more stress.

Proposition 2: As people experience more stress, their health declines.

Now, take a minute and see if you can link together these two propositions to generate a new idea. In doing so, follow a sequence like that diagrammed in Figure 2-2.

As you can see, it was not particularly difficult to generate the new, third proposition: "People living in societies with greater social inequality experience poorer health." In following this process you have developed a rudimentary theory. You began with two ideas and, by thinking logically, you generated a new, third proposition. The three propositions are logically linked together. This set of interrelated propositions constitutes a theory.

You should now have a real sense of what it means to say that theories are composed of abstract propositions that are logically related to one another. When this occurs, theories tell a coherent story that systematically takes us from one idea to the next, from known propositions to new ones. All of which leads us to appreciate one final feature of theories: The object of scientific theories is to tell a story about events in the real world. Although the theories might be imaginary (abstract), they are directed at helping us understand real things. In this way, scientific theories differ from other kinds of theories. J. R. R. Tolkien's magnificent *The Lord of the Rings* is a wonderful, coherent story, but it is not about existing, empirical reality. You've never seen a real hobbit, have you?

Remember, a scientific theory is a story directed at helping us understand reality. Reality, as you learned previously, emerges where the abstract and concrete levels of experience merge. This has an important implication for scientific theories. It means that the concepts in Figure 2-2 must refer to empirical things. One way this is accomplished is by linking concepts to variables.

Variables are properties of objects that can change; they can be used as indicators of the imaginary concepts we have in mind. The result

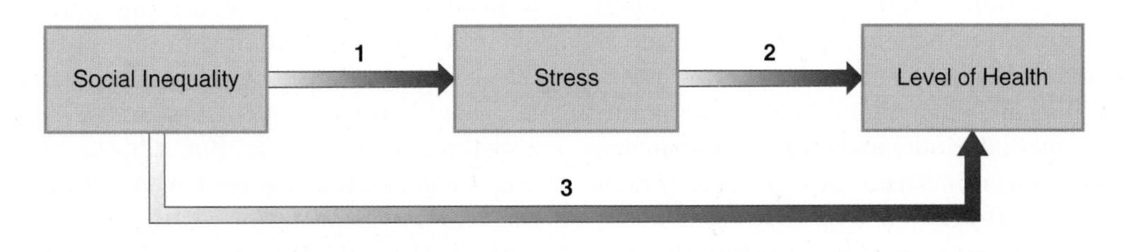

Proposition #	Concepts	Relationship
1	Social Inequality; Stress	More Social Inequality → More Stress
2	Stress; Level of Health	More Stress → Less Health
3	Social Inequality; Health	More Social Inequality → Less Health

FIGURE 2-2 **Interrelating Theoretical Propositions.** This set of propositions connecting concepts constitutes a theory.

of the theoretical thinking in the example in Figure 2-2 is the following idea: "People living in societies with greater social inequality experience poorer health." To be clear, the concepts in this theoretical proposition are (i) national inequality and (ii) community health, and the relationship is "the more of one, the less of the other." This theoretical proposition relating national inequality and community health is a fine idea, but, like all ideas, it is imaginary. Have you ever seen a national inequality or touched a community health? Of course not, which is just another way of emphasizing that these are abstract concepts.

For scientific theories to be connected to the real world, we must find a way of translating the concepts and relationships into observable, empirical experience. This is where variables enter the picture. Variables are used in theories as indicators of the concepts under consideration. The process of linking concepts to variables is called **operationalization**.

Let's stick with our example using national inequality and community health. By themselves, these concepts are meaningful yet abstract. We certainly have some idea in mind when we use either of these terms, but their referents are vague. Clarification occurs if we specify a variable that indicates what we have in mind when we use the concept. For example, "national inequality" might be indicated by a variable such as "the proportion of national wealth controlled by the richest 10 percent of the population." Societies where the richest people control a greater proportion of resources are more unequal than societies where they control a smaller share. Likewise, "community health" might be indicated by a variable such as rates of cancer. Societies with high cancer rates are less healthy than ones with lower rates. By operationalizing concepts, scientific theories are pointed in the direction of reality. Figure 2-3 takes the theoretical proposition "People living in societies with greater social inequality experience poorer health" and diagrams its operationalization.

Several things about this diagram are worth noting. First, we begin with the two concepts (national inequality, community health) and the proposition that relates them at the abstract level. Second, each of the concepts is indicated by a variable. The vertical arrows in the figure are operationalizations; they tell us what we might examine in the real world to get a sense of the concepts under consideration. Notice that the variables are below the concepts in the diagram, which indicates they are directed toward concrete experience.

Figure 2-3 indicates another very important process related to the development and testing of scientific theories. This process relates to the numbers connected to each of the arrows. Let's begin at the top, with the horizontal arrow labelled "1." This relationship is the original, abstract theoretical proposition. The vertical arrows (labelled "2") connecting each of the proposition's concepts to variables are operationalizations. Notice that there is another horizontal arrow ("3") in the figure. This arrow expresses a relationship between variables and is called a hypothesis.

Most students in school learn to call a hypothesis an "educated guess." Figure 2-3 lets you understand what this catchy phrase actually means. A hypothesis is not a wild guess; it is an educated one. The "education" part of the hypothetical anticipation comes from the fact that it is derived from a theory. A hypothesis is informed by theoretical thinking; it is backed by a systematic set of ideas. But still, the hypothesis is a guess. It is a guess because it exists at the realm of expectation. A **hypothesis** provides a theoretically informed expectation about empirical patterns. But it is "hypothetical"; whether the hypothetical expectation is confirmed by concrete experience is another matter.

Figure 2-3 shows how a theoretical proposition (arrow 1) uses operationalization (arrows 2) to generate a hypothesis (arrow 3). This translation of a theoretical proposition into a research

operationalization The process of translating abstract concepts into variables that indicate the concepts.

hypothesis A theoretically informed expectation about empirical patterns expressed as a relationship between variables.

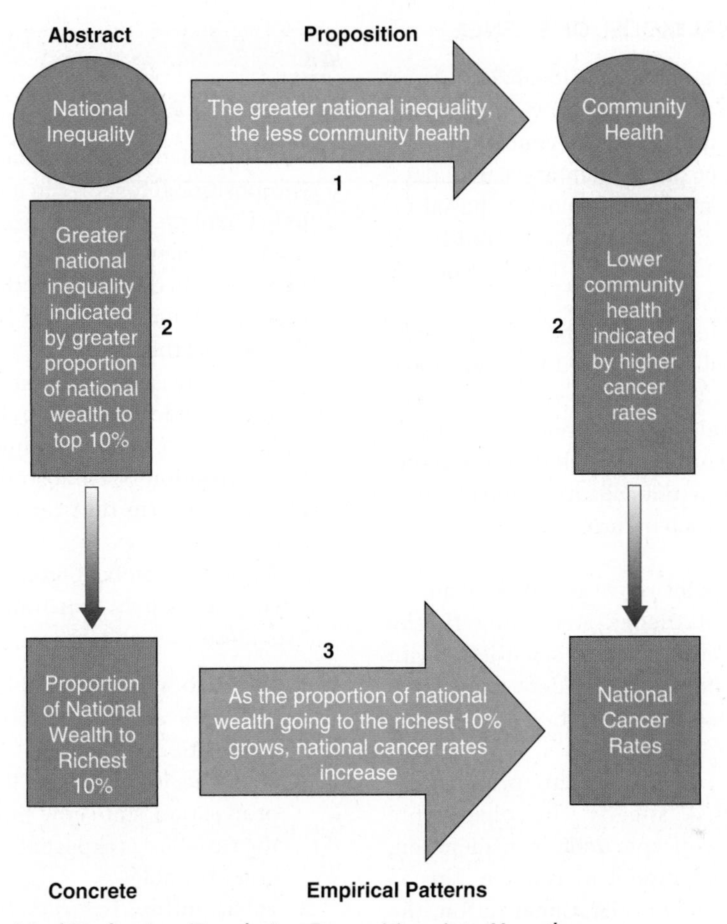

FIGURE 2-3 **Empirical Deduction: Translating Propositions into Hypotheses.**

hypothesis occurs through a process called **empirical deduction.** To see how this works, let's list the propositions in Figure 2-3.

1. Societies with greater national inequality experience poorer community health.

2.1. Greater national inequality is indicated by a greater proportion of the society's wealth going to the richest 10 percent of the population.

2.2. Greater community health is indicated by lower rates of cancer.

Can you see how these three ideas can be joined to produce the following hypothesis? *As the proportion of a society's wealth going to the richest 10 percent grows, the national rates of cancer grow.* This empirical deduction used the following logic:

- **If** societies with greater national inequality experience poorer community health, and
- **If** greater national inequality is indicated by a greater proportion of national wealth going to the richest 10 percent, and
- **If** poorer community health is indicated by higher national cancer rates,
- **Then** we expect that societies with a greater proportion of national wealth going to the richest 10 percent will have higher cancer rates.

TWO LOGICAL SYSTEMS REVISITED

In Chapter 1, we introduced deductive and inductive theory with a promise that we would return to them later. It's later.

empirical deduction The logical process for transforming a theoretical proposition into a research hypothesis.

THE TRADITIONAL MODEL OF SCIENCE

Most of us have a somewhat idealized picture of the "scientific method." It is a view gained as a result of the physical science education we've received ever since our elementary-school days. This traditional model of science is based on **hypothesis testing**. Although this traditional model of science tells only a part of the story, it's helpful to understand its logic.

The discussion of elements of a scientific theory in the last section used the traditional model of science. There are three main elements in the traditional model of science, typically presented in the order in which they are implemented: theory, operationalization, and observation. Let's review each in turn.

Theory At this point you're already acquainted with the idea of theory. According to the traditional model of science, scientists begin with a theory, from which they derive new ideas (propositions) that they can test.

Operationalization To test any proposition, researchers must specify the observable indicators of the concepts under consideration. In the traditional model of science, this is accomplished through operationalization, the process that selects variables as indicators of concepts. Once appropriate indicators (variables) are selected, the process of empirical deduction is used to translate an abstract theoretical proposition into a research hypothesis. (See the How to Do It box "Framing a Research Hypothesis" for more on hypothesis creation.)

Observation Look at the diagram in Figure 2-3 again and notice that the empirical deduction process moves the focus of attention from the abstract level toward the concrete level. Although empirical deduction inches us toward the patterns of empirical experience, we are still not there. In order to observe the operation of variables in the real world, we need some way

hypothesis testing Determining whether the expectations specified in a hypothesis are confirmed by concrete, empirical patterns.

HOW TO DO IT

Framing a Research Hypothesis

Scientific theories systematically link ideas (propositions) together in a narrative that helps explain empirical observations. In doing so, scientific theories often generate new ideas. In deciding whether or not new theoretical ideas are worth keeping, scientists subject them to empirical testing. Since scientific ideas are imaginary, they need to be translated into a researchable form in order to be tested. Hypotheses represent the translation of an abstract theoretical idea into a form that can be empirically tested.

Given a theoretical proposition, the following steps help you frame a research hypothesis:

1. **Indicators:** Select variables that are good indicators of the concepts in the proposition.
2. **Hypothesis statement:** Based on the proposition, state how changing one of the variables is expected to change the other variable.
3. **Falsifiability:** To ensure falsifiability, imagine empirical evidence that would disconfirm the hypothesis (i.e., that would permit a "test" of the hypothesis).

Let's apply this to the proposition "Educated people are wealthier people."

1. **Indicators:** "Highest grade completed" to indicate education; "Reported taxable income" to indicate wealth.
2. **Hypothesis:** As highest grade completed increases, the reported taxable income increases.
3. **Falsifiability:** It is possible to imagine that the empirical evidence might show some pattern other than that predicted by the hypothesis.

of connecting them to the concrete level. This is what traditional science means by observation.

Measurement involves quantifying observations by assigning numbers to attributes composing a variable. If I observe you have blue eyes, I have determined what attribute (numerical score or value) you (the object under consideration) have on the variable "eye colour." Similarly, if you answer "10 hours" to the survey question "How many hours a week did you spend studying for school last week?" then that score is your measurement on the variable "hours spent studying," and it can be compared to another respondent's score on the same variable.

An **operational definition** spells out the procedures ("operations") for measuring a concept. Since concepts are at the abstract level and measurements are at the concrete level, operational definitions are the procedures used for linking these levels of experience.

Note that when an operational definition is complete, the abstract, conceptual level has been linked to the concrete, empirical level. Through operational definition something imaginary is expressed as something concrete. The traditional methods of scientific research rely heavily on operational definitions, since their model is deductive and organized around the idea of hypothesis testing. We will have much more to say about operationalization in Chapter 5. For now, we can give you a sense of what these procedures mean by way of example.

To solidify your understanding of the steps in an operational definition, let's revisit the example in Figure 2-3. Recall that the theoretical proposition in Figure 2-3 was that societies with greater *national inequality* experience poorer *community health*. These two concepts were then operationalized. "National inequality" was operationally defined as the proportion of national wealth controlled by the richest 10 percent of the population. "Community health" was operationally defined as rates of cancer. Each country will have a score on the national inequality indicator variable (i.e., the proportion of national wealth concentrated in the top 10 percent), and each country will have a score on the community health indicator variable (e.g., the number of cancer cases per 100,000 people). A country's score on an indicator variable is a measurement.

Thus, at the empirical level, the hypothesis is between indicator variables: *As the proportion of a society's wealth going to the richest 10 percent increases, the national rate of cancer increases.* If the data fit this pattern, it suggests that the hypothesized relationship between the variables is true.

It is important to note that for the researcher testing a hypothesis, the meaning of variables is exactly and only what the operational definition specifies.

In this respect, scientists are very much like Humpty Dumpty in Lewis Carroll's *Through the Looking Glass*. "When I use a word," Humpty Dumpty tells Alice, "it means just what I choose it to mean—neither more nor less."

"The question is," Alice replies, "whether you can make words mean so many different things." To which Humpty Dumpty responds, "The question is, which is to be master—that's all" (1872/1999).

Scientists have to be "masters" of their operational definitions for the sake of precision in observation, measurement, and communication. Otherwise, we would never know whether a study that contradicted ours did so only because it used a different set of procedures to measure one of the variables and thus changed the meaning of the hypothesis being tested. Of course, this also means that to evaluate a study's conclusions about national inequality and community health, or any other variables, we need to know the operational definitions of the concepts under consideration.

Exactly how were the concepts operationalized? For example, there are other possible ways to operationalize national inequality and community health (each with particular strengths and limitations). Other possible community health indicators you could choose include incidence of low birth weight, obesity, or life expectancy. A researcher may decide to use one of these or a combination of these to operationalize

---

measurement The process of quantifying observations by assigning numbers to attributes composing a variable.

operational definition The specific steps ("operations") of measuring abstract concepts at the concrete level.

---

community health rather than cancer rates. Similarly, national inequality could also be measured by alternative or additional indicators, such as income inequality or poverty rate. There are many operationalization choices to be made. We'll consider such issues, including the merits of using multiple indicators, in detail in Part 2.

Disconfirmability or the possibility of falsification is an essential quality of a good hypothesis in the traditional model of science. **Falsification** refers to the possibility of evidence negating the hypothesis. The basic idea is this: If there is no chance that a hypothesis can be disconfirmed, it hasn't said anything meaningful. In other words, a hypothesis must be testable; it must make predictions (relationships between variables) that we can test against observation (i.e., the empirical evidence). You can't test whether a hypothesis is true unless your test contains the possibility of deciding it's false (i.e., disconfirmed by the evidence). The hypothesis in Figure 2-3 met this criterion because it predicted a relationship between variables that could be measured and tested.

DEDUCTIVE AND INDUCTIVE REASONING: AN ILLUSTRATION

The traditional model of science just described uses deductive reasoning. From a general theoretical understanding, the researcher derives (deduces) expectations and finally testable hypotheses. It's neat and clean. But, in reality, science uses inductive reasoning also. W. I. B. Beveridge (1950:113), a philosopher of science, describes these two systems of logic in a way that should already seem familiar to you:

> Logicians distinguish between inductive reasoning (from particular instances to general principles, from facts to theories) and deductive reasoning (from the general to the particular, applying a theory to a particular case). In induction one starts from observed data and develops a generalization which explains the relationships between the objects observed. On the other hand, in deductive reasoning one starts from some general law and applies it to a particular instance.

falsification The criterion that it is possible for empirical evidence to disconfirm a hypothesis.

Let's consider a real research example as a vehicle for comparing the deductive and inductive linkages between theory and research. Years ago, Charles Glock, Benjamin Ringer, and Earl Babbie set out to discover what caused differing levels of church involvement among U.S. Episcopalians. Several theoretical or quasi-theoretical positions suggested possible answers. We'll focus on only one here, which came to be called the Comfort Hypothesis.

In part, we took our lead from the Christian injunction to care for "the halt, the lame, and the blind" and those who are "weary and heavy laden." At the same time, ironically, we noted the Marxist assertion that religion is an "opiate for the masses." Given both, it made sense to expect the following, which was our hypothesis: "Parishioners whose life situations most deprive them of satisfaction and fulfillment in the secular society turn to the church for comfort and substitute rewards" (Glock et al. 1967:107–108).

Having framed this general proposition, we set about testing it. Were those deprived of satisfaction in the secular society in fact more religious than those who received more satisfaction from the secular society? To answer this, we needed to distinguish who was deprived. The questionnaire, which was constructed to test the Comfort Hypothesis, included variables that seemed to offer indicators of whether parishioners were relatively deprived or gratified in secular society.

To start, we reasoned that men enjoyed more status than women in our generally male-dominated society. Though hardly a novel conclusion in itself, it laid the groundwork for testing the Comfort Hypothesis. If the proposition was correct, women should appear more religious than men. Once the survey data had been collected and analyzed, the expectation about gender and religion was clearly confirmed. On three separate measures of religious involvement—*ritual* (such as church attendance), *organizational* (such as belonging to church organizations), and *intellectual* (such as reading church publications)—women were more religious than men. On the overall measure, women scored 50 percent higher than men.

In another test of the Comfort Hypothesis, we reasoned that in a youth-oriented society, old people would be more deprived of secular gratification than would the young. Once again, the data confirmed our expectation. The oldest parishioners were more religious than the middle aged, who were more religious than the young adults.

Social class—measured by *education* and *income*—afforded another test of the Comfort Hypothesis. Once again, the test was successful. Those with low social status were more involved in the church than those with high social status.

The hypothesis was even confirmed in a test that went against everyone's common-sense expectations. Despite church posters showing worshipful young families and bearing the slogan "The Family That Prays Together Stays Together," the Comfort Hypothesis suggested that parishioners who were married and had children—the clear American ideal at that time—would enjoy secular gratification in that regard. As a consequence, they should be *less* religious than those who lacked one or both family components. Thus, we hypothesized that parishioners who were both single and childless should be the most religious, those with either spouse or child should be somewhat less religious, and those married with children—representing the ideal pictured on all those posters—should be least religious of all. That's exactly what we found!

Finally, the Comfort Hypothesis suggested that the various kinds of secular deprivation should be cumulative: those with all the characteristics associated with deprivation should be the most religious, and those with none should be the least. When the four individual measures of deprivations were combined into a composite measure, the theoretical expectation was exactly confirmed. Comparing the two extremes, we found that single, childless, old, lower-class female parishioners scored more than three times as high on the measure of church involvement than did young, married, upper-class fathers. Thus, the Comfort Hypothesis was confirmed.

This research example clearly illustrates the logic of the deductive model. Beginning with general, theoretical propositions about the impact of social deprivation on church involvement, it was possible to derive concrete hypotheses linking specific measurable variables, such as age and church attendance. The actual empirical data were then analyzed to determine whether the deductive expectations were supported by empirical reality.

This example shows how it was possible to do it that way, but, alas, we've been fibbing a little bit just now. To tell the truth, although the study began with an interest in discovering what caused variations in church involvement among Episcopalians, it wasn't actually begun with a Comfort Hypothesis, or any other hypothesis for that matter. A questionnaire was designed to collect information from parishioners that *might* shed some light on why some participated in the church more than others, but questionnaire construction was not guided by any precise, deductive theory. In fact, the original investigation was exploratory and used an inductive approach.

Once the data were collected, the task of explaining differences in religiosity began with an analysis of variables that have a wide impact on people's lives, including *gender, age, social class,* and *family status.* Each of these four variables was found to relate strongly to church involvement in the ways already described. Indeed, they had a cumulative effect, also already described. Rather than being good news, this presented a dilemma.

Glock discussed his findings with colleagues. Once he had displayed the tables illustrating the impact of each individual variable as well as their powerful composite effect, a colleague asked, "What does it all mean, Charlie?" Glock was at a loss. Why were those variables so strongly related to church involvement?

That question launched a process of reasoning about what the several variables had in common, aside from their impact on religiosity. Eventually, there was recognition that each of the four variables also reflected *differential status in the secular society,* and then the thought developed that perhaps the issue of comfort was involved. Thus, the inductive process had moved from concrete observations to a general theoretical explanation.

A GRAPHIC CONTRAST

Theory and research can usefully be done both inductively and deductively, as the preceding illustration shows. Figure 2-4 presents a graphic comparison of the two approaches applied to an investigation of study habits and exam performance. In both cases, we are interested in the relationship between the number of hours spent studying for an exam and the grade earned on that exam. Using the deductive method, we would begin by examining the matter logically. Doing well on an exam reflects a student's ability to recall and manipulate information. Both of these abilities should be increased by exposure to the information before the exam. In this fashion, we would arrive at a hypothesis suggesting a positive relationship between the number of hours

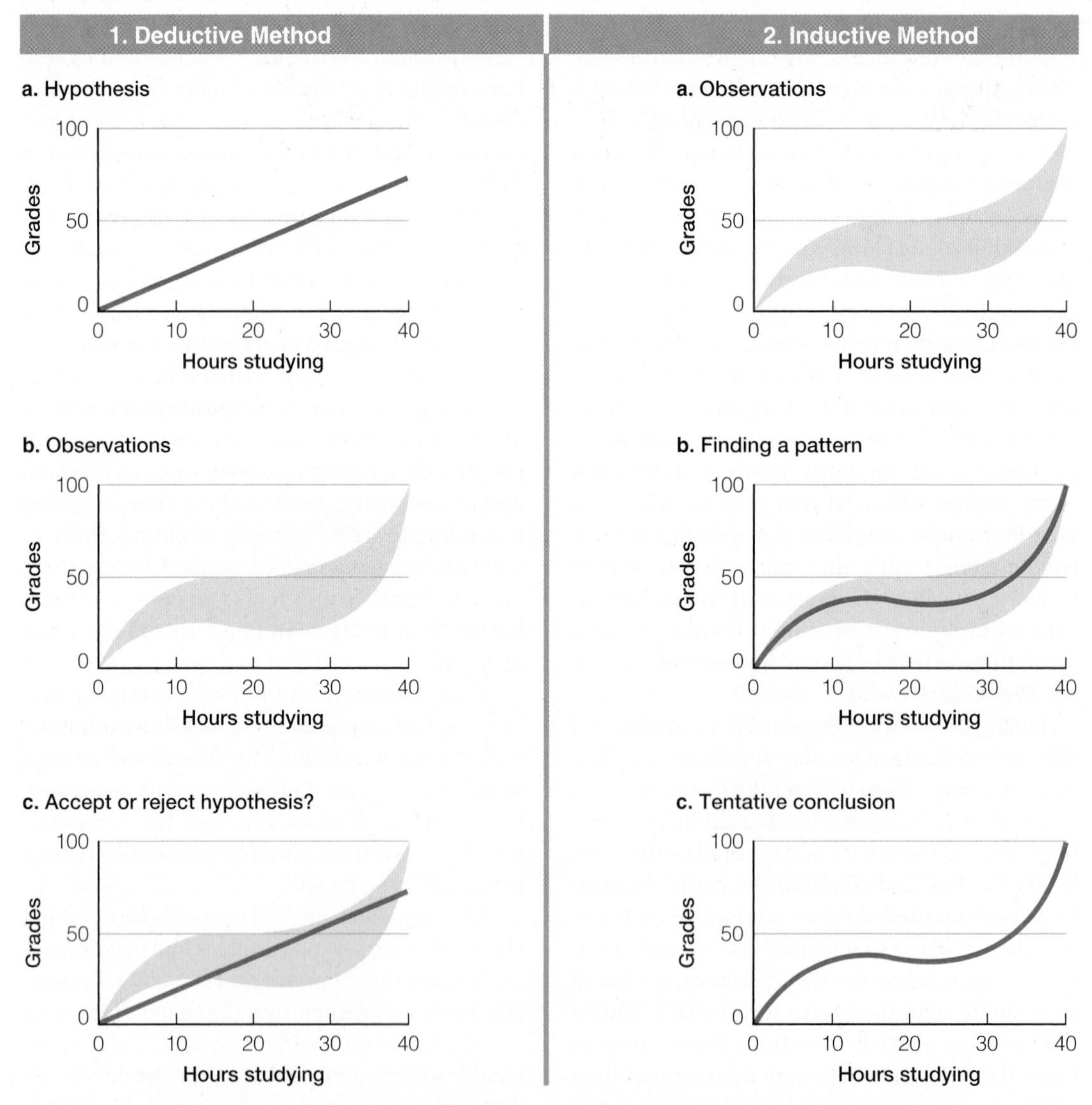

FIGURE 2-4 Deductive and Inductive Methods. "Both deduction and induction are legitimate and valuable approaches to understanding. Deduction begins with an expected pattern that is tested against observations, whereas induction begins with observations and seeks to find a pattern within them."
Source: © Cengage Learning

spent studying and the grade earned on the exam. We say *positive* because we expect grades to increase as the hours of studying increase. If increased hours produced decreased grades, that would be called a *negative*, or inverse, relationship. The hypothesis is represented by the line in part 1(a) of Figure 2-4.

Our next step would be to make observations relevant to testing our hypothesis. The shaded area in part 1(b) of the figure represents perhaps hundreds of observations of different students, noting how many hours they studied and what grades they received. Finally, in part 1(c), we compare the hypothesis and the observations. Because observations in the real world seldom if ever match our expectations perfectly, we must decide whether the match is close enough to consider the hypothesis confirmed. Put differently, can we conclude that the hypothesis describes the general pattern that exists, granting some variations in real life? To determine this, it is sometimes necessary to conduct a statistical analysis (we will look at this type of analysis in Part 4 of this book).

Now suppose we used the inductive method to address the same research question. In this case we would begin with a set of observations, as in Figure 2-4, part 2(a). Curious about the relationship between hours spent studying and grades earned, we might simply arrange to collect relevant data. Then we'd look for a pattern that best represented or summarized our observations. In part 2(b) of the figure, the pattern is shown as a curved line running through the centre of the curving mass of points.

The pattern found among the points in this case suggests that with 1 to 15 hours of studying, each additional hour generally produces a higher grade on the exam. With 15 to about 25 hours, however, more study seems to slightly lower the grade. Studying more than 25 hours, on the other hand, results in a return to the initial pattern: more hours produce higher grades. Using the inductive method, then, we end up with a *tentative* conclusion about the pattern of the relationship between the two variables. The conclusion is tentative because the observations we have made cannot be taken as a test of the pattern—those observations are the *source* of the pattern we've created.

In practice, theory and research interact through a never-ending alternation of deduction and induction. Walter Wallace (1971) has represented this process nicely as a circle, which is presented in a modified form in Figure 2-5. Émile Durkheim's classic work on suicide ([1897] 1951) provides a good example of this. When he pored over table after table of official statistics on suicide rates in different areas, he was struck by the fact that Protestant countries consistently had higher suicide rates than Catholic ones. Why should that be the case? His initial observations led him to create, inductively, a theory of religion, social integration, anomie, and suicide. His theoretical explanations then led deductively to further hypotheses and further observations.

In summary, the scientific norm of logical reasoning provides a two-way bridge between theory and research. In practice, scientific inquiry typically involves alternating between deduction and induction. During the deductive phase, we reason *toward* observations; during the inductive phase, we reason *from* observations. Both approaches involve an interplay of logic and observation. And both are routes to the construction of social theories.

Although both inductive and deductive methods are valid in scientific inquiry, individuals may feel more comfortable with one approach than the other. Consider this exchange in Sir Arthur Conan Doyle's *A Scandal in Bohemia*,

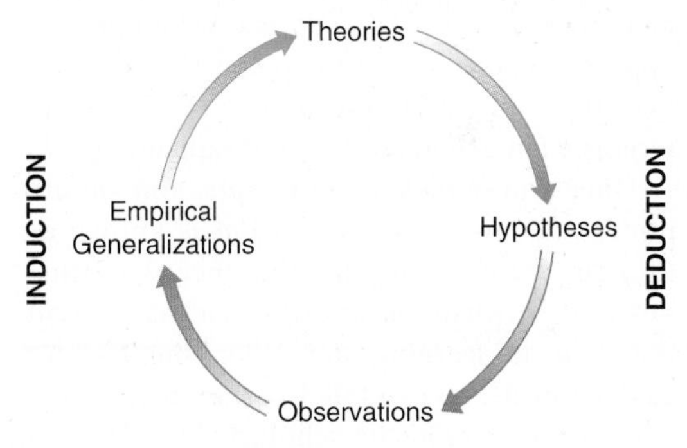

FIGURE 2-5 The Wheel of Science. The theory and research cycle can be compared to a relay race; although all participants do not necessarily start or stop at the same point, they share a common goal—to examine all levels of social life.

Source: Adapted from Walter Wallace, *The Logic of Science in Sociology* (Hawthorne, NY: Aldine, 1971).

as Sherlock Holmes answers Dr. Watson's inquiry (Doyle [1891] 1892:13):

> "What do you imagine that it means?"
>
> "I have no data yet. It is a capital mistake to theorise before one has data. Insensibly one begins to twist facts to suit theories, instead of theories to suit facts."

Some social scientists would more or less agree with this inductive position (see especially the discussions of grounded theory in Chapters 10 and 13), while others would take a more deductive stance. Most, however, concede the legitimacy of both approaches.

Now that we've completed our overview of the deductive and inductive linkages between theory and research, let's look a little deeper into how theories are constructed using these two different approaches.

DEDUCTIVE THEORY CONSTRUCTION

What's involved in deductive theory construction and hypothesis testing? Let's look at how you might go about constructing such a theory.

GETTING STARTED

The first step in deductive theory construction is to pick a topic that interests you. It can be very broad, such as "What's the structure of society?" or narrower, as in "Why do people support or oppose a woman's right to an abortion?" Whatever the topic, it should be something you're interested in understanding and explaining.

Once you've picked your topic, you should undertake an inventory of what is known or thought about it. In part, this means writing down your own observations and ideas. Beyond that, it means learning what other scholars have said about it. You can talk to other people, and you'll want to read the scholarly literature on the topic.

Your preliminary research will probably uncover consistent patterns discovered by prior scholars. For example, religious and political variables will stand out as important determinants of attitudes about abortion. Findings such as these will be very useful to you in creating your own theory.

In this process, don't overlook the value of introspection. If you can look at your own personal processes—including reactions, fears, and prejudices—you may be able to gain important insights into human behaviour in general. We are by no means saying that everyone thinks like you, but introspection can be a useful source of insights that may inform our inquiries.

CONSTRUCTING YOUR THEORY

With knowledge of previous work on the topic, you can begin constructing your theory. Although theory construction is not a lockstep affair, the following steps should help organize the activity for you:

1. Specify the topic.
2. Specify the range of phenomena your theory addresses. Will your theory apply to all of human social life, only to Canadian citizens, only to young people, and so on.
3. Identify and specify your major concepts and variables.
4. Find out what is known (propositions) about the relationships among those variables.
5. Reason logically from those propositions to the specific topic you are examining.

We've already discussed items (1) through (3), so let's focus now on (4) and (5). As you identify the relevant concepts and discover what has already been learned about them, you can begin to create a propositional structure that explains the topic under study.

Let's look now at an example of how these building blocks fit together in actual deductive theory construction and empirical research.

AN EXAMPLE OF DEDUCTIVE THEORY: DISTRIBUTIVE JUSTICE

A topic of central interest to scholars is the concept of *distributive justice*, people's perceptions of whether they're being treated fairly by life—whether they are getting "their share." Guillermina Jasso describes the theory of distributive justice more formally, as follows:

> The theory provides a mathematical description of the process whereby individuals, reflecting on their holdings of the goods they value (such as beauty, intelligence, or wealth), compare themselves to others, experiencing a fundamental instantaneous magnitude of the justice evaluation (*J*), which captures their sense of being fairly or unfairly treated in the distributions of natural and social goods.
>
> (Jasso 1988:11)

Notice that Jasso has assigned a symbolic representation for her key variable: *J* will stand for distributive justice. She does this to support her intention to state her theory in mathematical formulas. Though theories are often expressed mathematically, we'll not delve too deeply into that practice here.

Jasso indicates that there are three kinds of postulates in her theory. "The first makes explicit the fundamental axiom which represents the substantive point of departure for the theory." She elaborates as follows:

> The theory begins with the received Axiom of Comparison, which formalizes the long-held view that a wide class of phenomena, including happiness, self-esteem, and the sense of distributive justice, may be understood as the product of a comparison process.
>
> (Jasso 1988:11)

Thus, your sense of whether you are receiving a "fair" share of the good things of life comes from comparing yourself with others. If this seems obvious to you, that's not a shortcoming of the axiom. **Axioms** are the taken-for-granted beginnings of theory.

Jasso continues to lay the groundwork for her theory. First, she indicates that our sense of distributive justice is a function of "Actual Holdings (*A*)" and "Comparison Holdings (*C*)" of some good. Let's consider money, for example. A person's sense of justice in this regard is a function of how much she actually has (*A*), compared with how much others have (*C*). By specifying the two components of the comparison, Jasso can use them as variables in her theory.

Jasso then offers a "measurement rule" that further specifies how the two variables, *A* and *C*, will be conceptualized. This step is needed because some of the goods to be examined are concrete and commonly measured (such as money) whereas others are less tangible (such as respect). The former kind, she says, will be measured conventionally, whereas the latter will be measured "by the individual's relative rank ... within a specially selected comparison group" (1988:13). The theory will provide a formula for making that measurement.

Jasso continues in this fashion to introduce additional elements, weaving them into mathematical formulas to be used in deriving predictions about the workings of distributive justice in a variety of social settings. Here is just a sampling of where her theorizing takes her (1988:14–15):

- Other things [being] the same, a person will prefer to steal from a fellow group member rather than from an outsider.
- The preference to steal from a fellow group member is more pronounced in poor groups than in rich groups.
- In the case of theft, informants arise only in cross-group theft, in which case they are members of the thief's group.
- Persons who arrive a week late at summer camp or for freshman year of college are more likely to become friends of persons who play games of chance than of persons who play games of skill.
- In wartime, the favorite leisure-time activity of soldiers is playing games of chance.
- A society becomes more vulnerable to deficit spending as its wealth increases.
- Societies in which population growth is welcomed must be societies in which the set of valued goods includes at least one quantity-good, such as wealth.

These propositions should provide a good sense of where deductive theorizing can take you. To gain a sense of how she reasons her way to these propositions, let's look briefly at the logic involved

axioms Theoretical propositions that are assumed to be true.

in the first and third propositions, relating to theft within and outside one's group.

Beginning with the assumption that thieves want to maximize their relative wealth, ask yourself whether that goal would be best served by stealing from those you compare yourself with or from outsiders. In each case, stealing will increase your Actual Holdings, but what about your Comparison Holdings? If you think about it, you'll see that stealing from people in your comparison group will *lower* their holdings, further increasing your *relative* wealth.

To simplify, imagine there are only two people in your comparison group: you and Sally. Suppose each of you has $100. If you steal $50 from someone outside your group, you will have increased your relative wealth by 50 percent compared with Sally: $150 versus $100. But if you steal $50 from Sally, you will have increased your relative wealth 200 percent: $150 to Sally's $50. Your goal is best served by stealing from within the comparison group; hence, the first proposition.

Regarding the third proposition, can you see why it would make sense for informants (1) to arise only in the case of cross-group theft and (2) to come from the thief's comparison group? This proposition again depends on the fundamental assumption that everyone wants to increase his or her relative standing. Suppose you and Sally are in the same comparison group, but this time the group contains more people. If you steal from someone else in your comparison group, Sally's relative standing in the group does not change. Although your wealth has increased, the average wealth in the group remains the same (because someone else's wealth has decreased by the same amount), so Sally's relative standing remains the same. Sally has no incentive to inform on you.

If you steal from someone outside your comparison group, however, your nefarious income increases the total wealth in your group. This means that Sally's wealth relative to that total is diminished. Since Sally's relative wealth has suffered, she's more likely to bring an end to your stealing by informing on you. Therefore, cross-group theft produces informants.

This last deduction also begins to explain why these informants are more likely to come from within the thief's comparison group. We've just seen how Sally's relative standing was decreased by your theft. How about members of the other group (other than the person you stole from)? Each of them would actually profit from the theft, since you would have reduced the total with which they compare themselves. Thus, they have no reason to inform on you. Hence, the theory of distributive justice predicts that informants arise from the thief's own comparison group.

This brief and selective look at Jasso's derivations should give you some sense of the enterprise of deductive theory. Of course, the theory doesn't guarantee the truth of any of the given predictions. The role of research is to test each of them empirically to determine whether what makes sense (logic) actually occurs in reality (observation).

There are two important elements in science, then: logical integrity and empirical verification. Both are essential to scientific inquiry and discovery. Logic alone is not enough, but on the other hand, the mere observation and collection of empirical facts does not provide understanding—the reading on your pedometer, for example, is not a scientific conclusion. Observation, however, can be the springboard for the construction of a social scientific theory, as we'll now see in the case of inductive theory.

INDUCTIVE THEORY CONSTRUCTION

As we've noted, social scientists often begin constructing a theory through the inductive method by observing aspects of social life and then seeking to discover patterns that may point to relatively universal principles.

Field research (see Chapter 10)—the direct observation of events in progress—is frequently used to develop theories using inductive reasoning (see Chapter 13 for further details on inductive approaches to qualitative data analysis).

Among contemporary social scientists, no one was more adept at seeing the patterns of human behaviour through observation than the Alberta-born sociologist Erving Goffman (1974:5):

> A game such as chess generates a habitable universe for those who can follow it, a plane

> of being, a cast of characters with a seemingly unlimited number of different situations and acts through which to realize their natures and destinies. Yet much of this is reducible to a small set of interdependent rules and practices. If the meaningfulness of everyday activity is similarly dependent on a closed, finite set of rules, then explication of them would give one a powerful means of analyzing social life.

In a variety of research efforts, Goffman uncovered the rules of such diverse behaviours as living in a mental institution (1961) and managing the "spoiled identity" of disfiguration (1963). In each case, Goffman observed the phenomenon in depth and teased out the rules governing behaviour. Goffman's research provides an excellent example of qualitative field research as a source of inductive theory construction.

As indicated by the search for causes of church involvement, qualitative field research is not the only method of observation appropriate to the development of inductive theory. Here's another example to illustrate further the construction of inductive theory using quantitative methods.

AN EXAMPLE OF INDUCTIVE THEORY: MULTIPLE KILLINGS

The news regularly reports incidents of multiple killings. Although most common in the United States, this tragic phenomenon is evident around the globe, including occurrences in Norway, Finland, Australia, Scotland, Germany, Canada, and England (Associated Press 2012). Each multiple killing is a unique event and its circumstances account for most of the news coverage. Reporters inform us about whatever details of the killer's life they can find on social media, in public records, and through interviews with neighbours, co-workers, friends, and family. Although fascinating and informative, these reports tell us little about what commonly drives these fatal acts. Telling that story requires a theory.

The sociologist Neil Websdale (2010) undertook the challenge of trying to discern the roots of multiple killings by carefully examining a large number of specific cases. The cases he chose were instances of familicide, the class of multiple killing in which one spouse or partner kills the other and one or more of their children. His approach was inductive and involved studying 211 cases from around the world. Although there were some earlier cases, most of the cases occurred since 1970. His work is documented in his insightful book *Familicidal Hearts: The Emotional Styles of 211 Killers.*

Websdale is a key researcher in the National Domestic Violence Fatality Review Initiative, which provided him access to a wide range of data sources. Although the early examples of familicide were documented through newspaper reports, the ones in recent decades included a rich range of data sources, including police investigation reports and persons who knew the family. From these data sources Websdale constructed a large database in which he rated, ranked, and reviewed each of the 211 cases on a wide range of variables. Websdale conducted the inductive search for patterns among familicidal killings from this database.

The details of the cases make for disturbing reading and the theoretical insights of Websdale's findings are nuanced. However, there are two core points of note. The first is the role of gender. Of the 211 cases, 196 of the killers were male and 15 were female. This stunning difference is in line with the central role gender plays in all forms of violence. The fact that it is largely a male phenomenon should give us pause to reflect on socialization patterns and gender roles. Digging deeper, Websdale found that the key drivers of familicidal killing were emotional. Although many emotions were present the central one was shame.

In all of the cases for which Websdale had sufficient data, deep shame was present. Shame is the "master emotion" because it is at the core of all social experience (Scheff 2014). Shame signifies disconnection—a break or threatened break in the social bond. Where shame is experienced, alienation is present. This second pattern found by Websdale's inductive analysis points to the important role earlier shame plays in violent outbursts. Shaming others severs the bonds through which we support and influence one another and, in doing so, provides a path to uncontrolled emotions, like rage, and uncontrolled conduct, like multiple killing.

Websdale's study illustrates how useful theoretical generalizations can be induced from carefully observing empirical evidence and search for common patterns. Through such investigations we come to understand the general structures that underwrite specific cases. This is important because it allows us to turn our attention to developing interventions that get at the root of the problem. In Websdale's case, there is a growing network of cities using his research findings to develop public policies aimed at reducing domestic violence.

THE LINKS BETWEEN THEORY AND RESEARCH

Before turning to inspirations for research agendas, we want to briefly consider the relationship between theory and research in social scientific inquiry. We have discussed the idealized, logical models of induction and deduction. These are highly useful, but in practice social scientific research has developed many variations on these themes. As you will see, sometimes theoretical issues are introduced merely as a backdrop for empirical analyses. Other studies cite selected empirical data to strengthen theoretical arguments. In neither case is there really an interaction between theory and research for the purpose of developing new explanations. Not all social science research is tightly linked to social theory—sometimes theory is more implicit. For example, some studies are conducted in order to determine whether a social program is effective or to find out the general public's opinion on any number of issues, like abortion or who is likely to win the next election. Still other research, like descriptive ethnography, is done to provide useful information and insights.

Most often, however, social science researchers are conscious of the implications of their research for social theories and vice versa. In practice, there are many ways of going about social inquiry and linking theory and research.

There's no simple recipe for conducting social science research. It is far more open-ended than the traditional view of science suggests. Ultimately, science rests on two pillars: logic and observation. As you'll see throughout this book, they can be fit together in many patterns.

INSPIRATIONS FOR RESEARCH AGENDAS

Sitting at a major junior hockey game in Alberta with her husband, psychologist Roger Barnsley, Paula Barnsley saw a potential pattern when looking at the game program. Reading the roster of players, she noticed that a disproportionate number of the boys on the team were born in the first few months of the year. After she and her husband looked into the matter a bit more, they and a colleague, A. H. Thompson, began to systematically investigate whether a pattern was evident, examining the birth months of members of the National Hockey League and two Canadian Junior A leagues. They discovered that the players were much more likely to be born in the early months of the year—the likelihood of playing on elite teams steadily decreasing from January to December (Barnsley and Thompson 1988; Thompson 2012).

Once the pattern was recognized, they attempted to explain what they found. They noted that the cut-off date between Canadian youth hockey levels was December 31. This meant that the difference in age for those playing together could be as much as a year. That is a relatively large difference for young boys. Therefore, where selection and differentiation is made at a young age, a rule such as a cut-off date provides a major advantage for some—those born earlier in the year. Instead of necessarily selecting the best players to move on to the elite teams, it is argued that they are often simply picking the older and therefore bigger, more mature and coordinated players. These players maintain this advantage, getting selected out for better teams—teams that play more games, get more and special coaching, and so on, helping to make these boys better players over time. Barnsley and Thompson (1988) also demonstrated that the younger boys (born in July through December) had a higher likelihood of dropping out of minor league hockey. The impact of this research finding is eye-opening. What they discovered is what is known as the relative age effect (RAE) in Canadian hockey. Malcolm Gladwell (2008) highlights this and other research findings of the relative age effect in his book *Outliers*, where he assesses the causes of success as perhaps having less to do with individual smarts, talent, or ambition than many might think.

Barnsley and Thompson pursued their research agenda for many years. The RAE has been studied and found to exist in baseball, American football, and academic achievement, among other things. Their findings with respect to Canadian hockey are the foundation of research on the topic to this day (Addona and Yates 2010).

What inspires social researchers and their research agendas? A variety of things. For some it may be an issue related to their family history. For others it may be their own experiences, something they saw or noticed, something they read, an injustice they have witnessed whether near or far, or perhaps a teacher's influence. Inspiration can come from any source. In broad strokes, this chapter has set out what it takes to approach a question of interest scientifically. Before proceeding with further details, it is important to establish that a proposed course of research is ethical. This issue is addressed in Chapter 3.

MAIN POINTS

- Social scientists use a variety of paradigms to organize how they understand and inquire into social life.
- Paradigms are theoretical perspectives including a set of assumptions about reality that guide research questions, methods selection, and results interpretation.
- A distinction between types of theories that cuts across various paradigms is macrotheory (theories about large-scale features of society) versus microtheory (theories about smaller units or features of society).
- Four common sociological paradigms include functionalism, conflict theory, symbolic interactionism, and feminism.
- Rationality and reasonableness are qualities that enhance scientific research. Rationality refers to linking ideas together logically, while reasonableness expresses an openness to changing one's mind based on new ideas and evidence.
- All individual observation is subjective. Objectivity occurs when there is consistency between different subjective reports.
- Positivism is the discredited belief that an independent reality awaits discovery.
- Scientific theories are composed of propositions that are logically linked together to explain observations of interest.
- Operationalization is the process of identifying variables that indicate concepts; empirical deduction is the process of translating a theoretical proposition into a researchable hypothesis.
- The traditional model of science centres on hypothesis testing that uses operational definitions. Operational definitions, in turn, specify exactly how a variable will be measured.
- In the traditional image of science, scientists proceed from theory through operational definitions to observation. However, this image is not an accurate picture of how scientific research is actually done.
- Social scientific theory and research are linked through two logical methods:
  - *Deduction* involves the derivation of expectations or hypotheses from theories.
  - *Induction* involves the development of generalizations from specific observations.
- In practice, science is a process involving an alternation of deduction and induction.
- Jasso's theory of distributive justice illustrates how formal reasoning can lead to a variety of theoretical expectations that can be tested by observation.
- Websdale's study of familicide illustrates how collecting observations can lead to generalizations and an explanatory theory.

- In practice, there are many possible links between theory and research, and many ways to conduct social inquiry.
- Social research is inspired by a variety of things, including family history, experiences, recognition of a pattern, a witnessed injustice, or something about which one has read.

REVIEW QUESTIONS AND EXERCISES

1. Consider a possible relationship between education and prejudice. Describe how that relationship might be examined through (a) deductive and (b) inductive methods.
2. Select a social problem that concerns you, such as war, pollution, overpopulation, prejudice, or poverty. Identify the key variables involved in the study of that problem, including variables that may cause it or hold the key to its solution. Feel free to draw on others' theoretical and empirical work.
3. State a proposition that describes the relationship between two concepts. Using the processes of operationalization and empirical deduction, translate the proposition into a research hypothesis.
4. How could an inductive approach be used to examine the credibility of the notion that "Canadians are characteristically polite"?

CONTINUITY PROJECT

THINKING ABOUT INEQUALITY

Theories are narratives, composed of ideas systematically linked together. Three concepts are prevalent in the research literature:

- inequality
- social cohesion
- violence

Review Figure 2-2 and create a model relating these three concepts. Write out the three propositions that connect the concepts in the model.

Imagine you are conducting a macrolevel study of the effects of inequality on violence. Now take the theoretical narrative you just created and, using Figure 2-3 as a guide, translate it into a set of testable hypotheses.

Repeat the process, this time imagining you are conducting a microlevel study of the effects of inequality on violence.

Africa Studio/Shutterstock.com

ETHICAL ISSUES FOR SOCIAL RESEARCHERS

No research study should be designed and implemented without careful thought concerning who might be affected and how. Therefore, researchers must take into account many ethical considerations alongside scientific ones. Clear-cut answers to thorny ethical issues, however, are often hard to come by.

IN THIS CHAPTER ...

INTRODUCTION

In order to communicate the various elements that go into a research study, it is necessary to discuss the process as a series of steps or phases. In practice, however, the steps involved in conducting research are interdependent. Researchers must understand the various modes of observation available when considering the operationalization of concepts, for example. Knowledge of the variety of techniques for data analysis is important at the stage of data gathering. In short, the phases of social research are highly interconnected. Ethical considerations must be attended to during all phases of the research process.

Most of this book focuses on scientific and administrative constraints. We'll see that the logic of science suggests certain research procedures, but we'll also see that some scientifically "perfect" study designs are not administratively feasible because they would be too expensive or take too long to execute. Researchers have to deal with workable compromises. Before we get to the scientific and administrative constraints on research, this chapter will explore the important consideration of ethics and its potential constraints when doing research in the real world.

THE ETHICAL DIMENSION OF SOCIAL RESEARCH

Imagine yourself working with a team of researchers trying to design a study to observe how individuals initially respond to hearing stressful news. News of the death of a loved one is considered to be highly stressful. So is hearing that you've just lost your job. Someone on your research team suggests that you draw a random sample of individuals in a community and inform each in turn that a member of their immediate family has just died—of course, ensuring that the family member is someplace else at the time—so you can watch their reactions when they hear the news. Likely, the moment you hear this suggestion it would strike you as being highly unethical.

How about working with an organization that is willing to randomly choose people in their employ and inform them that they have been fired, because the organization's managers want to learn more about how to cope with people's responses under such circumstances? We imagine that this approach to researching the topic would strike you as unethical also.

Perhaps someone then suggests that instead of creating a false stressful experience, the research team should try to gain access to a hospital where they could observe real-life situations of people being informed about the death of a loved one. Would it be ethical to observe them at that moment in their lives, ask them questions, or hand them a questionnaire? How about gaining access to a company that is about to lay off thousands of workers? What kind of observation and inquiry might be ethical to engage in then?

Just as certain procedures are too impractical to use, others are either ethically prohibitive or politically difficult or impossible. The problem with ethical considerations, however, is that they are not always self-evident. While some situations may appear to be black and white, there are also many shades of grey. Here's a story to show you what we mean.

Several years ago, Earl Babbie was invited to sit in on a planning session to design a study of legal education in California. The joint project was to be conducted by a university research centre and the state bar association. The purpose of the project was to improve legal education by learning which aspects of the law school experience were related to success on the bar exam. Here is a brief account of his experience.

Essentially, the plan was to prepare a questionnaire that would get detailed information about the law school experiences of individuals. People would be required to answer the questionnaire when they took the bar exam. By analyzing how people with different kinds of law school experiences did on the bar exam, we could find out what sorts of things worked and what didn't. The findings of the research could be made available to law schools, and ultimately legal education could be improved.

The exciting thing about collaborating with the bar association was that all the normally irritating logistical hassles would be handled. There would be no problem getting permission to administer questionnaires in conjunction with the exam, for example, and the problem of nonresponse could be eliminated altogether.

Earl recalls leaving the meeting excited about the prospects for the study. When he told a colleague about it, he glowed about the absolute handling of the nonresponse problem. Her immediate comment turned everything around completely. "That's unethical. There's no law requiring the questionnaire, and participation in research has to be voluntary." The study wasn't done. In retelling this story, it is now obvious that requiring participation would have been inappropriate. You may have seen that before you read the colleague's comment. Earl still feels a little embarrassed over the matter. However, there is a specific purpose in the telling of this story.

All of us consider ourselves ethical—not perfect perhaps, but more ethical than most of humanity. The problem in social research, as probably in life, is that ethical considerations are not always apparent to us. As a result, we often plunge into things without seeing ethical issues that may be apparent to others and may even be obvious to us when pointed out.

Any of us can immediately see that a study that requires the torturing of small children is unethical. You'd no doubt speak out immediately if we suggested you interview people about their sex lives and then publish what they said in the local newspaper. But, as ethical as you are, you'd totally miss the ethical issue in some other situations not because you're bad, but because we all do that.

Concern with ethical standards and guidelines in research gained momentum in North America in the second half of the 20th century. Much of the impetus for greater attention to research ethics had to do with medical experimentation on human subjects. We have all heard horrifying stories of tortures on Jews and others in concentration camps conducted by Nazi Germany in the name of medical experimentation.

North America is not exempt from horrifying tales of research conducted in the name of science. The Tuskegee Syphilis Study (Jones 1981) is an infamous example. The study began in the United States around 1930. It examined the long-term consequences of untreated syphilis. Although no treatment was available for syphilis at the time the study began, it was allowed to run until 1972, well after a cure for the disease was available, so that the study would not be ruined. The sample was made up entirely of African-American males. Public pressure forced the termination of the study once it was exposed by the news media.

Canada also has its share of scandalous medical research stories. At the Allan Memorial Institute in Montreal, Dr. Evan Cameron oversaw LSD experiments (sponsored by the U.S. Central Intelligence Agency) conducted on unwitting psychiatric patients in the 1960s. These patients were subjected to mind-altering drugs—for government experiments concerning such issues as brainwashing—without their knowledge or consent, and they were not even told that this had been done to them. Not only did the experiments have no relationship to their illnesses—hence devoid of any potential therapeutic value—but some subjects experienced severe, sometimes life-long, psychological impairment as a result of the drugs administered.

Experimentation on Canadian prisoners provides another illustration. Much of this research—for example, drug testing, tests to determine the toxicity of food additives, and sensory deprivation studies—was conducted between 1955 and 1975 (Osborne 2006). This research gained attention following allegations by Dorothy Proctor (a former inmate) in the mid-1990s and a series of stories in 1998 in the *Ottawa Citizen* on the use of prisoners in experimental research. As a result, the Correctional Service of Canada commissioned an ethics report from McGill University and an independent researcher to review how extensive such inmate research was in Canada (see Osborne 2006).

Other cases in Canada have involved issues of falsification of data, informed consent, and potential harm to subjects. The breast cancer research scandal in the 1990s is an example. Dr. Roger Poisson, who was part of a larger study, was conducting clinical trials concerning lumpectomies followed by chemotherapy and radiation versus mastectomy at L'Hôpital Saint-Luc in Montreal for over a decade beginning in the 1970s. His research contributed to the conclusion that the outcome of the former was as effective as a total mastectomy in the treatment of many instances of breast cancer. The reporting of these results had a great impact on the choice of lumpectomies in women's breast cancer treatments. In the 1990s, it was determined that Dr. Poisson had falsified the medical records of a number of patients he enrolled so that they would fit the trial's eligibility requirements, including reports of lab tests that were never completed. He maintained two sets of files for the women, one labelled as true and the other false. Progress reports were even submitted on a woman who had died. Although the fraud was detected in 1990, the case didn't gain public attention until 1994, when officials and scientists finally went public with it. Thankfully, when Poisson's cases were removed, the results of the study were unchanged and subsequent studies confirmed the conclusions, although reports of the scandal did cause concern for many women who had undergone lumpectomies (Gorman 2001; Park 2012).

Social scientific research also has the potential to harm research subjects. The possibility of psychological harm and stress is one major concern. Milgram's famous obedience to authority experiment (discussed later in this chapter) is often used to illustrate such concerns. But physical harm, while much more rare, is a possibility that must be guarded against as well. The Zimbardo prison experiment is a good illustration of this concern (discussed in Chapter 7). There is the potential of putting subjects into legal jeopardy, particularly when one is researching underground or deviant activities. In addition to placing subjects at legal risk, other major forms of risk to the research subject must be attended to, such as loss of job, destruction of family life, and even blackmail. The *Tearoom Trade* study by Humphreys will also be discussed later in this chapter to illustrate the need to guard against such possibilities.

ETHICAL CODES, REBs, AND THE TRI-COUNCIL POLICY STATEMENT

To guard against the variety of potential harms that can come to human subjects, codes of ethics and other guidelines for moral conduct in research became prevalent during the second half of the 20th century. Most professions and disciplines have their own ethical guidelines, as do many organizations, institutions, and granting agencies. Nonetheless, with the passing of each decade, greater attention has been given to ethical reviews of research. In Canada, for example, a national set of ethical guidelines was established in the 1990s for institutions that receive federal funding. These guidelines are applicable across disciplines to all types of research concerning human subjects.

In 1994, the three major granting agencies in Canada—the Medical Research Council (MRC) (recently renamed the Canadian Institutes of Health Research [CIHR]), the Natural Science and Engineering Research Council (NSERC), and the Social Sciences and Humanities Research Council (SSHRC)—formed the Tri-Council Working Group to create a joint policy concerning ethical standards for research involving humans. The goal was to create a standard of ethical norms that transcended disciplinary boundaries. In 1998, after several draft reports, they issued the *Tri-Council Policy Statement: Ethical Conduct for Research Involving Humans* (TCPS), which articulated their standards. This statement was revised and issued asTCPS 2 in 2010. TCPS 2 was further revised and published in 2014 and again in 2018. A condition of their funding is that researchers and their institutions must follow the principles and policies laid out in the statement.

Because ethical issues in research are both important and ambiguous, formal codes of conduct describing what is considered acceptable and unacceptable professional behaviour are by themselves not adequate. Gaining ethical approval of proposed research projects by an ethics or human subjects committee has been required by many institutions and granting agencies for decades. The organization and composition of such ethical review boards, however, have varied greatly. The TCPS 2 (2018) has laid out rules for the standardization of the ethics review process. Research ethics boards (REBs) now have common procedures and follow the same ethical guidelines. The minimum five-person REB must include a member from the community, a person knowledgeable in ethics, and someone with knowledge about the relevant law. Universities establish their own REBs according to the standards laid out and mandate these REBs to review all research that involves human subjects to ensure they meet the minimum ethical standards of the policy. The REB has the right to approve, reject, or request modifications to research involving human subjects that is proposed or ongoing. If they reject the research, they must provide reasons why, and the researcher may appeal. Ethical review is required of all research involving human subjects conducted by researchers associated with institutions eligible for funding from these agencies, including research conducted by undergraduate students. The researchers' job in designing a study is to carefully consider ethical issues and to explain the goals and methods of their proposed research clearly so the review board can make an informed decision in their particular case.

Figure 3-1 contains an abridged section of the TCPS 2 (2018) that lays out the three core principles guiding the common standards and values adopted: Respect for Persons, Concern for Welfare, and Justice. The core principles "are relevant to the full range of research covered by this policy" (p. 6).

Article 1.1 The guidelines in this Policy are based on the following three core principles:

- Respect for Persons
- Concern for Welfare
- Justice

These principles are complementary and interdependent. How they apply and the weight accorded to each will depend on the nature and context of the research being undertaken.

Respect for Persons: Respect for Persons recognizes the intrinsic value of human beings and the respect and consideration that they are due ... Respect for Persons incorporates the dual moral obligations to respect autonomy and to protect those with developing, impaired or diminished autonomy.

An important mechanism for respecting participants' autonomy in research is the requirement to seek their free, informed and ongoing consent ... An informed choice is one that is based on as complete an understanding as is reasonably possible of the purpose of the research, what it entails, and its foreseeable risks and potential benefits, both to the participant and to others. Respect for Persons also includes a commitment to accountability and transparency in the ethical conduct of research.

Some people may be incapable of exercising autonomy because of youth, cognitive impairment, other mental health issues or illness ... For those prospective participants, additional measures are needed to protect their interests and to ensure that their wishes (to the extent that these are known) are respected. These measures will generally include seeking consent from an authorized third party who is entrusted to make decisions on behalf of the prospective participant ... Even when the requirements of free, informed and ongoing consent cannot be met, Respect for Persons requires involving individuals in circumstances of vulnerability in decision making where possible. This may include asking about their feelings regarding participation and/or for their assent.

Concern for Welfare: The welfare of a person is the quality of that person's experience of life in all its aspects. Welfare consists of the impact on individuals of factors such as their physical, mental and spiritual health, as well as their physical, economic and social circumstances. Thus, determinants of welfare can include housing, employment, security, family life, community membership, and social participation, among other aspects of life. Other contributing factors to welfare are privacy and the control of information about the person, and the treatment of human biological materials according to the free, informed and ongoing consent of the person who was the source of the information or materials. A person's or group's welfare is also affected by the welfare of those who are important to them. Harm includes any negative effects on welfare, broadly construed.

Concern for Welfare means that researchers and REBs should aim to protect the welfare of participants [including minimizing risk], and, in some circumstances, to promote that welfare in view of any foreseeable risks associated with the research. They are to provide participants with enough information to be able to adequately assess risks and potential benefits associated with their participation in the research ...They should attempt to achieve the most favourable balance of risks and potential benefits in a research proposal.

FIGURE 3-1 Tri-Council Policy Statement: Ethical Conduct for Research Involving Humans 2018.
Source: Canadian Institutes of Health Research, Excerpts from *Tri-Council Policy Statement: Ethical Conduct for Research Involving Humans*, 2018, http://www.pre.ethics.gc.ca/eng/policy-politique_tcps2-eptc2_2018.html.

The welfare of groups can also be affected by research. Groups may benefit from the knowledge gained from the research, but they may also suffer from stigmatization, discrimination, or damage to reputation. Engagement during the design process with groups whose welfare may be affected by the research can help to clarify the potential impact of the research and indicate where any negative impact on welfare can be minimized. Researchers must also consider the risks and potential benefits of their research and the knowledge it might generate for the welfare of society as a whole. Where research on individuals may affect the welfare of a group(s), the weight given to the group's welfare will depend on the nature of the research being undertaken, and the individuals or group in question. This consideration does not imply, however, that the welfare of a group should be given priority over the welfare of individuals.

Justice: Justice refers to the obligation to treat people fairly and equitably. Fairness entails treating all people with equal respect and concern. Equity requires distributing the benefits and burdens of research participation in such a way that no segment of the population is unduly burdened by the harms of research or denied the benefits of the knowledge generated from it.

Treating people fairly and equitably does not always mean treating people in the same way ... People or groups whose circumstances cause them to be vulnerable or marginalized may need to be afforded special attention in order to be treated justly in research ...

An important threat to Justice is the imbalance of power that may exist in the relationship between researcher and participant. Participants will generally not understand the research in the same way and in the same depth as does the researcher. Historically, there have been instances in which this power imbalance has been abused, with resulting harm to participants.

FIGURE 3-1 *(Continued)*

The TCPS 2 (2018) addresses a number of issues in more depth, as well as some that the first edition did not. Shortly after the implementation of the initial policy, there was recognition that the different contexts and needs of disciplines in the social sciences and humanities required attention (SSHWC Report 2008). As a result, the revised policy devotes an entire chapter (10) to ethical issues that may arise in qualitative research. The policy states,

> Qualitative research may pose special ethical issues around gaining access, building rapport, using data and publishing results. Researchers and REBs should consider issues of consent, confidentiality and privacy, and relationships between researchers and participants in the design, review and conduct of the research.[1]
>
> (TCPS 2 (2018:136)

It also says that "REBS should consider the range of strategies for documenting the consent process that may be used by researchers using qualitative research approaches" (p. 144), noting that a signed written consent is not always appropriate in qualitative research. How consent is sought and confirmed, however, has to be documented. The Qualitative Research chapter of the TCPS 2 is rich with information about the variety of situations qualitative researchers may face and the ethical guidelines that apply.

The TCPS 2 (2018) also has a chapter devoted to research about the First Nations, Inuit, and Métis peoples of Canada and places greater emphasis on issues of confidentiality (see the Applying Concepts in Everyday Life box "Ethics of Indigenous Research"). For example, it states that when researchers promise confidentiality, it is their "ethical duty" to maintain it. It also states that "institutions shall support their researchers in maintaining promises of confidentiality" (p. 60).

These and many other issues are addressed. The TCPS 2 is complex, and it is not without potential problems (for a critique, see Palys and Lowman 2011). The full policy statement (as well as a summary highlighting key changes

1 Canadian Institutes of Health Research, Excerpts from *Tri-Council Policy Statement: Ethical Conduct for Research Involving Humans*, 2018, http://www.pre.ethics.gc.ca/eng/policy-politique_tcps2-eptc2_2018.html.

to the 2018 edition) may be obtained from www.pre.ethics.gc.ca/eng/policy-politique_tcps2-eptc2_2018.html.

USING STATISTICS CANADA DATA

Guidelines for ethical use are not limited to the collection of new data. For example, Statistics Canada has a great concern for maintaining the confidentiality of those from whom it gathers data. It has a large number of safeguards in place to protect the confidentiality of research subjects. Figure 3-2 provides a segment of the "Guide for Researchers under Agreement with Statistics Canada" (2005), which reports three types of disclosure about which researchers must be concerned. One major way that Statistics Canada protects the confidential information of individual subjects is by restricting disclosure of information when there are too few cases, helping to avoid inadvertent identification of a research respondent. For instance, Fikretoglu et al. (2006:851) used a Statistics Canada survey to study treatment sought for post-traumatic stress disorder by those in the Canadian military. In reporting their findings, the researchers had to leave some table cells without data. In explanation of this they noted: "To protect confidentiality, Statistics Canada prohibits release of output which, in its unweighted version, contains fewer than five participants in a cell. For cumulative lifetime trauma, there was at least one such cell when descriptive statistics were calculated separately for each gender."

APPLYING CONCEPTS IN EVERYDAY LIFE

Ethics of Indigenous Research

Three core principles govern the Tri-Council Policy Statement (TCPS) on research ethics. These principles include respect for persons, concern for welfare, and justice. Beyond these basic principles, the TCPS has special requirements for research involving Indigenous (First Nations, Métis, Inuit) peoples. For instance, beyond individual consent, when proposed research may affect the welfare of the community to which participants belong, community consultation is required. Such community engagement must recognize and respect Indigenous organizations and their leaders, as well as their "cultural traditions, customs and codes of practice" (TCPS 2 2018:108). The reason for these special considerations is rooted in the history of unethical treatment for the advancement of science. Here is an example. (Unless otherwise identified, the quoted passages are from Brym et al. 2019:44.)

In the 1940s relatively little was known about all kinds of nutritional issues. Vitamins and minerals had been discovered only a decade before, and little was known about their effects.

In 1942 federal government researchers visiting remote reserve communities in northern Manitoba found the Aboriginal populations in bad shape. They were malnourished and demoralized. One researcher characterized these Aboriginal populations as marked by "shiftlessness, indolence, improvidence and inertia" (Mosby 2013:147).

Although the obvious response to malnourished populations under government care is to provide increased support, government researchers saw this situation as an opportunity for a field experiment. The researchers had encountered a ready-made laboratory. By defining Aboriginal malnourishment and demoralization as dependent variables and vitamin supplements as independent variables, the design was set to learn how different nutrient supplements affected health. The first experiments were conducted in 1942 on a population of 300 Norway House Cree in northern Manitoba. The experimental group of 125 received vitamin supplements. These supplements were withheld from the control group.

(*Continued*)

APPLYING CONCEPTS IN EVERYDAY LIFE (*CONTINUED*)

Recognizing that Aboriginal children in government-controlled residential schools provided ideal experimental subjects, the research program spread. By 1947 experiments involving 1,300 Aboriginal students in six residential schools were in place in British Columbia, Alberta, Manitoba, Ontario, and Nova Scotia. In some experiments, milk rations were reduced to half the recommended levels for two years to observe the effects. In other research different kinds of vitamin and mineral supplement combinations were provided to one group and not another. Since an important indicator of the dependent variable (health) was measured by observing the health of students' gums, dental services were withdrawn from participating students since fixing the children's teeth and gums would contaminate the results.

When these experiments were conducted in the 1940s, codified ethics for the treatment of human subjects in scientific research were just beginning.[2]

Even today the lead researcher's son defends his father's actions by rationalizing "He was just trying to do good work" (Livingstone 2013). As Canadians, this research legacy is part of our heritage. How does it stack up against the current standards of respect for persons, concern for welfare, and justice? Do you think that the effects of this research were confined to the individual participants, or did they have broader impacts on the Indigenous community? If so, are the additional ethical standards for Indigenous research justified?

2 From Brym/Roberts/Strohschein/Lie. *Sociology: Your Compass for a New World*, 5E. © 2016 Nelson Education Ltd. Reproduced by permission. www.cengage.com/permissions

ETHICAL ISSUES IN SOCIAL RESEARCH

As the councils themselves acknowledge, ethical considerations concerning "human subjects are complex and continually evolving." We, therefore, cannot possibly cover all the ethical issues that might arise or provide standard solutions to those we do highlight. First, there's not always agreement on what is or is not ethical. Second, any given research situation may present researchers with new, challenging ethical dilemmas. Our goal here, therefore, is to *sensitize* you to the ethical component in research so that you'll look for it whenever you plan a study. Even when the ethical aspects of a situation are debatable, you should know there's something to argue about. Toward this end, we'll discuss some of the broadly agreed-upon norms describing what's ethical and what's not.

In most dictionaries and in common usage, *ethics* is typically associated with morality, and both deal with matters of right and wrong. But what is right and what is wrong? What is the source of the distinction? For individuals the sources vary. They may be religions, political ideologies, or the pragmatic observation of what seems to work and what doesn't.

Webster's New World Dictionary is typical among dictionaries in defining *ethical* as "conforming to the standards of conduct of a given profession or group." Although the idea may frustrate those in search of moral absolutes, what we regard as morality and ethics in day-to-day life is a matter of agreement among members of a group. And, not surprisingly, different groups have agreed on different codes of conduct. Part of living successfully in a particular society is knowing what that society considers ethical and unethical. The same holds true for the social research community.

Anyone involved in social scientific research, then, needs to be aware of the general agreements shared by researchers about what's proper and improper in the conduct of scientific inquiry.

3.1 What Is Disclosure?

Disclosure occurs when data that can be attributed to individual respondents (e.g., persons, households, businesses, other organizations) are released.

3.1.1 Types of Disclosure

There are three types of disclosure: identity, attribute, and residual.

Identity disclosure occurs when an individual can be identified from the released output, leading to information being provided about that identified subject.

Attribute disclosure occurs when confidential information is revealed and can be attributed to an individual. It is not necessary for a specific individual to be identified or for a specific value to be given for attribute disclosure to occur. For example, publishing a narrow range for the salary of persons exercising a particular profession in one region may constitute a disclosure.

Residual disclosure can occur when released information can be combined to obtain confidential data. Care must be taken to examine all output to be released. While a table on its own might not disclose confidential information, disclosure can occur by combining information from several sources, including external ones (e.g., suppressed data in one table can be derived from other tables).

3.1.2 Some Examples of Disclosure in Survey Data

- A well-known personality (e.g., a professional athlete) is selected in a survey and information is published about her community, such as the highest reported income in that community, which almost certainly was reported by her. (Identity disclosure.)
- Results from a longitudinal survey highlight one household with a highly unusual migration pattern, leading to its identification. (Identity disclosure.)
- The parents of a 16-year-old selected in the sample see a table showing that all sampled 16-year-old respondents in their region have tried drugs. (Attribute disclosure.)
- A newspaper article relates a 37-year-old widower's complaints about being surveyed, and there are only two sampled 30- to 39-year-old widowers in survey cross-tabulations. (Eventually leading to identity and/or attribute disclosure.)
- By combining several results, a person identified information that was purposely excluded from the Public Use Microdata File (PUMF) because it presented too high a disclosure risk (e.g., the country of birth of recent immigrants). (Residual disclosure.)

FIGURE 3-2 Disclosure Issues from the Guide for Researchers under Agreement with Statistics Canada.
Source: Adapted from Statistics Canada, *Guide for Researchers under Agreement with Statistics Canada*, pp. 22–23. This does not constitute an endorsement by Statistics Canada of this product.

Note that "anyone" includes you. For example, if you collect data from human subjects for any of your term papers or projects, you are not excluded. This section summarizes some of the most important ethical agreements that prevail in social research.

VOLUNTARY PARTICIPATION

Social research often, though not always, represents an intrusion into people's lives. The interviewer's knock on the door or the arrival of a questionnaire in the mail signals the beginning of an activity that the respondent has not requested and one that may require a significant portion of his or her time and energy. Participation in a social experiment disrupts the subject's regular activities.

Social research, moreover, often requires that people reveal personal information about themselves—information that may be unknown to their friends and associates. And social research often requires that such information be revealed to strangers. Other professionals, such as physicians and lawyers, also require such information. Their requests may be justified, however, because the information is required for them to serve the personal interests of the individual. Social researchers can seldom make this claim. Like medical scientists, they can only argue that the research effort may ultimately help all humanity.

A major tenet of medical research ethics—rooted in the three core principles—is that participant involvement in research must be **voluntary**. The same norm applies to social research. No one should be forced to participate. This norm is far easier to accept in theory than to apply in practice, however.

Again, medical research provides a useful parallel. Many experimental drugs have been tested on prisoners. In the most rigorously ethical cases, the prisoners were told the nature and the possible dangers of the experiment; they were told that participation is completely voluntary; and they were further instructed that they could expect no special rewards, such as early parole, for participation. Even under these conditions, it's often clear that volunteers are motivated by the belief that they will personally benefit from their cooperation.

When the instructor in an introductory sociology class asks students to fill out a questionnaire that he or she hopes to analyze and publish, students should always be told that their participation in the survey is completely voluntary. Even so, most students fear that nonparticipation will somehow affect their grade. The instructor should, therefore, be especially sensitive to the implied sanctions and make special provisions to obviate them. For example, the instructor could leave the room while the questionnaires are being completed. Or students could be asked to return the questionnaires by mail or to drop them in a box near the door just before the next course meeting.

This norm of voluntary participation, though, goes directly against a number of scientific concerns. In the most general terms, the scientific goal of **generalizability** is threatened if experimental subjects or survey respondents are only the kinds of people who willingly participate in such things. Because this orientation probably reflects more general personality traits, the results of the research might not be generalizable to all kinds of people. Most clearly, in the case of a descriptive survey, a researcher cannot generalize the sample survey findings to an entire population unless a substantial majority of the scientifically selected sample actually participates—the willing respondents and the somewhat unwilling.

Field research has its own ethical dilemmas in this regard (see Chapter 10). Very often, the researcher cannot even reveal that a study is being done, for fear that that revelation might significantly affect the social processes being studied. Clearly, the subjects of study in such cases are not given the opportunity to volunteer or refuse to participate.

Although the norm of voluntary participation is important, it's often impossible to follow it. In cases where you feel ultimately justified in violating it, it's all the more important that you observe the other ethical norms of scientific research, such as bringing no harm to the people under study.

voluntary participation The ethical norm requiring that participants be free to choose whether or not to participate in a study.

generalizability The goal of research findings being applicable to as broad a population as possible.

NO HARM TO THE PARTICIPANTS

Social research should never injure the people being studied, regardless of whether they volunteer for the study. Perhaps the clearest instance of this norm in sociological practice concerns the revealing of information that would embarrass them or endanger their home life, friendships, jobs, and so forth. This aspect of the norm is discussed more fully below.

Because subjects can be harmed psychologically in the course of a study, the researcher must look for the subtlest dangers and guard against them. Quite often, research subjects are asked to reveal deviant behaviour, attitudes they feel are unpopular, or personal characteristics that may seem demeaning, such as low income, the receipt of welfare payments, and the like. Revealing such information usually makes them feel at least uncomfortable.

Social research projects may also force participants to face aspects of themselves they don't normally consider. This can happen even when the information is not revealed directly to the researcher. In retrospect, a certain past behaviour may appear unjust or immoral. The project, then, can be the source of a continuing, personal agony for the subject. If the study concerns codes of ethical conduct, for example, the subject may begin questioning his or her own morality, and that personal concern may last long after the research has been completed and reported. For instance, probing questions can injure a fragile self-esteem.

It should be apparent from these observations that just about any research you might conduct runs the risk of injuring other people somehow. It's not possible to insure against all these potential injuries; however, some study designs make such injuries more likely than others. If a particular research procedure seems likely to produce unpleasant effects for subjects—asking survey respondents to report deviant behaviour, for example—the researcher should have the firmest of scientific grounds for doing it. If the research design is essential and also likely to be unpleasant for subjects, you'll find yourself in an ethical netherworld and may go through some personal agonizing. Although agonizing has little value in itself, it may be a healthy sign that you've become sensitive to the problem.

Increasingly, the ethical norms of voluntary participation and no harm to participants have become formalized in the concept of **informed consent**. This means that voluntary participation must be decided on the basis of a full understanding of the possible risks involved. For example, prospective subjects of a medical experiment will be presented with a discussion of the experiment and all the possible risks to themselves. They'll be required to sign a statement indicating that they are aware of the risks and choose to participate anyway. While the value of such a procedure is obvious when subjects will be injected with drugs designed to produce physical effects, for example, it's hardly appropriate when a researcher rushes to the scene of urban rioting to study deviant behaviour. While the researcher in this latter case is still required to do no harm to those observed, gaining informed consent is not the means to achieving that end.

Although the fact often goes unrecognized, subjects can be harmed by the analysis and reporting of data. Every now and then, research subjects read the books published about the studies they participated in. Reasonably sophisticated subjects can locate themselves in the various indexes and tables. Having done so, they may find themselves characterized, though not identified by name, as bigoted, unpatriotic, irreligious, and so forth. At the very least, such characterizations are likely to trouble them and threaten their self-images. Yet the whole purpose of the research project may be to explain why some people are prejudiced and others are not.

Like voluntary participation, avoiding harm to people is easy in theory but often difficult in practice. Sensitivity to the issue and experience with its applications, however, should improve the researcher's tact in delicate areas of research.

In recent years, social researchers have been getting greater support for abiding by this norm. The requirement of independent evaluation of the treatment of human subjects for research proposals by review committees, such as the REBs we just discussed, serves this function. Although sometimes troublesome and inappropriately applied, such requirements not only guard against unethical research but also can reveal ethical issues overlooked by the most scrupulous of researchers.

ANONYMITY AND CONFIDENTIALITY

The clearest concern in the protection of the subjects' interests and well-being is the protection of their identity. Two techniques, *anonymity* and *confidentiality*, assist researchers in this regard, although the two are often confused.

Anonymity A subject may be guaranteed **anonymity** only when both the researcher and the people who read about the research cannot identify a given response with a given subject. This means an interview survey respondent,

informed consent The ethical norm requiring research subjects to base their voluntary participation on a full understanding of the potential risks involved.

anonymity The guarantee that neither the researchers nor the readers of research can link individuals to their responses.

for example, can never be considered anonymous, since an interviewer collects the information from an identifiable individual. (We assume here that standard sampling methods are followed.) An example of anonymity would be the mail survey in which no identification numbers are put on the questionnaires before their return to the research office (see Chapter 8).

Ensuring anonymity makes it difficult to keep track of who has or hasn't returned the questionnaires. Despite this problem, there are some situations in which you may be advised to pay the necessary price. In studies seeking information on sensitive topics or illegal behaviour such as sexual practices or drug use, some researchers feel that honestly ensuring anonymity would increase the likelihood and accuracy of responses. In addition, the researcher may not want to be in the position of being asked by authorities for the names of the respondents when illegal behaviour is the topic of study.

Confidentiality A respondent is guaranteed **confidentiality** when the researcher can identify a given person's responses but essentially promises not to do so publicly. In an interview survey, for example, the researcher would be in a position to make public the income reported by a given respondent, but the respondent is assured that this will not be done.

Whenever a research study is confidential rather than anonymous, it's the researcher's responsibility to make that fact clear to the subject. Moreover, researchers should never use the term *anonymous* to mean *confidential.*

With few exceptions (such as surveys of public figures who agree to have their responses published), the information research participants give must at least be kept confidential. This is not always an easy norm to follow, since the courts (at least until recently in Canada), have not recognized social research data as constituting the kind of "privileged communication" accepted in the case of priests and lawyers.

confidentiality The guarantee that although researchers can link individuals to their responses, they promise not to do so publicly.

This unprotected guarantee of confidentiality was challenged in Canada in 1994 in the case of Russel Ogden. Ogden was a graduate student at Simon Fraser University (SFU) in the early 1990s conducting research for his master's thesis on assisted death among people with HIV/AIDS. Investigating underground practices such as these necessarily involves gaining knowledge of illegal activities. The ethical rules he followed were to protect his subjects from harm. In order to do this, he had to maintain strict confidentiality, a promise he made to those who volunteered to participate in his study. He obtained ethical approval of his proposed research from the university's ethics committee—a proposal that stated his commitment to complete confidentiality.

When Ogden completed his thesis in 1994, his research received a great deal of attention. This attention brought with it a subpoena issued in a coroner's inquest. He was asked to report his knowledge of practices of assisted death and provide names. Refusing to comply, he faced contempt of court charges. He sought support and assistance from the university administration but was denied it.

Ogden chose to maintain his ethical responsibilities and fight for the right of privileged communication between the researcher and subject, bearing the risks and the legal costs himself. He was successful in defending the confidentiality of his research participants and thus established a common-law precedent in Canada concerning academic privilege.

This case brought to light not only the responsibilities of and risks to researchers in maintaining ethical standards, but also those of universities to protect the rights and interests of research participants and the rights of academic freedom and research. Although Ogden ultimately succeeded, he was left to defend the ethical principle of confidentiality on his own. The university gave him $2,000 on "compassionate" grounds to assist in his legal expenses but refused to become involved in the case on any level. Ogden sued the university and was awarded $34,000 and an official apology (Hager 2015).

Ogden's problems researching this topic with support for protecting the confidentiality of participants did not end, however. In 1995, Ogden moved to the University of Exeter in England to pursue his PhD, with assurances that the university would support him and his research subjects. Three years later, Exeter reneged on its promise, fearing the university might be liable. Early in 2003, the University of Exeter was ordered to pay Ogden $140,000 for breaking the agreement (Hager 2015).

After returning to Canada to continue his research, Ogden had further troubles. He was once again subpoenaed by the Crown in January 2003, and the circumstances appeared to be even worse than the time before. His previous subpoena came from an inquest—this one was from a criminal legal proceeding. Fearful that a search warrant might result, he hid his data, still maintaining his promise of confidentially to his research participants. In February 2003, the subpoena was dropped without explanation, but he was left without guarantees of protection against future subpoenas.

Ogden began teaching at Kwantlen Polytechnic University in British Columbia in 1999. In 2004, the university research ethics board approved his right to maintain participant confidentiality in research on assisted suicide. By 2007, however, the university reconsidered its commitment and in 2008 signed an agreement with Ogden forbidding him from teaching on the campus or using the university's name on his academic publications. They continue, however, to pay his salary (Todd 2015).

Professor Ogden's case raised the profile of research ethics considerations in Canada. The SFU administration, for instance, came to recognize the importance of confidentiality guarantees and announced that they would provide the same legal support for graduate students that is afforded faculty when issues of research confidentiality are challenged. As noted earlier, the TCPS 2 has also expanded its discussion of confidentiality, emphasizing how important maintaining confidentiality is to research and stating that it is a researcher's duty to maintain it. This has proved useful as researchers face challenges to their maintenance of a participant's confidence. For example, two criminologists at the University of Ottawa (Bruckert and Parent) conducted an interview with convicted killer Luka Magnotta. The police demanded access to the taped interview and the researchers refused, citing researcher–participant confidentiality privilege. In a groundbreaking decision, the Quebec Superior Court upheld the confidentiality rights (CAUT 2014).

Techniques are available to ensure better performance on the guarantee of confidentiality. To begin, interviewers and others with access to respondent identifications should be trained in their ethical responsibilities. Beyond training, the most fundamental technique is to remove all identifying information as soon as it's no longer necessary. In surveys, for instance, names and addresses should be removed from questionnaires and replaced by identification numbers. An identification file should be created that links numbers to names to permit the later correction of missing or contradictory information, but this file should not be available except for legitimate purposes.

The same technique holds for interviews. You may need to identify survey respondents initially so you can recontact them to verify that the interview was conducted and perhaps to get information that was missing in the original interview. As soon as you've verified an interview and assured yourself that you don't need any further information from the respondent, however, you can safely remove all identifying information from the interview booklet. Often, interview booklets are printed so that the first page contains all the identifiers. It can be torn off once the respondent's identification is no longer needed.

This technique is no less true for data gathered in field research. Using codes for people and places instead of real identifying information when typing up your notes and organizing your data is an excellent precaution. Keep in mind, however, that even without the identifying information, if someone has access to all of your data, however they are gathered, it may still be possible to identify an individual, especially if the information has been gathered from a small, defined population of people.

In cases where you intended to remove the identifying information but haven't yet done so, what do you do when the police or a court orders you to provide the responses given by your research subjects? This is the kind of ethical dilemma that researchers must be prepared to face. Gaining the prior approval of institutional ethics boards and executing ethical research protocols helps make these challenges easier, but it doesn't make them disappear.

DECEPTION

We've seen that the handling of subjects' identities is an important ethical consideration. Handling your own identity as a researcher can be tricky also. Sometimes it's useful and even necessary to identify yourself as a researcher to those you want to study. You'd have to be a master con artist to get people to participate in a laboratory experiment or complete a lengthy questionnaire without letting on that you were conducting research.

On other occasions it is necessary to either conceal your own identity or the purposes of your research. This requires acts of **deception**. Even when you must conceal your research identity, you need to consider the following. Because deceiving people is unethical, deception within social research needs to be justified by compelling scientific or administrative concerns. Even then, the justification will be arguable.

Sometimes researchers admit that they're doing research but fudge about why they're doing it or for whom. Suppose you've been asked by a public welfare agency to conduct a study of living standards among aid recipients. Even if the agency is looking for ways of improving conditions, the recipient-subjects are likely to fear a witch hunt for "cheaters." They might be tempted, therefore, to give answers making themselves seem more destitute than they really are. Unless they provide truthful answers, however, the study will not produce accurate data that will contribute to an effective improvement of living conditions. What do you do?

deception When respondents are misled about either the identity of the researcher or the nature of the research.

debriefing Interviewing subjects following their participation in a research project to ensure they are both fully informed and not harmed by their participation.

One solution would be to tell subjects that you're conducting the study as part of a university research program, concealing your affiliation with the welfare agency. Doing that improves the scientific quality of the study, but it raises a serious ethical issue.

Lying about research purposes is common in laboratory experiments. Although it's difficult to conceal the fact that you're conducting research, it's usually simple, and sometimes appropriate, to conceal your purpose. Many experiments in social psychology, for example, test the extent to which subjects will abandon the evidence of their own observations in favour of the views expressed by others.

If deception is necessary for the experiment to work, how do we deal with the ethical issue of deceit? One solution researchers have found appropriate is to debrief subjects following the experiment. **Debriefing** involves interviewing the subjects to determine whether the research experience generated any problems and then attempting to correct such problems. Even though subjects can't be told the true purpose of the study prior to their participation in it, there's usually no reason they can't know afterward. Telling them the truth afterward may make up for having to lie to them at the outset. This must be done with care, however, making sure the subjects aren't left with bad feelings or doubts about themselves based on their performance in the experiment. If this seems complicated, it's simply the price we pay for using other people's lives as the subject matter for our research.

ANALYSIS AND REPORTING

Researchers have ethical obligations to their colleagues in the scientific community in addition to their ethical obligations to their subjects. These obligations concern the analysis of data and the way results are reported.

In any rigorous study, the researcher should be more familiar than anyone else with the technical shortcomings and failures of the study. Researchers have an obligation to make such shortcomings known to their readers, even if admitting mistakes and qualifications makes them feel foolish.

Negative findings, for example, should be reported if they're at all related to the analysis. There is an unfortunate myth in scientific reporting that only positive discoveries are worth reporting (journal editors are sometimes guilty of believing this as well). In science, however, it is often as important to know that two variables are *not* related as to know that they are.

Similarly, researchers must avoid the temptation to save face by describing their findings as the product of a carefully planned analytical strategy when that's not the case. Many findings arrive unexpectedly, even though they may seem obvious in retrospect. So an interesting relationship is uncovered by accident. So what? Embroidering such situations with descriptions of fictitious hypotheses is dishonest. It also does a disservice to less experienced researchers. It misleads them into thinking that all scientific inquiry is rigorously planned and organized.

In general, science progresses through honesty and openness; ego defences and deception retard it. Researchers can best serve their peers, and scientific discovery as a whole, by telling the truth about all the pitfalls and problems they've experienced in a particular line of inquiry. Perhaps they'll save others from the same problems. Some topics of research provoke more attention to ethical concerns than do others. For example, given the highly sensitive nature of research on human sexuality, it is quite noticeable that articles reporting such research often explicitly address concerns the readers might have about the ethical precautions the researchers have taken and the impact such precautions may have on their findings. This is often true of research concerning vulnerable populations such as children, prisoners, mental patients, and the homeless. When a research study happens to combine such topics and populations, these concerns are even greater. Some examples help to illustrate the point.

Stephen Baron (1997) researched homeless Canadian skinhead youths. Here's what he said about the consideration of ethical issues when designing his study and the impact of his choices: "[O]nly male youths were approached, so that ethical concerns surrounding questions directed at respondents' sexual and physical victimization were minimized" (1997:131). He described the thinking that surrounded this choice in a footnote.

> [T]he female population created a number of ethical dilemmas in designing the research. In research of this nature, a number of questions necessarily tap into delicate areas of the respondents' lives. For example, areas of the interview required details concerning physical and sexual victimization in childhood histories. It also included questions concerning various types of victimization outside the home (sexual assault), as well as probed for participation in illegal activities, including prostitution. These questions are sensitive in character, and the fact that the primary researcher was male would likely have made them even more so for female respondents.
>
> (Baron 1997:131)

Baron concluded, "along with the ethics board," that it wasn't proper for a male researcher to ask such questions of females. He acknowledged that while these questions could have been removed, past research indicated such factors to be important in explaining street youths' behaviour. Because the author felt the questions were essential to his research, he chose to limit his study to males.

Baron further revealed how he obtained contact and informed consent, his appearance in the field, and the fact that respondents were given $10 in food coupons for their participation. Because such a population is likely to have problems with illiteracy, Baron offered to help the participants read the consent forms and questioned them about their understanding of the forms after they had reviewed them.

Shelley Young (1997) addressed the care taken in her study on the sexual exploitation of children. She gathered data from case files concerning child sexual assault at a victim/witness assistance program. She reported, for example, that she had "to swear an oath of confidentiality" concerning the information to which she was given access. In addition, she discussed her strategy for protecting the identities of those involved in potentially identifiable cases:

> Although highly unusual or unique cases were included in the sample, they were not presented in totality; only elements of these cases which fit with other scenarios were used in the final presentation. Data were presented as profiles or aggregate scenarios to prevent the identification of any particular case or individual involved.
>
> (1997:288)

Ethical approval of the project from the University of Windsor Department of Sociology and Anthropology Ethics Committee was noted as well.

TWO ETHICAL CONTROVERSIES

Even with the adoption of many professional codes of conduct and other guidelines, ethical issues in research have not been resolved. There is some disagreement on general principles by social researchers, and those who agree in principle often debate specifics.

We'll briefly describe two research studies in this section because of the controversy they have provoked and the roles many believe they have played in heightening ethical concerns in social research. The first research project studied homosexual behaviour in public restrooms; the second examined obedience in a laboratory setting.

TEAROOM TRADE

The Tearoom Trade (1970) study by Humphreys is often used to illustrate some key ethical concerns. Humphreys was interested in the study of homosexual behaviour. He became particularly interested in researching casual same-sex acts engaged in by male strangers who met in public restrooms in parks, referred to as "tearooms" by participants. He was able to study the sexual encounters between these men because they usually included a third person. He, therefore, pretended to participate as the voyeur/lookout, known as the "watchqueen," whenever possible—a perfect opportunity to make field observations as a participant observer.

In order to find out more about these men and the lives they led (since they probably would not have been receptive to being interviewed), he secretly took down their licence plate numbers when possible and used the police registers to obtain their names and addresses. In disguise, Humphreys then went to these men's homes on the pretence that he was conducting a health survey in order to gather further information about them.

This controversial study has provoked a great deal of argument and debate over what is or is not acceptable, ethical behaviour in social research. Some of the key issues this study raised concern invasion of privacy, deceit, lack of consent, and risk of harm to the research subjects.

There were those who argued that the study was valuable and could not have been done any other way. They argued that not only was observing the behaviour engaged in publicly within ethical bounds but that the deceit was essentially harmless. They noted that he was careful to protect the men's identities, and that his research did not result in any personal harm to the men. Arguments in support of the research also noted that the research revealed previously unknown information about men who engaged in these casual, homosexual encounters. For instance, the tearoom participants were otherwise living rather conventional family lives and were accepted community members.

While some praised his research as worthwhile, many others disapproved of the deceit and invasion of privacy the study entailed, particularly the follow-up survey. Even some who felt that observing the participants in the restrooms was OK because they used a public facility felt the follow-up survey was unethical—tracking people to their homes and interviewing them under false pretences. Others expressed concern that the information had the potential to seriously harm the subjects in any number of ways, including the risk of criminal charges, since such acts were at that time and place illegal. This study continues to provoke debate over what research practices, under what circumstances, are ethical.

OBSERVING HUMAN OBEDIENCE

This next study by Stanley Milgram was unlike Humphreys's in a couple of major ways. The "tearoom" study was a participant observation study while Milgram's study was a laboratory experiment. Humphreys's study was sociological, while Milgram's was psychological.

In the early 1960s, Milgram's study generated debate about ethical practices in research soon after he completed it. Stimulated by the atrocities committed during World War II, his research concerned how willing people were to obey authority even when they were told to engage in wrongful or immoral behaviour, including the potential of killing someone.

Milgram advertised for men to participate in a study concerning memory and learning. The research participant (experimental subject) was cast in the role of "teacher." As "teacher," he was asked to test the "learner's" memory of word lists and administer electric shocks of increasing intensity to him each time he gave an incorrect answer. The "learner" (believed by the research subject to be a study participant as well) was placed in an adjacent room. He was not visible to the "teacher," but he was audible. As the shock levels increased, the "learner's" indication of discomfort increased from noises of pain and discomfort to screaming, begging that the experiment be stopped, kicking the wall, and ultimately silence.

Milgram reported his findings in his book *Obedience to Authority* (1969). When the research subjects indicated concern about the "learner" and a desire to stop administering shocks, the researcher would tell him that he must continue—and most did. All of the first 40 men in Milgram's experiment continued to administer the shocks until the "learner" began to kick the wall, and the majority of the subjects (26 of the 40) continued the shocks to their highest level—clearly marked as highly dangerous. Nonetheless, many of them experienced a great deal of stress when doing so, exhibited by sweating, groaning, and pressing their fingernails into their skin; some had uncontrollable seizures.

The learner was a confederate, and the shocks being administered by the teacher were not real, although he didn't know this, of course, as the teacher was the real subject of the experiment. The experiment was designed to test the subject's willingness to follow orders to the point of presumably killing someone. Ironically, in trying to determine the conditions under which people will obey authority even in situations regarded as immoral, the study, while praised by many as one of the most important pieces of social psychological research conducted in its time, was also condemned by others on grounds of unethical practices.

The criticism focused on the effects of the experiment on the human subjects. Is it right to (deceptively) subject research participants to this degree of psychological stress and pain? In weighing the human costs and benefits of this research, many believe that the research was worthwhile—what was learned about human behaviour was important. Others believe the risk to the human subjects crossed the ethical line.

In defence of the research, Milgram wrote that despite the unexpected degree of stress experienced by many of the subjects during the experiment, they themselves reported overwhelmingly that they were glad they had participated. After his participation, each subject was debriefed. They were immediately informed that no one was actually harmed in the experiment. Once the experiment was complete, the subjects received a report detailing the procedures and the results. After receiving the report, they were sent a follow-up questionnaire concerning participation. As Milgram (1969:195) reported: "In its quantitative aspect ... 84 percent of the subjects stated they were glad to have been in the experiment; 15 percent indicated neutral feelings; and 1.3 percent indicated negative feelings." While acknowledging the need to interpret such information with caution, he noted that such data should not be ignored either. He further reported that 80 percent believed that further experiments of this nature should be conducted, and nearly three-quarters said "that they had learned something of personal importance as a result of being in the study."

This raises interesting questions as well. The vast majority of the subjects were not condemning of the research. Do we protect people from what they themselves may want to know more about and better understand? Perhaps there was a different research design that could have been used to investigate obedience?

The Milgram experiment illustrates the ambiguity that surrounds ethical issues in research. None of the issues raised has an easy solution, but they certainly warrant much consideration and debate.

INTERNET-MEDIATED RESEARCH: NEW ETHICAL CONSIDERATIONS

Have you ever used social media? Bought something online? Or used a debit card or credit card to buy something at a store in your neighbourhood? Chances are you have done all of these and do so most days. This means there are data out there about you—a veritable digital trail. Someone who has the skills and access can easily find out a lot about you by following your digital trail. The question is, should they be allowed to? What data should be protected as part of our right to personal privacy? And what data are public domain, fair game for third parties like corporations, governments, or academic researchers?

The technological capabilities for producing, analyzing, and disseminating digital data online have grown rapidly in recent years. But the societal norms, rules, and laws regulating these activities have struggled to keep pace. This leaves significant ethical and legal grey areas, and social science researchers must be particularly sensitive to the pros and cons of such ambiguities. On one hand, we are optimistic about Internet-mediated research (IMR) (Hewson 2016) as an exciting new frontier for understanding human behaviour. We are drawn by its potential to facilitate and augment existing *obtrusive* data collection methods such experiments (see Chapter 7) and surveys (see Chapter 8). We are also intrigued by its potential to allow new *unobtrusive* (nonreactive) data collection techniques that enable us to study digital traces of people's online activity without their awareness (see Chapter 9). On the other hand, there are serious ethical concerns related to informed consent, privacy, and protecting people from harm due to misuse of personal information.

Although the basic ethical standards of voluntary participation, harm minimization, and respect for privacy hold for social research online, there are additional complications that arise in the online context. Procedures for obtaining participants' informed consent for online surveys and experiments are similar to their traditional off-line counterparts. But the ability to observe people's online behaviour without their awareness raises new ethical issues and complexities. What are the boundaries between public and private places online, and when/where do people have a reasonable expectation of privacy? Online information is accessible, but does that make it public? For example, people may interact in a public space such as an online chat room from a private space such as their bedroom—what expectation of privacy are they due? Related to this is the question of what level of awareness people have about how public their online activity is. Are they aware of the extent to which their online activity is logged and made available to third parties (e.g., online retailers or marketers)? The level of disclosure that people practise in their interactions and activities may differ significantly depending on their level of awareness about the accessibility of their data. (How closely do you read the fine print of every user agreement you have agreed to?) A person may share much less personal or sensitive information in their chat room interactions if they are aware of the public nature of their data. It is also possible that your data may become available without your consent because of your interactions with someone else who has consented (e.g., a social networking friend). Or that data you consented to having collected for one purpose (e.g., improving the functionality of a mobile app) may be used for another purpose you were unaware of.

These last two possibilities are illustrated by the recent Facebook controversy involving Cambridge Analytica. Cambridge Analytica, a political data firm hired by the 2016 Trump presidential election campaign, obtained access to 50 million Facebook users' private information. The data included details on users' identities, friend networks, and "likes." The objective was to profile voters' personalities based on what they liked on Facebook, and to influence their behaviour by targeting them with digital advertising based on those profiles. How did they gain access to all those Facebook users' private information? In 2014, a researcher asked Facebook users (as permitted by Facebook policy at the time) to take a personality survey and to download an app. The app harvested some private information from those users and their friends. Thus, although only 270,000 users (who had been told it was for academic use) had originally consented to participate in the survey and have their data collected, the database that was ultimately generated contained information from 50 million users (Granville 2018).

What if neither you nor any of your friends consented to having your data collected? It is possible that online activity traces (such as Web browsing or social media activity) or personal details (e.g., website registration) that are initially private may become public later when different sources of information are combined (see Figure 3-2 on types of disclosure). Much of the optimism about the usefulness of access to ever-increasing amounts of online data is based on the idea of anonymity. The data have been de-identified (stripped of all information that may identify a person). In theory, de-identified data cannot be linked to any particular individual, poses no risk to privacy, and thus can be shared online without threat of harm to individuals (Ohm 2010). But as a number of recent examples have revealed, this assumption is increasingly suspect. Three prominent examples are discussed below (for more detail see Ohm 2010; Salganik 2018).

In the 1990s, the Massachusetts Group Insurance Commission (GIC) released de-identified data on state employees' hospital visits. The state government assured the public that the de-identified nature of the data meant people's privacy was safe. Researcher Latanya Sweeney revealed that this was not the case. She was easily able to re-identify the hospital records of then-governor William Weld by linking the GIC data with publicly available voter records, using name, date of birth, zip code, and sex. It turns out that only six people in the city where he lived shared his birth date; only three were men, and of those three, only one lived in his ZIP code—the governor himself!

In 2006, America Online (AOL) as part of its AOL Research initiative, posted the anonymized (de-identified) data of 650,000 AOL users. Identifiers such as username and IP address were removed, but, in order to maintain the analytical usefulness, were replaced with unique user numbers. AOL executives thought they were committing a public good by releasing user data for study, while at the same time protecting the privacy of users. But, within days the anonymity illusion was shown for what it was. Two *New York Times* reporters demonstrated how easy it was to re-identify users. They used records of AOL search queries such as "landscapers in Lilburn, Ga," and "homes sold in shadow lake subdivision gwinnett county Georgia," to track down and identify User 4417749 as Thelma George, a 62-year-old widow from Lilburn, Georgia.

Later that same year, Netflix released 100 million movie ratings from 500,000 subscribers. These data, which Netflix "anonymized" beforehand, were released as part of the Netflix Prize. This was a contest that aimed to crowdsource the refinement of Netflix's movie recommendation system by allowing 50,000 contestants to use the free data to create and test their own algorithms (mathematical instructions that help computers calculate answers to problems). Again, the shakiness of the anonymity assumption was quickly exposed. Two researchers were able to identify specific users by linking so-called anonymous Netflix movie ratings to ratings and personal data posted publicly on the Internet Movie Data Base website. Their strategy was similar to Sweeney's and involved linking two data sets, each of which seemed fairly safe on its own. The resulting disclosures included identifying users' personal attributes such as political leanings and sexual orientation (Singel 2009).

These examples of people being re-identified from their supposedly anonymous data illustrate that "all data are potentially identifiable, and all data are potentially sensitive" (Salganik 2018:311). Relevant TCPS 2 (2018) guidelines reflect attempts to weigh these various complexities for IMR. Ethics (REB) approval is not required for "[r]esearch that is non-intrusive, and does not involve direct interaction between the researcher and individuals through the Internet." Nor is REB approval required for use of "[c]yber-material such as documents, records, performances, online archival materials or published third party interviews to which the public is given uncontrolled access on the Internet [and] for which there is no expectation of privacy," as it "is considered to be publicly available information." But for IMR that involves "accessing identifiable information in digital sites, such as online groups with restricted membership, the privacy expectation of contributors of these sites is much higher" and requires ethics (REB) approval. Also requiring REB approval is research "[w]here data linkage of different sources of publicly available information is involved, [that] could give rise to new forms of identifiable information that would raise issues of privacy and confidentiality" (TCPS 2 (2018) Ch 2:16). Of course, it should be noted that nonacademic online researchers (such as retailers, marketers, and political data firms) are not subject to TCPS 2 (2018) or institutional REB review and may follow much less stringent ethical guidelines (e.g., see Chapter 7 for a discussion of the Emotional Contagion study conducted on Facebook users).

Research ethics, then, is an important though ambiguous topic. The difficulty of resolving ethical issues should not be an excuse for ignoring them. To sensitize you further to the ethical component in social research, the first review question provides a variety of examples to contemplate and discuss. With the numerous issues raised kept in mind, you can evaluate some of the research examples presented in the following chapters with regard to ethical considerations. Ethical considerations are prominent in research design from its inception, and they remain prominent throughout every phase of the process, down to the reporting of the research and application of findings.

MAIN POINTS

- Social research projects are shaped not only by technical scientific considerations but also by administrative, political, and ethical considerations.
- What is ethical and unethical in research is ultimately a matter of what a community of people agrees is right and wrong.
- Over the past several decades, codes of ethics to guide researchers have increasingly been created by government agencies and professional associations. While helpful, such codes do not resolve all ethical questions. Much research must now be approved by a research ethics committee.
- The Tri-Council Policy Statement (TCPS) was established in 1998 by the three major granting agencies in Canada as a joint policy concerning ethical standards for research involving humans. The policy statement was revised in 2018. The TCPS 2 establishes rules for the creation of research ethics boards (REBs) in institutions receiving research funding, to review and approve studies involving human subjects before they may be conducted.
- Statistics Canada is very conscientious about protecting the confidentiality of those from whom they gather data. Among other things, researchers who are given permission to use Statistics Canada data must adhere to specific guidelines when reporting their findings, taking great care to avoid various forms of disclosure.
- Researchers agree that participation in research should normally be voluntary. This norm, however, can conflict with the scientific need for generalizability.
- Research should not harm those who participate in it, unless they willingly and knowingly accept the risks of harm, giving their informed consent.
- Anonymity refers to the situation in which even the researcher cannot identify specific information with the individuals it describes;

however, confidentiality refers to the situation in which the researcher promises to keep information about subjects private. The most straightforward way to ensure confidentiality is to destroy identifying information as soon as it's no longer needed.

- Deception of subjects is involved in many research designs. Because deceiving people violates common standards of ethical behaviour, deception in research requires a strong justification. Even then the justification may be challenged.
- Social researchers have ethical obligations to the community of researchers as well as to subjects. These obligations include reporting results fully and accurately as well as disclosing errors, limitations, and other shortcomings in the research.
- Humphreys's study of "tearoom" encounters and Milgram's study of obedience raise ethical issues that are debated to this day.
- The ever-expanding volume of digital information available online brings many exciting opportunities for Internet-mediated social research, but along with this come many new ethical issues and considerations related to informed consent and privacy.

REVIEW QUESTIONS AND EXERCISES

1. Consider the following real and hypothetical research situations. See if you can find the ethical component in each. How do you feel about it? Do you believe the procedures described are ultimately acceptable or unacceptable? You might find it useful to discuss some of these with classmates.
   a. After a field study of deviant behaviour during a riot, law enforcement officials demand that the researcher identify those people who were observed looting. Rather than risk arrest as an accomplice after the fact, the researcher complies.
   b. After completing the final draft of a book reporting a research project, the researcher-author discovers that 25 of the 2,000 survey interviews were falsified by interviewers but chooses to ignore that fact and publish the book anyway.
   c. Researchers obtain a list of right-wing radicals they wish to study. They contact the radicals with the explanation that each has been selected "at random" from among the general population to take a sampling of "public opinion."
   d. A university instructor who wants to test the effect of unfair berating administers an hour-long exam to both sections of a specific course. The overall performance of the two sections is essentially the same. The grades of one section are artificially lowered, however, and the instructor berates them for performing so badly. The instructor then administers the same final exam to both sections and discovers that the performance of the unfairly berated section is worse. The hypothesis is confirmed, and the research report is published.
   e. A researcher studying dorm life on campus discovers that 60 percent of the residents regularly violate restrictions on alcohol consumption. Publication of this finding would probably create a furor in the campus community. Because no extensive analysis of alcohol use is planned, the researcher decides to ignore the finding and keep it quiet.
   f. To test the extent to which people may try to save face by expressing attitudes on matters they are wholly uninformed about, the researcher asks for their attitudes regarding a fictitious issue.
   g. A research questionnaire is circulated among students as part of their university registration packet. Although students are not told they must complete the questionnaire, the hope is that they will believe they must, thus ensuring a higher survey completion rate.
   h. A researcher interested in studying an online community plans to enter the community's chat room to observe and record their discussions. Does the researcher need consent? What concerns should she weigh when considering reproducing conversations verbatim in her research report?

i. A researcher pretends to join a radical political group in order to study it and is successfully accepted as a member of the inner planning circle. What should the researcher do if the group makes plans for the following?
   (i) a peaceful, though illegal, demonstration
   (ii) the bombing of a public building during a time it is sure to be unoccupied
   (iii) the assassination of a public official
2. Review the discussion of the Milgram experiment on obedience. How would you design a study to accomplish the same purpose while avoiding the ethical criticisms levelled at Milgram? Would your design be equally valid? Would it have the same effect?
3. Review the "nutritional experiments" research conducted on Indigenous peoples (see the Applying Concepts in Everyday Life box "Ethics of Indigenous Research"). How does this research stack up against the current standards of respect for persons, concern for welfare, and justice? Do you think that the effects of this research were confined to the individual participants, or did the research have broader impacts on the Indigenous community?

CONTINUITY PROJECT

■ AVOIDING EXPLOITATION

Scientific work carries a high value in modern societies, and researchers doing scientific work are awarded high prestige. Prestige inequalities are reflected in power differences, which means that researchers must be careful about exploiting participants. This is especially true when participants are from vulnerable populations.

Review the research on nutritional issues (reported previously in this chapter in Applying Concepts in Everyday Life, "Ethics of Indigenous Research"). If you require them, here is a source for more details about the original research:

Mosby, Ian. 2013. "Administering Colonial Science: Nutrition Research and Human Biomedical Experimentation in Aboriginal Communities and Residential Schools, 1942–1952." *Social History* 46(91):145–172.

If this research were to be replicated today, what specific ethical issues would have to be addressed? Describe approaches that could be used to meet each of these ethical obligations.

PART 2

THE STRUCTURING OF INQUIRY

Posing questions properly is often more difficult than answering them. Indeed, a properly phrased question often seems to answer itself. You may have discovered the answer to a question just in the process of making the question clear to someone else.

Part 2 considers the posing of proper scientific questions—the structuring of inquiry. Part 3 will describe some of the specific methods of social scientific observation.

Chapter 4 addresses the beginnings of research. It examines some of the purposes of inquiry, including explanation, in social science, which rests on the logic of causation. It then considers units of analysis and reasons scientists get involved in research projects.

Chapter 5 deals with the specification of what it is you want to study—the processes of conceptualization and operationalization. It looks at some of the terms we use quite casually in everyday life—prejudice, liberalism, happiness, and so forth—and shows how essential it is to clarify what we really mean by such terms when we do research. This process of clarification is called conceptualization. Once we clarify what we mean by certain terms, we can then measure the referents of those terms. The process of devising steps or operations for measuring concepts that we want to study is called operational definition.

The chapter ends with a brief discussion of techniques for measuring variables in quantitative research through the combination of several indicators: indexes and scales. As an example, we might ask survey respondents five different questions about their attitudes toward gender equality and then combine the answers to all five questions into a composite measure of gender-based egalitarianism. Although such measures are constructed during the analysis of data (see Part 4), the raw materials for them must be provided for in the design and execution of data collection. (A more detailed discussion is available in the Online Chapter—Indexes and Scales.)

Finally, we'll look at how social scientists select people or things for observation. Chapter 6 addresses the fundamental scientific issue of generalizability. As you'll see, we can select a few people or things for observation and then apply what we observe to a much larger group of people or things. This chapter examines techniques that increase the generalizability of what we observe.

What you learn in Part 2 will bring you to the verge of making controlled research observations. Part 3 will show you how to take that next step.

RESEARCH DESIGN AND THE LOGIC OF CAUSATION

A wide variety of research designs are available to social science researchers. Designing a study involves specifying exactly who or what is to be studied, when, how, and for what purpose. Explanation is one of the main goals of researchers. An understanding of how causality is established in social research is needed in order to evaluate and conduct explanatory research.

IN THIS CHAPTER ...

INTRODUCTION

Science is an enterprise dedicated to "finding out." No matter what you want to find out, though, there will likely be a great many ways of doing it. That's true in life generally. Suppose that you want to find out whether a particular automobile—say, the new Burpo-Blasto—would be a good car for you. You could, of course, buy one and find out that way. You could talk to a lot of B-B owners or to people who considered buying one and didn't. You might check the online ads to see if there are a lot of B-Bs being sold cheap. You could study online consumer evaluations of Burpo-Blastos, and so on. You might combine several of these ways of finding out. A similar situation occurs in scientific inquiry.

Ultimately, scientific inquiry comes down to making observations and interpreting what you've observed, the subjects of Parts 3 and 4 of this book. Before you can observe and analyze, however, you need a plan. You need to determine what you're going to observe and analyze why and how. That's what research design is all about.

Although the details vary according to what you wish to study, there are two major tasks in any research design. First, you must specify as clearly as possible what you want to find out. Second, you must determine the best way to do it. Interestingly, if you can handle the first consideration fully, you'll probably handle the second in the same process. As mathematicians say, a properly framed question contains the answer. Of course, issues of ethics are integral to your determination of the best way to design your research as well.

Let's say you're interested in studying corruption in government. That's certainly a worthy and appropriate topic for social research. But what do you mean by *corruption*? Specifically, what kinds of behaviours do you have in mind? And what do you mean by *government*? Whom do you want to study—all public employees? Elected officials? Civil servants? Finally, what is your purpose? Do you want to find out *how much* corruption there is? Do you want to learn *why* corruption exists? These are the kinds of questions that need to be answered in the course of research design.

This chapter provides a general introduction to research design, while the other chapters in Part 2 elaborate on specific aspects. In practice, all aspects of research design are interrelated. How these parts interrelate will become clearer as you move through Part 2. Remember from Chapter 2 that the purpose of a research design is to find a defensible way of linking abstract and concrete levels of experience. We'll begin by briefly examining the three main purposes of social research that help define what kind of study to undertake. Then we'll consider units of analysis—the *what* or *whom* you want to study. We will then elaborate on the logic of causation in the context of explanation, because typically researchers explain things by specifying the causes of the phenomena they observe. The idea of causation has been implicit in much of our discussion in Chapters 1 and 2. We would like to address a few issues about causation directly here before moving ahead to discuss other aspects of research design. We'll look at causation in the context of the nomothetic and idiographic models of explanation introduced in Chapter 1, discussing the criteria for deciding that one thing causes another. Next we'll consider alternative ways of handling time in social research. Some studies examine a static cross-section of social life, but others follow social processes over time.

THREE PURPOSES OF RESEARCH

Social research, of course, serves many purposes. Three of the most common and useful purposes are *exploration*, *description*, and *explanation*. Although a given study can have more than one of these purposes—and most do—examining them separately is useful because each has different implications for other aspects of research design.

EXPLORATION

Much of social research is conducted to explore a topic, or to begin to familiarize the researcher with that topic. This approach typically occurs when a researcher examines a new interest or when the subject of study itself is relatively new.

As an example, let's suppose that widespread taxpayer dissatisfaction with the government erupts into a taxpayers' revolt. People begin refusing to pay their taxes, and they organize themselves around that issue. You might like to learn more about the movement: How widespread is it? What levels and degrees of support are there within the community? How is the movement organized? What kinds of people are active in it? You might undertake an exploratory study to obtain at least approximate answers to some of these questions. You might check figures with tax-collecting officials, collect and study the literature of the movement, attend meetings, and interview leaders.

Exploratory studies are also appropriate for more persistent phenomena. Suppose you're unhappy with your university's graduation requirements and want to help change them. You might study the history of such requirements at the university and meet with university officials to learn the reasons for the current standards. You could talk to several students to get a rough idea of their sentiments on the subject. Though this last activity would not necessarily yield a precise and accurate picture of student opinion, it could suggest what the results of a more extensive study might be.

Sometimes exploratory research is pursued through the use of *focus groups*, or guided small-group discussions. This technique is frequently used in market research; we'll define and examine it further in Chapter 11.

Exploratory studies are most typically done for three purposes: (1) to satisfy the researcher's curiosity and desire for better understanding, (2) to test the feasibility of undertaking a more extensive study, and (3) to develop the methods to be employed in any subsequent study.

Exploratory studies are quite valuable in social scientific research. They're essential whenever a researcher is breaking new ground, and they almost always yield new insights into a topic for research. Exploratory studies are also a source of grounded theory rooted in induction, as discussed in Chapter 2.

The chief shortcoming of exploratory studies is that they seldom provide satisfactory answers to research questions, though they can hint at the answers and can give insights into which research methods could provide definitive answers. The reason exploratory studies are seldom definitive in themselves has to do with representativeness—that is, the people studied in exploratory research may not be typical of the larger population of interest. (Representativeness is discussed at length in Chapter 6.) Once you understand representativeness, you will be able to know whether a given exploratory study actually answered its research problem or only pointed the way toward an answer.

DESCRIPTION

A major purpose of many social scientific studies is to describe situations and events. The researcher observes and then describes what was observed. Because scientific observation is careful and deliberate, however, scientific descriptions are typically more accurate and precise than casual ones.

The Canadian census is an excellent example of descriptive social research. The goal of the census is to describe accurately and precisely a wide variety of characteristics of the Canadian population, as well as the populations of smaller areas such as provinces and cities. Other examples of descriptive studies are the computation of age–gender profiles of populations done by demographers, the computation of crime rates for different cities, and a product marketing survey that describes the people who use, or would use, a particular product. A researcher who carefully chronicles the events that take place on a labour union picket line has a descriptive purpose. A researcher who computes and reports the distribution of wages for men and women over several decades also fulfills a descriptive purpose. Many qualitative studies aim primarily at description. An anthropological ethnography, for example, may try to detail the particular culture of some preliterate society. At the same time, such studies are seldom limited to a merely descriptive purpose. Researchers usually go on to examine *why* the observed patterns exist and what they imply.

EXPLANATION

The third general purpose of social scientific research is to explain things. Descriptive studies answer questions of who, what, where, and when;

explanatory studies answer questions of how and why. The term **explanation** literally means "to make plain." We explain an occurrence when we make the event clear—when we make it understandable. When explanations are successful, the curiosity that led to our asking how or why is satisfied. Imagine asking for an explanation of an unexpected event, such as a friend cheating on his or her partner. Reciting the descriptive details of the escapade (who, what, where, when) will not be satisfactory. For a satisfactory explanation, how or why questions must be answered.

So when William Sanders (1994) set about characterizing the varieties of gang violence, he also wanted to reconstruct the process that brought about violent episodes among the gangs of different ethnic groups.

Reporting the voting intentions of an electorate is a descriptive activity, but reporting why some people plan to vote for Candidate A and others for Candidate B is an explanatory activity. Reporting the crime rates of different cities is a case of description, but identifying variables that explain why some cities have higher crime rates than others involves explanation. A researcher who sets out to discover *why* an anti-abortion demonstration ended in a violent confrontation with police, as opposed to simply describing what happened, has an explanatory purpose.

Although it's useful to distinguish the three purposes of research, it bears repeating that many studies will have elements of all three. Suppose, for example, that you have set out to evaluate a new form of psychotherapy. Your study will have exploratory aspects, as you explore potentially relevant variables and map out the effects of the therapy. You'll want to describe things like recovery rates, and you'll undoubtedly seek to explain why the therapy works better for some types of people (or problems) than for others.

UNITS OF ANALYSIS

Chapter 2 emphasized that the hallmark of scientific investigation is a defensible merger of abstract conceptualizations (theory) and empirical patterns (evidence). Whether an investigation is conducted for exploratory, descriptive, or explanatory purposes, every investigation tries to draw conclusions about something. The "things" that are the object of a study's attention are called **units of analysis**.

To draw research-based conclusions about something, evidence must be collected from or about some cases. **Cases** are the specific objects to which evidence (data) refer. The kinds of objects from which evidence is collected are called **units of observation**.

The distinction between units of observation and units of analysis can be confusing, since what you are studying (units of analysis) is sometimes the same as, and sometimes different from, what you are collecting evidence from (units of observation). A couple of examples will help clarify your understanding. Imagine you want to investigate whether students who complete their homework do better in a French course. In this example, your unit of analysis (what you want to draw conclusions about) is the *same as* your unit of observation (what you want to collect data from). In both instances it is individuals (students). To complete your study, you would collect data from *individual* students about their homework behaviour and their course performance, and then you would compare *individuals* to determine whether those who complete their homework perform better.

Now consider an investigation in which you wanted to determine whether Grade 10 math classes with male teachers do better than those taught by females. What is your unit of analysis? It is "class," because this is what you want to know about. You are inquiring whether male-taught *classes* do better than female-taught ones. What is your unit of observation; that is, what do you have to collect evidence from? It is "individuals," since you will have to determine the sex of *individual* teachers and the math performance of

explanation The satisfaction of curiosity by successfully clarifying how or why an event occurred.

unit of analysis The object of a study's interest.

case A specific object to which evidence refers.

unit of observation The kinds of objects from which evidence is collected.

individual students. In this example, the units of analysis and units of observation are *different.*

In this second example, if you collect math-performance data from individual students (units of observation), how do you get math-performance evidence about classes (units of analysis)? Well, you would probably create an average math score using all the students in the class. Note that although these average scores use data from individuals (units of observation), they refer to classes (units of analysis). Individuals don't have class averages; classes do.

In social research, the most common "things" studied (units of observation) are people. When individuals are being observed and our interest is in talking about specific persons, the resulting evidence is called **individual data**. Gathering data from specific individuals, however, does not restrict us to only studying individuals. People can be observed in larger units than individuals (e.g., families, teams, and nations). When the cases studied are assemblies of individuals, the evidence is called **aggregate data**.

In designing a research study, it is important that you be clear about what units of analysis are being used. Here's an example of what can go wrong. Let's say you conduct a survey of inner-city youth with the intention of understanding what characteristics are related to gang membership. In this case both your units of observation and analysis are individuals. Analysis of your interesting findings leads you to wonder how male gangs differ from female ones. This research question shifts your focus to a different unit of analysis, since you want to compare gangs (groups). If you haven't been clear about this group unit of analysis in designing your study, you probably won't be able to follow this lead, since you will not have enough cases of female gang members to conduct the analysis.

To solidify your understanding of units of analysis, let's look at several common ones in more detail.

individual data Evidence gathered about cases that are specific individuals.

aggregate data Evidence gathered about cases that are collections of individuals.

INDIVIDUALS

Individual human beings are the most typical unit of observation and unit of analysis in social scientific research. When researchers shift to aggregate units of analysis (like groups and organizations) they commonly do so based on individual levels of observation.

Any type of individual may be the unit of analysis for social scientific research. This point is more important than it may seem at first. Since social science seeks to understand human behaviour in general, this suggests that scientific findings are most valuable when they apply to all kinds of people. In practice, however, social scientists seldom study all kinds of people. At the very least, their studies are typically limited to the people living in a single country, though some comparative studies stretch across national boundaries. Often, though, studies are quite circumscribed.

Examples of classes of individuals that might be chosen for study are university students, gays and lesbians, autoworkers, Canadian voters, single parents, and professional athletes. Notice that each of these terms implies some population of individual persons. Descriptive studies with individuals as their units of analysis typically aim to describe the population that comprises those individuals, whereas explanatory studies aim to discover the social dynamics operating within that population.

As the units of analysis, individuals may be characterized by their membership in social groupings. Thus, an individual may be described as belonging to a rich family or to a poor one, or as having a university-educated mother or not. We might conduct a research project to examine whether people with university-educated mothers are more likely to attend university than those with nonuniversity-educated mothers, or whether high school graduates in rich families are more likely to attend university than those in poor families. In each case, the unit of analysis—the "thing" whose characteristics we are seeking to describe or explain—is the individual. We can then aggregate these individuals and make generalizations about the population they belong to.

GROUPS

Social groups can also be the units of analysis for social scientific research. That is, we may be interested in characteristics that belong to one group that is considered as a single entity. If you were to study criminals by looking at members of a criminal gang, the individual (criminal) would be the unit of analysis. But if you studied all the gangs in a city to learn the differences, say, between big gangs and small ones, between uptown and downtown gangs, and so forth, you would be interested in gangs rather than their individual members. In this case, the unit of analysis would be the gang, a social group.

Here's another example. Suppose your interest was in the question of access to computers in different parts of society. You might describe families by total annual income and according to whether they had computers. You could then aggregate families and describe the mean income of families and the percentage of families who have computers. You would then be in a position to determine whether families with higher incomes were more likely to have computers than those with lower incomes. In this case, the unit of analysis would be families.

As with other units of analysis, we can derive the characteristics of social groups from those of their individual members. Thus we might describe a family by the age, race, or education of the parents. In a descriptive study, we might find the percentage of all families that have a university-educated head of family. In an explanatory study, we might determine whether such families have, on average, more or fewer children than families headed by people who have not graduated from university. In each of these examples, the family would be the unit of analysis. In contrast, had we asked whether university-educated individuals have more or fewer children than their less educated counterparts, then the individual person would have been the unit of analysis.

Social groups may be characterized in other ways, such as according to their environments or their membership in larger groupings. Families, for example, might be described by their dwelling: we might want to determine whether rich families are more likely to reside in single-family houses (as opposed to, say, apartments) than poor families. It's worth noting that some attributes apply only to collectivities, just as some apply only to individuals. For instance, families or gangs can be characterized by "number of members"—this factor varies among families or gangs but does not characterize individuals.

Other units of analysis at the group level could be friendship cliques, married couples, cities, or geographic regions. As in the case of individuals, each of these terms also implies some population. Street gangs implies some population that includes all street gangs, perhaps in a given city. The population of street gangs could be described, say, in terms of its geographical distribution throughout a city. In an explanatory study of street gangs, you might discover whether large gangs are more likely than small ones to engage in intergang warfare.

ORGANIZATIONS

Formal social organizations may also be the units of analysis in social scientific research. For example, a researcher might study corporations, by which he or she implies a population of all corporations. Individual corporations might be characterized by their number of employees, net annual profits, gross assets, number of defence contracts, percentage of employees from racial or ethnic minority groups, and so forth. We might determine whether large corporations hire a larger or smaller percentage of minority-group employees than small corporations. Other examples of formal social organizations suitable as units of analysis would be church congregations, universities, academic departments, and supermarkets.

SOCIAL ARTIFACTS

Another unit of analysis is the **social artifact**, which is a product of human activity. One class of artifacts includes concrete objects such as books, poems, paintings, automobiles, buildings, songs, pottery, jokes, student excuses for missing exams,

social artifact Any product of human activity.

and scientific discoveries. For example, studying the depiction of coverage of Indigenous people in the media, Grenier's (1994) units of analysis were daily newspapers. In order to examine how the English–Canadian press covered Indigenous issues, he did a content analysis of all regular *Montreal Gazette* daily newspapers prior to and during a major Indigenous protest known as the Oka Crisis (January 2–July 31, 1990).

Just as individuals and social groups imply populations, each social artifact implies a set of all objects of the same class: all books, all novels, all biographies, all introductory sociology textbooks, all cookbooks. In a study using books as the units of analysis, a book might be characterized by its size, weight, length, price, content, number of pictures, number sold, or description of its author. Then the population of all books or of a particular kind of book could be analyzed for the purpose of description or explanation: what kinds of books sell best and why, for example.

Similarly, a social scientist could analyze whether paintings by Russian, Chinese, or Canadian artists showed the greatest degree of working-class consciousness, taking paintings as the units of analysis and describing each, in part, by the nationality of its creator. Or you might examine a local newspaper's editorials regarding a local university, for the purpose of describing, or perhaps explaining, changes in the newspaper's editorial position on the university over time. In this example, individual editorials would be the units of analysis.

Social interactions form another class of social artifacts suitable for social scientific research. For example, we might characterize weddings as racially or religiously mixed or not, as religious or secular in ceremony, as resulting in divorce or not, or by descriptions of one or both of the marriage partners (such as "previously married"). When a researcher reports that weddings between partners of different religions are more likely to be performed by secular authorities than those between partners of the same religion, weddings are the units of analysis, not the individuals involved.

Other social interactions that might be units of analysis are friendship choices, court cases, traffic accidents, divorces, fist fights, ship launchings, sporting events, race riots, and student demonstrations. The student demonstrations could be characterized by whether or not they occurred during an election campaign, whether the demonstration leaders were male or female, whether the leaders had been convicted of a felony or not, and so on. Notice that even if we characterized and compared the demonstrations in terms of the leaders, the demonstrations themselves, not the individual leaders, would be our units of analysis.

Figure 4-1 provides a graphic illustration of some different units of analysis and the statements that might be made about them.

UNITS OF ANALYSIS IN REVIEW

The examples in this section suggest the nearly infinite variety of possible units of analysis for social scientific research. Although individual human beings are typical objects of study, many research questions can be answered more appropriately through the examination of other units of analysis. Social scientists can study just about anything that bears on social life.

Moreover, the types of units of analysis named in this section don't begin to exhaust the possibilities. Morris Rosenberg (1968:234–248), for example, speaks of individual, group, organizational, institutional, spatial, cultural, and societal units of analysis. Lofland and colleagues (2006:122–132) speak of practices, episodes, encounters, roles, relationships, groups, organizations, settlements, lifestyles, and subcultures as suitable units of study. What's important here is to grasp the logic of units of analysis.

Categorizing possible units of analysis may make the concept seem more complicated than it needs to be. What you call a given unit of analysis—a group, a formal organization, or a social artifact—is irrelevant. The key is to be clear about what your unit of analysis is. When you begin a research project, you must decide whether you are studying marriages or marriage partners, crimes or criminals, corporations or corporate executives. Otherwise, you run the risk of drawing invalid conclusions because your assertions about one unit of analysis are actually based on the examination of another. We'll see an example of this issue as we look at the ecological fallacy.

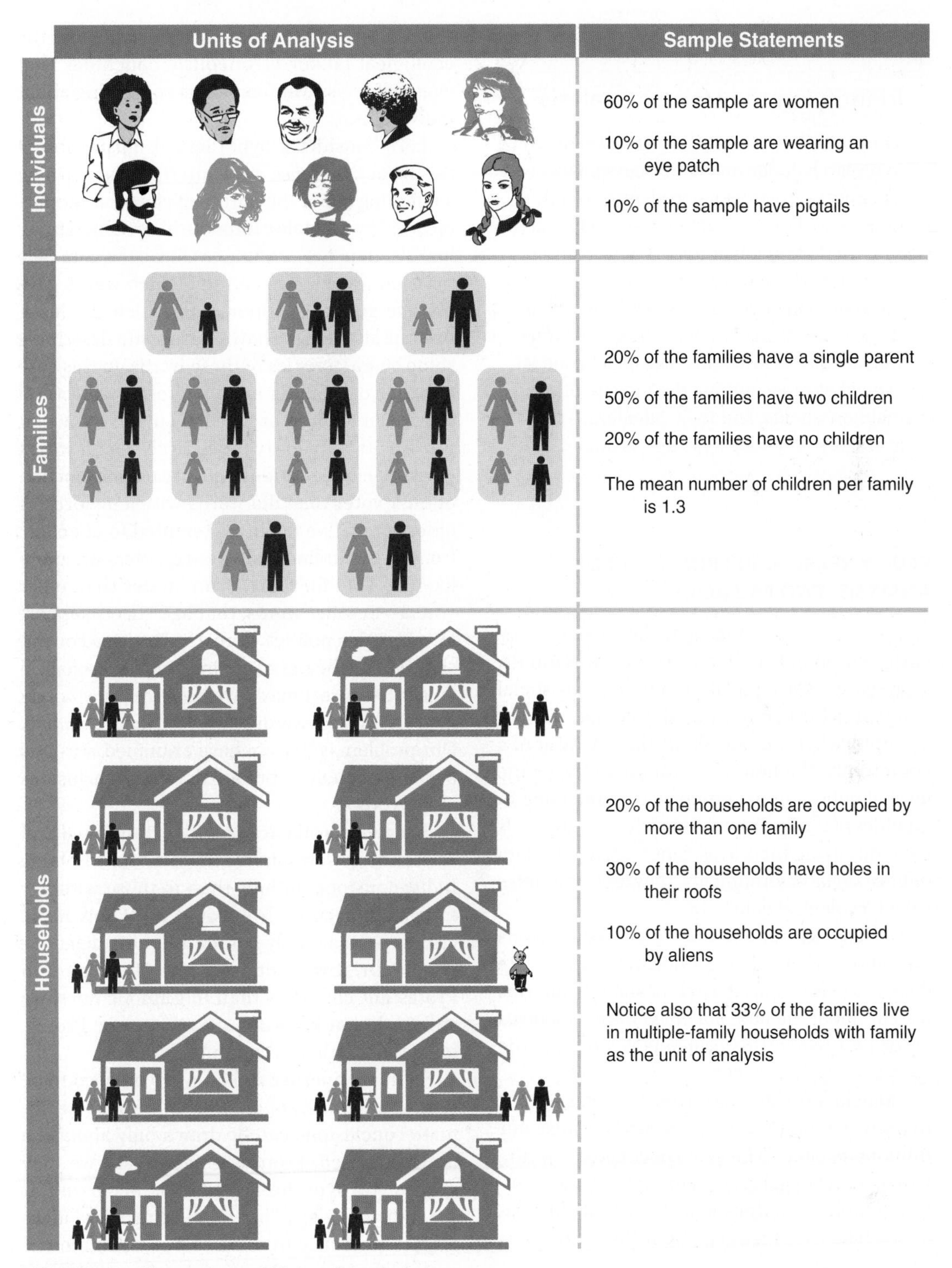

FIGURE 4-1 **Illustrations of Units of Analysis.** Units of analysis in social research can be individuals, groups, or even nonhuman entities.
Source: © Cengage Learning

HOW TO DO IT

Identifying the Unit of Analysis

The unit of analysis is an important element in research design and data analysis. Here is a helpful way of thinking to identify a study's units of analysis: determine who or what has the attribute being studied. For example, consider the statement "The average household income was $60,000." Income is the variable of interest, but who or what *has* the income? Households. The conclusion is arrived at by examining the income of several households, and then calculating their average. Household is the unit of analysis.

FAULTY REASONING FROM UNITS OF ANALYSIS: TWO FALLACIES

Ecological Fallacy Aggregate data are evidence gathered about collections of individuals. Aggregate data typically report on the social reality in which an individual is embedded. For example, when we talk about the sex ratio of a community, the homicide rate in a city, or the level of cohesion in a group, we are referring to qualities of the environment in which individuals go about living their lives. Since aggregate data refer to social environments, they are sometimes called "ecological data."

Evidence about any unit of analysis tells us only about what is being studied. For aggregate data, evidence about the unit of analysis informs us only about the unit, *not about the components of the unit.* When this principle is violated, the **ecological fallacy** occurs.

Fallacies are thinking errors. Fallacies lead us to draw inappropriate conclusions because our thinking is faulty. The ecological fallacy occurs when we use aggregate data about some collective unit of analysis and think that this evidence tells us something about the individuals that compose the aggregate. Specifically, the ecological fallacy erroneously concludes that aggregate observations tell us something about individuals.

Let's consider a hypothetical illustration of this fallacy. Suppose we're interested in learning something about the nature of electoral support received by a female candidate in a recent municipal election. Let's assume we have the vote tally for each ward so we can tell which wards gave her the greatest support and which the least. Assume also that we have census data describing some characteristics of these wards. In this case our unit of analysis is an aggregate, "electoral ward." Our analysis of such data might show that wards with a majority of relatively young voters gave the female candidate a greater proportion of their votes than did wards with a majority of older voters. We might be tempted to conclude from these findings that young voters are more likely to vote for female candidates than older voters—in other words, that age affects support for women in politics. In reaching such a conclusion, we run the risk of committing the ecological fallacy because it may have been the older voters in those "young" wards who voted for the woman. Our problem is that we have examined wards as our unit of analysis but are drawing conclusions about voters.

The same problem arises if we discovered that crime rates were higher in cities having large Indigenous populations than in those with few Indigenous people. We would not know if the crimes were actually committed by Indigenous people. Or, if we found suicide rates higher in Protestant countries than in Catholic ones, we still could not know for sure that more Protestants than Catholics committed suicide.

So this is another reason why you need to be clear on the units of analysis in a study. Legitimate conclusions can be drawn only about the units analyzed. From aggregate data we may suspect or hypothesize what is occurring at the individual level, but confirming these ideas requires evidence from that level. Communities with higher proportions of young people may have higher crime rates—but whether it is actually the youth committing the crimes is a separate question.

ecological fallacy The reasoning error that occurs when conclusions about individuals are based solely on group observations.

Exception Fallacy The ecological fallacy rests on confusion about units of analysis. Another common confusion is related to describing a unit of analysis. This reasoning error is called the **exception fallacy**.

Often observed aggregate patterns challenge people's common sense. For example, most people believe that reality is given, rather than constructed (Bredemeier 1998). Or they believe that violence is easy and common, when it is actually difficult and infrequent (Collins 2008). Findings like these are confounding, since they question everyday assumptions about social experience. A common response is to challenge the aggregate reports with evidence—specifically, with evidence from individual experience. All of us have probably heard someone defend themselves against an assertion they found surprising by saying something like, "Well, in my experience...." When such individualist evidence is used to counter aggregate findings, the exception fallacy is at play.

The exception fallacy occurs when individual evidence is used to draw conclusions about aggregate phenomena. Many people think that if their individual experience differs from the aggregate pattern, then the aggregate pattern is negated. Here, the exception fallacy is operating. Identifying an exceptional case does not dismiss an aggregate finding. Those who think it does are committing a thinking error. Individual exceptions are just that; they should not be confused with aggregate patterns. Your knowledge of someone who got rich without any formal education doesn't deny the general pattern relating higher education to higher income.

So far you have seen that, in designing a research study, you need to be clear about the study's purpose (exploration, description, or explanation) and its units of analysis. Next, we turn our attention to how studies are designed to provide explanatory answers.

THE LOGIC OF CAUSATION

While studies conducted for exploratory and descriptive purposes have their place, most compelling research is explanatory. These are the studies that satisfy our curiosity about something by making clear either how or why an outcome of interest occurred. In doing so, these studies rely on identifying **causes**. Causes are the mechanisms (how) or reasons (why) some event occurred.

Identifying causes is challenging and has the best chance of success when a study's design supports causal exploration. This requires understanding the logic of causation. The logic of causation differs among types of studies. First, we shall explore how explanation operates in studies that connect abstract and concrete levels of experience through deductive reasoning. Then we shall look at the model of explanation used in research that begins at the concrete level and works inductively to the abstract one.

CAUSAL LOGIC IN NOMOTHETIC EXPLANATIONS

Chapter 1 introduced you to the idea that scientific research focuses on linking abstract ideas (theory) with concrete findings (evidence) to create a defensible understanding of reality. In the traditional model of science, the process begins at the abstract level, moves down toward concrete testing, and then up again for interpretation. This research model is typically used in quantitative research that seeks nomothetic (general) explanations by identifying a key number of operating considerations (variables).

The causal logic of nomothetic explanation centres on variables (i.e., properties of objects that can change). The dependent variable is the event whose differences are to be explained. For example, perhaps we are interested in explaining "permissiveness in abortion attitudes." In designing a quantitative, nomothetic study we are interested in identifying what independent (explanatory) variables are most important to explaining why some people have more permissive and others less permissive attitudes. Let's say we have good reason to think (theoretically) that abortion attitudes are affected by religious

exception fallacy The reasoning error that occurs when conclusions about aggregates are drawn from individual cases.

causes The mechanisms or reasons leading to an outcome.

commitment, education, and permissiveness of attitudes toward premarital sex.

Using this collection of independent and dependent variables, a quantitative study proceeds to do all those things discussed in Chapter 2, including hypothesis creation (through empirical deduction) and empirical testing (through instrumentation and measurement). With your empirical evidence collected, you are left with the causal question: What explains differences in attitudes toward abortion? Answering this question requires analyzing the data, which will be discussed later in this book. For now, it is important to understand what criteria quantitative researchers use in establishing a causal connection between variables.

CRITERIA FOR NOMOTHETIC CAUSALITY

First, we need to be clear that when discussing causality we are talking about a particular form of relationship between variables. A relationship exists when a change in one thing is identified with a systematic change in another thing. In quantitative research, the "things" are independent and dependent variables. In social life, the "things" are people. So the quantitative search for causes is a search for a systematic connection between variables.

It is important to appreciate that observing variables that have some relationship does not establish that the relationship is one of cause and effect. Imagine we found that people affiliated with the Liberal Party prefer strawberry to vanilla ice cream (i.e., a relationship exists between political party and ice cream preference). This does not mean that party preference causes a preference for strawberry flavour—or, alternatively, that a preference for strawberry causes people to become Liberals. Establishing causality requires more than observing that variables are related. In fact, it requires that three criteria be demonstrated to exist: (1) the variables are correlated, (2) the cause occurs before the effect, and (3) the connection between the variables is nonspurious. Let's discuss each of these criteria.

Correlation/Association To say that a causal relationship exists there must be an actual, observed relationship—or **correlation**—between two variables. Literally, *correlation* means "change together." A correlation (association) exists between variables when they are observed to be related—that is, when one occurs or changes, the other does so systematically. It would make no sense to say that exploding gunpowder causes bullets to leave muzzles of guns if, in observed reality, bullets did not come out after the gunpowder exploded (or if they came out even when it didn't explode).

Correlation is a challenging criterion to demonstrate. Since correlations are rarely perfect, researchers debate about how strong a correlation must exist for a connection to be causal. We will discuss this kind of technical issue later. For now, what is important to appreciate is this: If variables do not change together systematically (i.e., are not associated), then they cannot have a causal connection.

Time Order/Sequence The second causal criterion is time order (sequence). We can't say that a causal relationship exists unless the independent (causal) variable precedes the effect (dependent variable) in time. It makes no sense to imagine something being caused by something else that happened later on. Clearly, a bullet leaving the muzzle of a gun does not cause the gunpowder to explode; it works the other way around. Owning a luxury car doesn't cause one to earn enough money to afford one.

As simple and obvious as this criterion may seem, you'll discover that it generates problems in the analysis of social science data. Often, the order of two variables is simply unclear. Which comes first: prejudice or the trait known as authoritarianism (excessive submissiveness to authority accompanied by rigid thinking)? Again, we will tackle the technical details later. For now, what's important is recognizing that the correct sequence must be demonstrated (not just asserted).

correlation Empirical evidence that a change in one variable is systematically identified with a change in another (association).

Nonspuriousness/Authenticity[1] The third causal criterion is nonspuriousness. The term *spurious* means phony; so a *non*spurious relationship is one that is not phony. In other words, nonspurious relationships are genuine or authentic. Remember, we are applying this criterion to the observed relationship between two variables. So what exactly are we talking about?

Remember, the first causal criterion requires demonstrating that a correlation (association) exists between the variables of interest. A correlation (association) is an observed relationship. The problem is that our observations may fool us, because appearances do not necessarily reflect reality. What appears genuine is sometimes phony. So this third causal criterion (nonspuriousness) requires that the observed correlation (in the first criterion) be demonstrably genuine. The following discussion will clarify how this is done.

Relationships between people do not exist in isolation, and neither do relationships between independent and dependent variables. Instead, connections between variables and people always exist in a context. In research, a **control variable** (or several control variables) specifies the context of a relationship. For example, an observed relationship between family income (independent variable) and educational attainment (dependent variable) may depend on the national context, such as whether the national postsecondary system is funded privately or by the state. Stated in research terms, high-quality state-funded schools (control variable) may influence the observed effect of family income (independent variable) on years of education attained (dependent variable).

Contexts affect relationships. Here are some example relationships that illustrate the need for not simply accepting evidence of correlation as a causal connection. Each lists the independent and dependent variables, followed by the actual empirical correlation:

- Storks and babies: Areas that have greater concentrations of storks have more babies.
- Fire engines and fire damage: As more fire engines appear on a scene, the amount of fire damage systematically increases.
- Shoe size and math ability: People with larger shoe sizes have greater math abilities.
- Ice cream sales and drowning deaths: Increasing ice cream sales are reliably correlated with the number of deaths due to drowning.

Do you actually believe that storks cause babies? Or that fire engines cause fire damage? Or that shoe size contributes to math competence, or ice cream consumption to drowning? Believing so would have you living in a bizarre world where you did not call 911 when your house is on fire because you prefer to limit fire damage! These are, of course, all spurious relationships; the variables appear correlated when, in actuality, they are not. Sorting out authentic from spurious connections is what the third causal criterion (nonspuriousness) is about. The following elaboration will assist your understanding of this important point.

Figure 4-2 diagrams a spurious relationship. To understand the diagram, you need to remember that variables have their effects on other variables *when they change*. With this in mind, look at the figure and note that no line connects the independent and dependent variables, suggesting that the two variables are not really connected. Follow the arrows and you will see how spuriousness operates. Variation in the third, control variable causes change in both the independent and dependent variables. Consequently, if you examined only the independent and dependent variables—if you ignored the context—you would see the independent and dependent variables changing together systematically. Under spurious circumstances, you would see that independent and dependent variables are related when, in fact, they are not. In doing so, you would be fooled by phony appearances.

Nobody likes to be fooled, least of all researchers. Therefore, in the quest to identify causes, researchers test for potential spuriousness in independent–dependent variable relationships.

1 From BRYM/ROBERTS/STROHSCHEIN/LIE. *Sociology: Your Compass for a New World*, 6E. © 2019 Nelson Education Ltd. Reproduced by permission. www.cengage.com/permissions

control variable A variable identifying the context for the relationship between independent and dependent variables.

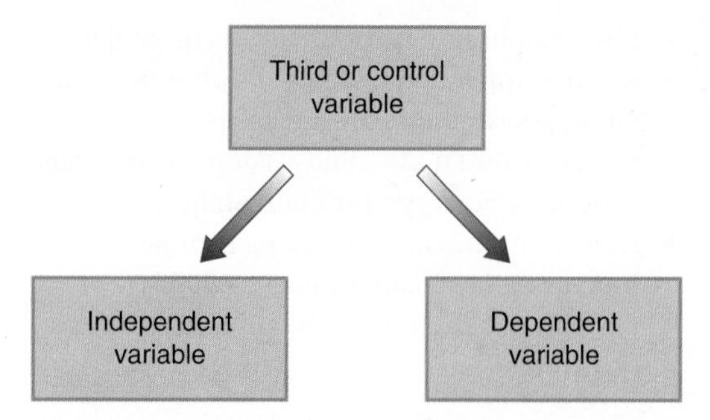

FIGURE 4-2 How Spurious Relationships Occur.
Source: From BRYM/ROBERTS/STROHSCHEIN/LIE. Sociology: *Your Compass for a New World*, 6E. © 2019 Nelson Education Ltd. Reproduced by permission. www.cengage.com/permissions

The easiest way to understand the test for spuriousness is to contrast Figure 4-2 with Figure 4-3, which illustrates what a genuine relationship looks like. In Figure 4-3, the independent and dependent variables are actually related, as evidenced by the double-headed arrow connecting them. Moreover, in this diagram, the third variable is unconnected to either the independent or dependent variable.

Comparing the two diagrams, we see that the operation of the control variable has either nothing to do with the independent–dependent variable connection (the authentic case, Figure 4-3), or everything to do with the appearance of such a connection (the spurious case, Figure 4-2). Based on this crucial difference between the authentic and inauthentic models, researchers have devised a test for determining the existence of spuriousness.

The key idea of the spuriousness test involves examining the independent–dependent variable relationship under two conditions—first, when the third variable is allowed to change and, second, when the third variable is held constant. Where a variable is held constant it is fixed and does not change. And when a variable is held constant, it cannot have any effect on other variables.

Third or control variable

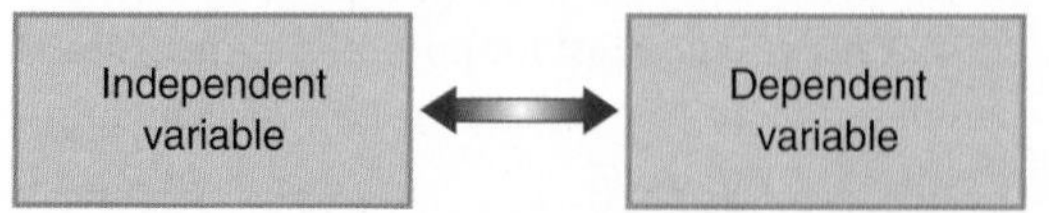

FIGURE 4-3 How Authentic Relationships Occur.
Source: From BRYM/ROBERTS/STROHSCHEIN/LIE. Sociology: *Your Compass for a New World*, 6E. © 2019 Nelson Education Ltd. Reproduced by permission. www.cengage.com/permissions

Using these comparisons, here is how the test for spuriousness works. If the independent–dependent variable relationship is authentic, then the original independent–dependent variable relationship remains the same under both conditions; that is, the relationship is evident both when the third (control) variable is allowed to vary and when it is held constant. By contrast, if the relationship is spurious, the independent–dependent variable connection is evident only when the control variable is changing (the first condition) and disappears when the control variable is held constant (the second condition).

You can better appreciate this logic by returning to our examples. If the connection between storks and babies were authentic (real), then it would be unaffected by the third variable, region. Here is how the test would occur. Under the first condition, the researcher would examine the connection between stork sightings and babies appearing for both rural and urban regions. In this condition, the control variable (region) is being allowed to change. As reported previously, the relationship between stork sightings and babies appearing is evident under this condition. Next, under the second condition, the researcher would examine the storks–babies connection *only* for rural regions and then *only* for urban regions. In doing so, the researcher would be examining the independent–dependent variable connection with the third variable being held constant. This second test would reveal no connection between stork sightings and babies appearing. The researcher would then conclude the storks–babies relationship is spurious because the relationship is evident in the first condition but disappeared in the second condition.

Here is how the test applies to the fire trucks–fire damage relationship. Condition 1: Examine the independent–dependent variable relationship for all kinds of fires. The evidence will indicate an apparent connection. Condition 2: Examine the fire trucks–fire damage connection only for small fires and then only for large fires. The evidence will show no connection between the independent and dependent variables. The inability to replicate the relationship under the two conditions leads to the conclusion that the apparent relationship is spurious.

To summarize, researchers conclude there is a causal connection between two variables when they successfully demonstrate three conditions:

1. The variables systematically change together (the correlation/association criterion).
2. The independent variable changed before observed changes in the dependent variable (the sequencing criterion).
3. The observed relationship is an authentic one (the nonspuriousness criterion).

These are the three criteria working researchers use to determine causal connections. Using these criteria differ somewhat from the way the term *cause* is used in contexts outside of research.

FALSE CRITERIA FOR NOMOTHETIC CAUSALITY

The idea of cause and effect is well entrenched in everyday language and logic. Therefore, it's important to specify some of the things social researchers do *not* mean when they speak of causal relationships. When they say one variable causes another, they do not necessarily mean to suggest complete causation, to account for exceptional cases, or to claim that the causation exists in a majority of cases.

Complete Causation Remember that the quantitative, nomothetic approach seeks to identify a relatively small set of the most prominent contributing causes that generally produce a specific outcome. Therefore, nomothetic explanations are both probabilistic and incomplete. For example, social researchers may say that political orientations cause attitudes toward legalizing marijuana, even though not all liberals approve nor all conservatives disapprove. Thus, we say that political orientation is one of the causes of the attitude, but not the only one.

Exceptional Cases In nomothetic explanations, exceptions do not disconfirm a causal relationship. For example, it has been found that women are more religious than men in both Canada and the United States. Thus gender may be a cause of religiosity, even if your uncle is a religious zealot or you know a woman who is an avowed atheist. Those exceptional cases do not disconfirm the overall causal pattern.

Majority of Cases Causal relationships can be true even if they do not apply in a majority of cases. For example, we say that children who are not supervised after school are more likely to become delinquent than are those who are supervised; hence, lack of supervision is a cause of delinquency. This causal relationship holds true even if only a small percentage of those not supervised become delinquent. As long as they are *more likely* than those who are supervised to be delinquent, we say there is a causal relationship.

The social scientific view of causation may vary from what you are accustomed to, since people commonly use the term *cause* to mean something that completely causes another thing. The somewhat different standard used by social researchers can be seen more clearly in terms of necessary and sufficient causes.

NECESSARY AND SUFFICIENT CONDITIONS

In addition to the three causal criteria conventional researchers use, nonresearchers commonly add two additional conditions, necessity and sufficiency. We need to be clear on what these conditions mean and what effect they would have on the interpretation of causes if they were adopted.

A **necessary condition** is one that *must* be present for the effect to follow. For example, it is necessary for you to take university courses in order to get a degree—without the courses, the degree never happens. But simply taking the courses is not a sufficient cause of getting a degree. You need to take the right ones and pass them.

Similarly, being female is a necessary condition of becoming pregnant, but it is not a sufficient cause. Otherwise all women would get pregnant. Figure 4-4 illustrates this relationship,

necessary condition A condition that must be present for a specific outcome to occur.

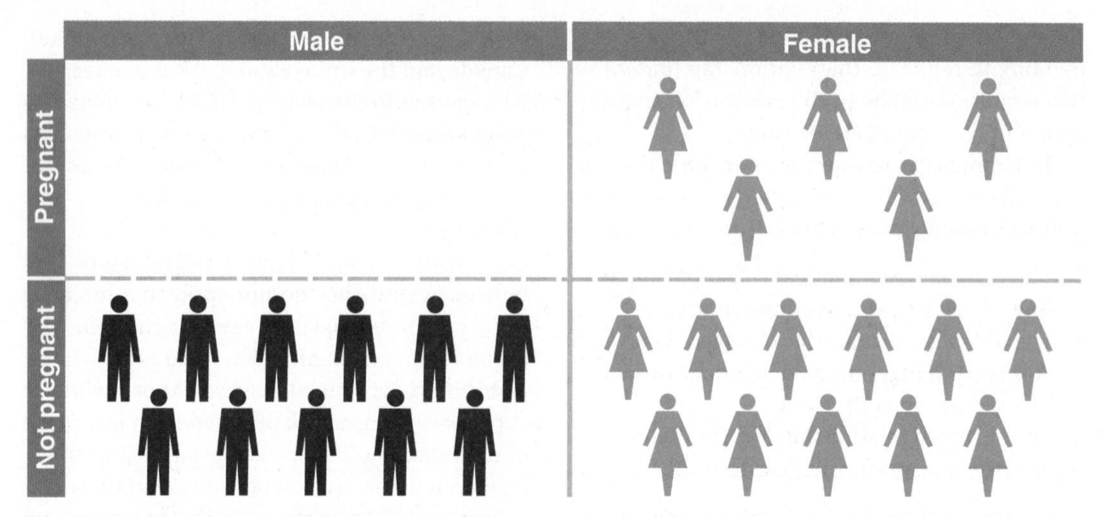

FIGURE 4-4 **Necessary Conditions.** Being female is a necessary condition of pregnancy; that is, you can't get pregnant unless you are female.
Source: © Cengage Learning

showing the possible outcomes of combining the variables of gender and pregnancy.

A **sufficient condition**, on the other hand, is one that, if it is present, guarantees the outcome in question. This does not mean that a sufficient condition is the *only* possible contributor a particular effect. For example, skipping an exam in this course would be a sufficient condition for failing it, though students could fail it other ways as well. Therefore, a condition can be sufficient but not necessary. Figure 4-5 illustrates the relationship between taking or not taking the exam and either passing or failing it.

Took the exam | Didn't take the exam | Failed the exam | Passed the exam

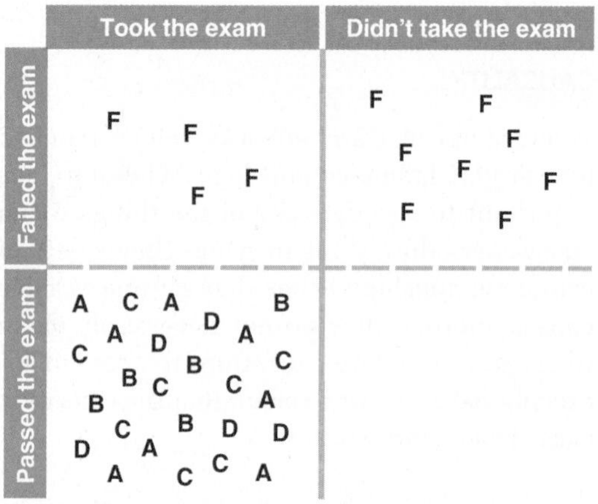

FIGURE 4-5 **Sufficient Conditions.** Not taking the exam is a sufficient condition for failing it, even though there are other ways of failing (such as answering randomly).
Source: © Cengage Learning

The identification of causes that meet both necessary and sufficient conditions would be a powerful demonstration. If juvenile delinquency were the effect under examination, it would be nice to discover a single variable that met the three conventional causal criteria and (1) must be present for delinquency to develop (necessity) and (2) always resulted in delinquency (sufficiency). In such a case, you would surely feel that you knew precisely what caused juvenile delinquency.

In practice, we never discover single causes that are absolutely necessary and absolutely sufficient when analyzing the nomothetic relationships among variables. If we did, the social world would be very different than it is. If necessity and sufficiency are operating, the social world would operate like a billiard table, where one ball's movement is necessary and sufficient to move another. For better or worse, the social world does not operate this way; it is not mechanistic but probabilistic. Sometimes we can identify variables that are necessary

sufficient condition A condition that, when present, produces a specific outcome.

(you must be female to become pregnant) or sufficient (pleading guilty will result in your conviction), but most of the time the causes identified through demonstrating correlation, sequence, and nonspuriousness generate understandings that improve the probabilities (not certainties) for effective action.

CAUSAL LOGIC IN IDIOGRAPHIC EXPLANATIONS

Research aimed at connecting abstract ideas (theory) to concrete patterns (empirical evidence) is not restricted to the nomothetic, traditional science model just discussed. Social researchers often employ a different type of causal logic when their interests are idiographic. Idiographic explanation seeks an exhaustive, comprehensive understanding of the causes producing events or situations in a single or limited number of cases. While idiographic explanations can take many forms, they generally rely on answering "how" (Becker 1998). In doing so, they typically focus on a restricted number of complete cases, rather than teasing out the effects of variables across a wide range of instances.

Understanding the causal logic of idiographic explanations rests on your appreciating how its general approach differs from the quantitative tradition just discussed. Here are some key differences, the first of which centres on viewpoint. Nomothetic researchers use an "outsider's" viewpoint, while idiographic research emphasizes an "insider's" view. The emphasis on variables and large samples in nomothetic studies allows researchers to gain a bird's-eye (outsider's) view of some phenomenon. While nomothetic research wants to see the forest, idiographic studies are interested in the trees. Idiographic research aims to provide a detailed understanding of what it is like to be part of a particular event or community, or in a particular kind of situation. Idiographic researchers understand, for example, that First Nations people living on reserves have a rich, detailed appreciation of reserve life that urban dwellers lack. Or that full-patch gang members understand the inner operations of the organization in ways that no outsider can appreciate.

Since many things are unknown at the outset, a researcher trying to develop an insider's appreciation of some event, group, or circumstances presents very different research constraints and challenges. Usually this means they are in the business of constructing a theoretical understanding (rather than theory testing). And with this process comes a research approach full of feedback (rather than the linear approach of quantitative researchers). Since contextualized understanding is key, inductive logic governs the approach.

Imagine you wished to understand why a student protest broke out on a particular university campus. In doing so you would seek to root out everything that contributed to that result. You would consider the history of the university, its organizational structure, the nature of the student body, the actions of influential individuals (administrators, faculty, students, others), the context of student activities nationally, triggering events (e.g., shutting down a student organization, arresting a student), and so forth. You'll know your analysis is complete when the explanatory factors you have assembled make it clear how the protest was inevitable, and how the absence of any of those factors might have kept it from happening.

In idiographic studies, there is no statistical test or specified set of procedures that tell you when you have achieved explanatory success. Idiographic explanations rest on the "art" of social research, which is achieved primarily through experience—by reading the analyses of others and by conducting your own. Here, however, are a few techniques commonly used in constructing idiographic explanations.

- Situate your case(s): Real-world events occur in some context, and that context is important to what occurs. Therefore, you should learn as much as you can about the historical and contemporary context of the cases you are studying. This will help ground your interpretations of what you observe.
- Focus on types of activities, rather than types of people: Idiographic studies emphasize process; that is, specifying chains of circumstances, events, and interactions that produced outcomes of interest.

This approach is assisted by paying close attention to what is actually occurring, rather than labelling actors into types such as deviants and non-deviants or sociopaths and normal.

- Pay attention to the explanations offered by the people living the social processes you are studying: This is necessary in order to gain an insider's appreciation of what's going on. It is important that you not believe everything you are told, of course, but don't make the opposite mistake of thinking you understand the situation better than those living there. If there is wide agreement as to the importance of a certain factor, that should increase your confidence that it was a cause of the event under study. This would be even more compelling if participants with very different points of view agree on that point. In the case of the student protest, administrators and students are likely to have very different opinions about what happened, but if they all agree that the arrest of a student activist was a triggering event, then it probably was an important cause.
- Compare your case with similar situations, either in different places or at different times in the same place: This procedure helps you gain a sense of perspective. Perhaps the campus in question has had previous protests, or perhaps there was a time when a protest almost occurred but didn't. Knowledge of such instances can provide useful comparisons and contrasts to the case under study. Similarly, protests or non-protests at other campuses can offer useful comparisons.
- Rely on analytic induction: Idiographic investigation helps us make sense of (explain) how events unfold in specific cases. This is a bottom-up approach. Researchers have to make sense of their empirical observations and reports, and doing so requires abstract concepts and propositions. In qualitative studies these concepts and propositions are developed as needed, which is the core of **analytic induction** (Ragin 1994). Analytic induction makes sense of events by creating meaningful categories from the observations at hand. After creating these sensitizing concepts, researchers make additional observations to see how well they fit actual conditions. Through this iterative (feedback) process, an understanding of events is progressively enlarged.

analytic induction A process for understanding events that relies on grounding concepts in empirical observation and progressively sharpening them through iteration.

Later chapters will explore the specific techniques associated with nomothetic and idiographic studies. While the approaches seem very different, they are flip sides of similar coins. Both approaches seek the same thing: greater knowledge of the social world. Quantitative studies do so by trying to detect general patterns through examining a relatively few attributes across a large number of cases, and qualitative studies do so by understanding the linkages among many attributes in a few cases. As Becker (1996:54) notes, the two approaches imply each other:

> Every analysis of a case rests, explicitly or implicitly, on some general laws, and every general law supposes that the investigation of particular cases would show that law at work. Despite the differing emphases, it all ends up with the same sort of understanding, doesn't it?

And, to be clear, remember that both approaches rest on making sense of empirical evidence. Both the numbers used by quantitative researchers and the narratives used by qualitative investigators come from observing concrete cases and trying to interpret the observed patterns.

Whether nomothetic or idiographic, all investigations must take time into account. They do so in different ways, as we shall see in the following section.

THE TIME DIMENSION

So far in this chapter, we have regarded research design as a process for deciding *what aspects* we shall observe, *of whom*, and *for what purpose.* Now we must consider a set of time-related options that cut across each of these earlier considerations. We can choose to make observations more or less at one time or over a long period.

Time plays many roles in the design and execution of research, quite aside from the time it takes to do research. In both nomothetic and idiographic designs, the time sequencing of events and situations is critical to determining causation among variables (a point we'll return to in Part 4). Time also affects the generalizability of research findings. Do the descriptions and explanations resulting from a particular study accurately represent the situation of ten years ago, ten years from now, or only the present? In dealing with the issue of time, researchers principally choose between cross-sectional and longitudinal study designs.

CROSS-SECTIONAL STUDIES

A **cross-sectional study** involves observations of a sample, or cross-section, of a population or phenomenon concerning one point in time. Exploratory and descriptive studies are often cross-sectional. For example, Taylor and Peter (2011) examined homophobia and transphobia in Canadian high schools by collecting data from 3,607 public school students. Students were questioned about school climate, harassment, school attachment, and institutional interventions. The researchers found that schools were neither safe nor respectful for sexual and gender minority students. They commented on their findings this way:

> What is striking is the gap students are experiencing between official school curriculum, which emphasizes human rights and diversity, and the curriculum of the hallways, where LGBTQ students feel unsafe, insulted or harassed. Students also see adults, including teachers, looking the other way rather than dealing with homophobic comments, and they express profound disappointment and cynicism about the adult world.[2]
>
> (Taylor 2011)

Many explanatory studies are also cross-sectional. A researcher conducting a large-scale national survey to examine the sources of racial and religious prejudice would, in all likelihood, be dealing with a single time frame, in essence taking a "snapshot" of the sources of prejudice at a particular point in history.

Explanatory cross-sectional studies have an inherent problem. Although their conclusions are based on observations made at only one time, they typically aim at understanding causal processes that occur over time. This problem is somewhat akin to that of determining the speed of a moving object on the basis of a high-speed, still photograph that freezes the movement of the object.

Yanjie Bian (1994), for example, conducted a survey of workers in Tianjin, China, to study stratification in contemporary, urban Chinese society. In undertaking the survey in 1988, however, he was conscious of the important changes brought about by a series of national campaigns, such as the Great Proletarian Cultural Revolution, dating from the 1949 Chinese Revolution (which brought the communists into power) and continuing into the present.

> These campaigns altered political atmospheres and affected people's work and nonwork activities. Because of these campaigns, it is difficult to draw conclusions from a cross-sectional social survey, such as the one presented in this book, about general patterns of Chinese workplaces and their effects on workers. Such conclusions may be limited to one period of time and are subject to further tests based on data collected at other times.
>
> (1994:19)

The problem of generalizations about social life from a snapshot in time is one this book addresses repeatedly. One solution is suggested by Bian's final comment about data collected "at other times." Social research often builds on the results of earlier research by revisiting phenomena and building on the results.

2 Courtesy of Dr. Catherine G. Taylor, The University of Winnipeg.

cross-sectional study A study based on observations representing a single point in time.

LONGITUDINAL STUDIES

In contrast, **longitudinal studies** are designed to permit observations of the same phenomena over an extended period. For example, a researcher can participate in and observe the activities of a radical political group from its inception to its demise. Other longitudinal studies use records or artifacts to study change over time. In analyses of newspaper editorials or Supreme Court decisions over time, for instance, the studies are longitudinal whether the researcher's observations and analyses are made at one time or over the course of the events under study.

Most field research projects, involving direct observation and perhaps in-depth interviews, are naturally longitudinal. For example, when Jacqueline Lewis (1998) studied the experiences of exotic dancers, her field observations and interviews in strip clubs in southern Ontario allowed her to examine the evolution of their occupational socialization over time—in other words, the process of becoming an exotic dancer.

In the classic study *When Prophecy Fails* (1956), Leon Festinger, Henry Reicker, and Stanley Schachter were specifically interested in learning what happened to a flying saucer cult when their predictions of an alien encounter failed to come true. Would the cult members close down the group or would they become all the more committed to their beliefs? A longitudinal study was required to provide an answer. (The cult redoubled their efforts to get new members.)

Longitudinal studies can be more difficult for quantitative studies such as large-scale surveys. Nonetheless, they are often the best way to study changes over time. There are three special types of longitudinal studies you should know about—trend, cohort, and panel studies.

Trend Studies A researcher who examines changes within a population over time engages in a **trend study**. Simple examples are a comparison of Canadian censuses over several decades showing shifts in the makeup of the national population, and a series of political polls during the course of an election campaign showing trends in the relative strengths and standing of different political parties.

For example, you could ask, as Galarneau and her colleagues (2013) did, what has changed for young people in Canada since their parents were young. Do today's youth face more social and economic challenges than their parents did? Or has social reality remained fairly stable between the generations? To address this issue the researchers examined several decades of trend data in Canada. In summary, here is what they found. On the issue of stability:

> Life today, both social and economic, for young Canadians is very different than it was for their parents at the same age. Today's young people represent an increasingly smaller proportion of the total population and are more likely to be born outside Canada or have parents who were born outside Canada. Young people are also more educated but are transitioning to the labour market later in life. (p. 8)

On the issue of level of challenges:

> The answer differs based on sex, age, and young people's place of residence. Women age 25 to 34 have experienced an improvement in unemployment, full-time employment and wages, while for their male counterparts living in non-oil-producing provinces, as well as for those age 24 and under, it was just the opposite. (p. 8)

Young and Dugas's (2011:1) research provides an example of a trend study conducted using qualitative content analysis. They looked at "longitudinal trends in media coverage of global climate change issues in Canada's national print media." They examined coverage by two national newspapers, *The Globe and Mail* and the *National Post*, over three time periods (1988–89, 1998–99, and 2007–08). They showed that the coverage has become less sophisticated over time. While climate change coverage has significantly increased, it has become less scientifically informative—paying less attention, for example, to the impact of climate change and potential causes of it. Instead, attention is focused more on issues of business and politics.

longitudinal study A study design involving the collection of data at different points in time.

trend study A type of longitudinal study in which a given characteristic of some population is monitored over time.

TABLE 4-1 Age and Political Liberalism

Survey dates	1972 to 1974	1977 to 1980	1982 to 1984	1987 to 1989
Age of cohort	20–24	25–29	30–34	35–39
Percent who would let the communist speak	72%	68%	73%	73%

Source: James Davis, "Changeable Weather in a Cooling Climate atop the Liberal Plateau: Conversion and replacements in Forty-Two General Social Survey Items 1972–1989," *Public Opinion Quarterly* 1992, Vol. 56: 261–306.

Cohort Studies

When researchers examine specific subpopulations, or *cohorts*, as they change over time, they engage in a **cohort study**. Typically, a cohort is an age group, such as those people born during the 1950s, but it can also be based on some other time grouping, such as people born during World War II, people who got married in 2000, and so forth. An example of a cohort study would be a series of national surveys, conducted perhaps every 20 years, to study the economic attitudes of the cohort born during the Great Depression. A sample of people 15 to 20 years of age might be surveyed in 1950, another sample of those 35 to 40 years of age in 1970, another sample of those 55 to 60 years of age in 1990, and another of those 75 to 80 years old in 2010. Although the specific set of people studied in each survey would differ, each sample would represent the survivors of the cohort born between 1930 and 1935.

James Davis (1992) turned to a cohort analysis in an attempt to understand shifting political orientations during the 1970s and 1980s in the United States. Overall, he found a liberal trend on issues such as race, gender, religion, politics, crime, and free speech. But did this trend represent people in general getting a bit more liberal, or did it merely reflect more liberal younger generations replacing the conservative older ones?

To answer this question, Davis examined national surveys conducted in four time periods beginning five years apart. In each survey, he grouped the respondents into age groups, also five years apart. This strategy allowed him to compare different age groups at any given point in time, as well as follow the political development of each age group over time.

One of the questions he examined was whether a person who admitted to being a communist should be allowed to speak in the respondents' communities. Consistently, the younger respondents in each period of time were more willing to let the communist speak than were the older ones. Among those aged 20 to 40 in the first set of the survey, for example, 72 percent took this liberal position, contrasted with 27 percent among respondents 80 and older. What Davis found when he examined the youngest cohort over time is shown in Table 4-1. This pattern of a slight conservative shift in the 1970s, followed by a liberal rebound in the 1980s, typifies the several cohorts Davis analyzed (Davis 1992:269).

Warman et al. (2006) analyzed data from 1970 through 2001 concerning professors at Canadian universities working full-time. They state, "We restrict the sample to people aged 30 to 65 who were born between 1930 and 1969 for the cohort analysis and use five-year birth cohorts. For example, our first cohort is the 1930–1934 birth cohort and our last cohort is the 1965–1969 birth cohort" (p. 8).

They found that the wage differences between male and female professors declined over time for the more recent birth cohorts, although female professors still earned, on average, less than male professors. They note that "cross cohort decline in the earnings of male professors" (p. 19), which was not experienced by female professors, accounts for the wage differential reduction more than any real salary increase for female professors.

cohort study A study in which some specific subpopulation, or cohort, is studied over time, although data may be collected from different members in each set of observations.

Panel Studies

Though similar to trend and cohort studies, **panel studies** examine the same set of people each time. For example, we could interview the same sample of voters every month during an election campaign, asking for whom they intended to vote. Though such a study would allow us to analyze overall trends in voter preferences for different candidates, it would also show the precise patterns of persistence and change in intentions. For example, a trend study that showed that Candidates A and B each had exactly half of the voters on September 1 and on October 1 could indicate that none of the electorate had changed voting plans, that all of the voters had changed their intentions, or something in between. A panel study would eliminate this confusion by showing what kinds of voters switched from A to B and what kinds switched from B to A, as well as other facts.

Edgerton and his associates (2014) used panel data to explore what happens to youth who begin gambling at an early age. The conventional view is that early gambling behaviour is a "downward spiral"; once you begin, your gambling worsens over time. To test this view, the researchers used a panel study of 679 youth in Manitoba between the ages of 18 and 20. The participants were interviewed about their gambling and other activities every year for four years. In the final cycle, the sample size included 517 respondents (which illustrates the retention problem associated with panel studies). By analyzing the data, the researchers were able to see how the gambling behaviour of the same people changed over time. The study's main finding challenged conventional wisdom; rather than rising, the risk of problem gambling among young adults diminished over time. This finding has the important policy implication that targeted prevention campaigns may be a cost-effective alternative for reaching treatment-resistant youth.

In another example, Clouston and Quesnel-Vallée (2012) explored the well-known finding that persons with partners live longer, healthier lives than those who are single. But why is this so? One hypothesis is that partners provide benefits, such as companionship and caring, which are healthful. This is the social causation hypothesis. A competing idea is the health selection hypothesis, which argues that healthier people are more successful in finding partners than less healthy persons. The researchers used panel data from Canada and the United States to test these competing hypotheses and found very different patterns between the nations. Among Canadians, social causation's effects were much stronger than health selection. Among Americans, the reverse was true. The authors explore how different social policies between our countries may account for these differences.

panel study A type of longitudinal study in which data are collected from the same set of people (the sample or panel) at several points in time.

Comparison of the Three Types of Longitudinal Studies

To reinforce the distinctions among trend, cohort, and panel studies, let's contrast the three study designs using the same variable: attitudes toward abortion. A trend study might look at shifts in attitudes of the general Canadian population, using polling data collected on a regular basis. A cohort study might follow shifts in attitudes among the "World War II generation," specifically, say, people who were between 20 and 30 in 1942. We could study a sample of people 30 to 40 years old in 1952, a new sample of people aged 40 to 50 in 1962, and so forth. A panel study could start with some special subset of the population and study those specific individuals over time. Notice that only the panel study would give a full picture of the shifts in attitudes toward abortion—from "against" to "in favour," from "in favour" to "against," and other possible in betweens—for example, "in favour only when the woman's life is at risk." Cohort and trend studies would uncover only net changes.

Longitudinal studies generally have an obvious advantage over cross-sectional ones in providing information describing processes over time. But this advantage often comes at a heavy cost in both time and money, especially in a large-scale survey. Observations may have to be made at the time events are occurring, and the method of observation may require many research workers.

Panel studies, which offer the most comprehensive data on changes over time, face a special problem: **panel attrition**. Some of the respondents studied in the first wave of the survey may not participate in later waves, whether by choice or circumstance. This was evident in the Edgerton et al. (2014) study on youth gambling. The sample size diminished from 679 to 517 participants over a four-year period. In panel studies, the danger is that those who drop out of the study may not be typical, thereby distorting the results of the study. These differences needed to be taken into account to avoid misleading conclusions in the interpretation of their results. For a further comparison of the three types of longitudinal studies, see the How to Do It box entitled "The Time Dimension and Aging."

APPROXIMATING LONGITUDINAL STUDIES

It's not always possible or practical to conduct longitudinal studies, and those that exist may not contain the information we need on the topic that we are interested in researching. However, researchers can often draw approximate conclusions about processes that take place over time, even when only cross-sectional data are available. Here are some ways to do that.

Sometimes cross-sectional data imply processes over time on the basis of simple logic. For example, in a study of student drug use conducted at the University of Hawaii (Takeuchi 1974), students were asked to report whether they had ever tried each of several illegal drugs. The study found that some students had tried both marijuana and LSD, some had tried only one, and others had tried neither. Because these data were collected at one time, and because some students presumably would experiment with drugs later on, it would appear that such a study could not tell whether students were more likely to try marijuana or LSD first.

A closer examination of the data showed, however, that although some students reported having tried marijuana but not LSD, there were no students in the study who had tried only LSD. From this finding it was inferred, as common sense suggested, that marijuana use preceded LSD use. If the process of drug experimentation occurred in the opposite time order, then a study at a given time should have found some students who had tried LSD but not marijuana, and it should have found no students who had tried only marijuana.

Logical inferences may also be made whenever the time order of variables is clear. If we discover in a cross-sectional study of university students that those educated in private high schools received better university grades than those educated in public high schools, we would conclude that the type of high school attended affected university grades, not the other way around. Thus, even though our observations were made at only one time, we would feel justified in drawing conclusions about processes that took place across time.

Very often, age differences discovered in a cross-sectional study form the basis for inferring processes across time. Suppose you're interested in the pattern of worsening health over the course of the typical life cycle. You might study the results of annual checkups in a large hospital. You could group health records according to the ages of those examined and rate each age group based on several health conditions: sight, hearing, blood pressure, and so forth. By reading across the age-group ratings for each health condition, you would have something approximating the health history of individuals. Thus, you might conclude that the average person develops vision problems before hearing problems. You would need to be cautious in this assumption, however, because the differences might reflect society-wide trends. Perhaps improved hearing examinations instituted in the schools had affected only the young people in your study.

Asking people to *recall* their pasts is another common way of approximating observations over time. Researchers use that method when they ask people where they were born, when they graduated from high school, or who they voted for in 2011. Qualitative researchers often conduct in-depth "life history" interviews. Teppo Sintonen (1993) used this technique in a study concerning

panel attrition The increase in participants' nonresponsiveness over time that reduces the accuracy of longitudinal changes.

HOW TO DO IT

The Time Dimension and Aging

Joseph J. Leon
Behavioral Science Department
California State Polytechnic University, Pomona

One way to identify the type of time dimension used in a study is to imagine a number of different research projects on growing older in Canadian society. If we studied a sample of individuals in 2000 and compared the different age groups, the design would be termed *cross-sectional*. If we drew another sample of individuals using the same study instrument in the year 2010 and compared the new data with the 2000 data, the design would be termed *trend*.

Suppose we wished to study only those individuals who were 51–60 in the year 2010 and compare them with the 2000 sample of 41–50-year-old persons (the 41–50 age cohort); this study design would be termed *cohort*. The comparison could be made for the 51–60 and 61–70 age cohorts as well. Now, if we desired to do a panel study on growing older in Canada, we would draw a sample in the year 2000 and, using the same sampled individuals in the year 2010, do the study again. Remember, there would be fewer people in the year 2010 study because some of the sampled individuals from 2000 would no longer be available to participate. For example, some would no longer be alive in the year 2010.

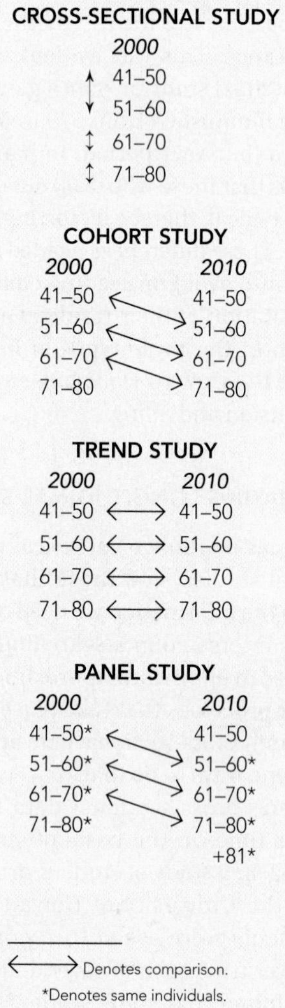

Source: Reprinted with permission from Joseph J. Leon. Behavioral Science Department. California State Polytechnic University, Pomona.

CROSS-SECTIONAL STUDY

2000
41–50
↕
51–60
↕
61–70
↕
71–80

COHORT STUDY

2000		*2010*
41–50	↘	41–50
51–60	↘	51–60
61–70	↘	61–70
71–80		71–80

TREND STUDY

2000		*2010*
41–50	⟷	41–50
51–60	⟷	51–60
61–70	⟷	61–70
71–80	⟷	71–80

PANEL STUDY

2000		*2010*
41–50*	↘	41–50
51–60*	↘	51–60*
61–70*	↘	61–70*
71–80*	↘	71–80*
		+81*

⟷ Denotes comparison.
*Denotes same individuals.

experiences of Canadian Finns who immigrated to Canada in the 1920s. Respondents were asked to reconstruct aspects of their life experiences, particularly those related to ethnicity. Answers to questions about experiences or events that happened a long time ago yield information that is sometimes called *retrospective* data.

Kemp (2004) used life history interviews to investigate relationships of grandparents and their adult grandchildren, exploring various aspects of their interactions over time by asking them to recount their earliest memories up to the time of the interview. Kemp found that there are some general norms concerning behavioural expectations for the grandparent and grandchild. For example, there was mutual respect for each other's independence.

Retrospective data can also be gathered through survey research. For example, Gaudet, Cooke, and Jacob (2011) used data from a

Canadian General Social Survey (GSS) cross-sectional survey that collected data on family history, including retrospective data on childbirth, work, and education, to conduct a cohort study of mothers who had their first child between 1970 and 1999. They used childbirth cohorts of five years beginning with 1970 to 1974 to investigate mothers' entry into the paid labour market after their first child was born. They found that the percentage of women entering the workforce within two years of their first child's birth increased with each successive cohort, going from 28.5 to 61.3 percent. They also investigated family and personal factors that may have had an impact on the difference between mothers who stayed out of the paid labour force for 24 months or longer after their first childbirth and those who did not. In this analysis they found, for example, that since the mid-1980s women with less education were much more likely to remain out of the labour force. The authors noted some of the potential problems of using retrospective data and thus made cautionary notes about their findings.

The danger in this technique is evident. Sometimes people have faulty memories; sometimes they lie. When people are asked in post-election polls who they voted for, the results inevitably show more people voting for the winner than actually did so on election day. As part of a series of in-depth interviews, such a report can be validated in the context of other reported details; however, results based on a single question in a survey must be regarded with caution.

These are some of the ways time figures into social research and some of the ways researchers confront the element of time in their studies. In designing any study, be sure to examine both the explicit and the implicit assumptions you're making about time. Are you interested in describing or explaining some process that occurs over time, or are you simply interested in what exists now? If you want to describe a process occurring over time, will you be able to make observations at different points in the process, or will you have to approximate such observations, drawing logical inferences from what you can observe now? If you decide on a longitudinal design, which method best serves your research purposes?

Now that you've had a broad overview of social research, let's move on to the remaining chapters in this book and learn exactly how to design and execute each specific step. If you've found a research topic that really interests you, you'll want to keep it in mind as you see how you might go about studying it.

HOW TO DO IT

Available Longitudinal Studies

The following are a few of the wide range of interesting longitudinal studies in Canada that are available for analysis:

- National Longitudinal Survey of Children and Youth (NLSCY) conducted by Statistics Canada between 1994 and 2009.
- The Survey of Labour and Income Dynamics (SLID), also produced by Statistics Canada.
- General Social Survey, which covers six themes (care giving and receiving; families; social identity; time use; giving, volunteering, and participating; victimization) on a rotating schedule.

International longitudinal studies are available at the Inter-university Consortium for Political and Social Research (ICPSR) website. There you can find archived data on a huge range of social science topics, including:

- World Values Survey
- International Social Survey Programme
- Programme for International Student Assessment

Links to all these sites are available on this book's MindTap site. New studies become available all the time, so check with your data librarian to see what is available to explore your interests.

MAIN POINTS

- Three major purposes of social research are exploration, description, and explanation. Research studies often combine more than one purpose.
- Exploration is the attempt to develop an initial, rough understanding of some phenomenon.
- Description is the precise reporting and/or measurement of the characteristics of some population or phenomenon under study.
- Explanation is the discovery and reporting of relationships among different aspects of the phenomenon under study. However, descriptive studies answer the question "What's so?" (i.e., "What is the situation, reality, or phenomenon?") explanatory ones tend to answer "Why is it so?" or "How did it become so?" questions.
- Units of analysis are the people or things whose characteristics social researchers observe, describe, and explain. Typically, the unit of analysis in social research is the individual person, but it may also be a social group, a formal organization, a social artifact, or some other phenomenon such as a lifestyle or social interaction.
- The ecological fallacy involves conclusions drawn from the analysis of the attributes of groups (e.g., cities) that are then assumed to apply to individuals (e.g., specific residents of different cities). The exception fallacy occurs when conclusions are drawn about groups based on individual data.
- Both idiographic and nomothetic models of explanation rest on the idea of causation. The idiographic model aims at a complete understanding of a particular phenomenon, using all relevant causal factors. The nomothetic model aims at a general understanding—not necessarily complete—of a class of phenomena, using a small number of relevant causal factors.
- Three basic criteria exist for establishing causation in nomothetic analyses: (1) the variables must be empirically associated, or correlated, (2) the causal variable must occur earlier in time than the variable it is said to affect, and (3) the observed effect cannot be explained as the effect of a different variable.
- Mere association, or correlation, does not in itself establish causation. A spurious causal relationship is an association that in reality is caused by one or more other variables.
- A perfect statistical relationship between two variables is not an appropriate criterion for causation in social research. Therefore, we may say that a causal relationship exists between X and Y even though X is not the total cause of Y. Most explanatory social research uses a probabilistic model of causation. X may be said to cause Y if it is seen to have some influence on Y.
- In theory, *necessary* and *sufficient* can be added to causal criteria; in practice, they are not. X is a necessary cause of Y if Y cannot happen without X. X is a sufficient cause of Y if Y always happens when X happens.
- Cross-sectional studies are based on observations made at one time. Although such studies are limited by this characteristic, researchers can sometimes make inferences about processes that occur over time.
- In longitudinal studies, observations are made at many times. Such observations may be made of samples drawn from general populations (trend studies), samples drawn from more specific subpopulations (cohort studies), or the same sample of people each time (panel studies).
- There are a number of ways to approximate longitudinal studies when such research studies are not feasible or practical.

■ REVIEW QUESTIONS AND EXERCISES

1. Here are some examples of real research topics. For each one, name the unit of analysis. (The answers are at the end of this chapter.)
   a. "We estimate the relative distribution of health stories using content analysis.... A total of 4,732 stories were analyzed from 13 Canadian daily newspapers (10 English, 3 French language).... Topics related to health care ... dominated newspaper stories, accounting for 65% of all stories" (Hayes et al. 2007:1842).
   b. "The present research is designed to test the hypothesis that the observed variation in provincial crime rates will be positively related to the amount of provincial geographic mobility" (Hartnagel 1997:391).
   c. "The sample was designed to represent the population of Canadian women between the ages of 18 and 65 who speak English or French.... Nearly 77 percent of respondents reported more than one form of harassment and most women experienced more than one incident of each type" (Lenton et al. 1999:523).
   d. "This study describes the reaction of different Toronto newspapers to the possibility of Quebec separation in the period from September 12, 1994 to November 15, 1995.... Editorials form the basis of analysis since they represent the official views of the paper and so act as an indirect glimpse into the general stance taken on the Quebec issue by ethnic and mainstream communities" (Bright et al. 1999:318).
   e. "As a first step in our data analysis, we examined the socio-demographic characteristics of employees who use and do not use computers in the job they held at the time of the GSS [Canadian General Social Survey]" (Hughes and Lowe 2000:36).
   f. "Using a detailed 33-category occupational classification, and inspecting the proportion of workers in each occupation who use computers and their mean weekly hours of use, we were able to identify six discrete clusters for comparison. Three fell at the high end of the computer use scale, while the other three were at the low end" (Hughes and Lowe 2000:37).
   g. "The aim of this exploratory study was to identify among a range of sociodemographic, health, and lifestyle variables, those that differ significantly between adolescents who have had sexual intercourse and those who have not" (Feldman et al. 1997:198).
   h. "The current article analyzes ... data from the Canadian National Longitudinal Survey of Children and Youth to examine the relevance of family structures to trajectories of parental reports on hyperactivity-inattention among elementary school aged children. We ... compare children living in intact families, lone-parent families, stepfamilies, and families where parents divorced or separated" (Kerr and Michalski 2007:85).
   i. "The typology is drawn from qualitative and quantitative data compiled by trained observers who conducted 1,056 nights of unobtrusive observations in 75 high-capacity nightclubs [in Toronto]. Ten club 'types' were constructed using the genre of music as the primary distinction" (Purcell and Graham 2005:131).
2. In 2010, women earned an average of 68.1 percent as much as men in Canadian society (Statistics Canada 2012a). What do you suppose "causes" that difference? Describe the procedures by which you might test your conjectures.
3. Review the logic of spuriousness. Can you think of an example where an observed relationship between two variables could be explained away by a third variable?
4. Find a research article that reports on a project using a cohort or panel study design. Describe the study design and discuss the major findings reported.
5. Both sociologists and historians are interested in war and peace. How might a sociologist's nomothetic explanation of war differ from a historian's idiographic explanation?

CONTINUITY PROJECT

RACE AND REJECTION

Discrimination is an important potential source of inequalities. Imagine you are asked to help design a study to determine if discrimination is contributing to unequal employment outcomes for Indigenous people in a Canadian city. The basics of your design are as follows.

Nearly identical applications will be submitted to advertised jobs. The only differences will be the applicant's name and current address. The application differences will rely on stereotypes. In one case, the applications will include an Indigenous-sounding name (Johnny Starblanket) and reserve location address. The alternative application will use a W.A.S.P. sounding name (William Ferguson) and a residential address in a middle-class area.

Pairs of applications will be submitted to a substantial number of advertised positions. Differences in the rates of positive response will be used as a measure of discrimination.

How does this study's design take into account the three causal criteria (association, sequence, nonspuriousness)? Are the criteria sufficiently well established that you would be confident in attributing any unequal results to discrimination?

ANSWERS TO REVIEW QUESTIONS AND EXERCISES, ITEM 1

a. newspaper stories (artifacts)
b. province (groups)
c. Canadian women (individuals)
d. editorials (artifacts)
e. employees (individuals)
f. occupations (groups)
g. adolescents (individuals)
h. families (groups)
i. nightclubs (organizations)

Dragon Images/Shutterstock.com

5

CONCEPTUALIZATION, OPERATIONALIZATION, AND MEASUREMENT

The interrelated steps of conceptualization, operationalization, and measurement allow researchers to turn a general idea for a research topic into useful and valid measurements in the real world. An essential part of this process involves transforming the relatively vague terms of ordinary language into precise objects of study with well-defined and measurable meanings.

IN THIS CHAPTER ...

INTRODUCTION

This chapter deals with how researchers move from a general idea about what they want to study to effective and well-defined reports about features of the real world. We emphasize a traditional view, using the interrelated processes of conceptualization, operationalization, and measurement. But we also highlight how realities can be explored by starting with observation. The chapter concludes with an introduction to more complex types of measurements, composite measures.

We begin by confronting the hidden concern people often have about whether it's possible to measure the stuff of life: love, hate, prejudice, radicalism, religiosity, alienation. To understand how this is possible, let's start by elaborating on our earlier understanding of concepts.

WHERE CONCEPTS COME FROM

Chapter 1 introduced you to concepts, which are the fundamental components of thinking. Thinking is imaginary; it occurs at the abstract level. Your mind is full of concepts, like Big Mac, pencil, orange, alienation, love. Concepts have two important features: they are non-empirical and they are meaningful. Let's be clear about each.

Empirical experiences are sensate ones; they involve sight, sound, smell, taste, or touch. To say that concepts are non-empirical is to say that they don't have these qualities. Imagine a concept like "power." Now ask yourself, "How does it taste, smell, sound?" This, of course, is a silly question because the concept of "power" (like every other concept) is tasteless, unscented, and soundless. Components of your mind don't have these properties. But they do contain meaning.

Although concepts are not empirical, they are loaded with meaning. Meaning is what gives concepts life. Imagine someone wants to share what is on their mind with you. Their statement takes the form "I ___ you." There is a world of difference between their filling the blank with the word "love" or filling it with "blaqxent." The difference occurs because the concept "love" is meaningful, while the term "blaqxent" is not. This is precisely what occurs when someone speaks in a language that is foreign to you. Since the terms are not meaningful, the talk is, from your viewpoint, nonsense.

In short, the concepts in your mind are what you use to make your life meaningful. This, by the way, is the great benefit of gaining more education. By filling your mind with more concepts, the potential meaning in your life expands. Your life contains more meaning now than it did when you were a child because you command more concepts and principles. You can identify the differences between steam and diesel locomotives, between shame and guilt, between winning and losing, between sex and love, between France and Germany. And your life is richer for being able to understand the meaning of these different concepts.

Since concepts are so important, it is worth understanding where they come from. The simple answer, of course, is to say they were given to you—by your culture, through your parents, and through other significant agents of socialization. But drilling a little deeper into the story of concept acquisition is revealing, since it shows the work you had to do.

Concepts are abstract categories for organizing sensory experience. They are a product. More specifically, concepts are the product of a process called **conceptualization**. Creating concepts through conceptualization requires mental effort. Here's an illustrative example. Randomly select any five pens you have lying around and place them in front of you. Pick up each and examine it very carefully. Notice its empirical properties (sensations); what it looks like, feels like, smells like, tastes like (yuck!), and so on. Each of the objects you examine will be empirically unique. Perhaps the pens are different colours, or different lengths, or use different types of ink. Perhaps some have teeth marks; others have a cap missing. The point of your examination is this: At the concrete level, these five objects are distinctively different things. But somehow you manage to recognize them as the same thing—that is, as pens.

conceptualization The process by which concepts are formed through the selective organization of sensory experience.

Your classification of the different concrete objects into the same abstract category (the concept "pen") occurs through conceptualization. Specifically, here is what you did. You used your mind to ignore most of the objects' empirical properties and focused on whether they had specific ones. In your example, you ignored whether the objects had teeth marks or not, whether they were long or short, whether they contained black or blue ink. Instead, you focused only on two properties, including (1) whether or not the object was a writing instrument, and (2) whether or not it used ink. Since each of the five objects before you was a writing instrument that used ink, you called (conceptualized) each as a "pen."

Of course, you take all this mental effort for granted because you are now expert at everyday conceptualization. But you weren't always so expert. The fact that young children make conceptualization errors all the time illustrates that this is no easy task. A young child may call pencils "pens," because he uses the first distinguishing characteristic of a pen (i.e., a writing instrument) but not the second (i.e., uses ink). But he will learn, as you did.

While you are expert in conceptualizing everyday things, you can easily have the same troubles as a young child when things become more complex. Lance Roberts recalls a time when he met a radiologist whose job it was to look at X-rays and other images to determine whether patients had a cancerous tumour. The radiologist let Lance look at a series of images with him one day and asked Lance to identify which contained cancer and which didn't. Lance's detection rate was less successful than guessing. His problem, of course, was one of conceptualization. All the different shapes, shadings, and ambiguities in the images overwhelmed him; he didn't know what to attend to and what to ignore. He was like a child in an incomprehensible world.

You probably have similar experiences. Is it always crystal clear to you whether you are in "love" with someone new? Do you really know whether your acquaintance's odd behaviour is "neurotic" rather than "psychotic"? Are you certain whether you are a "liberal"?

Like everyone else, social researchers use concepts to organize and understand their empirical experiences. And the concepts they use rely on conceptualization. Here's an example.

As we've wandered down the road of life, we've observed and heard reports from others about a lot of things, such as the following:

- We have personally heard people say nasty things about minority groups.
- We have heard people say women are inferior to men.
- We have read that women and minorities have earned less than white males for the same work.
- We have read about homosexuals and minorities being beaten and killed.
- We have learned about ethnic cleansing and wars in which one ethnic group tried to eradicate another.

With additional experience, we have noticed something more. People who participated in beatings and killings were also quite likely to call homosexuals and minorities ugly names. A lot of them, moreover, seem to want women to "stay in their place." Eventually, it dawned on us that these several tendencies often appeared together and had something in common. At some point, someone had the bright idea: "Let's use the word *prejudiced* for people like that. We can use the term even if they don't do all those things, as long as they're pretty much like that." That's where "prejudice" came from. We agreed to use it as a shortcut, a name (concept) that represents a collection of apparently related phenomena that we've each observed in the course of life.

It's important to recognize that prejudice (like all concepts) is something we made up. It's not "out there" waiting to be discovered; it's something we created through conceptualization. When we use the word *prejudice*, it evokes a mental image in your mind, just as it evokes one in ours. It's as though file drawers in our minds contained thousands of sheets of paper, with each sheet of paper labelled in the upper right-hand corner. A sheet of paper in each of our minds has the term *prejudice* on it. On your sheet are all the things you were told about prejudice and everything you've observed that seemed to be an example of it. Someone else's sheet has what she was told about it plus all the things she has observed that seem to be examples of it—and her sheet isn't the same as yours.

This example illustrates the central problem associated with conceptualization, which involves communication. Your concepts make your experience meaningful. When you want to meaningfully communicate with others you use the concepts in your mind. But there is no guarantee that when you use a specific concept it has the same meaning in another person's mind. After all, the conceptualization process is different for each of us. We don't share parents, teachers, books read, movies watched, loves lost, places visited. So there are many reasons to expect an imperfect alignment of meanings among persons who use the same concept.

CONCEPTS, MEANINGS, AND DEFINITIONS

To review, concepts are the fundamental components of thinking. They are the abstract categories we use for organizing sensory (empirical) experience. When we use our minds to express relationships between concepts, we are creating ideas (propositions). Whatever meaning life has for us derives from its interpretation through concepts. A little story helps solidify these points.

The story is about how animals got their names. So, imagine the setup in the Garden of Eden. There are all these animals roaming around but none has a name. This presents a real conceptualization problem, say, if Eve wants to tell Adam there is a lion about to pounce, or if Adam wants to point out a beautiful bird in a tree. So Eve takes up the challenge of naming all the animals, and does so very quickly. When asked how she did it her reply was, "Well, it was easy, really. I called this one a rabbit, because it looks like a rabbit, and that one a lion because it looks like a lion, and so on" (quoted in Bredemeier 1998:5). This story, of course, is incredible because that's not how conceptualization works. There is nothing in or about a rabbit or a lion, or anything else, that signifies what it should be called. The concept and meaning are not there waiting to be discovered. We actively and deliberately put the name (concept) on and meaning into objects and experiences.

And social researchers follow exactly the same process in this regard. There is nothing intrinsic about certain thoughts, feelings, actions, or observations that require them to be labelled "discrimination," or "love," or "genocide," or "happiness," or anything else. Social researchers decide, for their purposes, what these concepts mean, what they refer to. Concepts are abstract, imaginary constructions. To treat them otherwise, to give them reality status, is to make an error called **reification**.

All of this just reinforces the understanding provided in Chapter 1 about levels of experience and the social construction of reality. But understanding that concepts, the fundamental carriers of meaning, are constructions reveals the fundamental problem of communication. It is risky to assume that when you use a concept the person receiving it shares its full meaning.

Everyone is familiar with such communication problems. We struggle with finding the right concepts to share our experience, and after we express ourselves, we can be baffled by how others misinterpret what we intended. Misunderstanding is more common than we typically recognize. To get on with our lives, we typically just assume that the intended meaning was the one received, and leave it at that. And that gets us by, more or less. But checking on whether the intended meanings are those received reveals much misalignment. Ask any lovers who have quarrelled about their situation. Ask any professor who looks at students' notes after a lecture. Ask any patient who has heard bad news from a medical doctor. Misunderstanding is everywhere.

Social researchers are in the business of deliberately trying to clarify our understanding of reality. Therefore, conceptual clarity is particularly important. So they take special measures to clarify the meaning of the concepts they use, using the general process of **specification**. These special measures take the form of definitions; specifically, two kinds of definitions, conceptual and operational. Understanding these types of

reification The mistake of treating a conceptual construction as something real.

specification The process of clarifying the meaning of concepts.

definitions is easiest if we connect them to the levels of experience (concrete and abstract) introduced in Chapter 1. But before we do, let's dispense with a third kind of definition, called "real definitions."

Real definitions are the type purportedly used by Eve in naming animals. They assume that there is something intrinsic in a thing that leads to its name. Real definitions uncover that essential meaning and its associated label. Real definitions are based on reification errors. Here is how the famous philosopher of science Carl Hempel (1952:6) dismissed these types of definitions:

> A "real" definition, according to traditional logic, is not a stipulation determining the meaning of some expression but a statement of the "essential nature" or the "essential attributes" of some entity. The notion of essential nature, however, is so vague as to render this characterization useless for the purposes of rigorous inquiry.

This leads social researchers interested in clarifying their terms to rely on conceptual and operational definitions.

Conceptual definitions (also called nominal definitions) clarify a term's meaning by relating it to other concepts. This, for example, is what dictionaries do. You look up a concept whose meaning you do not know and find an understanding of that concept expressed in terms of concepts you (hopefully) do know. Let's say you don't understand what the concept "intelligence" means and ask for a conceptual definition. You read the conceptual definition: "Intelligence is the ability to think abstractly." Assuming you understand what the terms "ability," "think," and "abstract" mean, this conceptual definition aids your understanding of what "intelligence" means.

Conceptual definitions are used by researchers all the time. You find them in every chapter of this book, where a term is highlighted in bold. The following important feature of conceptual definitions is worth noting: They operate entirely at the abstract level. In conceptual definitions, an abstract term is described using other abstract terms. The key to successful understanding of the new term is to understand the meaning of the words in the definition. If, in the earlier example, you don't know what "ability," "think," and "abstract" mean, the conceptual definition of "intelligence" won't assist your understanding.

Since conceptual definitions are constructions, they can be used to define a concept as the author prefers. That is why it is important in everyday experience, and particularly important for researchers, to provide conceptual definitions. Otherwise, the risk of misunderstanding is high. Of course, conceptual definitions are not completely arbitrary—we don't just make up definitions as we go. You can give yourself a nickname, but if no one else uses it, it will not be recognized by others and will soon disappear. Similarly, conceptual definitions in social science are usually rooted in some shared community of usage, such as a particular theoretical framework or a specialized body of previous research on the phenomena of interest.

Furthermore, although conceptual definitions are constructions, not all are created equal. Useful conceptual definitions are ones that specify clear boundaries. In other words, a useful conceptual definition informs us both what is included and what is excluded from the concept. For example, a useful definition of "role strain" will clearly distinguish it from "role conflict," will help us clarify how "culture" differs from "social structure," or will allow us to identify how "shame" differs from "guilt."

So pay careful attention to conceptual definitions—and if none are provided be wary, since the author is dubiously assuming that her mind is aligned with yours. And if the conceptual definitions provided are muddled, don't be shy about realizing what this means: The author is not clear on what he is talking about. Of course, even if conceptual definitions are clear, you are welcome to disagree with the meaning being assigned to the term. Researchers routinely argue about the meaning of terms like "genocide," "violence," and "discrimination." That's fine, since this kind of clear disagreement helps sharpen our thinking.

Since conceptual definitions do their work in the abstract level, they are "all talk." They are full acts of the imagination. Because social

conceptual definition A statement that indicates the meaning of an abstract term by expressing it in other abstract terms.

researchers are interested in linkages between the abstract and concrete levels of experience, they use a second way of clarifying the meaning of terms, **operational definitions**. Operational definitions were introduced in Chapter 2. They get their name from the fact that they specify a set of steps (operations) for connecting an abstract concept with concrete observations. In other words, an operational definition specifies the meaning of a concept by showing how it is experienced empirically. Operational definitions are of the "show me" type.

Look up the term "lemon soufflé" and you will find a conceptual definition such as "a light, slightly sour dessert containing a lot of air and made mainly from eggs." This definition gives you one kind of understanding. But is very different from a recipe, which provides the steps for producing (experiencing) a lemon soufflé. The recipe is an operational definition. Similarly, an understanding of what "guilt" means (conceptual definition) is quite different from knowing what it is like to experience guilt (operational definition).

To summarize, social researchers (like everyone else) use concepts to think about experience. The concepts they use as labels organize and give meaning to experience. To be clear about what they have in mind, researchers need to define their concepts; in other words, they need to tell us what they mean. They do so through conceptual and operational definitions. Conceptual definitions specify meaning by expressing a concept in terms of other concepts. Operational definitions provide meaning by specifying the steps used to concretely experience the concept.

While separate, conceptual and operational definitions are linked in research. Here's how. The steps (operations) in an operational definition must be about something; they aren't just an arbitrary set of steps. Conceptual definitions provide the **dimensions** of the concept that need to be articulated in an operational definition. Dimensions are specifiable aspects of a concept. For example, an initial conceptual definition of "religiosity" might refer to the degree of a person's commitment to their faith. But such commitment might take several forms, including belief, ritual, and devotional. In this case, belief, ritual, and devotional would be dimensions of religiosity.

dimension A specifiable aspect or facet of a concept.

AN EXAMPLE OF CONCEPTUALIZATION AND DEFINITION: THE CONCEPT OF ANOMIE

To bring together this discussion of conceptualization and definition in research, let's look briefly at the history of a specific social scientific concept. Researchers studying deviance are often interested in the part played by feelings of social dislocation. Social scientists sometimes use the concept "anomie" in this context. This term was first introduced into social science by Émile Durkheim, the great French sociologist, in his classic 1897 study *Suicide*.

Using only government publications on suicide rates in different regions and countries, Durkheim produced a work of analytical genius. To determine the effects of religion on suicide, he compared the suicide rates of predominantly Protestant countries with those of predominantly Catholic ones, Protestant regions of Catholic countries with Catholic regions of Protestant countries, and so forth. To determine the possible effects of the weather, he compared suicide rates in northern and southern countries and regions, and he examined the different suicide rates across the months and seasons of the year. Thus, he could draw conclusions about a supremely individualistic and personal act without having any data about the individuals engaging in it.

At a more general level, Durkheim suggested that suicide also reflected the extent to which a society's agreements were clear and stable. Noting that times of social upheaval and change often present individuals with grave uncertainties about what is expected of them, Durkheim suggested that such uncertainties cause confusion, anxiety, and even self-destruction. To describe this societal condition of normlessness, Durkheim chose the term *anomie*. Durkheim did not make this word up. Used in both German and French, it literally meant "without law." The English term *anomy* had been used for at least three centuries before Durkheim to mean disregard for divine law. However, Durkheim created the social scientific concept of anomie.

Since the publication of *Suicide*, social scientists have found anomie a useful concept, and many have expanded on Durkheim's use. Robert Merton, in a classic article entitled "Social Structure and Anomie" (1938), concluded that anomie results from a disparity between the goals and means prescribed by a society. Monetary success, for example, is a widely shared goal in our society, yet not all individuals have the resources to achieve it through acceptable means. An emphasis on the goal itself, Merton suggested, produces normlessness, because those denied the traditional avenues to wealth go about getting it through illegitimate means. Merton's discussion, then, could be considered a further conceptualization of the concept of anomie.

Although Durkheim originally used the concept of anomie as a characteristic of societies, as did Merton after him, other social scientists have used it to describe individuals. To clarify this distinction, some scholars have chosen to use *anomie* in reference to its original, societal meaning and to use *anomia* in reference to the individual characteristic. In a given society, then, some individuals experience anomia, and others do not. Elwin Powell (1958:132), writing twenty years after Merton, provided the following conceptualization of anomia (though using the term *anomie*) as a characteristic of individuals:

> When the ends of action become contradictory, inaccessible or insignificant, a condition of anomie arises. Characterized by a general loss of orientation and accompanied by feelings of "emptiness" and apathy, anomie can be simply conceived as meaninglessness.

Powell went on to suggest that there were two distinct kinds of anomia and to examine how the two rose out of different occupational experiences to result at times in suicide. In his study, however, Powell did not measure anomia per se; he studied the relationship between suicide and occupation, making inferences about the two kinds of anomia. Thus, the study did not provide an operational definition of anomia, only a further conceptualization.

Although many researchers have offered operational definitions of anomia, one name stands out over all. Two years before Powell's article appeared, Leo Srole (1956) published a set of questionnaire items that he said provided a good measure of anomia as experienced by individuals. It consists of five statements that subjects are asked to agree or disagree with.

1. In spite of what some people say, the lot of the average man is getting worse.
2. It's hardly fair to bring children into the world with the way things look for the future.
3. Nowadays a person has to live pretty much for today and let tomorrow take care of itself.
4. These days a person doesn't really know who he can count on.
5. There's little use writing to public officials because they aren't really interested in the problems of the average man. (p. 713)

In the decades following its publication, the Srole scale has become a research staple for social scientists. You'll likely find this particular operationalization of anomia used in many of the research projects reported in academic journals.

This abbreviated history of anomie and anomia as social scientific concepts illustrates several points. First, it's a good example of the process through which general concepts become operationalized measurements. This is not to say that the issue of how to operationalize anomie/anomia has been resolved once and for all. Scholars will surely continue to reconceptualize and reoperationalize these concepts for years to come, continually seeking more useful measures.

The Srole scale illustrates another important point. Letting conceptualization and operationalization be open-ended does not necessarily produce anarchy and chaos, as you might expect. Order often emerges. For one thing, although we could define anomia any way we chose—in terms of, say, shoe size—we're likely to define it in ways not too different from other people's mental images. If you were to use a really offbeat definition, people would probably ignore you.

A second source of order is that as researchers discover the utility of a particular conceptualization and operationalization of a concept, they're likely to adopt it, which leads to standardized definitions of concepts. Besides the Srole scale, examples include IQ tests and a host of demographic and economic measures developed by Statistics Canada. Using such established measures has two advantages: they have been extensively pretested and debugged, and studies using the same scales can be compared. If two researchers do separate studies of two different groups and use the Srole scale, they can compare the two groups on the basis of anomia.

Social researchers, then, can come to terms with anything that is grounded in empirical experience. This "coming to terms" occurs through the conceptualization process, which provides meaning and understanding. Clarifying meanings occurs through conceptual and operational definitions. As always, for researchers there is a continuing link between concrete and abstract to make sense of reality.

CREATING CONCEPTUAL ORDER

The clarification of concepts is a continuing process in social research. Catherine Marshall and Gretchen Rossman (1995:18) speak of a "conceptual funnel" through which a researcher's interest becomes increasingly focused. Thus, a general interest in social activism could narrow to "individuals who are committed to empowerment and social change" and further focus on discovering "what experiences shaped the development of fully committed social activists." This focusing process is inescapably linked to the language we use.

In many forms of quantitative research, researchers begin with concepts and propositions (theory) that they are eager to test with empirical experience. By contrast, in many forms of qualitative research, the clarification of concepts is a key element in data collection. Remember, using induction, you begin with empirical observations and work your way toward concepts and propositions that capture the meaning of your experience. The How to Do It box "Creating Conceptual Order through Induction" illustrates this point.

HOW TO DO IT

Creating Conceptual Order through Induction

This chapter emphasizes the traditional, deductive model of science to help you understand the key ideas of conceptualization, operationalization, and measurement. Later chapters will show how these concepts are applied using qualitative research techniques. For now, here's an example of how induction generates useful concepts.

Recall the example in Chapter 2 about the emotional styles of multiple killers. In that research, Websdale (2010) demonstrated the place and importance of shame as a driver of familicide. His findings supported the common view that shame leads to anger and, ultimately, to violence. This understanding is known as the shame–rage cycle of violence (Scheff and Retzinger 1991).

While this understanding covered the majority of the 211 cases of familicide Websdale studied, it did not fit the pattern in a substantial minority of cases. This substantial other category was composed of cases where the killers had no history of violence, and where the killings were carefully planned over an extended period. Interestingly, while almost all male multiple killers fell into the shame–rage pattern, most of the female cases followed the premediated pattern.

From a careful examination of his cases, Websdale detected a clear difference in the patterns and styles of multiple killers. To characterize these different patterns, Websdale conceptualized them differently. He called the almost exclusively male, history-of-violence, shame–rage killers the "livid-coercive" type. By contrast, he labelled the premeditated style the "civil-reputable" type.

Websdale had no idea of these concepts before he began his study. The livid-coercive versus civil-reputable types emerged through induction as he examined his evidence and tried to make sense of the patterns that he found.

Suppose you were conducting interviews and observations in a radical political group devoted to combating oppression in Canadian society. Imagine how the meaning of *oppression* would shift as you delved more and more deeply into the members' experiences and worldviews. For example, you might start out thinking of oppression in physical and perhaps economic terms. The more you learned about the group, however, the more you might appreciate the possibility of psychological oppression.

The same point applies even to contexts where meanings might seem more fixed. In the analysis of textual materials, for example, social researchers sometimes speak of the "hermeneutic circle," a cyclical process of ever-deeper understanding.

> The understanding of a text takes place through a process in which the meaning of the separate parts is determined by the global meaning of the text as it is anticipated. The closer determination of the meaning of the separate parts may eventually change the originally anticipated meaning of the totality, which again influences the meaning of the separate parts, and so on.
>
> (Kvale 1996:47)

Consider the concept "prejudice." Suppose you needed to write a definition of the term. You might start out thinking about racial prejudice. At some point you would realize you should probably allow for gender prejudice, ethnic prejudice, religious prejudice, anti-gay prejudice, and the like in your definition. Examining each of these specific types of prejudice would affect your overall understanding of the general concept. As your general understanding changed, however, you would likely see each of the individual forms somewhat differently.

The continual refinement of concepts occurs in all social research methods. Often you'll find yourself refining the meaning of important concepts even as you write up your final report.

Although conceptualization is a continuing process, it's vital that you address it specifically at the beginning of any study design, especially rigorously structured research designs such as surveys and experiments. In a survey, for example, operationalization results in a commitment to a specific set of questionnaire items that will represent the concepts under study. Without that commitment, the study could not proceed further.

Even in less structured research methods, however, it's important to begin with an initial set of anticipated meanings that can be refined during data collection and interpretation. No one seriously believes we can observe life with no preconceptions; for this reason, scientific observers must be conscious of and explicit about these starting points.

DEFINITIONS IN DESCRIPTIVE AND EXPLANATORY STUDIES

As you recall from Chapter 4, two general purposes of research are *description* and *explanation.* It's easy to see the importance of clear and precise definitions for descriptive research. If we want to describe and report the unemployment rate in a city, our definition of *being unemployed* is critical. That definition will depend on our definition of another term: the *labour force.* If it seems patently absurd to regard a three-year-old child as being unemployed, it is because such a child is not considered a member of the labour force. Thus, we might follow Statistics Canada's convention for the census and exclude all people under 15 years of age from the labour force. (Statistics Canada 2011)

This convention alone, however, would not give us a satisfactory definition, because it would count as unemployed such people as high school students, the retired, the disabled, and homemakers. We might follow Statistics Canada's convention further by defining the labour force as "all persons 15 years of age and over, excluding institutional residents, who were either employed or unemployed during the week (Sunday to Saturday) prior to Census Day."[1] Unemployed is further defined as those who were "without paid work and were available for work."[2] If a student, homemaker, or retired person is not available for work, such a person would not be included in the labour force. Unemployed people, then, would be those members of the labour force, as defined, who are not employed (Statistics Canada 2011).

1,2 Statistics Canada, 2011. *Census Dictionary.* https://www12.statcan.gc.ca/census-recensement/2011/ref/dict/index-eng.cfm. Reproduced and distributed on an "as is" basis with the permission of Statistics Canada.

But what does "available for work" mean? Would it be sufficient for a person to be open to an offer of employment or to desire work? Perhaps a person must go from door to door letting everyone know about his or her availability for employment? Or maybe a person must register with a government employment service. The 2006 Canadian census definition stated clearly exactly what "available for work" means. Those considered unemployed had to be without paid work and available for work the week prior to the census. They also "(a) had [to have] actively looked for paid work in the past four weeks; or (b) were on temporary lay-off and expected to return to their job; or (c) had definite arrangements to start a new job in four weeks or less" (Statistics Canada 2011).[3]

As you can see, the conclusion of a descriptive study about the unemployment rate depends directly on how each issue is resolved. Increasing the period of time during which people are counted as looking for work would have the effect of adding more unemployed people to the labour force as defined, thereby increasing the reported unemployment rate. On the other hand, decreasing the time period would decrease the reported unemployment rate. Thus, the descriptive statement that the unemployment rate in a city is 3 percent, or 9 percent, or whatever it might be, depends directly on the conceptual and operational definitions used.

This example is relatively clear because there are several accepted conventions relating to the labour force and unemployment. Consider how difficult it would be to get agreement about the definitions you'd need in order to say, "Forty-five percent of the students at this institution are politically conservative." Like the unemployment rate, this percentage would depend directly on the definition of what is being measured, in this case political conservatism. A different definition might result in the conclusion "Five percent of the student body is politically conservative."

The same issues of conceptual and operational definition present themselves in explanatory studies, except that now the focus shifts from single to multiple concepts. It is important to remember that description is not explanation. Descriptive studies use concepts to classify and give meaning to observations under consideration. While describing some phenomenon is important, descriptions do not help us understand why the phenomenon exists or how it occurred. These *why* and *how* questions are embedded in explanation, not description.

Providing explanations requires systematically linking *different* concepts together. Notice the emphasis on the word "different." To explain something, you must account for it by linking it to something else. An event or experience does not explain itself. Attempts to do so result in the thinking error called a **tautology**, the error of "circular reasoning." For example, a conceptual definition of "anti-Semitic" will make reference to the hatred of Jews. Understanding that, if you ask why some people are anti-Semitic, it is a tautology if your explanation refers to them hating Jews. Sometimes tautologies are obvious, but often they are not. Here is the famous sociologist Howard Becker's explanation of why some people smoke marijuana:

> "A person, then, cannot begin to use marijuana for pleasure, or continue its use for pleasure, unless he learns to define its effects as enjoyable, unless it becomes and remains an object which he conceives as capable of producing pleasure."
>
> (Becker 1953:241)

Can you spot the tautology here?[4]

In short, definitions are necessary for us to be clear on what we are thinking and talking about. In order to be clear, we should try to be explicit. Otherwise, in descriptive studies we misunderstand what the reports tell us, and in explanatory studies we can confuse naming with explaining. Clear conceptual and operational definitions help us avoid these errors.

3 Statistics Canada, 2011. Census Dictionary. https://www12.statcan.gc.ca/census-recensement/2011/ref/dict/index-eng.cfm. Reproduced and distributed on an "as is" basis with the permission of Statistics Canada.

tautology The thinking error that claims to explain something by referring to itself.

4 Hint: Are pleasurable and enjoyable different things? This example comes from Stark and Roberts (1996).

OPERATIONALIZATION CHOICES

In social research conceptualization and operationalization are intimately linked. To recap: conceptualization is the refinement and specification of abstract concepts, and operationalization is the development of specific research procedures (operations) that will result in empirical observations representing those concepts.

As with the methods of data collection, social researchers have a variety of choices when operationalizing a concept. Although the several choices are closely interconnected, we've separated them for the sake of discussion. Realize, though, that operationalization does not proceed through a systematic checklist.

RANGE OF VARIATION

In operationalizing any concept, researchers must be clear about the range of variation that interests them in their research. The question is, to what extent are we willing to combine attributes in fairly gross categories?

Let's suppose you want to measure people's incomes in a study by collecting the information from either records or interviews. The highest annual incomes people receive run into the millions of dollars, but not many people get that much. Unless you're studying the very rich, it probably wouldn't add much to your study to keep track of extremely high categories. Depending on who you study, you'll probably want to establish a highest income category with a much lower floor, maybe $100,000 or more. Although this decision will lead you to group together people who earn a trillion dollars a year with those earning a mere $100,000, they'll survive it, and that mixing probably won't hurt your research any, either. The same decision faces you at the other end of the income spectrum. In studies of the general Canadian population, a cut-off of $10,000 or less would probably work just fine.

In studies of attitudes and orientations, the question of range of variation has another dimension. Unless you're careful, you may end up measuring only half an attitude without really meaning to. Here's an example of what we mean.

Suppose you're interested in people's attitudes toward the expanded use of nuclear power generators. You'd anticipate that some people consider it the greatest thing since the wheel, whereas other people have absolutely no interest in it. Given that anticipation, it would make sense to ask people how much they favour expanding the use of nuclear energy and to give them answer categories ranging from "Favour it very much" to "Don't favour it at all."

This operationalization, however, conceals half the attitudinal spectrum regarding nuclear energy. Many people have feelings that go beyond simply not favouring it: they are, with greater or lesser degrees of intensity, actively opposed to it. In this instance, there is considerable variation on the left side of zero. Some oppose it a little, some quite a bit, and others a great deal. To measure the full range of variation, then, you'd want to operationalize attitudes toward nuclear energy with a range from favouring it very much, through no feelings one way or the other, to opposing it very much.

This consideration applies to many of the variables social scientists study. Virtually any public issue involves both support and opposition, each in varying degrees. Political orientations range from very liberal to very conservative, and depending on the people you're studying, you may want to allow for radicals on one or both ends. Similarly, people are not just more or less religious; some are positively antireligious.

The point is not that you must measure the full range of variation in every case. You should, however, consider whether you need to, given your particular research purpose. If the difference between not religious and antireligious isn't relevant to your research, forget it. Someone has defined pragmatism as "any difference that makes no difference is no difference." Be pragmatic.

Finally, decisions on the range of variation should be governed by the expected distribution of attributes among the subjects of the study. In a study of university professors' attitudes toward the value of higher education, you could probably stop at no value and not worry about those who might consider higher education dangerous to students' health. (If you were studying students, however....)

VARIATIONS BETWEEN THE EXTREMES

Degree of precision is a second consideration in operationalizing terms. What it boils down to is how fine you will make distinctions among the various possible attributes composing a given variable. Does it matter for your purposes whether a person is 17 or 18 years old, or could you conduct your inquiry by grouping them together in a category labelled 10 to 19 years old? Don't answer too quickly. If you wanted to study rates of voter registration and participation, you'd definitely want to know whether the people you studied were old enough to vote. In general, if you're going to measure age, you must look at the purpose and procedures of your study and decide whether fine or gross differences in age are important to you. In a survey, you'll need to make these decisions in order to design an appropriate questionnaire. In the case of in-depth interviews, these decisions will condition the extent to which you probe for details.

The same thing applies to other variables. If you measure religious affiliation, is it enough to know that a person is a Protestant, or do you need to know the denomination? Do you simply need to know whether a person is married, or will it make a difference to know if he or she has never married or is separated, widowed, or divorced?

There is, of course, no general answer to such questions. The answers come out of the purpose of a given study, or why we are making a particular measurement. We can give you a useful guideline, though. Whenever you're not sure how much detail to pursue in a measurement, get too much rather than too little. When a subject in an in-depth interview volunteers that she is 37 years old, record "37" in your notes, not "in her 30s." When you're analyzing the data, you can always combine precise attributes into more general categories, but you can never separate out any variations you lumped together during observation and measurement.

A NOTE ON DIMENSIONS

We've already discussed dimensions as a characteristic of concepts. When researchers get down to the business of creating operational measures, they often discover—or worse, never notice—that they're not exactly clear about which dimensions of a concept they're really interested in. Here's an example.

Let's suppose you're studying people's attitudes toward government, and you want to include an examination of how people feel about corruption. Here are just a few of the dimensions you might examine:

- Do people think there is corruption in government?
- How much corruption do they think there is?
- How certain are they in their judgment of how much corruption there is?
- How do they feel about corruption in government as a problem in society?
- What do they think causes it?
- Do they think it's inevitable?
- What do they feel should be done about it?
- What are they willing to do personally to eliminate corruption in government?
- How certain are they that they would be willing to do what they say they would do?

The list could go on and on. How people feel about corruption in government has many dimensions. It's essential to be clear about which ones are important in your inquiry; otherwise, you may measure how people *feel* about corruption when you really wanted to know how much they think there is, or vice versa.

Once you've determined how you're going to collect your data (e.g., survey, field research) and have decided on the relevant range of variation, the degree of precision needed between the extremes of variation, and the specific dimensions of the variables that interest you, you may have another choice: a mathematical–logical one. That is, you may need to decide what *level* of measurement to use. This point is of central importance in quantitative research. To discuss this point, we need to take another look at attributes and their relationship to variables.

DEFINING VARIABLES AND ATTRIBUTES

As you will recall from Chapter 1, an **attribute** is a characteristic or quality of something. "Female" is an example of an attribute. So is "old" or "student." **Variables**, on the other hand, are logical sets of attributes. Thus, *gender* is a variable composed, for example, of the attributes female, male, and non-binary.

The conceptualization and operationalization processes can be seen as the specification of variables and the attributes composing them. Thus, in the context of a study of unemployment, *employment status* is a variable having the attributes employed and unemployed; the list of attributes could also be expanded to include the other possibilities discussed earlier, such as homemaker.

Every variable must have two important qualities. First, the attributes composing it should be **exhaustive**. For the variable to have any utility in research, we must be able to classify every observation in terms of one of the attributes composing the variable. We'll run into trouble if we conceptualize the variable *political party affiliation* in terms of the attributes Liberals, Conservatives, and Bloc Québécois, because some of the people you set out to study will identify with the New Democratic Party, the Green Party, or some other organization, and some (often a large percentage) will tell you they have no party affiliation. We could make the list of attributes exhaustive by adding "other" and "no affiliation." Whatever we do, we must be able to classify every observation.

At the same time, attributes composing a variable must be **mutually exclusive**. Every observation must be able to be classified in terms of one and only one attribute. For example, we need to define "employed" and "unemployed" in such a way that nobody can be both at the same time. That means being able to classify the person who is working at a job but is also looking for work. (We might run across a fully employed mud wrestler who is looking for the glamour and excitement of being a social researcher.) In this case, we might define the attributes so that employed takes precedence over unemployed, and anyone working at a job is employed regardless of whether he or she is looking for something better.

LEVELS OF MEASUREMENT

Attributes operationalized as mutually exclusive and exhaustive may be related in other ways as well. For example, the attributes composing variables may represent different levels of measurement. In this section, we'll examine four levels of measurement applied to variables: nominal, ordinal, interval, and ratio.

Nominal Measures

Variables whose attributes have only the characteristics of exhaustiveness and mutual exclusiveness are **nominal measures**. Examples include *gender*, *religious affiliation*, *national political party affiliation*, *birthplace*, *university major*, and *hair colour*. Although the attributes composing each of these variables—as NDP, PC, Liberal, Green, and Other compose the variable *national political party affiliation*—are distinct from one another (and exhaust the possibilities of national political party affiliation among Canadians), they have no additional features. Nominal measures merely offer names or labels for characteristics.

Imagine a group of people being characterized in terms of one such variable and physically grouped by the applicable attributes. For example, say we've asked a large gathering of people to stand together in groups according to the provinces in which they were born: all those born in British Columbia in one group, those born in Newfoundland and Labrador in another, and so forth. The variable is *place of birth*; the attributes are "born in British Columbia," "born in Newfoundland and Labrador," and so on. All the people standing in a given group have at least one thing in common and differ from the people in all other groups in that same regard. Where the individual groups form, how close they are to one another, or how the groups are arranged in the room would be irrelevant. All that matters is that all the members of a given group share the same province of birth and that each group has a different shared province of birth. All we can say

exhaustive A property of a variable ensuring that all objects can be classified.

mutually exclusive A property of a variable ensuring that every object can be classified into only one attribute.

nominal measure A variable whose attributes have only the characteristics of being jointly exhaustive and mutually exclusive. In other words, a level of measurement describing a variable that has attributes that are merely different from each other, as distinguished from ordinal, interval, or ratio measures. *Political party affiliation* is an example of a nominal measure.

about two people in terms of a nominal variable is that they are either the same or different.

Ordinal Measures Variables with attributes we can logically rank-order are **ordinal measures**. The different attributes of ordinal variables represent relatively more or less of the variable. Variables of this type are *social class, conservatism, alienation, prejudice, intellectual sophistication,* and the like. In addition to saying that two people are the same or different in terms of an ordinal variable, you can also say one is "more" than the other—that is, more conservative, more religious, more prejudiced, and so forth. Prestige rating scales, like those of Pineo–Porter (Pineo et al. 1977) or Goyder and Frank (2007), are good sociological illustrations. There is agreement that "employed professionals" rate higher prestige than "unskilled manual labourers," but how much more is an open question.

In the physical sciences, *hardness* is the most frequently cited example of an ordinal measure. We may say that one material (e.g., diamond) is harder than another (say, glass) if the former can scratch the latter and not vice versa. By attempting to scratch various materials with other materials, we might eventually be able to arrange several materials in a row, ranging from the softest to the hardest. We could never say how hard a given material is in absolute terms; we could only say how hard in relative terms—which materials it is harder than and which it is softer than.

Let's pursue the earlier example of grouping the people at a social gathering. This time imagine that we asked all the people with a post-secondary degree to stand in one group, all those whose highest degree is a high school diploma to stand in another group, and all those who had not graduated from high school to stand in a third group. This manner of grouping people satisfies the requirements for exhaustiveness and mutual exclusiveness discussed earlier. In addition, however, we might logically arrange the three groups by the relative amount of formal education (the shared attribute) each had. We might arrange the three groups in a row, ranging from most to least formal education. This arrangement would provide a physical representation of an ordinal measure. If we knew which groups two individuals were in, we could determine that one had more, less, or the same formal education as the other.

Notice in this example that it is irrelevant how close or far apart the educational groups are from one another. The postsecondary and high school groups might be a metre apart, and the less-than-high-school group 100 metres farther down the line. These actual distances don't have any meaning. The high school group, however, should be between the less-than-high-school group and the postsecondary group, or else the rank order would be incorrect.

Interval Measures For the attributes composing some variables, the actual distance separating those attributes does have meaning. Such variables are **interval measures**. For these, the logical distance between attributes can be expressed in meaningful standard intervals.

For example, in the Celsius temperature scale, the difference, or distance, between 30°C and 40°C is the same as that between 10°C and 20°C. However, 40°C is not twice as hot as 20°C, because the zero points in the Celsius (and Fahrenheit) scales are arbitrary; 0°C does not mean lack of heat. Similarly, –30° on either scale doesn't represent 30° less than no heat. (In contrast, the Kelvin scale is based on an absolute zero, which does mean a complete lack of heat.)

About the only interval measures commonly used in social scientific research are constructed measures such as standardized intelligence tests that have been more or less accepted. The interval separating IQ scores of 100 and 110 may be regarded as the same as the interval separating scores of 110 and 120 by virtue of the distribution of observed scores obtained by many thousands of people who have taken the tests over the years.

ordinal measure A level of measurement describing a variable with attributes one can rank-order along some dimension. An example would be *socioeconomic status* as composed of the attributes high, medium, low.

interval measure A level of measurement describing a variable whose attributes are rank-ordered and have equal distances between adjacent attributes. The *Celsius temperature scale* is an example of this, because the distance between 17 and 18 is the same as that between 39 and 40.

But it would be incorrect to infer that someone with an IQ of 150 is 50 percent more intelligent than someone with an IQ of 100. (A person who received a score of 0 on a standard IQ test could not be regarded, strictly speaking, as having no intelligence, although we might feel he or she was unsuited to be a university professor or even a university student.)

When comparing two people using an interval variable, we can say they are different from each other (nominal), and that one is more than another (ordinal). In addition, we can say how much more.

Ratio Measures Most of the social scientific variables that meet the minimum requirements for interval measures also meet the requirements for ratio measures. In **ratio measures**, the attributes composing a variable, besides having all the structural characteristics mentioned previously, are based on a true zero point. The Kelvin temperature scale is one such measure. Examples from social scientific research would include *age, income, length of residence in a given place, number of organizations belonged to, number of times married,* and *number of Australian friends.*

Returning to the illustration of methodological party games, we might ask a gathering of people to group themselves by age. All the one-year-olds would stand (or sit or lie) together, the two-year-olds together, the three-year-olds, and so forth. The fact that members of a single group share the same age and that each different group has a different shared age satisfies the minimum requirements for a nominal measure. Arranging the several groups in a line from youngest to oldest meets the additional requirements of an ordinal measure and lets us determine whether one person is older than, younger than, or the same age as another. If we space the groups equally far apart, we satisfy the additional requirements of an interval measure and will be able to say how much older one person is than another. Finally, because one of the attributes included in age represents a true zero (babies carried by women about to give birth), the phalanx of hapless partygoers also meets the requirements of a ratio measure, permitting us to say that one person is twice as old as another. Another example of a ratio measure is income, which extends from an absolute zero to approximately infinity, if you happen to be the founder of Microsoft.

Comparing two people using a ratio variable, then, allows us to conclude (1) they are different (or the same), (2) one is more than the other, (3) how much they differ, and (4) the ratio of one to another. Figure 5-1 summarizes this discussion by presenting a graphic illustration of the four levels of measurement.

IMPLICATIONS OF LEVELS OF MEASUREMENT

Because it's unlikely you will undertake the physical grouping of people just described (try it once, and you won't be invited to many parties), we should draw your attention to some of the practical implications of the differences that have been distinguished. These implications primarily appear in the analysis of data (discussed in Part 4), but you need to anticipate such implications when you're structuring any research project.

Certain quantitative analysis techniques require variables that meet certain minimum levels of measurement. To the extent that the variables to be examined in a research project are limited to a particular level of measurement—say, ordinal—you should plan your analytical techniques accordingly. More precisely, you should anticipate drawing research conclusions appropriate to the levels of measurement used in your variables. For example, you might reasonably plan to determine and report the mean age of a population under study (add up all the individual ages and divide by the number of people), but you should not plan to report the mean religious affiliation, because that is a nominal variable, and the mean requires ratio-level data. (You could report the modal—the most common—religious affiliation.)

As you go up the levels of measurement from nominal to ratio, additional features are being added. To be specific, an ordinal measure is a

ratio measure A level of measurement describing a variable whose attributes have all the qualities of nominal, ordinal, and interval measures, and in addition are based on a "true zero" point. *Age* is an example of a ratio measure.

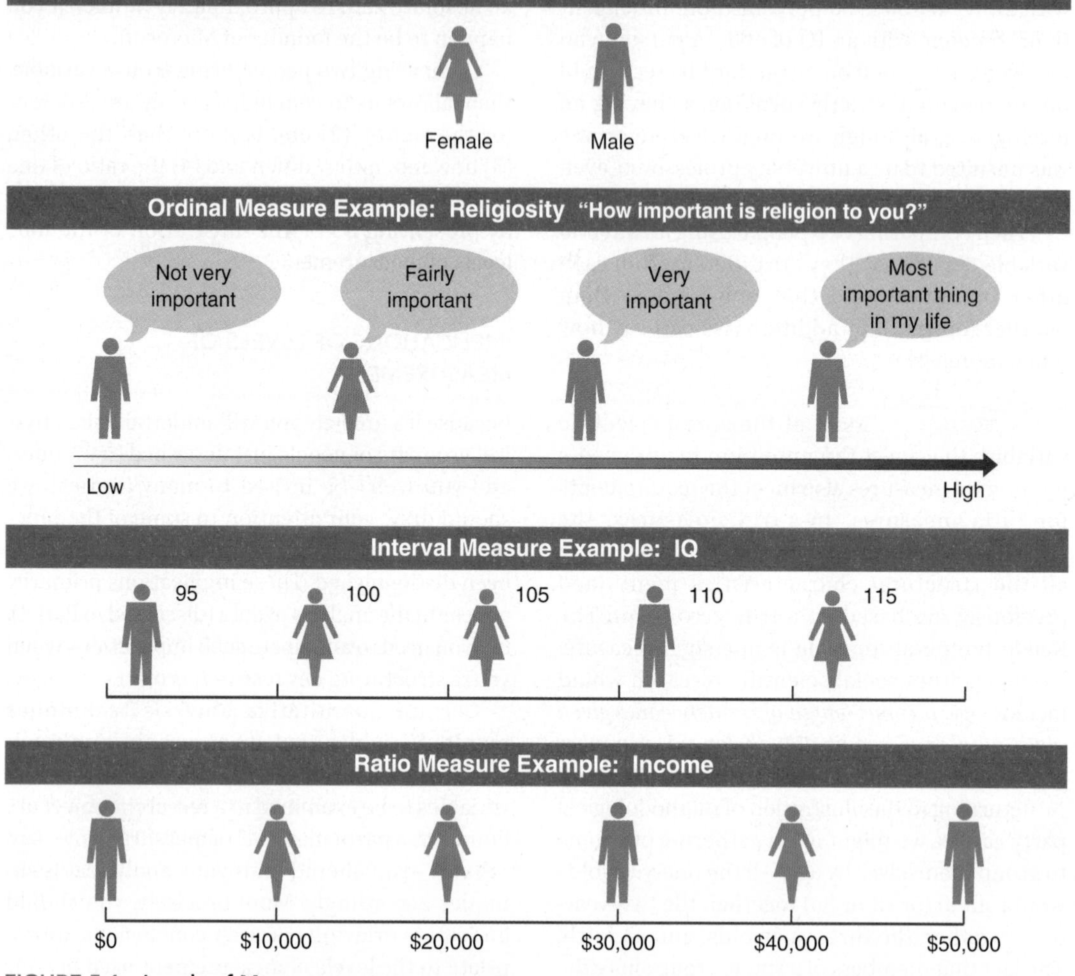

FIGURE 5-1 **Levels of Measurement.** Often you can choose among different levels of measurement—nominal, ordinal, interval, or ratio—carrying progressively more amounts of information.
Source: © Cengage Learning

nominal measure with the additional feature that the attributes can be rank ordered. An interval measure is an ordinal one with the added feature that the distance between the categories is fixed. And a ratio measure is an interval one with the additional feature that the zero point is absolute (rather than arbitrary). Like Russian dolls, the levels of measurement are embedded in one another. This fact has the important implication that higher levels of measurement can be converted to lower ones. In other words, you can always make a measure less complex. Take the variable "earned annual income." If we measure it as "number of dollars per year," then its measurement is ratio. (If you earn zero dollars per year, your annual income is literally nothing.) If we have this information from a sample of subjects, we can convert it to an ordinal level of measure by grouping the incomes into categories such as low, medium, and high.

The level of measurement you'll seek, then, is determined by the analytical uses you've planned for a given variable, keeping in mind that some variables are inherently limited to a certain level. If a variable is to be used in a variety of ways, requiring different levels of measurement, the study should be designed to achieve the highest level required. For example, if the subjects in a study are asked their exact ages, they can later be organized into ordinal or nominal groupings.

You need not necessarily measure variables at their highest level of measurement, however. If you're sure to have no need for ages of people at higher than the ordinal level of measurement, you may simply ask people to indicate their age range, such as 20 to 29, 30 to 39, and so forth. In a study of the wealth of corporations, rather than seek more precise information you may use Dun & Bradstreet ratings to rank corporations. Whenever your research purposes are not altogether clear, however, seek the highest level of measurement possible. Again, although ratio measures can later be reduced to ordinal ones, you cannot convert an ordinal measure to a ratio one. More generally, you cannot convert a lower-level measure to a higher-level one. This is a one-way street worth remembering.

The level of measurement is significant in terms of the arithmetic operations that can be applied to a variable and the statistical techniques using those operations. The accompanying table summarizes some of the implications, including ways of stating the comparison of two incomes.

Level of Measurement	Arithmetic Operations	How to Express the Fact That Jan Earns $80,000 a Year and Andy Earns $40,000
Nominal	$= \neq$	Jan and Andy earn different amounts.
Ordinal	$> <$	Jan earns more than Andy.
Interval	$+ -$	Jan earns $40,000 more than Andy.
Ratio	$\div \times$	Jan earns twice as much as Andy.

Source: © Cengage Learning

Typically a research project will tap variables at different levels of measurement. For example, William and Denise Bielby (1999) set out to examine the world of film and television using a nomothetic, longitudinal approach (take a moment to remind yourself what this means). In what they referred to as the "culture industry," the authors found that *reputation* (an ordinal variable) is the best predictor of screenwriters' future productivity. More interestingly, they found that screenwriters who were represented by core (or elite) agencies were far more likely not only to find *jobs* (a nominal variable), but also to find jobs that *paid more* (a ratio variable). In other words, the researchers found that an agency's *reputation* (ordinal) was a key independent variable for predicting screenwriters' success. The researchers also found that being older (*age*, ratio), being female (*gender*, nominal), belonging to an ethnic minority (*ethnicity*, nominal), and having more *years of experience* (ratio) were disadvantageous to a screenwriter. On the other hand, higher *earnings from previous years* (measured in ordinal categories) led to more success in the future. In the researchers' terms, "success breeds success" (Bielby and Bielby 1999:80). See the Applying Concepts in Everyday Life box "On to Hollywood" for more on the Bielby study.

SINGLE OR MULTIPLE INDICATORS

With so many alternatives for operationalizing variables in social research, you may find yourself worrying about making the right choices. To counter this feeling, let us add a momentary dash of certainty and stability.

Many social scientific variables have fairly straightforward measures. With some exceptions (genderqueer), *gender* usually turns out to be a matter of male or female: a nominal-level variable that can be measured by a single observation—either looking (well, not always) or asking a question (usually). In a study involving the size of

APPLYING CONCEPTS IN EVERYDAY LIFE

On to Hollywood

Say you want to be a Hollywood screenwriter. How might you use the results of the Bielby and Bielby (1999) study to enhance your career? Say you didn't do so well and instead started a school for screenwriters. How could the results of the study be used to plan courses? Finally, how might the results be useful to you if you were a social activist committed to fighting discrimination in the "culture industry"?

families, you'll want to think about adopted and foster children, as well as blended families, but it's usually pretty easy to find out how many children a family has. For most research purposes, the reported resident population of a country is the resident population of that country. You can find the number in an almanac. A great many variables, then, have obvious single indicators. If you can get one piece of information, you have what you need.

Sometimes, however, there is no single indicator that will give you the measure of a variable you really want. As discussed earlier in this chapter, many concepts are subject to varying interpretations, each with several possible indicators. In these cases, you'll want to make several observations for a given variable. You can then combine the several pieces of information you've collected to create a composite measurement of the variable in question. Ways of doing this will be discussed further shortly, so let's just consider one simple illustration here.

Consider the concept "university performance." All of us have noticed that some students perform well in university and others do not. In studying these differences, we might ask what characteristics and experiences are related to high levels of performance; many researchers have done just that. How should we measure overall performance? Each grade in any single course is a potential indicator of university performance, but a single course grade may not typify the student's general performance. The solution to this problem is so firmly established that it is, of course, obvious: the *grade point average* (GPA). We assign numerical scores to each letter grade, total the points earned by a given student, and divide by the number of courses taken to obtain a composite measure. (If the courses vary in number of credits, we adjust the point values accordingly.) It's often appropriate to create such composite measures in social research.

SOME ILLUSTRATIONS OF OPERATIONALIZATION CHOICES

To bring together all the operationalization choices available to the social researcher and to show the potential in those possibilities, let's look at some of the distinct ways you might address various research problems. The alternative ways of operationalizing the variables in each case should demonstrate the opportunities that social research can present to our ingenuity and imaginations. To simplify matters, we have not attempted to describe all the research conditions that would make one alternative superior to the others, though in a given situation they would not all be equally appropriate.

Here are specific research questions, then, and some of the ways you could address them. We'll begin with an example discussed earlier in this chapter. It has the added advantage that one of the variables is straightforward to operationalize.

1. Are women more compassionate than men?
   a. Select a group of subjects for study, with equal numbers of men and women. Present them with hypothetical situations that involve someone being in trouble. Ask them what they would do if they were confronted with that situation. What would they do, for example, if they came across a small child who was lost and crying for his or her parents? Consider any answer that involves helping or comforting the child as an indicator of compassion. See whether men or women are more likely to indicate they would be compassionate.
   b. Set up an experiment in which you pay a small child to pretend that he or she is lost. Put the child to work on a busy sidewalk, and observe whether men or women are more likely to offer assistance. Also, be sure to count the total number of men and women who walk by, because there may be more of one than the other. If that's the case, simply calculate the percentage of men and the percentage of women who help.
   c. Select a sample of people and do a survey in which you ask them what organizations they belong to. Calculate whether women or men are more likely to belong to those that seem to reflect compassionate feelings. To take account of men belonging to more organizations than women in general or vice versa, do this: for each person you study, calculate the percentage of his or her organizational memberships

that reflect compassion. See if men or women have a higher average percentage.

2. Are sociology students or chemistry students better informed about world affairs?
   a. Prepare a short quiz on world affairs and arrange to administer it to the students in a sociology class and in a chemistry class at a comparable level. If you want to compare sociology and chemistry majors, be sure to ask students what they are majoring in.
   b. Get the instructor of a course in world affairs to give you the average grades of sociology and chemistry students in the course.
   c. Take a petition to sociology and chemistry classes that urges that "the UN headquarters be moved to New York City." Keep a count of how many in each class sign the petition and how many inform you that the UN headquarters is already located in New York City.
3. Who are the most popular instructors on your campus: those in the social sciences, the natural sciences, or the humanities?
   a. If your school has a provision for student evaluation of instructors, review some recent results and compare the average ratings given to the three groups.
   b. Begin visiting the introductory courses given in each group of disciplines and measure the attendance rate of each class.
   c. In December, select a group of faculty in each of the three divisions and ask them to keep a record of the numbers of holiday greeting cards and presents they receive from admiring students. See who wins.

The point of these examples is not necessarily to suggest respectable research projects but to illustrate the many ways variables can be operationalized.

OPERATIONALIZATION GOES ON AND ON

Although we've discussed conceptualization and operationalization as activities that precede data collection and analysis—for example, you must design questionnaire items before you send out a questionnaire—these two processes continue throughout any research project, even if the data have been collected in a structured mass survey. As we've seen, in less structured methods such as field research, the identification and specification of relevant concepts is inseparable from the ongoing process of observation.

As a researcher, always be open to re-examining your concepts and definitions. The ultimate purpose of social research is to clarify the nature of social life. The validity and utility of what you learn in this regard doesn't depend on when you first figured out how to look at things any more than it matters whether you got the idea from a learned textbook, a dream, or your brother-in-law.

CRITERIA FOR MEASUREMENT QUALITY

This chapter has come some distance. It began by introducing how meaningful concepts are constructed and then explored tools and techniques researchers use for determining the existence of conceptual properties in reality. Now we will discuss some of the yardsticks against which we judge our relative success or failure in measuring things.

PRECISION AND ACCURACY

To begin, measurements can be made with varying degrees of **precision**. As we saw in the discussion of operationalization, precision concerns the fineness of distinctions made between attributes composing a variable. The description of a woman as "43 years old" is more precise than "in her 40s." Saying a street gang was formed in the summer of 1996 is more precise than saying "during the 1990s."

As a general rule, precise measurements are superior to imprecise ones, as common sense would dictate. There are no conditions under which imprecise measurements are intrinsically superior to precise ones. Even so, exact precision is not always necessary or desirable. If knowing

precision The property that refers to the fineness of measurement distinctions.

that a woman is in her 40s satisfies your research requirements, then any additional effort invested in learning her precise age is wasted. The operationalization of concepts, then, must be guided partly by an understanding of the degree of precision required. If your needs are not clear, be more precise rather than less.

Don't confuse precision with **accuracy**, however. Describing someone as "born in the Maritimes" is less precise than "born in New Brunswick"—but suppose the person in question was actually born on Prince Edward Island. The less precise description, in this instance, is more accurate—a better reflection of the real world.

Precision and accuracy are obviously important qualities in research measurement, and they probably need no further explanation. When social scientists construct and evaluate measurements, however, they pay special attention to two technical considerations: reliability and validity.

RELIABILITY

In the abstract, **reliability** is a matter of whether a particular technique, applied repeatedly to the same object, yields the same result each time. Let's say you want to know how much your postal carrier weighs. (No, we don't know why.) As one technique, you might ask two different people to estimate his or her weight. If the first person estimated 55 kilograms and the other estimated 110, we have to conclude the technique of having people estimate your carrier's weight isn't very reliable.

Suppose, as an alternative, that you use a bathroom scale as your measurement technique. Your carrier steps on the scale twice, and you note the result each time. The scale reported the same weight both times, indicating that the scale provided a more reliable technique for measuring a person's weight than did asking people to estimate it.

Reliability, however, does not ensure accuracy any more than precision does. Suppose your father set the bathroom scale to shave two kilograms off his weight just to make himself feel better. Although you would (reliably) report the same weight for your carrier each time, you would always be wrong. This new element, called bias, is discussed in Chapter 6. For now, just be warned that reliability does not ensure accuracy.

Let's suppose we're interested in studying morale among factory workers in two different kinds of factories. In one set of factories, workers have specialized jobs, reflecting an extreme division of labour. Each worker contributes a tiny part to the overall process performed on a long assembly line. In the other set of factories, each worker performs many tasks, and small teams of workers complete the whole process.

How should we measure *morale*? Following one strategy, we could observe the workers in each factory, noticing such things as whether they joke with one another, whether they smile and laugh a lot, and so forth. We could ask them how they like their work and even ask them whether they think they would prefer their current arrangement or the other one being studied. By comparing what we observed in the different factories, we might reach a conclusion about which assembly process produced the higher morale.

Now let's look at some reliability problems inherent in this method. First, how we are feeling when we do the observing will likely colour what we see. We may misinterpret what we see. We may see workers kidding each other but think they're having an argument. We may catch them on an off day. If we were to observe the same group of workers several days in a row, we might arrive at different evaluations on each day. If several observers evaluated the same behaviour, on the other hand, they too might arrive at different conclusions about the workers' morale.

Here's another strategy for assessing morale. Suppose we check the company records to see how many grievances have been filed with the union during some fixed period of time. Presumably this would be an indicator of morale: the

accuracy The property that refers to the correctness of measurements.

reliability That quality of measurement method that suggests that the same data would have been collected each time in repeated observations of the same phenomenon. In the context of a survey, we would expect that the question "Did you attend religious services last week?" would have higher reliability than the question "About how many times have you attended religious services in your life?" This is not to be confused with *validity*.

more grievances, the lower the morale. This measurement strategy would appear to be more reliable: counting up the grievances over and over, we should keep arriving at the same number.

If you find yourself thinking that the number of grievances doesn't necessarily measure morale, you're worrying about validity, not reliability. We'll discuss validity in a moment. The point for now is that the last method is more like your bathroom scale—it gives consistent results.

In social research, reliability problems crop up in many forms. Reliability is a concern every time a single observer is the source of data, because we have no certain guard against the impact of that observer's subjectivity. We can't tell for sure how much of what's reported originated in the situation observed and how much in the observer.

Subjectivity is not only a problem with single observers, however. Survey researchers have known for a long time that different interviewers, because of their own attitudes and demeanours, get different answers from respondents. Or, if we were to conduct a study of newspapers' editorial positions on some public issue, we might create a team of coders to take on the job of reading hundreds of editorials and classifying them by their position on the issue. Unfortunately, different coders will code the same editorial differently. Or we might want to classify a few hundred specific occupations using some standard coding scheme—say, a set of categories created by Statistics Canada for the census. Working independently, we would not place all those occupations in the same categories.

Each of these examples illustrates problems of reliability. Similar problems arise whenever we ask people to give us information about themselves. Sometimes we ask questions that people don't know the answers to: How many times have you been to religious services this year? Sometimes we ask people about things they consider totally irrelevant: Are you satisfied with China's current relationship with Albania? In such cases, people will answer differently at different times because they're making up answers as they go. Sometimes we explore issues so complicated that a person who had a clear opinion on the matter might arrive at a different interpretation of the question when asked a second time.

So how do you create reliable measures? If your research design calls for asking people for information, you can be careful to ask only about things the respondents are likely to know the answer to. Ask about things relevant to them, and be clear in what you're asking. Of course, these techniques don't solve every possible reliability problem. Fortunately, social researchers have developed several techniques for cross-checking the reliability of the measures they devise.

Test-Retest Method Sometimes it's appropriate to make the same measurement more than once, a technique called the test-retest method. If you do not expect the information sought to change, then you should expect the same response both times. If answers vary, the measurement method may, to the extent of that variation, be unreliable. Here's an illustration.

In their research on health hazard appraisal (HHA), a part of preventive medicine, Jeffrey Sacks, W. Mark Krushat, and Jeffrey Newman (1980) wanted to determine the risks associated with various background and lifestyle factors, making it possible for physicians to counsel their patients appropriately. By knowing patients' life situations, physicians could advise them on their potential for survival and on how to improve it. This purpose, of course, depended heavily on the accuracy of the information gathered about each subject in the study.

To test the reliability of their information, Sacks and his colleagues had all 207 subjects complete a baseline questionnaire that asked about their characteristics and behaviour. Three months later, a follow-up questionnaire asked the same subjects for the same information, and the results of the two surveys were compared. Overall, only 15 percent of the subjects reported the same information in both studies.

Sacks and his colleagues report (1980:730) the following:

> Almost 10 percent of subjects reported a different height at follow-up examination. Parental age was changed by over one in three subjects. One parent reportedly aged 20 chronologic years in three months. One in five ex-smokers and ex-drinkers have apparent difficulty in reliably recalling their previous consumption pattern.

Some subjects erased all trace of previously reported heart murmur, diabetes, emphysema, arrest record, and thoughts of suicide. One subject's mother, deceased in the first questionnaire, was apparently alive and well in time for the second. One subject had one ovary missing in the first study but present in the second. In another case, an ovary present in the first study was missing in the second study—and had been for ten years! One subject was reportedly 55 years old in the first study and 50 years old three months later. (You have to wonder if the physician-counsellors could ever have nearly the impact on their patients that their patients' memories did.) Thus, the test-retest revealed that this data-collection method was not especially reliable.

Split-Half Method As a general rule, it's always good to make more than one measurement of any subtle or complex social concept, such as prejudice, alienation, or social class. This procedure lays the groundwork for another check on reliability. Let's say you've created a questionnaire that contains ten items you believe measure prejudice against women. Using the split-half technique, you would randomly assign those ten items to two sets of five. Each set should provide a good measure of prejudice against women, and the two sets should classify respondents in the same way. If the two sets of items classify people differently, you likely have a problem of reliability in your measure of the variable.

Using Established Measures Another way to help ensure reliability in getting information from people is to use measures that have proven their reliability in previous research. If you want to measure anomia, for example, you might want to follow Srole's (1956) lead.

validity A term describing a measure that accurately reflects the concept it is intended to measure. For example, your IQ would seem a more valid measure of your intelligence than would the number of hours you spend in the library. Though the ultimate validity of a measure can never be proven, we may agree to its relative validity on the basis of face validity, criterion-related validity, content validity, construct validity, internal validation, and external validation. This must not be confused with reliability.

The heavy use of measures, though, does not guarantee their reliability. For example, the Minnesota Multiphasic Personality Inventory (MMPI) has been accepted as a standard in the psychological assessment of individuals for decades. In recent years, though, it has needed fundamental overhauling to reflect changes in society.

Reliability of Research Workers As we've seen, it's possible for measurement unreliability to be generated by research workers: interviewers and coders, for example. There are several ways to check on reliability in such cases. To guard against interviewer unreliability, it is common practice in surveys to have a supervisor call a subsample of the respondents on the telephone and verify selected pieces of information.

Replication works in other situations also. If you're worried that newspaper editorials or occupations may not be classified reliably, you could have each independently coded by several coders. Those cases that are classified inconsistently can then be evaluated more carefully and resolved.

Finally, clarity, specificity, training, and practice can prevent a great deal of unreliability and grief. If you and your professor spent some time reaching a clear agreement on how to evaluate editorial positions on an issue—discussing various positions and reading through several together—you could probably do a good job of classifying them in the same way independently.

The reliability of measurements is a fundamental issue in social research, and we'll return to it more than once in the chapters ahead. For now, however, let's recall that even total reliability doesn't ensure that our measures measure what we think they measure. Now let's plunge into the question of validity.

VALIDITY

In conventional usage, the term **validity** refers to the extent to which an empirical measure adequately reflects the *real meaning* of the concept under consideration. Whoops! We're already committed to the view that concepts don't have real meanings. So how can we ever say whether a particular measure adequately reflects the concept's meaning? Ultimately, of course, we can't. At the same time, as we've already seen, all of social life, including social research, operates on agreements about the terms we use and the concepts they represent. There are several criteria of success in making measurements that are appropriate to these agreed-upon meanings of concepts.

First, there's something called **face validity**. Particular empirical measures may or may not jibe with our common agreements and our individual mental images concerning a particular concept. For example, you might quarrel with us about the adequacy of measuring worker morale by counting the number of grievances filed with the union. Still, we'd surely agree that the number of grievances has *something* to do with morale. That is, the measure is valid "on its face," even if it's not entirely adequate for the purpose of our study. If we were to suggest that morale be measured by finding out how many books the workers took out of the library during their off-duty hours, you'd undoubtedly raise a more serious objection: that measure wouldn't have much face validity.

Second, we've already pointed to many of the more formally established agreements that define some concepts. Statistics Canada, for example, has created operational definitions of such concepts as family, household, and employment status that seem to have a workable validity in most studies using these concepts.

Three additional types of validity also specify particular ways of testing the validity of measures. The first, **criterion-related validity**, sometimes called *predictive validity*, is based on some external criterion. For example, many occupations have qualifying exams. The validity of the exam is shown in its ability to predict future evaluations of the individuals' job performances. The validity of a written driver's test is determined, in this sense, by the relationship between the scores people get on the test and their subsequent driving records. In these examples, job performance and driving record are the criteria.

To test your understanding of this concept, see if you can think of behaviours that might be used to validate each of the following attitudes:

- is very religious
- supports equality of men and women
- is concerned about the environment

Some possible validators would be, respectively, attends religious services, votes for women candidates, and belongs to the Sierra Club.

Sometimes it's difficult to find behavioural criteria that can be taken to validate measures as directly as in such examples. In those instances, however, we can often approximate such criteria by applying a different test. We can consider how the variable in question ought, theoretically, to relate to other variables. **Construct validity** is based on the logical relationships among variables.

Let's suppose, for example, that you want to study the sources and consequences of marital satisfaction. As part of your research, you develop a measure of marital satisfaction, and you want to assess its validity.

In addition to developing your measure, you'll have developed certain theoretical expectations about the way the variable *marital satisfaction* relates to other variables. For example, you might reasonably conclude that satisfied husbands and wives will be less likely than dissatisfied ones to cheat on their spouses. If your measure relates to marital fidelity in the expected fashion, that constitutes evidence of your measure's construct validity. If satisfied marriage partners are as likely to cheat on their spouses as are the dissatisfied ones, however, that would challenge the validity of your measure.

Tests of construct validity, then, can offer a weight of evidence that your measure either does or doesn't tap the quality you want it to measure, without providing definitive proof. Although we have suggested that tests of construct validity are less compelling than those of criterion validity,

face validity That quality of an indicator that makes it seem a reasonable measure of some variable. That the frequency of attendance at religious services is some indication of a person's religiosity seems to make sense without a lot of explanation. It has face validity.

criterion-related validity The degree to which a measure relates with some external criterion. For example, the validity of occupational qualifying examinations is shown in their ability to predict future evaluations of the individuals' job performances. Also called *predictive validity*.

construct validity The degree to which a measure relates to other variables as expected within a system of theoretical relationships.

there is room for disagreement over which kind of test a particular comparison variable (driving record, marital fidelity) represents in a given situation. It's less important to distinguish the two types of validity tests than to understand the logic of validation that they have in common: if we have been successful in measuring some variable, then our measures should relate in some logical fashion to other measures.

Finally, **content validity** refers to how much a measure covers the range of meanings included within the concept. For example, a test of mathematical ability cannot be limited to addition alone but also needs to cover subtraction, multiplication, division, and so forth. Or, if we are measuring prejudice, do our measurements reflect all types of prejudice, including prejudice against racial and ethnic groups, religious minorities, women, the elderly, and so on?

Figure 5-2 illustrates the difference between validity and reliability.

WHO DECIDES WHAT'S VALID?

Our discussion of validity began with a reminder that we depend on agreements to determine what's real, and we've just seen some of the ways social scientists can agree among themselves that they have made valid measurements. There is yet another way of looking at validity.

Social researchers sometimes criticize themselves and each other for implicitly assuming they are somewhat superior to those they study. For instance, researchers often seek to uncover motivations that the social actors themselves are unaware of. You *think* you bought that new Burpo-Blasto because of its high performance and good looks, but *we know* you're really trying to achieve a higher social status.

This implicit sense of superiority would fit comfortably with a totally positivistic approach (the biologist feels superior to the frog on the lab table), but it clashes with the more humanistic and typically qualitative approach taken by many social scientists. This issue will be explored more deeply in Chapter 10.

In seeking to understand the way ordinary people make sense of their worlds, ethnomethodologists have urged all social scientists to pay more respect to these natural social processes of conceptualization and shared meaning. At the very least, behaviour that may seem irrational from the scientist's paradigm may make logical sense when viewed from the actor's/subject's paradigm.

Ultimately, social researchers should look both to their colleagues and to their subjects as sources of agreement on the most useful meanings and measurements of the concepts they study. Sometimes one source will be more useful,

content validity The degree to which a measure covers the range of meanings included within a concept.

Reliable but not valid

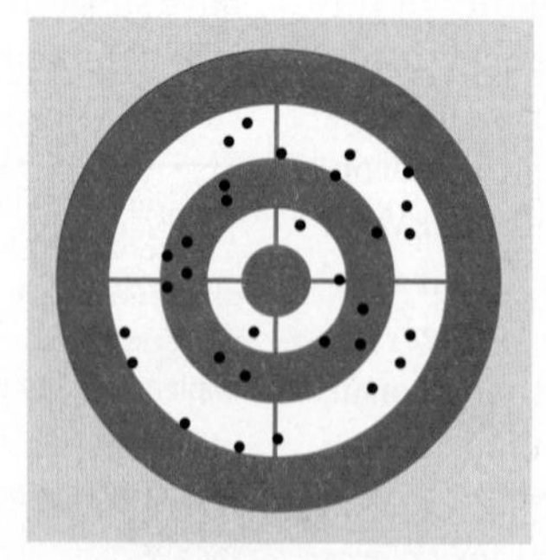

Valid but not reliable

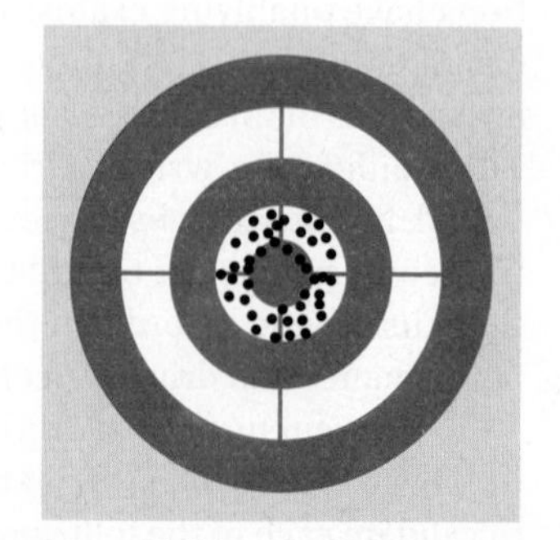

Valid *and* reliable

FIGURE 5-2 **An Analogy to Validity and Reliability.** A good measurement technique should be both valid (measuring what it is intended to measure) and reliable (yielding a given measurement dependably).
Source: © Cengage Learning

sometimes the other. But neither should be dismissed. For an example of how subjects' and researchers' perspectives may both help inform the construction and validation of a measurement instrument, see the Spotlight on Mixed Methods Research Box later in this chapter.

TENSION BETWEEN RELIABILITY AND VALIDITY

Clearly we want our measures to be both reliable and valid. However, there is often a tension between the criteria of reliability and validity, forcing a trade-off between the two.

Recall the example of measuring morale in different factories. The strategy of immersing yourself in the day-to-day routine of the assembly line, observing what goes on, and talking to the workers would seem to provide a more valid measure of morale than counting grievances. It just seems obvious that we'd get a clearer sense of whether the morale was high or low using this first method.

As we pointed out earlier, however, the counting strategy would be more reliable. This situation reflects a more general strain in research measurement. Most of the really interesting concepts we want to study have many subtle nuances, and it's hard to specify precisely what we mean by them. Researchers sometimes speak of such concepts as having a "richness of meaning." Although scores of books and articles have been written on the topic of anomie/anomia, for example, they still haven't exhausted its meaning.

Very often, then, specifying reliable operational definitions and measurements seems to rob concepts of their richness of meaning. Positive morale is much more than a lack of grievances filed with the union; anomie is much more than what's measured by the five items created by Leo Srole. Yet the more variation and richness we allow for a concept, the more opportunity there is for disagreement on how it applies to a particular situation, thus reducing reliability.

To some extent, this dilemma explains the persistence of two quite different approaches to social research: quantitative, nomothetic, structured techniques such as surveys and experiments on the one hand, and qualitative, idiographic methods such as field research and historical studies on the other. In the simplest generalization, the former methods tend to be more reliable, the latter more valid.

By being forewarned, you'll be effectively forearmed against this persistent and inevitable dilemma. If there is no clear agreement on how to measure a concept, measure it several different ways. If the concept has several dimensions, measure them all. Above all, know that the concept does not have any meaning other than what we give it. The only justification for giving any concept a particular meaning is utility. Measure concepts in ways that help us understand the world around us.

INDICATORS, INDEXES, AND SCALES

Our discussion of levels of measurement, reliability, and validity has been organized around variables. You may recall from Chapter 2 that *variable* is a concept used largely in the quantitative research tradition. Before we cover some final topics related to variables we should note that concepts like reliability and validity are just as much a concern to qualitative researchers. Researchers from both quantitative and qualitative traditions struggle to ensure that their reports provided a consistent picture of what is occurring (reliability) and that the results are accurate reflections (validity).

Whether generated inductively or used deductively, both qualitative and quantitative reports use concepts to express and interpret their understanding of social reality. Since concepts are abstract, empirical investigation must rely on things that reflect what the concepts mean. These empirical specifications of abstract concepts are called **indicators**. In quantitative research, variables are used as indictors which are spelled out through the process of operationalization (see Figure 2-5 in Chapter 2). In qualitative research, the indicators are generated from observation and the interpretive task is one of constructing concepts that capture their meaning.

indicator An empirical specification of some abstract concept.

Most concepts are rich with meaning. Think of concepts like alienation, love, power, happiness, and discrimination. This richness implies that finding appropriate indicators is challenging. Indicators are intended to capture the meaning of the concept, and if a concept is rich with meaning, multiple indicators are likely necessary. Can you think of a single indicator that captures when you have fallen in (or out of) romantic love? How about one that captures how happy you are (or aren't)?

The methodological point is that researchers should regularly be looking for multiple indicators of the concepts they are using. Using multiple indicators provides the best chance of capturing concepts reliably and validly. Here is an example.

Bhutan is a small Himalayan country with a big idea. Its king believes that society should be organized around making its citizens happy. This idea stands in stark contrast to the Western notion that material well-being, as indicated by gross domestic product (GDP), is most important. In order to track how well the country is doing, Bhutan developed an alternative to GDP, which they labelled gross national happiness (GNH). The Bhutan conceptualization of happiness includes nine dimensions, ranging from psychological well-being through health to community diversity. These dimensions were measured with thirty-three indicators. More recently, the United Kingdom took up this idea and developed its own conceptualization and measure of national happiness. It includes ten indicators covering issues such as personal health, relationships with loved ones, trust in political institutions, and satisfaction with education and employment (Beaumont 2011).

In both Bhutan and the United Kingdom, researchers expended considerable effort trying to develop or locate measures that validly and reliably captured the multiple indicators of happiness.

Using multiple indicators allows researchers the opportunity to more adequately capture the richness of meaningful concepts, since different indicators are capturing different facets of the concept. It also allows researchers to explore how the multiple indicators might be combined into overall, summary measures in the form of indexes and scales.

Indexes and scales are useful composite measures made up of several indicators of variables. As we have seen in this chapter, many social scientific concepts have complex and varied meanings. Making measurements that capture such concepts can be a challenge. Recall our discussion of content validity, which concerns whether we've captured all the different dimensions of a concept. Researchers often need to use multiple indicators to measure a variable adequately and validly.

To achieve broad coverage of the various dimensions of a concept, we usually need to make multiple observations pertaining to that concept. Thus, for example, Bruce Berg (2007:100) advises in-depth interviewers to prepare essential questions that are "geared toward eliciting specific, desired information." In addition, the researcher should prepare "questions roughly equivalent to certain essential ones, but worded slightly differently."

Multiple indicators are used with quantitative data as well. Suppose you're designing a survey. Although you can sometimes construct a single questionnaire item that captures the variable of interest—"Gender: ❑ Male ❑ Female ❑ Non-binary" is an example—other variables may require you to use several questionnaire items to measure them adequately.

Quantitative data analysts have developed specific techniques for combining indicators into a single measure. This section discusses two types of composite measures of variables: indexes and scales. Although these measures can be used in any form of social research, they are most common in survey research and other quantitative methods.

Composite measures are frequently used in quantitative research, for several reasons. First, social scientists often wish to study variables that do not have clear and unambiguous single indicators. Single indicators are sufficient for some variables, like age. We may determine a survey respondent's age by asking "How old are you?" We may determine a city's population by looking at census data. In the case of complex concepts, however, researchers can seldom develop single indicators before they actually do the research. This is especially true with regard to attitudes and orientations. Rarely can survey researchers, for example, devise single questionnaire items that adequately tap respondents' degrees of prejudice, religiosity, political orientations, alienation, and the like. More likely, they will devise several items, each of which provides some indication of the variables. Taken individually, each of these is likely to prove invalid or unreliable for many respondents. A composite measure, however, can overcome this problem.

Second, researchers may wish to use a rather refined ordinal measure of a variable—alienation, say—such as arranging cases in several ordinal categories from very low to very high. A single data item might not have enough categories to provide the desired range of variation, but an index or scale formed from several items can provide the desired range.

Finally, indexes and scales are efficient devices for data analysis. If considering a single data item gives us only a rough indication of a given variable, considering several data items may give us a more comprehensive and more accurate indication. For example, a single newspaper editorial may give us some indication of the political orientations of that newspaper. Examining several editorials would probably give us a better assessment, but the manipulation of several data items simultaneously could be very complicated. Indexes and scales are efficient *data-reduction devices*: they allow us to summarize several indicators in a single numerical score, even while very nearly maintaining the specific details of all the individual indicators.

INDEXES VERSUS SCALES

The terms *index* and *scale* are typically used imprecisely and interchangeably in social research literature. Before considering the distinctions we'll make in this book between these two types of measures, let's see what they have in common.

Both scales and indexes are ordinal measures of variables. Both rank-order the units of analysis using specific variables such as religiosity, alienation, socioeconomic status, prejudice, or intellectual sophistication. A person's score on either a scale or an index of religiosity, for example, gives an indication of his or her religiosity relative to the religiosity of other people.

Further, both scales and indexes are composite measures of variables—that is, measurements based on more than one data item. Thus, a survey respondent's score on an index or scale of religiosity is determined by the responses given to several questionnaire items, each of which provides some indication of religiosity. Similarly, a person's IQ score is based on answers to a large number of test questions. The political orientation of a newspaper might be represented by an index or scale score reflecting the newspaper's editorial policy on various political issues.

Despite these shared characteristics, it's useful to distinguish between indexes and scales. In this book we'll distinguish them by the way scores are assigned in each. An **index** is constructed by simply accumulating scores assigned to individual indicators. The indicators do not typically need to be in a specific order, and each item is given the same weight, or importance, in scoring. We might measure prejudice, for example, by adding up the number of prejudiced statements each respondent agreed with. A **scale**, however, is constructed by assigning scores to patterns of responses, recognizing that some items reflect a relatively weak degree of the variable while others reflect something stronger; hence, different items may be assigned different weight, or importance, in scoring. For example, agreeing that "Women are different from men" is, at best, weak evidence of sexism compared with agreeing that "Women should not be allowed to vote." A scale takes advantage of differences in intensity among the attributes of the same variable to identify distinct patterns of response.

An examination of actual social science research reports will show that researchers use indexes much more frequently than they do

index A type of composite measure that combines multiple items that, when aggregated, are intended to represent some more general dimension.

scale A type of composite measure composed of several items that have a logical or empirical structure among them. Examples of scales are Bogardus social distance and the Guttman, Likert, and Thurstone scales.

scales. Ironically, however, the methodological literature contains little if any discussion of index construction, while discussions of scale construction abound. There appear to be two reasons for this disparity. First, indexes may be used more frequently because scales are often difficult or impossible to construct from the data at hand. Second, methods of index construction seem so obvious and straightforward that they aren't discussed much.

Constructing indexes, however, is not a simple undertaking. The general failure to develop index construction techniques has resulted in many bad indexes in social research. With this in mind, we have an online chapter devoted to the methods of index and scale construction. We begin with the construction of indexes. With a solid understanding of the logic of this activity, you'll be better equipped to try constructing scales. Indeed, a carefully constructed index may turn out to be a scale. To further pursue index and scale construction, go to the MindTap site for this textbook to find the chapter titled "Indexes and Scales."

Figure 5-3 provides an example of a composite index—the Problem Gambling Severity Index (PGSI). The PGSI is a sub-index of the Canadian Problem Gambling Index (Ferris and Wynne 2001) and has been widely used in studies of problem gambling in Canada and abroad (Williams and Volberg 2010). The PGSI does not try to measure problem gambling risk with a single question, such as "How frequently do you gamble?" or "How much money have you lost gambling in the last 12 months?" The PGSI assesses the problem gambling risk using multiple indicators that reflect a number of aspects of gambling-related problems. Respondents are asked to indicate how often in the past twelve months these situations have occurred to them.

PGSI scores range from a minimum score of 0 (someone who answered "never" to all 9 questions) and a maximum score of 27 (someone who answered "all the time" to all 9 questions).

	Never	Sometimes	Most of the time	All of the time
a) Have you bet more than you could really afford to lose?	❑ 0	❑ 1	❑ 2	❑ 3
b) Have you needed to gamble with larger amounts of money to get the same feeling of excitement?	❑ 0	❑ 1	❑ 2	❑ 3
c) When you gambled did you go back another day to try and win back the money you lost?	❑ 0	❑ 1	❑ 2	❑ 3
d) Have you borrowed money or sold anything to get money to gamble?	❑ 0	❑ 1	❑ 2	❑ 3
e) Have you felt that you might have a gambling problem?	❑ 0	❑ 1	❑ 2	❑ 3
f) Has gambling caused you health problems, including stress or anxiety?	❑ 0	❑ 1	❑ 2	❑ 3
g) Have people criticized your betting or told you that you had a gambling problem, regardless of whether or not you thought it was true?	❑ 0	❑ 1	❑ 2	❑ 3
h) Has your gambling caused any financial problems for you or your household?	❑ 0	❑ 1	❑ 2	❑ 3
i) Have you felt guilty about the way you gamble or what happens when you gamble?	❑ 0	❑ 1	❑ 2	❑ 3

FIGURE 5-3 **The Problem Gambling Severity Index.** All items are given the same weight and responses are simply summed across all nine items to produce and overall index score for each respondent.
Source: Ferris, J. and Wynne, H. 2001. *The Canadian Problem Gambling Index: Final Report.* Ottawa, ON: Canadian Centre on Substance Abuse.

SPOTLIGHT ON MIXED METHODS

Incorporating Qualitative Evidence into the Validation of Quantitative Instruments

There has been growing recognition of the importance of qualitative evidence in the development and validation of quantitative instruments (AERA et al. 2014). Onwuegbuzie and colleagues (2010) propose the Instrument Development and Construct Validation (IDCV) process, which consists of ten interactive phases. These phases are not strictly sequential, but rather unfold as an iterative process in which researchers may move back and forth between phases. A key component is crossover analysis, which involves combining qualitative and quantitative data analysis techniques, such as using one or more analysis procedures associated with one approach (e.g., quantitative analyses) to analyze data associated with the other approach (e.g., qualitative analyses). This approach takes advantage of a number of mixed methods research (MMR) strengths (discussed in Chapter 1). One example would be to compare qualitative and quantitative observations to check for divergent and convergent validity (triangulation). Another example would be to use one method to elaborate, enhance, or clarify the analyses of another method (complementarity), or help shape or inform the analyses of another method (development).

Koskey et al. (2018) recently applied the IDCV framework to develop the Transformative Experience Questionnaire (TEQ) for students. They outline ten stages:

1. *Conceptualize the construct of interest*
   Transformative experience (TE) is conceptualized as a "representation of student engagement with academic content extending beyond the classroom to everyday life" (Koskey et al. 2018:98) that is associated with numerous positive academic outcomes.
2. *Identify and describe behaviours that underlie the construct*
   TE is evident along three main dimensions: behavioural (e.g., motivated use, such as spontaneously—and on their own initiative—applying learning outside the classroom), cognitive (e.g., expansion of perception—understanding and perceiving the world through the lens of learned content), and affective (e.g., experiential value—enhanced appreciation for how new learning enriches everyday life).
3. *Develop initial instrument*
   Survey items were developed to represent an underlying continuum of student engagement, from in-class to out-of-class, with out-of-class engagement indicative of a greater level of TE. Koskey and colleagues developed two forms of the instrument to assess TE in two content areas relevant to the middle- and high-school science curricula: genetics and properties of matter.
4. *Pilot-test initial instrument*
   They first pilot-tested items with two individuals from the target population. Then they revised according to their interview feedback.
5. *Design and field-test revised instrument*
   In the second stage of pilot-testing, 49 students filled out the revised survey with four-point Likert-type response options (strongly disagree to strongly agree). Items (i.e., survey questions) that were a poor fit as indicated by quantitative (Rasch modelling) and qualitative (expert review) criteria were removed.
6. *Validate revised instrument: Quantitative-dominant analysis phase*
   A sample of middle- and high-school students (n = 196) were administered the revised survey. Quantitative tests of reliability (e.g., test-retest) and validity (e.g., concurrent validity, construct validity) were conducted on the response data.

(*Continued*)

SPOTLIGHT ON MIXED METHODS (*CONTINUED*)

7. *Validate revised instrument: Qualitative-dominant analysis phase*
   A subsample of student volunteers participated in a "think-aloud" validity check: they read each question aloud as they completed it; an interviewer asked what they thought each question was asking and which response they were choosing and why. The idea was to help developers determine whether students interpreted questions as intended by designers (i.e., a good question) or not (i.e., a question in need of revision or removal).

8.&9. *Crossover analyses*
   Results from the quantitative Rasch analysis and the qualitative think-aloud interview were combined to corroborate (i.e., cross-validate) that the instrument and items were functioning as intended. This is part of a broader sense of validation that Onwuegbuzie and colleagues (2010:59) term instrument fidelity, which entails developing an instrument "to maximize its appropriateness and/or utility."

10. *Evaluate the instrument development/construct evaluation process and product*

The research team consisted of multiple members with a variety of expertise who engaged regularly in debriefing to review their decisions and procedures during the instrument development process.

Rasch modelling is a quantitative test development technique built on the basic idea that a person's score on an item is a function of two things: (1) their ability or competence and (2) the item's difficulty. Accordingly, the ability of an individual is determined by how many items they get right, while the difficulty of an item is determined by how many individuals get it right. Instrument developers are typically looking for a balance of items along the difficulty continuum in order to differentiate individuals with differing levels of ability or competency. For example, easy items should be answered correctly by students at all ability levels, moderately difficult items should differentiate weak students from average (and above) students, and difficult items should differentiate between strong students and average (or below) students.

The higher the summed PGSI score, the more severe a person's risk for problem gambling. These PGSI continuous scores (0–27) can also be recoded into a four-category ordinal variable using the following cut-off points (Currie et al. 2013): "non-problem gambler" (continuous PGSI score of 0), "low-risk gambler" (continuous PGSI score of 1 to 4), "moderate-risk gambler" (continuous PGSI score of 5 to 7), and "problem gambler" (continuous PGSI score of 8 or more). For example, in a recent study of a Canadian sample of young adults, Sanscartier and colleagues (2018) found that the mean continuous PGSI score was .93, and that 70.2 percent of young adults were non-problem gamblers, 24 percent were low-risk, 2.8 percent were moderate-risk, and 3 percent were problem gamblers.

ETHICS AND MEASUREMENT

When devising operational procedures, the measures researchers choose are limited by both practical and ethical considerations. As we noted, the researcher is continually searching for better measures of concepts, but there are trade-offs that must be made between choosing the "better" measure and choosing the more ethical measure.

Suppose we were asked to study how women respond to sexual harassment. Some indicators of sexual harassment might be derogatory statements about women, misogynistic jokes, unwanted touching, and stalking. Perhaps the best way for us to ensure exact uniformity across research subjects would be to supply a research assistant with a script and instructions to confront the research subjects. Subjecting women to such acts to determine their response would clearly be unethical. Therefore, the ethical researcher would devise other means of conducting such a study.

There are endless examples of trade-offs that might be considered in designing an effective and ethical research study. Many issues of interest to social scientists involve topics that people are sensitive about or tap into events that people have experienced that caused them pain and trauma. Given that there are many ways that researchers can manipulate subjects, they must consider how much discomfort or harm a particular measure may cause a person. Could a measure put people at risk, such as tracking criminal activities that may get them in trouble with the law? How much deception is allowable for the sake of gathering more accurate data? Is it OK to lie to people or spy on them because the data collected will be better—a more accurate reflection of the concept or issue under study? If we want to learn how corporate executives make decisions, tapping their phones and bugging their boardrooms might supply the best information. Most would agree, however, that such strategies would be unethical (and probably illegal).

Many ethical concerns in measurement are more subtle, and there is often disagreement over what is or is not risky or harmful to the subjects of study. For example, let's reconsider one of the ways we discussed measuring compassion. Recall that we suggested we might measure compassion by putting a child on the street and having her pretend to be lost so we could observe who comes to her aid and how. Some ethical concerns we might take into account are the potential stress to those who witness this, the major intrusion of such an event on people's lives, the lack of voluntary participation, the deception involved, and the risk to the child actor. What impact might such an experience have on someone rushing by on her or his way to the hospital to attend to a family emergency? Has an unnecessary dilemma been posed for some people that may cause them anxiety or harm? And what about the risk to the child actor who might be whisked off by some malevolent being?

How about creating studies where people might act in ways they might be ashamed of afterward—for example, provoking them to anger or pointing out their weakness in the face of authority? Demonstrating people's flaws and frailties in social experiments could cause them psychological harm or worse. Even in a questionnaire or an interview, some questions might be rude, insulting, or demeaning. Consideration of the research participants must be taken into account here as well.

How social scientists approach their research is therefore not guided merely by the quest for ever-better measures. The validity and reliability of a measure must be weighed against the potential harm, inconvenience, and intrusion these measures might have on those who they wish to study. Yet there is often disagreement and debate over what actions are considered harmful and what topics are important enough to warrant some degree of potential risk or harm to subjects. Therefore, the determination of what is or is not ethical practice in research is now made collegially, as we discussed in Chapter 3.

MAIN POINTS

- Concepts are mental images we use as summary devices for bringing together observations and experiences that seem to have something in common.
- Concepts are created through the process of conceptualization.
- Conceptualization involves mentally ignoring most attributes of a set of concrete objects or experiences and concentrating on a selected set of attributes.
- The meaning of any concept is not intrinsic; it is assigned.
- Definitions inform us of the meaning of a concept and are central to understanding and communication.
- Researchers rely on two types of definition—conceptual and operational.

- Conceptual definitions provide the meaning of a new concept by expressing it in terms of other concepts whose meanings are known.
- Operational definitions provide the meaning of a concept by expressing its linkage to concrete experience.
- Precise definitions are important in both descriptive and explanatory studies. The degree of precision needed varies with the type and purpose of a study.
- Operational definitions are extensions of conceptualization that specify the exact procedures that will be used to measure the attributes of variables.
- Operational definitions involve a series of interrelated choices: specifying the range of variation that is appropriate for the purposes of a study, determining how precisely to measure variables, accounting for relevant dimensions of variables, clearly defining the attributes of variables and their relationships, and deciding on an appropriate level of measurement.
- Researchers must choose from four levels of measurement that capture increasing amounts of information: nominal, ordinal, interval, and ratio. The most appropriate level depends on the purpose of the measurement.
- A given variable can sometimes be measured at different levels. When in doubt, researchers should use the highest level of measurement appropriate to that variable so they can capture the greatest amount of information.
- Operationalization begins in the design phase of a study and continues through all phases of the research project, including the analysis of data.
- Criteria of the quality of measures include precision, accuracy, reliability, and validity.
- Reliability means getting consistent results from the same measure. Validity refers to getting results that accurately reflect the concept being measured.
- Researchers can test or improve the reliability of measures through the test-retest method, the split-half method, the use of established measures, and the examination of work performed by research workers.
- The yardsticks for assessing a measure's validity include face validity, criterion-related validity, construct validity, and content validity.
- Creating specific, reliable measures often seems to diminish the richness of meaning our general concepts have. This problem is inevitable. The best solution is to use several different measures, tapping the different aspects of the concept.
- Single indicators of variables seldom capture all the dimensions of a concept, have sufficiently clear validity to warrant their use, or permit the desired range of variation to allow ordinal rankings. Composite measures, such as scales and indexes, solve these problems by including several indicators of a variable in one summary measure.
- Although indexes are based on the simple accumulation of indicators of a variable, scales take advantage of any logical or empirical intensity structures that exist among a variable's indicators.
- Ethical considerations are an important element of a researcher's choice of measures.

■ REVIEW QUESTIONS AND EXERCISES

1. Pick a social science concept such as liberalism or alienation, and then specify that concept so that it could be studied in a research project. How would you specify the indicators you would use? Be sure to specify the dimensions you wish to include and those you wish to exclude in your conceptualization.
2. What level of measurement—nominal, ordinal, interval, or ratio—describes each of the following variables?
   a. race (white, Indigenous, Asian, and so on)
   b. order of finish in a race (first, second, third, and so on)
   c. number of children in families

d. populations of nations

e. attitudes toward nuclear energy (strongly approve, approve, disapprove, strongly disapprove)

f. province of birth (Alberta, British Columbia, Manitoba, and so on)

3. In a Web article or magazine, find an instance of invalid and/or unreliable measurement. Justify your choice.

4. Use the Web to locate several reports of scientific findings concerning causes of the difference between men's and women's earnings. State what variables the researchers used and how they operationalized and tested them. State their findings and discuss whether you accept the conclusions they reported and why.

5. In your own words, describe the difference between an index and a scale.

CONTINUITY PROJECT

■ COUNTING INEQUALITY

Income inequality is in the news and on the political agenda of parties in Canada and the United States. The heated debates about this issue often focus on issues related to values. But they also can relate to issues of conceptualization and measurement.

The Fraser Institute, a conservative-leaning think tank, recently reported that "income inequality in Canada is often treated simplistically, is poorly defined, and presented without proper context, which can paint a flawed picture" (Fraser Institute 2015).

The image from the report, shown here, summarizes their point.

What conceptual definition of inequality is used in each of these alternatives?

How does the measurement of income inequality differ between the cases? What accounts for the substantial differences in outcomes?

The Fraser Institute claims that their nonconventional alternative is "more appropriate." Explain why you agree or disagree.

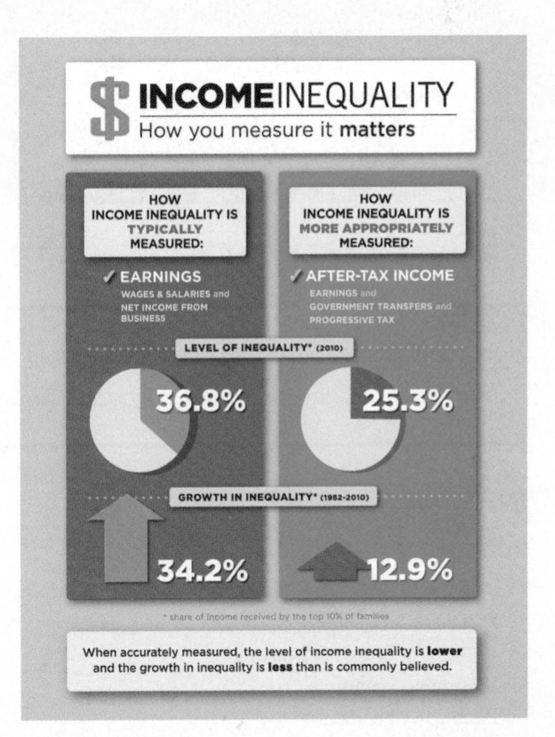

Source: From Christopher Sarlo, Jason Clemens, and Joel Emes (2015). *Income Inequality Measurement Sensitivities*. The Fraser Institute, www.fraserinstitute.org. Reprinted with permission.

THE LOGIC OF SAMPLING

How can social scientists select a few people for discussion and make discoveries that apply to hundreds of millions of people they don't observe? The logic of sampling provides the answer.

IN THIS CHAPTER ...

INTRODUCTION

In October 2015, the Liberal Party won the largest percentage of the popular vote in the Canadian federal election. With a plurality of the vote, the party got a majority of seats, ushering Justin Trudeau into his position as prime minister of Canada. The Liberal Party got 39.5 percent of the popular vote, the Conservative Party 31.9 percent, the New Democratic Party (NDP) 19.7 percent, the Bloc Québécois (BQ) 4.7 percent, and the Green Party 3.4 percent. The remaining 0.8 percent of the vote went to others. Prior to the election, the vast majority of political polls had predicted the Liberal Party victory.

Table 6-1 shows the results of several national polls conducted just days before the election. The majority of the polls were within a couple of percentage points of the actual votes cast for most of the political parties. The Nanos poll conducted the day prior to the election was very accurate, with only a small underestimation of the Conservative vote.

Now, how many interviews do you suppose it took for each of these pollsters to come within a couple of percentage points in estimating the behaviour of about 15 million voters? Fewer than 2,500! In fact, many of the polls were based on less than 2,000 interviews, with the smallest based on 800. In this chapter, we're going to find out how social researchers can pull off such wizardry.

Political polling, which is one of the most visible uses of survey sampling, is subsequently tested by the results of elections. Like other forms of social research, political polling rests on observations. But neither pollsters nor other social researchers can observe everything that might be relevant to their interests. A critical part of social research, then, is deciding what to observe and what not to observe. If you want to study voters, for example, which voters should you study?

The process of selecting observations is called *sampling*. Although sampling can mean any procedure for selecting units of observation—for example, interviewing every tenth passerby on a busy street—the key to generalizing from a sample to a larger population is *probability sampling*, which involves the important idea of *random selection*.

Much of this chapter is devoted to the logic and skills of probability sampling. This topic is more rigorous and precise than some of the other topics in this book. Although social research as a whole is both art and science, sampling leans toward science. Although this subject is somewhat technical, the basic logic of sampling is not difficult to understand. In fact, the logical neatness of this topic can make it easier to comprehend than, say, conceptualization.

Although probability sampling is central to social research today, we'll take some time to examine a variety of nonprobability methods as well. These methods have their own logic and can provide useful samples for some social research purposes.

TABLE 6-1 Polls Predicting Federal Election Outcomes (percent of votes)

Poll Date	*Pollster*	Liberal	Conservative	NDP	Bloc	Green
October 18	Nanos	39.5	30.5	19.7	4.7	3.4
October 18	Forum	40.0	30.0	20.0	6.0	3.0
October 18	EKOS	35.8	31.9	20.4	4.9	5.6
October 17	Ipsos Reid	38.0	31.0	22.0	4.0	4.0
October 16	Leger	38.0	30.0	22.0	6.0	4.0
October 19	Election Results	39.5	31.9	19.7	4.7	3.4

Note: Totals may not add up to 100 percent because of rounding errors and persons voting for other parties.

Source: Author's compilations from various sources.

Before we discuss the two major types of sampling, we'll introduce you to some basic ideas by way of a brief history of sampling. As you'll see, the pollsters who correctly predicted the Conservative Party's victory in the popular vote in 2011 did so in part because researchers had learned to avoid some pitfalls that earlier pollsters had not.

A BRIEF HISTORY OF SAMPLING

Sampling in social research has developed hand in hand with political polling. This is the case, no doubt, because political polling is one of the few opportunities social researchers have to discover the accuracy of their estimates. On election day, they find out how well or how poorly they did. A brief look at the history of the successes and failures of political polling in the United States and Canada helps to illustrate some important lessons learned from them about sampling.

PRESIDENT ALF LANDON

Was there a U.S. president named Alf Landon? No—but Alf Landon would have been president if a famous poll conducted by the *Literary Digest* had proved to be accurate. The *Literary Digest* was a popular news magazine published between 1890 and 1938 in the United States. In 1920, *Digest* editors mailed postcards to people in six states, asking them who they were planning to vote for in the presidential race between Warren Harding and James Cox. Names were selected for the poll from telephone directories and automobile registration lists. Based on the postcards sent back, the *Digest* correctly predicted that Harding would be elected. In the elections that followed, the *Literary Digest* expanded the size of its poll and made correct predictions in 1924, 1928, and 1932.

In 1936, the *Digest* conducted its most ambitious poll: 10 million ballots were sent to people listed in telephone directories and on lists of automobile owners. Over 2 million people responded, giving the Republican contender, Alf Landon, a stunning 57 percent to 43 percent landslide over the incumbent, President Franklin Roosevelt. The editors modestly cautioned,

> We make no claim to infallibility. We did not coin the phrase "uncanny accuracy" which has been so freely applied to our Polls. We know only too well the limitations of every straw vote, however enormous the sample gathered, however scientific the method. It would be a miracle if every State of the forty-eight behaved on Election Day exactly as forecast by the Poll.
>
> (Literary Digest 1936a:6)

Two weeks later, the *Digest* editors knew the limitations of straw polls even better: the voters gave Roosevelt a second term in office by the largest landslide in history, with 61 percent of the vote. Landon won only 8 electoral votes to Roosevelt's 523.

The editors were puzzled by their unfortunate turn of luck. How could their poll be so wrong? A part of the problem surely lay in the 22 percent return rate garnered by the poll. The editors asked,

> Why did only one in five voters in Chicago to whom the *Digest* sent ballots take the trouble to reply? And why was there a preponderance of Republicans in the one-fifth that did reply? ... We were getting better cooperation in what we have always regarded as a public service from Republicans than we were getting from Democrats. Do Republicans live nearer to mailboxes? Do Democrats generally disapprove of straw polls?
>
> (Literary Digest 1936b:7)

Actually, there was a better explanation—what is technically called the *sampling frame* used by the *Digest.* In this case, the sampling frame consisted of telephone subscribers and automobile owners. In the context of 1936, this design selected a disproportionately wealthy sample of the voting population, especially coming on the tail end of the worst economic depression in the nation's history. The sample effectively excluded poor people, and the poor voted predominantly for Roosevelt's New Deal recovery program. The *Digest*'s poll may or may not have correctly represented the voting intentions of telephone subscribers and automobile owners. Unfortunately for the editors, it decidedly did not represent the voting intentions of the population as a whole.

PRESIDENT THOMAS E. DEWEY

The 1936 election also saw the emergence of a young pollster whose name has become synonymous with public opinion. In contrast to the *Literary Digest*, George Gallup correctly predicted that Roosevelt would beat Landon. Gallup's success in 1936 hinged on his use of *quota sampling*, which we'll look at more closely later in the chapter. For now, it's enough to know that quota sampling is based on a knowledge of the characteristics of the population being sampled: what proportion are men, what proportion are women, what proportions are of various incomes, ages, and so on. Quota sampling selects people to match a set of these characteristics: the right number of poor, white, rural men; the right number of rich, black, urban women; and so on. The quotas are based on those variables most relevant to the study. In the case of Gallup's poll, the sample selection was based on levels of income; the sample procedure ensured the right proportion of respondents at each income level.

Gallup and his American Institute of Public Opinion used quota sampling to good effect in 1936, 1940, and 1944, correctly picking the presidential winner in each of those years. Then, in 1948, Gallup and most political pollsters suffered the embarrassment of predicting that Governor Thomas Dewey of New York would win the election over the incumbent, President Harry Truman. The pollsters' embarrassing miscue continued right up to election night. A famous photograph shows a jubilant Truman—whose followers' battle cry was "Give 'em hell, Harry!"—holding aloft a newspaper with the banner headline "Dewey Defeats Truman."

Several factors accounted for the pollsters' failure in 1948. First, most pollsters stopped polling in early October despite a steady trend toward Truman during the campaign. In addition, many voters were undecided throughout the campaign, and they went disproportionately for Truman when they stepped in the voting booth.

More important, Gallup's failure rested on the unrepresentativeness of his samples. Quota sampling, which had been effective in earlier years, was Gallup's undoing in 1948. This technique requires that the researcher know something about the total population—in this case, the population of voters. For national political polls, such information came primarily from census data. By 1948, however, World War II had produced a massive movement from the country to the cities, radically changing the character of the U.S. population from what the 1940 census showed, but Gallup relied on 1940 census data. City dwellers, moreover, tended to vote Democratic; hence the overrepresentation of rural voters in his poll had the effect of underestimating the number of Democratic votes. As you'll see shortly, quota sampling and straw polls (as just discussed) are both nonprobability samples.

CLINTON VS. TRUMP

The 2016 U.S. presidential election provides a more recent example. Leading up to the vote, most polls showed Hillary Clinton ahead of Donald Trump in a number of battleground states that are traditionally pivotal in deciding presidential elections. Pre-election forecasts based on these polls set the likelihood of Clinton winning the presidency at about 90 percent. Yet, as we now know, it was Trump who emerged as the 45th president of the United States. Public confidence in political polls was greatly shaken. How did polls miss this? Is polling defective? A subsequent review by the American Association for Public Opinion Research (AAPOR) (2017) identified at least three key issues that biased the poll results in Clinton's favour: (1) a higher than expected number of "undecided" voters broke for Trump at the last minute, (2) turnout among Trump supporters was higher than expected, and (3) many polls, especially at the state level, failed to adjust for education (Cohn 2017).

The first two issues are difficult for pollsters to address. First, some portion of the undecided voters who broke late for Trump was due to actual changes in voting preference, but some may have been due to a "Shy Trump" effect (although definitive evidence of this is lacking). That is, they misrepresented their preference (indicated themselves as being undecided or a Clinton supporter) in pre-election polls before actually voting for Trump at election time. (See Chapter 8 and "social desirability" bias in surveys.) The late-revealing

APPLYING CONCEPTS IN EVERYDAY LIFE

Compulsory Census or Voluntary Survey?

Between 1871 and 1956, the Canadian census was conducted every ten years. Then it changed to every five years. Government legislation required mandatory completion of the census. Renowned for its breadth, depth, and accuracy, the Canadian census was used by academics, businesses, government, and nongovernment agencies for strategic planning.

In 2011, the federal Conservative government dictated that the mandatory long-form census be replaced with a voluntary National Household Survey (NHS) distributed to 33 percent of households. This policy change produced predictable results. While the 2006 long-form census had a response rate of 98.3 percent, the 2011 NHS response rate was 68.6 percent. In Statistics Canada's own assessment, "in some areas with smaller populations and for some population groups, the response rate may be insufficient to provide a valid statistical picture" (quoted in Paperny 2013).

This difference in participation has important consequences for estimating the social profiles of Canadian communities. In particular, since disadvantaged communities have lower survey participation rates, their number and characteristics are underestimated, while the opposite is true for privileged communities.

Traditional census users are questioning the NHS data (Isfeld 2015). Are changes observed between 2006 (and earlier) findings and 2011 results real social trends, or do they result from low-quality data? Does less reliable evidence about disadvantaged Canadian communities give governments more freedom to make policies based on ideology rather than evidence? Such questions underscore the importance of high-quality empirical evidence for shaping public policy in this country. Fortunately, the federal government reinstated the long-form census in 2016 and reported a response rate of 97.8 percent.[1] Nonetheless, the issues that affect the 2011 NHS data will remain.

1 https://www12.statcan.gc.ca/census-recensement/2016/ref/response-rates-eng.cfm

Trump supporters markedly outnumbered the late-revealing Clinton supporters. Second, based on data from the 2012 election, pollsters overestimated the voter turnout rates for some groups that traditionally support Democratic candidates (e.g., African-Americans) and underestimated turnout for some traditionally Republican-leaning groups (e.g., rural whites). The faulty turnout rate projections were used to weight their predictions and thus produced estimates biased in Clinton's direction. (Weighting is a technique for adjusting survey estimates to account for sample characteristics; it is discussed in detail later in this chapter.) Third, there was a strong correlation between level of education and preferred presidential candidate in a number of key states. Those with higher levels of education were more likely to vote for Clinton. This effect was further compounded by the fact that those with higher levels of education are also significantly more likely than the less educated to participate in surveys. A number of polls—especially at the state level—failed to adjust (i.e., weight) for the overrepresentation of college-educated voters in their samples, and thus overestimated the level of support for Clinton.

POLLING IN CANADA

Political polling began in Canada in the early 1940s, when the Gallup organization arrived. The prime minister at the time, Mackenzie King, was not keen on their arrival. He worried about the potential effect that reporting the opinions of the Canadian population might have. He was concerned that the French–English divide could be made more visible, and that embarrassing information, such as how many Canadians were really against conscription in World War II, might be revealed. He was also worried about the potential misuse of information, like the number of Canadians who thought Hitler was a great man, by people such as Nazi propagandists. Although Prime Minister King publicly claimed a disdain for polls, those close to him were advocating the commission of secret polls. In recent decades, polling has become a key component of successful campaigns in all major institutional sectors.

Polls provide us with much useful information, but there has always been concern expressed about who conducts them, how they are conducted, and their potential impact and misuse, among other things. Thus, polls and polling are often the subjects of debate. Nonetheless, they are the means by which we may obtain useful information. Learning about sampling and other issues raised in this chapter will help you in your assessment of the information reported by polls and other forms of information you read and hear about.

TWO TYPES OF SAMPLING METHODS

By 1948, some academic researchers had been experimenting with a form of sampling based on probability theory. This technique involves the selection of a "random sample" from a list containing the names of everyone in the population under study. By and large, the probability sampling methods used in 1948 were far more accurate than quota sampling techniques.

Today, probability sampling remains the primary method for selecting large, representative samples for social science research, including national political polls. At the same time, many research situations make probability sampling impossible or inappropriate. Therefore, before turning to the logic and techniques of probability sampling, we'll first look at nonprobability sampling techniques and how they're used in social research.

Before we look at either type of sampling, we need to be clear about types of error. **Errors** are mistakes. In an ideal world, when researchers select subjects for their study, they would conduct a **census**. A census includes all the relevant cases in a set. We are used to the idea of using the term *census* to talk about all the cases in a national population, but for researchers *census* applies more broadly. It can apply to any population. You could have a census of students at your university, employees in an organization, or members of a religion. But researchers don't live in a utopia and, for the most part, conduct their research on a selection of cases; that is, on a **sample**. Because they rely on samples, researchers risk committing errors, since the parts selected may not reflect the whole. The 2010 Conservative government policy mandating a change from a compulsory census to a voluntary survey illustrates the difficulties. (See the Applying Concepts in Everyday Life box "Compulsory Census or Voluntary Survey?") With the election of a Liberal government in 2015, a return to the traditional mandatory long-form census was reinstated for the 2016 census.

Research is prone to different types of errors, and they are not equal. One type of error is random. **Random error** refers to mistakes that are equally likely. For example, when asking people whether they were victims of crime in the past year, if it is equally likely that those who were not victims report they were, and that those who were victims report they weren't, then random error is present. In the overall results, random errors tend to cancel out their effects. This is not the case when bias is present.

Bias refers to error that is systematic; that is, where some pattern of mistake is more likely than others. This, in fact, is what occurs in victimization surveys. People are far more likely to not report victimization than to falsely report it.

error Any difference between reported results and true scores.

census All the members of a population.

sample A selection of members from a population.

random error Refers to mistakes that are equally likely to occur.

bias A form of systematic error.

Errors of bias do not tend to cancel themselves out and consequently can seriously distort research results.

All sampling methods are prone to error simply because they are examining some cases rather than all cases. As we shall see, however, they differ in their risk of different types of error.

NONPROBABILITY SAMPLING

Social research is often conducted in situations that don't permit the kinds of probability samples used in large-scale social surveys. Suppose you wanted to study homelessness: there is no list of all homeless individuals, nor are you likely to create such a list. Moreover, as you'll see, there are times when probability sampling wouldn't be appropriate even if it were possible. Many such situations call for **nonprobability sampling**. We'll examine four types in this section: reliance on available subjects, purposive or judgmental sampling, snowball sampling, and quota sampling. We'll conclude with a brief discussion of the use of informants as a technique for gathering information about social groups.

RELIANCE ON AVAILABLE SUBJECTS

Relying on available subjects, such as stopping people at a street corner or some other location, is an extremely risky sampling method, yet it's used all too frequently. Such a method doesn't allow control over the representativeness of a sample. It's justified only if the researcher wants to study the characteristics of people passing the sampling point at specified times, or if less risky sampling methods are not feasible. Even when use of this method is justified on grounds of feasibility, researchers must exercise great caution in generalizing from their data. Also, they should alert readers to the risks associated with this method.

University researchers frequently conduct surveys among the students enrolled in large lecture classes. The ease and low cost of such a method explains its popularity, but it seldom produces data of any general value. It may be useful for pretesting a questionnaire, but such a sampling method should not be used for a study purportedly describing students as a whole.

Consider this report on the sampling design of a research study:

> Participants were recruited for a study of sexual thoughts and experiences by way of sign-up sheets, class announcements and advertisements in university residences.
>
> (Renaud and Byers 1999:20)

After all is said and done, what will the results of this study represent? The study consisted of 292 volunteer undergraduate students. They do not provide a meaningful representation of students in Canada or even in their university. Is there anything different about students who are willing to volunteer for studies? We can guess that these students were probably more comfortable with issues of sex than were other students, but we can't say for sure. While such studies can be the source of useful insights, we must take care not to overgeneralize from them. The authors of this study do address the lack of generalizability to the general population, concluding that further research should be conducted using non-student samples.

PURPOSIVE OR JUDGMENTAL SAMPLING

Sometimes it's appropriate for you to select your sample on the basis of your own knowledge of the population and the purpose of the study. This type of sampling is called **purposive sampling** or *judgmental sampling*. In the initial design of a questionnaire, you might wish to select the widest variety of respondents to test the broad applicability of questions. Although the study findings would not represent any meaningful population,

nonprobability sampling Any technique in which samples are selected in some fashion not suggested by probability theory. Examples are purposive (judgmental), snowball, and quota sampling, as well as reliance on available subjects.

purposive sampling A type of nonprobability sampling in which you select the units to be observed on the basis of your own judgment about which ones will be the most useful or representative. Another name for this is *judgmental sampling*.

the test run might effectively uncover any unforeseen defects in your questionnaire. This situation would be considered a pretest, however, rather than a final study.

In some instances, you may wish to study a small subset of a larger population in which many members of the subset are easily identified, but the enumeration of all of them would be nearly impossible. For example, you might want to study the leadership of a student protest movement—many of the leaders are easily visible, but it would not be feasible to define and sample *all* leaders. In studying all or a sample of the most visible leaders, you may collect data sufficient for your purposes.

Or let's say you want to compare left-wing and right-wing students. Because you may not be able to enumerate and sample from all such students, you might decide to sample the memberships of left- and right-leaning groups, such as campus organizations of the New Democratic Party and the Conservative Party. Although such a sample design would not provide a good description of either left-wing or right-wing students as a whole, it might suffice for general comparative purposes.

Selecting deviant cases for study is another example of purposive sampling. Field researchers are often particularly interested in studying *deviant cases*—cases that don't fit into the fairly regular patterns of, for instance, attitudes and behaviours—in order to improve their understanding of the more regular pattern. For example, you might gain important insights into the nature of school spirit as exhibited at a pep rally by interviewing people who did not appear to be caught up in the emotions of the crowd or by interviewing students who did not attend the rally at all.

Nazilla Khanlou (2005) used a purposive sample to study the cultural identity and self-concept of Canadian high school students. She wanted to be sure that her study sample had adequate cultural variation. As she said,

> The sample population consisted of students in Grades 9–13 who attended four urban secondary schools in Ontario's Hamilton-Wentworth Region in Canada. Purposive, non-random sampling was used to ensure that adolescents from different cultural backgrounds and acculturating groups were included. At least three of the four schools were identified as having a culturally diverse student population.
>
> (2005:4)

SNOWBALL SAMPLING

Another nonprobability sampling technique, which some consider to be a form of accidental sampling, is called **snowball sampling**. This procedure is appropriate when the members of a special population are difficult to locate, such as homeless individuals, prostitutes, or undocumented immigrants. In snowball sampling, researchers collect data on the few members of the target population they can locate, and then ask those individuals to provide the information needed to locate other members of that population whom they happen to know. *Snowball* refers to the process of accumulation as each located subject suggests other subjects. Because this procedure also results in samples with questionable representativeness, it's used primarily for exploratory purposes.

Suppose you want to learn the pattern of recruitment to a community organization over time; you might begin by interviewing fairly recent recruits, asking them who introduced them to the group. You might then interview the people named, asking them who introduced *them* to the group. You might then interview those people named, asking, in part, who introduced *them*. In studying a loosely structured political group, you might ask one of the participants who he or she believes to be the most influential members of the group. You might interview those people and, in the course of the interviews, ask who *they* believe to be the most influential. In each of these examples, your sample would "snowball" as each of your interviewees suggested others to interview.

snowball sampling A nonprobability sampling method often used in field research in which each person interviewed may be asked to suggest additional people for interviewing.

Nancy Netting (2006:129) used a snowball sample when examining "how Indo-Canadian young people negotiate love and arranged marriages in Canada." She started with a few individuals she knew, and then each interviewee was asked to recommend others who might be interviewed on the topic. A sample of another population that would be hard to locate, "entrepreneurs who entered Canada through the Business Immigration Programme," was also obtained using snowball sampling (Ley 2006:750). Ninety interviews with entrepreneurs who originally came from Hong Kong, Taiwan, and Korea (30 interviews from each group) were conducted in Vancouver using snowball samples with multiple entry points.

QUOTA SAMPLING

Quota sampling is the method that helped George Gallup avoid disaster in 1936 but set up the polling disaster of 1948. Like probability sampling, quota sampling addresses the issue of representativeness, although the two methods approach the issue quite differently.

Quota sampling begins with a matrix, or table, describing the characteristics of the target population. Depending on your research purposes, you need to know what proportion of the population is male and what proportion female, as well as what proportions of each gender fall into various age categories, educational levels, ethnic groups, and so forth. In establishing a national quota sample, you would need to know what proportion of the national population is urban, eastern, male, under 25, white, working class, and so on, and all the other possible combinations of these attributes.

Once such a matrix is created and a relative proportion assigned to each cell in the matrix, you proceed to collect data from people having all the characteristics of a given cell. You then assign a weight to all the people in a given cell that is appropriate to their portion of the total population. When all the sample elements are so weighted, the overall data should provide a reasonable representation of the total population.

Quota sampling has several inherent problems. First, the *quota frame* (the proportions that different cells represent) must be accurate, and it is often difficult to get up-to-date information for this purpose. The U.S. presidential polling failures in 1948 and 2016 were partly due to this problem. Second, the selection of sample elements within a given cell may be biased even though their proportion of the population is accurately estimated. Instructed to interview five people who meet a complex set of characteristics, an interviewer might introduce bias in a sample by avoiding people who have particularly rundown homes or who own vicious dogs.

In recent years, attempts have been made to combine probability and quota sampling methods, but the effectiveness of these efforts remains to be seen. At present, you would be advised to treat quota sampling warily if your purpose is statistical description.

At the same time, the logic of quota sampling can sometimes be applied usefully to a field research project. In the study of a formal group, for example, you might wish to interview both leaders and nonleaders. In studying a student organization, you might want to interview radical, moderate, and conservative members of that group. You may be able to achieve sufficient representativeness in such cases by using quota sampling to ensure that you interview both men and women, both younger and older people, and so forth.

SELECTING INFORMANTS

When field research involves the researcher's attempt to understand some social setting—a juvenile gang or local neighbourhood, for example—much of that understanding comes from collaboration with some members of the group being studied. However, social researchers speak of *respondents* as people who provide information about themselves, allowing the researcher to construct a composite picture of the group

quota sampling A type of nonprobability sampling in which units are selected into the sample on the basis of prespecified characteristics, so that the total sample will have the same distribution of characteristics assumed to exist in the population being studied.

those respondents represent. An **informant** is a member of the group who can talk directly about the group.

Especially important to ethnography, informants can be very helpful to other social researchers as well. If you wanted to learn about informal social networks in a local public housing project, for example, you would do well to locate individuals who could understand what you were looking for and help you find it.

When Young and Craig (1997:179) did a study on Canadian skinhead subculture, they discussed the important role of informants in their research:

> Ongoing contact with the group and smooth relations in the field were facilitated through the assistance of three key informants, two of whom were current members, and one who maintained frequent contact with SHARP [Skinheads Against Racial Prejudice] and neo-Nazi skinheads through his work with an anti-racist organization. All key informants tirelessly addressed our questions and requests for interviews, and provided additional sources of data such as skinhead newspapers, books, magazines and musical tapes.

Usually, you'll want to select informants somewhat typical of the groups you're studying. Otherwise, their observations and opinions may be misleading. Interviewing only physicians will not give you a well-rounded view of how a community medical clinic is working, for example. Along the same lines, a researcher who interviews only men in a society where women are sheltered from outsiders will get a biased view. Similarly, while informants fluent in English are convenient for English-speaking researchers, they do not typify the members of many societies or even many subgroups within English-speaking countries.

Simply because they're the ones willing to work with outside investigators, informants will sometimes be somewhat "marginal" or atypical within their group. At times this is obvious. Other times, however, you'll learn about their marginality only in the course of your research. Informants' marginality may bias the view you get, and their marginal status may also limit their access (and hence yours) to the different sectors of the community you wish to study.

These comments should give you some sense of the concerns involved in nonprobability sampling. We'll conclude with the following injunction (Lofland et al. 2006:15):

> Your overall goal is to collect the *richest possible data*. By rich data, we mean a wide and diverse range of information collected over a relatively prolonged period of time in a persistent and systematic manner.... You achieve this primarily through sustained and direct face-to-face interaction with the participants in some social location or circumstance.

In conclusion, nonprobability samples have a place in social research. However, their use in the traditional, deductive, quantitative approach to science is not a good fit. In such studies, the design hinges on eliminating sampling bias and estimating random error. Nonprobability samples allow neither to occur. But in qualitative, inductive research studies, it is a different story.

In qualitative research, the goal is to understand the meaningful experience of selected persons, events, or places. For these ends the sampling goals are different; the purpose of sample selection is illustrative. Commonly, qualitative studies aim to give voice to a specific community, interpret a historically or culturally significant phenomenon, or advance theoretical understanding by closely examining some atypical cases (Ragin 1994). For these purposes, qualitative studies carefully select cases that will illustrate community voices, provide insight into culturally or historically significant phenomena, or advance theoretical understanding.

Qualitative researchers rarely know how large their sample will be. Given their interests in a nuanced, comprehensive understanding of the cases under consideration, qualitative researchers know their sample will be relatively small. But how small?

---

informant Someone well versed in the social phenomenon that you wish to study and who is willing to tell you what he or she knows. If you were planning participant observation among the members of a religious sect, you would do well to make friends with someone who already knows about them—possibly a member of the sect—who could give you some background information about them. Not to be confused with a respondent.

In qualitative research, the general rule for determining sample size uses the principle of **saturation**. Qualitative researchers select initial cases and gather narratives. At some point, the key points (insights) in these narratives begin to overlap; commonalities emerge. This is the point of saturation. In other words, qualitative researchers typically continue gathering evidence from illustrative cases until it is evident that new insights are unlikely to occur from studying additional cases. At that point the basic narrative of the study is in place.

Nonprobability samples are particularly useful in qualitative research studies. When they are used in quantitative studies, they usually detract from the central goal of creating accurate representations of populations. This point will become clearer as we discuss the logic and techniques of probability sampling.

THE THEORY AND LOGIC OF PROBABILITY SAMPLING

While appropriate to some research purposes, nonprobability sampling methods cannot guarantee that the sample we observed is representative of the whole population. When researchers want precise, statistical descriptions of large populations—for example, the percentage of the population that is unemployed, plans to vote for Candidate X, or feels a rape victim should have the right to an abortion—they turn to **probability sampling**. Large-scale surveys, therefore, use probability sampling methods.

The basic logic of probability sampling is not hard to understand, even though the application of probability sampling involves some sophisticated use of statistics. If all members of a population were identical in all respects—all demographic characteristics, attitudes, experiences, behaviours, and so on—there would be no need for careful sampling procedures. In this extreme case of homogeneity, in fact, any single case would suffice as a sample to study characteristics of the whole population.

saturation A sampling principle used in qualitative studies that encourages adding cases until new insights are unlikely.

probability sampling The general term for samples selected in accord with probability theory, typically involving some random selection mechanism. Specific types of probability sampling include EPSEM, PPS, simple random sampling, and systematic sampling.

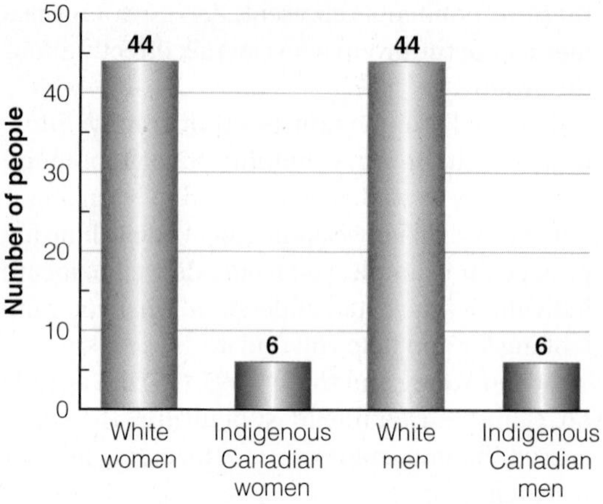

FIGURE 6-1 A Population of 100 Individuals.
Typically, sampling aims at reflecting the characteristics and dynamics of large populations. For the purpose of some simple illustrations, let's assume our total population has only 100 members.
Source: © Cengage Learning

In fact, of course, the human beings who make up real populations are quite heterogeneous, varying in many ways. Figure 6-1 offers a simplified illustration of a heterogeneous population: the 100 members of this small population differ by gender and ethnic origin. We'll use this hypothetical micropopulation to illustrate various aspects of sampling.

The fundamental idea behind probability sampling is this: to provide useful descriptions of the total population, a sample of individuals from a population must contain essentially the same variations that exist in the population. This isn't as simple as it might seem, however. Let's take a minute to look at some of the ways researchers might go astray. Then we'll see how probability sampling provides an efficient method for selecting a sample that should adequately reflect variations that exist in the population.

CONSCIOUS AND UNCONSCIOUS SAMPLING BIAS

At first glance, it may look as though sampling is pretty straightforward. To select a sample of 100 university students, you might simply interview

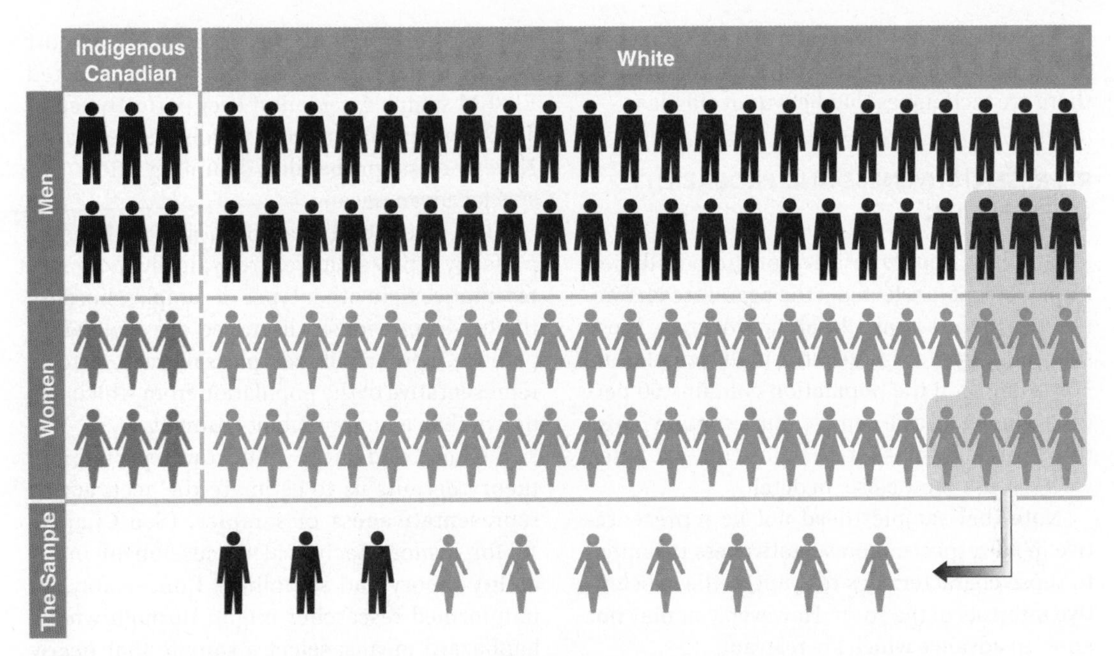

FIGURE 6-2 **A Sample of Convenience: Easy, but Not Representative.** Selecting and observing those people who are most readily at hand is the simplest method, but it's unlikely to provide a sample that accurately reflects the total population.
Source: © Cengage Learning

the first 100 students you find walking around campus. Untrained researchers often use this kind of sampling method, but the risk is very high that biases will be introduced into the samples. **Sampling bias** means that those selected are not typical or representative of the larger populations they have been chosen from—and such bias need not be intentional. This kind of bias is virtually inevitable when you pick people by the seat of your pants.

Figure 6-2 illustrates what can happen when you simply select people who are convenient for study. Although women are only 50 percent of our micropopulation, the group closest to the researcher (in the upper-right corner) happens to be 70 percent women, and although the hypothetical population is 12 percent Indigenous Canadian, none were selected into the sample.

Beyond the risks inherent in simply studying people who are convenient, other problems can arise. To begin with, researchers' personal leanings may affect the sample to the point where it does not truly represent the target population. Suppose you're a little intimidated by students who look like they might ridicule your research effort. You might consciously or unconsciously avoid interviewing such people. Or you might feel that the attitudes of "super-straight-looking" students would be irrelevant to your research purposes and so avoid interviewing them.

Even if you sought to interview a "balanced" group of students, you wouldn't know the exact proportions of different types of students making up such a balance, and you wouldn't always be able to identify the different types just by watching them walk by.

Even if you made a conscientious effort to interview every tenth student entering the university library, for example, you could not be sure of a *representative* sample, because different types of students visit the library with different frequencies. Your sample would overrepresent students who visit the library more often.

sampling bias Systematic error derived from using nonprobability samples that produces unrepresentative results.

The possibilities for inadvertent sampling bias are endless and not always obvious. Fortunately, there are techniques that help us avoid bias.

REPRESENTATIVENESS AND PROBABILITY OF SELECTION

A sample is **representative** of the population from which it is selected if the aggregate characteristics of the sample closely approximate those same aggregate characteristics in the population. For example, if the population contains 50 percent women, then a sample must contain "close to" 50 percent women to be representative. Later, we'll discuss "how close" in detail.

Note that samples need not be representative in all respects; representativeness is limited to those characteristics relevant to the substantive interests of the study. However, you may not know in advance which are relevant.

A basic principle of probability sampling is that a sample will be representative of the population from which it is selected if all members of the population have an equal chance of being selected in the sample. (We'll see shortly that the size of the sample selected also affects the degree of representativeness.) Samples that have this quality are often labelled **EPSEM (equal probability of selection method)** samples. Later we'll discuss variations of this principle—a principle that forms the basis of probability sampling.

representativeness That quality of a sample of having the same distribution of characteristics as the population from which it was selected. By implication, descriptions and explanations derived from an analysis of the sample may be assumed to represent similar ones in the population. Representativeness is enhanced by *probability sampling* and provides for *generalizability* and the use of *inferential statistics*.

EPSEM (equal probability of selection method) A sample design in which each member of a population has the same chance of being selected into the sample.

sampling error The discrepancy between the characteristics of a probability sample and the characteristics of the population. The more representative the sample, the smaller the sampling error, and the more accurate the sample-derived estimates of population characteristics will be.

element The unit of which a population is composed and which is selected in a sample. Distinguished from *units of analysis*, which are used in data analysis.

Moving beyond this basic principle, we must realize that samples, even carefully selected EPSEM samples, seldom if ever perfectly represent the populations from which they're drawn. Nevertheless, probability sampling offers two special advantages.

First, probability samples, although never perfectly representative, are typically more representative than other types of samples, because the biases previously discussed are avoided. In practice, a probability sample is more likely to be representative of the population from which it is drawn than a nonprobability sample.

Second, and more important, probability theory permits us to estimate the accuracy or representativeness of samples. (See Chapter 16 for a more technical discussion of probability theory and sampling.) Conceivably, an uninformed researcher might, through wholly haphazard means, select a sample that nearly perfectly represents the larger population. The odds are against doing so, however, and we would be unable to estimate the likelihood that he or she has achieved representativeness. The probability sampler, on the other hand, can provide an accurate estimate of the probability of how close he or she will come. This estimate of the accuracy or representativeness of samples is called the **sampling error**. The more representative a sample is, the smaller the sampling error, and the better the job it does estimating population characteristics.

Probability sampling ensures that samples are representative of the population we desire to study, as we've said. Probability sampling is based on the use of a random selection procedure, as you'll see in a moment. To develop this idea, however, we must give more precise meaning to two important terms: element and population.

An **element** is that unit about which information is collected and that provides the basis of analysis. Typically, in survey research, elements are people or certain types of people. However, other kinds of units can constitute the elements for social research: families, social clubs, or corporations might be the elements of a study. In a given study, elements are often the same as units of analysis, but the former are used in sample selection and the latter in data analysis.

So far we've used the term *population* to mean the group or collection that we're interested in generalizing about. More technically, a **population** is the theoretically specified aggregation of the elements in a study. Although the vague term *Canadians* might be the target for a study, the delineation of the population would include the definition of the element *Canadians* (e.g., citizenship, residence) and the time referent for the study (Canadians as of when?). Translating the abstract "adult Torontonians" into a workable population would require a specification of the age defining *adult* and the boundaries of Toronto. Specifying the term *university student* would include a consideration of full- and part-time students, degree candidates and non-degree candidates, undergraduate and graduate students, and so forth.

A **study population** is that aggregation of elements from which the sample is actually selected. As a practical matter, researchers are seldom in a position to guarantee that every element meeting the theoretical definitions laid down actually has a chance of being selected in the sample. Even when lists of elements exist for sampling purposes, the lists are usually somewhat incomplete. Some students are always inadvertently omitted from student rosters. Many people only have a cellphone instead of a land line, and so their names and phone numbers are not listed in the telephone directory (i.e., the "phone book").

Often, researchers decide to limit their study populations more severely than indicated in the preceding examples. National polling firms and other organizations may limit their national samples to the ten provinces, omitting the territories for practical reasons. This is done, for example, by Statistics Canada in conducting the General Social Survey. A researcher wishing to sample psychology professors may limit the study population to those in psychology departments, omitting those in other departments (such as gender studies and family studies). Such redefinitions of the population under examination must be made clear to readers.

RANDOM SELECTION

With these definitions in hand, we can define the ultimate purpose of sampling: to select a set of elements from a population in such a way that descriptions of those elements accurately portray the total population from which the elements are selected. Probability sampling enhances the likelihood of accomplishing this aim and provides methods for estimating the degree of probable success.

Random selection is the key to this process. In random selection, each element has an equal chance of selection independent of any other event in the selection process. Flipping a coin is the most frequently cited example. Provided that the coin is perfect (i.e., equally likely to come up heads or tails), the "selection" of a head or a tail is independent of previous selections of heads or tails. It doesn't matter how many tails turn up in a row—the chance that the next flip will produce "tails" is exactly 50–50. Rolling a perfect set of dice is another example.

Such images of random selection are useful but seldom apply directly to sampling methods in social research. Social researchers more typically use tables of random numbers (see Appendix A) or computer programs that provide a random selection of sampling units. A **sampling unit** is that element or set of elements considered for selection in some stage of sampling. In Chapter 8 on survey research, we'll see how computers are used to select random telephone numbers for interviewing, a process called *random-digit dialling*.

The reasons for using random selection methods are twofold. First, this procedure serves as a check on conscious or unconscious bias on the part of the researcher. The researcher who selects cases on an intuitive basis might very well select cases that would support his or her research expectations or hypotheses. Random selection erases this danger. Second and more important, random selection offers access to the

population The theoretically specified aggregation of the elements in a study.

study population The aggregation of elements from which a sample is actually selected.

random selection A sampling method in which each element has an equal chance of selection independent of any other event in the selection process.

sampling unit The element or set of elements considered for selection in some stage of sampling.

body of probability theory, which provides the basis for estimating the characteristics of the population as well as estimates of the accuracy of samples. Let's now examine the mechanics of using random sampling.

POPULATIONS AND SAMPLING FRAMES

Random selection is used to increase the chances that the sample results reflect the population. Random selection specifies the criteria from which sample cases are selected from a population. Using random selection, however, requires a list of cases (called a sampling frame) that constitutes the population. In real research, this is often a problem.

The preceding section has introduced the theoretical model for social research sampling. Simply put, a **sampling frame** is the list or quasi-list of elements from which a probability sample is selected. If a sample of students is selected from a student roster, the roster is the sampling frame. If the primary sampling unit for a complex population sample is the census block, the list of census blocks composes the sampling frame—in the form of a printed booklet or some computerized record. Here are some reports of sampling frames appearing in research journals, with the actual sampling frames italicized in each:

> The sample used in that study was drawn from the *Directory of the Korean Society of Toronto*.... First a simple random sample of households was drawn and then one adult from each household was randomly selected.
>
> (Noh and Avison 1996:196)

> A random cluster sample was chosen by grade and home room from *class lists submitted by the principals of the three [Ontario] high schools.*
>
> (Feldman et al. 1997:199)

sampling frame The list or quasi-list of units that make up a population from which a sample is selected. If the sample is to be representative of the population, it is essential that the sampling frame include all (or nearly all) members of the population.

> The lawyers were randomly sampled from the *Directory of Lawyers, 2003, volume 15, and the online subscription service of the directory*. The BC branch of the Canadian Bar Association routinely updates both directories.
>
> (Brown and MacAlister 2006:553)

> Data were collected in a telephone survey with a random sample of Chinese family caregivers in Calgary, Alberta.... First, a comprehensive ethnic Chinese surnames list was used as the basis for identifying *Chinese surnames in the local telephone directory*.... Second, from this sampling frame, 3,545 were randomly selected and contacted by trained interviewers to identify eligible participants.
>
> Daniel Lai (2007:46)

Properly drawn samples provide information appropriate for describing the population of elements composing the sampling frame—nothing more. We emphasize this point in view of the all-too-common tendency for researchers to select samples from a given sampling frame and then make assertions about a population that is similar, but not identical to, the population defined by the sampling frame.

For example, take a look at this report, which discusses the drugs most frequently prescribed by U.S. physicians:

> Information on prescription drug sales is not easy to obtain. But Rinaldo V. DeNuzzo, a professor of pharmacy at the Albany College of Pharmacy, Union University, Albany, NY, has been tracking prescription drug sales for 25 years by polling nearby drugstores. He publishes the results in an industry trade magazine, *MM&M.*
>
> DeNuzzo's latest survey, covering 1980, is based on reports from 66 pharmacies in 48 communities in New York and New Jersey. Unless there is something peculiar about that part of the country, his findings can be taken as representative of what happens across the country.
>
> (Moskowitz 1981)

What's striking in the excerpt is the casual comment about whether there is anything peculiar about New York and New Jersey. There is.

The lifestyle in these two states hardly typifies the other forty-eight. We cannot assume that residents in these large, urbanized, Eastern seaboard states necessarily have the same drug-use patterns as residents of Mississippi or Nebraska.

Does the survey even represent prescription patterns in New York and New Jersey? To determine that, we would have to know something about the way the 48 communities and the 66 pharmacies were selected. We should be wary in this regard, in view of the reference to "polling nearby drugstores." As we'll see, there are several methods for selecting samples that ensure representativeness, and unless they are used, we shouldn't generalize from the study findings.

A sampling frame, then, must be consonant with the population we wish to study. In the simplest design, the sampling frame is a list of the elements making up the study population. In practice, though, existing sampling frames often define the study population rather than the other way around. That is, we often begin with a population in mind for our study, then we search for possible sampling frames. The frames available for our use are examined and evaluated, and we decide which frame presents a study population most appropriate to our needs.

Studies of organizations are often the simplest from a sampling standpoint because organizations typically have membership lists. In such cases, the list of members constitutes an excellent sampling frame. If a random sample is selected from a membership list, the data collected from that sample may be taken as representative of all members—if all members are included in the list.

Populations that can be sampled from good organizational lists include elementary school, high school, and university students and faculty; factory workers; fraternity or sorority members; members of social, service, or political clubs; and members of professional associations.

The preceding comments apply primarily to local organizations. Often province-wide or national organizations do not have a single membership list. There is, for example, no single list of high school students. However, a slightly more complex sample design could take advantage of local high school student lists by first sampling high schools and then subsampling the student lists of those schools selected. (More about that later.)

Other lists of individuals can be relevant to the research needs of a particular study. Government agencies maintain lists of registered voters, for example, that might be used to conduct a pre-election poll or an in-depth examination of voting behaviour, but the researcher would have to be satisfied that the list is up to date. In some countries, similar lists contain the names of automobile owners, welfare recipients, taxpayers, business permit holders, licensed professionals, and so forth. Although it may be difficult to gain access to some of these lists, they provide excellent sampling frames for specialized research purposes.

The sampling elements in a study need not be individual persons. Lists of other types of elements also exist: universities, businesses of various types, cities, academic journals, newspapers, unions, professional associations, and so forth.

Telephone directories are frequently used for "quick and dirty" public opinion polls. Undeniably they're easy and inexpensive to use—no doubt the reason for their popularity. And, if you want to make assertions about telephone subscribers, the directory is a fairly good sampling frame. (Realize, of course, that a given directory will not include new subscribers or those who have requested unlisted numbers. Sampling is further complicated by the directories' inclusion of nonresidential listings.) Unfortunately, telephone directories are all too often used as a listing of a city's population or of its voters. Of the many defects in this reasoning, the chief one involves a social-class bias. Poor people are less likely to have telephones; rich people may have more than one line. A telephone directory sample, therefore, is likely to have a middle- or upper-class bias. Additionally, concerns have arisen about potential bias in the use of a telephone directory sample due to the greater use of cellphones. An increasing number, especially of young people, have only cellphones—a potential for an age bias. We will discuss these issues further in Chapter 8 when we talk about survey research and ways of sampling that have evolved to help resolve some of these problems.

In some countries, street directories and tax maps are often used for easy samples of households, but they may also suffer from incompleteness and possible bias. For example, in strictly zoned urban regions, illegal housing units are unlikely to appear on official records. As a result, such units could not be selected, and sample findings could not be representative of those units, which are often poorer and more overcrowded than the average.

Though most of these comments apply to Canada and the United States, the situation is different in some other countries. In Japan, for example, the government maintains quite accurate population registration lists. Moreover, citizens are required by law to keep their information up to date, such as changes in residence or births and deaths in the household. As a consequence, you can select simple random samples of the Japanese population more easily.

TYPES OF PROBABILITY SAMPLING DESIGNS

Up to this point, we've focused on simple random sampling (SRS). And, indeed, the body of statistics typically used by social researchers assumes such a sample. As you'll see shortly, however, researchers have several options in choosing a sampling method, and they seldom if ever choose simple random sampling. There are two reasons for this. First, with all but the simplest sampling frame, simple random sampling is not feasible. Second, and probably surprisingly, simple random sampling may not be the most accurate method available. Let's turn now to a discussion of simple random sampling and the other options available.

simple random sampling A type of probability sampling in which the units composing a population are assigned numbers. A set of random numbers is then generated, and the units having those numbers are included in the sample. Although probability theory and the calculations it provides assume this basic sampling method, it's seldom used, for practical reasons. An equivalent alternative is the systematic sample (with a random start).

systematic sampling A type of probability sampling in which every *k*th unit in a list is selected for inclusion in the sample—for example, every 25th student in the university directory of students. You compute *k* by dividing the size of the population by the desired sample size; *k* is called the *sampling interval*. Within certain constraints, systematic sampling is a functional equivalent of simple random sampling and usually easier to do. Typically, the first unit is selected at random.

SIMPLE RANDOM SAMPLING

As noted, **simple random sampling** is the basic sampling method assumed in the statistical computations of social research. Because the mathematics of random sampling are especially complex, we'll detour around them in favour of describing the ways of using this method in the field.

Once a sampling frame has been properly established, to use simple random sampling the researcher assigns a single number to each element in the list, not skipping any number in the process. A random number generator can then be used to select elements for the sample. If your sampling frame is in a machine-readable form, a simple random sample can be selected automatically by computer. (In effect, the computer program numbers the elements in the sampling frame, generates its own series of random numbers, and prints out the list of elements selected.) If not, you might find the following website useful for generating lists of random numbers when creating samples: https://www.randomizer.org. The How to Do It box entitled "Using a Random Number Generator" explains its use.

Figure 6-3 offers a graphic illustration of simple random sampling. Note that the members of our hypothetical micropopulation have been numbered from 1 to 100. We generated a unique set of ten random numbers using the online random number generator https://www.randomizer.org. This yields person number 30 as the first one selected into the sample. Number 67 is next, and so forth.

SYSTEMATIC SAMPLING

Simple random sampling is seldom used in practice. As you'll see, it's not usually the most efficient method, and it can be laborious if done manually. SRS typically requires a list of elements. When such a list is available, researchers often employ systematic sampling instead.

In **systematic sampling**, every *k*th element in the total list is chosen (systematically)

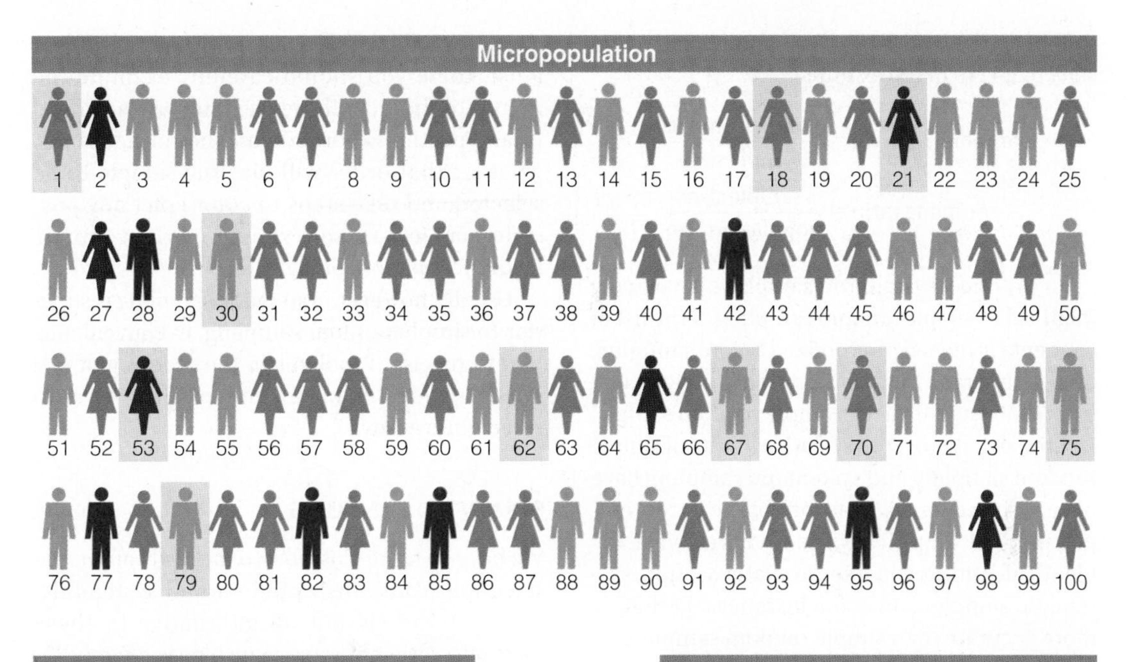

RESULTS

1 Set of 10 Unique Numbers
Range: From 1 to 100

Set #1

30, 67, 70, 21, 62, 1, 79, 75, 18, 53

30 67 70 21 62
1 79 75 18 53

FIGURE 6-3 **A Simple Random Sample.** Having numbered everyone in the population, we can use a random number generator to select a representative sample from the overall population. Anyone whose number appears in the randomly generated list is then selected to the sample.
Source: © Cengage Learning

for inclusion in the sample. If the list contains 10,000 elements and you want a sample of 1,000, you select every tenth element for your sample. To ensure against any possible human bias in using this method, you should select the first element at random. Thus, in the preceding example, you would begin by selecting a random number between 1 and 10. The element having that number is included in the sample, plus every tenth element following it. This method is technically referred to as a *systematic sample with a random start.* Two terms are frequently used in connection with systematic sampling. The **sampling interval** is the standard distance between elements selected in the sample: 10 in the preceding sample. The **sampling ratio** is the

sampling interval The standard distance (k) between elements selected from a population for a sample.

sampling ratio The proportion of elements in the population that are selected to be in a sample.

proportion of elements in the population that are selected: 1/10 in the example.

$$\text{sampling interval} = \frac{\text{population size}}{\text{sample size}}$$

$$\text{sampling ratio} = \frac{\text{sample size}}{\text{population size}}$$

In practice, systematic sampling is virtually identical to simple random sampling. If the list of elements is indeed randomized before sampling, one might argue that a systematic sample drawn from that list is, in fact, a simple random sample. By now, debates over the relative merits of simple random sampling and systematic sampling have been resolved largely in favour of the latter, simpler method. Empirically, the results are virtually identical. And, as you'll see in a later section, systematic sampling, in some instances, is slightly more accurate than simple random sampling.

There is one danger involved in systematic sampling. The arrangement of elements in the list can make systematic sampling unwise. Such an arrangement is usually called *periodicity.* If the list of elements is arranged in a cyclical pattern that coincides with the sampling interval, a grossly biased sample may be drawn. For example, suppose we select a sample of apartments in an apartment building. If the sample is drawn from a list of apartments arranged in numerical order (e.g., 101, 102, 103, 104, 201, 202, and so on), there is a danger of the sampling interval coinciding with the number of apartments on a floor or some multiple thereof. Then the samples might include only northwest-corner apartments or only apartments near the elevator. If these types of apartments have some other particular characteristic in common (e.g., higher rent), the sample will be biased. The same danger would appear in a systematic sample of houses in a subdivision arranged with the same number of houses on a block.

stratification The grouping of the units making up a population into homogeneous groups (or strata) before sampling. This procedure, which may be used in conjunction with simple random, systematic, or cluster sampling (covered in the next section) improves the representativeness of a sample, at least with regard to the variables used for stratification.

In considering a systematic sample from a list, then, you should carefully examine the nature of that list. If the elements are arranged in any particular order, you should figure out whether that order will bias the sample to be selected and take steps to counteract any possible bias (e.g., take a simple random sample from cyclical portions).

Usually, however, systematic sampling is superior to simple random sampling, in convenience if nothing else. Problems in the ordering of elements in the sampling frame can usually be remedied quite easily.

STRATIFIED SAMPLING

We have so far discussed two methods of sample selection from a list: random and systematic. **Stratification** is not an alternative to these methods; rather, it represents a possible modification in their use.

Simple random sampling and systematic sampling both ensure a degree of representativeness and permit an estimate of the error present. Stratified sampling is a method for obtaining a greater degree of representativeness—decreasing the probable sampling error. To understand this method, we must say a few words about the basic theory of sampling.

In theory, sampling error is reduced by two factors in sample design. First, a large sample produces a smaller sampling error than a small sample. Second, a homogeneous population produces samples with smaller sampling errors than does a heterogeneous population. If 99 percent of the population agrees with a certain statement, it's extremely unlikely that any probability sample will greatly misrepresent the extent of agreement. If the population is split 50–50 on the statement, then the sampling error will be much greater.

Stratified sampling is based on this second factor in sampling theory. Rather than selecting a sample from the total population at large, the researcher ensures that appropriate numbers of elements are drawn from homogeneous subsets of that population. To get a stratified sample of undergraduate university students, for example, you would first organize your population by university class (i.e., year of study) and then draw

HOW TO DO IT

Using a Random Number Generator

There are a number of software programs available to generate random sets of numbers, including some available free online. Here is how to use one.

Suppose you want to select a simple random sample of 100 people (or other units) out of a population totalling 980.

1. To begin, number the members of the population: in this case, from 1 to 980. Now the problem is to select 100 random numbers.
2. Go to https://www.randomizer.org/ . Answer the questions in the boxes provided as shown below.

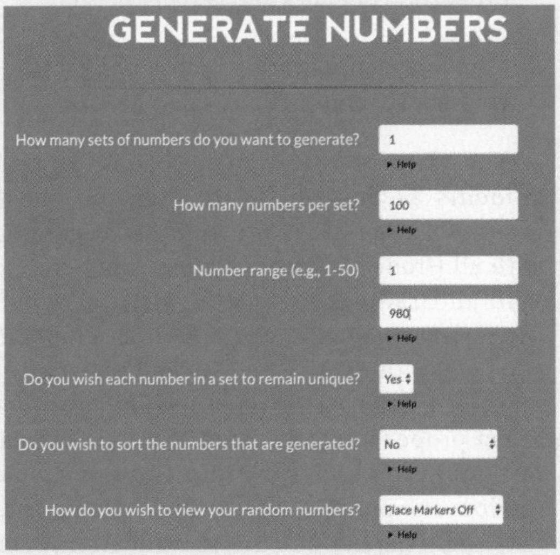

GENERATE NUMBERS

How many sets of numbers do you want to generate? 1
How many numbers per set? 100
Number range (e.g., 1-50) 1 980
Do you wish each number in a set to remain unique? Yes
Do you wish to sort the numbers that are generated? No
How do you wish to view your random numbers? Place Markers Off

Source: Courtesy of Dr. Scott Plous, randomizer.org

3. Then press the *Randomize Now!* button at the bottom of the page. Then a little window, as below, will appear with a unique set of 100 random numbers (your set of numbers will differ of course, as you've generated another set of unique numbers).

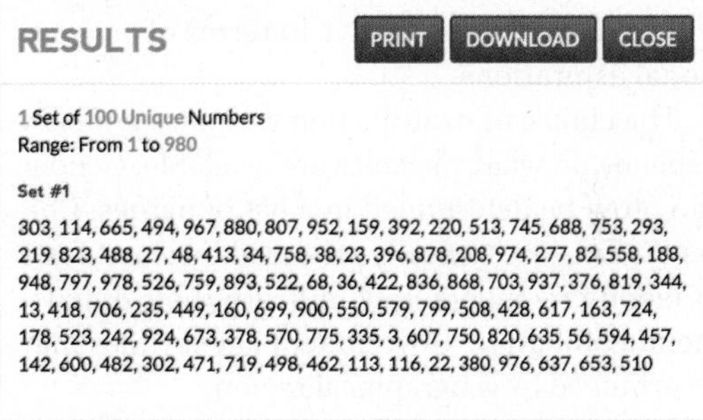

RESULTS PRINT DOWNLOAD CLOSE

1 Set of 100 Unique Numbers
Range: From 1 to 980

Set #1

303, 114, 665, 494, 967, 880, 807, 952, 159, 392, 220, 513, 745, 688, 753, 293, 219, 823, 488, 27, 48, 413, 34, 758, 38, 23, 396, 878, 208, 974, 277, 82, 558, 188, 948, 797, 978, 526, 759, 893, 522, 68, 36, 422, 836, 868, 703, 937, 376, 819, 344, 13, 418, 706, 235, 449, 160, 699, 900, 550, 579, 799, 508, 428, 617, 163, 724, 178, 523, 242, 924, 673, 378, 570, 775, 335, 3, 607, 750, 820, 635, 56, 594, 457, 142, 600, 482, 302, 471, 719, 498, 462, 113, 116, 22, 380, 976, 637, 653, 510

Source: https://www.randomizer.org/

4. Your sample will consist of the people (or units) having the numbers corresponding to the list you've generated. (*Note*: You can select to have the numbers sorted from least to greatest or greatest to least if you wish; this would be useful if your list of people/units is numbered sequentially. But it's not essential to actually number the people on your list, as long as you're sure of the total. If you have them in a list, for example, you can always count through the list after you've generated the unique set of numbers. For example, selecting the 344th name on the list, then the 128th, 258th, and so on)

appropriate numbers of first-, second-, third-, and fourth-year students. In a nonstratified sample, representation by class would be subjected to the same sampling error as other variables. In a sample stratified by class, the sampling error on this variable is reduced to zero.

More complex stratification methods are possible. In addition to stratifying by class, you might also stratify by gender, by grade point average (GPA), and so forth. In this fashion, you might be able to ensure that your sample will contain the proper numbers of second-year male students with a 3.0 average, second-year female students with a 4.0 average, and so forth.

The ultimate function of stratification, then, is to organize the population into homogeneous subsets (with heterogeneity between subsets) and to select the appropriate number of elements from each. To the extent that the subsets are homogeneous on the stratification variables, they may be homogeneous on other variables as well. Because *age* is related to *university class*, a sample stratified by class will be more representative in terms of age as well, compared with an unstratified sample. To the extent that occupational aspirations are still related to gender, a sample stratified by gender will be more representative in terms of occupational aspirations.

The choice of stratification variables typically depends on what variables are available. Gender can often be determined in a list of names. University lists are typically arranged by class. Lists of faculty members may indicate their departmental affiliation. Government agency files may be arranged by geographical region.

In selecting stratification variables from among those available, however, you should be concerned primarily with those that are presumably related to variables you want to represent accurately. Because gender is related to many variables and is often available for stratification, it is often used. Education is related to many variables, but it is often not available for stratification. Geographical location within a city, province, or nation is related to many things. Within a city, stratification by geographical location usually increases representativeness in social class, ethnic group, and so forth. Within a nation, it increases representativeness in a broad range of attitudes as well as in social class and ethnicity.

When you're working with a simple list of all elements in the population, two methods of stratification predominate. In one method, you sort the population elements into discrete groups based on whatever stratification variables are being used. On the basis of the relative proportion of the population represented by a given group, you select—randomly or systematically—several elements from that group constituting the same proportion of your desired sample size. For example, imagine we wanted to draw a simple random sample of 30 students in a high school (using Grades 10 to 12) and are interested in differences between genders and grades. Our sampling design, as illustrated in Figure 6-4, would include the following steps:

1. Obtain a list of students in the school.
2. Sort it into grade groups.
3. Sort grade groups into gender groups.

(Stratifying by gender within grade produces 6 homogenous strata; a male and female grouping in each of 3 grades.)

4. Draw a simple random sample from the list of females in each grade and from the list of males in each grade. In our example we are drawing a proportionate sample, so each strata will be represented in the sample in relative proportion to its occurrence in the population. Each grade has 30 students, so we will draw a sample of 10 students from each grade, and this sample will reflect the proportion of males and females in each grade.
5. Combine all the stratified subsamples into your final overall sample.

The other stratification method is to group students as described and then put those groups together in a continuous list, beginning with all Grade 10 female students and ending with all Grade 12 male students. You would then select a systematic sample, with a random start, from the entire list. Given the arrangement of the list, a systematic sample would select proper numbers (within an error range of 1 or 2) from each subgroup. (*Note:* A simple random sample drawn from such a composite list would cancel out the stratification.) For a detailed example of a stratified, systematic sampling see the online appendix that accompanies this chapter ("More Examples of Complex Sampling Designs").

Stratified sampling ensures the proper representation of the stratification variables. This, in turn, enhances representation of other variables related to them. Taken as a whole, then, a stratified sample is likely to be more representative on several variables than a simple random sample. Although the simple random sample is still regarded as somewhat sacred, it should now be clear that you can often do better.

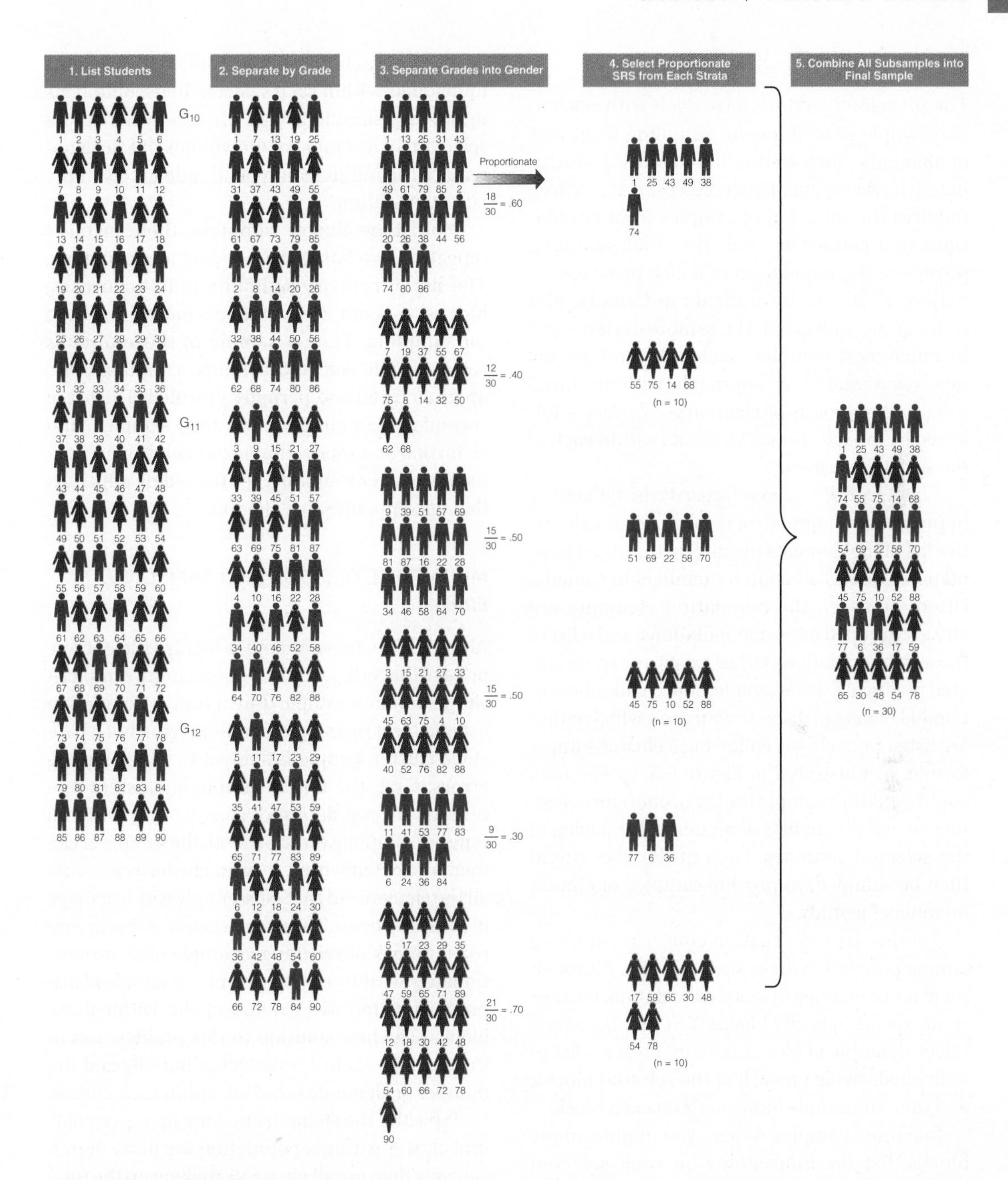

FIGURE 6-4 **A Stratified, Simple Random Sample.** Members of the population are gathered into homogeneous strata. This example merely uses grade and gender, but more could be used. Then an SRS is drawn from each strata and these are combined into an overall sample.
Source: Author created

MULTISTAGE CLUSTER SAMPLING

The preceding sections have dealt with reasonably simple procedures for sampling from lists of elements. Such a situation is ideal. Unfortunately, however, much interesting social research requires the selection of samples from populations that cannot be easily listed for sampling purposes: the population of a city, province, or nation; all university students in Canada; and so forth. In such cases, the sample design must be much more complex. Such a design typically involves a multistage approach, with an initial sampling of groups of elements—*clusters*— followed by the selection of elements within each of the selected clusters.

Cluster sampling may be used when it's either impossible or impractical to compile an exhaustive list of the elements making up the target population, such as all church members in Canada. Often, however, the population elements are already grouped into subpopulations, and a list of those subpopulations either exists or can be created practically. For example, church members in Canada belong to discrete churches, which either are listed or could be. Following a cluster sample format, as illustrated in Figure 6-5, researchers could randomly sample the list of churches. Next, they would obtain lists of members from each of the selected churches. Each of the lists would then be sampled, to provide samples of church members for study.

Another typical situation concerns sampling among population areas such as a city. Although there is no single list of a city's population, citizens reside on discrete city blocks. You can, therefore, select a sample of blocks initially, create a list of individuals living on each of the selected blocks, and then subsample individuals on each block.

In a more complex design, you might sample blocks, list the households on each selected block, sample the households, list the individuals residing in each household, and, finally, sample individuals within each selected household. This multistage sample design ultimately leads to a selection of a sample of individuals but does not require the initial listing of all individuals in the city's population.

Multistage cluster sampling, then, involves repeating two basic steps: listing and sampling. The list of primary sampling units (churches, blocks) is compiled and, perhaps, stratified for sampling. Then a sample of those units is selected. The selected primary sampling units are then listed and perhaps stratified. The list of secondary sampling units is then sampled, and so forth. For a more complex illustration of multistage cluster sampling, see the online appendix that accompanies this chapter.

cluster sampling A multistage sampling approach in which natural groups (clusters) are sampled initially, with the members of each selected group being subsampled afterward. For example, you might select a sample of Canadian universities from a directory, get lists of the students at all the selected schools, and then draw samples of students from each.

MULTISTAGE DESIGNS AND SAMPLING ERROR

Although cluster sampling is highly efficient, the price of that efficiency is a less accurate sample. A simple random sample drawn from a population list is subject to a single sampling error, but a two-stage cluster sample is subject to two sampling errors. First, the initial sample of clusters represents the population of clusters only within a range of sampling error. Second, the sample of elements selected within a given cluster represents all the elements in that cluster only within a range of sampling error. Thus, for example, a researcher runs the risk of selecting a sample of disproportionately wealthy city blocks, plus a sample of disproportionately wealthy households within those blocks. The best solution to this problem lies in the number of clusters selected initially and the number of elements selected within each cluster.

Typically, the elements making up a given natural cluster within a population are more homogeneous than are all elements making up the total population. The members of a given church are more alike than are all church members; the residents of a given city block are more alike than are the residents of a whole city. As a result, relatively few elements may be needed to represent a given natural cluster adequately, although a larger number of clusters may be needed to adequately represent the diversity found among the clusters.

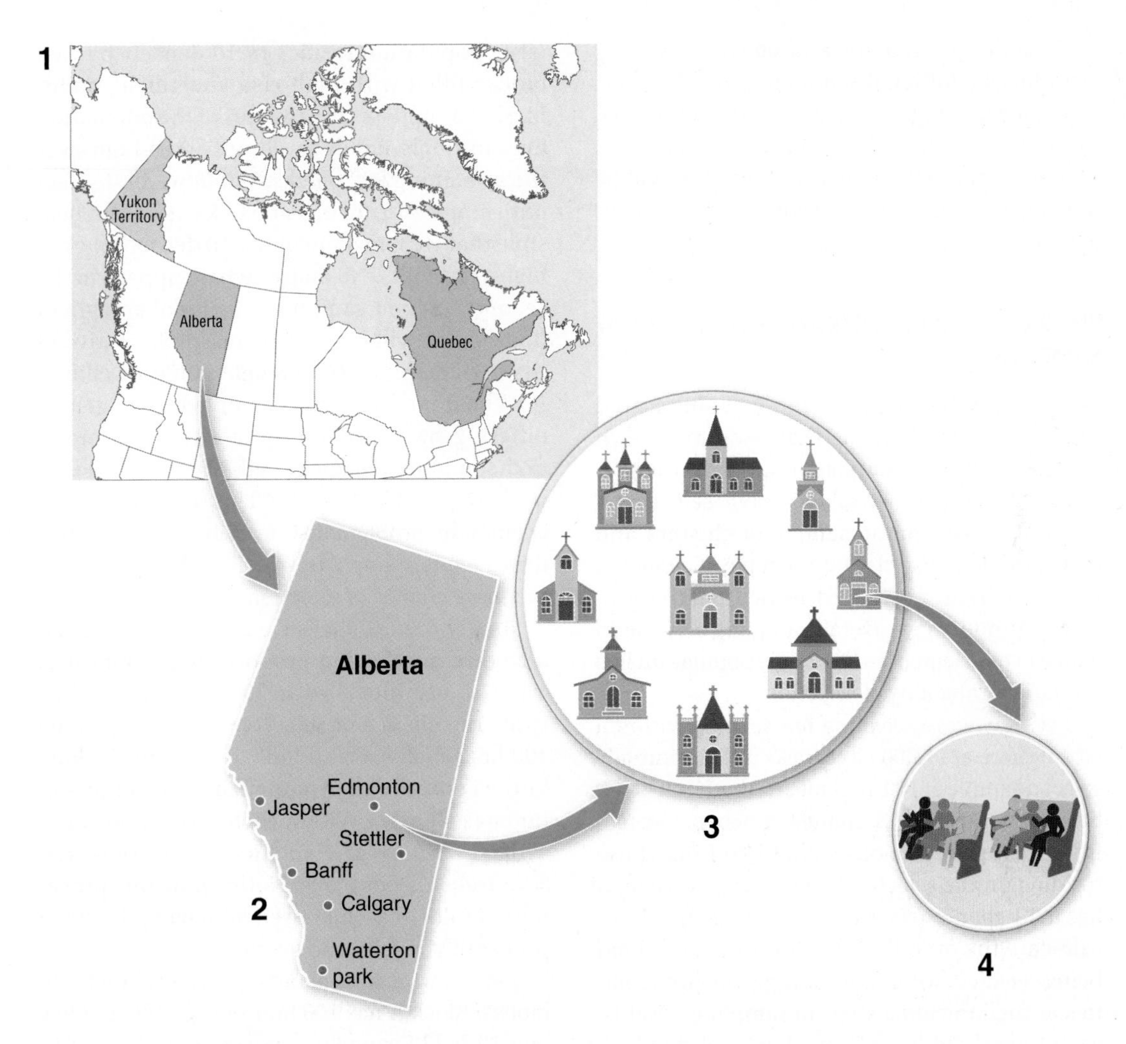

FIGURE 6-5 **An example of multistage sampling. Stage 1: Draw a sample of provinces/territories. Stage 2: Draw a sample of cities/towns within each selected province/territory. Stage 3: Draw a sample of churches from within each selected city/town. Stage 4: Draw a sample of congregants from within each selected church.**
Source: Author created

The general scientific guideline for cluster design, then, is to maximize the number of clusters selected while decreasing the number of elements within each cluster. But balanced against this is the logistical reality that the efficiency of cluster sampling is based on the ability to minimize the listing of population elements. By initially selecting clusters, you need only list the elements making up the selected clusters, not all elements in the entire population. Increasing the number of clusters, however, works directly against this efficiency factor. The final sample design will need to balance these two constraints. In effect, you'll probably select as many clusters as your study budget can afford. See the Spotlight on Mixed Methods Research Box for an example of researchers finding innovative solutions to cluster sampling challenges that incorporate both quantitative and qualitative clustering criteria.

To sum up, each stage of cluster sampling introduces additional sampling error. Furthermore, at each stage elements are typically drawn from among relatively homogeneous clusters. Therefore, the estimated sampling error will be too optimistic and must be adjusted in the light of the cluster sample design.

PROBABILITY PROPORTIONATE TO SIZE (PPS) SAMPLING

This section introduces a more sophisticated form of cluster sampling that is often used in large-scale survey sampling projects. In the preceding discussion, we talked about selecting a random or systematic sample of clusters and then a random or systematic sample of elements within each cluster selected. Notice that this procedure produces an overall sampling scheme in which every element in the whole population has the same probability of selection.

Let's say we're selecting households within a city. If there are 1,000 city blocks and we initially select a sample of 100, that means that each block has a 100/1,000 or 0.1 chance of being selected. If we next select 1 household in 10 from those residing on the selected blocks, each household has a 0.1 chance of selection within its block. To calculate the overall probability of a household being selected, we simply multiply the probabilities at the individual steps in sampling. That is, each household has a 1/10 chance of its block being selected and a 1/10 chance of that specific household being selected if the block is one of those chosen. Each household, in this case, has a $1/10 \times 1/10 = 1/100$ chance of selection overall. Because each household has the same chance of selection, the sample so selected should be representative of all households in the city.

There are dangers in this procedure, however. In particular, the variation in the size of blocks (measured in numbers of households) presents a problem. Let's suppose that half the city's population resides in 10 densely packed blocks filled with high-rise apartment buildings, and suppose that the rest of the population lives in single-family dwellings spread out over the remaining 900 blocks. When we first select our sample of 1/10 of the blocks, it's quite possible that we'll miss all of the 10 densely packed high-rise blocks. No matter what happens in the second stage of sampling, our final sample of households will be grossly unrepresentative of the city, comprising only single-family dwellings.

Whenever the clusters sampled are of greatly differing sizes, it's appropriate to use a modified sampling design called **PPS (probability proportionate to size)**. This design guards against the problem just described and still produces a final sample in which each element has the same chance of selection.

As the name suggests, each cluster is given a chance of selection proportionate to its size. Thus a city block with 200 households has twice the chance of selection as one with only 100 households. (We'll look at how this is done in the context of a hypothetical study of prison inmates shortly.) Within each cluster, however, a fixed *number* of elements is selected—say, 5 households per block. Notice how this procedure results in each household having the same probability of selection overall.

Let's look at households of two different city blocks. Block A has 100 households; Block B has only 10. In PPS sampling, we would give Block A 10 times as good a chance of being selected as Block B. So if, in the overall sample design, Block A has a 1/20 chance of being selected, that means Block B would have only a 1/200 chance. Notice that this means that all the households on Block A would have a 1/20 chance of having their block selected; Block B households have only a 1/200 chance.

If Block A is selected and we're taking 5 households from each selected block, then the households on Block A have a 5/100 chance of being selected into the block's sample. Since we can multiply probabilities in a case like this, we see that every household on Block A had an overall chance of selection equal to $1/20 \times 5/100 = 5/2{,}000 = 1/400$.

If Block B happens to be selected, on the other hand, its households stand a much better chance

PPS (probability proportionate to size) A type of multistage *cluster sample* in which clusters are selected, not with equal probabilities (see EPSEM), but with probabilities proportionate to their sizes—as measured by the number of units to be subsampled.

of being among the 5 chosen there: 5/10. When this is combined with their relatively poorer chance of having their block selected in the first place, however, they end up with the same chance of selection as those on Block A: $1/200 \times 5/10 = 5/2{,}000 = 1/400$.

Further refinements to this design make it a very efficient and effective method for selecting large cluster samples. For now, however, it's enough for you to understand the basic logic involved.

DISPROPORTIONATE SAMPLING AND WEIGHTING

You will recall from earlier in the chapter that one of the problems with many state-level polls leading up to the 2016 U.S. presidential election was the failure to adjust for the overrepresentation of college graduates in survey samples. In other words, pollsters' estimates failed to account for the fact that different segments of the population had different chances of being selected into the sample. Ultimately, a probability sample is representative of a population only if all elements in the population have an equal chance of selection in that sample. Thus, in each of the preceding discussions, we've noted that the various sampling procedures result in an equal chance of selection—even though the ultimate selection probability is the product of several partial probabilities.

More generally, however, a probability sample is one in which each population element has a *known nonzero* probability of selection—even though different elements may have different probabilities. If controlled probability sampling procedures have been used, any such sample may be representative of the population from which it is drawn if each sample element is assigned a weight equal to the inverse of its probability of selection. Thus, where all sample elements have had the same chance of selection, each is given the same weight: 1. This is called a *self-weighting sample.*

It's sometimes appropriate to give some cases more weight than others, a process called **weighting**. Disproportionate sampling and weighting come into play in two basic ways. First, you may sample subpopulations disproportionately to ensure sufficient numbers of cases from each for analysis. For example, when Fiona Kay was interested in examining causal factors that "push" lawyers out of law firm practice as well as those that "pull" them toward other options, she used "[a] disproportionately stratified random sample of lawyers ... selected from the membership lists of the Law Society of Upper Canada" (1997:309). Given her interest in gender issues, she stratified the sample by gender and oversampled women so she would have equal numbers of women and men.

In another example, a given city may have a suburban area containing one-fourth of its total population. Yet you might be especially interested in a detailed analysis of households in that area and may feel that one-fourth of this total sample size would be too few. As a result, you might decide to select the same number of households from the suburban area as from the remainder of the city. Households in the suburban area, then, are given a disproportionately better chance of selection than those located elsewhere in the city.

As long as you analyze the two area samples separately or comparatively, you need not worry about the differential sampling. If you want to combine the two samples to create a composite picture of the entire city, however, you must take the disproportionate sampling into account. If n is the number of households selected from each area, then the households in the suburban area had a chance of selection equal to n divided by one-fourth of the total city population. Because the total city population and the sample size are the same for both areas, the suburban households should be given a weight of $1/4n$, and the remaining households should be given a weight of $3/4n$. This weighting procedure could be simplified by merely giving a weight of 3 to each of the households selected outside the suburban area. (This procedure gives a proportionate representation to each sample element. The population figure would have to be included in the weighting if population estimates were desired.)

weighting A procedure used in connection with sampling whereby units selected with unequal probabilities are assigned weights in such a manner as to make the sample *representative* of the population from which it was selected. When all cases have the same chance of selection, no weighting is necessary.

For example, when studying public support for electoral reforms in Alberta, Johnston et al. (2006) used a disproportionate sample for the purpose of achieving regional representation. Their goal was to oversample the two metropolitan areas of Edmonton and Calgary. They noted that they weighted the results they reported from their survey in order to correct for the small degree of oversampling in the two metropolitan areas.

Here's an example of the problems that can be created when disproportionate sampling is not accompanied by a weighting scheme. When the *Harvard Business Review* (HBR) decided to survey its subscribers on the issue of sexual harassment at work, for example, it seemed appropriate to oversample women. Here's how G. C. Collins and Timothy Blodgett (1981:78) explained the matter:

> We also skewed the sample another way: to insure a representative response from women, we mailed a questionnaire to virtually every female subscriber, for a male/female ratio of 68% to 32%. This bias resulted in a response of 52% male and 44% female (and 4% who gave no indication of gender) compared to HBR's U.S. subscriber proportion of 93% male and 7% female.

Notice a couple of things in this quotation. First, it would be nice to know a little more about what "virtually every female" means. Evidently, they didn't send questionnaires to all female subscribers, but there's no indication of who was omitted and why. Second, they didn't use the term *representative* in its normal social science usage. What they meant, of course, is that they wanted to get a substantial or "large enough" response from women; oversampling was a perfectly acceptable way of accomplishing that.

By sampling more women than a straightforward probability sample would have produced, they were able to get enough women (812) to compare with the men (960). Thus, when the authors report, for example, that 32 percent of the women and 66 percent of the men agree that "the amount of sexual harassment at work is greatly exaggerated," we know that the female response is based on a substantial number of cases. That's good. There are problems, however.

To begin, subscriber surveys are always problematic. In this case, the best the researchers can hope to talk about is "what subscribers to HBR think." In a loose way, it might make sense to think of that population as representing the more sophisticated portion of corporate management. Unfortunately, the overall response rate was 25 percent. Although that's quite good for subscriber surveys, it's a low response rate with regard to generalizing from probability samples.

Beyond that, however, the disproportionate sample design creates a further problem. When the authors state that 73 percent of respondents favour company policies against harassment (Collins and Blodgett 1981:78), that figure is undoubtedly too high, because the sample contained a disproportionately high percentage of women, who were more likely to favour such policies. Further, when the researchers report that top managers are more likely to feel that claims of sexual harassment are exaggerated than are middle and lower-level managers (1981:81), that finding is also suspect. As the researchers report, women are disproportionately represented in lower management. That alone might have accounted for the apparent differences in different levels of management. In short, the failure to take account of the oversampling of women confounds all survey results that don't separate findings by gender. The solution to this problem would have been to weight the responses by gender, as described earlier in this section.

SOME REALITIES OF SAMPLING

Sampling can be much more complicated than the examples we've presented here. Some populations are extremely difficult to determine. Clever sampling designs are often a major component of a research project. For example, Bill Reimer (2001) and colleagues are involved in a long-term project concerning research and education in Canadian rural communities. In 1995, he proposed a systematic design for rural research: a national sample frame of 32 selected rural sites that allow researchers to compare important dimensions.

Part of the research project is the ongoing evaluation of this national sample frame and its refinement (see http://www.concordia.ca/artsci/sociology-anthropology/research/nre.html, accessed July 12, 2019). The basis for the site selections was the census subdivisions (CSD) in the 1991

Canadian census, which provided an exhaustive set of possible locations. Although this research design is too intricate to briefly describe here, we mention it as an illustration of the time and skill involved in developing useful sampling frames for extensive research on important topics. See Reimer (2011) for an example of an analysis using these data.

Sometimes the complications and difficulties are not in determining the sample but in making contact with those selected to be in the sample. There are situations when the sample one would like to gather is not possible due to the reality of the circumstances the researcher faces.

PROBABILITY SAMPLING IN REVIEW

Much of this chapter has been devoted to the key sampling method used in controlled survey research: probability sampling. In each of the variations examined, we've seen that elements are chosen for study from a population on a basis of random selection with known nonzero probabilities.

Depending on the field situation, probability sampling can be very simple or it can be very difficult, time-consuming, and expensive. Whatever the situation, however, it remains the most effective method for the selection of study elements. There are two reasons for this.

First, probability sampling avoids researchers' conscious or unconscious biases in element selection. If all elements in the population have an equal (or unequal and subsequently weighted) chance of selection, there is an excellent chance that the sample so selected will closely represent the population of all elements.

Second, probability sampling permits estimates of sampling error. Although no probability sample will be perfectly representative in all respects, controlled selection methods permit the researcher to estimate the degree of expected error.

Up to this point in the chapter, we have been considering the general issue of selecting observations, and our primary focus has been on selecting participants or informants whose responses or actions will constitute our observations. But sometimes rather than directly asking or observing people, we indirectly observe the artifacts or content of their communication. Thus, this chapter will conclude with a brief discussion of issues related to the sampling of content.

HOW TO DO IT

Sample Weighting

The Problem: In order to get sufficient cases of minority groups, researchers need to oversample. For example, Indigenous people constitute about 4 percent of the population. Therefore, in a random sample of 2,000 Canadian adults, we would expect to select 80 Indigenous cases. Let's say we need 160 Indigenous cases and include that many in the sample. Now our sample overrepresents Indigenous people.

The Solution: To make our sample representative, it needs to be weighted. Indigenous Canadians comprise 8 percent of the sample, when they should be 4 percent; non-Indigenous Canadians comprise 92 percent, when they should be 96 percent. To achieve representativeness, an appropriate weight (multiplying factor) needs to be applied to each group.

The Steps:

1. Determine the weight for each group by dividing desired (population) proportion by actual (sample) proportion.

   Indigenous weight: $0.04/0.08 = 0.50$

   Non-Indigenous weight: $0.96/0.92 = 1.04348$

2. Apply the weights by multiplying each group sample size by its weight.

   Indigenous weighted sample:
   $0.50000 \times 160 = 80$

   Non-Indigenous weighted sample:
   $1.04348 \times 1{,}840 = 1{,}920$

The weighted sample now reflects the correct proportions of Indigenous and non-Indigenous Canadians in the population.

SPOTLIGHT ON MIXED METHODS

A Multisite Case Study Sampling Design

Often in real-world research, it is not viable to randomly select samples and/or to randomly assign participants to experimental and control groups (see Chapter 7 on experiments). Sharp et al. (2012) were confronted with such a reality when they decided to study the effects of state-mandated policy reform in South Carolina. South Carolina's *Education and Economic Development Act* (EEDA) of 2005 was intended to improve levels of student engagement, achievement, and high school completion, as well as successful transition to postsecondary education and/or the labour market. Toward advancement of these goals, EEDA required "the creation of locally relevant career pathways or programs of study in high schools. Among other requirements, these pathways or programs must align with postsecondary education, pertain to local economic realities and industry, and provide workbased learning opportunities for students" (p. 35).

At the time—still in the data collection phase of a five- year longitudinal examination of this project—Sharp et al. (2012) detailed the mixed methods sampling strategy they were using. They designed a four-stage sequential mixed methods site selection strategy to select eight sites that were broadly representative of South Carolina, but which could also inform them of the local nuances and complexities of policy implementation. Sharp et al. (2012:49) note that in order to enhance generalization of results when random samples are not possible, researchers should use purposive sampling to "select sites that vary across policy implementation levels and should control for major contextual variables."

Their site selection strategy integrated quantitative and qualitative data and methods at various stages of sampling:

Stage 1: Researchers used quantitative data and analyses (selected economic measures) to select four economic districts in South Carolina (out of twelve districts) that reflected a cross-section of economic and regional diversity.

Stage 2: They used the economic data to cluster schools from these regions into high and low-to-moderate poverty schools.

Stage 3: They used a combination of qualitative and quantitative data to score and rank schools on level of EEDA policy implementation. Ten schools (representing a mix across dimensions of urban-rural, high-low poverty, and high-low policy implementation) were identified to receive site visits.

Stage 4: Researchers visited schools to verify level of policy implementation via interviews with key school personnel, including principals, assistant principals, guidance directors, guidance counsellors, and teachers. Based on interviews and on-site observations, the policy implementation scores and rankings were revised.

The final eight high schools were selected to represent variation in the level of policy implementation (high and low-to-moderate) as well as variation in levels of poverty, urbanicity, and regional economic characteristics.

Looking forward to the next steps in their study, the authors noted that their mixed methods sampling strategy (combining quantitative and qualitative components) "will allow us to draw comparisons and contrasts across several dimensions that are important for addressing our research questions, including the level of policy implementation and the availability of various community resources." And, in the end, will "increase internal validity and trustworthiness and the generalizability/transferability of [the] results" (Sharp et al. 2012: 49).

SAMPLING CONTENT

In the study of communications, as in the study of people, you often can't observe directly all you would like to explore. Imagine you were interested in studying TV violence and sponsorship; we'd advise against attempting to watch everything that's broadcast. It wouldn't be possible, and your brain would probably short-circuit before you came close to discovering that for yourself. Usually, then, it's appropriate to sample. Let's begin by revisiting the idea of units of analysis. We'll then review some of the sampling techniques that might be applied to them in content analysis.

UNITS OF ANALYSIS

As we discussed in Chapter 4, determining appropriate units of analysis—the individual units that we make descriptive and explanatory statements about—can be a complicated task. It's essential that you as a researcher be clear on this issue, because sample selection depends largely on what the unit of analysis is. If individual writers are the units of analysis, your sample design should select all or a sample of the writers appropriate to the research question. If books are the units of analysis, you should choose a sample of books, regardless of their authors. Bruce Berg (2007:312–313) points out that even if you plan to analyze some body of textual materials, the units of analysis might be words, themes, characters, paragraphs, items (such as books or letters), concepts, semantics, or combinations of these (see Figure 6-6).

We're not suggesting that sampling should be based solely on the units of analysis. Indeed, we may often *subsample*—select samples of subcategories—for each individual unit of analysis. Thus, if writers are the units of analysis, we might (1) select a sample of writers from the total population of writers, (2) select a sample of books written by each writer selected, and (3) select portions of each selected book for observation and coding.

Finally, let's look at a trickier example: the study of TV violence and sponsors. What's the unit of analysis for the research question "Are the manufacturers of men's products more likely to sponsor violent shows than other sponsors?" Is it the TV show? The sponsor? The instance of violence?

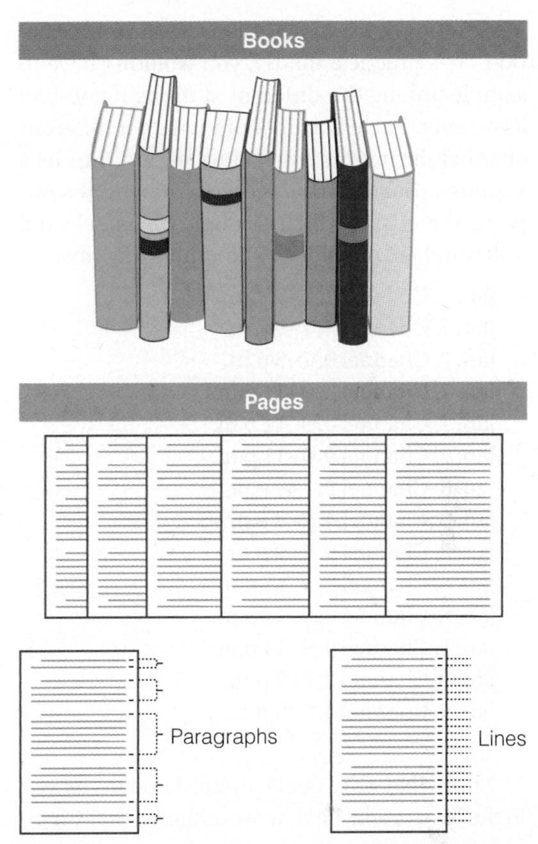

FIGURE 6-6 A Few Possible Units of Analysis for Content Analysis.
Source: © Cengage Learning

In the simplest study design, it would be none of these. Though you might structure your inquiry in various ways, the most straightforward design would be based on the commercial as the unit of analysis. You would use two kinds of observational units: the commercial and the program (the show that gets squeezed in between commercials). You'd want to observe both units. You would classify commercials by whether they advertised men's products and the programs by their violence.

In designing the sample, you would need to establish the universe to be sampled from. In this case, what TV stations will you observe? What will be the period of the study—number of days? And during which hours of each day will you observe? Then how many commercials do you want to observe and code for analysis? Watch TV for a while and find out how many commercials occur each hour; then you can figure out how many hours of observation you'll need (and can stand).

Now you're ready to design the sample selection. As a practical matter, you wouldn't have to sample among the different stations if you had assistants. Each of you could watch a different channel during the same time period. But let's suppose you're working alone. Your final sampling frame, from which a sample will be selected and watched, might look something like this:

Jan. 7, Channel 2, 7–9 p.m.
Jan. 7, Channel 4, 7–9 p.m.
Jan. 7, Channel 9, 7–9 p.m.
Jan. 7, Channel 2, 9–11 p.m.
Jan. 7, Channel 4, 9–11 p.m.
Jan. 7, Channel 9, 9–11 p.m.
Jan. 8, Channel 2, 7–9 p.m.
Jan. 8, Channel 4, 7–9 p.m.
Jan. 8, Channel 9, 7–9 p.m.
Jan. 8, Channel 2, 9–11 p.m.
Jan. 8, Channel 4, 9–11 p.m.
Jan. 8, Channel 9, 9–11 p.m.
Jan. 9, Channel 2, 7–9 p.m.
Jan. 9, Channel 4, 7–9 p.m.
etc.

Notice that we've made several decisions for you in the illustration. First, we've assumed that Channels 2, 4, and 9 are the ones appropriate to your study. We've assumed that you found the 7 p.m. to 11 p.m. prime-time hours to be the most relevant and that two-hour periods would do the job. We picked January 7 out of the hat for a starting date. In practice, of course, all these decisions should be based on your careful consideration of what would be appropriate to your particular study.

Once you have become clear about your units of analysis and the observations best suited to those units and have created a sampling frame like the one we've illustrated, sampling is simple and straightforward.

SAMPLING TECHNIQUES

As we've seen, in the content analysis of written prose, sampling may occur at any or all of several levels, including the contexts relevant to the works. Other forms of communication may also be sampled at any of the conceptual levels appropriate to them.

In content analysis, we could employ any of the conventional sampling techniques discussed earlier in the chapter. We might select a random or systematic sample of French and Canadian novelists, of laws passed in the province of Alberta, or of Shakespearean soliloquies. We might select (with a random start) every 23rd paragraph in Tolstoy's *War and Peace.* Or we might number all of the songs recorded by Beyoncé and select a random sample of 25.

Stratified sampling is also appropriate to content analysis. To analyze the editorial policies of Canadian newspapers, for example, we might first group all newspapers by region of the country or size of the community in which they are published, frequency of publication, or average circulation. We might then select a stratified random or systematic sample of newspapers for analysis. Having done so, we might select a sample of editorials from each selected newspaper, perhaps stratified chronologically.

Cluster sampling is equally appropriate to content analysis. Indeed, if individual editorials are our units of analysis, then the selection of newspapers at the first stage of sampling would be a cluster sample. In an analysis of political speeches, we might begin by selecting a sample of politicians; each politician would represent a cluster of political speeches. In the TV commercial study described previously, the initial sample of TV stations would be a cluster sample.

It deserves repeating that sampling need not end when we reach the unit of analysis. If novels are the unit of analysis in a study, we might select a sample of novelists, subsamples of novels written by each selected author, and a subsample of paragraphs within each novel. We would then analyze the content of the paragraphs for the purpose of describing the novels themselves. (*Note*: Researchers speak of samples within samples as "subsamples.")

In this lengthy chapter, we've taken on a basic issue that arises in much social research: how to select observations that will tell us something more general than the specifics we've actually observed. For example, this issue confronts field researchers, who face more action and more actors than they can observe and fully record; political pollsters, who want to predict an election but can't interview all voters; and content analysts confronted by hundreds of hours of TV or thousands of websites or pages of text. As we continue through the book, we'll see in greater detail how social researchers have found ways to deal with this issue.

MAIN POINTS

- Social researchers must select observations that will allow them to generalize to people and events not observed. Often, this involves a selection of people to observe—sampling.
- Social researchers have developed several sampling techniques appropriate to different research situations. Sometimes you can and should select probability samples using precise statistical techniques, but other times nonprobability techniques are more appropriate.
- Nonprobability sampling techniques include relying on available subjects, purposive (judgmental) sampling, snowball sampling, and quota sampling.
- In quota sampling, you begin with a detailed description of the characteristics of the total population (quota matrix) and then select your sample members so that they include different composite profiles that exist in the population. The representativeness of a quota sampling depends in large part on how accurately the quota matrix reflects the characteristics of the population.
- Nonprobability techniques are useful, but none of them ensures that the resulting sample is representative of the population being sampled.
- Researchers studying a social group may make use of informants. Informants should be selected in such a way that they provide a broad, diverse view of the group under study.
- Probability sampling methods provide an excellent way of selecting representative samples from large, known populations. These methods counter the problems of conscious and unconscious sampling bias by giving each element in the population a known, nonzero probability of being selected into the sample.
- The key to probability sampling is random selection.
- The most carefully selected sample will never provide a perfect representation of the population from which it was selected. There will always be some degree of sampling error.
- A sampling frame is a list or quasi-list of the members of a population. It is the resource used in the selection of a sample. A sample's representativeness depends directly on the extent to which a sampling frame contains all the members of the total population that the sample is intended to represent.
- Several sampling designs are available to researchers.
- Logically, simple random sampling is the most fundamental technique in probability sampling, although it is seldom used in practice.
- Systematic sampling involves the selection of every *k*th member from a sampling frame. This method is more practical than simple random sampling and, with a few exceptions, is functionally equivalent.
- Stratification is the process of grouping the members of a population into relatively homogeneous strata before sampling. This practice improves the representativeness of a sample by reducing the degree of sampling error.
- Multistage cluster sampling is a relatively complex sampling technique frequently used when a list of all the members of a population does not exist. Typically, researchers must balance the number of clusters and the size of each cluster to achieve a given sample size.
- PPS (probability proportionate to size) is a special, efficient method for multistage cluster sampling.
- If the members of a population have unequal probabilities of selection into the sample, researchers must assign weights to the different observations made, in order to provide a representative picture of the total population. Basically, the weight assigned to a particular sample member should be the inverse of its probability of selection.

- Common units of analysis in content analysis include elements of communication: words, paragraphs, books, and so forth. Standard probability sampling techniques are sometimes appropriate in content analysis.

REVIEW QUESTIONS AND EXERCISES

1. Using https://www.randomizer.org, select a simple random sample of 10 numbers in the range from 1 to 9,876. Describe each step in the process.
2. The Canadian General Social Survey uses careful sampling methods. Use the Web to find out the sizes of the original samples for the two most recent surveys and the number of completed interviews ("completed cases") achieved in each survey. Start at the Statistics Canada homepage (http://www.statcan.gc.ca/start-debut-eng.html).
3. Using the Web, find a study that uses a systematic sample and write a few paragraphs describing the study and the sample. Then locate a study using a quota sample and do the same.
4. Describe the steps involved in selecting a multistage cluster sample of students taking first-year English in Canadian universities.
5. Using the Web, find two Canadian newspaper articles that report the results of national surveys. For each, write down what the article reports about how the survey was conducted. Then critique the description with regard to the survey results reported in the article and the information provided to the reader about the way the survey was conducted. Were you given enough information to assess the worth of the study and the accuracy of the claims?

CONTINUITY PROJECT

POLLING PUBLIC OPINION

The Broadbent Institute surveyed 3,000 Canadians about their perceptions of inequality and the distribution of wealth in our nation. Their findings are published in the report *The Wealth Gap: Perceptions and Misconceptions in Canada* (Broadbent Institute 2014). Here is what the report says about its sampling method:[2]

> On behalf of the Broadbent Institute, Greenberg Quinlan Rosner Canada conducted a nationwide survey among 3,000 Canadians age 18 years and older. The survey was conducted online from September 10 to 23, 2014, and reflects the demographic composition of Canada's population 18 years of age and older. If the survey had been conducted using random sample on the telephone, the margin of error would be ± 1.79 percent. The margin of error would be higher for subgroups. (p. 12)

What kind of sample was used in this study? Based on the information provided, what sampling problems are evident? What confidence do you have that this sample's results are representative of Canadian adults?

2 From Broadbent Institute, 2014. *The Wealth Gap: Perceptions and Misconceptions in Canada*, http://www.broadbentinstitute.ca/the_wealth_gap. Reprinted with permission.

PART 3

MODES OF OBSERVATION: QUANTITATIVE AND QUALITATIVE APPROACHES

Having explored the structuring of inquiry in some depth, we're now ready to dive into the various observational techniques available to social scientists. We'll cover both quantitative and qualitative techniques and interactive and unobtrusive (nonreactive) methods of observing. It is, of course, possible to gather both qualitative and quantitative data using most modes of observation. However, as you'll see, some methods are more suited to a qualitative approach to research and others to a quantitative one. Therefore, Chapters 7 and 8 focus on methods well suited to producing quantitative data and Chapters 10 and 11 cover methods that are highly suited to generating qualitative data.

Many methods of observation, such as experiments, surveys, and many forms of field research, are interactive. They necessarily involve intrusion of varying degrees on whatever is under study. In the case of an interactive technique, the method of observing has the potential to change or affect what is being studied. There are modes of observing, however, where the method does not affect what is being studied. Discussion of such unobtrusive methods is concentrated in Chapter 9. Many nonreactive methods are equally suited to a qualitative or quantitative approach to research.

As we'll discuss, each method of research has its strengths and weaknesses, so it's often best to think of the various alternatives as complementary. In the end, the ideal method is the one that best fits the research problem at hand.

Experiments are usually thought of in connection with the physical sciences. In Chapter 7, we'll see how social scientists use experiments. This is the most rigorously controllable of the methods we'll examine. Understanding experiments is also a useful way to enhance your understanding of the general logic of social scientific research.

Chapter 8 will describe survey research, one of the most popular methods in social science. This type of research involves collecting data by asking people questions, either in self-administered questionnaires or through interviews, which, in turn, can be conducted face to face or over the telephone.

Chapter 9 discusses three forms of unobtrusive data collection that take advantage of some of the data available all around us. The analysis of existing statistics offers a way of studying people without having to talk to them. Governments and a variety of private organizations regularly compile great masses of data that you often can use with little or no modification to answer properly posed questions. Content analysis is a method of collecting social data through carefully specifying a coding scheme and applying it to social artifacts such as books, songs, speeches, and paintings. Without making any personal contact with people, you can use this method to examine a wide variety of social phenomena. Finally, historical documents are another valuable resource for social scientific analysis.

Chapter 10, on field research, examines perhaps the most natural form of data collection used by social scientists: the direct observation of social phenomena in natural settings. As you'll see, some researchers go beyond mere observation to participate in what they're studying, because they want a more intimate view and fuller understanding.

Chapter 11 looks at different forms and goals of qualitative interviewing. It begins with a general discussion of in-depth interviews and moves to a group interview format known as focus groups. It ends with a discussion of oral history, a method of gathering data about the past through in-depth interviewing of informants.

Chapter 12, on evaluation research, looks at a rapidly growing subfield in social science that involves the application of experimental and quasi-experimental models to the testing of social interventions in real life. You might use evaluation research, for example, to test the effectiveness of a drug rehabilitation program or the efficiency of a new school cafeteria. In the same chapter, we'll look briefly at social indicators as a way of assessing broader social processes.

When reading these chapters, you'll probably discover that you've been using these scientific methods casually in your daily life for as long as you can remember. You use some form of field research every day. You employ a crude form of content analysis every time you judge an author's motivation or orientation from his or her writings. You engage in at least casual experiments frequently. The chapters in Part 3 will show you how to improve your use of these methods to avoid the pitfalls of casual, uncontrolled observation.

None of the data-collection methods described in the following chapters is appropriate to all research topics and situations. We have tried to give you some ideas, early in each chapter, of when a given method might be appropriate. Still, we could never anticipate all the possible research topics that may one day interest you. As a general guideline, you should always use a variety of techniques in the study of any topic. Because each method has its weaknesses, the use of several methods can help fill in any gaps. If the different, independent approaches to the topic all yield the same conclusion, you've achieved a form of replication.

Jacobs Stock Photography/Photodisc/Getty Images

EXPERIMENTS

An experiment is a mode of observation that enables researchers to probe causal relationships. Many experiments in social research are conducted under the controlled conditions of a laboratory, but experiments can also take advantage of natural occurrences to study the effects of events in the social world.

IN THIS CHAPTER ...

INTRODUCTION

This chapter addresses the research method probably most frequently associated with structured science in general—the experiment. Here we'll focus on the experiment as a mode of scientific observation in social research. At the most basic level, experiments involve (1) taking action and (2) observing the consequences of that action. Social scientific researchers typically select a group of subjects, do something to them, and observe the effect of what was done. In this chapter, we'll examine the logic and some of the techniques of social scientific experiments.

It's worth noting at the outset that we often use experiments in nonscientific inquiry. In preparing a stew, for example, we add salt, taste, add more salt, and taste again. In defusing a bomb, we clip the red wire, observe whether the bomb explodes, clip another, and . . . .

We also experiment copiously in our attempts to develop generalized understandings about the world we live in. All skills are learned through experimentation: eating, walking, riding a bicycle, and so forth. Through experimentation, students discover how much studying is required for academic success. This chapter discusses some ways social researchers use experiments to develop generalized understandings. We'll see that, like other methods available to the social researcher, experimenting has its special strengths and weaknesses.

TOPICS APPROPRIATE TO EXPERIMENTS

Experiments are more appropriate for some topics and research purposes than others. Experiments are especially well suited to research projects involving relatively limited and well-defined concepts and propositions. With regard to the traditional image of science, discussed earlier in this book, the experimental model is especially appropriate for hypothesis testing. Because experiments focus on determining causation, they're also better suited to explanatory than to descriptive purposes.

Let's assume, for example, that we want to study prejudice against Indigenous Canadians. We hypothesize that learning about the contribution of Indigenous Canadians to Canadian history will reduce prejudice, and we decide to test this hypothesis experimentally. To begin, we might test a group of experimental subjects to determine their levels of prejudice against Indigenous Canadians. Next, we might show them a documentary film depicting the many important ways in which Indigenous Canadians have contributed to the scientific, literary, political, and social development of the country. Finally, we would measure our subjects' levels of prejudice against Indigenous Canadians again to determine whether the film has actually reduced prejudice.

Experimentation has also been successful in the study of small group interaction. Thus, we might bring together a small group of experimental subjects and assign them a task, such as making recommendations for popularizing car pools. Then we observe how the group organizes itself and deals with the problem. Over the course of several such experiments, we might systematically vary the nature of the task or the rewards for handling the task successfully. By observing differences in the way groups organize themselves and operate under these varying conditions, we can learn a great deal about the nature of small group interaction and the factors that influence it.

We typically think of experiments as being conducted in laboratories. Indeed, most of the examples in this chapter will involve such a setting. This need not be the case, however. Social researchers often study what are called *natural experiments*: "experiments" that occur in the regular course of social events. In addition, social researchers are increasingly using the Web as a vehicle for conducting experiments. The latter portion of this chapter will deal with such research.

THE CLASSICAL EXPERIMENT

In both the natural sciences and the social sciences, the most conventional type of experiment involves three major pairs of components: (1) independent and dependent variables, (2) pretesting and posttesting, and (3) experimental and control groups. This section looks at each of these components and the way they're put together in the execution of the experiment.

INDEPENDENT AND DEPENDENT VARIABLES

Essentially, an experiment examines the effect of an independent variable on a dependent variable. Typically, the independent variable takes the form of an experimental stimulus, which is either present or absent. That is, the stimulus is a **dichotomous variable**, having two attributes, present or not present. In this typical model, the experimenter compares what happens when the stimulus is present with what happens when it is not.

In the example concerning prejudice against Indigenous Canadians, *prejudice* is the dependent variable and *exposure to Indigenous Canadian history* is the independent variable. The researcher's hypothesis suggests that prejudice depends, in part, on a lack of knowledge of Indigenous Canadian history. The purpose of the experiment is to test the validity of this hypothesis by presenting some subjects with an appropriate stimulus, such as a documentary film. In other terms, the independent variable is the cause and the dependent variable is the effect. Thus, we might say that watching the film caused a change in prejudice or that reduced prejudice was an effect of watching the film.

The independent and dependent variables appropriate to experimentation are nearly limitless. Moreover, a given variable might serve as an independent variable in one experiment and as a dependent variable in another. For example, *prejudice* is the dependent variable in our example, but it might be the independent variable in an experiment examining the effect of prejudice on voting behaviour.

To be used in an experiment, both independent and dependent variables must be operationally defined. Such operational definitions might involve a variety of observation methods. Responses to a questionnaire, for example, might be the basis for defining prejudice. Speaking to or ignoring Indigenous Canadians, or agreeing or disagreeing with them in conversation, might be elements in the operational definition of interaction with Indigenous Canadians in a small group setting.

Conventionally, in the experimental model, dependent and independent variables must be operationally defined before the experiment begins. However, as you'll see in connection with survey research and other methods, it's sometimes appropriate to make a wide variety of observations during data collection and then determine the most useful operational definitions of variables during later analyses. Ultimately, however, experimentation, like other quantitative methods, requires specific and standardized measurements and observations.

PRETESTING AND POSTTESTING

In the simplest experimental design, **pretesting** occurs first, whereby subjects are measured in terms of a dependent variable. Then the subjects are exposed to a stimulus representing an independent variable. Finally, in **posttesting**, they are remeasured in terms of the dependent variable. Any differences between the first and last measurements on the dependent variable are then attributed to the independent variable.

In the example of prejudice and exposure to Indigenous Canadian history, we'd begin by pretesting the extent of prejudice among our experimental subjects. Using a questionnaire asking about attitudes toward Indigenous Canadians, for example, we could measure both the extent of prejudice exhibited by each individual subject and the average prejudice level of the whole group. After exposing the subjects to the film on Indigenous Canadian history, we could administer the same questionnaire again. Responses given in this posttest would permit us to measure the later extent of prejudice for each subject and the average prejudice level of the group as a whole. If we discovered a lower level of prejudice during the second administration of the questionnaire, we might conclude that the film had indeed reduced prejudice.

In the experimental examination of attitudes such as prejudice, we face a special practical

dichotomous variable A variable that has only two attributes; also called a binomial variable.

pretesting The measurement of a dependent variable among subjects before they are exposed to a stimulus representing an independent variable.

posttesting The remeasurement of a dependent variable among subjects after they have been exposed to a stimulus representing an independent variable.

problem relating to validity. As you may already have imagined, the subjects might respond differently to the questionnaires the second time even if their attitudes remained unchanged. During the first administration of the questionnaire, the subjects may be unaware of its purpose. By the time of the second measurement, they may have figured out that we are interested in measuring their prejudice. Because no one wishes to seem prejudiced, the subjects may "clean up" their answers the second time around. Thus, the film will seem to have reduced prejudice although, in fact, it has not.

This is an example of a more general problem that plagues many forms of social research. The very act of studying something may change it. The techniques for dealing with this problem in the context of experimentation will be discussed in various places throughout the chapter. The first technique involves the use of control groups.

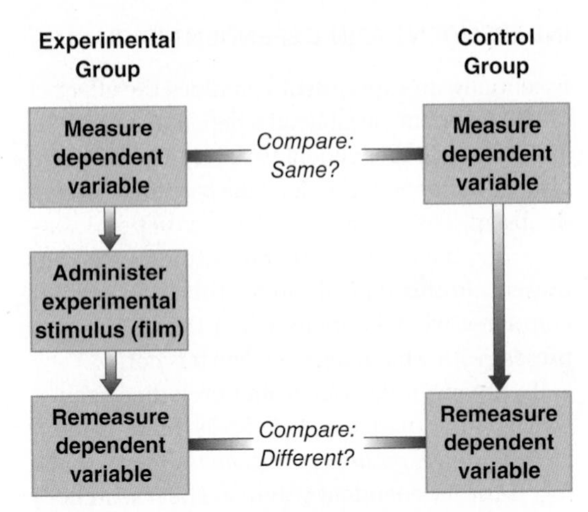

FIGURE 7-1 Diagram of Basic Experimental Design. The fundamental purpose of an experiment is to isolate the possible effect of an independent variable (called the *stimulus* in experiments) on a dependent variable. Members of the experimental group(s) are exposed to the stimulus and those in the control group(s) are not.

Source: © Cengage Learning

EXPERIMENTAL AND CONTROL GROUPS

Laboratory experiments seldom, if ever, involve only the observation of an **experimental group** to which a stimulus has been administered. In addition, the researchers also observe a **control group**, which does not receive the experimental stimulus.

In the example of prejudice and Indigenous Canadian history, we might examine two groups of subjects. To begin, we give each group a questionnaire designed to measure their prejudice against Indigenous Canadians. Then the experimental group is shown the film. Later the researcher administers a posttest of prejudice to *both* groups. Figure 7-1 illustrates this basic experimental design, where the major goal is the isolation of the possible effect of the independent variable (called the stimulus in an experiment) on the dependent variable. As the figure shows, those included in the experimental group are exposed to the stimulus; those in the control group are not.

Using a control group allows the researcher to detect any effects of the experiment itself. If the posttest shows that the overall level of prejudice exhibited by the control group has dropped as much as that of the experimental group, then the apparent reduction in prejudice must be a function of the experiment or of some external factor rather than a function of the film. If, on the other hand, prejudice were reduced *only* in the experimental group, such reduction would seem to be a consequence of exposure to the film, because that's the only difference between the two groups. Alternatively, if prejudice were reduced in both groups but to a greater extent in the experimental group than in the control group, that would also be grounds for assuming that the film reduced prejudice.

The need for control groups in social research became clear in connection with a series of studies of employee satisfaction conducted by Roethlisberger and Dickson (1939) in the late 1920s and early 1930s. These two researchers studied working conditions in the telephone "bank wiring room" of the Western Electric

experimental group In experimentation, a group of subjects to whom an experimental stimulus is administered.

control group In experimentation, a group of subjects to whom no experimental stimulus is administered and who should resemble the experimental group in all other respects. The comparison of the control group and the experimental group at the end of the experiment points to the effect of the experimental stimulus.

Works in the Chicago suburb of Hawthorne, Illinois. They were interested in discovering what changes in working conditions would improve employee satisfaction and productivity.

To the researchers' great satisfaction, they discovered that making working conditions better consistently increased satisfaction and productivity. As the workroom was brightened up through better lighting, for example, productivity went up. When lighting was further improved, productivity went up again. To further substantiate their scientific conclusion, the researchers then *dimmed* the lights: *productivity again improved!*

It became evident then that the wiring room workers were responding more to the attention given them by the researchers than to improved working conditions. As a result of this phenomenon, often called the **Hawthorne effect**, social researchers have become more sensitive to and cautious about the possible effects of experiments themselves. The use of a proper control group in the wiring room study—one that was studied intensively without any other changes in the working conditions—would have pointed to the existence of this effect.

The need for control groups in experimentation has been nowhere more evident than in medical research. Time and again, patients who participate in medical experiments have appeared to improve, and it has been unclear how much of the improvement has come from the experimental treatment and how much from the experiment. In testing the effects of new drugs, then, medical researchers frequently administer a *placebo*—a "drug" that actually should have no effect, like sugar pills—to a control group. Thus the control-group patients believe they, like the experimental group, are receiving an experimental drug. Often, they improve. If the new drug is effective, however, those receiving the actual drug will improve more than those receiving the placebo.

In social scientific experiments, control groups guard against not only the effects of the experiments themselves but also the effects of any events outside the laboratory during the experiments. In the example of the study of prejudice, suppose that a popular leader of an Indigenous Canadian community was beaten by the police in the middle of, say, a week-long experiment. Such an event might very well horrify the experimental subjects, requiring them to examine their own attitudes toward Indigenous Canadians, with the result of reduced prejudice. Because such an effect should happen about equally for members of the control and experimental groups, a *greater* reduction of prejudice among the experimental group would, again, point to the impact of the experimental stimulus: the documentary film.

Sometimes an experimental design requires more than one experimental or control group. In the case of the documentary film, for example, we might also want to examine the impact of reading a book about Indigenous Canadian history. In that case, we might have one group see the film and read the book; another group only see the movie; still another group only read the book; and the control group do neither. With this kind of design, we could determine the impact of each stimulus separately, as well as their combined effect.

THE DOUBLE-BLIND EXPERIMENT

Like patients who improve when they merely *think* they're receiving a new drug, sometimes experimenters tend to prejudge results. In medical research, the experimenters may be more likely to "observe" improvements among patients receiving the experimental drug than among those receiving the placebo. (This would be most likely, perhaps, for the researcher who developed the drug.) A **double-blind experiment** eliminates this possibility, because neither the subjects nor the experimenters know which is the experimental group and which is the control. In the medical case, those researchers responsible for administering the drug and for noting improvements would not be told which subjects

hawthorne effect A term coined in reference to a series of productivity studies at the Hawthorne plant of the Western Electric Company in Chicago, Illinois. The researchers discovered that their presence affected the behaviour of the workers being studied. The term now refers to any impact of research on the subject of study.

double-blind experiment An experimental design in which neither the subjects nor the experimenters know which is the experimental group and which is the control.

were receiving the drug and which the placebo. Conversely, the researcher who knew which subjects were in which group would not administer the experiment.

In social scientific experiments, as in medical experiments, the danger of experimenter bias is further reduced to the extent that the operational definitions of the dependent variables are clear and precise. For example, medical researchers would be less likely to unconsciously bias their reading of a patient's temperature than they would to bias their assessment of how lethargic the patient was. For the same reason, the small group researcher would be less likely to misperceive which subject spoke, or to whom he or she spoke, than whether the subject's comments sounded cooperative or competitive. The latter is a more subjective judgment that is difficult to define in precise behavioural terms.

As we've indicated several times, seldom can we devise operational definitions and measurements that are wholly precise and unambiguous. This is another reason it may sometimes be appropriate to employ a double-blind design in social research experiments.

SELECTING SUBJECTS

The logic of sampling was discussed in Chapter 6. We talked at length about selecting samples that are representative of some population. Similar considerations apply to experiments. Many social scientific laboratory experiments are conducted with university undergraduates as subjects because a large number of social researchers work in universities. Typically, the experimenter asks students enrolled in his or her classes to participate in experiments or advertises for subjects in a university newspaper. Subjects may or may not be paid for participating in such experiments.

In relation to the norm of **generalizability** in science, this tendency clearly represents a potential defect in social scientific research. Simply put, university undergraduates do not typify the public at large. There is a danger, therefore, that we may learn much about the attitudes and actions of university undergraduates but not about social attitudes and actions in general.

However, this potential defect is less significant in explanatory research than in descriptive research. True, having noted the level of prejudice among a group of university undergraduates in our pretesting, we would have little confidence that the same level existed among the public at large. On the other hand, if we found that a documentary film reduced the level of prejudice that existed among those undergraduates, we would have more confidence—without being certain—that it would have a comparable effect in the community at large. Social processes and patterns of causal relationships appear to be more generalizable and more stable than specific characteristics like an individual's prejudice level.

Aside from the question of generalizability, the cardinal rule of subject selection and experimentation concerns the comparability of experimental and control groups. Ideally, the control group represents what the experimental group would be like if it had *not* been exposed to the experimental stimulus. Therefore, the logic of experiments requires that experimental and control groups be as similar as possible. There are several ways to accomplish this.

PROBABILITY SAMPLING

The discussions of the logic and techniques of probability sampling in Chapter 6 provide one method for selecting two groups of people similar to each other. Beginning with a sampling frame composed of all the people in the population under study, the researcher might select two probability samples. If these samples each resemble the total population from which they're selected, they'll also resemble each other.

Recall also, however, that the degree of resemblance (representativeness) achieved by probability sampling is largely a function of the sample size. As a general guideline, probability samples of less than 100 are not likely to be terribly representative, and social scientific experiments seldom involve that many subjects in either experimental or control groups. As a result, then, probability

generalizability Refers to how broadly applicable results are to different populations.

sampling is seldom used in experiments to select subjects from a larger population. Researchers do use the logic of randomization, however, when assigning subjects to groups.

RANDOM ASSIGNMENT

Having recruited, by whatever means, a total group of subjects, the experimenter may randomly assign those subjects to either the experimental or the control group. Such **random assignment** may be accomplished by numbering all of the subjects serially and selecting numbers by means of a random number table or a random number generator. Alternatively, the experimenter might assign the odd-numbered subjects to the experimental group and the even-numbered subjects to the control group.

Let's return again to the basic concept of probability sampling. If we recruit 40 subjects altogether in response to a newspaper advertisement, there's no reason to believe that the 40 subjects represent the entire population from which they've been drawn. Nor can we assume that the 20 subjects randomly assigned to the experimental group represent that larger population. We may have greater confidence, however, that the 20 subjects randomly assigned to the experimental group will be reasonably similar to the 20 assigned to the control group.

Following the logic of our earlier discussions of sampling, we can view the 40 subjects as a population from which we select two probability samples, each consisting of half the population. Because each sample reflects the characteristics of the total population, the two samples will mirror each other.

As we saw in Chapter 6, our assumption of similarity in the two groups depends in part on the number of subjects involved. In the extreme case, if we recruited only two subjects and assigned, by the flip of a coin, one as the experimental subject and one as the control, there would be no reason to assume that the two subjects are similar to each other. With larger numbers of subjects, however, random assignment makes good sense. For example, in studying the impact of personal choice on children's learning, D'Ailly (2004) conducted a cross-cultural experiment with subjects from Canada and Taiwan. In Canada, 130 children in Grades 5 and 6 participated in the experiment, and in Taiwan, there were 153 children in the experiment. These subjects were randomly assigned to one of three different experimental groups or a control group. Although the logic of random selection underlies the process of randomization, random assignment should not be confused with a probability sample such as the simple random sample. The probability sample ensures that the subjects from whom actual data are gathered will be as representative as possible of some larger population.

Random assignment ensures that the subjects exposed to the test factor (experimental group) are as comparable as possible to those exposed to the control factor (control group). Just as random selection reduces the likelihood of bias in sampling, random assignment reduces the likelihood of bias in allocation of subjects to experimental and control groups. Similar to how a representative probability sample reflects the heterogeneity of the population, randomly assigned experimental and control groups should reflect the heterogeneity in the overall sample (and hence also reflect each other).

MATCHING

Another way to achieve comparability between experimental and control groups is through **matching**. This process is similar to the quota sampling methods discussed in Chapter 6. If 12 of our subjects are young white men, we might

---

random assignment The procedure of randomly assigning experimental subjects to experimental and control groups, such that each subject has an equal probability of being in either group. Random assignment increases the likelihood that all known and unknown characteristics (i.e., variable attributes) in the sample will be equally distributed between the experimental and control groups. Not to be confused with probability sampling techniques such as a simple random sample.

matching In connection with experiments, the procedure whereby pairs of subjects are matched on the basis of their similarities on one or more variables; then one member of the pair is assigned to the experimental group and the other to the control group.

assign 6 of those at random to the experimental group and the other 6 to the control group. If 14 are middle-aged Indigenous Canadian women, we might assign 7 to each group.

The overall matching process could be most efficiently achieved through the creation of a *quota matrix* constructed of all the most relevant characteristics. Figure 7-2 provides a simplified illustration of such a matrix. The experimenter in this example decided that age, race, and gender are the relevant characteristics. Ideally, the quota matrix is constructed to result in an even number of subjects in each cell of the matrix. Then half the subjects in each cell would go into the experimental group and half into the control group.

Alternatively, we might recruit more subjects than our experimental design requires. We might then examine many characteristics of the large initial group of subjects. Whenever we discover a pair of quite similar subjects, we would assign one to the experimental group and the other to the control group. Potential subjects who are unlike anyone else in the initial group would be left out of the experiment altogether.

Whatever method we use, the desired result is the same. The overall average description of the experimental group should be the same as that of the control group. For example, on average each group should have about the same ages, the same gender composition, the same racial composition, and so forth. This same test of comparability should be used whether the two groups are created through matching or through probability sampling with random assignment.

Thus far, we've referred to the "relevant" variables without saying clearly what those variables are. Of course, these variables can't be specified in any definite way, any more than we could specify in Chapter 6 which variables should be used in stratified sampling. Which variables are relevant ultimately depends on the nature and purpose of an experiment. As a general rule, however, the experimental and control groups should be comparable in those variables most likely to be related to the dependent variable under study. In a study of prejudice, for example, the two groups should be alike in education, ethnicity, and age, among other factors. In some cases, moreover, we may delay assigning subjects to experimental and control groups until we have initially measured the dependent variable. Thus, for example, we might administer a questionnaire measuring subjects' prejudice and then match the experimental and control groups on this variable to assure ourselves that the two groups exhibit the same overall level of prejudice.

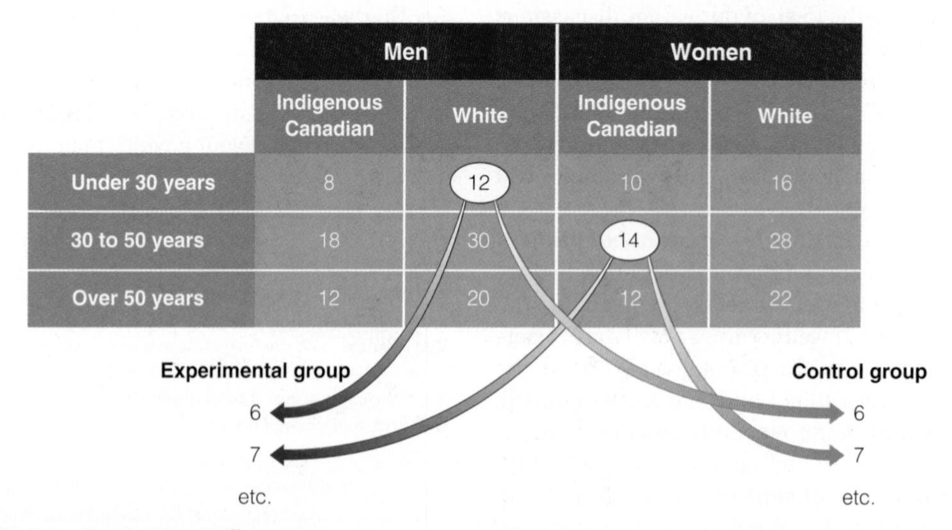

FIGURE 7-2 **Quota Matrix Illustration.** Sometimes the experimental and control groups are created by finding pairs of matching subjects and assigning one to the experimental group and the other to the control group.
Source: © Cengage Learning

MATCHING OR RANDOM ASSIGNMENT?

When assigning subjects to the experimental and control groups, you should be aware of two arguments in favour of random assignment over matching. First, you may not be in a position to know in advance which variables are relevant for the matching process. Second, most of the statistics used to analyze the results of experiments assume randomization. Failure to design your experiment that way, then, makes your later use of those statistics less meaningful. On the other hand, random assignment makes sense only if you have a fairly large pool of subjects, so that the laws of probability sampling apply. With only a few subjects, matching would be a better procedure.

Sometimes researchers combine matching and random assignment. When conducting an experiment on the educational enrichment of young adolescents, Yinger and colleagues (1977) needed to assign a large number of students, aged 13 and 14, to several different experimental and control groups to ensure the comparability of students making up each of the groups. They achieved this goal by the following method.

Beginning with a pool of subjects, the researchers first created strata of students nearly identical to one another with respect to some 15 variables. From each of the strata, students were randomly assigned to the different experimental and control groups. In this fashion, the researchers actually improved on conventional random assignment. Essentially, they used a stratified sampling procedure (Chapter 6), except that they used far more stratification variables than are typically used in, say, survey sampling.

VALIDITY ISSUES IN EXPERIMENTAL RESEARCH

At this point we want to present in a more systematic way the factors that affect the validity of experimental research. We'll first look at what Campbell and Stanley call the sources of *internal invalidity*, reviewed and expanded in a follow-up book by Thomas Cook and Donald Campbell (1979). Then we'll discuss the problem of generalizing experimental results to the "real" world, referred to as *external invalidity*. Having examined these, we'll be in a position to appreciate the advantages of some of the more sophisticated experimental and quasi-experimental designs social science researchers sometimes use.

Sources of Internal Invalidity The problem of **internal invalidity** refers to the possibility that the conclusions drawn from experimental results may not accurately reflect what has gone on in the experiment itself. The threat of internal invalidity is present whenever anything other than the experimental stimulus can affect the dependent variable.

Campbell and Stanley (1963:5–6) and Cook and Campbell (1979:51–55) point to over a dozen sources of internal invalidity. Here are the ones they identify that are not managed by control groups, pretesting, and so on:

1. *History.* During the course of the experiment, historical events may occur that will confound the experimental results. The beating by police of an Indigenous Canadian leader during the course of an experiment on reducing anti-Indigenous Canadian prejudice would be an example.
2. *Maturation.* People are continually growing and changing, and such changes affect the results of the experiment. In a long-term experiment, the fact that the subjects grow older (and wiser?) may have an effect. In shorter experiments, they may grow tired, sleepy, bored, or hungry, or change in other ways that may affect their behaviour in the experiment.
3. *Testing.* Often the process of testing and retesting will influence people's behaviour, thereby confounding the experimental results. Suppose we administer a questionnaire to a group as a way of measuring their prejudice. Then we administer an experimental stimulus and remeasure their prejudice. By the time we conduct the posttest, the subjects will

internal invalidity Refers to the possibility that the conclusions drawn from experimental results may not accurately reflect what went on in the experiment itself.

probably have become more sensitive to the issue of prejudice and will be more thoughtful in their answers. In fact, they may have figured out that we're trying to find out how prejudiced they are, and, because few people like to appear prejudiced, they may give answers that they think we want or that will make them look good.

4. *Instrumentation.* The process of measurement in pretesting and posttesting brings to light some of the issues of conceptualization and operationalization discussed earlier in the book. If we use different measures of the dependent variable in the pretest and posttest (say, different questionnaires about prejudice), how can we be sure they're comparable to one another? Perhaps prejudice will seem to have decreased simply because the pretest measure was more sensitive than the posttest measure. Or if the experimenters are making the measurements, their standards or their abilities may change over the course of the experiment.
5. *Statistical regression.* Sometimes it's appropriate to conduct experiments on subjects who start out with extreme scores on the dependent variable. If you were testing a new method for teaching math to hardcore failures in math, you'd want to conduct your experiment on people who previously have done extremely poorly in math. But consider for a minute what's likely to happen to the math achievement of such people over time without any experimental interference. They're starting out so low that they can only stay at the bottom or improve: they can't get worse. Even without any experimental stimulus, then, the group as a whole is likely to show some improvement over time. Referring to a *regression to the mean,* statisticians often point out that extremely tall people as a group are likely to have children shorter than themselves, and extremely short people as a group are likely to have children taller than themselves. There's a danger, then, that changes occurring by virtue of subjects starting out in extreme positions will be attributed erroneously to the effects of the experimental stimulus.
6. *Selection biases.* We discussed bias in selection earlier when we examined different ways of selecting subjects for experiments and assigning them to experimental and control groups. Comparisons don't have any meaning unless the groups are *comparable.*
7. *Experimental mortality.* Although some social experiments could, we suppose, kill subjects, *experimental mortality* refers to a more general and less extreme problem. Often, experimental subjects will drop out of the experiment before it's completed, which can affect statistical comparisons and conclusions. In the classical experiment involving an experimental and a control group, each with a pretest and posttest, suppose that the bigots in the experimental group are so offended by the Indigenous Canadian history film that they leave before it's over. Those subjects sticking around for the posttest will have been less prejudiced to start with, so the group results will reflect a substantial "decrease" in prejudice.
8. *Causal time order.* Though rare in social research, ambiguity about the time order of the experimental stimulus and the dependent variable can arise. Whenever this occurs, the research conclusion that the stimulus caused the dependent variable can be challenged with the explanation that the "dependent" variable actually caused changes in the stimulus (see Chapter 4).
9. *Diffusion or imitation of treatments.* When experimental and control-group subjects can communicate with each other, experimental subjects could pass on some elements of the experimental stimulus to the control group. If, for example, there is a time lapse between the showing of the film on Indigenous Canadian history and the administration of the posttest, members of the experimental group might tell control-group subjects about the film. In that case, the control group becomes affected by the stimulus and is not a real control. Sometimes we speak of the control group as having been "contaminated."

10. *Compensation.* As you'll see in Chapter 12, in experiments in real-life situations, such as a special educational program, subjects in the control group are often deprived of something considered to be of value. In such cases, there may be pressures to offer some form of compensation. For example, hospital staff might feel sorry for control-group patients and give them extra "tender loving care." In such a situation, the control group is no longer a genuine control group.
11. *Compensatory rivalry.* In real-life experiments, the subjects deprived of the experimental stimulus may try to compensate for the missing stimulus by working harder. Suppose an experimental math program is the experimental stimulus; the control group may work harder than before on their math to try to beat the "special" experimental subjects.
12. *Demoralization.* On the other hand, feelings of deprivation within the control group may result in their giving up. In educational experiments, demoralized control-group subjects may stop studying, act up, or get angry.

These, then, are some of the sources of internal invalidity in experiments. Aware of these, experimenters have devised designs aimed at handling them. The classical experiment, if coupled with proper subject selection and assignment, addresses each of these problems. Let's look again at that study design, presented graphically in Figure 7-3.

If we use the experimental design shown in Figure 7-3 in our study of prejudice against Indigenous Canadians, we should expect two findings. For the experimental group, the level of prejudice measured in their posttest should be less than was found in their pretest. In addition, when the two posttests are compared, less prejudice should be found in the experimental group than in the control.

This design also guards against the problem of history in that anything occurring outside the experiment that might affect the experimental group should also affect the control group. Therefore, there should still be a difference in the two posttest results. The same comparison guards against problems of maturation as long as the subjects have been randomly assigned to the two groups. Testing and instrumentation

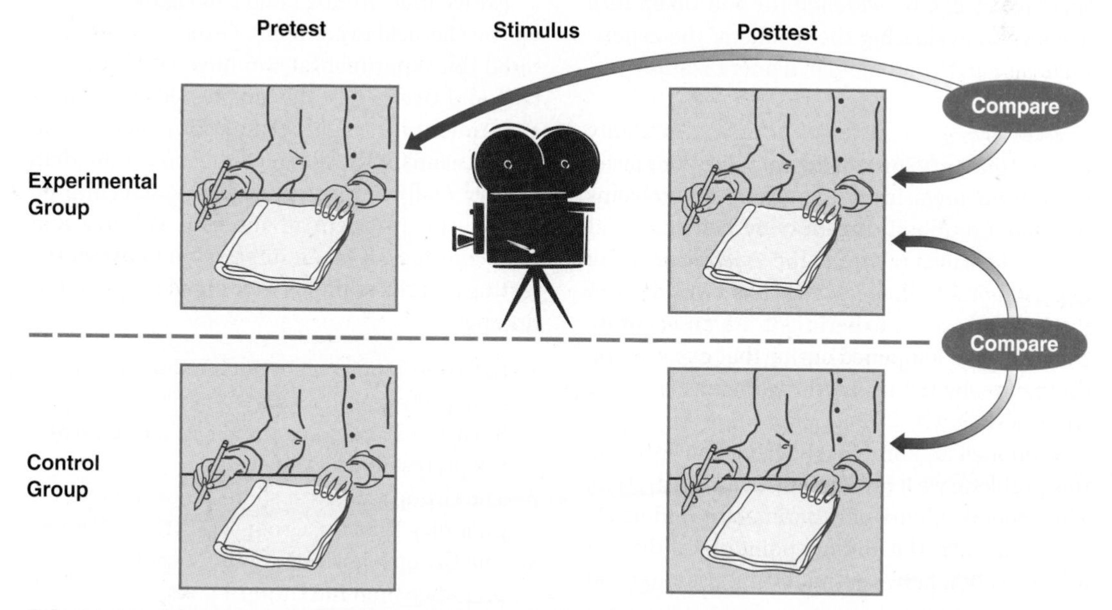

FIGURE 7-3 **The Classical Experiment: Using an Indigenous Canadian History Film to Reduce Prejudice.** This diagram illustrates the basic structure of the classical experiment as a vehicle for testing the impact of a film on prejudice. Notice how the control group, the pretesting, and the posttesting function.
Source: © Cengage Learning

can't be problems, since both the experimental and control groups are subject to the same tests and experimenter effects. If the subjects have been assigned to the two groups randomly, statistical regression should affect both equally, even if people with extreme scores on prejudice (or whatever the dependent variable is) are being studied. Selection bias is ruled out by the random assignment of subjects. Experimental mortality is more complicated to handle, but the data provided in this study design offer several ways to deal with it. Slight modifications to the design—administering a placebo (such as a film having nothing to do with Indigenous Canadians) to the control group, for example—can make the problem even easier to manage.

The remaining five problems of internal invalidity are avoided through the careful administration of a controlled experimental design. The experimental design we've been discussing facilitates the clear specification of independent and dependent variables. Experimental and control subjects can be kept separate, reducing the possibility of diffusion or imitation of treatments. Administrative controls can avoid compensations given to the control group, and compensatory rivalry can be watched for and taken into account in evaluating the results of the experiment, as can the problem of demoralization.

Sources of External Invalidity Internal invalidity accounts for only some of the complications faced by experimenters. In addition, there are problems of what Campbell and Stanley call **external invalidity**, which relates to the *generalizability* of experimental findings to the "real" world. Even if the results of an experiment are an accurate gauge of what happened during that experiment, do they really tell us anything about life in the wilds of society?

Campbell and Stanley describe four forms of this problem; we'll present one as an illustration. The generalizability of experimental findings is jeopardized, as the authors point out, if there is an interaction between the testing situation and the experimental stimulus (1963:18). Here's an example of what they mean.

external invalidity Refers to the possibility that conclusions drawn from experimental results may not be generalizable to the "real" world.

Staying with the study of prejudice and the Indigenous Canadian history film, let's suppose that our experimental group in the classical experiment has less prejudice in its posttest than in its pretest, and that its posttest shows less prejudice than that of the control group. We can be confident that the film actually reduced prejudice among our experimental subjects. But would it have the same effect if the film were shown in theatres or on TV? We can't be sure, since the film might be effective only when people have been sensitized to the issue of prejudice, as the subjects may have been in taking the pretest. This is an example of interaction between the testing and the stimulus. The classical experimental design cannot control for that possibility. Fortunately, experimenters have devised other designs that can.

The Solomon four-group design (Campbell and Stanley 1963:24–25) addresses the problem of testing interaction with the stimulus. As the name suggests, it involves four groups of subjects, assigned randomly from a pool. Figure 7-4 presents this design graphically.

Notice that Groups 1 and 2 in Figure 7-4 make up the classical experiment. Group 3 is administered the experimental stimulus without a pretest, and Group 4 is only posttested. This latest experimental design permits four meaningful comparisons. If the film on Indigenous Canadian history really reduces prejudice—unaccounted for by the problem of internal validity and unaccounted for by an interaction between the testing and the stimulus—we should expect four findings:

1. In Group 1, posttest prejudice should be less than pretest prejudice.
2. In Group 2, prejudice should be the same in the pretest and the posttest.
3. The Group 1 posttest should show less prejudice than the Group 2 posttest.
4. The Group 3 posttest should show less prejudice than the Group 4 posttest.

Notice that finding (4) rules out any interaction between the testing and the stimulus. And remember that these comparisons are

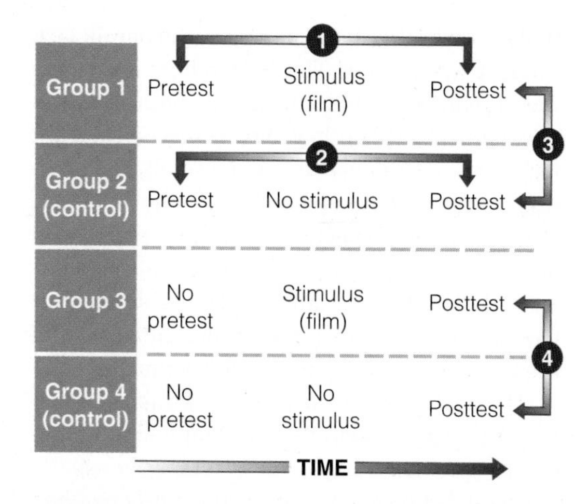

Expected Findings

1. In Group 1, posttest prejudice should be less than pretest prejudice.
2. In Group 2, prejudice should be the same in the pretest and the posttest.
3. The Group 1 posttest should show less prejudice than the Group 2 posttest does.
4. The Group 3 posttest should show less prejudice than the Group 4 posttest does.

FIGURE 7-4 **The Solomon Four-Group Design.** The classical experiment runs the risk that pretesting will have an effect on subjects, so the Solomon four-group design adds experimental and control groups that skip the pretest. Thus, the Solomon four-group design combines the classical experiment and the after-only design or "static-group comparison."
Source: © Cengage Learning

meaningful only if subjects have been assigned randomly to the different groups, thereby providing groups of equal prejudice initially, even though their pre-experiment prejudice is measured only in Groups 1 and 2.

There is a side benefit to this research design, as the authors point out. Not only does the Solomon four-group design rule out interactions between testing and the stimulus; it also provides data for comparisons that will reveal the amount of such interaction that occurs in the classical experimental design. This knowledge allows a researcher to review and evaluate the value of any prior research that used the simpler design.

The last experimental design we'll mention is what Campbell and Stanley (1963:25–26) call the *posttest-only control group design*; it consists of the second half (Groups 3 and 4) of the Solomon design. As the authors argue persuasively, with proper randomization only Groups 3 and 4 are needed for a true experiment that controls for the problems of internal invalidity as well as for the interaction between testing and stimulus. With randomized assignment to experimental and control groups, the subjects will be initially comparable on the dependent variable—comparable enough to satisfy the conventional statistical tests used to evaluate the results—so it's not necessary to measure them. Indeed, Campbell and Stanley suggest that the only justification for pretesting in this situation is tradition. Experimenters have simply grown accustomed to pretesting and feel more secure with research designs that include it. Be clear, however, that this point applies only to experiments in which subjects have been assigned to experimental and control groups *randomly*, because that's what justifies the assumption that the groups are equivalent—without actually measuring them to find out.

This discussion has introduced the intricacies of experimental design, its problems, and some solutions. There are, of course, a great many other possible experimental designs in use. Some involve more than one stimulus and combinations of stimuli. Others involve several tests of the dependent variable over time and the administration of the stimulus at different times for different groups. If you're interested in pursuing this topic, you might look at the Campbell and Stanley book.

ILLUSTRATIONS OF EXPERIMENTATION

Experiments have been used to study a wide variety of topics in the social sciences. Some experiments have been conducted within laboratory situations; others occur in the "real world." The following discussion provides a glimpse of both.

In George Bernard Shaw's well-loved play *Pygmalion*, the basis for the musical *My Fair Lady*, Eliza Doolittle speaks of the powers others have in determining our social identity. Here's how she distinguishes the way she's treated by her tutor, Professor Higgins, and by Higgins's friend, Colonel Pickering:

> You see, really and truly, apart from the things anyone can pick up (the dressing and the proper way of speaking, and so on), the difference between a lady and a flower girl is not how she behaves, but how she's treated. I shall always be a flower girl to Professor Higgins, because he always treats me as a flower girl, and always will, but I know I can be a lady to you, because you always treat me as a lady, and always will.
>
> (Act V)

The sentiment Eliza expresses here is basic social science, addressed more formally by sociologists such as Charles Horton Cooley ("looking-glass self") and George Herbert Mead ("the generalized other"). The basic point is that who we think we are—our *self-concept*—and how we behave are largely a function of how others see and treat us. Further, the way others perceive us is largely conditioned by expectations they have in advance. If they've been told we're stupid, for example, they're likely to see us that way, and we may come to see ourselves that way and actually act stupidly. "Labelling theory" addresses the phenomenon of people acting in accord with the ways they are perceived and labelled by others.

The tendency to see in others what we've been led to expect takes its name from Shaw's play and is called the **Pygmalion effect**. The effect is nicely suited to controlled experiments. In one of the best-known experiments on this topic, Robert Rosenthal and Lenore Jacobson (1968) administered what they called the "Harvard Test of Inflected Acquisition" to students in a school on the west coast of the United States. Subsequently, they met with the students' teachers to present the results of the test. In particular, Rosenthal and Jacobson identified certain students as very likely to exhibit a sudden spurt in academic abilities during the coming year, based on the results of the test.

When IQ test scores were compared later, the researchers' predictions proved accurate. The students identified as "spurters" far exceeded their classmates during the following year, suggesting that the predictive test was a powerful one. In fact, the test was a hoax! The researchers had made their predictions randomly among both good and poor students. What they told the teachers did not really reflect students' test scores at all. The progress made by the "spurters" was simply a result of the teachers expecting the improvement and paying more attention to those students, encouraging them, and rewarding them for achievements. (Notice the similarity between this situation and the Hawthorne effect, mentioned earlier.)

The Rosenthal–Jacobson study attracted a great deal of popular as well as scientific attention. Subsequent experiments have focused on specific aspects of what has become known as the *attribution process*, or the *expectations communication model*. This research, largely conducted by psychologists, parallels research done primarily by sociologists, which takes a slightly different focus and is often gathered under the label *expectations-states theory*. The psychological studies focus on situations in which the expectations of a dominant individual affect the performance of subordinates, as in the case of a teacher and students, or a boss and employees. The sociological research has tended to focus more on the role of expectations among equals in small, task-oriented groups. In a jury, for example, how do jurors initially evaluate each other, and how do those initial assessments affect later interactions?

Here are examples from a pair of recent Canadian experiments whose results may give you pause. The experiments were conducted at York University and concern the use of computers in the university classroom (Sana et al. 2013).

The first experiment was aimed at determining what effect multitasking during a lecture has on learning. The design was aimed at simulating what every university student either sees or does—cruising about different websites when a laptop is purportedly being used to take lecture notes. Here's the experimental setup. All students attending a standardized lecture had laptops. One group was directed to use the laptop exclusively for taking lecture notes. The other group was assigned an additional set of tasks; specifically to, at convenient moments, use the Internet browser to answer 12 simple questions (e.g., "What is on Channel 3 tonight at 10 p.m.?"). At the lecture's close, students completed a multiple-choice comprehension test.

pygmalion effect Differences in study outcomes attributable to the researcher's expectations of participants.

What effect do you think multitasking had on the test results? Does multitasking—like checking Facebook, Google searching, and the like—affect learning positively, negatively, or not at all?

Before we review the results, here is the design of the researchers' second experimental study. Like the first study, the second one was about the effects of distraction. In the first study, the distraction was from using the computer for its designated purpose (note taking). In the second study, the distraction focused on what effect surrounding laptops had on traditional (i.e., pen-and-paper) note takers. In this experiment, students were subjected to the same standardized lecture and multiple-choice comprehension test. The two groups in the second study were traditional note takers who were either (1) seated so that their view included only other traditional note takers or (2) seated so their view included multitasking laptop users. The photographs in Figure 7-5 illustrate the different perspectives.

What effect do you think being surrounded by laptop multitaskers had on traditional note takers' learning? Here are the results of the two experiments. In Experiment 1, laptop users who multitasked achieved 11 percent *lower* learning scores than those who did not allow themselves to be distracted. In Experiment 2, traditional note takers who were distracted by laptop multitaskers scored 17 percent *lower* than their counterparts who were not distracted.

How do these findings fit with your predictions? Remembering that a typical difference in a letter grade (e.g., between a C and a B) is about 10 percent, do you need to reconsider how you discipline your use of the laptop during lectures? What implications do these findings have for the obligations of traditional note takers and laptop multitaskers to one another?

Not in view of a multitasking peer

Source: Ivan Froese

View 1: No Distraction from a Multitasking Peer.

Source: Ivan Froese

FIGURE 7-5 Traditional Note-Takers' Viewpoints.

View 2: Distraction from a Multitasking Peer.

"NATURAL" AND FIELD EXPERIMENTS

Although we tend to equate the terms *experiment* and *laboratory experiment* (as we will soon discuss, the Web is now included as a laboratory), many important social scientific experiments occur outside controlled settings, often in the course of normal social events. Sometimes nature designs and executes experiments that we can observe and analyze; sometimes social and political decision-makers serve this natural function.

Imagine, for example, that a hurricane has struck a particular town. Some residents of the town suffer severe financial damages while others escape relatively lightly. What, we might ask, are the behavioural consequences of suffering a natural disaster? Are those who suffer most more likely to take precautions against future disasters than those who suffer least? To answer these questions, we might interview residents of the town sometime after the hurricane. We might question them regarding their precautions before the hurricane and the ones they're currently taking, comparing the people who suffered greatly from the hurricane with those who suffered relatively little. In this fashion, we might take advantage of a **natural experiment**, which we could not have arranged even if we'd been perversely willing to do so.

A similar example comes from the annals of social research concerning World War II. After the war ended, social researchers undertook retrospective surveys of wartime morale among civilians in several German cities. Among other things, they wanted to determine the effect of mass bombing on the morale of civilians. They compared the reports of wartime morale of residents in heavily bombed cities with reports from cities that received relatively little bombing. (Bombing did not reduce morale.)

Because the researcher must take things pretty much as they occur, natural experiments raise many of the validity problems discussed earlier. Thus, taking special care in the study design is an important step.

Coldevin (1976) was able to take advantage of a unique opportunity to study the impact of the introduction of television into a Canadian Inuit community. In 1972, the CBC initiated the four-hour-a-day Frontier Coverage Package into the Frobisher Bay (now called Iqaluit) community on lower Baffin Island. The study was conducted in 1973 during a break in the programming, prior to the introduction of full-service television in the community:

> The initial survey was intended as both an evaluation of the impact of the Frontier Service and as baseline data toward monitoring the developmental effects of full service television.
> (1976:34)

The goal of the study was to assess whether such television exposure increased the level of national and international information among the community members and to evaluate the effect of television exposure on socioeconomic aspirations, desire for lifestyle change, and preference to travel to a wider range of destinations, among other things. The foundation of the study was open-ended interview questionnaires administered in Inuktitut.

Since the community had access to television for nearly a year, how could any changes due to the effects of television be determined? Coldevin found a control community, Fort Chimo (now called Kuujjuaq), in northern Quebec, to which he could make comparisons. Fort Chimo/Kuujjuaq was a community without television, and it was predominantly Inuit like Frobisher Bay/Iqaluit. In addition, its access to direct outside information was limited.

Coldevin's study design was necessarily based on the idea that the two communities were equivalent to each other except for the existence of television. Since he could not, of course, randomly assign his subjects to the experimental and control groups, he could not assume this. Instead, he compared characteristics of the two communities to see whether they were equivalent. He concluded that "the two samples closely parallel each other on a variety of demographic dimensions and accordingly were considered as

natural experiment An experimental approximation in which group assignment and administration of the independent variable are outside the researcher's control (i.e., occur "naturally").

highly satisfactory for comparison of the primary variables under consideration" (p. 36).

There were other problems that Coldevin had to deal with in trying to control factors in this natural setting. For example, his sample was selected from heads of households on the following basis:

> [T]hey represent the existing link between the traditional, nomadic hunting and fishing culture and the present day relatively stationary community and for the most part have not been exposed to the information resources of the school currently available to their children. It was therefore assumed that the thrust from a relatively information poor to information rich home environment would primarily accrue to the adult segment of the family.
>
> (p. 35)

His analysis also had to take into account the potential impact of the introduction, one month before his survey began, of a weekly bilingual newspaper (English and Inuktitut) in the television community (Iqaluit) but not the community without television (Kuujjuaq).

This example points both to the special problems involved in natural experiments and to the possibility of taking those problems into account. Social research generally requires ingenuity and insight; natural experiments call for a little more than the average.

For those of you who are curious about the outcome, Coldevin found, among other things, that the first year of the Frontier television "had little effect on information levels ... but did affect socioeconomic aspirations" (p. 34). The adults interviewed showed increased aspirations for their children's employment but not for themselves. These increased aspirations were "particularly prominent for daughters" (p. 38).

One advantage of natural experiments is their external validity. Since they occur in natural settings they have fewer problems with generalizability than laboratory experiments conducted in artificial settings. This external validity advantage also occurs with **field experiments**. Field experiments execute experimental designs in real-world conditions. Here's an example related to crime and deviance.

Criminologists argue that social surroundings are an important determinant of deviant conduct. In neighbourhoods with a strong sense of community, the higher level of integration discourages deviance. The opposite situational effect occurs in environments characterized by anonymity and low levels of integration. Philip Zimbardo tested effects of low and high levels of social integration (the independent variable) on deviance (the dependent variable) by abandoning good-condition, used cars in two neighbourhoods. The first neighbourhood, representing low social integration, was a block away from New York University. The second neighbourhood, representing high social integration, was one block away from Stanford University in Palo Alto, California. The cars had their licence plates removed and their hoods raised slightly. At a distance, hidden researchers watched and recorded what happened. Here is Zimbardo's (2007) report:[1]

> The bait worked swiftly in the Bronx [New York]; we had barely gotten our equipment set up from a vantage point in the psychology laboratory across the street, when the first vandals took something from the car. Within 10 minutes of officially beginning this study, the next vandals surfaced—a father, mother and son who stopped their car and proceeded calmly to strip our car of its battery, radiator and the contents of the glove compartment and trunk. The parade of vandals continued for several days, some jacking up the car to steal its tires, or removed its seats or dashboard parts. When there was nothing of value left to strip, random destruction began. In 48 hours, we recorded 23 separate destructive acts by individuals or groups, who either took something from the abandoned vehicle or did something to wreck it.

By contrast, the abandoned car in the high social integration community of Palo Alto experienced no vandalism in the five-day observation period. The fact that this study was conducted on real streets in real communities (external validity) adds to the intuitive appeal of the observed

1 Excerpt of deleted material from *The Lucifer Effect*, by Philip Zimbardo. http://www.lucifereffect.com/about_content.htm. Reprinted by permission of the author.

field experiment The execution of an experimental design in real-world conditions.

differences in how social environments affect deviance. (For a further example of how field experiment results can help increase confidence in the external validity of laboratory results, see the Spotlight on Mixed Methods Research box later in this chapter).

These examples anticipate the subject of Chapter 12, evaluation research, which can be seen as a type of field experiment. As you'll see, evaluation research involves taking the logic of experimentation into the field to observe and evaluate the effects of stimuli in real life. Because this is an increasingly important form of social research, we devote an entire chapter to it.

WEB-BASED EXPERIMENTS

In recent years, Internet use has exploded. The huge number of people connected to the Internet makes it an obvious location for social research. Note, however, that Internet access and use are not equally distributed across groups. A digital divide continues, with different Internet access and use based on age, region, socioeconomic status, and other variables (CIRA 2014). This divide affects the external validity of Web-based experimental findings. Still, Web-based experiments are one important use of this resource. Like all research methods, Web-based experiments have strengths and limitations (Reips 2000).

On the positive side, Web experiments significantly broaden the range of potential participants. Internet users span the international spectrum of genders, races, ethnicities, nationalities, religions, social classes, ages, and the like. This range, assuming it can be captured for participation, gives Web-based experiments an enormous advantage over conventional experiments, which rely on either university students or significantly restricted participant pools. This advantage contains the seeds of a significant disadvantage, which relates to participation. It is challenging for researchers to verify the identities of participants, or to control dropout rates or the seriousness of participation. Online "always-on" digital systems (e.g., Facebook, Amazon) do provide the possibility of enhanced control (including access to background information via administrative and/or user data) to increase internal validity, process data, and cost-effective longitudinal tracking (Salganik 2018). Of course, as discussed in Chapter 1, such unprecedented data availability is accompanied by a host of new and emerging ethical issues.

There are a number of possible forms of Web-based experiment. (For more detailed introductions see, for example, Chen and Konstan (2015) or Salganik, 2018). In this section, we will discuss examples of four basic approaches that involve using an existing online environment, building your own environment, collaborating with an online media company, or using crowdsourcing to conduct your own experiment.

USING EXISTING ONLINE ENVIRONMENTS

We live in a society where success is in large measure determined by the market. For instance, whether you get a good job is determined by how you are evaluated relative to others. How much of such individual success is based on luck and how much is a reflection of meritorious qualities is a matter of serious debate. Conservatives generally think the marketplace provides true reflections of value, while liberals are more skeptical. Inspired by this debate, van de Rijt et al. (2014) used four existing online environments to examine the phenomenon of "cumulative advantage." That is, why do apparently similar individuals experience very different success trajectories, one excelling and succeeding at a much higher level than the other? For example, two artists graduate from the same art school; one toils in relative obscurity, working odd jobs to make ends meet, while the other hits it big, showing their work in major galleries and selling pieces for top dollar. Is it solely due to actual differences in artistic merit between the two? Or might there be some arbitrary initial advantage (e.g., a lucky break) that has set the more successful artist on their favourable path? Van de Rijt and colleagues examined this second possibility, that an early initial success (i.e., positive social feedback) increases the chances of subsequent success (the "success-breeds-success" hypothesis). They conducted random field experiments in four existing online social environments, each with its own market-like reward system (funding, ratings, status, endorsement). In each system, they allocated signals of success (social feedback) to randomly chosen members, as follows:

1. On the crowdfunding website kickstarter.com, where creators of technology and arts or entertainment ventures vie for donations from the general public, the research team sampled 200 new unfunded projects and made donations to 100 randomly selected projects.
2. On the website epinions.com, where reviewers are paid for posting reviews of new products, their rate of pay per review, determined by how helpful their reviews are rated by website visitors, the research team sampled 305 new unrated reviews. Of these, they gave a randomly selected subset a "very helpful" review rating.
3. On the collaborative online encyclopedia website wikipedia.org, where highly productive article editors receive status awards from the community to recognize their contributions to the site, the researchers sampled 521 editors who belonged to the top 1 percent of most productive editors and gave an award to a random subset of them.
4. On the petition website change.org, petitioners seek support for political or social issues by starting petitions that can be signed electronically by supporters. The researchers sampled 200 early-stage campaigns and gave 12 signatures to 100 randomly chosen campaigns.

In each experiment, after randomly selecting the experimental group (those receiving the stimulus, an early initial signal of success), the researchers kept track of all subsequent donations, ratings, awards, and signatures given by the public for both the experimental and control groups. The overall results indicated "that different kinds of success (money, quality ratings, awards and endorsements)," when allocated to randomly chosen recipients, "all produced significant improvements in subsequent rates of success as compared with the control group of nonrecipients" (van de Rijt et al. 2014:6934). But this initial advantage diminished, rather than magnified, across time, suggesting that the cumulative advantage effect might be more modest than thought over the long term.

In another example of working within an existing online environment, Ayres et al. (2015) examined the effect of race of the seller on the sale of baseball cards on eBay. They opened accounts on eBay and auctioned 394 baseball cards (that they had bought there a few weeks earlier). The independent variable was the colour of the hand holding the card in each photo posted on eBay—either a dark-skinned/African-American hand or a light-skinned/Caucasian hand. Their results showed that cards held by African-American sellers sold for approximately 20 percent ($0.90) less than cards held by Caucasian sellers. Similarly, other studies have used existing online social environments to examine a number of interesting phenomena, such as gender differences in mate income preferences on an online dating site (Ong and Wang 2015), the effect of race of guest on Airbnb rentals (Edelman et al. 2016), and the effect of neighbourhood stigma on online classified market sales (Besbris et al. 2015).

CREATING YOUR OWN ONLINE ENVIRONMENT

Another research team interested in examining the social feedback dynamics of cultural markets chose to create their own artificial music market (Salganik et al. 2006; Watts 2012).

The researchers created a website called Music Lab. The site included four dozen songs by new indie bands. Participants in the control group could download any of the songs for free in exchange for their rating of a song's quality. These ratings provided evidence of the "objective" value of each song, since their ratings were independent of any social influence.

In the experimental group, participants could also download and rate songs of their choosing, but beside each selection were two pieces of information. The information included how frequently others had downloaded the song and how the song was rated by others. In this circumstance, ratings were not independent judgments of song quality—they were potentially affected by social feedback.

The researchers found that others' behaviour did affect participants' ratings. In their words, "the 'best' songs never do very badly, and the 'worst' songs never do extremely well, but almost any other result is possible" (Salganik et al. 2006:855). Specifically, for those outside the extremes, the ratings produced enhanced inequalities. The objectively popular songs became much more popular and the least popular songs became much less popular. This finding is important because it indicates that, while objective qualities are important at the extremes, random considerations can otherwise have enormous effects on success.

In another example of building a custom online environment for the purpose of experimental study, Centola (2010) was interested in studying how behaviour spread in an online social network, so he built a Web-based health forum—The Healthy Lifestyle Network—that offered access and ratings tools for online health resources. Participants who joined the network were randomly assigned to one of two experimental conditions—a clustered-lattice network or a random network. This difference in network structure was all that distinguished the two groups. In the clustered network condition, connections were more localized (smaller but tighter/denser networks); in the random network condition, connections were more equally distributed (broader, but thinner/looser networks). Centola introduced different health behaviour messages (e.g., registering for a health forum website) into the networks to observe how they spread. He found, contrary to some prominent theories, that behaviour spread wider and faster across clustered networks than random networks. This finding is significant in that it suggests efforts aimed at spreading public health behaviour messages may do better to focus on clustered residential networks rather than more casual contact networks.

COLLABORATING WITH EXISTING ONLINE ORGANIZATIONS OR COMPANIES

Where van de Rijt et al. (2014) and similar studies simply used information available to consumers/members from social media websites, some researchers have partnered with social media companies or other organizations that run online platforms. Such collaborations have produced studies on a wide range of phenomena, including the effect of anonymity on online dating behaviour (Bapna et al. 2016), the effect of public tweets versus private messages on political mobilization (Coppock et al. 2016), the relationship between trust and participation in the online sharing economy (Abrahao et al. 2017), and the effect of popularity (information on the number of applicants) on job application rates (Gee 2018).

A more high profile and controversial example of collaborating with an existing online platform can be seen in the Kramer et al. (2014) "Emotional Contagion" study on Facebook. Jamie Kramer was a Facebook data scientist and his two co-authors were from Cornell University. This experiment tested whether emotional contagion occurs through social networks. The research asked: Without in-person interaction and nonverbal cues, does the emotional content expressed by others affect your feelings? Here is how the experiment was designed. A sample of 689,003 Facebook users were randomly selected. Then the news feeds of users were manipulated. One group received more positive messages and the other more negative messages. Then the subsequent posts of participants were monitored to see whether those who received more positive messages posted more positive messages, and vice versa. The results were affirmative and provided experimental confirmation for "massive-scale contagion via social networks" (Kramer et al. 2014:8788).

When these interesting results were reported in a leading scientific journal, they provoked a storm of ethical controversy related to the issue of informed consent (Goel 2014; Schuklenk 2014). In the experiment, Facebook users had no idea that their news feeds were being manipulated one way or the other. The ethical debate turned on the following section of the standard Facebook user agreement:

> [W]e may use the information we receive about you . . . for internal operations, including troubleshooting, data analysis, testing, research and service improvement.
>
> (quoted in Schuklenk 2014)

As a user of Facebook, do you think this agreement meets the informed consent criterion? Are you comfortable with your Facebook postings being confidentially monitored based on this disclaimer? Whether conducted on the Web or in the field, in a natural setting or in a laboratory, experiments, like all forms of research, are subject to ethical scrutiny. In this case, the study was conducted by Facebook for internal purposes, and so was not subject to approval by a Cornell University research ethics board.

USING CROWDSOURCING TO CONDUCT ONLINE EXPERIMENTS

Creating your own online environment or partnering with an existing online platform is not always a suitable or feasible option to social researchers. Increasingly, social researchers are using crowdsourcing platforms to select participants for their online surveys and experiments. At base, crowdsourcing involves breaking large or complex tasks into many smaller or simpler pieces of work that can be distributed across many workers. Amazon's Mechanical Turk (MTurk) is arguably the most well-known task crowdsourcing platform. It provides an online marketplace for recruiting workers to accomplish small tasks for pay. MTurk users must register either as a "requester" (task creator) or a "worker" (paid task completer) and it contains a wide variety of tasks that can be completed online, including participating in surveys and experiments (Buhrmester et al. 2011). The use of MTurk to recruit participants in social sciences has grown rapidly in recent years, from 50 papers using MTurk sourced data in 2011 to over 500 articles in 2015 (Chandler and Shapiro 2016).

MTurk enables access to pools of participants in a more timely and cost-effective manner than would otherwise be possible for many researchers (Buhrmester et al. 2018). Researchers can use MTurk's own workspace to set up an internal task (e.g., a survey), or they can provide a link to an external website containing the task (e.g., an experiment). Research has shown that MTurk samples are more demographically diverse than the typical undergraduate convenience samples often used in social science research, although they are still not fully representative of the general population (Chandler and Shapiro 2016). There are a number of tools and strategies that can be used to ensure that the quality of data from MTurk is comparable to other modes of nonprobability sampling (Buhrmester et al. 2011; Chandler and Shapiro, 2016).

MTurk also enables sampling of specific or hard to reach populations (i.e., those with specific characteristics, experiences, conditions). For example, Wohl et al. (2018) used MTurk to recruit participants for two experiments examining whether discontinuity-induced nostalgia affected self-reported willingness to seek help for problem drinking and problem gambling. The basic premise was that cues that induced nostalgia for their former (pre-problem) self would cause individuals with addiction to be more likely to want to change their problematic behaviour in an attempt to recapture their former self. They recruited 180 gamblers for one study and 202 drinkers for the other. In each study, participants were randomly assigned to either the self-discontinuity (experimental) or non-self-discontinuity (control) condition. Self-discontinuity involved reading a short article summarizing the ostensible results of a number of top-tier academic studies. In addition to describing various negative consequences associated with the problem behaviour (heavy gambling or heavy drinking), the article explained "that people who gambled [or drank] heavily reported that their behavior and mood had fundamentally worsened, and that their gambling [or drinking] had led them to dislike the person they had become compared to the person they were before engaging in gambling [or drinking] activities" (p. 85). Individuals in the non-self-discontinuity condition read that "despite heavy gambling [or heavy drinking] leading to an array of negative consequences (e.g., financial and interpersonal problems), gambling [or drinking] does not change people's personalities and behaviors." The results indicated that discontinuity-induced nostalgia did increase reported willingness to change, but only for those with more severe addictive behaviour.

There are also other less well-known platforms for crowdsourcing study participants.

(See Peer et al. 2017 for a review.) For example, LabintheWild is an alternative platform for running online experiments (Reinecke and Gajos, 2015). But unlike MTurk and its ilk, LabintheWild does not pay participants. Instead, in exchange for participating, it provides participants with personalized feedback, including the ability to compare themselves to others (the incentive is entertaining self-knowledge). LabintheWild also purports to attract a more diverse pool of participants from a greater range of countries than MTurk, where the vast majority of respondents are from the United States or India (Paolacci et al. 2010).

SPOTLIGHT ON MIXED METHODS RESEARCH

Mixing Laboratory and Field Experiments within the Same Study

As discussed in Chapter 1, mixing research methods typically refers to some combination of quantitative and qualitative approaches within the same study. But it is also possible to mix different quantitative (or qualitative) methods within the same study. For example, Correll et al. (2007) combined two different quantitative approaches (a laboratory experiment and a field experiment) to study the sources of the "motherhood penalty" on wages. There is evidence of bias against mothers in the labour market, since mothers tend to earn less than women who have no children, even when controlling for skill and job type. (Interestingly, the opposite appears true for men, with fathers typically out-earning their childless counterparts).

First, Correll and colleagues (2007) conducted a lab experiment in which participants (university undergrads) were tasked with making recommendations to a company looking to fill a management position. The participants were asked to review resumés and to rate candidates on a number of dimensions, including intelligence, commitment, and whether they would recommend hiring a candidate. They were also asked to suggest a starting salary. The independent variable was whether the candidate was a mother or not—the resumés were the same except some signalled motherhood (listed participation in a parent-teacher association) while others did not. They found that participants were less likely to recommend hiring mothers and also suggested lower starting salaries for mothers. Furthermore, the statistical analysis suggested that this discrepancy was due to the fact that mothers tended to be rated lower on both competence and commitment.

Given concerns about the external validity of a lab experiment with a couple of hundred undergrads, the researchers followed up with an audit study. An audit study is a field study that combines aspects of experimental design with real-world settings, but the participants are real people who make real decisions, such as whether to hire someone. Audit studies have often been used to study forms of discrimination (Baldassarri and Abascal 2017). The idea is that audit studies can provide greater external validity by allowing in-context insight into the social and cognitive processes of real-world participants who are unaware they are participating in a study. Increasingly, such audit studies are being conducted using the Internet (e.g., Blommaert et al. 2014; Gaddis 2015; Lauster and Easterbrook 2011).

In their audit study, Correll and colleagues (2007) responded to hundreds of advertised job openings with fabricated cover letters and resumés. Consistent with the lab experiment, all the resumés and cover letters were the same except some signalled motherhood and some did not. They found that mothers were less likely to receive job interview offers than were equally qualified nonmothers. Thus, the decisions of real employers in the actual job market converged with those of the undergrads in the laboratory study, increasing the degree of confidence researchers can place in their results.

ETHICAL CONSIDERATIONS

In Chapter 3, we provided illustrations of ethical concerns arising from experiments. Potential for harm in some research methods is higher than in others. Experiments are particularly vulnerable to ethical breaches due to the degree of manipulation of subjects by researchers.

We discussed the Milgram experiment at length in Chapter 3, a psychological study concerning obedience to authority that raised many ethical issues, including the potential for psychological harm. Almost a decade after Milgram's study, Zimbardo led what is called the Stanford Prison Experiment. This experiment also raised many ethical concerns. An experiment regarding the psychology of imprisonment was supposed to last for two weeks. Student volunteers, chosen for their "normal" scores on personality tests, were assigned the roles of guards and prisoners in a mock prison. The researchers stopped the experiment after six days due to the risk of long-term psychological harm and immediate physical harm to the research subjects. A 50-minute documentary, *Quiet Rage* (Zimbardo and Musen 1992), illustrates the transformation of the research subjects over the six days through edited clips of the experiment. The film also presents follow-up interviews with some of the subjects, and it explores the ethical dimension of the study. It's a good documentary that is worth watching and discussing. You may also learn more about this experiment and some of the problems the researchers encountered when conducting it at http://www.prisonexp.org/.

The rise of online experimental research brings additional ethical considerations to the fore. For example, when using crowdsourcing platforms such as MTurk to sample participants, it is difficult to provide access to local mental health support if needed, or to debrief participants. There are also issues related to poor pay for workers, and the fact that MTurk workers are not actually anonymous—their worker ID is their Amazon ID and may be linked to personal identifying information accessible via profiles or product reviews on Amazon (Chandler and Shapiro 2016).

Finally, consider the experiments used as illustrations in this chapter. Did any ethical concerns cross your mind when you were reading about them? For example, what did you think when you read about Rosenthal and Jacobson's study? It's likely that you thought about the effect of such a study on the students. Did you stop to weigh the importance of their findings against the impact of their hoax on the subjects? If you were sitting on a review ethics board, what might your response be to the proposal of such a study?

STRENGTHS AND WEAKNESSES OF THE EXPERIMENTAL METHOD

The great strength of experiments is that they are a model method for studying causal relationships. Causal relationships, in turn, are the gold standard for explanation within quantitative research. As you learned in Chapter 4, demonstrating that an independent variable "causes" changes in a dependent variable requires that three criteria be met. The first criterion is sequence or time-ordering, which states that the independent variable must change prior to observed changes in the dependent variable. This criterion is met within the experimental design because the researcher administers the independent variable before observing dependent variable changes. The second causal criterion is association or correlation, which states that the variables must change together systematically. This is evident in experimental designs by detecting systematic differences in the experimental and control groups attributable to the administration of the independent variable. The third causal criterion is nonspuriousness or authenticity, which states that the observed association between the independent and dependent variable is not due to any other variables. Experimental designs meet this criterion by ensuring that experimental and control groups are initially equivalent on all relevant variables, so that later posttesting differences are attributable only to changes in the independent variable.

In addition, since individual experiments are often rather limited in scope, requiring relatively little time and money and relatively few subjects, we can often replicate a given experiment several times using several different groups of subjects.

(This isn't always the case, of course, but it's usually easier to repeat experiments than, say, surveys.) As in all other forms of scientific research, replication of research findings strengthens our confidence in the validity and generalizability of those findings.

Despite the power of experiments in meeting causal criteria and their replicability, the method carries serious limitations. The greatest weakness of laboratory experiments lies in their artificiality. Social processes that occur in a laboratory setting might not necessarily occur in more natural social settings. For example, a film on the history of Indigenous Canadians might genuinely reduce prejudice among a group of experimental subjects. This would not necessarily mean, however, that the same film shown in neighbourhood movie theatres throughout the country would reduce prejudice among the general public. Artificiality is not as much of a problem, of course, for natural experiments as for those conducted in the laboratory. Experiments are also limited in their units of analysis. Most social science experiments use microlevel units—individuals—as subjects. But much of sociology concerns larger-scale units of analysis such as cities, regions, or nations. These more macro-scale units are rarely available to experimentation.

When research conditions allow, experiments are powerful research tools in the quantitative research tradition. Experiments establish credible causal links between independent and dependent variables better than any other approach. That is why they are the gold standard in natural science fields (e.g., biology, medicine) and in social science fields (e.g., psychology) that aspire to the natural science model. Experimental research is less common in sociology, although, as we have seen, important work is being done where this method is appropriate. As we shall see in Chapter 8, the widely prevalent use of survey methods uses an approximation of the experimental model.

MAIN POINTS

- Experiments are an excellent vehicle for the controlled testing of causal processes.
- The classical experiment tests the effect of an experimental stimulus (the independent variable) on a dependent variable through the pretesting and posttesting of experimental and control groups.
- It's generally less important that a group of experimental subjects be representative of some larger population than that experimental and control groups be similar to each other.
- A double-blind experiment guards against experimenter bias because neither the experimenter nor the subject knows which subjects are in the control and experimental groups.
- Probability sampling, random assignment, and matching are all methods of achieving comparability in the experimental and control groups. Random assignment is the generally preferred method. In some designs, it can be combined with matching.
- Campbell and Stanley list 12 of the sources of internal invalidity in experimental design. The classical experiment with random assignment of subjects guards against each of these 12 sources of internal invalidity.
- Experiments also face problems of external invalidity: experimental findings may not reflect real life.
- The interaction of testing with the stimulus is an example of external invalidity that the classical experiment does not guard against.
- The Solomon four-group design and other variations on the classical experiment can safeguard against external invalidity.
- Campbell and Stanley suggest that, given proper randomization in the assignment of subjects to the experimental and control groups, there is no need for pretesting in experiments.

- Natural experiments often occur in the course of social life in the real world, and social researchers can implement them in somewhat the same way they would design and conduct laboratory experiments.
- It is becoming increasingly common for researchers to use the Web as a place to conduct social science experiments.
- Experiments are particularly vulnerable to ethical breaches due to the degree of manipulation of subjects by researchers.
- Experiments, like all research methods, have both strengths and weaknesses. Their primary weakness is artificiality. What happens in an experiment may not reflect what happens in the outside world. Their strengths include scientific rigour; the isolation of the independent variable, which permits causal inferences; and the relative ease of replication.

REVIEW QUESTIONS AND EXERCISES

1. Find an article that reports the results of an experiment. Briefly state the goal of the experiment, and then identify the stimulus and dependent variable.
2. Think of a recent natural disaster you've witnessed or read about. Frame a research question that might be studied by treating that disaster as a natural experiment. In two or three paragraphs, outline how the study might be done.
3. Pick 6 of the 12 sources of internal invalidity discussed in the book and make up examples (not discussed in the book) to illustrate each.
4. In this chapter, we looked briefly at the problem of the effects of using placebos in experiments. On the Web, find a study in which the effect of using a placebo figured importantly. Write a brief report on the study, including the source of your information. (*Hint*: You might want to do a search for *placebo*.)

CONTINUITY PROJECT

"LOSERS" AND STRESS

At all levels, systems that generate inequalities create winners and losers. This is as true of international systems like globalization as it is of a local hockey game. The labels "winner" and "loser" designate inequality.

Losing is stressful and stress is not good for well-being. Researchers have determined that cortisol levels in saliva are a reliable marker of stress. Simple swabs in a person's mouth are a sufficient measurement tool.

Evaluation in university classes is a notorious source of stress for students. Imagine you are tasked with conducting an experiment to determine whether different kinds of assessment affect levels of student stress. The independent variable is "kind of assessment," where the conditions are "high stress" and "low stress." The dependent variable is "student stress."

Design a classical experiment to determine whether different kinds of assessment affect stress levels. Specifically, answer the following questions:

1. How will you create "high stress" and "low stress" assessment conditions?
2. What steps will you take to ensure the subjects in each group are comparable?
3. What justification do you have for thinking your design has external validity?

Chris Ryan/OJO Images/Getty Images

SURVEY RESEARCH

Researchers have many methods for collecting data through surveys, such as mail questionnaires, personal interviews, or online surveys conducted over the Internet. Social researchers should know how to select an appropriate method and how to implement it effectively.

IN THIS CHAPTER ...

INTRODUCTION

Survey research is a very old research technique. The oldest known census was conducted by the Babylonians nearly 6000 years ago in 3800 BCE. Ancient Persian and Egyptian rulers took censuses to help them administer their domains, as did the Roman Empire. The oldest existing census data is from the Han Dynasty, taken two millennia ago in the year 2 CE. William the Conqueror undertook a comprehensive survey—known as the *Domesday Book*—of his newly acquired kingdom (England) in 1086 CE.

Relatively more recently, a little-known survey was attempted among French workers in 1880. A German political sociologist mailed some 25,000 questionnaires to workers to determine the extent of their exploitation by employers. The rather lengthy questionnaire included items such as these:

> Does your employer or his representative resort to trickery in order to defraud you of a part of your earnings?
>
> If you are paid piece rates, is the quality of the article made a pretext for fraudulent deductions from your wages?

The survey researcher in this case was not George Gallup but Karl Marx ([1880] 1956:208). Though 25,000 questionnaires were mailed out, there is no record of any being returned.

Today, survey research is a frequently used mode of observation in the social sciences. In a typical survey, the researcher selects a sample of respondents and administers a standardized questionnaire to them. Chapter 6 discussed sampling techniques in detail. This chapter discusses how to prepare a questionnaire and describes the various options for administering it so that respondents answer your questions adequately.

Let's begin by looking at the kinds of topics that researchers can appropriately study using survey research.

TOPICS APPROPRIATE TO SURVEY RESEARCH

Chapter 2 introduced you to the qualitative and quantitative research traditions. The qualitative tradition is interpretive, uses small samples, and relies on a flexible, inductive approach to generate authentic, context-specific narratives of people, situations, and events. By contrast, the quantitative tradition rests on a traditional model of science. It uses a structured, deductive approach to empirically test theoretical propositions and hypotheses using large, representative samples.

Survey methods are embedded in the quantitative research tradition, where the focus is on identifying and measuring variables for descriptive or explanatory purposes. Surveys are chiefly used in studies that have individual people as the units of analysis. Although this method can be used for other units of analysis, such as groups or interactions, some individual persons must serve as **respondents** or informants. We could undertake a survey in which divorces were the unit of analysis, but we would need to administer the survey questionnaire to the participants in the divorces (or to some other respondents).

Survey research is probably the best method available to the social scientist interested in collecting original data for describing a population too large to observe directly. Careful probability sampling provides a group of respondents whose characteristics may be taken to reflect those of the larger population, and carefully constructed standardized questionnaires provide data in the same form from all respondents.

Surveys are also excellent vehicles for measuring attitudes and orientations in a large population. Public opinion polls—such as Léger, Ipsos, Nanos, EKOS, Harris/Decima, and Environics—are well-known examples of this use.

Indeed, polls have become so prevalent that at times the public seems unsure what to think of them. Pollsters are criticized by those who don't think (or don't want to believe) that polls are accurate (candidates who are "losing" in polls often tell voters not to trust the polls). But polls are also criticized for being *too* accurate—for example, when exit polls on election day are used to predict a winner before the voting is complete.

The general attitude toward public opinion research is further complicated by scientifically

respondent A person who provides data for analysis by responding to a survey questionnaire.

unsound "surveys" that nonetheless capture people's attention because of the topics they cover and/or their findings. A good example may be found in the Hite Reports on human sexuality. While enjoying considerable attention in the popular press, the writer Shere Hite was roundly criticized by the research community for her data-collection methods. For example, a 1987 Hite report was based on questionnaires completed by women around the United States— but *which* women? Hite reported that she distributed some 100,000 questionnaires through various organizations, and around 4,500 were returned. Now 4,500 and 100,000 are large numbers in the context of survey sampling. However, given Hite's research methods, her 4,500 respondents didn't necessarily represent American women any more than the *Literary Digest*'s enormous 1936 sample represented the U.S. electorate when their 2 million sample ballots indicated Landon would bury Roosevelt in a landslide.

Sometimes, people use the pretence of survey research for quite different purposes. For example, you may have received a telephone call indicating you've been selected for a survey, only to find the first question was "How would you like to make thousands of dollars a week right there in your own home?" Unfortunately, a few unscrupulous telemarketers do try to prey on the general cooperation people have given to survey researchers.

By the same token, political parties and charitable organizations have begun conducting phony surveys. Often under the guise of collecting public opinion about some issue, callers ultimately ask respondents to donate money.

Political campaigns have produced another form of bogus survey, called the **push poll**. Push polls seem like surveys, but they aren't. Rather than gathering information, their goal is to influence respondents' attitudes and opinions. These are not scientific tools; they are political marketing instruments.

push poll A telephone survey designed to influence respondents' attitudes and opinions for political purposes.

questionnaire A research instrument containing questions and other types of items designed to gather information about specific variables.

In short, the labels "survey" and "poll" are sometimes misused. When done properly, however, survey research is one of the most valuable tools of social inquiry. For example, there are countless survey studies conducted concerning issues such as public attitudes toward crime and justice, abortion, and government. Large surveys are conducted to determine the amount of victimization in a society, the degree of violence against women, the use of public services, perceptions of satisfaction and happiness, engagement in cultural activities, and participation in sports, for example. They are also conducted to collect information on issues of employment, income, job benefits, healthcare experiences, the use of alcohol, smoking, support networks, division of household work, occupational and emotional health, and so forth. Statistics Canada conducts a large number of national surveys, some annually, concerning issues such as these.

Designing useful (and trustworthy) survey research begins with formulating good questions. Let's turn to that topic now.

GUIDELINES FOR ASKING QUESTIONS

In quantitative social research, concepts are identified to express what the researcher has in mind. Concepts are then translated into variables through the process of operationalization. In survey research, operationalization involves the construction of a **questionnaire**—an instrument specifically designed to elicit information to measure the variables under consideration.

To illustrate the process of operationalization in survey research, imagine that you wanted to measure "alienation." For sociologists, the conceptual definition of alienation specifies that it is the experience of "estrangement of individuals from one another, or from a specific situation or process" (Scott and Marshall 2005:12). Several variables are available to indicate alienation. For example, in his classic study, Seeman (1959) proposes five dimensions of alienation: powerlessness, meaninglessness, normlessness, isolation, and self-estrangement. Our example will focus on the powerlessness variable. In surveys, the instrument that contains the variables is the questionnaire, specifically the items on the questionnaire. In our example, five questions are used to measure the variable "powerlessness." Figure 8-1 lists the possible response categories. When the survey questionnaire is administered, each respondent's answers to the questions constitute a measure of powerlessness. The collection of respondents' answers comprises the empirical data used for quantitative analysis.

Given the centrality of the questionnaire, careful construction of this instrument is critical to effective survey research. While some of the specific points to follow are more appropriate to structured questionnaires than to the interview guides used in qualitative, in-depth interviewing, the underlying logic is valuable whenever we ask people questions in order to gather data.

Before moving on to consider the details of questionnaire items, we must highlight an important point. In Figure 8-1, notice that questionnaire items included on a survey occur in a context. Specifically, the questionnaire items are carefully constructed measures of a variable. Moreover, the variable is a carefully considered reflection of a concept a researcher has in mind. In short, survey questions are part of the larger operational definition process of trying to measure an abstract concept. Without this context, what the questionnaire items (and the associated responses gathered from respondents) mean is up for grabs. Which leads to the following advice: *Questionnaire items should never be included "because they are interesting."* Neglecting this advice is a common fault in many surveys. To their chagrin, many organizations have learned how useless questionnaire results can be unless they are embedded in a process that links the items to variables and the variables to concepts. Questionnaire items should always be justified by their links to variables and associated concepts. Without this linkage, surveys are being conducted without clear purpose, which is a waste of everyone's valuable resources.

With this advice in mind, let's consider several general guidelines to help you frame and ask questions that serve as excellent measures of variables while avoiding pitfalls that can result in useless or even misleading information.

CHOOSE APPROPRIATE QUESTION FORMS

Let's begin with some of the options available to you in creating questionnaires. These options include using questions or statements and choosing open-ended or closed-ended questions.

Possible respondent scores in brackets:	Questions	Answer
1) Do you feel that most things that happen to you are a result of your own decisions or of things over which you have no control?	Own decisions ❑ [0]	No control ❑ [1]
2) I generally have confidence that when I make plans I will be able to carry them out.	Agree ❑ [0]	Disagree ❑ [1]
3) There are things that I can do that might affect national policy.	Agree ❑ [0]	Disagree ❑ [1]
4) How often do you feel powerless to get what you want out of life?	Rarely ❑ [0]	Frequently ❑ [1]

FIGURE 8-1 **Operational Definition in Surveys.**
*Example questionnaire items from Kohn and Schooler (1983) "Powerlessness Scale."

Questions and Statements Although the term *questionnaire* suggests a collection of **questions**, an examination of a typical questionnaire will probably reveal as many **statements** as questions. This is not without reason. Often, the researcher is interested in determining the extent to which respondents hold a particular attitude or perspective. If you can summarize the attitude in a fairly brief statement, you can present that statement and ask respondents whether they agree or disagree with it. Rensis Likert greatly formalized this procedure through the creation of the Likert scale (see Chapter 5), a format in which respondents are asked to strongly agree, agree, disagree, or strongly disagree, or perhaps strongly approve, approve, and so forth.

Both questions and statements may be used profitably. Using both in a given questionnaire gives you more flexibility in the design of items, and it can make the questionnaire more interesting.

OPEN-ENDED AND CLOSED-ENDED QUESTIONS

In asking questions, researchers have two options. They may ask **open-ended questions**, in which case the respondent is asked to provide their own answer to the question. For example, the respondent may be asked, "What do you feel is the most important issue facing Canada today?" and be provided with a space to write in the answer (or be asked to report it verbally to an interviewer). As we'll see in Chapter 11, in-depth, qualitative interviewing relies almost exclusively on open-ended questions. However, this type of question is also used in survey research.

In the case of **closed-ended questions**, the respondent is asked to select an answer from among a list provided by the researcher. Closed-ended questions are very popular in survey research because they provide a greater uniformity of responses and are more easily processed.

Open-ended responses must be coded before they can be processed for computer analysis, as will be discussed in Chapter 14. This coding process often requires that the researcher interpret the meaning of responses, raising the possibility of misunderstanding and researcher bias. There is also a danger that some respondents will give answers that are essentially irrelevant to the researcher's intent. Closed-ended responses, on the other hand, can often be transferred directly into a computer format.

The chief shortcoming of closed-ended questions lies in the researcher's structuring of responses. When the relevant answers to a given question are relatively clear, there should be no problem. In other cases, however, the researcher's structuring of responses may overlook some important responses. In asking about "the most important issue facing Canada," for example, his or her checklist of issues might omit certain issues that respondents would have said were important.

The construction of closed-ended questions should be guided by two structural requirements, initially introduced in Chapter 5. First, the response categories provided should be **exhaustive**: they should include all the possible responses that might be expected. Often, researchers ensure this by adding a category such as "Other (Please specify: ______)." Second, the answer categories must be **mutually exclusive**: the respondent should not feel compelled to select more than one. (In some cases, you may wish to solicit multiple answers, but these may create difficulties in data processing and analysis later on.) To ensure that your categories are

question An interrogative sentence that asks for information or clarification.

statement A declarative sentence that provides an opinion or observation.

open-ended questions Questions to which respondents are asked to provide their own answers. Qualitative in-depth interviewing relies heavily on open-ended questions, but they are sometimes used in other forms of data collection such as telephone surveys and self-administered questionnaires.

closed-ended questions Questions to which the respondent is asked to select an answer from among a list provided by the researcher. These are popular in survey research because they provide a greater uniformity of responses and are more easily processed than open-ended questions.

exhaustive A property of a variable ensuring that all objects can be classified.

mutually exclusive A property of a variable ensuring that every object can be classified into only one attribute.

mutually exclusive, carefully consider each combination of categories, asking yourself whether a person could reasonably choose more than one answer. In addition, it's useful to add an instruction to the question asking the respondent to select the one best answer, but such an instruction should not be used as a substitute for a carefully constructed set of responses.

MAKE ITEMS CLEAR

It should go without saying that questionnaire items should be clear and unambiguous, but the broad proliferation of unclear and ambiguous questions in surveys makes the point worth emphasizing. Often, we can become so deeply involved in the topic under examination that opinions and perspectives are clear to us but not to our respondents, many of whom have paid little or no attention to the topic. Or if we have only a superficial understanding of the topic, we may fail to specify the intent of a question sufficiently. The question "What do you think about the proposed peace plan?" may evoke in the respondent a counter-question: "Which proposed peace plan?" Questionnaire items should be precise so that the respondent knows exactly what the researcher is asking.

The possibilities for misunderstanding are endless and no researcher is immune. For example, a study to determine the accuracy of a survey conducted by the U.S. Census Bureau found that some questions used to determine the nation's employment patterns were ambiguous. When the Census Bureau asked questions about activities during the "last week," they meant Sunday through Saturday. Yet more than half the respondents took "last week" to include only Monday through Friday. By the same token, whereas they define "working full-time" as 35 or more hours a week, the same evaluation studies showed respondents using the more traditional definition of 40 hours per week. These findings resulted in modification of the questions to specify the Census Bureau's definitions. A look at the *Canadian Census Dictionary* shows that many employment questions concern information about a respondent's activities during the "last week," which Statistics Canada also defines as Sunday through Saturday. When inquiring about full- versus part-time employment, however, a full-time week is defined by Statistics Canada as 30 or more hours.

AVOID DOUBLE-BARRELLED QUESTIONS

Frequently, researchers ask respondents for a single answer to a question that actually has multiple parts. That seems to happen most often when the researcher has personally identified with a complex question. For example, you might ask respondents to agree or disagree with the statement "Canada should spend less money on welfare programs and more money on education." Although many people would unequivocally agree with the statement and others would unequivocally disagree, still others would be unable to answer. For example, some would want to cut welfare spending and use the money to reduce taxes. Others would want to continue spending the same amount on welfare programs and spend more money on education. These latter respondents could neither agree nor disagree without misleading you.

As a general rule, whenever the word *and* appears in a question or questionnaire statement, check whether you're asking a double-barrelled question.

RESPONDENTS MUST BE COMPETENT TO ANSWER

In asking respondents to provide information, you should continually ask yourself whether they are able to do so reliably. In a study of childrearing, you might ask respondents to report the age at which the child first talked back to their parents. Quite aside from the problem of defining *talking back to parents*, it's doubtful that most respondents would remember with any degree of accuracy.

As another example, student government leaders occasionally ask their constituents to indicate how students' fees ought to be spent. Typically, respondents are asked to indicate the percentage of available funds that should be devoted to a long list of activities. Without a fairly good knowledge of the activities and their costs, the respondents cannot provide meaningful answers.

One group of researchers examining the driving experience of teenagers insisted on asking an open-ended question concerning the number of kilometres driven since receiving a licence. Although consultants argued that few drivers would be able to estimate such information with any accuracy, the question was asked nonetheless. In response, some teenagers reported driving hundreds of thousands of kilometres.

RESPONDENTS MUST BE WILLING TO ANSWER

Often, we would like to learn things from people that they are unwilling to share with us. For example, Yanjie Bian indicated that it has often been difficult to get candid answers from people in China:

> [Here] people are generally careful about what they say on nonprivate occasions in order to survive under authoritarianism. During the Cultural Revolution between 1966 and 1976, for example, because of the radical political agenda and political intensity throughout the country, it was almost impossible to use survey techniques to collect valid and reliable data inside China about the Chinese people's life experiences, characteristics, and attitudes towards the Communist regime.
>
> (Bian 1994:19–20)

Sometimes, North American respondents may say they are undecided when, in fact, they have an opinion but think they are in a minority. Under that condition, they may be reluctant to tell a stranger (the interviewer) what that opinion is. Given this problem, the Gallup Organization, for example, has used a "secret ballot" format, which simulates actual election conditions, in that the "voter" enjoys complete anonymity. In an analysis of the Gallup poll election data from 1944 to 1988, Andrew Smith and G. F. Bishop (1992) found that this technique substantially reduced the percentage saying they were undecided about how they would vote.

The emergence of computer tablets provides an alternative approach to dealing with respondents' reluctance to provide face-to-face answers to sensitive questions. Using computer-assisted personal interviewing (CAPI), the interviewer simply hands the tablet containing the sensitive question to the respondent, who then answers privately. The tablet is then returned to the interviewer, who proceeds to complete the survey. We discuss CAPI in more detail later in this chapter.

QUESTIONS SHOULD BE RELEVANT

Similarly, questions asked in a questionnaire should be relevant to most respondents. When attitudes are requested on a topic that few respondents have thought about or really care about, the results are not likely to be very useful. Of course, because the respondents may express attitudes even though they've never given any thought to the issue, you run the risk of being misled.

This point is illustrated occasionally when researchers ask for responses relating to fictitious people and issues. In one political poll a Canadian colleague conducted, respondents were asked whether they were familiar with each of 15 political figures in the community. As a methodological exercise, the fictitious candidate Tom Sakumoto was included. In response, 9 percent of the respondents said they were familiar with him. About half of the respondents reporting familiarity with him also reported seeing him on TV and reading about him in the newspapers.

When you obtain responses to fictitious issues, you can disregard those responses. But when the issue is real, you may have no way of telling which responses genuinely reflect attitudes and which reflect meaningless answers to an irrelevant question.

Ideally, we would like respondents to simply report that they don't know, have no opinion, or are undecided in instances where that is the case. Unfortunately, however, they often make up answers.

SHORT ITEMS ARE BEST

In the interests of being unambiguous, being precise, and pointing to the relevance of an issue, researchers tend to create long and complicated items. This should be avoided. Respondents are often unwilling to study an item in order to understand it. The respondent should be able to read an item quickly, understand its intent, and select or provide an answer without difficulty.

In general, assume that respondents will read items quickly and give quick answers. Accordingly, provide clear, short items that will not be misinterpreted under those conditions.

AVOID NEGATIVE ITEMS

The appearance of a negation in a questionnaire item paves the way for easy misinterpretation. Asked to agree or disagree with the statement "Canada should not support UN peacekeeping missions," a sizeable portion of the respondents will read over the word *not* and answer on that basis. Thus, some will agree with the statement when they're in favour of support, and others will agree when they oppose it. And you may never know which is which.

Similar considerations apply to other negative-type words. In a study of civil liberties support, respondents were asked whether they felt "the following kinds of people should be *prohibited* from teaching in public schools" and were presented with a list including such items as a Communist, a Ku Klux Klansman, and so forth. The response categories "yes" and "no" were given beside each entry. A comparison of the responses to this item with other items reflecting support for civil liberties strongly suggested that many respondents gave the answer "yes" to indicate willingness for such a person to teach, rather than to indicate that such a person should be prohibited from teaching. (A later study in the series giving as answer categories "permit" and "prohibit" produced much clearer results.)

AVOID BIASED ITEMS AND TERMS

Recall from our discussion of conceptualization and operationalization in Chapters 2 and 5 that there are no ultimately true meanings for any of the concepts we typically study in social science. *Prejudice* has no ultimately true definition; whether a given person is prejudiced depends on our definition of that term. This same general principle applies to the responses we get from people completing a questionnaire.

The meaning of someone's response to a question depends in large part on its wording. This is true of every question and answer. Some questions seem to encourage particular responses more than do other questions. When this happens, bias enters the research. Recall from Chapter 6 that bias refers to systematic error. **Questionnaire bias** occurs when a property of questions or statements encourages respondents to answer in a particular way. Questions that contain bias are also referred to as "loaded questions" or "leading questions."

Most researchers recognize the likely effect of a question that begins "Don't you agree with the prime minister of Canada that ..." and no reputable researcher would use such an item. Unhappily, the biasing effect of items and terms is far subtler than this example suggests.

The mere identification of an attitude or position with a prestigious person or agency can bias responses. The item "Do you agree or disagree with the recent Supreme Court decision that ..." would have a similar effect. Such wording may not produce consensus or even a majority in support of the position identified with the prestigious person or agency, but it will likely increase the level of support over what would have been obtained without such identification.

Sometimes the impact of different forms of question wording is relatively subtle. For example, the use of certain words or terms can affect the outcome of responses. As a result, different ways of asking questions are often tested and evaluated. There have been several demonstrations, for instance, that people are less likely to indicate support for "welfare" programs and more likely to indicate support for social programs that are intended to assist the "poor" or reduce "poverty."

Statistics Canada illustrates how the wording of a question can affect the results as follows:[1]

1 Statistics Canada, *Toronto Area Survey 1991*, an annual survey conducted by the Institute for Social Research at York University. http://www.statcan.gc.ca/edu/power-pouvoir/ch2/questionnaires/5214775-eng.htm. Accessed July 1, 2015. Reproduced and distributed on an "as is" basis with the permission of Statistics Canada.

questionnaire bias A form of systematic error that occurs when properties of questions or statements encourage responses in a particular direction.

In your opinion, should Sunday shopping be allowed in Ontario; that is, should stores that want to stay open on Sunday be allowed to stay open on Sundays if they want to?

Results:

73%	In favour of Sunday shopping
25%	Opposed to Sunday shopping
2%	No opinion

In your opinion, should a Sunday pause day be adopted in Ontario; that is, should the government make Sunday the one uniform day a week when most people do not have to work?

Results:

50%	Opposed to a Sunday pause day
44%	In favour of a Sunday pause day
6%	No opinion

Questions are often tested to determine the quality of data obtained from them. Statistics Canada has published numerous reports detailing the outcome of their research on potential questions for use in the Canadian census and other surveys they conduct. Reading through such reports provides valuable insights into the kinds of issues that must be considered in developing useful questions. For example, a series of questions directed at measuring the impact on labour market participation of giving and getting unpaid care were tested in the Survey of Labour and Income Dynamics (SLID) interview. The researchers were concerned with both the respondents' reactions to and understanding of the questions. The research report, therefore, discussed issues such as the following:[2]

> Respondents did not like to say how many hours they helped others who needed help and could not understand why we asked. They didn't like to call it "unpaid help" and did not want anyone to think that they would have wanted to work rather than help those in need.
>
> (Saint-Pierre 1995)

In this context, be wary of what researchers call the **social desirability** of questions and answers. Whenever you ask people for information, they answer through a filter of what will make them look good. This is especially true if they're interviewed face to face. Thus, for example, a particular man may feel that things would be a lot better if women were kept in the kitchen, not allowed to vote, forced to be quiet in public, and so forth. Asked whether he supports equal rights for women, however, he may want to avoid looking sexist. Recognizing that his views are out of step with current thinking, he may choose to say "yes."

In research conducted by Kreuter and colleagues (2008), respondents were found to be most likely to provide information that did not reflect well on them via an Internet survey, less likely when interviewed by an interactive recording, and least likely to provide such information when questioned in a conventional telephone interview.

The best way to guard against this problem is to imagine how you would feel giving each of the answers you intend to offer to respondents. If you would feel embarrassed, perverted, inhumane, stupid, irresponsible, or otherwise socially disadvantaged by any particular response, give serious thought to how willing others will be to give those answers.

The biasing effect of particular wording is often difficult to anticipate. In both surveys and experiments, it's sometimes useful to ask respondents to consider hypothetical situations and say how they think they would behave in such situations. Because those situations often involve other people, the names used can affect responses. For example, researchers have long known that male names for the hypothetical people may produce different responses than do female names. Research by Joseph Kasof (1993) points to the importance of what the specific names are whether they generally evoke positive or negative images with regard to attractiveness, age, intelligence, and so forth. Kasof's review of

2 Yves Saint-Pierre, *Household Surveys Division, Statistics Canada, Questions Relating to Social Support: Results from the SLID January 1993 Test*, Catalogue No. 93-13. Reproduced and distributed on an "as is" basis with the permission of Statistics Canada.

social desirability A form of bias occurring when respondents answer with socially acceptable views rather than their own.

past research suggests there has been a tendency to use more positively valued names for men than for women.

As in all other research, carefully examine the purpose of your inquiry and construct items that will be most useful to it. You should never be misled into thinking there are ultimately "right" and "wrong" ways of asking the questions. When in doubt about the best question to ask, moreover, remember that you should ask more than one.

These, then, are some general guidelines for writing questions to elicit data for analysis and interpretation. Before we turn to how to construct questionnaires, a bit of caution is advised. Writing good questions is important, but interpreting responses, even when a clear, straightforward question is asked, requires logic and thought. For example, when asked whether Canada should be a leader in peacekeeping efforts around the world, 82 percent of Canadians agreed, according to the *Maclean's* year-end poll. Does this translate into support for greater military spending? Well, as *Maclean's* points out, not necessarily. In the same poll when the public was asked to choose between putting more money into strengthening and updating the military versus investing in housing for Canada's homeless population, 75 percent chose housing for the homeless over the military (*Maclean's* 2000–2001:30).

QUESTIONNAIRE CONSTRUCTION

Questionnaires are used in connection with many modes of observation in social research. Although structured questionnaires are essential to and most directly associated with survey research, they're also widely used in experiments, field research, and other data-collection activities. For this reason, questionnaire construction can be an important practical skill for researchers. Until recently, questionnaires were constructed and administered on paper. Now they are offered through a variety of platforms, including online versions. The fundamentals of good questionnaire construction are largely independent of format. As we discuss the established techniques for constructing questionnaires, let's begin with some issues of questionnaire format.

GENERAL QUESTIONNAIRE FORMAT

The format of a questionnaire is just as important as the nature and wording of the questions asked. An improperly laid out questionnaire can lead respondents to miss questions. It can also confuse them about the nature of the data desired, and even lead them to throw the questionnaire away.

As a general rule, the questionnaire should be spread out and uncluttered. Inexperienced researchers tend to fear that their questionnaire will look too long; as a result, they squeeze several questions onto a single line, abbreviate questions, and try to use as few pages as possible. These efforts are ill-advised and even dangerous. Putting more than one question on a line will cause some respondents to miss the second question altogether. More generally, respondents who find that they have spent considerable time on the first page of what seemed a short questionnaire will be more demoralized than respondents who quickly complete the first several pages of what initially seemed a rather long form. Moreover, the latter will have made fewer errors and will not have been forced to reread confusing, abbreviated questions. Nor will they have been forced to write a long answer in a tiny space.

Problems of this nature are not exclusive to respondents with a self-administered questionnaire. Interviewers in telephone or face-to-face interviews could miss questions, lose their place, and become frustrated when working from an ill-designed questionnaire. Interview questionnaires need to be laid out in a way that supports the interviewer's work, with special instructions and guidelines for them clearly distinguished.

The desirability of spreading out questions in the questionnaire cannot be overemphasized. Squeezed-together questionnaires are disastrous, whether completed by the respondents themselves or administered by trained interviewers. And the processing of such questionnaires is another nightmare. (The processing of questionnaire data will be discussed in Chapter 14.)

FORMATS FOR RESPONDENTS

In one of the most common types of questionnaire items, the respondent is expected to check one response from a series. For this purpose, boxes adequately spaced apart seem to be the best format. Modern software makes the use of boxes a practical technique these days; setting boxes in type can also be accomplished easily and neatly. Here are some easy examples:

Rather than providing boxes to be checked, you might print a code number beside each response and ask the respondent to circle the appropriate number (see Figure 8-2). This method has the added advantage of specifying the code number to be entered later in the processing stage. If numbers are to be circled, however, you should provide clear and prominent instructions to the respondent, because many will be tempted to cross out the appropriate number, which makes data processing even more difficult. (Note that this technique can be used more safely when interviewers administer the questionnaires, for they can specially instruct and supervise the respondents.)

Did you happen to vote in the last federal election?

1. Yes (circled)
2. No
3. Don't know

Have you ever felt you were the victim of sexual discrimination?

1. Yes
2. No (circled)
3. Don't know

FIGURE 8-2 **Circling the Answer.**
Source: © Cengage Learning

CONTINGENCY QUESTIONS

Quite often in questionnaires, certain questions will be relevant to some of the respondents and irrelevant to others. In a study of birth control methods, for instance, you would probably not want to ask men if they take birth control pills.

This sort of situation often arises when researchers wish to ask a series of questions about a certain topic. You may want to ask whether your respondents belong to a particular organization and, if so, how often they attend meetings, whether they have held office in the organization, and so forth. Or you might want to ask whether respondents have heard anything about a certain political issue and then learn the attitudes of those who have heard of it.

Each subsequent question in series such as these is called a **contingency question**: whether it is to be asked and answered is contingent on responses to the first question in the series. The proper use of contingency questions can facilitate the respondents' task in completing the questionnaire, because they are not faced with trying to answer questions irrelevant to them.

There are several formats for contingency questions. The one shown in Figure 8-3 is probably the clearest and most effective. Note two key elements in this format. First, the contingency question is isolated from the other questions by being set off to the side and enclosed in a box. Second, an arrow connects the contingency question to the answer on which it is contingent. In the illustration, only those respondents answering "yes" are expected to answer the contingency question. The rest of the respondents should simply skip it.

Note that the questions shown in Figure 8-3 could have been dealt with in a single question. The question might have read, "How many times, if any, have you smoked marijuana?" The response categories, then, might have read: "Never," "Once," "2 to 5 times," and so forth. This single question would apply to all respondents, and each would find an appropriate answer category. Such a question, however, might put some

contingency question A survey question intended for only some respondents, determined by their responses to some other question. For example, all respondents might be asked whether they watch sports on TV, and only those who id yes would be asked which sports they watch, and how n. The latter would be contingency questions.

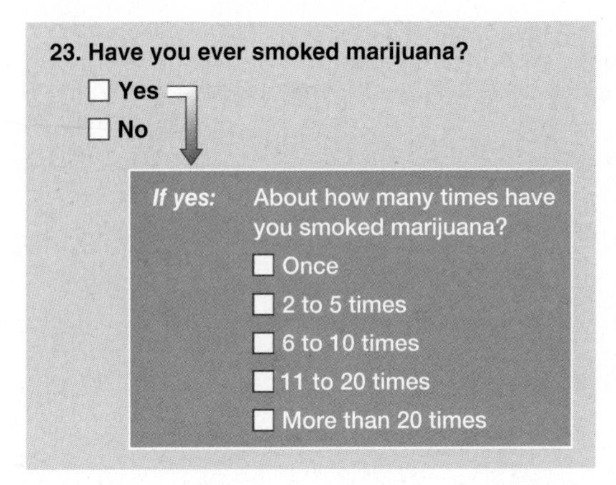

FIGURE 8-3 **Contingency Question Format.** Contingency questions offer a structure for exploring subject areas logically in some depth.
Source: © Cengage Learning

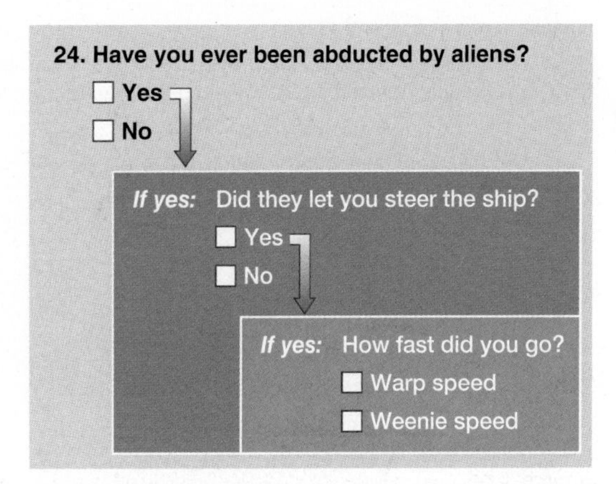

FIGURE 8-4 **Contingency Table.** Sometimes it will be appropriate for certain kinds of respondents to skip over inapplicable questions. To avoid confusion, you should provide clear instructions to that end.
Source: © Cengage Learning

pressure on respondents to report having smoked marijuana, because the main question asks how many times they have smoked it, even though it allows for those *exceptional* cases *who have never smoked marijuana even once.* (The emphases used in the previous sentence give a fair indication of how respondents might read the question.) The contingency question format illustrated in Figure 8-3 should reduce the subtle pressure on respondents to report having smoked marijuana.

Used properly, even rather complex sets of contingency questions can be constructed without confusing the respondent. Figure 8-4 illustrates a more complicated example.

Sometimes a set of contingency questions is long enough to extend over several pages. Suppose you're studying political activities of university students, and you wish to ask a large number of questions of those students who had voted in a federal, provincial, or local election. You could separate out the relevant respondents with an initial question such as "Have you ever voted in a federal, provincial, or local election?" but it would be confusing to place the contingency questions in a box stretching over several pages. It would make more sense to enter instructions in parentheses after each answer telling respondents to answer or skip the contingency questions. Figure 8-5 provides an illustration of this method.

In addition to these instructions, it's worthwhile to place an instruction at the top of each page containing only the contingency questions. For example, you might say, "This page is only for respondents who have voted in a federal, provincial, or local election." Clear instructions such as these spare respondents the frustration of reading and puzzling over questions that are irrelevant to them and increase the likelihood of responses from those for whom the questions are relevant.

MATRIX QUESTIONS

Quite often, you'll want to ask several questions that have the same set of answer categories. This is typically the case whenever the Likert response categories are used. In such cases, it's often possible to construct a matrix of items and answers, as illustrated in Figure 8-6.

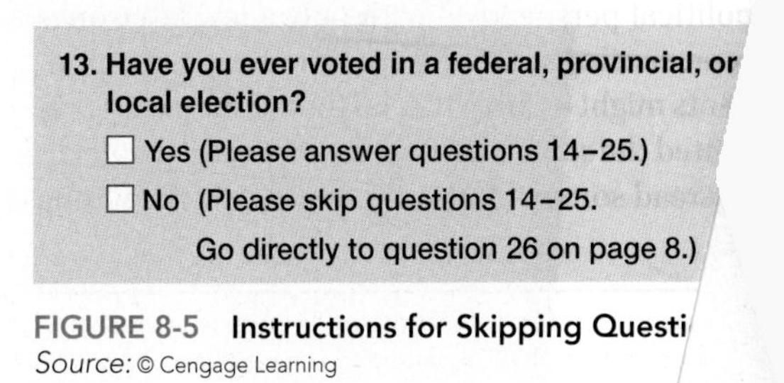

FIGURE 8-5 **Instructions for Skipping Questi**
Source: © Cengage Learning

17. Beside each of the statements presented below, please indicate whether you Strongly Agree (**SA**), Agree (**A**), Disagree (**D**), Strongly Disagree (**SD**), or are Undecided (**U**).

	SA	**A**	**D**	**SD**	**U**
a. What this country needs is more law and order..........	☐	☐	☐	☐	☐
b. The police should be disarmed in Canada...........	☐	☐	☐	☐	☐
c. The death penalty should be made legal in Canada..........	☐	☐	☐	☐	☐
etc.					

FIGURE 8-6 Matrix Question Format. Matrix questions offer an efficient format for presenting closed-ended questionnaire items that have the same response categories.
Source: © Cengage Learning

This format offers several advantages over other formats. First, it uses space efficiently. Second, respondents will probably find it faster to complete a set of questions presented in this fashion. In addition, this format may increase the comparability of responses given to different questions for the respondent as well as for the researcher. Because respondents can quickly review their answers to earlier items in the set, they might choose between, say, "strongly agree" and "agree" on a given statement by comparing the strength of their agreement with their earlier sponses in the set.

There are some dangers inherent in using this at, however. Its advantages may encourage structure an item so that the responses the matrix format when a different, more atic set of responses might be more e. Also, the matrix question format can **ponse set** among some respondents: evelop a pattern of, say, agreeing with ments. This would be especially likely statements began with several that particular orientation (e.g., a liberal spective) with only a few later ones g the opposite orientation. Respon- assume that all the statements repre- me orientation and, reading quickly, e of them, thereby giving the wrong answers. This problem can be reduced somewhat by alternating statements representing different orientations and by making all statements short and clear.

form of bias occurring when respondents physical pattern to answer questions or

ORDERING ITEMS IN A QUESTIONNAIRE

The order in which questionnaire items are presented can also affect responses. First, the appearance of one question can affect the answers given to later ones. For example, if several questions have been asked about the dangers of crime in Canada and then a question asks respondents to volunteer (open-ended) what they believe to be the most severe social problems facing Canada, crime will receive more citations than would otherwise be the case. In this situation, it is preferable to ask the open-ended question first.

Similarly, if respondents are asked to assess their overall religiosity ("How important is your religion to you in general?"), their responses to later questions concerning specific aspects of religiosity will be aimed at consistency with the prior assessment. The converse is true as well. If respondents are first asked specific questions about different aspects of their religiosity, their subsequent overall assessment will reflect the earlier answers.

The impact of item order is not uniform. When J. Edwin Benton and John Daly (1991) conducted a local government survey, they found that the less-educated respondents were more influenced by the order of questionnaire items than were those with more education.

Some researchers attempt to overcome this effect by randomizing the order of items. This effort is usually futile. In the first place, a randomized set of items will probably strike respondents as chaotic and worthless. The random order also makes it more difficult for respondents to answer because they must continually switch their attention from one topic to another. Finally, even a randomized ordering of items will have the effect discussed previously—except that you'll have no control over the effect.

The safest solution is sensitivity to the problem. Although you cannot avoid the effect of item order, try to estimate what that effect will be so you can interpret results meaningfully. If the order of items seems especially important in a given study, you might construct more than one version of the questionnaire with different orderings of the items. You will then be able to determine its effects by comparing responses to the various versions. At the very least, you should pretest your questionnaire in the different forms. (We'll discuss pretesting in a moment.)

The desired ordering of items differs between interviews and self-administered questionnaires. In the latter, it's usually best to begin the questionnaire with the most interesting set of items. The potential respondents who glance casually over the first few items should want to answer them. Perhaps the items will ask for attitudes they're aching to express. At the same time, however, the initial items should not be threatening. (It might be a bad idea to begin with items about sexual behaviour or drug use.) Requests for duller, demographic data (age, gender, and the like) should generally be placed at the end of a self-administered questionnaire. Placing these items at the beginning, as many inexperienced researchers are tempted to do, gives the questionnaire the initial appearance of a routine form, and the person receiving it may not be motivated to complete it.

Just the opposite is generally true for interview surveys. When the potential respondent's door first opens, the interviewer must begin gaining rapport quickly. After a short introduction to the study, the interviewer can best begin by enumerating the members of the household, getting demographic data about each. Such items are easily answered and generally nonthreatening. Once the initial rapport has been established, the interviewer can then move into the area of attitudes and more sensitive matters. An interview that began with the question "Do you believe in witchcraft?" would probably end rather quickly.

QUESTIONNAIRE INSTRUCTIONS

Every questionnaire, whether it is to be completed by respondents or administered by interviewers, should contain clear instructions and introductory comments where appropriate. (We'll further discuss information that should be included in an introduction to respondents, written or oral, in the "Ethical Considerations" section later in this chapter.)

It's useful to begin every self-administered questionnaire with basic instructions for completing it. Although many people have experience with forms and questionnaires, begin by telling them exactly what you want: they are to indicate their answers to certain questions by placing a check mark or an X in the box beside the appropriate answer or by writing in their answer when asked to do so. If many open-ended questions are used, respondents should be given some guidelines about whether brief or lengthy answers are expected. If you wish to encourage your respondents to elaborate on their responses to closed-ended questions, that should be noted.

If a questionnaire has subsections—political attitudes, religious attitudes, background data—introduce each section with a short statement concerning its content and purpose. For example, "In this section, we'd like to know what people consider the most important community problems." Demographic items at the end of a self-administered questionnaire might be introduced thus: "Finally, we would like to know just a little about you so we can see how different types of people feel about the issues we have been examining."

Short introductions such as these help the respondent make sense of the questionnaire. They make the questionnaire seem less chaotic, especially when it taps a variety of data. And they help put the respondent in the proper frame of mind for answering the questions.

Some questions may require special instructions to facilitate proper answering. This is especially true if a given question varies from the general instructions pertaining to the whole questionnaire. Some specific examples will illustrate this situation.

Despite attempts to provide mutually exclusive answer categories in closed-ended questions, often more than one answer will apply for respondents. If you want a single answer, you should make this perfectly clear in the question. An example would be "From the list below, please check the primary reason for your decision to attend university." Often, the main question can be followed by a parenthetical note: "Please check the one best answer." If, on the other hand, you want the respondent to check as many answers as apply, you should make this clear.

When a set of answer categories are to be rank-ordered by the respondent, the instructions should indicate this, and a different type of answer format should be used (e.g., blanks instead of boxes). These instructions should indicate how many answers are to be ranked (e.g., all, only the first and second, only the first and last, the most important and least important). These instructions should also spell out the order of ranking (e.g., "Place a 1 beside the most important, a 2 beside the next most important, and so forth"). Rank-ordering of responses is often difficult for respondents, however, because they may have to read and reread the list several times, so this technique should be used only in those situations where no other method will produce the desired result.

PRETESTING THE QUESTIONNAIRE

No matter how carefully researchers design a data-collection instrument such as a questionnaire, there is always the possibility—indeed the certainty—of error. They will always make some mistake: an ambiguous question, one that people cannot answer, or some other violation of the rules just discussed.

precoding Embedding numerical translation of questionnaire responses into the instrument.

The surest protection against such errors is to pretest the questionnaire in full or in part. Give the questionnaire to a diverse set of ten people, for example. It's not usually essential that the pretest subjects comprise a representative sample, although you should use people to whom the questionnaire is at least relevant.

By and large, it's better to ask people to complete the questionnaire rather than to read through it looking for errors. All too often, a question seems to make sense on a first reading, but it proves to be impossible to answer. Stanley Presser and Johnny Blair (1994) describe several different pretesting strategies and reported on the effectiveness of each. Later, Presser and colleagues (2004) discuss problems with survey questions that conventional pretests may not adequately determine. Describing cognitive interviewing, they talk about collecting information from respondents as they answer questions (or just after they answer a question) in an attempt to determine whether the questions being asked are gathering the information the researchers aim to gather.

There are more tips and guidelines for questionnaire construction, but covering them all would take a book in itself. We'll complete this discussion with an illustration of a real questionnaire, showing how some of these comments find substance in practice.

Before turning to the illustration, however, we want to mention a critical aspect of questionnaire design—**precoding**. Because the information collected by questionnaires is typically transformed into quantitative formats, it's usually appropriate to include data-processing numerical codes into the questionnaire itself. These instructions indicate how specific pieces of information will be stored in the machine-readable data files. The precodes are placed on the questionnaire near question and answer categories. While such precoding makes data entry easier and often more accurate, care should be taken that the data-processing instructions not interfere with the respondent's ability to understand and easily respond to the questions on the questionnaire. After all, it would be of little value to more easily and accurately enter data that are flawed due to the inclusion of such data-processing instructions.

A COMPOSITE ILLUSTRATION

Figure 8-7 is part of a questionnaire used by Statistics Canada in 2011. It is a segment of the voluntary National Household Survey (NHS) that deals with information about labour market activities. The NHS replaced the previously mandatory long-form census questionnaire. For other examples of questionnaires, go to the Statistics Canada website or see the data librarian at your university.

SELF-ADMINISTERED QUESTIONNAIRES

So far we've discussed how to formulate questions and how to design effective questionnaires. As important as these tasks are, the labour will be wasted unless the questionnaire produces useful data—which means that respondents actually complete the questionnaire. We turn now to the major methods for getting responses to questionnaires.

We've referred several times in this chapter to interviews versus self-administered questionnaires. Actually, there are three main methods of administering survey questionnaires to a sample of respondents: self-administered questionnaires, in which respondents are asked to complete the questionnaires themselves; surveys administered by interviewers in face-to-face encounters; and surveys conducted by telephone. This section and the next two discuss each of these methods in turn.

Until very recently, the most common form of self-administered questionnaire was the mail survey. As Internet access and usage rose, the prevalence of hard-copy mailout and return surveys quickly declined. Hard copy distribution and return is still used where a group of respondents is gathered at the same place at the same time. A survey of students taking introductory sociology might be conducted in this manner during class. High school students might be surveyed during home-room period. Employees of a business at a retreat might be surveyed this way. But, generally, self-administered questionnaires are completed online.

ONLINE SURVEYS

Online survey research involves the use of the Internet and the World Wide Web—two of the most far-reaching developments of the late 20th century. Mick Couper and Peter Miller (2008:831) give an excellent introduction to the timeline of this new face of social research:

> Despite their relatively short history, Web surveys have already had a profound effect on survey research. The first graphic browser (NCSA Mosaic) was released in 1992, with Netscape Navigator following in 1994 and Internet Explorer in 1995. The first published papers on Web surveys appeared in 1996. Since then, there has been a virtual explosion of interest in the Internet generally, and World Wide Web specifically, as a tool for survey data collection.

Some researchers believe that the Internet can be used to conduct meaningful survey research. This technique has been getting especially popular in market research, for example. Some online surveys are conducted completely via email; others are conducted via websites. Commonly, potential respondents will receive an email asking them to go to a weblink where the survey resides.

One immediate objection that many social researchers make to online surveys concerns representativeness: Will the people who can be surveyed online be representative of meaningful populations, such as all Canadian adults, all voters, and so on? This is the criticism that researchers have previously raised with regard to telephone surveys.

Camilo Wilson (1999) points out that some populations are ideally suited to online surveys: specifically, those who visit a particular website. For example, Wilson indicates that market research for online companies should be conducted online. Although website surveys could easily collect data from all who visit a particular site, Wilson suggests that survey sampling techniques can provide sufficient consumer data without irritating thousands or millions of potential customers.

But what about general population surveys? What about political polling? Not everyone of

2011 National Household Survey Questions

Note:
Many of the following questions refer to ***the week from Sunday, May 1 to Saturday, May 7, 2011.***

LABOUR MARKET ACTIVITIES

34. During the week of **Sunday, May 1 to Saturday, May 7, 2011,** how many hours did this person spend working for pay **or** in self-employment?

Please enter the total number of hours worked for pay or in self-employment at all jobs held during the week of May 1 to May 7.

Include:

- *working for wages, salary, tips or commission;*
- *working in his/her own business, farm or professional practice, alone or in partnership;*
- *working directly towards the operation of a family farm or business without formal pay arrangements (e.g., assisting in seeding, doing accounts).*

Number of hours (to the nearest hour)

________ → **Go to Question 40**

OR

❍ None → **Continue with the next question**

35. During the week of **May 1 to May 7,** was this person on temporary lay-off or absent from his/her job or business?

Mark one circle only.

❍ No
❍ Yes, on temporary lay-off from a job to which this person expects to return
❍ Yes, on vacation, ill, on strike or locked out, or absent for other reasons

36. During the week of **May 1 to May 7,** did this person have definite arrangements to start a new job within the next four weeks?

❍ No
❍ Yes

37. Did this person look for paid work during the **four weeks from April 10 to May 7, 2011?**

For example, did this person contact an employment centre, check with employers, place or answer newspaper ads, etc.?

Mark one circle only.

❍ No → **Go to Question 39**
❍ Yes, looked for full-time work
❍ Yes, looked for part-time work (less than 30 hours per week)

FIGURE 8-7 A Sample Questionnaire: Excerpt from the National Household Survey 2011.
Source: Statistics Canada, *2011 National Household Survey Questions.* Found at: http://www.statcan.gc.ca/survey-enquete/household-menages/pdf/nhs-enm-quest-eng.pdf. Reproduced and distributed on an "as is" basis with the permission of Statistics Canada.

2011 National Household Survey Questions

38. Could this person have started a job during the week of **Sunday, May 1 to Saturday, May 7, 2011** one been available?

Mark one circle only.

- ❍ Yes, could have started a job
- ❍ No, already had a job
- ❍ No, because of temporary illness or disability
- ❍ No, because of personal or family responsibilities
- ❍ No, going to school
- ❍ No, other reasons

39. When did this person last work for pay **or** in self-employment, even for a few days?

Mark one circle only.

- ❍ In 2011
- ❍ In 2010

▶ **Continue with the next question**

- ❍ Before 2010
- ❍ Never

▶ **Go to Question 53**

Note: Questions 40 to 49 refer to this person's job or business during the week of May 1 to May 7, 2011. *If this person held no job, answer for the job of longest duration since January 1, 2010. If this person held more than one job, answer for the job at which he or she worked the* ***most hours.***

40. For whom did this person work?

For self-employed persons, enter the name of their business. If the business does not have a name, enter the person's name.

Print in capital letters as follows:

A B C C O N C R E T E P R O D U C T S L I M I T E D

Name of firm, government agency, etc.	Section, plant, department, etc. (if applicable)
____________________	____________________
____________________	____________________
____________________	
____________________	

FIGURE 8-7 **(Continued)**

2011 National Household Survey Questions

41. What kind of business, industry or service was this?

Please give details. For example:
- *primary school*
- *municipal police*
- *wheat farm*
- *shoe store*

Kind of business, industry or service

____
____
____

42. What was this person's work or occupation?

Please be specific. For example:
- *plumber*
- *fishing guide*
- *wood furniture assembler*
- *secondary school teacher*

(If in the Armed Forces, give rank.)

Occupation

____
____
____

43. In this work, what were this person's main activities?

Please give details. For example:
- *installed residential plumbing*
- *guided fishing parties*
- *made wood furniture products*
- *taught mathematics*

Main activities

____
____
____

44. In this job or business, was this person mainly:

Mark one circle only.

- ○ working for wages, salary, tips or commission? → **Go to Question 46**
- ○ working without pay for his/her spouse or another relative in a family farm or business? → **Go to Question 46**
- ○ self-employed without paid help (alone or in partnership)?
- ○ self-employed with paid help (alone or in partnership)?

FIGURE 8-7 ***(Continued)***

interest can be reached by Internet, nor does everyone feel comfortable using it. Moreover, those less available for online surveys are not a random segment of the overall population. The poor and the elderly, for example, are likely to be underrepresented by online surveys. At the same time, as more and more people gain access to the Internet, this problem is reduced.

In one solution to this problem, the National Opinion Research Center, which conducts the periodic General Social Survey (GSS), used probability-sampling methods to create a representative sample of potential respondents (Smith 2001). Each person in the sample was provided with WebTV access to the Internet, with an agreement that they would participate in polls from time to time. While these online respondents were demographically representative, there were differences in their responses on survey issues that will require further study. For example, the online respondents were more likely to choose extreme responses (such as "strongly agree") than were those surveyed in face-to-face interviews.

Commercial polling and market research firms report that they have developed large-scale panels of online respondents from whom they can select samples that are representative of whatever populations are of interest for study. Because their specific methods are proprietary and secret, it's difficult to assess their methodological strengths and weaknesses. As discussed in Chapter 7, online crowdsourcing platforms like MTurk are also growing in popularity, allowing survey researchers to sample respondents in a cost-effective manner. Although not as representative of the general population as well-designed probability samples, MTurk samples are more demographically diverse than many other forms of convenience sampling, such as relying on undergraduate university students.

As online survey methods develop, researchers continue to accumulate lessons for increasing success. Here are some best practices for creating an effective online survey:

- Provide a clear, compelling reason for participation in survey completion.
- Use simple, direct language.
- Restrict the survey length to under 20 minutes (15 is better).
- Offer to share a summary of the results with interested participants.
- Use appropriate design and colour to help respondents navigate the survey.
- Use radio buttons and drop-down boxes to reduce response errors.
- In grid-design questions, make sure response labels are continuously visible.
- Take full advantage of skip pattern preprogramming.

Leah Christian and colleagues (2007) provide a wealth of guidance on formatting Web surveys. Their aim is, as their article title suggests, "helping respondents get it right the first time."

The relative youth of online surveys makes them a fertile ground for innovation and experimentation. For example, survey researchers have often worried that respondents to self-administered questionnaires may spend more of their attention on the first responses in a list, skipping quickly over those farther down. To test this possibility, Mirta Galesic and colleagues (2008) used a special eye-tracking computer monitor that unobtrusively followed respondents' eye movements as they completed an online survey. The result: respondents did, in fact, spend more time on the early choices, sometimes failing to read the whole list before clicking their choice on the screen.

The years ahead will see many more experiments aimed at improving the effectiveness of online surveys. In the meantime, several books (e.g., Couper 2008; Sue and Ritter 2012; Toepoel 2016) offer comprehensive guides to this new technique, based on what we have learned about it to date. If you are interested in experimenting with Web surveys on your own, see the How to Do It box "Conducting an Online Survey."

In recent years, several firms have developed excellent online platforms for mounting and managing Web surveys. In addition to being able to construct professional-looking surveys with every level of sophisticated question format (e.g., contingent questions, matrix questions), the platforms include excellent management tools. For example, after respondents receive access to a

HOW TO DO IT

Conducting an Online Survey

If you're interested in testing the waters of online surveys, *SurveyGizmo* will give you the opportunity to try your hand at this emerging technique. Just go to their website (http://www.surveygizmo.com) and you can register to try out their impressive software for a week. The program is user-friendly and full of sophisticated options for designing questionnaires. The online technical support is excellent, as is their toll-free support service. You can also manually pretest your questionnaire. Or if you prefer, you can have the "robots" generate random responses to your survey.

After creating your survey you can enter email addresses of your intended respondents, and they'll receive an email invitation to visit the survey Web page and participate. The data are stored in a variety of conventional formats so you can analyze the results yourself. Or use their online analysis tools to explore the data you collected.

This introduction will give you a sense of the scope and power of online survey tools, since *SurveyGizmo* is used by professional researchers across North America.

survey, the question arises regarding when they should be nudged to complete the survey. Obviously, respondents must be given some time to provide their responses, but how much time? The answer comes from monitoring returns through a **rate of return graph**. Better online platforms provide this monitoring ability. A rate of return graph plots the total number of completed surveys every day since the survey opened. This is a cumulative number. In other words, each day the rate of return graph increases as that day's completed surveys are added to the total. At some point, the rate of return graph levels off, which indicates that additional daily completions are few. This flattening of the rate of return graph also indicates when follow-up reminders should be distributed to those who have not completed the survey. Online survey platforms allow sending reminder nudges easily and only to those who have not responded.

RESPONSE RATES

A question that new survey researchers frequently ask concerns the percentage return rate, or **response rate**, that should be achieved. In the quantitative research tradition, the inferential statistics used in survey analysis assume that all members of the initial sample complete and return their questionnaires. Because this almost never happens, response bias becomes a concern, with the researcher testing (and hoping) for the possibility that the respondents look essentially like a random sample of the initial sample, and thus constitute a somewhat smaller random sample of the total population.

Overall, response rate is one guide to the representativeness of the sample respondents. If a high response rate is achieved, there's less chance of significant response bias than in a low rate. Conversely, a low response rate is a danger signal, because the nonrespondents are likely to differ from the respondents in ways other than just their willingness to participate in your survey. Richard Bolstein (1991), for example, found that those who did not respond to a pre-election political poll were less likely to vote than those who did participate. Estimating the turnout rate from the survey respondents, then, would have overestimated the number who would show up at the polls. However, given that those who did not respond were less likely to vote, those who did respond might provide a good election results poll.

But what is an acceptable response rate? A quick review of the survey literature will uncover a wide range of response rates. While the goal is to get a 100 percent response rate, in practice most survey response rates fall well below that. Therefore, testing for nonresponse bias whenever possible is important.

Online surveys appear to have response rates approximately comparable to mail surveys, according to a large-scale study of Michigan State University students (Kaplowitz et al. 2004), especially when the online survey is accompanied by a reminder encouraging respondents to participate. While producing a comparable response rate, the cost of an online survey is substantially less than traditional mail surveys.

In another study of ways to improve response rates in online surveys, Stephen Porter and Michael Whitcomb (2003) found that some of the techniques effective in older mail surveys, such as personalizing the appeal or varying the apparent status of the researcher, had little or no impact in the new medium. At the same time, specifying that the respondents had been specially selected for the survey and setting a deadline for participation did increase response rates.

As you can imagine, one of the more persistent discussions among survey researchers concerns ways of increasing response rates. Survey researchers have developed many ingenious techniques addressing this problem. Some have experimented with novel formats. Others have tried paying respondents to participate. The problem with paying, of course, is that it's expensive to make meaningfully high payments

rate of return graph A daily plot of the total (cumulative) number of completed surveys.

response rate The number of people participating in a survey divided by the number selected in the sample, in the form of a percentage; also called the completion rate or, in self-administered surveys, the return rate.

to hundreds or thousands of respondents. As online survey methodologies develop, improved methods of soliciting representative samples and higher participation will be pursued.

Let us conclude this section with a brief mention of some cutting edge techniques for attempting to increase response rates. Responsive and adaptive survey designs use paradata to help improve response rates (Laflamme and Wagner 2016). Paradata is any data that provide information about data collection throughout the data collection process. Records of call/visit attempts (e.g., date, time, result of call or visit) and interviewer observations about the neighbourhood, sampled unit, or person are important sources of such information. Paradata are usually available for respondents and nonrespondents and can be used to try to make strategic adjustments (e.g., change time of attempted contact, change survey mode, change interviewer) to improve data collection for subsequent cases to raise response rates. "Responsive design generally refers to a strategy that can be modified during collection while the adaptive design approach takes advantage of the lessons learned from previous collection cycles to improve the next one" (Laflamme and Wagner 2016:398). Not only can paradata be used to help improve subsequent data collection, but it can be used to weight estimates in order to correct for nonresponse bias (Bethlehem and Schouten 2016).

Finally, sequential mixed-mode surveys have also shown some success in improving response rates (Leeuw & Berzelak 2016). In these the respondent is first contacted using one mode of survey administration, followed by a second or even a third mode if necessary. Usually, the first mode is the least expensive one, such as regular mail or Internet. The second phase may move to CATI or, if no phone number is available (or there is still no response), in-person visits to attempt interviews may be made.

AN ILLUSTRATION OF AN ONLINE SURVEY

A recent example of a large-scale online survey is the National Student Climate Survey on Homophobia, Biphobia, and Transphobia in Canadian Schools (Taylor, Peter, et al. 2011b:4). It was the first national survey of Canadian high school students intended "to identify the forms and extent of students' experiences of homophobic, [biphobic], and transphobic incidents at school, the impact of those experiences, and the efficacy of measures being taken by schools to combat these common forms of bullying."

The student climate survey was hosted on its own website. It asked students (N = 3,700) a series of questions about their school climate in the previous 12 months, including questions specific to experiences of hostile climate and targeted harassment as well as related impacts and interventions. The survey took two forms: (1) an open-access online survey advertised widely through news releases, website notices, and Facebook notices, as well recruitment via contacting organizations Canada-wide that the authors identified as having LGBTQ youth membership; and (2) a controlled access (login only) survey system administered through in-school sessions in 15 randomly selected school districts (except Quebec). The survey had 54 questions, 7 of which were open-ended. The in-school findings were used to validate the open-access findings.

Previous to this survey, there had been little solid empirical data on the experiences of LGBTQ youth in Canadian schools. By addressing this knowledge gap and statistically documenting the prevalence and impact of LGBTQ-hostile climates in Canadian schools (see Figure 8-8), the student climate survey—and subsequent surveys of teachers and superintendents (Taylor, Meyer, et al. 2016; Taylor, Peter, et al. 2016)—has shone light on the magnitude of this issue and the importance of addressing it. Taylor, Peter and colleagues (2016) made a number of recommendations aimed at making schools more LGBTQ-inclusive, including policy and curriculum development, teacher education, and institutional promotion and support of gay–straight student alliances (or similar LGBTQ-inclusive student-led initiatives). Has the LGBTQ-inclusiveness of Canadian schools changed in the decade since this survey? That is the focus of the second national student climate study, which is underway at the time of this writing (see https://egale.ca/schools-survey/).

- 70% of all participating students, LGBTQ and non-LGBTQ reported hearing expression such as "That's so gay" every day in school, and almost half (48%) reported hearing remarks such as "faggot," "lezbo" and "dyke" every day in school.
- 74% of trans students, 55% of sexual minority students, and 26% on non-LGBTQ students reported having been verbally harassed about their gender expression.
- 37% of trans students, 32% of female sexual minority students, and 20% of male sexual minority students reported being verbally harassed daily or weekly about their sexual orientation.
- More than one in five (21%) LGBTQ students reported being physically harassed or assaulted due to their sexual orientation.
- 20% of LGBTQ youth and almost 10% of non-LGBTQ youth reported being physically harassed or assaulted about their perceived sexual orientation or gender identity.
- The percent of students that reported having experienced sexual harassment was high across all LGBTQ subgroups, ranging between 33% for lesbian student to 49% for trans students.
- Almost two-thirds (64%) of LGBTQ students and 61% of students with LGBTQ parents reported that they feel unsafe at school, with washrooms and Phys Ed. change rooms being the most commonly identified unsafe spaces.

FIGURE 8-8 **Selected Findings from the National Student Climate Survey.**
Source: Taylor, C. & Peter, T., with McMinn, T. L., Elliott, T. Beldom, S., Ferry, A., Gross, Z., Paquin, S., & Schacter, K. (2011). *Every class in every school: The first national climate survey on homophobia, biphobia, and transphobia in Canadian schools.* Final report. Toronto, ON: Egale Canada Human Rights Trust, 151 pp.

INTERVIEW SURVEYS

The **interview** is an alternative method of collecting survey data. Rather than asking respondents to read questionnaires and enter their own answers, researchers send interviewers to ask the questions orally and record respondents' answers. Interviewing is typically done in a face-to-face encounter, but telephone interviewing, discussed in the next section, follows most of the same guidelines. Traditionally, survey interviewers recorded responses on a paper copy of the questionnaire. Today, **computer-assisted personal interviewing (CAPI)** is more common. In CAPI, questionnaire content is included on a tablet or computer, the interviewer reads the questions, and the responses are recorded by the interviewer directly onto the computer. By comparison, in **computer-assisted self-interviewing (CASI)**, there is typically no interviewer present. The respondent uses a computer/digital device (they read the questions or the computer dictates the questions out loud) and answers by typing in precoded response options (e.g., multiple choice) or composing answers to open questions. Additionally, **computer-assisted Web interviewing (CAWI)** is a form of CASI in which the interviewee reads and fills out the interview questionnaire online (e.g., online questionnaires hosted by platforms like SurveyGizmo or Qualtrics).

Most interview surveys require more than one interviewer, although you might undertake a small-scale interview survey yourself. Portions

interview A data-collection encounter in which one person (an interviewer) asks questions of another (a respondent). Interviews may be conducted face-to-face or by telephone.

computer-assisted personal interviewing (CAPI) A face-to-face interview system in which questions are provided on a computer or tablet device and interview responses are entered into the computer by the interviewer.

computer-assisted self-interviewing (CASI) An interview system in which there is no interviewer; instead, the participant reads or listens to questions on a computer or mobile digital device and types their answers directly into the computer or device.

computer-assisted Web interviewing (CAWI) A form of CASI in which the interviewee reads and fills out the interview questionnaire online (e.g., online questionnaires hosted by platforms like SurveyGizmo or Qualtrics).

of this section will discuss methods for training and supervising a staff of interviewers assisting you with a survey.

This section deals specifically with survey interviewing. Chapter 10 discusses the less structured, in-depth interviews often conducted in field research.

THE ROLE OF THE SURVEY INTERVIEWER

There are several advantages to having a questionnaire administered by an interviewer rather than the respondent. To begin with, interview surveys commonly attain higher response rates than self-administered surveys. A properly designed and executed interview survey ought to achieve a completion rate of at least 80 to 85 percent. Respondents seem more reluctant to turn down an interviewer standing on their doorstep.

The presence of an interviewer also generally decreases the number of "don't knows" and "no answers." If minimizing such responses is important to the study, the interviewer can be instructed to probe for answers. ("If you had to pick one of the answers, which do you think would come closest to your feelings?")

Interviewers can also serve as a guard against confusing questionnaire items. If the respondent clearly misunderstands the intent of a question or indicates that he or she does not understand, the interviewer can clarify matters, thereby obtaining relevant responses. (As we'll discuss shortly, such clarifications must be strictly controlled through formal specifications.)

Finally, the interviewer can observe respondents as well as ask questions. For example, the interviewer can note the quality of the dwelling, the presence of various possessions, the respondent's general reactions to the study, and so forth. In one survey of students, respondents were given a short, self-administered questionnaire concerning political attitudes and voting behaviour to complete during the course of the interview. While a student completed the questionnaire, the interviewer made detailed notes regarding the dress and grooming of the respondent.

This procedure raises an ethical issue. Some researchers have objected that such practices violate the spirit of the agreement by which the respondent has allowed the interview. If the respondent is not aware that such information is being collected, then he or she has not been fully informed about the study. This puts into question whether the respondent has truly been given the choice of voluntary participation. Although ethical issues are seldom clear-cut in social research, it's important to be sensitive to them.

Survey research is of necessity based on an unrealistic stimulus-response theory of cognition and behaviour. Researchers must assume that a questionnaire item will mean the same thing to every respondent, and every given response must mean the same when given by different respondents. Although this is an impossible goal, survey questions are drafted to approximate the ideal as closely as possible.

The interviewer must also fit into this ideal situation. The interviewer's presence should not affect a respondent's perception of a question or the answer given. In other words, the interviewer should be a neutral medium through which questions and answers are transmitted.

Thus, different interviewers should obtain exactly the same responses from a given respondent. (Recall earlier discussions of reliability.) This neutrality has a special importance in area samples. To save time and money, a given interviewer is typically assigned to complete all the interviews in a particular geographical area such as a city block or a group of nearby blocks. If the interviewer does anything to affect the responses obtained, the bias thus interjected might be interpreted as a characteristic of that area.

Let's suppose that a survey is being done to determine attitudes toward low-cost housing to help in the selection of a site for a new government-sponsored development. An interviewer assigned to a given neighbourhood might, through word or gesture, communicate his or her own distaste for low-cost housing developments. Respondents might therefore tend to give responses in general agreement with the interviewer's own position. The results of the survey would indicate that the neighbourhood in question strongly resists construction of the development in its area, when in fact their apparent resistance simply reflects the interviewer's attitudes.

GENERAL GUIDELINES FOR SURVEY INTERVIEWING

The manner in which interviews ought to be conducted varies somewhat by survey population and is affected to some degree by the nature of the survey content. Nevertheless, some general guidelines apply to most if not all interviewing situations.

Appearance and Demeanour As a rule, interviewers should dress in a fashion similar to that of the people they'll be interviewing. Although middle-class neatness and cleanliness may not be accepted by all sectors of Canadian society, they remain the primary norm and are the most likely to be acceptable to the largest number of respondents.In demeanour, interviewers should be pleasant if nothing else. Because they'll be prying into a respondent's personal life and attitudes, they must communicate a genuine interest in getting to know the respondent without appearing to spy. They must be relaxed and friendly without being too casual or clinging.

If an interviewer is unfamiliar with the questionnaire, the study suffers and an unfair burden is placed on the respondent. The interviewer must take care to know the questions well. The lines must be read as though they constituted a natural conversation, but that conversation must follow exactly the language set down in the questionnaire.

Following Question Wording Exactly The first part of this chapter discussed the significance of question wording for the responses obtained. A slight change in the wording of a given question may lead a respondent to answer "yes" rather than "no." Therefore, interviewers must be instructed to follow the wording of questions exactly. Otherwise, all the effort that the developers have put into carefully phrasing the questionnaire items to obtain the information they need and to ensure that respondents will interpret items precisely as intended will be wasted.

Recording Responses Exactly Whenever the questionnaire contains open-ended questions that solicit the respondent's own answer, the interviewer must record that answer exactly as given. No attempt should be made to summarize, paraphrase, or correct bad grammar.

This exactness is especially important because the interviewer will not know how the responses are to be coded. Indeed, the researchers may not know the coding until they've read a hundred or so responses. For example, the questionnaire might ask respondents how they feel about the traffic situation in their community. One respondent might answer that there are too many cars on the roads and that something should be done to limit their numbers. Another might say that more roads are needed. If the interviewer recorded these two responses with the same summary—"congested traffic"—the researchers would not be able to take advantage of the important differences in the original responses.

Sometimes, verbal responses are too inarticulate or ambiguous to permit interpretation. However, the interviewer may be able to understand the intent of the response through the respondent's gestures or tone. In such a situation, the interviewer should still record the exact verbal response but also add marginal comments giving both the interpretation and the reasons for arriving at it.

More generally, researchers can use any marginal comments explaining aspects of the response not conveyed in the verbal recording, such as the respondent's apparent anger, embarrassment, uncertainty in answering, and so forth. In each case, however, the exact verbal response should also be recorded.

Probing for Responses Sometimes respondents in an interview will give an inappropriate or incomplete answer. In such cases a **probe**, or request for an elaboration, can be useful. For example, a closed-ended question may present an attitudinal statement and ask the respondent to strongly agree, agree somewhat, disagree somewhat, or strongly disagree. The respondent,

probe A technique used in interviewing to solicit a more complete answer to a question. It is a nondirective phrase or question used to encourage a respondent to elaborate on an answer. Examples include "Anything more?" and "How is that?"

however, may reply "I think that's true." The interviewer should follow this reply with "Would you say you strongly agree or agree somewhat?" If necessary, interviewers can explain that they must check one or the other of the categories provided. If the respondent adamantly refuses to choose, the interviewer should write in the exact response given by the respondent.

Probes are more frequently required in eliciting responses to open-ended questions. For example, in response to a question about traffic conditions, the respondent might simply reply, "Pretty bad." The interviewer could obtain an elaboration on this response through a variety of probes. Sometimes the best probe is silence; if the interviewer sits quietly with pencil poised, the respondent will probably fill the pause with additional comments. (This technique is used effectively by newspaper reporters.) Appropriate verbal probes might be "How is that?" or "In what ways?" Perhaps the most generally useful probe is "Anything else?"

Often, interviewers need to probe for answers that will be sufficiently informative for analytical purposes. In every case, however, such probes *must* be completely neutral; they must not in any way affect the nature of the subsequent response. Whenever you anticipate that a given question may require probing for appropriate responses, you should provide one or more useful probes next to the question in the questionnaire. This practice has two important advantages. First, you'll have more time to devise the best, most neutral probes. Second, all interviewers will use the same probes whenever they're needed. Thus, even if the probe isn't perfectly neutral, all respondents will be presented with the same stimulus. This is the same logical guideline discussed for question wording. Although a question should not be loaded or biased, it's essential that every respondent be presented with the same question, even if it's biased.

SPECIFICATIONS

It's always a good idea to prepare specifications to accompany an interview questionnaire. **Specifications** are explanatory and clarifying comments about handling difficult or confusing situations that might occur with regard to particular questions in the questionnaire. When drafting the questionnaire, try to think of all the problem cases that might arise—the bizarre circumstances that might make a question difficult to answer. The survey specifications should provide detailed guidelines on how to handle such situations. For example, even as simple a matter as age might present problems. Suppose a respondent says he or she will be 25 next week. The interviewer might not be sure whether to take the respondent's current age or the nearest one. The specifications for that question should explain what should be done. (Probably, you would specify that the age as of last birthday should be recorded in all cases.)

TELEPHONE SURVEYS

For years telephone surveys had a rather bad reputation among professional researchers. Telephone surveys are limited by definition to people who have telephones. Years ago, this method produced a substantial social-class bias by excluding poor people from the surveys. This was vividly demonstrated by the *Literary Digest* fiasco of 1936. Recall that even though voters were contacted by mail, the sample was partially selected from telephone subscribers, who were hardly typical in a nation just recovering from the Great Depression. Over time, however, the telephone became a standard fixture in almost all Canadian homes. Therefore, "a surveyor's use of the telephone does not bias respondent selection as it would have a few decades ago" (Guppy and Gray 2008:143).

A related sampling problem involves unlisted numbers, which includes cellphones. The impact of not including cellphones in telephone surveys has received much attention. When cellphones are excluded, there is a potential bias due to the fact that younger people are more likely to use only cellphones. Reporting results of its Residential Telephone Service Survey (*The Daily* 2014), Statistics Canada found that in 2013 Canadian

specification An explanatory or clarifying comment about handling a difficult or confusing situation that might occur regarding particular questions in an interview.

households with cellphones had increased to 83 percent. They also found more households with only cellphones, 21 percent. However, in households where all members are under age 35, 60 percent were cellphone-only households while only 6 percent of households made up of those ages 55 and older used cellphones only.

A survey sample selected from the pages of a local telephone listings would totally omit all those people, typically richer, who requested that their numbers not be published. It would also exclude large segments of younger people who only use cellphones. These potential biases are corrected through a technique that advanced telephone sampling substantially: **random-digit dialling (RDD)**.

RDD begins by specifying the operating telephone prefixes (area codes and telephone banks) in an area. Random digits are then assigned to these prefixes to create phone numbers. When these randomly generated phone numbers are dialled, a large proportion of them are not operational. But that is the price paid in order to ensure that all operating phone numbers are equally included in a sample. Because it dramatically reduces selection bias, RDD is a widely used technique in telephone surveys.

Telephone surveys have many advantages that underlie their popularity. Probably the greatest advantages are money and time, in that order. It's cheaper and quicker (not to mention potentially safer) to make phone calls than to make trips to do face-to-face interviews. In addition, social cues, such as the interviewer's appearance, are less likely to affect the answers respondents give over the phone. And sometimes respondents are more honest in giving socially disapproved answers if they don't have to look you in the eye. Similarly, it may be possible to probe into more sensitive areas, though this isn't necessarily the case. People are, to some extent, more suspicious when they can't see the person asking them questions.

Telephone surveys can allow greater control over data collection if several interviewers are engaged in the project. If all the interviewers are calling from the research office, they can get clarification from the person in charge whenever problems occur, as they inevitably do. Alone in the boondocks, an interviewer may have to wing it between weekly visits with the interviewing supervisor.

There are problems involved in telephone interviewing, however. Not getting through to people at all is a potential problem that telephone interviewers face due to the prevalence of voicemail and caller ID that allow people to screen their calls. Telephone methodology is also hampered by the proliferation of bogus "surveys" that are actually sales campaigns disguised as research. For the researcher, the ease with which people can hang up is a serious shortcoming of telephone surveys. Once you've been let inside someone's home for an interview, the respondent is unlikely to order you out of the house in mid-interview. It's much easier to terminate a telephone interview abruptly, saying something like "Whoops! Someone's at the door. I gotta go." or "OMIGOD! Someone is outside beating my car with a bat." (That sort of thing is much harder to fake when the interviewer is sitting in your living room.)

There are many issues and trade-offs that researchers must consider when selecting the best method of collecting survey data for their particular studies. While people are often more willing to report their views about sensitive issues over the telephone, there are those for which the opposite might be true. There are no certain guidelines for how best to ask personal questions and get honest responses, or for that matter, any response.

COMPUTER-ASSISTED TELEPHONE INTERVIEWING (CATI)

In Part 4, we'll be looking at some of the ways computers influence the conduct of social research, particularly data processing and analysis. Computers have also changed the nature of telephone interviewing. **Computer-assisted telephone interviewing (CATI)** is a major method used by

random-digit dialling (RDD) A telephone number generation system that ensures the equal inclusion of listed and unlisted numbers, as well as cellphones.

computer-assisted telephone interviewing (CATI) A survey research technique in which the telephone interviewer reads the questions from the computer monitor and enters the answers directly into the computer.

academic, government, and commercial survey researchers. Though there are variations in practice, CATI is like CAPI except the interview takes place over the phone instead of face-to-face.

In addition to the obvious advantages for data collection, CATI automatically prepares the data for analysis; in fact, the researcher can begin analyzing the data before the interviewing is complete, thereby gaining an advanced view of how the analysis will turn out.

Further, there is the telephone survey interview that does not require a human at all. Interactive voice recognition allows for the "robo-poll." Computers are programmed to both ask questions and record the answers. They are able to interpret answers that respondents give and then proceed with the interview.

RESPONSE RATES IN TELEPHONE SURVEYS

Telephone survey response rates have been reduced over time due to several factors. Some believe that increased telemarketing has contributed in a major way to the reduction in response rates. There is also the impact of factors such as caller ID and voicemail that contribute to the decline in rates (Tuckel and O'Neill 2002). And people contacted on their cellphones are less likely to agree to a survey than those reached by land line (Pew Research Center 2012). These are various types of difficulties that modern survey researchers must consider. However, Pew Research Center (2012:1) reported in "Assessing the Representativeness of Public Opinion Surveys" that

> despite declining response rates, telephone surveys that include landlines and cell phones and are weighted to match the demographic composition of the population continue to provide accurate data on most political, social and economic measures. This comports with the consistent record of accuracy achieved by major polls when it comes to estimating election outcomes, among other things.

As they stated, this does not mean that the decline in response rate has no consequence. They noted, for example, that people who volunteer more are more likely to respond to surveys. This, as well as other characteristics of people who are more likely to respond, potentially has an impact on survey results. For example, volunteer-related behaviours could be overestimated in telephone surveys. The report detailed a number of characteristics of likely respondents and other important issues.

As we noted earlier, while response rate will continue to be of great concern, a demonstrated lack of response bias can be more important than a high response rate. The relationship between response rate and accuracy of survey estimates of the population under study is a complicated one and, therefore, difficult to easily summarize. Useful information about surveys and response rates can be found on the Web by searching Nate Silver of the *New York Times* and the Pew Research Center's publication index.

COMPARISON OF THE DIFFERENT SURVEY METHODS

Now that we've seen several ways to collect survey data, let's take a moment to compare them directly.

Self-administered questionnaires are generally cheaper and quicker than face-to-face interview surveys. These considerations are likely to be important for an unfunded student wishing to undertake a survey for a term paper or thesis. Moreover, if you use the self-administered format, it costs no more to conduct a national survey than a local one of the same sample size. In contrast, a national interview survey (either face to face or by telephone) would cost far more than a local one. Also, online surveys, for example, typically require a small staff. Further, respondents are sometimes reluctant to report controversial or deviant attitudes or behaviours in interviews but are willing to respond to an anonymous self-administered questionnaire.

Interview surveys also offer many advantages. For example, they generally produce fewer incomplete questionnaires. Although respondents may skip questions in a self-administered questionnaire, interviewers are trained not to do so. However, computer-assisted surveys often offer a check on this by not allowing the respondent

SPOTLIGHT ON MIXED METHODS

Mixing Self-Administered Surveys and In-Depth Interviews

Epidemiological data indicates that Indigenous Canadians are nearly three times as likely as non-Indigenous Canadians to be infected with HIV, and that Indigenous youth are particularly at risk (Boulos et al. 2006). HIV testing and counselling have been identified as key components of any prevention program aimed at reducing HIV transmission among marginalized and vulnerable groups. Given the importance of early detection on the course of care and treatment of HIV infection, it is critical to understand what factors motivate individuals' decisions to seek HIV testing or not.

In light of these concerns, Mill et al. (2008) sought to investigate why Indigenous youth choose or don't choose to be tested; what types of services they use; and what the relationship is between testing and the decision to initiate treatment. To do so they conducted a mixed methods study using a cross-sectional, self-administered survey (n = 413) and in-depth interviews (n = 28) with Indigenous Canadians between the ages of 15 and 30. Eleven community-based organization in seven provinces and one territory helped with recruitment. The study was guided by a community-based research (CBR) approach, incorporating the principles of ownership, control, access, and possession (OCAP) for research involving Indigenous communities. This included guidance in all phases of the research from a community advisory committee (CAC) that included Indigenous youth, Elders, and representatives from community-based organizations (CIHR, 2007).

> The use of a MMR design allowed the researchers to describe HIV testing behaviours and care decisions in a large sample of Canadian [Indigenous] youth, while at the same time develop[ing] a more in-depth understanding of factors influencing youths' decision to have an HIV test and access care" (p. 11).[3]

They found that 51 percent of survey respondents reported being tested for HIV, as did 89 percent of interview respondents. The most commonly reported reason to seek testing was having sex without a condom (43.6 percent) or pregnancy (35.4 percent), while the most commonly identified reasons for not getting tested were the belief they were low risk for HIV (45.3 percent) or that they had not had sex with an infected person (34.5 percent). A prominent reason identified by interviewees for not getting tested was the feeling of "invulnerability" and that "it can't happen to me."

Of those youth who reported being tested, 12.7 percent of surveyed youth and 36 percent of interviewed youth indicated that they were HIV-positive. Delays in care-seeking after diagnosis were common, ranging from a few months to seven years after testing. Some of the reasons for delaying care-seeking that interviewees identified include "being scared or not wanting to think about their disease; being preoccupied with drugs or alcohol; not wanting to live; not knowing anything about care" (p. 9). Understanding their reasons for not getting tested and for delaying treatment after diagnosis have important implications for future efforts to deliver comprehensive HIV testing services to Indigenous youth.

3 Copyright © 2008 Mill et al., HIV Testing and Care in Canadian Aboriginal Youth: A community based mixed methods study; licensee BioMed Central Ltd. https://www.ncbi.nlm.nih.gov/pmc/articles/PMC2573888/

to leave a page or submit their questionnaire until they have answered all the questions. Still, interview surveys have typically achieved higher completion rates than self-administered questionnaires.

Although self-administered questionnaires may be more effective for sensitive issues, interview surveys are definitely more effective for complicated ones. Prime examples are the enumeration of household members and the determination of whether a given address corresponds to more than one housing unit. Although the concept of housing unit has been refined and standardized by those responsible for the census and interviewers can be trained to deal with the concept, it's extremely difficult to communicate in a self-administered questionnaire. This advantage of interview surveys pertains generally to all complicated contingency questions.

With interviewers, you can conduct a survey based on a sample of addresses or phone numbers rather than on names. An interviewer can arrive at an assigned address, or call the assigned number, introduce the survey, and even, following instructions, choose the appropriate person at that address to respond to the survey.

Finally, as we've seen, interviewers questioning respondents face to face can make important observations aside from responses to questions asked in the interview. In a household interview, they may note the characteristics of the neighbourhood, the dwelling unit, and so forth. They may also note characteristics of the respondents or the quality of their interaction with the respondents—whether the respondent had difficulty communicating, was hostile, and so forth.

The chief advantages of telephone surveys over those conducted face to face relate primarily on time and money. Telephone interviews are much cheaper and can be mounted and executed quickly. Also, interviewers are safer when interviewing in high-crime areas. Moreover, the impact of the interviewers on responses is somewhat lessened when they can't be seen by the respondents.

Online survey research continues to grow, with CAWI being the predominant form of questionnaire administration. Some of the advantages of self-administered online surveys include ease and convenience of survey completion and greater sampling reach, and technological innovation has allowed increased flexibility for online surveys with respect to question formatting (e.g., questions types, fonts, visuals, randomization of questions, enhanced capacity to restrict or eliminate invalid responses) and accessibility on various mobile digital devices. Also, data collection is simplified, since survey responses are automatically formatted into data files for ease of analysis. There are, of course, issues associated with online surveys as well. Prominent among these are lower response rates, sampling bias (e.g., online convenience samples are typically younger and more educated than the general population), and data privacy issues (Evans and Mathur 2018; Kim et al. 2010; Sowa et al. 2015).

Clearly, each survey method has its place in social research. Ultimately, you must balance the advantages and disadvantages of the different methods in relation to your research needs and your resources.

STRENGTHS AND WEAKNESSES OF SURVEY RESEARCH

Regardless of the specific method used, surveys, like other modes of observation in social scientific research, have special strengths and weaknesses. You should keep these in mind when determining whether the survey is appropriate for your research goals.

Surveys are particularly useful in describing the characteristics of a large population. A carefully selected probability sample in combination with a standardized questionnaire offers the possibility of making refined descriptive assertions about a student body, a city, a nation, or any other large population. Surveys determine unemployment rates, voting intentions, and the like with uncanny accuracy. Although the examination of official documents such as marriage, birth, or death records can provide equal accuracy for a few topics, no other method of observation can provide this general capability.

Surveys, especially self-administered ones, make large samples feasible. Surveys of 2,000 respondents are not unusual. A large number of cases is important for both descriptive and explanatory analyses, especially wherever several variables are to be analyzed simultaneously.

In one sense, surveys are flexible. Many questions may be asked on a given topic, giving you considerable flexibility in your analyses. Although an experimental design may require you to commit yourself in advance to a particular operational definition of a concept, surveys let you develop operational definitions from actual observations.

Finally, standardized questionnaires have an important strength in regard to measurement generally. Earlier chapters have discussed the ambiguous nature of most concepts: they have no ultimately real meanings. One person's religiosity is quite different from another's. Although you must be able to define concepts in those ways most relevant to your research goals, you may not find it easy to apply the same definitions uniformly to all subjects. The survey researcher is bound to this requirement by having to ask exactly the same questions of all subjects and having to impute the same intent to all respondents giving a particular response.

Survey research also has several weaknesses. First, the requirement for standardization often seems to result in the fitting of round pegs into square holes. Standardized questionnaire items often represent the least common denominator in assessing people's attitudes, orientations, circumstances, and experiences. By designing questions that will be at least minimally appropriate to all respondents, you may miss what is most appropriate to many respondents. In this sense, surveys often appear superficial in their coverage of complex topics. Although this problem can be partly offset by sophisticated analyses, it is inherent in survey research.

Similarly, survey research can seldom deal with the context of social life. Although questionnaires can provide information in this area, the survey researcher rarely develops the feel for the total life situation in which respondents are thinking and acting that, say, the participant observer can (see Chapter 10).

In many ways, surveys are inflexible. Studies involving direct observation can be modified as field conditions warrant, but surveys typically require that an initial study design remain unchanged throughout. As a field researcher, for example, you can become aware of an important new variable operating in the phenomenon you're studying and begin making careful observations of it. The survey researcher would probably be unaware of the new variable's importance and could do nothing about it in any event.

Finally, surveys are subject to the artificiality mentioned earlier in connection with experiments. Finding out that a person gives conservative answers to a questionnaire does not necessarily mean the person is conservative; finding out that a person gives prejudiced answers to a questionnaire does not necessarily mean the person is prejudiced. This shortcoming is especially salient in the realm of action. Surveys cannot measure social action; they can only collect self-reports of recalled past action or of prospective or hypothetical action.

The problem of artificiality has two aspects. First, the topic of study may not be amenable to measurement through questionnaires. Second, the act of studying that topic—an attitude, for example—may affect it. A survey respondent may have given no thought to whether a member of parliament should resign until asked for his or her opinion by an interviewer. He or she may, at that point, form an opinion on the matter.

Survey research is generally weak on validity and strong on reliability. In comparison with field research, for example, the artificiality of the survey format puts a strain on validity. As an illustration, people's opinions on issues seldom take the form of strongly agreeing, agreeing, disagreeing, or strongly disagreeing with a specific statement. Their survey responses in such cases must be regarded as approximate indicators of what the researchers had in mind when they framed the questions. This comment, however, needs to be held in the context of earlier discussions of the ambiguity of validity itself. To say something is a valid or an invalid measure assumes the existence of a "real" definition of what's being measured, and many scholars now reject that assumption.

Reliability is a clearer matter. By presenting all subjects with a standardized stimulus, survey research goes a long way toward eliminating unreliability in observations made by the researcher. Moreover, careful wording of the questions can also significantly reduce the subject's own unreliability.

As with all methods of observation, a full awareness of the inherent or probable weaknesses of survey research can partially resolve them in some cases. Ultimately, though, researchers are on the safest ground when they can use several research methods in studying a given topic.

ETHICAL CONSIDERATIONS

The ethical issues discussed in Chapter 3 apply to survey research as they do to all forms of research. We've mentioned several ethical considerations in the course of this chapter as well. Whether a survey is conducted face to face, over the telephone, or online, the researcher must provide for voluntary, informed consent from each participant. Participants should be told the purposes of the study through an introductory letter, or orally when it's a telephone or face-to-face interview survey. In the case of an online survey, whether the responses will be anonymous or confidential should be clearly indicated. In the case of interview surveys, assurances of confidentiality should be indicated, if that is the intent. If such assurances are not intended, that too should be clearly indicated. If a researcher plans to tape an interview, over the phone or in person, the respondent must be made aware of this and his or her permission must be sought. Information about how the respondents were selected for the study, the auspices under which the study is being conducted, and contact information should be provided for those who might want more information about the study. In the case of a mail survey, information about the mechanisms of how to return the questionnaire is also often included in the letter.

When seeking ethical approval for a survey research project, the letter or speech of introduction must be submitted to the review board. As you can see, such introductions may vary, depending on the study's design and purpose. An illustration of a short telephone introduction used in the 2000 General Social Survey follows:[4]

> Hello I'm ... from Statistics Canada. We are calling you for a study on new technology. The purpose of the study is to better understand people's use of technology and how it has affected their daily lives.
>
> All information we collect in this voluntary survey will be kept strictly confidential. Your participation is essential if the survey results are to be accurate.
>
> **Optional:**
>
> My supervisor is working with me today and may listen to the interview to evaluate the survey.
>
> (Statistics Canada, June 2001:B2)

Some of the ethical responsibilities of the survey researcher are initially rather subtle. When research is conducted from afar, as in mail surveys for example, the impact of the research on the respondent may not be as salient. The absence of face-to-face interaction may make the researcher less sensitive to respondents' needs and concerns. We want to emphasize, therefore, the researchers' moral and ethical responsibility to be considerate of respondents—of their time, their interests, their feelings, and their experience with the survey—when conducting any type of survey. In interview surveys, the interviewers should be familiar with the questionnaire so that the interview runs smoothly. In mail or online surveys, the questionnaires should be easy to understand and fill out.

As Guppy and Gray (2008) note—in a chapter in their book on surveys devoted to ethical issues—researchers must show respect for respondents and must be sure to represent accurately the information provided to them. The potential risks of a study to participants must be thoughtfully considered, and a plan should be made concerning how confidentiality or anonymity will be maintained. Survey researchers must carefully consider ethical concerns when designing, implementing, and reporting their research.

4 Statistics Canada, *2000 General Social Survey, Cycle 14: Access to and use of Information and Technology.* Catalogue no. 12M0014GPE. B2, June, 2001. Reproduced and distributed on an "as is" basis with the permission of Statistics Canada.

MAIN POINTS

- Survey research, a popular social research method, involves administering questionnaires to a sample of respondents selected from some population.
- Survey research is especially appropriate for making descriptive studies of large populations; survey data may also be used for explanatory purposes.
- Questionnaires provide a method of collecting data by (1) asking people questions or (2) asking them to agree or disagree with statements representing different points of view.
- Questions may be open-ended (respondents supply their own answers) or closed-ended (they select from a list of provided answers).
- There are several guidelines for questionnaire items:
  - Items should be clear and precise.
  - They should ask about a single thing (avoiding double-barrelled questions).
  - Short items are usually best.
  - Questions should be directed to respondents who are competent to answer.
  - Items should be relevant to the respondent.
  - Respondents must be willing to answer.
  - Items should avoid negative terms because they may confuse respondents.
  - Items should be worded to avoid biasing responses (i.e., encouraging respondents to answer in a particular way or to support a particular point of view).
  - Questionnaire formats can influence the quality of data collected.
- A clear format for contingency questions is needed to ensure that respondents answer all questions intended for them.
- The matrix question is an efficient format for presenting several items sharing the same response categories.
- The order of items in a questionnaire can influence the responses given.
- Clear instructions are important for getting appropriate responses to a questionnaire.
- Questionnaires should be pretested before being administered to the study sample.
- Questionnaires are usually administered in three basic ways: self-administered questionnaires, face-to-face encounters, or telephone surveys.
- Online surveys are the most common form of self-administered surveys. Properly monitoring completed returns provides a good guide to when a follow-up nudging is appropriate.
- A great deal of marketing research is done using online surveys. Care must be taken, however, when conducting online surveys because of concerns about representativeness. They are better at tapping targeted populations such as online shoppers or university students than general populations such as all Canadian adults.
- The essential characteristic of interviewers is that they be neutral; their presence in the data-collection process must not have any effect on the responses given to questionnaire items.
- Interviewers must be carefully trained to be familiar with the questionnaire, to follow the question wording and question order exactly, and to record responses exactly as they are given.
- Probes can be used by interviewers to elicit an elaboration on an incomplete or ambiguous response. Ideally, all interviewers should use the same probes and the probes should be neutral.
- Telephone surveys are often cheaper and more efficient than face-to-face interviews.
- A useful technique for eliminating potential bias in telephone number selections is random-digit dialling (RDD).
- The development of computer-assisted telephone interviewing (CATI) has been

beneficial and permits greater control over data collection.

- The advantages of a self-administered questionnaire over an interview survey are economy, speed, lack of interviewer bias, and the possibility of anonymity and privacy to encourage candid responses on sensitive issues.
- The advantages of an interview survey over a self-administered questionnaire are fewer incomplete questionnaires, fewer misunderstood questions, generally higher return rates, and greater flexibility in sampling and special observations.
- The principal advantages of telephone surveys over face-to-face interviews are the savings in cost and in time. Telephone interviewers may also have a smaller impact on the interview itself, and they are safer for the interviewer than in-person interviews.
- Online surveys have many of the strengths and weaknesses of older mail surveys. Although they are cheaper to conduct, they must be used with caution because it can be difficult to ensure that the respondents represent a more general population. When the population being studied is readily accessible on the Web, however, online surveys can be very efficient and cost effective.
- In general, survey research offers advantages in economy, the amount of data that can be collected, and the chance to sample a large population. The standardization of the data collected represents another special strength of survey research.
- Survey research has several weaknesses. It is somewhat artificial, potentially superficial, and relatively inflexible. It's difficult to use surveys to gain a full sense of social processes in their natural settings. In general, survey research is comparatively weak on validity and strong on reliability.
- When conducting surveys, the researcher must provide for voluntary, informed consent from each respondent. Introductions should include information such as the study's purpose and whether the data collected will be confidential.

REVIEW QUESTIONS AND EXERCISES

1. What closed-ended questions can you construct from each of the following open-ended questions?
   a. What was your family's total income last year?
   b. How important is religion in your life?
   c. What was your main reason for attending university?
   d. What do you feel is the biggest problem facing your community?
2. Construct a set of contingency questions for use in a self-administered questionnaire that would solicit the following information:
   a. Is the respondent employed?
   b. If unemployed, is the respondent looking for work?
   c. If the unemployed respondent is not looking for work, is he or she retired, a student, or a homemaker?
   d. If the respondent is looking for work, how long has he or she been looking?
3. Locate a survey being conducted on the Web. Briefly describe the survey and discuss its strengths and weaknesses.
4. Look at your appearance right now. What aspects of your attire, hairstyle, or hygiene might create a problem if you were interviewing a general cross-section of the public?

CONTINUITY PROJECT

PERCEPTIONS OF INEQUALITY

The Broadbent Institute is committed to fostering progressive change in Canadian society. They commissioned a survey of 3,000 Canadians about their perceptions of inequality and the distribution of wealth in our nation. Their findings are published in the report *The Wealth Gap: Perceptions and Misconceptions in Canada* (Broadbent Institute 2014).

Here are two main survey questions asked of the respondents:[5]

- What percent of Canada's wealth do you think each group controls?

  Wealthiest 20% _____
  2nd wealthiest 20% _____
  Middle 20% _____
  2nd poorest 20% _____
  Poorest 20% _____

- What percent of Canada's wealth should each group control?

  Wealthiest 20% _____
  2nd wealthiest 20% _____
  Middle 20% _____
  2nd poorest 20% _____
  Poorest 20% _____

1. Critically evaluate each of these questions against the guidelines for asking questions. What deficiencies can you identify in these questions?
2. What suggestions for improving the questions can you offer?

5 From Broadbent Institute, 2014. *The Wealth Gap: Perceptions and Misconceptions in Canada*, http://www.broadbentinstitute.ca/the_wealth_gap. Reprinted with permission.

Ermolaer Alexander/Shutterstock.com

NONREACTIVE RESEARCH

This chapter will present overviews of three unobtrusive research methods: the analysis of existing statistics and secondary analysis, content analysis, and historical and comparative research. Each of these methods allows researchers to study social life from afar, without influencing it in the process.

IN THIS CHAPTER...

INTRODUCTION

The modes of observation discussed so far require the researcher to intrude to some degree on whatever he or she is studying. This is most obvious in the case of experiments, followed closely by survey research. Even the field researcher, as we'll see, can change things in the process of studying them.

At least one previous example in this book, however, was totally exempt from that danger. Durkheim's analysis of suicide did nothing to affect suicides one way or the other (see Chapter 5). His study is an example of **nonreactive research**, or methods of studying social behaviour without affecting it. As you'll see, nonreactive research can be qualitative or quantitative.

This chapter examines four types of nonreactive research methods: analysis of existing statistics (including the secondary analysis of survey data), content analysis, unobtrusive online research, and historical and comparative research. The Durkheim study is an example of the *analysis of existing statistics.* As you'll see, there are great masses of data all around you, awaiting your use in the understanding of social life. Of particular note is the large number of high-quality survey data sets available for *secondary analysis.* In *content analysis,* researchers examine a class of social artifacts that are usually written documents, such as newspaper editorials. *Unobtrusive online research* involves observing our activities online, either in real time (e.g., chat rooms) or via digital traces (e.g., online purchases). Big data techniques are used to examine patterns and make connections from the masses of user data collected online. Social network analysis aims to understand the highly interconnected nature of our social world, relying increasingly on digital data and online traces to do so. Finally, *historical and comparative research,* a form of research with a venerable history in the social sciences, is currently enjoying a resurgence of popularity. Historical and comparative research is for many a qualitative method, one in which the main resources for observation and analysis are historical records. There are also, however, a number of historical and comparative analysts who use quantitative techniques. The method's name often includes the word *comparative* because social scientists—in contrast to historians who may simply describe a particular set of events—look for common patterns that recur in different times and places.

To set the stage for our examination of these four research methods, we want to draw your attention to an excellent book that should sharpen your senses about the potential for nonreactive measures in general. It is a classic work that uses a synonym for nonreactive research, labelled "unobtrusive research."

In 1966, Eugene Webb and three colleagues published an ingenious little book on social research (revised in 2000) that has become a classic: *Unobtrusive Measures.* It focuses, as you likely surmised, on the idea of unobtrusive or nonreactive research. Webb and his colleagues have played freely with the task of learning about human behaviour by observing what people inadvertently leave behind them. Do you want to know what exhibits are the most popular at a museum? You could conduct a poll, but people might tell you what they thought you wanted to hear or what might make them look more intellectual and serious. You could stand by different exhibits and count the viewers that came by, but people might come over to see what you were doing. Webb and his colleagues suggest you check the wear and tear on the floor in front of various exhibits. Those where the tiles have been worn down the most are probably the most popular. Want to know which exhibits are popular with little kids? Look for mucus on the glass cases. To get a sense of the most popular radio stations, you could arrange with an auto mechanic to check the radio settings for cars brought in for repair.

The possibilities are limitless. Like a detective investigating a crime, the social researcher looks for clues. If you stop to notice, you'll find that clues of social behaviour are all around you. In a sense, everything you see represents the answer to some important social scientific question. All you have to do is think of the question.

nonreactive research Methods of studying social behaviour without affecting it. This includes analysis of existing statistics, secondary analysis, content analysis, and historical and comparative research.

Although problems of validity and reliability crop up in unobtrusive measures, a little ingenuity can either handle them or put them in perspective. We encourage you to look at Webb's book. It's enjoyable reading, and it can be a source of stimulation and insight for social inquiry through data that already exist. For now, let's turn our attention to four unobtrusive methods often used by social scientists.

ANALYZING EXISTING STATISTICS AND SECONDARY ANALYSIS

Frequently, you can or must undertake social scientific inquiry through the use of official or quasi-official statistics. We begin by looking at ways of drawing on data analyses reported by others, such as government agencies. This differs from secondary analysis, in which you obtain a copy of someone else's data and undertake your own statistical analysis. Nonetheless, there is a great deal of overlap between secondary analysis and the use of existing statistics. Many of the data problems and limitations that apply to the use of existing statistics also apply to secondary analysis. For example, the researcher must often face the limitations and constraints of available measures, and sound judgment often requires knowledge of exactly how the measures were devised, collected, and coded—and thus what they incorporate. There are other similarities as well—for example, ethical approval is almost never required when using existing statistics or conducting a secondary analysis. However, the data available to you may at times be constrained because of promises of confidentiality in the initial data collections.

The method of using existing statistics is particularly significant because existing statistics should always be considered at least as a supplemental source of data. If you were planning a survey of political attitudes, for example, you would do well to examine and present your findings within a context of voting patterns, rates of voter turnout, or similar statistics relevant to your research interest. Or if you were doing evaluation research on an experimental morale-building program on an assembly line, statistics on absenteeism, sick leave, and so on, would probably be interesting and revealing in connection with the data your own research would generate. Existing statistics, then, can often provide a historical or conceptual context within which to locate your original research. For example, Sosteric (1996) did a participant observation study in a nightclub in a small Canadian city. In support of his claim that the club's workers made above-average incomes, he reported data from Statistics Canada on industry averages for full- and part-time waitresses and bartenders.

Existing statistics can also provide the main data for a social scientific inquiry. For example, Kiepal and colleagues (2012) compare data from the police on missing persons with Canadian census data for the same city to determine whether those reported missing are more likely to be from groups who are disadvantaged socially and economically. They find, for example, that Indigenous people, the unemployed, and youth from disadvantaged backgrounds are "overrepresented among people reported missing" (p. 137).

Another excellent example of existing statistics providing the main data for a social scientific inquiry is the classic study mentioned at the beginning of this chapter, the French sociologist Émile Durkheim's *Suicide* ([1897] 1951). Let's take a closer look at Durkheim's work before considering some of the special problems this method presents.

DURKHEIM'S STUDY OF SUICIDE

Why do people kill themselves? Undoubtedly, every suicide case has a unique history and explanation, yet all such cases could no doubt be grouped according to certain common causes: financial failure, trouble in love, disgrace, and other kinds of personal problems. Émile Durkheim had a slightly different question in mind when he addressed the matter of suicide, however. He wanted to discover the environmental conditions that encouraged or discouraged it, especially social conditions.

The more Durkheim examined the available records, the more patterns of differences became apparent to him. One of the first things to attract his attention was the relative *stability* of suicide rates. Looking at several countries, he found suicide rates to be about the same year after year. He also discovered that a disproportionate number of suicides occurred in summer, leading him to hypothesize that temperature might have something to do with suicide. If this were the case, suicide rates should be higher in the southern European countries than in the temperate ones. However, Durkheim discovered that the highest rates were found in countries in the central latitudes, so temperature couldn't be the answer.

He explored the role of age (35 was the most common suicide age), gender (men outnumbered women around four to one), and numerous other factors. Eventually, a general pattern emerged from different sources.

With regard to the stability of suicide rates over time, for instance, Durkheim found the pattern was not totally stable. He found spurts in the rates during times of political turmoil, which occurred in several European countries around 1848. This observation led him to hypothesize that suicide might have something to do with "breaches in social equilibrium." Put differently, social stability and integration seemed to be a protection against suicide.

This general hypothesis was substantiated and specified through Durkheim's analysis of a different set of data. The countries of Europe had radically different suicide rates. The rate in Saxony (now part of Germany), for example, was about 10 times that of Italy, and the relative ranking of various countries persisted over time. As Durkheim considered other differences among the various countries, he eventually noticed a striking pattern: predominantly Protestant countries had consistently higher suicide rates than Catholic countries. The predominantly Protestant countries had 190 suicides per million population; mixed Protestant–Catholic countries had 96; and predominantly Catholic countries had 58 (Durkheim [1897] 1951:152).

Although suicide rates therefore seemed to be related to religion, Durkheim reasoned that some other factor, such as level of economic and cultural development, might explain the observed differences. If religion had a genuine effect on suicide, then the religious difference would have to be found *within* given countries as well. To test this idea, Durkheim first noted that the German state of Bavaria had both the most Catholics and the lowest suicide rates in that country, whereas heavily Protestant Prussia had a much higher suicide rate. Not content to stop there, however, Durkheim examined the provinces making up each of those states.

Figure 9-1 shows what he found. As you can see, in both Bavaria and Prussia, provinces with the highest proportion of Protestants, also had the highest suicide rates. Increasingly, Durkheim became confident that religion played a significant role in the matter of suicide.

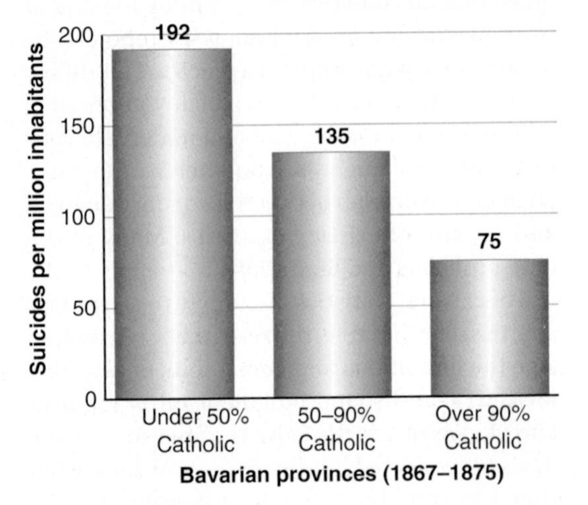

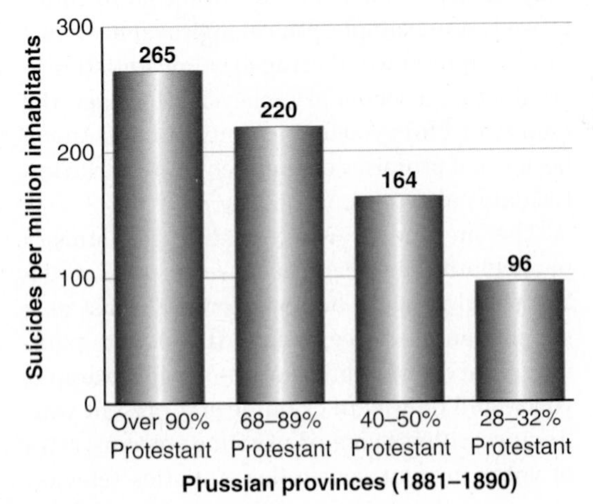

FIGURE 9-1 Suicide Rates in Various German Provinces, Arranged in Terms of Religious Affiliation.
Source: Durkheim (1951).

Returning eventually to a more general theoretical level, Durkheim combined the religious findings with the earlier observation about increased suicide rates during times of political turmoil. Put most simply, Durkheim suggested many suicides are a product of *anomie*, "normlessness," or a general sense of social instability and disintegration. During times of political strife, people may feel that the old ways of society are collapsing. They become demoralized and depressed, and suicide is one answer to the severe discomfort. Seen from the other direction, social integration and solidarity—reflected in personal feelings of being part of a coherent, enduring social whole—offer protection against depression and suicide. That was where the religious difference fits in. Catholicism, as a far more structured and integrated religious system, gave people a greater sense of coherence and stability than did the more loosely structured Protestantism.

From these theories, Durkheim created the concept of *anomic suicide*. More important, as you know, he added the concept of *anomie* to the lexicon of the social sciences.

This account of Durkheim's classic study is greatly simplified, of course. Anyone studying social research would profit from studying the original. For our purposes, though, Durkheim's approach provides a good illustration of the possibilities for research contained in the masses of data regularly gathered and reported by government agencies and other organizations.

UNITS OF ANALYSIS

The unit of analysis involved in the analysis of existing statistics is often *not* the individual. Durkheim, for example, was required to work with political-geographical units: countries, regions, states, and cities. The same situation would probably arise if you were to undertake a study of crime rates, accident rates, or disease. By their nature, most existing statistics are aggregated—they describe groups.

The aggregate nature of existing statistics can present a problem, though not an insurmountable one. As we saw, for example, Durkheim wanted to determine whether Protestants or Catholics were more likely to commit suicide. The difficulty was that none of the records available to him indicated the religion of those people who committed suicide. Ultimately, then, it was not possible for him to say whether Protestants committed suicide more often than Catholics, though he inferred as much. Because Protestant countries, regions, and states had higher suicide rates than Catholic countries, regions, and states, he drew the obvious conclusion.

There's danger in drawing this kind of conclusion, however. It's always possible that patterns of behaviour at a group level may not reflect corresponding patterns on an individual level. Such errors are said to be due to an ecological fallacy, which was discussed in Chapter 4. In the case of Durkheim's study, it was altogether possible, for example, that it was Catholics who committed suicide in the predominantly Protestant areas. Perhaps Catholics in predominantly Protestant areas were so badly persecuted that they were led into despair and suicide. In that case, it would be possible for Protestant countries to have high suicide rates without any Protestants committing suicide.

Durkheim avoided the danger of ecological fallacy in two ways. First, his general conclusions were based as much on rigorous theoretical deductions as on the empirical facts. The correspondence between theory and fact made a counter-explanation, such as the one we just made up, less likely. Second, by extensively retesting his conclusions in a variety of ways, Durkheim further strengthened the likelihood that they were correct. Suicide rates were higher in Protestant countries than in Catholic ones, higher in Protestant regions of Catholic countries than in Catholic regions of Protestant countries, and so forth. The replication of findings added to the weight of evidence in support of his conclusions.

PROBLEMS OF VALIDITY

Whenever we base our research on an analysis of data that already exist, we're obviously limited to what exists. Often, the existing data do not cover exactly what we're interested in, and our measurements may not be altogether valid representations of the variables and concepts we want to draw conclusions about.

Two characteristics of science are used to handle the problem of validity in analysis of existing statistics: *logical reasoning* and *replication.* Durkheim's strategy provides an example of logical reasoning. Although he could not determine the religion of people who committed suicide, he reasoned that most of the suicides in a predominantly Protestant region would be Protestants.

Replication can be a general solution to problems of validity in social research. Crying in sad movies isn't necessarily a valid measure of compassion, nor is putting little birds back in their nests or giving money to charity. None of these things, taken alone, would prove that one group (women, say) was more compassionate than another (men). But if women appeared more compassionate than men by all these measures, that would create a weight of evidence in support of the conclusion. In the analysis of existing statistics, a little ingenuity and reasoning can usually turn up several independent tests of a given hypothesis. If all the tests seem to support the hypothesis, then the weight of evidence supports the validity of the measure.

PROBLEMS OF RELIABILITY

The analysis of existing statistics depends heavily on the quality of the statistics themselves: Are they accurate reports of what they claim to report? This can be a substantial problem at times, because the weighty tables of government statistics are sometimes grossly inaccurate.

Consider research into crime. Because a great deal of the research into crime depends on official crime statistics, this body of data has come under critical evaluation. The results have not been too encouraging. As an illustration, suppose you were interested in tracing the long-term trends in violence against women in Canada since the late 1960s, specifically the crime of rape. Official statistics on the numbers of people arrested for rape or attempted rape would seem to be a reasonable measure to use. Right? Not necessarily.

To begin, you face a hefty problem of validity. The first thing you would become aware of in attempting to gather official statistics is that there is no longer a legally defined crime of "rape" in Canada. Laws can change, and therefore so do the definitions of what constitutes a given criminal act. "The sections of the *Criminal Code* dealing with rape were repealed and replaced in a process begun in 1980, partly as a result of the modern feminist movement" (Silverman et al. 2000:8). Since the legal reform of 1983, sexually aggressive acts are covered under three levels of seriousness of sexual assault (sections 271–273 of the *Criminal Code*). As Roberts and Gebotys (1992:558–559) stated, prior to 1983 the offence of rape "had a degree of conceptual clarity that is absent from the sexual assault offenses. If a victim reported a coerced sexual act involving penetration, the incident was by definition rape and not indecent assault. Sexual Assault is undefined in the current *Criminal Code* of Canada, leaving the courts free to resolve the question of what kinds of behaviours are included in the offense." Thus, "there is no direct, one-to-one correspondence between the prereform and postreform offenses (i.e., rape does not correspond exclusively to any particular level of sexual assault)" (p. 560).

Because there is no direct correspondence between the old and new offences, you would not be able to get a valid measure of rape in Canada from the 1960s to the present using official crime statistics. But even if you limited your study to the period prior to the change in law, for example, you would still have problems of reliability, stemming from the nature of law enforcement and crime record keeping. As Kong (2000:63) warns, "Many factors could influence official crime statistics. These include reporting by the public to the police; reporting by police to the CCJS [Canadian Centre for Justice Statistics]; and the impact of new initiatives such as changes in legislation, policies or enforcement practices."

Law enforcement, for example, is subject to various pressures. A public outcry against the poor handling of rape cases and the negative treatment of rape victims by the criminal justice system could affect reporting and the processing of cases by the police, for example, increasing the number of cases the police find credible and hence in which charges are laid. A sensational story in the press can have a similar effect. In addition, the volume of overall business facing the police can affect the handling of offences more generally.

As analyses of victimization surveys and data concerning police processing of cases demonstrate, the official records present a far less accurate history of the occurrence of rape and other forms of sexual assaults than actually exist in our society. Most sexual assaults are not reported to the police, and a high percentage of reported incidents are classified as unfounded, indicating the police investigation declared the crime did not occur (Roberts and Gebotys 1992). On a different level of analysis, Donald Black (1970) and others have analyzed the factors influencing whether an offender is actually arrested by police or let off with a warning. Ultimately, official crime statistics are influenced by whether specific offenders are well or poorly dressed, whether they are polite or abusive to police officers, and so forth. When we consider unreported crimes in general, sometimes estimated to be as much as ten times the number of crimes known to police, the reliability of crime statistics gets even shakier.

Finally, the process of record keeping affects the records that are kept and reported and, therefore, the data available to researchers. Whenever a law enforcement unit improves its record-keeping system—computerizes it, for example—the apparent crime rates always increase dramatically. This can happen even if the number of crimes committed, reported, and investigated does not increase.

Researchers' first protection against the problems of reliability in the analysis of existing statistics is being aware that the problem may exist. Investigating the nature of the data collection and tabulation may enable you to assess the nature and degree of unreliability so you can judge its potential impact on your research interest. If you also use logical reasoning and replication, you can usually cope with the problem.

SOURCES OF EXISTING STATISTICS

It would take a whole book just to list the sources of data available for analysis. We want to mention a few sources and point you in the direction of finding others relevant to your research interest.

One of the most valuable sources of data for Canada is Statistics Canada, the statistics bureau of the federal government. As its website (2016) states, "Under the Statistics Act, Statistics Canada is required to collect, compile, analyse, abstract and publish statistical information relating to the commercial, industrial, financial, social, economic and general activities and conditions of the people of Canada."

Statistics Canada develops and conducts statistical surveys and other types of studies (discussed in Chapter 8). It is responsible for the census, labour statistics, and statistics on health and welfare, finance, agriculture, and industry. It is also responsible for the collection and reporting of official crime statistics in Canada. "Since 1962, all criminal incidents are reported by police agencies to the Uniform Crime Reporting [UCR] Survey at the Canadian Centre for Justice Statistics" (CCJS) located within Statistics Canada (CCJS 1999: vi). Thus, Statistics Canada is responsible for providing population information, economic data, data on crime and justice, and indicators such as the unemployment rate and the consumer price index. The list of information that is gathered and reported by Statistics Canada is nearly endless.

Statistics Canada publishes numerous analytic periodicals and series of reports, such as Canadian Social Trends, Canadian Economic Observer, Perspectives on Labour and Income, Juristat, Health Reports, and Focus on Culture, which present statistics and analyses on a wide range of topics. It has also made available an electronic edition of Historical Statistics of Canada (second edition), jointly produced with the Social Science Federation of Canada, that can be viewed online or downloaded from its Internet site without charge. "This volume contains about 1,088 statistical tables on the social, economic, and institutional conditions of Canada from the start of the Confederation in 1867 to the mid-1970s" (Statistics Canada 2012b). Other information about available statistics and data may be located on Statistics Canada's website at http://www.statcan.gc.ca/eng/help/options. Information about the Data Liberation Initiative (DLI), which provides affordable access to a wide range of Statistics Canada data for research and teaching, may also be obtained on the Statistics Canada website. A large number of Canadian universities subscribe to it. You can check the site to see if yours subscribes to it and then obtain the DLI contact information for your university as well—or you can check with the data librarian at your university. In addition, the website contains a large socioeconomic database available for exploration, called CANSIM, which is updated daily. It contains more than 43 million time series. A quick tutorial at the site helps you learn how to use the database.

The only way to truly gain a sense of the information available to you from Statistics Canada is to explore its website.

A vast majority of governments have highly developed institutions for gathering statistics, and most produce annual volumes reporting a wide range of information about their countries. For example, there is the annual *Statistical Abstract of the United States*, *Annuaire Statistique de la France*, *Annuario Statistico Italiano*, and the *Japan Statistical Yearbook* (published in English). Collection of data—official statistics—by governments provides some of the best sources of available data.

Government agencies at all levels publish countless data series. World statistics are available through the United Nations. Its *Demographic Yearbook* presents annual vital statistics (births, deaths, and other data relevant to population) for the individual nations of the world. Other publications report a variety of other kinds of data. To find out some of what's available, spend a few hours searching the Web. Here are just a few websites to illustrate the richness of this resource:

- Library and Archives Canada: http://www.collectionscanada.gc.ca/electroniccollection/
- UK National Statistics Publication Hub: https://www.gov.uk/government/statistics
- Canadian Institute for Health Information: http://www.cihi.ca/
- The World Bank: http://www.worldbank.org/
- Eurostat: http://ec.europa.eu/eurostat/help/new-eurostat-website
- Australian Bureau of Statistics: http://www.abs.gov.au/

The amount of data provided by nongovernmental agencies is as staggering as the amount your taxes buy. Chambers of commerce often publish data reports on business, as do private consumer groups. Nonprofit organizations such as the Canadian Council on Social Development (http://www.ccsd.ca) provide free access to statistics concerning poverty, welfare, and income, for example. George Gallup publishes reference volumes on public opinion as tapped by Gallup Polls since 1935. Statistical and other types of data can be found in such places as the genealogy website for Prince Edward Island (http://www.islandregister.com/) as well.

Organizations such as the Population Reference Bureau (http://www.prb.org/) publish a variety of international demographic data that a researcher could use. Its *World Population Data Sheet* and *Population Bulletin* are resources heavily used by social scientists.

The sources listed here are only a tiny fraction of the thousands that are available. With so much data already collected, the lack of funds to support expensive data collection is no reason for not doing good and useful social research.

SECONDARY ANALYSIS

Chapter 8 introduced you to the rich quantitative tradition of survey research. **Secondary analysis** is a form of research in which the data collected and processed by one researcher are reanalyzed—often for a different purpose—by another. Beginning in the 1960s, survey researchers became aware of the potential value that lay in archiving survey data for analysis by scholars who had nothing to do with the survey design and data collection. Even when one researcher had conducted a survey and analyzed the data, others with slightly different interests could further analyze those same data. Thus, if you were interested in the relationship between political attitudes and attitudes toward gender equality, you could examine that research question through the

secondary analysis A form of research in which the data collected and processed by one researcher are reanalyzed—often for a different purpose—by another. This is especially appropriate in the case of survey data. Data archives are repositories or libraries for the storage and distribution of data for secondary analysis.

analysis of any dataset that happened to contain questions relating to those two variables. Data archives, therefore, contain data sets available to others for secondary analysis. There are now a large number of archives containing a wide range of data sets. Once you have obtained such data from the archive, it's yours to keep and use again and again if you desire.

Available Data for Secondary Analysis Statistics Canada has a number of data sets available for secondary analysis. For example, it has conducted the General Social Survey (GSS) on an annual basis since 1985 (with two exceptions, 1987 and 1997), gathering national information on a wide range of topics. Statistics Canada also conducts special surveys on a wide variety of issues. The information generated from these surveys is a great source of secondary data for social researchers. For example, Rosemary Gartner and Ross Macmillan (2000) used Statistics Canada's Violence Against Women (VAW) survey to investigate whether the relationship between the offender and female victim has an impact on the reporting of violence against women to the police. They noted that the VAW survey was "the most comprehensive survey data set" on the topic currently available (p. 128). Other examples of surveys conducted by Statistics Canada are the National Population Health Survey, the National Longitudinal Survey of Children and Youth (NLSCY), the Workplace and Employee Survey, and the Survey of Labour and Income Dynamics (SLID).

Survey data for secondary analysis may be obtained in a number of places. The Inter-university Consortium for Political and Social Research (ICPSR) at the University of Michigan, for example, has an excellent data archive (http://www.icpsr.umich.edu/) and information on data resources on the Web. Researchers can access a number of surveys from ICPSR, and many Canadian universities are ICPSR member institutions. The U.S. General Social Survey (GSS) is a major survey of American residents (funded by the U.S. federal government) and has been conducted since 1972, nearly annually. The surveys gather numerous social science variables and are readily accessed on the Web at http://www3.norc.org. Canada has its own version of the GSS (http://www.statcan.gc.ca/pub/89f0115x/89f0115x2013001-eng.htm) and includes a wealth of longitudinal data for analysis.

If you desire a list of public opinion polls in Canada by such groups as Gallop Canada and Angus Reid, for example, you can go to the Roper Center for Public Opinion Research website (https://ropercenter.cornell.edu/) at Cornell University, which contains information on Canadian opinion polls and much more. If you would like readily available opinion poll data from companies such as Environics and CROP, go to the Canadian Opinion Research Archive (CORA) at http://www.queensu.ca/cora/, where analyses may be conducted directly on the website.

If you are interested in finding available data sources for a particular research question or for a given country, a Web search may prove very useful. There are a number of international archives available to social researchers. In addition, many universities have data librarians who are highly knowledgeable about sources of archived data available to scholars at little or no cost.

Advantages and Disadvantages of Secondary Analysis The advantages of secondary analysis are obvious and enormous: it's cheaper and faster than doing original surveys, and, depending on who did the original survey, you may benefit from the work of top-flight professionals. With the relative ease of secondary analysis, the likelihood of gathering together a body of past research in order to, for example, pursue an issue or relationship—that is, conduct a meta-analysis—is more likely. In a meta-analysis, similar data from many studies can be analyzed.

There are, however, disadvantages to secondary analysis. A key problem involves the recurrent question of validity. When one researcher collects data for one particular purpose, you have no assurance that those data will be appropriate for your research interests. Typically, you'll find that the original researcher asked a question that "comes close" to measuring what you're interested in, but you'll wish the question had been asked just a little differently or that another related question had also been asked. Your question, then, is whether the question that was asked provides a valid measure of the variable you want to analyze. Nonetheless, secondary analysis can be very useful. While no single method unlocks all puzzles, there is no limit to the ways you can find out about things. And when you zero in on an issue from several independent directions, you gain that much more expertise.

Let's move from the analysis of existing statistics and secondary analysis to content analysis. In content analysis, communications rather than numbers are the substance analyzed.

CONTENT ANALYSIS

Human experience is guided by that set of shared, meaningful symbols called culture. Culture is abstract; it exists in people's minds. But the products of culture are concrete and subject to observation and research. A central product of culture is **artifacts**. Artifacts are material products of culture. Artifacts are everywhere: think iPads, the Mona Lisa, *Duck Dynasty*, *Fifty Shades of Grey*, automobiles, blockbuster movies, sofas, clothes, food. All this material is a concrete expression of culture.

If culture is abstract and artifacts are concrete, then a connection exists between these two levels of experience. Artifacts are concrete *expressions* of abstract culture. If the connection is reversed, then the interpretation of artifacts provides insights into culture. The methodology of content analysis does just that; it seeks to study and interpret what artifacts tell us about the culture that produced them.

Content analysis is the systematic study and interpretation of cultural products (artifacts). The artifacts can be books, websites, magazines, poems, newspapers, songs, paintings, speeches, letters, email messages, laws, and constitutions. Any cultural artifacts are fair game. We will begin by giving extended consideration to a common expression of content analysis, communications research. We will then discuss other uses of content analysis, including discourse analysis and visual sociology.

artifacts Concrete objects that are expressions of abstract culture.

content analysis The systematic study and interpretation of cultural products.

TRADITIONAL CONTENT ANALYSIS

Content analysis is particularly well suited to the study of communications and to answering the classic question of communications research: "Who says what, to whom, why, how, and with what effect?" Are popular French novels more concerned with love than Canadian ones? Was the popular British music of the 1960s more politically cynical than the popular German music during that period? Do political candidates who primarily address "bread and butter" issues get elected more often than those who address issues of high principle? Each of these questions addresses a social scientific research topic: the first might address national character, the second political orientations, and the third political process. Although such topics might be studied by observing individual people, content analysis provides another approach.

Tremblay used content analysis to examine the legislative behaviour of female and male members of the Canadian Parliament. Her goal was to determine whether female members of the House of Commons have an impact on politics and, in particular, whether they are more likely than male MPs to represent women by promoting women's issues. In addition to a survey, a "content analysis was conducted specifically on the Index of the Debates in the House of Commons [Hansard Index] during the first session of the 35th Parliament. This Index covered over 17,700 pages of debate. Both MPs (who spoke on women's issues) and themes (which women's issues were raised) were analyzed" (1998:444). What Tremblay found was that a higher percentage of the female MPs addressed women's issues than did the male MPs, but that MPs of both genders acted to support women's issues—although such issues were a relatively minor area of interest for both.

Bright et al. conducted a content analysis of newspaper editorials in Toronto. They were interested in the accessibility of public discourse in a multicultural society; for example, whether "the voices of a variety of ethnic communities are heard on issues of general interest" (1999:317).

They assessed the views expressed on Quebec independence in both mainstream and "marginal 'ethnic'" newspaper editorials in the year preceding the 1995 Quebec referendum. (Interviews with editorialists were also conducted to determine what factors influenced editorial opinion.) From their qualitative content analysis, they concluded that

> Editorials in both the mainstream and marginal presses are steadfastly anti-separatist, a stance evident both in the predictions of economic doom in the event of Quebec independence and the focus on and vilification of the sovereigntist forces. At the same time, the ethnic presses demonstrate a measure of autonomy in their discourse, emphasizing the cultural aspects of the Quebec issue and focussing on the reaction of minority communities.
>
> (1999:319)

Some topics are more appropriately addressed by content analysis than by any other method of inquiry. Suppose you're interested in violence on television. Maybe you suspect that the manufacturers of men's products are more likely to sponsor violent TV shows than are other kinds of sponsors. Content analysis would be the best way of finding out.

Briefly, here's what you would do. First, you'd develop operational definitions of the two key variables in your inquiry: *men's products* and *violence*. The section on coding, later in this chapter, will discuss some of the ways you could do that. Ultimately, you'd need a plan that would allow you to watch TV, classify sponsors, and rate the degree of violence on particular shows.

Next you'd have to decide what to watch. Probably you'd decide (1) what stations to watch, (2) for what period, and (3) at what hours. (It may be useful here to briefly go to Chapter 6 for a refresher on sampling in content analysis) Then you'd stock up on beer and potato chips and start watching, classifying, and recording. Once you had completed your observations, you'd be able to analyze the data you collected and determine whether men's product manufacturers sponsored more blood and gore than did other sponsors.

As a mode of observation, content analysis requires a thoughtful handling of the "what" that is being communicated. The analysis of data collected in this mode, as in others, addresses the "why" and "with what effect."

Let's turn now to the coding or classification of material being observed. The next section discusses the manipulation of such classifications to draw descriptive and explanatory conclusions.

CODING IN CONTENT ANALYSIS

Content analysis is essentially a coding operation. **Coding** is the process of transforming raw data into a standardized form. In content analysis, communications—oral, written, or other—are coded or classified according to some conceptual framework. Thus, for example, TV shows may be coded as violent or nonviolent. Novels may be coded as romantic or not, paintings as representational or not, and political speeches as containing character assassinations or not. Recall that terms such as these are subject to many interpretations, and the researcher must specify definitions clearly.

Coding in content analysis involves the logic of conceptualization and operationalization, as discussed in Chapter 5. As in other research methods, you must refine your conceptual framework and develop specific methods for observing in relation to that framework.

Manifest and Latent Content In field research (Chapter 10), the researcher faces a fundamental choice between depth and specificity of understanding. Often, this represents a choice between validity and reliability, respectively. Typically, field researchers opt for depth, preferring to base their judgments on a broad range of observations and information, even at the risk that another observer might reach a different judgment of the same situation. Survey research, through the use of standardized questionnaires, represents the other extreme: total specificity, even though the specific measures of variables may not be fully satisfactory as valid reflections

coding The process whereby raw data are transformed into standardized form suitable for machine processing and analysis.

of those variables. The content analyst has some choice in this matter, however.

Coding the **manifest content**—the visible, surface content—of a communication is analogous to using a standardized questionnaire. To determine, for example, how erotic certain novels are, you might simply count the number of times the word *love* appears in each novel or the average number of appearances per page. Or you might use a list of words, such as *love, kiss, hug,* and *caress,* each of which might serve as an indicator of the erotic nature of the novel. This method would have the advantage of ease and reliability in coding and of letting the reader of the research report know precisely how eroticism was measured. It would have a disadvantage, on the other hand, with regard to validity. Surely the phrase *erotic novel* conveys a richer and deeper meaning than the number of times the word *love* is used.

Alternatively, you may code the **latent content** of the communication: its underlying meaning. In the present example, you might read an entire novel or a sample of paragraphs or pages and make an overall assessment of how erotic the novel was. Although your total assessment might very well be influenced by the appearance of words such as *love* and *kiss,* it would not depend fully on their frequency.

Clearly, this second method seems better designed for tapping the underlying meaning of communications, but its advantage comes at a cost of reliability and specificity. Especially if more than one person is coding the novel, somewhat different definitions or standards may be used. A passage that one coder regards as erotic may not seem erotic to another. Even if you do all the coding yourself, there's no guarantee that your definitions and standards will remain constant throughout the enterprise. Moreover, the reader of your research report will likely be uncertain about the definitions you've used.

manifest content In connection with content analysis, the concrete terms contained in a communication, as distinguished from latent content.

latent content As used in connection with content analysis, the underlying meaning of communications as distinguished from their manifest content.

The differences between manifest and latent coding can be summarized as follows. Manifest coding of materials (objective) involves the counting of specific elements, such as the word *love,* to determine whether and to what degree the passage should be judged "erotic." Latent coding of materials (subjective) calls for the researcher to view the entire unit of analysis (a paragraph in this example) and make a subjective assessment regarding whether and to what degree it is "erotic."

Given their respective strengths and limitations, the best strategy generally is to use both coding methods. For example, Carol Auster was interested in changes in the socialization of young women in the Girl Scouts. To explore this, she undertook a content analysis of the Girl Scout manuals as revised over time. In particular, Auster was interested in the view that women should be limited to homemaking. Her analysis of the manifest content suggested a change: "I found that while 23 percent of the badges in 1913 centered on home life, this was true of only 13 percent of the badges in 1963 and 7 percent of the badges in 1980" (1985:361).

An analysis of the latent content also pointed to an emancipation of the Girl Scouts, similar to that occurring in North American society at large. The change of uniform was one indicator: "The shift from skirts to pants may reflect an acknowledgement of the more physically active role of women as well as the variety of physical images available to modern women" (Auster 1985:362). Supporting evidence was found in the appearance of badges such as "Science Sleuth," "Aerospace," and "Ms. Fix-It."

Clarke and Everest (2006) used both manifest and latent coding in their content analysis of the role the print media play in reporting about cancer. Examining the magazines available in Canada (published in Canada or the United States) that had the highest circulation during three time periods, cancer stories were coded for manifest content such as frequency of stories concerning breast cancer versus other types of cancer. Their latent content analysis meant categorizing the content of articles into themes.

The authors used, for example, the medical, political economy, and lifestyle frames to distinguish among the articles. Issues such as an emphasis on the fear of cancer were examined through latent content analysis also.

Conceptualization and the Creation of Code Categories For all research methods, conceptualization and operationalization typically involve the interaction of theoretical concerns and empirical observations. If, for example, you believe some newspaper editorials to be liberal and others to be conservative, ask yourself why you think so. Read some editorials and try to pick out the cues or details that are prompting you to categorize some as liberal and others as conservative. Was the political orientation of a particular editorial most clearly indicated by its manifest content or by its tone? Was your decision based on the use of certain terms (e.g., *leftist*, *fascist*) or on the support or opposition given to a particular issue or political personality?

Both inductive and deductive methods should be used in this activity. If you're testing theoretical propositions, your theories should suggest empirical indicators of concepts. If you begin with specific empirical observations, you should attempt to derive general principles relating to them and then apply those principles to the other empirical observations.

Bruce Berg (2007:311) places code development in the context of grounded theory and likens it to solving a puzzle:[1]

> Coding and other fundamental procedures associated with grounded theory development are certainly hard work and must be taken seriously, but just as many people enjoy finishing a complicated jigsaw puzzle, many researchers find great satisfaction in coding and analysis. As researchers ... begin to see the puzzle pieces come together to form a more complete picture, the process can be downright thrilling.

1 BERG, BRUCE L., QUALITATIVE RESEARCH METHODS FOR THE SOCIAL SCIENCES, 6th, © 2007, pp. 311, 324. Reprinted by permission of Pearson Education, Inc., New York, New York.

Throughout this activity, remember that the operational definition of any variable is composed of the attributes included in it. Such attributes, moreover, should be mutually exclusive and exhaustive. A newspaper editorial, for example, should not be described as both liberal and conservative, though you should probably allow for some to be middle of the road. It may be sufficient for your purposes to code novels as erotic or nonerotic, but you may also want to consider that some could be anti-erotic. Paintings might be classified as representational or not, if that satisfied your research purpose, or you might wish to classify them as impressionistic, abstract, allegorical, and so forth.

Realize further that different levels of measurement may be used in content analysis. You may, for example, use the nominal categories of liberal and conservative for characterizing newspaper editorials, or you might wish to use a more refined ordinal ranking, ranging from extremely liberal to extremely conservative. Bear in mind, however, that the level of measurement implicit in your coding methods—nominal, ordinal, interval, or ratio—does not necessarily carry over to the interpretation of the variables that are your ultimate interest. If the word *love* appeared 100 times in Novel A and 50 times in Novel B, you would be justified in saying that the word *love* appeared twice as often in Novel A, but not that Novel A was twice as erotic as Novel B. Similarly, agreeing with twice as many anti-Semitic statements in a questionnaire does not necessarily make one twice as anti-Semitic.

Counting and Record Keeping If you plan to evaluate your content analysis data quantitatively, your coding operation must be amenable to data processing. This means, first, that the end product of your coding must be numerical. If you're counting the frequency of certain words, phrases, or other manifest content, the coding is necessarily numerical. But even if you're coding latent content on the basis of overall judgments, it will be necessary to represent your coding decision numerically: 1 = very liberal, 2 = moderately liberal, 3 = moderately conservative, and so on.

Second, your record keeping must clearly distinguish between units of analysis and units of observation, especially if these are different. The initial coding, of course, must relate to the units of observation. If novelists are the units of analysis, for example, and you wish to characterize them through a content analysis of their novels, your primary records will represent novels as the units of observation. You may then combine your scoring of individual novels to characterize each novelist, the unit of analysis.

Third, while you're counting, it will normally be important to record the base from which the counting is done. It would tell us little that the word *love* appeared 87 times in a novel if we didn't know about how many words there were in the entire novel. Similarly, it would probably be useless to know the number of realistic paintings produced by a given painter without knowing the total number of all paintings he or she has done; the painter would be regarded as a realistic painter if a high percentage of his or her total output of paintings were of that genre. The issue of observational bias is most easily resolved if every observation is coded in terms of one of the attributes making up a variable. Rather than simply counting the number of liberal editorials in a given collection, for example, code each editorial by its political orientation, even if it must be coded "no apparent orientation."

Let's suppose we want to describe and explain the editorial policies of different newspapers. Figure 9-2 presents part of a tally sheet that might result from the coding of newspaper editorials. Note that newspapers are the units of analysis. Each newspaper has been assigned an identification number to facilitate mechanized processing. The second column has a space for the number of editorials coded for each newspaper. This will be an important piece of information, since we want to be able to say, for example, "Of all the editorials, 22 percent were pro–United Nations," not just "There were eight pro–United Nations editorials."

One column in Figure 9-2 is for assigning a subjective overall assessment of the newspapers' editorial policies. (Such assignments might later be compared with several objective measures.) Other columns provide space for recording numbers of editorials reflecting specific editorial positions. In a real content analysis, there would be spaces for recording other editorial positions plus

Newspaper ID	Number of editorials evaluated	SUBJECTIVE EVALUATION 1. Very liberal 2. Moderately liberal 3. Middle-of-road 4. Moderately conservative 5. Very conservative	Number of "isolationist" editorials	Number of "pro–United Nations" editorials	Number of "anti–United Nations" editorials
001	37	2	0	8	0
002	26	5	10	0	6
003	44	4	2	1	2
004	22	3	1	2	3
005	30	1	0	6	0

FIGURE 9-2 **Sample Tally Sheet (Partial).**
Source: © Cengage Learning

noneditorial information about each newspaper, such as the region in which it is published, its circulation, and so forth.

Qualitative Data Analysis Not all content analysis results in counting. Sometimes a qualitative assessment of the materials is most appropriate, as in Carol Auster's examination of changes in Girl Scout uniforms and handbook language.

Bruce Berg (2007:323–325) discusses **deviant case testing** as a technique for qualitative idea generation. First, in the grounded theory tradition, you begin with an examination of the data, which might yield a general idea. Let's say you're examining the leadership of a new community association by reviewing the minutes of meetings to see who made motions that were subsequently passed. Your initial examination of the data suggests that the wealthier members are the most likely to assume this leadership role.

The second stage in the analysis is to search your data to find all the cases that would contradict the initial hypothesis. In this instance, you would look for poorer members who made successful motions and wealthy members who never did. Third, you must review each of the disconfirming cases and either (1) give up the idea or (2) see how it needs to be fine-tuned.

Let's say that in your analysis of disconfirming cases, you notice that each of the unwealthy leaders has a graduate degree, while each of the wealthy nonleaders has very little formal education. You may revise your hypothesis to consider both education and wealth as routes to leadership in the association. Perhaps you'll discover some threshold for leadership (a white-collar job, a level of income, and a university degree) beyond which those with the most money, education, or both are the most active leaders.

This process is an example of what Barney Glaser and Anselm Strauss (1967) call **analytic induction**. It is inductive in that it primarily begins with observations, and it is analytic because it goes beyond description to find patterns and relationships among variables.

There are, of course, dangers in this form of analysis, as in all others. The chief risk here is misclassifying observations to support an emerging hypothesis. For example, you may erroneously conclude that a nonleader didn't graduate from university or you may decide that the job of factory supervisor is "close enough" to being white collar.

Berg and Lune (2011:324) offer techniques for avoiding these errors:[2]

1. If there are sufficient cases, select some at random from each category in order to avoid merely picking those that best support the hypothesis.
2. Give at least three examples in support of every assertion you make about the data.
3. Have your analytic interpretations carefully reviewed by others uninvolved in the research project to see whether they agree.
4. Report whatever inconsistencies you do discover—any cases that simply do not fit your hypotheses. Realize that few social patterns are 100 percent consistent, so you may have discovered something important even if it doesn't apply to absolutely all of social life. However, you should be honest with your readers in that regard.

A variety of computer software programs can assist with content analysis. For online information about such programs, publications, and other resources useful to content analysis and text analysis, go to https://www.terry.uga.edu/management/contentanalysis/resources/. Discussion of some of the computer-assisted qualitative data analysis software programs used in content analysis can be found in Chapter 13 of this book, in the "Computer Programs for Qualitative Data" section.

2 BERG, BRUCE L., QUALITATIVE RESEARCH METHODS FOR THE SOCIAL SCIENCES, 6th, © 2007, pp. 311, 324. Reprinted by permission of Pearson Education, Inc., New York, New York.

deviant case testing Examining outliers (negative cases) in comparison to typical cases to gain a sense of how generalized an insight is.

analytic induction Searching for general insights by systematically looking for patterns among individual cases.

Before moving on, we should mention one other very useful tool, **discourse analysis**. Although there are numerous variants of discourse analysis, the term refers broadly to methods for examining texts to explore how meaning, knowledge, and power are created and recreated in everyday experience. Through careful reading and rereading of texts informed by thoughtful consideration, discourse analysis searches for thematic patterns and seeks to improve understanding of how language works in its social and cultural contexts. Many specific discourse analysis tools exist (Ruiz 2009), with some specialized for sociological insight (Keller 2011). Discourse analysis has produced many useful insights into how social structures are perpetuated. Using discourse analysis tools, valuable insights have recently been gained into topics such as the perpetuation of discrimination (Boyd and Kerr 2015), the place and importance of shame in identity construction (Scheff 2014), and the place of power in public education (Lim 2014). Discourse analysis, and related approaches—conversation analysis and narrative analysis—will be described in more detail in Chapter 13 (on qualitative data analysis).

SOME ILLUSTRATIONS OF CONTENT ANALYSIS

As we have seen, content analysis can take both quantitative and qualitative forms. Research by Charis Kubrin (2005) illustrates the qualitative tradition and draws on popular culture. Kubrin focused on the themes put forth in rap music, particularly gangsta rap, and the relationship of those themes to neighbourhood culture and "the street code."[3]

3 Charis E. Kubrin, "I See Death around the Corner: Nihilism in Rap Music," *Sociological Perspectives* (48, 7), pp. 433-459, copyright © 2005 by SAGE Publications, Inc. Reprinted by Permission of SAGE Publications, Inc.

discourse analysis Qualitative methods for examining texts to explore how meaning, knowledge, and power are created and recreated in everyday experience.

> In response to societal and neighborhood conditions, black youth in disadvantaged communities have created a substitute social order governed by their own code—a street code—and rituals of authenticity.... This social order reflects the subcultural locus of interests that emerges from pervasive race and class inequality and the social isolation of poor black communities.
>
> (2005:439)

She began her study by identifying all the platinum-selling rap albums released between 1992 and 2000: 130 albums containing 1,922 songs. She then drew a simple random sample of one-third of the songs (632) and set about the task of listening to each. She did this twice with each song.

> First, I listened to a song in its entirety while reading the printed lyrics to determine what the song was about. Second, I listened to the song again and coded each line to determine whether the street code elements described earlier were present: (1) respect, (2) willingness to fight or use violence, (3) material wealth, (4) violent retaliation, (5) objectification of women, and (6) nihilism.
>
> (2005:443)

Kubrin was particularly interested in the theme of nihilism, the rejection of traditional moral principles, and a fundamental skepticism about the meaning of life. She wanted to know how that theme was portrayed in gangsta rap music and how it fit into the street code.

Though she began with a sample of 632 songs, she found that no new themes appeared to be showing up after about 350 songs had been analyzed. To be safe, she coded another 50 songs and found no new themes, completing her coding process at that point.

Kubrin notes that rap music is typically regarded as antisocial and resistant to organized society, but her in-depth analysis of lyrics suggested something different.

> Rap music does not exist in a cultural vacuum; rather it expresses the cultural crossing, mixing, and engagement of black youth culture with the values, attitudes and concerns of the white majority. Many of the violent (and patriarchical,

> materialistic, sexist, etc.) ways of thinking that are glorified in gangsta rap are a reflection of the prevailing values created and sustained in the larger society.
>
> (2005:454)

She traces the implications of this for understanding street life as well as for the likely success of various crime-control strategies.

A good illustration of quantitative content analysis is Savage's (2011) examination of gender bias in newspaper op-eds. He examined a large sample of op-ed contributions from Canada's two largest newspapers and found that only 20 percent were authored by women. Moreover, he found that women's voices were even more underrepresented (only 10 percent) in "hard news" opinions including economics, politics, and international affairs. This extensive bias is particularly troubling since the purported purpose of op-eds is "to nurture a range of new voices bringing diversity of insight on a range of matters of public concern" (Savage 2011:181).

The rapid rise of digitization has produced rich sources of auditory and visual content for sociologists to analyze (Rose 2012). The ease of production and availability of photographs, video, closed circuit television (CCTV), films, and images of all sorts has sparked a growth in **visual sociology** (Mitchell 2011). Visual sociology is "devoted to the visual study of society, culture, and social relationships" (IVSA 2015). The scope of topics explored through visual sociology is restricted only by the availability of artifacts for interpretation and the practitioner's sociological imagination.

Randall Collins's research provides wonderful illustrations of the insights to be gained from careful visual analysis. In one example, he takes on the mysterious Mona Lisa (Collins 2012). Perhaps the most famous painting in the world, the Mona Lisa has been subject to endless interpretation and speculation (PBS 2014). Collins provides a micro-sociological interpretation of the famous painting, starting from the understanding that Mona Lisa is sending viewers a sign. Read Collins's (2012) blog for the full story, and you will see that if "we examine the Mona Lisa face, zone by zone, the reason for its mysteriousness becomes clear: there are different emotions expressed in different facial zones" (Collins 2012). Collins uses micro-sociological content analysis tools across a wide range of visual products. His book on violence (Collins 2008), for example, analyzes a large number of photographs at the moment of face-to-face violence. Through careful analysis and interpretation he shows how "expressions of anger on the part of the attacker turn into tension and fear [which] leads to a new theory of what makes violence happen, or not" (Collins 2008:44).

As these examples illustrate, content analysis provides a rich possibility space for research.

STRENGTHS AND WEAKNESSES OF CONTENT ANALYSIS

Probably the greatest advantage of content analysis is its economy in both time and money. A single university student might undertake a content analysis, whereas undertaking a survey, for example, might not be feasible. There is no requirement for a large research staff; no special equipment is needed. As long as you have access to the material to be coded, you can undertake content analysis.

Allowing the correction of errors is another advantage of content analysis. If you discover you've botched up a survey or an experiment, you may be forced to repeat the whole research project with all its attendant costs in time and money. If you botch up your field research, it may be impossible to redo the project; the event under study may no longer exist. In content analysis, it's usually easier to repeat a portion of the study than it is in other research methods. You might be required, moreover, to recode only a portion of your data rather than all of it.

A third advantage of content analysis is that it permits the study of processes occurring over a long time. You might focus on the imagery of women conveyed in Canadian magazines from 1960 to 1970, for example, or you might examine changing imagery from 1960 to the present.

---

visual sociology The study of society, culture, and social relationships through the analysis of audio-visual artifacts.

Finally, content analysis has the advantage of all unobtrusive measures—namely, that the content analyst seldom has any effect on the subject being studied. Because the novels have already been written, the paintings already painted, the speeches already presented, content analyses can have no effect on them.

Content analysis has disadvantages as well. For one thing, it's limited to the examination of *recorded* communications. Such communications may be oral, written, or graphic, but they must be recorded in some fashion to permit analysis.

As we've seen, content analysis has both advantages and disadvantages with regard to validity and reliability. Problems of validity are likely unless you happen to be studying communication processes per se. However, the concreteness of materials studied in content analysis strengthens the likelihood of reliability. You can always code and recode and even recode again if you want, making certain that the coding is consistent. In field research, by contrast, there's probably nothing you can do after the fact to ensure greater reliability in observation and categorization.

UNOBTRUSIVE ONLINE RESEARCH

Previous chapters have looked at obtrusive online data collection methods such as experiments and surveys, where responses are elicited from participants for the purposes of observation. But as more and more of our activities occur online (emailing, social networking, shopping, etc.) and/or are mediated by online digital technologies (credit card and debit card purchases, smartphones, GPS, etc.), we are leaving an ever richer trail of digital footsteps. Hewson et al. (2016) group unobtrusive Internet-mediated research methods into *observation* and *document analysis*. Although the distinction can be somewhat blurred, as a working definition they classify *observational methods* as those that study online behaviour and interactions either in real time or as digital traces; in contrast, *document analysis* involves studying published documents or static media placed on the Internet, often as a finished/authored product. Observational data include text-based linguistic or conversational content (archived or real time) harvested from mailing lists, discussion forums, online chat software, and so on, or information about other online activities (such as searches on Google) and the structures and processes of interactions and behaviour (such as friendship networks on Facebook). Researchers may also go beyond linguistic interactions to study virtual reality environments and extralinguistic interactions.

BIG DATA

According to a recent estimate, about 2.5 exabytes (Eb)[4] of data are generated daily worldwide (Holmes 2017). Some of these data are structured (in database or spreadsheet formats amenable to traditional quantitative analysis techniques), such as the large amounts of digital data created and stored by companies and governments in the process of providing services, generating profits, and administering laws (Salganik, 2018). But much of them are unstructured (in forms not amenable to traditional data analytical methods) such as photos, videos, tweets, or word-processor documents, and some of them are semi-structured (have identifiers or tags that can be structured) like emails and hashtags (Holmes, 2017). Given their unsuitability for traditional data storage and analysis techniques, new tools have been and are being developed to "extract useful information" from the masses of unstructured data available online.

Although a precise definition is difficult to arrive at, the combining of these various forms of digital data and repurposing them to answer questions that they were not originally intended to answer is generally what is meant by the term *big data* (Salganik, 2018). Key characteristics of big data include the high *volume* of data being produced, the *velocity* of data production (including real-time streaming data), and the great *variety* "of production sources (messages, updates, and images from social networks, readings from sensors, GPS signals from cell phones, and others) that provide enormous streams of

4 An Eb is 1 million terabytes, a typical laptop hard drive is around 1 or 2 terabytes.

data tied to people, activities, and locations" (Amaturo and Punziano p. 39, 2017).

The basic stages of big data approaches involve collecting or capturing data from multiple sources, linking those data sets, storing and organizing the data, and then analyzing them (Foster et al. 2017). Online data can be collected numerous ways, such as from email server logs, by harvesting information directly from websites via Web scraping, and by using APIs (application programming interfaces), which are computer programming tools that make different computer systems interoperable. APIs are increasingly used to gather social media data, such as information about "likes" on Facebook or followers on Twitter. Then all these different data sets have to be linked. A key component to data linkage (or record linkage) is finding unique identifiers (e.g., birth date, postal code, Amazon customer number) that can be cross-referenced and matched across data sets. Powerful computer algorithms are integral to this process. Once the data sets have been linked the data must be stored and organized. This is typically accomplished with the use of a DBMS (database management system), which makes large data sets more manageable. Big data is too large to store and analyze on a single computer and so typically involves innovative programming techniques to take advantage of the power of parallel computing. The programs allow tasks to be distributed across multiple computers to organize, store, and analyze big data (the most popular of these software frameworks is Apache Hadoop). When it comes to modelling or analyzing these massive data sets, two of the most noteworthy approaches are data mining and social network analysis (discussed later in the chapter).

Data mining is the automated discovery of patterns in large databases; it is rooted in computer science and statistics. Fundamentally, it involves applying algorithms to discover patterns, such as partitioning the data into groups (e.g., grouping Internet users based on their website visiting habits), describing relationships between variables (e.g., 60 percent of people who purchased book A also purchased book B), determining sequences in data (e.g., news coverage about a mass recall of romaine lettuce is followed by increased searches on Google about *E. coli*), classifying data items into predetermined classes (e.g., political party affiliation based on website visits), or predicting continuous outcomes (e.g., predicting monthly spending based on income) (Baram-Tsabari et al. 2017).

Related to data mining are computer-aided text/content techniques that provide a number of useful tools for researchers, such as finding relevant information in large databases or topic modelling. The latter can help researchers understand "the contents of thousands of documents in a comprehensible format by discovering only the most important words and phrases in those documents" (Klochikhin and Boyd-Graber, 2017:188). Machine learning is also being developed to apply to content analysis. Machine learning algorithms (such as those underlying speech and facial recognition software, autonomous cars, personalized Netflix or Amazon recommendation systems) are "trained" using example documents and then applied to code large volumes of textual content (Popping, 2017).

Baram-Tsabari et al. (2017) provide a useful categorization of data mining research studies. Based on differences in research focus, data-mining strategies used, and the source of data, they sort data-mining studies into three groups: those interested in mainstream media (e.g., popular news sites); those focused on user-generated content (e.g., social media, online forums, reader comments, Wikipedia, blogs), and those focused on user activity (e.g., queries to search engines). Many studies primarily use one of these approaches. For example, Jones and colleagues (2013) used online archives to study changes over 57 years in two American newspapers; Anderson and colleagues (2014) data-mined user-generated content (personal profiles and activity logs from a popular dating website) to investigate the persistence of same-race dating preferences; Choi and Varian (2012) used Google Trends data (data about trends in Google search activity) to predict consumer behaviour such as automobile, home, and retail sales.

An example of a study combining aspects of all three approaches is Wolfsfeld and colleagues' (2013) investigation of the role of social media in collective action using the Arab Spring as a case study. The Arab Spring was a series of anti-government, pro-democracy political protests that took place in several Middle Eastern countries in 2010. Wolfsfeld et al. (2013) were interested in whether social media activity could predict or explain collective action or political protest as well as, or better than, traditional variables, and whether increased social media activity preceded or followed the political uprising. In addition to data on traditional economic (e.g., GDP), political (e.g., Democracy Index), and technological (e.g., Internet penetration) variables, they used various digital data sources to operationalize social media variables. For example, they assessed the extent (and arc) of uprisings in each of 22 Arab countries using several mainstream newspapers and online sources, they assessed changes in social media use through variables like growth in new Facebook accounts and number of Google searches for Facebook, and they assessed trend data on popular Google search terms (related to political and current events) before, during, and after the uprising. By triangulating their different data sources, the researchers found that the traditional variables were better predictors of the uprisings, and that social media activity was more likely to increase after, not before, a political uprising. Thus, social media use was more effect than cause of political activism. (See the Spotlight on MMR box for another example of triangulation, where unobtrusive observation of company websites was used to help validate a survey questionnaire).

Although unobtrusive Internet-mediated research methods offer an exciting new array of data sources and research possibilities, there are a number of questions related to data quality in addition to the ethical concerns discussed in Chapter 3 and the selection bias issues discussed in Chapter 6. As Janetzko (2017) points out, although unobtrusive online data may be available in massive quantities, it also tends to be rather limited in the information it provides. For example, data on number of Facebook friends, Google search terms, or time spent on a website don't tell us much about underlying motivations or other factors related to a person's behaviour. Unobtrusive data gathered online usually only lends itself to *thin description* (Geertz 1973) and lacks the contextual information required for deeper, more meaningful understanding (or *thick description*) on the part of the observer. This has to do with "the narrow coding schemas implemented by most data-recording devices used on the Internet" (Janetzko 2017:3), because the data generated online is intended for technical rather than research purposes.

In fact, a number of steps and procedures are required before the data are rendered (data capture and cleaning, linkage, storage) into a form usable for modelling or analysis. The more clever (and convoluted) the procedures, the more possibility for noise to enter into the data (which lessens validity and reliability). For example, Salganik (2018) discusses the impact of *algorithmic confounding* and *dirty* data. A number of the features programmed into online platforms such as Facebook or Amazon are based on computer algorithms that operate in accordance with social science research findings (e.g., how to draw users to your webpage or service and then keep them there using it). Thus, the human behaviour we observe online in environments like Facebook may be less spontaneous or natural than we think and more an artifact of how Facebook works. For example, people's Facebook friend networks may in part be a result of how Facebook prompts people to add new friends, and those prompts are informed by existing social science theory. By *dirty data*, Salganik is referring to the fact that many online big data sources are "always on" and collect data automatically. Consequently, the data collected may contain much irrelevant data that do not "reflect real actions of interest to researchers." Thus, the researcher is confronted with a formidable data cleaning challenge before he or she can proceed to gather potentially useful knowledge from big data.

SOCIAL NETWORK ANALYSIS

If you go to https://oracleofbacon.org/ you can enter any movie actors' name, (e.g., Emma Watson) and it will tell you how many steps separate that actor from Kevin Bacon in the Hollywood movie industry. The number of steps (connections) equals the Bacon number (see Figure 9-3).

SPOTLIGHT ON MIXED METHODS

Using Unobtrusive Observational Data to Assess Nonresponse Bias in Surveys

Nonresponse bias due to low response rates is a growing concern in survey research (see Chapter 6 for review). Of central concern is that there are systematic differences between respondents and nonrespondents. A good way to test this would be to get data from nonrespondents to compare with respondents; of course, this is not usually possible. But what if you could get comparable data on nonrespondents through other means? Rasmussen and Thimm (2015) took a novel approach to this problem. Interested in validating their survey of small- and medium-sized enterprises (SMEs), they sought to use unobtrusive observational data collected from company websites to test for nonresponse bias.

Rasmussen and Thimm were interested in surveying SMEs about their information technology (IT) capabilities. They expected that companies that were less interested in, and thus less invested in, IT would be less likely to respond to the survey, hence biasing the survey toward more IT savvy companies. They hypothesized that (1) there would be a positive relationship between companies' level of IT capability and the quality (i.e., functionality and aesthetics) of their website; and (2) that companies that responded to the IT survey would, on average, have higher quality websites.

To measure website quality two indices were developed that involved researchers visiting company websites ($N = 851$) and coding them according to 16 functionality criteria and 8 aesthetic criteria. A website either met a criterion (scored a 1) or didn't (scored a 0), the more criteria a website met the higher it's score on each index.

They found that, although scores on the aesthetic index were not correlated with IT capacity (as measured by an IT use index in the survey), functionality scores were. Thus, the hypothesized relationship between IT capacity and website quality was partially supported, in that there was a positive relationship between website functionality (how useful in terms of services and features provided) and company IT capability. The second hypothesis, however, was not supported: there was no significant difference between respondent and nonrespondent companies in the average level of website functionality. Thus, the authors conclude that, despite a rather high nonresponse rate (87.4 percent), the survey is indeed a "valid representation of the small and medium-sized manufacturing companies in the two northern European regions" from which it was sampled, and that unobtrusive website observation is an effective data collection method.

This is a fun illustration of what Stanley Milgram (1967) termed the "small world problem." Also known more popularly as the "six degrees of separation" phenomenon, it holds that any two people in the world are separated by no more than six intermediaries. Milgram (1967) found evidence of this in his famous postcard experiments, and subsequent studies using email chains (Dodds et al. 2003) and Facebook contacts (Backstrom et al. 2012) have confirmed it. Understanding the highly interconnected nature of peoples' social worlds is at the root of social network analysis (SNA).

Basic SNA Concepts "A social network is a set of socially relevant nodes connected by one or more relations. Nodes, or network members, are the units that are connected by the relations whose patterns we study" (Marin and Wellman, 2014:13). The nodes (actors/members) that make up social networks can be individuals, companies, families, online accounts, and so on. The links interconnecting these nodes are called *ties*. Ties vary in intensity between *strong* (closer, long-standing relationships characterized by deeper levels of trust and obligation) and *weak* (more

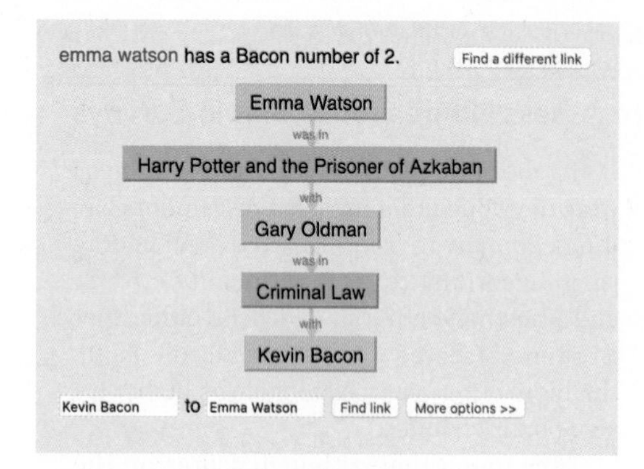

FIGURE 9-3 The Oracle of Bacon.
Source: Courtesy of Patrick Reynolds, oracleofbacon.org

casual/superficial relationships with lesser levels of expectation and obligation). The structural characteristics of networks can vary along a number of dimensions including *size* (the number of nodes in a network) and *cohesion/density* (how tightly interconnected nodes of a network are). More dense networks have a shorter average *path length* among members. That is, the average number of ties (paths) a member must follow to reach another member is less in denser networks. Interconnected subsets of members within a larger network are called *cliques*, gaps that exist in networks between subsets of members are *structural holes*, and members who connect otherwise isolated cliques together are *bridges*. The characteristics of members within networks can also vary along a number of dimensions, including *degree centrality* (the number of ties a member has) and *closeness centrality* (how closely tied to other members an actor is, as indicated by the average path length between them and other members).

Analytical Approaches A key distinction in SNA research is between whole (sociocentric) and egocentric network designs. *Whole network* designs take a "bird's-eye" view of social networks. In these types of studies, researchers collect all the information about all the actors in a network. This enables them to measure the characteristics and relationships of each member of a network, as well as network-level characteristics such as cliques and structural holes. *Egocentric network* designs are interested in examining networks from the perspective of individual actors. That is, the researcher is interested in the local network of individual nodes (the network of ties directly connected to an actor) rather than the larger network as a whole.

Data Collection There are both obtrusive and unobtrusive approaches to data collection in social network analysis. Obtrusive approaches include survey interviews (where the respondents answer a number of questions designed to elicit information about their social networks), contact diaries (respondents are asked to record all their contacts within a given period of time, such as a day, and researchers use the diaries to construct a profile of their networks), and ecological momentary assessment or EMA (smartphone apps are used to generate real-time data by intermittently prompting participants to answer questions pertaining to their social activity, such as "Who are you with at this moment?"). Given the purpose of this chapter, we focus on unobtrusive approaches.

One common unobtrusive approach to data collection relies on archives (e.g., news reports, personnel files, and legal and/or official records) to reconstruct social networks. For example, Padgett and Ansell (1993) relied on detailed historical accounts of the interrelations of elite Florentine families in the 15th century to show how the Medici family rose to influence. The Medici were able to shrewdly bridge gaps in the Florentine power structure by forging different connections with different unconnected families (e.g., economic alliances with neighbours and marriage or friendship alliances with more distant families). In this way, they were able to put their family at the centre of numerous important relations (to be a bridge between structural gaps) while consolidating their interests and outflanking their rivals.

More recently, Carroll (2017) used publicly accessible online data on Canadian companies, directors, and executives to map the organization of corporate power in the carbon-capital elite (companies involved directly or indirectly with oil and gas industries). He found the carbon-capital elite power structure in Canada is characterized by networks of "interlocking directorates" as well as ties to the financial and corporate sectors at the national and transnational level. Interlocking directorates refers to interconnections (ties) between corporations, such as when directors or executives of one corporation sit on the board of directors of another. His analysis reveals that a tight-knit group of directors and executives sit on multiple corporate boards within the carbon-capital and financial sectors. He concludes that this concentration of unaccountable corporate power "privileges short-term private profit over public and ecological concerns" and thus presents significant obstacles to our ability to deal effectively with the ecological threats to our collective future.

There are also numerous unobtrusive sources of social network data online such as weblogs and other linked pages, threaded conversations on the Web (e.g., forums or comment sections of newspaper or blogs), email traffic, Twitter networks, and social network sites more generally (Hogan, 2017). For example, Kossinets and Watts (2006) combined email logs with other data on the affiliations and attributes (gender, age, friendship links, and joint activities) of network members to identify factors that influence the development of social networks over time. Lewis and colleagues (2012) conducted social network analysis with Facebook data (linked to other user background data) to investigate the impact of selection versus influence mechanisms on the development of cultural "tastes." The influence hypothesis is that people's tastes (in music, movies, books, etc.) are influenced by their social networks, while the selection hypothesis suggests that people affiliate with those who have similar tastes. For the most part their analysis supports the selection hypothesis that friends tend to have tastes in common not because they influence each other, but because similar tastes are part of what attracted them together in the first place. Interestingly, one exception to this was a taste for classical/jazz music, which appeared more likely to spread among Facebook friends in part due to its perceived high status value.

It is important to note that online social network data are characterized by the same general advantages and limitations as many other online methods. Data collection can be relatively easy and inexpensive, and it can be automated and potentially linkable with multiple databases. On the other hand, skewed online populations (younger, better educated) limit generalizability, and legal and ethical concerns about data privacy persist.

HISTORICAL AND COMPARATIVE RESEARCH

Historical and comparative research differs substantially from the methods discussed so far, though it overlaps somewhat with content analysis and the analysis of existing statistics. It involves the use of historical methods by sociologists, political scientists, and other social scientists.

The discussion of longitudinal research designs in Chapter 4 notwithstanding, our examination of research methods so far has focused primarily on studies anchored in one point in time and in one locale, whether a particular small group or a nation. Although accurately portraying the main thrust of contemporary social scientific research, this focus conceals the fact that social scientists are also interested in tracing the development of social forms over time and comparing those developmental processes across cultures. Mahoney and Rueschemeyer (2003:4) suggest that current historical and comparative researchers "focus on a wide range of topics, but they are united by a commitment to providing historically grounded explanations of large-scale and substantively important outcomes." Therefore, you find historical and comparative studies dealing with such topics as social class, capitalism, religion, revolution, and the like.

After describing some prominent examples of historical and comparative research, this section discusses some of the key elements of this method.

historical and comparative research The examination of societies (or other social units) over time and in comparison with one another.

EXAMPLES OF HISTORICAL AND COMPARATIVE RESEARCH

August Comte, who coined the term *sociologie*, saw that new discipline as the final stage in a historical development of ideas. With his broadest brush, he painted an evolutionary picture that took humans from a reliance on religion to metaphysics to science. With a finer brush, he portrayed science as evolving from the development of biology and the other natural sciences to the development of psychology and, finally, to the development of scientific sociology.

A great many later social scientists have also turned their attention to broad historical processes. Several have examined the historical progression of social forms from the simple to the complex, from rural–agrarian to urban–industrial societies. The anthropologist Robert Redfield, for example, wrote about a shift from "folk society" to "urban society" (1941). Émile Durkheim saw social evolution largely as a process of ever-greater division of labour ([1893] 1964). In a more specific analysis, Karl Marx examined economic systems progressing historically from primitive to feudal to capitalistic forms ([1867] 1967). All history, he wrote in this context, was a history of class struggle: the "haves" struggling to maintain their advantages and the "have-nots" struggling for a better lot in life. Looking beyond capitalism, Marx saw the development of socialism and finally communism.

Not all historical studies in the social sciences have had this evolutionary flavour, however. Some social scientific readings of the historical record, in fact, point to grand cycles rather than to linear progressions. No scholar better represents this view than Pitirim A. Sorokin. A participant in the Russian Revolution of 1917, Sorokin served as secretary to Prime Minister Kerensky. Both Kerensky and Sorokin fell from favour, however, and Sorokin began his second career as an American sociologist.

Although Comte read history as a progression from religion to science, Sorokin (1937–1940) suggested that societies alternate cyclically between two points of view, which he called "ideational" and "sensate." Sorokin's sensate point of view defines reality in terms of sense experiences. The ideational, by contrast, places a greater emphasis on spiritual and religious factors. Sorokin's reading of the historical record further indicated that the passage between the ideational and sensate was through a third point of view, which he called the "idealistic." This third view combined elements of the sensate and ideational in an integrated, rational view of the world.

These examples indicate some of the topics historical and comparative researchers have examined. To get a better sense of what historical and comparative research entails, let's look at a few examples in somewhat more detail.

Weber and the Role of Ideas In his analysis of economic history, Karl Marx put forward a view of economic determinism. That is, he believed that economic factors determined the nature of all other aspects of society. For example, Marx's analysis showed that a function of European churches was to justify and support the capitalist status quo. Religion was a tool of the powerful in maintaining their dominance over the powerless. "Religion is the sigh of the oppressed creature," Marx wrote in a famous passage, "the sentiment of a heartless world, and the soul of soulless conditions. It is the opium of the people" (Bottomore and Rubel [1843] 1956:27).

Max Weber, a German sociologist, disagreed. Without denying that economic factors could and did affect other aspects of society, Weber argued that economic determinism did not explain everything. Indeed, Weber said, economic forms could come from noneconomic ideas. In his research in the sociology of religion, Weber examined the extent to which religious institutions were the source of social behaviour rather than mere reflections of economic conditions. His most noted statement of this side of the issue is found in *The Protestant Ethic and the Spirit of Capitalism* ([1905] 1958). Here's a brief overview of Weber's thesis.

John Calvin (1509–1564), a French-born Swiss theologian, was an important figure in the Protestant reformation of Christianity. Calvin taught that the ultimate salvation or damnation of every individual had already been decided by God; this idea is called *predestination*. Calvin also suggested that God communicated his decisions to people by making them either successful or unsuccessful during their earthly existence. God gave each person an earthly "calling"—an occupation or profession—and manifested his or her success or failure through that medium. Ironically, this point of view led Calvin's followers to seek proof of their coming salvation by working hard, saving their money, and generally striving for economic success.

In Weber's analysis, Calvinism provided an important stimulus for the development of capitalism. Rather than "wasting" their money on worldly comforts, the Calvinists reinvested it in their economic enterprises, thus providing the capital necessary for the development of capitalism. In arriving at this interpretation of the origins of capitalism, Weber researched the official doctrines of the early Protestant churches, studied the preaching of Calvin and other church leaders, and examined other relevant historical documents.

In three other studies, Weber conducted detailed historical analyses of Judaism ([1934] 1952) and the religions of China ([1934] 1951) and India ([1934] 1958). Among other things, Weber wanted to know why capitalism had not developed in the ancient societies of China, India, and Israel. In none of the three religions did he find any teaching that would have supported the accumulation and reinvestment of capital, thus strengthening his conclusion about the role of Protestantism in that regard.

Japanese Religion and Capitalism Weber's thesis regarding Protestantism and capitalism has become a classic in the social sciences. Not surprisingly, other scholars have attempted to test it in other historical situations. In *Tokugawa Religion* (1957), Robert Bellah examined the growth of capitalism in Japan during the late 19th and early 20th centuries.

As both an undergraduate and a graduate student, Bellah had developed interests in Weber and in Japanese society. Thus, in 1951, he first conceived his PhD thesis topic as "nothing less than an 'Essay on the Economic Ethic of Japan' to be a companion to Weber's studies of China, India, and Judaism: *The Economic Ethic of the World Religions*" (recalled in Bellah 1967:168). Originally, Bellah sketched his research design as follows:

> Problems would have to be specific and limited—no general history would be attempted—since time span is several centuries. Field work in Japan on the actual economic ethic practiced by persons in various situations, with, if possible, controlled matched samples from the U.S. (questionnaires, interviews, etc.).
>
> (1967:168)

Bellah's original plan, then, called for surveys of contemporary Japanese and Americans. However, he did not receive the financial support necessary for the study as originally envisioned. So, instead, he immersed himself in the historical records of Japanese religion, seeking the roots of the rise of capitalism in Japan.

In the course of several years' research, Bellah uncovered numerous leads. In 1952, he believed he had found the answer in the samurai code of Bushido and in the Confucianism practised by the samurai class:

> Here I think we find a real development of this worldly asceticism, at least equaling anything found in Europe. Further, in this class the idea of duty in occupation involved achievement without traditionalistic limits, but to the limits of one's capacities, whether in the role of bureaucrat, doctor, teacher, scholar, or other role open to the Samurai.
>
> (quoted in Bellah 1967:171)

The samurai, however, made up only a portion of Japanese society. So Bellah kept looking at the religions among Japanese generally. His understanding of the Japanese language was not yet very good, but he wanted to read religious texts in the original. Under these constraints and experiencing increased time pressure, Bellah decided to concentrate his attention on a single group: Shingaku, a religious movement among merchants in the 18th and 19th centuries. He found that Shingaku had two influences on the development of capitalism. It offered an attitude toward work similar to the Calvinist notion of a "calling," and it had the effect of making business a more acceptable calling for Japanese. Previously, commerce had had a very low standing in Japan.

In other aspects of his analysis, Bellah examined the religious and political roles of the emperor and the economic impact of periodically appearing emperor cults. Ultimately, Bellah's research pointed to the variety of religious and philosophical factors that laid the groundwork for capitalism in Japan. It seems unlikely that he would have achieved anything approaching that depth of understanding if he had been able to pursue his original plan to interview matched samples of U.S. and Japanese citizens.

These examples of historical and comparative research should have given you some sense of the potential power in the method. Let's turn now to an examination of the sources and techniques used in this method.

SOURCES OF HISTORICAL AND COMPARATIVE DATA

As we saw in the case of existing statistics, there is no end of data available for analysis in historical research. To begin, historians may have already reported on whatever it is you want to examine, and their analyses can give you an initial grounding in the subject, a jumping-off point for more in-depth research.

Most likely, you'll want to go beyond others' conclusions and examine some "raw data" to draw your own conclusions. These data vary, of course, according to the topic under study. In Bellah's study of Tokugawa religion, raw data included the sermons of Shingaku teachers. When W. I. Thomas and Florian Znaniecki (1918) studied the adjustment process for Polish peasants who went to the United States in the early 20th century, they examined letters written by the immigrants to their families in Poland. (They obtained the letters through newspaper advertisements.) Other researchers have analyzed old diaries. Such personal documents only scratch the surface, however. In discussing procedures for studying the experience of women in the settlement of Canada's Prairie region, Sandra Rollings-Magnusson (2000:228) listed the following sources:[5]

> In analyzing the work done and contributions made by women in the process of prairie development, contemporaneous historical sources were utilized. Newspapers, government publications and brochures, advertisements printed by private companies, and women settlers' autobiographies, writings, diaries, letters and other materials held in the Saskatchewan Archives in Regina, were reviewed. The most informative material was discovered in letters, poems and articles written by prairie women and submitted to newspapers for publication. Weekly issues of *The Grain Grower's Guide* and *The Nor'-West Farmer*, cumulatively covering a period extending from 1888 to 1913, were examined for comments relating to the farm experience of women. While most of these sources are anecdotal forms of self-reporting and thus potentially biased, advice columns proved to be a key source of candid information. Women, many writing under pseudonyms, sent in questions and comments on topics ranging from earning their own money, to baking tips, child rearing, property rights and complaints of hardship on the farm. It is recognized that these source materials provide information on a subset of the female rural population, as only those individuals with the education to read and write English and the financial ability to purchase newspapers and pay for correspondence would be included. As such, the information contained in this article cannot be taken as representative of the experiences of all women settlers.

Organizations generally document themselves, so if you're studying the development of some organization as Bellah studied Shingaku, for example, you should examine its official documents: charters, policy statements, speeches by leaders, and so on.

5 Sandra Rollings-Magnusson, "Canada's Most Wanted: Pioneer Women on the Western Prairies," *Canadian Review of Sociology and Anthropology* (37, 2), p. 228, Copyright © 2008 John Wiley and Sons. Canadian review of sociology by Canadian Sociological Association. Reproduced with permission of BLACKWELL PUBLISHING in the format Book via Copyright Clearance Center.

Often, official government documents provide the data needed for analysis. Howlett (1986) examined legal–historical records to illustrate their importance in interpreting the intentions of governments in policymaking decisions in a federal state. He points to conflicting interpretations in the literature concerning whether policy decisions made by the Canadian federal government at the turn of the 20th century had "the objective of creating and fostering the development of a national capitalist market economy" (p. 366). In trying to establish what, if any, the financial policies of the Canadian government were, he argues that one cannot simply look at federal legislation where the government took action (acts of commission).

As Howlett notes, to establish intentionality, the researcher must establish that an alternative course of action was a possibility that was actively considered but was rejected by the government (acts of omission). In a federal system, legislative policies can be proposed at different levels of government. When there is disagreement over such policies, this may result in conflict over who has the jurisdictional authority to act. Constitutional arbitration is often used to settle the matter, leaving behind some legal record of the policy issues over which there was conflict. Thus, for example, when the provincial government initiates policies that are overturned by the federal government, such information is likely to be contained in the legal–historical record, positively demonstrating "acts of omission." Howlett concludes: "By pointing out the existence of a fiscal and monetary act of omission, the legal–historical evidence tends to support Naylor's argument that the federal government pursued a financial policy with direct and foreseeable consequences in terms of favouring certain interests over others" (p. 370).

Using historical records of individual cases considered by the Alberta Eugenics Board and official minutes from the meetings of the board, Grekul and colleagues (2004) examined the practice of the sterilization of the "feebleminded" from 1929 until 1972. They used individual board files that

> included a short standardized "presentation summary" containing all the information the Board would have seen for each case (e.g., gender, birth date, ethnicity, place of residence, family and medical history, psychiatric diagnosis, IQ test information). Most of the files also contained several other standardized forms that recorded the Board's decision, its recommendation for a particular operation and, if sterilization did eventually take place, a medical document providing details of the operation.
>
> (Grekul et al. 2004:365)

They also had access to the official minutes from all 398 meetings of the board over this period of time.

Among research questions assessed, they looked at the relative amount of sterilization that took place in Alberta compared to other places, such as the United States, and whether some groups were overrepresented in the decision to sterilize. They found, for example, that Alberta was aggressive in the degree to which it chose to sterilize, with a higher rate of sterilization compared with the United States overall. They also found that groups such as Indigenous people and women had a higher chance of being targeted by the board.

The sources of data for historical analysis are too extensive to cover even in outline here, though the few examples we've looked at should suggest some ideas. Whatever resources you use, however, a couple of cautions are in order.

As you saw in the case of existing statistics, you can't trust the accuracy of records, official or unofficial, primary or secondary. Your protection lies in replication. In the case of historical research, that means corroboration. If several sources point to the same set of "facts," your confidence in them might reasonably increase.

At the same time, you need always to be wary of bias in your data sources. If all your data on the development of a political movement are taken from the movement itself, you're unlikely to gain a well-rounded view of it. The diaries of well-to-do gentry of the Middle Ages may not give you an accurate view of life in general during those times. Note the recognition of possible bias by Rollings-Magnusson in the earlier example when discussing her data sources. Where possible, obtain data from a variety of sources, representing different points of view. Here's what

HOW TO DO IT

Reading and Evaluating Documents

by Ron Aminzade and Barbara Laslett
University of Minnesota

The purpose of the following comments is to give you some sense of the kind of interpretive work historians do and the critical approach they take toward their sources. It should help you to appreciate some of the skills historians develop in their efforts to reconstruct the past from residues, to assess the evidentiary status of different types of documents, and to determine the range of permissible inferences and interpretations. Here are some of the questions historians ask about documents:

1. Who composed the documents? Why were they written? Why have they survived all these years? What methods were used to acquire the information contained in the documents?
2. What are some of the biases in the documents and how might you go about checking or correcting them? How inclusive or representative is the sample of individuals, events, and so on, contained in the document? What were the institutional constraints and the general organizational routines under which the document was prepared? To what extent does the document provide more of an index of institutional activity than of the phenomenon being studied? What is the time lapse between the observation of the events documented and the witnesses' documentation of them? How confidential or public was the document meant to be? What role did etiquette, convention, and custom play in the presentation of the material contained within the document? If you relied solely upon the evidence contained in these documents, how might your vision of the past be distorted? What other kinds of documents might you look at for evidence on the same issues?
3. What are the key categories and concepts used by the writer of the document to organize the information presented? What selectivities or silences result from these categories of thought?
4. What sorts of theoretical issues and debates do these documents cast light on? What kinds of historical and/or sociological questions do they help to answer? What sorts of valid inferences can one make from the information contained in these documents? What sorts of generalizations can one make on the basis of the information contained in these documents?

Bellah (1967:179) said regarding his analysis of Shingaku:

> One could argue that there would be a bias in what was selected for notice by Western scholars. However, the fact that there was material from Western scholars with varied interests from a number of countries and over a period of nearly a century reduced the probability of bias.

The issues raised by Bellah are important ones. As Ron Aminzade and Barbara Laslett have indicated in the How to Do It box "Reading and Evaluating Documents," there's an art in knowing how to regard such documents and what to make of them. Incidentally, the critical review that they urge for the reading of historical documents is useful in many areas of your life.

ANALYTICAL TECHNIQUES

The analysis of historical and comparative data is another large subject that we can't cover exhaustively here. Moreover, because historical and comparative research is frequently approached qualitatively, there are no easily listed steps to follow in the analysis of historical data. Nevertheless, a few comments are in order.

Max Weber used the German term **Verstehen**, which means "empathic understanding," in reference to an essential quality of social research. He meant that the researcher must be able to take on, mentally, the circumstances, views, and feelings of those being studied, so that the researcher can interpret their actions appropriately. Certainly this concept applies to historical and comparative research.

The historical and comparative researcher must find patterns among the voluminous details describing the subject matter being studied. Often, this takes the form of what Weber called *ideal types*: conceptual models composed of the essential characteristics of social phenomena. Thus, for example, Weber himself did considerable research on bureaucracy. Having observed numerous actual bureaucracies, Weber ([1925] 1946) detailed those qualities essential to bureaucracies in general: jurisdictional areas, hierarchically structured authority, written files, and so on. Weber did not merely list those characteristics common to all the actual bureaucracies he observed. Rather, to create a theoretical model of the "perfect" (ideal type) bureaucracy, he needed to understand fully the essentials of bureaucratic operation.

Often, historical and comparative research is informed by a particular theoretical paradigm. Marxist scholars may undertake historical analyses of particular situations such as the history of black minorities in Canada to determine whether they can be understood in terms of the Marxist version of conflict theory. Sometimes, historical and comparative researchers attempt to replicate prior studies in new situations—for example, Bellah's study of Tokugawa religion in the context of Weber's studies of religion and economics.

While historical and comparative research is often regarded as a qualitative rather than quantitative technique, this is by no means necessary. Historical analysts sometimes use *time-series* data to monitor changing conditions over time, such as data on population, crime rates, unemployment, and infant mortality rates. A. R. Gillis has done extensive research on France between 1852 and 1914. His work provides good examples of the combination of historical and quantitative research skills. He has grappled with key issues and factors related to historical changes in rates of crime. He has examined the impact of various forms of social control, such as the amount of state policing, and other factors believed to affect the rates of both major and minor crimes and crimes of violence versus property crimes (1989). His research and analyses on 19th-century France have brought to light novel findings on the relationships between literacy and violence (1994) and marital dissolution and domestic violence (1996). His tests of key hypotheses derived from the literature have shown that expectations were not always borne out in reality and that potentially more subtle relationships are worthy of attention.

To provide an illustration, Gillis (1994) analyzed time-series data to examine the impact of literacy on major crimes of violence. He shows that, although major crimes of violence and "passion-inspired homicide" decreased as literacy increased, there's more to the story if one delves a little deeper. His analysis shows that while rates of passionate violence against others declined, violence against self, as indicated by rates of suicide, greatly increased. As he states, "In fact between 1852 and 1914, the increase in rates of suicide in France was almost eight times greater than the decline in homicide, suggesting that literacy transformed rather than depressed death by violence" (p. 371).

Many historical analysts combine methods in addressing research questions. Mosher and Hagan's (1994:613) "study combines qualitative and quantitative data in an examination of historical patterns in the sentencing of narcotics offenders in five Upper Canadian cities for the years 1908 to 1953." They used jail records as their quantitative data source and daily police court reports in the local newspapers as their primary source of qualitative historical data. Using the jail records to obtain offender names and court appearance dates, they then searched local newspapers for reports on individual cases. In this way,

Verstehen A method that seeks to understand the meaning of actions from the viewpoint of the participants.

they gathered qualitative information on almost 1,000 cases and included the data in their statistical analysis. In addition, they systematically examined a vast amount of qualitative historical data concerning police courts from sources such as annual police department reports, parliamentary debates, local newspapers, and popular magazines to gain local knowledge of the legal culture over this extended period. As they note, understanding the contemporary context of the actors who generated the data is necessary to more accurately interpret patterns. One key finding they report is that despite changes in judicial decision-making patterns, "sensitivity" to class remained constant in the sentencing of narcotics offenders over this period. The brunt of harsh treatment was experienced by the working class while the upper-class offenders received "disproportionately lenient treatment" by mid-century.

In another study that focused on the French criminal justice system in the 19th century, analysis of official documents was supplemented by judicial statistics to gain insights into the use of state repression in the transition from the authoritarian regime of Napoleon III's Second Empire to France's Third Republic (Benaquisto and Couton 2001). It might be expected that state repression would decline in the onset of a liberal regime. However, examination of official documents such as circulars, pamphlets, letters, reports, and official bulletins of the ministries of Justice and the Interior, and laws and legislative debates, helped demonstrate that, if anything, state repression was enhanced in the establishment of the Third Republic.

As you can see, unobtrusive research methods can be used to gather and assess both qualitative and quantitative data. Like all methods, some are more suitable to generating one type of data as opposed to another. In the next two chapters, we'll turn our attention once again to interactive modes of observation and focus on methods that are particularly suited to a qualitative approach to research.

MAIN POINTS

- Nonreactive (unobtrusive) measures are ways of studying social behaviour without affecting it in the process.
- A variety of governmental and nongovernmental agencies provide aggregate statistical data for studying aspects of social life.
- Problems of validity in the analysis of existing statistics can often be handled through logical reasoning and replication.
- Existing statistics often have problems of reliability, so they must be used with caution.
- Archived survey data sets offer rich research opportunities through the secondary analysis of the data.
- Content analysis is a social research method appropriate for studying human communications through social artifacts. Researchers can use it to study not only communication processes, but other aspects of social behaviour as well.
- Content analysis involves coding—transforming raw data into categories based on some conceptual scheme. Coding may attend to both manifest and latent content. The determination of latent content requires judgments on the part of the researcher.
- Both quantitative and qualitative techniques are appropriate for interpreting content analysis data.
- The advantages of content analysis include economy, safety, and the ability to study processes occurring over a long time. Its disadvantages are that it is limited to recorded communications and can raise issues of reliability and validity.
- Unobtrusive online data can be collected on a massive scale, which has led to new research approaches—such as data mining and online social network analysis—each of which presents new possibilities and new problems.

- Social scientists use historical and comparative methods to discover patterns in the histories of different cultures.
- Although often regarded as a qualitative method, historical and comparative research can make use of quantitative techniques.

REVIEW QUESTIONS AND EXERCISES

1. Using the Web, find out how many countries have a higher life expectancy than Canada. (*Hint*: You might want to try the Population Reference Bureau at http://www.prb.org/.)
2. In two or three paragraphs, outline a content analysis design (including a coding scheme) to determine whether the Liberal Party or the Conservative Party is the more supportive of free speech.
3. The Aboriginal Peoples Survey is a rich source of information about an important community in Canada. Go to the archived data set and determine what percentage of Indigenous peoples have completed various levels of education: http://search1.odesi.ca/#/details?uri=%2Fodesi%2Faps-89653-E-2012.xml. Select three other variables from the survey that interest you and look at graphs of the evidence.
4. Select a major controversial event that is in the news. Go to a conservative news organization's publication (e.g., newspaper, magazine, website) and a liberal one's and look at the photographs selected to portray the event. What kind of values and ideology do you see embedded in the photographs?
5. Go to Google Trends and enter the search term "women's hockey." Use the buttons on the toolbar to choose a five-year time range and Canada. You will see a distinct spike in the "interest over time" line in February of 2018. How do you account for this uptick in searches? Try the same (five years, Canada) with "cannabis" as the search term. Try some other interesting search terms to explore in Google Trends. (Also try varying the time range and the country.)

CONTINUITY PROJECT

INEQUALITY AND SHAME

Inequality is everywhere and affects our emotional states. Thomas Scheff (2011) argues that shame is the emotion at the centre of social life. Shame (and its opposite, pride) are rooted in the social bond; they signal how we imagine others perceive us. To experience shame is to feel as if the social bond is weakened or broken. When you are shamed, the social signal is you are no longer an equal. Shame is operating when you report feeling foolish, inadequate, incompetent, embarrassed, humiliated, awkward, stupid, ridiculous, vulnerable, insecure, exposed, and the like.

Because it is so powerful, Scheff argues that feeling shame directly is avoided; hence "hidden shame" is common.

Here are references to lyrics from some popular songs. In all cases, the writers are referring to shame. Check out each song and conduct a content analysis of each lyric and determine where the emotion of shame is present. How is shame being implied in each lyric?

- Chorus of Keith Urban's 2004 "Tonight I Wanna Cry."
- Opening lines of Kevin Sharp's 1996 "Nobody Knows."
- John Lennon and Paul McCartney's 1965 "You've Got to Hide Your Love Away."

Hint: These examples come from a paper by Scheff ("Shame as the Master Emotion: Examples from Pop Songs"). If you are stuck, you might want to check out this paper on his website: http://www.soc.ucsb.edu/faculty/scheff/80.pdf.

CREATISTA/Shutterstock.com

FIELD RESEARCH

Field research allows researchers to observe social life in its natural habitat: to go where the action is and watch. The observational techniques used in this type of research enable the properly skilled researcher to collect rich, detailed data.

IN THIS CHAPTER ...

INTRODUCTION

Earlier chapters introduced you to the idea that social research focuses on systematically trying to connect observed concrete (empirical) patterns with abstract (meaningful) interpretations. In this way, research is a systematic type of reality construction. These chapters also highlighted that research methods can use either a "top-down" (abstract to concrete) or a "bottom-up" (concrete to abstract) approach, or both. Traditional, quantitative models of scientific research emphasize the top-down approach—theory leading to hypothesis and testing. The qualitative tradition, in which field research is a key method, stresses beginning with careful observation and moving systematically toward the construction of meaningful concepts and interpretations.

The following classic example (Wynne 1996) helps solidify your understanding of the differing insights provided by traditional, quantitative research and situated qualitative understanding. In 1986, a catastrophic nuclear accident occurred at Chernobyl, which was then part of the Soviet Union in the Ukraine. The accident sent up a nuclear cloud that enveloped much of northern and western Europe. Part of the cloud covered Cumbria, a rural area in northwest England where sheep farming is a central economic activity.

Natural scientists were sent in to determine the risks to the community of radioactive waste. They followed traditional sampling and measurement techniques, and as a result they initially told residents there was little to worry about since the effects would dissipate shortly. Contamination readings a few months later were still high, but the scientists predicted a return to normal in short order. It didn't happen. As a result, scientists encouraged an open-ended ban on sheep farming in the region, which produced harsh economic consequences.

It turned out that the natural scientists' predictions about the sources and consequences of contamination were wrong. Had they consulted local sheep farmers, who have an intimate knowledge of local soil composition and conditions, they would have come to a very different, benign conclusion. In this case, the complex, situated, qualitative understanding of local conditions provided a more accurate account of radioactivity in the region than traditional science (Wynne 1996).

This example illustrates the contrast between the generalized, one-size-fits-all approach of traditional quantitative research and the context-specific, in-depth, specialized understanding of a qualitative approach. These approaches take different views and, accordingly, yield different insights. The approaches are complementary (Mazzocchi 2006). With this in mind let's turn to field research, which is largely qualitative.

Field observation differs from some other models of observation in that it's not just a data-collecting activity. Frequently, perhaps typically, it's a theory-generating activity as well. As a field researcher, you'll seldom approach your task with precisely defined hypotheses to be tested. More typically, you'll attempt to make sense out of an ongoing process that can't be predicted in advance—making initial observations, developing tentative general conclusions that suggest particular types of further observations, making those observations and thereby revising your conclusions, and so forth. The alternation of induction and deduction discussed in Part 1 of this book is perhaps nowhere more evident and essential than in good field research. Although in qualitative research, data collection, theory, and analysis are tightly intertwined, for expository purposes this chapter focuses primarily on some of the theoretical foundations of field research and on techniques of data collection. The analysis of qualitative data will be discussed in Chapter 13.

TOPICS APPROPRIATE TO FIELD RESEARCH

One of the key strengths of field research is the comprehensiveness of perspective it gives researchers. By going directly to the social phenomenon under study and observing it as completely as possible, researchers can develop a deeper and fuller understanding of it. Therefore, this mode of observation is especially, though not exclusively, appropriate to research topics and social studies that appear to defy simple quantification. Field researchers may recognize several nuances of attitude and behaviour that might escape researchers using other methods.

Field research is especially appropriate to the study of those attitudes and behaviours best understood within their natural setting, as opposed to the somewhat artificial settings of experiments and surveys. For example, field research provides a superior method for studying the dynamics of religious conversion at a revival meeting, just as a statistical analysis of membership rolls would be a better way of discovering whether men or women were more likely to convert.

Finally, field research is well suited to the study of social processes over time. Thus, the field researcher might be in a position to examine the rumblings and final explosion of a riot as events actually occur rather than afterward in a reconstruction of the events.

In *Analyzing Social Settings* (Lofland et al. 2006:123–132), the authors discuss several elements of social life appropriate to field research:

1. *Practices.* Various kinds of behaviour such as talking.
2. *Episodes.* A variety of events such as divorce, crime, and illness.
3. *Encounters.* Two or more people meeting and interacting in immediate proximity with one another.
4. *Roles and Social Types.* The analysis of the positions people occupy and the behaviour associated with those positions: occupations, family roles, ethnic groups. Social types (which overlap with roles), such as the bully or bookworm, may also be analyzed.
5. *Social and Personal Relationships.* Behaviour appropriate to pairs or sets of roles: mother–son relationships, friendships, and the like.
6. *Groups and Cliques.* Small groups, such as friendship cliques, athletic teams, and work groups.
7. *Organizations.* Formal organizations, such as hospitals or schools.
8. *Settlements and Habitats.* It's difficult to study large societies such as nations, but field researchers often study smaller-scale "societies" such as villages, ghettos, and neighbourhoods.
9. *Subcultures and Lifestyle.* How large numbers of people adjust to life in groups such as a "ruling class" or an "urban underclass."

In all these social settings, field research can reveal things that would not otherwise be apparent.

Field research offers the advantage of probing social life in its natural habitat. Although some things can be studied adequately in questionnaires or in the laboratory, others cannot. And direct observation in the field lets you observe subtle communications and other events that might not be anticipated or measured otherwise.

METHODOLOGICAL TERMS IN FIELD RESEARCH

If you read much of the literature on qualitative inquiry—either reports of qualitative research or texts on how to do it—you're likely to encounter a "terminological jungle" (Lofland et al. 2006:5). In this jungle, authors often use different labels for research approaches that can seem confusingly similar.

Field research incorporates a number of data-gathering techniques and variations in perspectives concerning what questions should be asked and how they should be answered—what we'll call puzzle solving—that are communicated through terms such as grounded theory, interpretivism, ethnomethodology, phenomenology, social constructionism, institutional ethnography, extended case study method, and participatory action research. For example, *phenomenology* is a term associated with the idea that reality is socially constructed. This perspective is prominent in qualitative research and emphasizes attention to the worldview of the people being observed and/or interviewed. A major aim is to discover subjects' experiences and how subjects make sense of them.

Data-gathering techniques in field research tend to cut across these various perspectives. Therefore, we will first talk about general aspects of field research and labels used to signify common data-gathering techniques. We'll then talk about some of the issues that field researchers must consider when preparing for and engaging in fieldwork. After presenting an illustration of a field research study, we'll discuss a few of the alternative frameworks to puzzle solving in field research just mentioned. We'll then look at some specific ideas and guidelines for conducting field research.

ETHNOGRAPHY AND PARTICIPANT OBSERVATION

When you read accounts of qualitative research, you'll see that many field researchers refer to their research method as **ethnography** or *participant observation.* Some use these terms synonymously, while others distinguish them in relation to their history, disciplinary association, and research orientation. Both research methods are rooted in the tradition of naturalism. As Schatzman and Strauss's 1973 book title—*Field Research: Strategies for a Natural Sociology*—indicates, ethnography and participant observation have in common the natural setting. When they speak of "observations of actual situations," they refer "directly to what is known as the field method—a generic term for observing events in a natural situation. The activities of the naturalist in sociology and anthropology have distinct similarities to those of naturalists in zoology, archeology and geology" (1973:13–14).

Thus, some see ethnography and participant observation as a way of studying any group, phenomenon, and so forth in its natural environment. For others ethnography is viewed as somewhat distinctive, referring to naturalistic observations and holistic understandings of cultures or subcultures. Still others use the term *ethnography* to refer more broadly to the set of activities engaged in while in the field, and participant observation is included within this set.

Ethnography is historically associated with anthropology, while participant observation has often been linked to sociology. The more traditional ethnography is associated with travel to a foreign land by anthropological researchers who immerse themselves in a different culture and report their investigations in a richly descriptive manner, providing readers with an intimate feel for the way of life they observed (e.g., the works of Bronislaw Malinowski, Margaret Mead, and E. E. Evans-Pritchard). Nonetheless, for many, contemporary ethnography has come to refer to any research conducted in the field. Finally, in addition to referring to a method of research, ethnography also refers to the written report of the research produced from the field.

Both ethnography and participant observation typically combine a variety of techniques for gathering data. As Reinharz (1992:46) states, "Contemporary ethnography or fieldwork is multimethod research. It usually includes observation, participation, archival analysis, and interviewing...." Others speak of participant observation in the same manner. Both terms connote researchers immersing themselves in a social setting and gathering data that lends itself to interpretation.

In summary, ethnography and participant observation are terms that refer to multimethod modes of data gathering in a natural setting (the field) and are used by researchers with differing orientations for qualitative social scientific puzzle solving. Another term you will frequently run across in your readings is *case study.*

CASE STUDY DESIGN

A **case study** is conducted when the social researcher focuses attention on a single instance of some social phenomenon, like a town, an industry, a community, an organization, or a person. An immediate variation is to study more than one such instance (case), usually a limited number like two, three, or four. Some use the term *case* when referring to a study that focuses on a particular process or period of time as well.

ethnography The term *ethnography* varies somewhat in its use by researchers. It generally refers to a report on social life that focuses on detailed and accurate description rather than explanation. For some, it refers also to data collected in the natural setting, while for others, it refers to naturalistic observations and holistic understandings of cultures or subcultures.

case study A focused, detailed investigation of a single instance of some social phenomenon such as a town, industry, community, organization, or person.

As indicated in Reinharz (1992:164), a case may refer to any unit of social life.

Although many researchers refer to the case study as a method, it is not a technique for gathering data such as observation, in-depth interviews, or self-administered questionnaires. It more appropriately refers to the design of a research study. It concerns what unit the researcher will focus upon—not how the data will be gathered.

We introduce the case study in this chapter because it is prominent in qualitative research studies and thus often associated with field research. The chief purpose of a case study is to focus on the specifics of the case, providing rich, detailed data. The greater time and energy that may be directed to the study of a single instance permits this more intensive investigation. This is an advantage of the case study approach, particularly when the case is a complex, multi-person social phenomenon such as an organization—for instance, a social problems agency like a welfare office or a private drug rehabilitation centre. The trade-off, of course, is between depth and breadth of cases—much more information on one instance as opposed to lesser information on a range of instances.

Sometimes a case study is used as a preliminary to a more elaborate study of many instances—in other words, it is exploratory. The goal of a case study is often descriptive as well—for example, an idiographic account of a particular street gang or an anthropologist's detailed depiction of a specific, nonliterate tribe. While case studies are often exploratory or descriptive, researchers whose goals are explanatory insight also use the design. This is often accomplished through comparison of several cases, but it is also attempted through the use of a single case considered to be typical of a set of cases of a given type.

Classic illustrations of case studies using field research are community studies such as Lynd and Lynd's study of Middletown (1929, 1937), Gans's study of a Boston West End working-class Italian community (1962), and Gans's *The Levittowners* (1967). To whet your appetite for case study–based field research and give you a sense of its broad range of application as a method, here are summaries of four recent studies.

Gang Leader for a Day As of 2016, Sudhir Venkatesh was a sociology professor at Columbia University in New York. But in 1989, he was a student with a ponytail and a tie-dyed T-shirt. His research job was to go to one of the toughest housing projects in Chicago and survey residents about their experience. A sample question on his survey was "How does it feel to be black and poor?" with the answer options "very bad, somewhat bad, neither bad nor good, somewhat good, very good." The actual answers were unprintable (Grimes 2008).

Venkatesh's experience transformed him. He became fascinated with the housing project and decided to conduct an ethnography. The housing project was largely controlled by a gang, the Black Kings, whose leader was J. T. He befriended J. T. and was allowed to carefully observe (and occasionally participate in) gang activities. Hence, the title of his best-selling ethnography, *Gang Leader for a Day* (Venkatesh 2008).

Through careful observation for more than seven years, Venkatesh constructed a vivid understanding of what gang life in the housing project was really like. For example, he learned that much of the day as a gang leader was spent sorting out petty squabbles, that the gang considered itself a social service organization rather than a criminal enterprise, that all community residents earning money were subject to gang extortion, that relationships between the gang, police, and politicians ran deep, and that regular gang members barely earned minimum wage (which explains why most lived with their mothers). Venkatesh's ethnography provides a rich example of how power and institutional corruption dominate the lives of the poor.

Dude, You're a Fag Before 2005, C. J. Pascoe, now a professor at the University of Oregon, spent 18 months conducting an ethnography in a California high school where she told students she wanted to "write a book about guys." Her real interests were in understanding the role of masculinity. Toward this goal, she carefully observed and interviewed dozens of students, faculty, and school administrators (Pascoe 2007).

Her observations took place in "gender neutral" sites (e.g., math class) and traditionally male ones (e.g., automotive repair). She observed drama classes, Gay/Straight Alliance meetings, and lunchrooms, and she attended dances, plays, and other school events. Her observations and interviews with everyone at the school centred on how the students constructed meanings of gender and sexuality.

Among her principal observations was the frequency with which boys would call one another "fag" or "faggot." This practice was so common that she wanted to know what it meant for boys to use this label. Her first impression was that they were labelling the other gay or homosexual. But she soon learned that the "fag" label had nothing to do with sexual preference. So she probed more deeply into what kinds of conduct would deserve the faggot label and a reliable list emerged—including dancing, caring about one's clothing, being too emotional, or being incompetent. All of these things were interpreted as being "unmasculine." In other words, the label "fag" was used as an insult to police the boundaries of masculinity. It wasn't about sexuality; it's a charge about "not being a real man."

Pascoe learned that, for these young men, although being homosexual was "not that bad," what was really devalued was being an "unmasculine man." What Pascoe's ethnography shows in vivid detail is that, through language, boys are continually reminding one another what the defined boundaries of masculinity are. Among the boys in her study, nonnormative masculinity was punished much more harshly than sexual orientation. But, not surprisingly, homosexual youth did not have an easy time of it. Pascoe's study provides insights into the everyday workings of high school culture and, from those insights, provides useful policy proposals about how to create a fairer, more welcoming school environment.

Flesh Hook Pulling Body modification is popular. Among your friends, what percentage of you have either a tattoo or some kind of piercing? Body modification can also be controversial. What was your parents' reaction when you proposed or displayed your first tattoo or piercing? Experiences vary, but a large proportion of youth encounter some level of resistance. Body modification can also be hip. What supportive responses did you get from your friends when you showed them your body modification?

But all practices are governed by social norms, which set limits. How do you think your parents and friends might respond if you told them you were going to attend a "flesh hook pulling" get-together? Here is a description for those unfamiliar with this practice:

> Flesh hook pulling involves a group of people literally pulling from hooks that are pierced into the flesh of their chests or backs. Participants are pierced on either side of their chest with two twelve-gauge needles that are followed immediately by eleven-gauge flesh hooks. Each of the hooks is then attached to a synthetic rope and a clip that can be clipped onto [an]other participant's clips or to ropes affixed to trees.
>
> (Horton 2013:119)

The flesh hooks are strategically positioned so that they don't come out under pressure. Participants can then use their own weight and strength to pull on the hooks and experience the consequences.

Do you have any guesses on why participants would organize and participate in such practices? How would you justify your participation if this practice interested you? Questions like these motivated the Canadian sociologist Alicia Norton. In her search for answers, she located and gained fieldwork access to an annual two-day flesh hook pulling event. In addition to observation, she conducted in-depth interviews with participants both during and after the event. The result is an engaging ethnographic description of what motivates and rewards participants. Her work provides an insider's view of the spiritual, personal, and social benefits associated with this extreme community ritual.

My Freshman Year A central principle in learning theory is that teachers need to empathize with the position and viewpoint of learners. A realistic sense of the challenges a student faces and the resources at their command makes it easier to communicate and calibrate expectations. Without such communication and calibration, frustration is more likely than learning. Look what happens if you try to teach a six-year-old geometry, or your grandparents how to rap.

With this in mind, do a quick review of the professors who are teaching your courses. They are likely older (often much older) than you, have much more education, and a set of interests that are very different from yours. Do you think they have a genuine sense of the realities of your situation? More than one professor has asked the same question and, if they are being honest with themselves, concluded that a big empathy gap exists between them and their students.

One professor, Rebekah Nathan, came to this realization after 15 years of teaching. And, to her credit, she decided to do something about it. She took a year off, enrolled as a first-year student, and immersed herself in the student experience. She moved into the dorm and took a full course load. She ate with students and participated wherever she could in undergraduate student life. Through it all she observed, conversed, and made notes about the student experience and its meaning. Afterward, she wrote up her experience in the ethnography My Freshman Year: What a Professor Learned by Becoming a Student (Nathan 2005).

Here is a roster of some of the things the professor learned about undergraduates:[1]

> Students who live in dorms take a dim view of forced community-building. Students these days devote lots of time to part-time (and full-time) jobs. Students use cellular telephones and instant messaging to communicate. Nathan's students don't seem to value college as a time of intellectual growth or exploration; instead, she notes, they quickly figure out to skip assignments for which they won't be quizzed.
>
> (Jones 2006)

Does any of this surprise you? If it doesn't, what does the fact that this is news to professors tell you about the empathy gap between professors and students?

Despite the diversity of application, these field studies share a methodological approach. Researchers select an illustrative case, go to the field and immerse themselves in the situation, and in doing so try to describe and interpret how the situation is experienced by those participating in it. With this in mind, we turn to the details of the fieldwork approach.

1 Reprinted by permission of PopMatters.

CONSIDERATIONS IN FIELD RESEARCH

When you use field research methods, there are decisions that you'll need to make about the role you'll play as an observer and your relations with the people you're observing. Here we'll examine some of the issues involved in these decisions.

THE VARIOUS ROLES OF THE OBSERVER

Observers in field research can play a variety of roles, including participating in what they want to observe. The term *participant observation* is sometimes used by researchers to describe their method as opposed to field research; this term need not mean that the researchers actively participated in what they studied, though it typically does indicate they studied it directly at the scene of the action. As Catherine Marshall and Gretchen Rossman (1995:60) point out:

> The researcher may plan a role that entails varying degrees of "participantness," that is, the degree of actual participation in daily life. At one extreme is the full participant, who goes about ordinary life in a role or set of roles constructed in the setting. At the other extreme is the complete observer, who engages not at all in social interaction and may even shun involvement in the world being studied. And, of course, all possible complementary mixes along the continuum are available to the researcher.

The complete participant, in this sense, may be a genuine participant in what he or she is studying (e.g., a participant in a campus demonstration) or may pretend to be a genuine participant. In any event, if acting as the complete participant, you let people see you *only* as a participant, not as a researcher. For instance, if you're studying a group made up of uneducated and inarticulate people, it wouldn't be appropriate for you to talk and act like a university professor or student.

This type of research introduces an ethical issue, one on which social researchers themselves are divided. Is it ethical to deceive the people you're studying in the hope that they will confide in you as they will not confide in an identified researcher? Do the potential benefits to be gained by the research offset such considerations? Although many professional associations have addressed this issue, the norms to be followed remain somewhat ambiguous when applied to specific situations.

Related to this ethical consideration is a scientific one. No researcher deceives his or her subjects solely for the purpose of deception. Rather, it's done in the belief that the data will be more valid and reliable, that the subjects will be more natural and honest if they don't know the researcher is doing a research project. If the people being studied know they're being studied, they might modify their behaviour in a variety of ways. This is known as the problem of **reactivity**.

First, they might expel the researcher. Second, they might modify their speech and behaviour to appear more "respectable" than would otherwise be the case. Third, the social process itself might be radically changed. Students making plans to burn down the university administration building, for example, might give up the plan altogether once they learn that one of their group is a social scientist conducting a research project.

On the other side of the coin, if you're a complete participant, you may affect what you're studying. To play the role of participant, you must participate. Yet your participation may importantly affect the social process you're studying. Suppose, for example, that you're asked for your ideas about what the group should do next. No matter what you say, you will affect the process in some fashion. If the group follows your suggestion, your influence on the process is obvious. If the group decides not to follow your suggestion, the process whereby the suggestion is rejected may affect what happens next. Finally, if you indicate that you just don't know what should be done next, you may be adding to a general feeling of uncertainty and indecisiveness in the group.

Ultimately, anything the participant observer does or does not do will have some effect on what is being observed; it's simply inevitable. More seriously, what you do or don't do may have an important effect on what happens. There is no complete protection against this effect, though sensitivity to the issue may provide a partial protection. (This influence, the Hawthorne effect, was discussed in Chapter 7.)

Because of these several considerations, ethical and scientific, the field researcher frequently chooses a different role from that of complete participant. You could participate fully with the group under study but make it clear that you were also undertaking research. As a member of the volleyball team, for example, you might use your position to launch a study in the sociology of sports, letting your teammates know what you're doing. There are dangers in this role also, however. The people being studied may shift much of their attention to the research project rather than focus on the natural social process, making the process being observed no longer typical. Or, conversely, you yourself may come to identify too much with the interests and viewpoints of the participants. If you do begin to over-identify, you might lose much of your scientific detachment.

At the other extreme, the complete observer studies a social process without becoming a part of it in any way. Quite possibly, because of the researcher's unobtrusiveness, the subjects of study might not realize they're being studied. Sitting at a bus stop to observe jaywalking at a nearby intersection would be an example. Although the complete observer is less likely to affect what's being studied and less likely to internalize the orientation of the subjects than the complete participant, she or he is also less likely to develop a full appreciation of what's being studied. Observations may be more sketchy and transitory.

Fred Davis (1973) characterizes the extreme roles that observers might play as "the Martian" and "the Convert." The latter involves delving deeper and deeper into the phenomenon under study, running the risk of over-identifying. We'll examine this further in the next section.

reactivity The change in attitudes and behaviour that may result when people know they are being observed.

To better appreciate the "Martian" approach, imagine that you were sent to observe some newfound life on Mars. Probably, you would feel yourself inescapably separate from the Martians. Some social scientists adopt this degree of separation when observing cultures or social classes different from their own.

Marshall and Rossman (1995:60–61) also note that the researcher can vary the amount of time spent in the setting being observed: you can be a full-time presence on the scene or just show up now and then. Moreover, you can focus your attention on a limited aspect of the social setting or seek to observe all of it—framing an appropriate role to match your aims.

Different situations ultimately require different roles for the researcher. Unfortunately, there are no clear guidelines for making this choice. You must rely on your understanding of the situation and your own good judgment. In making your decision, however, you must be guided by both methodological and ethical considerations. Because these often conflict, your decision will frequently be difficult, and you may find sometimes that your role limits your study.

RELATIONS TO SUBJECTS

Having introduced the different roles field researchers might play in connection with their observations, we're now going to focus more specifically on how researchers may relate to the subjects of their study and to the subjects' points of view. We will discuss techniques for conducting field research—for example, gaining access, preparing for the field, and recording observations—later in the chapter.

We've already mentioned the possibility of pretending to occupy social statuses we don't really occupy. Now consider how you would think and feel in such a situation.

Suppose you've decided to study a religious cult that has enrolled many people in your neighbourhood. You might study the group by joining it or pretending to join it. Take a moment to ask yourself what the difference is between "really" joining and "pretending" to join. The main difference is whether you actually take on the beliefs, attitudes, and other points of view shared by the "real" members. If the cult members believe that Jesus will come next Thursday night to destroy the world and save the members of the cult, do you believe it or do you simply pretend to believe it?

Traditionally, social scientists have tended to emphasize the importance of "objectivity" in such matters. In this example, that injunction would be to avoid getting swept up in the beliefs of the group. Without denying the advantages associated with such objectivity, social scientists today also recognize the benefits gained by immersing themselves in the points of view they're studying, what Lofland et al. (2006:70) refer to as "insider knowledge, skill or understanding." Ultimately, you won't be able to fully understand the thoughts and actions of the cult members unless you can adopt their points of view as true, at least temporarily. To fully appreciate the phenomenon you've set out to study, you need to *believe* that Jesus is coming Thursday night.

Adopting an alien point of view is an uncomfortable prospect for most people. It's often difficult enough simply to learn about views that seem strange to you. At times you may find it hard just to tolerate certain views. But to take those views on as your own is ten times worse. Robert Bellah (1970, 1974) has offered the term *symbolic realism* to indicate the need for social researchers to treat the beliefs they study as worthy of respect rather than as objects of ridicule. If you seriously entertain this prospect, you may appreciate why William Shaffir and Robert Stebbins (1991:1) concluded that "fieldwork must certainly rank with the more disagreeable activities that humanity has fashioned for itself."

There is, of course, a danger in adopting the points of view of the people that you're studying. When you abandon your objectivity in favour of adopting such views, you lose the possibility of seeing and understanding the phenomenon within frames of reference unavailable to your subjects. On the one hand, accepting the belief that the world will end on Thursday night allows you to appreciate aspects of that belief available only to believers. However, stepping outside that view makes it possible for you to consider some reasons why people might adopt such a view. You may discover that some did so as a consequence of personal trauma (such as unemployment or divorce), while others were brought into the fold through their participation in particular social networks (e.g., their whole soccer team or all of their Facebook friends joined the cult). Notice that the cult members might disagree with those "objective" explanations, and group members might not feel that you had operated legitimately.

The apparent dilemma here is that both of these postures offer important advantages but seem to be mutually exclusive. In fact, it is possible to assume both postures. Sometimes you can simply shift viewpoints at will. When appropriate, you can fully assume the beliefs of the cult; later, you can step outside those beliefs (more accurately, you step inside the viewpoints associated with social science). As you become more adept at this kind of research, you may come to hold contradictory viewpoints simultaneously, rather than switch back and forth. Allowing yourself to remain open to various possibilities helps in this regard. For example, as a researcher with the cult you might try to suspend your beliefs while in that realm, neither believing that the world will end on Thursday night (like most of the other participants) nor disbelieving it (like most scientists).

The problem we've just been discussing could be seen as psychological, occurring mostly inside the researcher's head. There is a corresponding problem at a social level, however. When you become deeply involved in the lives of the people you're studying, you're likely to be moved by their personal problems and crises. Imagine, for example, that one of the cult members becomes ill and needs a ride to the hospital. Should you provide transportation? Sure. Suppose someone wants to borrow money to buy a stereo. Should you lend it? Probably not. Suppose they need the money for food?

There are no black-and-white rules for resolving situations such as these; however, you should realize that you'll need to deal with them regardless of whether you reveal yourself as a researcher. Such problems do not tend to arise in other types of research—surveys and experiments, for example—but they are part and parcel of field research.

SOME ILLUSTRATIONS OF FIELD RESEARCH

Books on qualitative methodology often refer to qualitative inquiry as a craft or a mindset and suggest that the best way to learn about the variety of ways of going about it is to become involved in several differing qualitative studies. Short of that, let's now examine some illustrations of field research studies to give you a better sense of the diverse and creative ways such research has been conducted. The following examples help to demonstrate the flexibility, adaptability, and dynamism of this method, as well as the types of problems and issues the field researcher confronts when observing and participating with research subjects in their natural habitat. Also see the Spolight on MMR box, which presents an example in which the field under study spanned both off-line and online environments.

OBSERVING OUTLAW BIKERS

Daniel Wolf (1990) was a graduate student in Alberta when he decided to engage in field research inside an outlaw motorcycle club. He understood how the bikers were perceived by the general society, but he wanted to learn about their own worldview: How did they see themselves and how did they collectively create their subculture?

Though he bought an appropriate motorcycle and biker clothing, Wolf found it particularly difficult to gain access to a club.[2]

> In Calgary, I met several members of the Kings Crew MC in a motorcycle show and expressed an interest in "hanging around." But I lacked patience and pushed the situation by asking too many questions. I found out quickly that outsiders, even bikers, do not rush into a club, and that anyone who doesn't show the proper restraint will be shut out.
>
> (Wolf 1991:10–11)

Notice that while his attempt to join up with the Kings Crew was unsuccessful, Wolf learned

2 *The Rebels: A Brotherhood of Outlaw Bikers*, by Daniel R. Wolf, © University of Toronto Press 1991. Reprinted with permission of the publisher.

something about biker clubs nonetheless. His rapport with the club was not helped, however, when he got into a barroom fight with a club member days later:

> He flattened my nose and began choking me. Unable to get air down my throat and breathing only blood through my nostrils, I managed a body punch that luckily found his solar plexus and loosened his grip. I then grabbed one of his hands and pulled back on the thumb until I heard the joint break. Mistake number two. It was time to move on.
>
> (Wolf 1991:11)

Eventually, Wolf made a successful contact with the Rebels, beginning with a casual conversation about motorcycles with a gang member. He was invited to drink with the club, then to ride with them. Gradually, he became a friend with more and more club members, and his participation increased steadily.

For three years, Wolf became more involved with the Rebels and came to grasp their worldview more fully. He experienced his friendship with club members as genuine; they became more his brothers than research subjects:

> Brotherhood, I came to learn, is the foundation of the outlaw club community. It establishes among members a sense of moral, emotional, and material interdependence and commitment. The enduring emotion of brotherhood is comradeship. To a patch holder, brotherhood means being there when needed; its most dramatic expression occurs when brothers defend each other from outside threats.
>
> (Wolf 1991:16)

As he felt himself more and more a full participant in the Rebels, his role as researcher became increasingly problematic. Doing secret research was a blatant betrayal of the men he now regarded as his friends. Moreover, Wolf knew that three police officers who had attempted to infiltrate the club previously had been murdered. He wanted to tell the club members about his research but was afraid to do so.

Then one day, he got a lucky break. Club members knew that Wolf was an anthropology graduate student, and one asked if he had ever considered doing research on the club. Wolf said he would be interested in doing that and now had an excuse for making a proposal to the club leadership and members. After some heated disagreements, the club agreed, and Wolf could conduct his research openly.

Wolf eventually completed his thesis and gave a copy to the club. His desire to publish his thesis as a book, however, raised more disagreements among club members. Ultimately, he worked with club members to create fictional names that would protect them as individuals. The club itself was well known, however, and Wolf made no attempt to disguise it.

While Wolf continued to feel a personal friendship with members of the Rebels, his emergence as a researcher steadily eroded that relationship:

> I continued to ride with the Rebels for another year and a half, during which time I carried out formal data procedures—structured interviews. As my role as an ethnographer became more evident, my role as a biker became more contrived and I began to be excluded from the brotherhood. My contact with members became less frequent and less intense. As an ethnographer, my relationship with the club lost its substance and meaning and I lost touch with the innermost core of Rebel reality; I simply faded away.
>
> (Wolf 1991:349)

PARKOUR IN A CANADIAN CITY

You probably have seen it in video or movie clips and may have seen it in your city—young persons negotiating the urban landscape as if it were an obstacle course. Running, leaping, climbing, swinging, and rolling rapidly from one point to the next. The participants, called "traceurs," are practising parkour, a form of "free running" that has become a subculture of physical activity.

What purpose drives traceurs to participate in the rigorous physical demands of these urban gymnastics? Michael Atkinson (2009) decided that a way to find out was to join a group of participants in Toronto.

Atkinson spent two years with the group, who shared the following social profile:[3]

> They are predominantly male, are of mixed ethnic background or national origin, are high school graduates (only a few members of the group have university or college experience), range in age from 18 to 31, and live in close proximity to one another in the downtown core of Toronto. They have limited life experiences with organized sport but do share common backgrounds and interests in outdoor physical pursuits. Although they do possess extensive friendship and familial bonds, they almost universally describe feelings of alienation and isolation in/from social networks in the city. Each expresses an interest in environmental awareness, politics, and protection—a lifestyle position mainly impressed on them by close parents and peers.
> A majority of them grew up outside of organized/institutionalized religious networks but express a keen interest in exploring spiritually centered lives. It is interesting that they overwhelming feel a stereotypically (at least historically) middle-class political/vocational duty to act in socially responsible and beneficial manners. To this end, they prefer physical cultural practices that seamlessly integrate their somatic preferences, ideological leanings, and social values.
> (Atkinson 2009:179)

In these social roots, Atkinson locates the meaning and importance of parkour to the practitioners' lives, captured in the concept of "post-sport" lifestyle. In contrast to traditional sports, "postsports are cooperative over competitive, socially inclusionary rather than hierarchical, process oriented, and holistic. A postsport physical culture values human spiritual, physical, and emotional development (or rather realization) through athleticism, beyond medical-technical or power and performance terms" (Atkinson 2009:180).

This theme was repeatedly found in the interviews conducted with participants and with the author's own participation. Here is one participant's construction of his experience:

> Being on the edge made me learn who I am at my core. When I look into myself and confront my humanity, I realize what makes me function. It's when my body and mind are punished that I learn about me. In the middle of a run, when nothing else in the world matters and I'm tired, I realize how controlled and forced the rest of my life is.
> (Atkinson 2009:186)

Here is Atkinson's (2009:169) summary of his own experience:

> My entire body ached at the end of the 8 miles, my mind had been exhausted, and my emotions had run wild. After nearly 6 months in the field participating with traceurs ..., I finally realized the essence of Parkour. Free running is a mode of bringing forth or revealing dimensions of the physical and spiritual self through a particular type of urban gymnastics. It destabilizes and disrupts techno-capitalist meanings of a city's physical and social landscape for its practitioners. Parkour is ultimately a communion with one's habitat, in the goal of exploring how one's body is shaped by the political geography of a late modern city.

This research illustrates how a researcher's engagement in a countercultural lifestyle can help outsiders better understand that what initially looks like an incomprehensible activity is rich with meaning for its participants.

BEING A POLICE OFFICER IN RURAL CANADA

Entry into a valuable occupation typically requires a significant investment of time, effort, and money. Commonly, recruits make their occupational choices and investments based on their imagined understanding of what, for example, it will be like to be a doctor, lawyer, teacher, or police officer. Only later, after the training and investments have been made, do participants learn about the realities of the job.

This misalignment between expectations and experience is the classic recipe for role strain and its associated frustration, dissatisfaction, and demoralization. Huey and Ricciardelli (2015)

3 Michael Atkinson, "Parkour, Anarcho-Environmentalism, and Poiesis," *Journal of Sport & Social Issues* (33, 2), pp. 169–194, copyright © 2009 SAGE Publications, Inc. Reprinted by Permission of SAGE Publications, Inc.

performed a field study to investigate the potential for role strain among police officers stationed in remote communities in Eastern Canada. Their study conducted semi-structured interviews with 20 police officers working in rural detachments. They also engaged in ethnographic fieldwork in which they sat with patrol officers and observed.

What they found is captured in the title of their research: "This isn't what I signed up for." The roles of police officers can include those of law enforcer, peacekeeper (for minor offences), social worker (related to nonpolicing matters), and knowledge worker (administrative paperwork). Not surprisingly, most police officers initially thought and continued to prefer their work be centred on law enforcement and peacekeeping activity. In the words of one police officer, this is "what I wanted to do: law enforcement and a lot of peacekeeping too" (Huey and Ricciardelli 2015:199).

By contrast, many police officers in the remote communities were frustrated and demoralized by the fact that much of their work was related to social work and administrative paperwork. Witness the cynical laughter at the end of this exchange (Huey and Ricciardelli 2015:200):

> Q: Of those four roles—law enforcement, peacekeeping, social work, and knowledge work—which one do you feel best reflects what you actually do?
> A: Social work.
> Q: And what did you sign up for?
> A: Exactly [laughs]

Or the frustration is this officer's report: "My job is data entry. That is my job. It is not to solve crime. I'll tell you, nobody cares if I solve the crime" (Huey and Ricciardelli 2015:200).

This field study clearly reveals a major source of job dissatisfaction among police officers. The methods used give a human face to their experience. Documenting the range and depth of frustration and demoralization associated with the misalignment between what officers expected and what they experience has important consequences for recruiting, orientation, work organization, and performance.

VARIOUS FRAMEWORKS FOR FIELD RESEARCH: POSING AND SOLVING PUZZLES

Although we've described field research as going where the action is and observing it, there are actually many different approaches to this research method. These alternatives concern the framework of the study: what puzzles (research questions) to pose and how to solve them. While there are many such variations, this section looks at only a few of these alternative approaches to field research—grounded theory, the extended case method, institutional ethnography, and participatory action research—to give you a sense of the possibilities. The distinctions among the numerous approaches are sometimes subtle for those newly exposed to field methods. However, the more qualitative research you read, the more variety of approaches you will run across, and the clearer the distinctions among these approaches will become.

Before we turn to our examination of some of these alternative frameworks in field research, let's briefly revisit our discussion of the relationship between the researcher and subject. In the conventional view of science, there are implicit differences of power and status separating the researcher from the subjects of research. For example, when talking about experimental designs, it's clear that the experimenter is in charge. It is the experimenter who organizes things and tells the subjects what to do. Many times the experimenter is the only one who knows what the research is truly about. Something similar might be said about survey research. The person running the survey designs the questions, decides who will be selected for questioning, and is responsible for making sense out of the data collected.

Sociologists often look at these kinds of relationships as power or status relationships. In experimental and survey designs, the researcher clearly has more power and a higher status than do the people being studied. The researchers have a special knowledge that the subjects don't enjoy. They're not so crude as to say they're superior to the subjects, but there's a sense in which that's implicitly assumed. This sense of superiority, however, does not necessarily translate into greater power and status in all social settings. For example, it would rarely apply in the study of elites. Thus, power and status differences must be evaluated as a variable possibility, taking the particularity of the research setting into account.

Nonetheless, implicit assumptions of researcher superiority can be problematic in field research. When the early European anthropologists set out to study what were originally called "primitive" societies, there was no question but that the anthropologists thought they knew best. Although the Indigenous people "believed" in witchcraft, for example, the anthropologists "knew" it wasn't really true. While the Indigenous people said some of their rituals would appease the gods, the anthropologists explained that the "real" functions of these rituals were the creation of social identity, the establishment of group solidarity, and so on. They never thought to question the intrinsic superiority of the European culture that they took for granted.

The more social researchers have gone into the field to study their fellow humans face to face, however, the more they have become conscious of these implicit assumptions about researcher superiority, and the more they have considered alternatives. As we now turn to the various approaches to field research, we'll see some of the ways in which that ongoing concern has worked itself out.

GROUNDED THEORY

Grounded theory originated from the collaboration of Barney Glaser and Anselm Strauss. This approach has evolved and developed since the first major presentation of it in their book *The Discovery of Grounded Theory* (1967). It has many facets; therefore, our goal here is simply to briefly introduce some of the key ideas associated with this approach.

Grounded theory is the attempt to derive theory from an analysis of the patterns, themes, and common categories discovered in observational data. This differs from hypothesis testing, in which theory is used to generate hypotheses to be tested through observations (revisit Chapters 1 and 2 to refresh your familiarity with inductive reasoning and how it differs from and complements deductive reasoning). According to Strauss and Corbin, "A researcher does not begin a project with a preconceived theory in mind (unless his or her purpose is to elaborate and extend existing theory). Rather, the researcher begins with an area of study and allows the theory to emerge from the data" (1998:12).

As an inductive approach, grounded theory involves an ongoing back and forth between data (and even data collection) and theory. This is exemplified by two key techniques typically used in grounded theory—theoretical sampling and constant comparative method. As we will discuss grounded theory in more depth in Chapter 13, we will contain ourselves now to just a brief description of these two techniques. In **theoretical sampling**, cases (e.g., persons, communities, and institutions) are selected based on their theoretical relevance (as such, it is related to purposive sampling). That is, if certain characteristics (e.g., processes, types, events, categories, and examples) are necessary to develop your theory, then you must sample cases accordingly. Related to this is the **constant comparative method**, an iterative process in which theory (codes, concepts, categories, and hypotheses) is constantly checked against the data and revised/elaborated in light of new data. Thus, as theory emerges and evolves, it may require the observer in the field to adjust mid-course in order to observe newly relevant cases and collect newly relevant data.

grounded theory An inductive approach to social research that attempts to derive theory from an analysis of the patterns, themes, and common categories discovered in observational data. This differs from hypothesis testing, in which theory is used to generate hypotheses to be tested through observations.

theoretical sampling The selection of cases based on illustrative, theoretical relevance.

constant comparative method Involves the researching moving back and forth between theory and data; concepts, categories, and hypotheses are constantly checked against, and elaborated in light of, new data/observations.

Clifton F. Conrad's (1978) study of academic change in universities is an early example of constant comparative method and theoretical sampling at work in the grounded theory approach. Conrad hoped to uncover the major sources of changes in academic curricula and at the same time understand the process of change. Using the grounded theory idea of theoretical sampling, whereby groups or institutions are selected on the basis of their theoretical relevance, Conrad chose four universities for the purpose of his study. In two, the main vehicle of change was the formal curriculum committee; in the other two, the vehicle of change was an ad hoc group.

Conrad explained, step by step, the advantage of using the grounded theory approach in building his theory of academic change. He described the process of systematically coding data in order to create categories that must "emerge" from the data and then assessing the fitness of these categories with each other. Going continuously from data to theory and theory to data (constant comparative method) allowed him to reassess the validity of his initial conclusions about academic change.

For instance, it first seemed that academic change was mainly caused by an administrator who was pushing for it. By re-examining the data and looking for more plausible explanations, Conrad found the pressure of interest groups a more convincing source of change. The emergence of these interest groups actually allowed the administrator to become an agent of change.

Assessing how data from each of the two types of universities fit with the other helped refine theory building. Conrad's conclusion was that changes in university curricula are based on the following process: Conflict and interest groups emerge because of internal and external social structural forces; they push for administrative intervention and recommendation to make changes in the current academic program; these changes are then made by the most powerful decision-making body.

extended case method A research technique developed by Michael Burawoy that uses case study observations to discover flaws in and to improve existing social theories.

Grounded theory can be described as an attempt to combine a naturalist approach with an explicit concern for a "systematic set of procedures" in doing qualitative research. But make no mistake—taking qualitative evidence and transforming it into a coherent, comprehensible narrative is not easy; it requires serious intellectual work. We will have more to say about the techniques of this work in Chapter 13.

EXTENDED CASE METHOD

As previously discussed, the case study design may be used by researchers for the purpose of generating in-depth description or explanatory insights. Thus, case study researchers may seek only an idiographic understanding of a particular case or they may use case studies as the basis for the development of more general, nomothetic theories—for example, using the grounded theory approach.

Michael Burawoy and colleagues (1991) suggest a somewhat different relationship between case studies and theory. For them, the **extended case method** has the purpose of discovering flaws in, and then modifying, existing social theories.

Although in the grounded theory approach researchers attempt to enter the field without preconceived theory in mind, Burawoy suggests the opposite approach: to try "to lay out as coherently as possible what we expect to find in our site *before* entry" (Burawoy et al. 1991:9). He sees the extended case method as a way to rebuild or improve theory instead of approving or rejecting it. The goal is to look for all the ways in which observations conflict with existing theories and for what Burawoy calls "theoretical gaps and silences" (1991:10). In this orientation to field research, becoming deeply familiar with the literature before entering the field appears to be essential, whereas grounded theorists, in their goal of generating knowledge, feel that being too deeply entrenched in the literature beforehand might block creativity and constrain or bias observations and theory development.

Here's an example of a study by one of Burawoy's students to illustrate the extended case method. Katherine Fox (1991) set out to study an agency whose goal was to fight the AIDS epidemic by bringing condoms and bleach for cleaning needles to intravenous drug users. It's a good example of finding the limitations of well-used models of theoretical explanation in the realm of understanding deviance—specifically, the "treatment model" that predicted that drug users would come to the clinic and ask for treatment. Fox's interactions with outreach workers, most of whom were part of the community of drug addicts or former prostitutes, contradicted that model.

To begin, it was necessary to understand the drug users' subculture and use that knowledge to devise more realistic policies and programs. The target users had to be convinced, for example, that the program workers could be trusted, that they were really interested only in providing bleach and condoms. The target users needed to be sure they were not going to be arrested.

Fox's field research didn't stop with an examination of the drug users. She also studied the agency workers, discovering that the outreach program meant different things to the research directors than to the outreach workers. Some of the volunteers who were actually providing the bleach and condoms were frustrated about the minor changes they felt they could make. Many thought the program was just a bandage on the AIDS and drug abuse problems. Some resented having to take field notes. Directors, on the other hand, needed reports and field notes so that they could validate their research in the eyes of the government agencies that financed the project. Fox's study showed how the AIDS research project developed the bureaucratic inertia typical of established organizations. Its goal became that of sustaining itself.

This study illustrates how the extended case method can operate. The researcher enters the field with full knowledge of existing theories but aims to uncover contradictions that require the modification of those theories.

INSTITUTIONAL ETHNOGRAPHY

Conducting research from the "standpoint of women" (and, more recently, other subordinated groups) is key to the **institutional ethnography** approach originally developed by Dorothy Smith (1987). Challenging conventional methodological approaches, Smith argued that closer attention to women's voices and experiences would open the door to greater understanding of how these experiences are organized and determined.

Smith and other social scientists believe that if researchers ask women or other members of subordinated groups about "how things work," they can discover the institutional practices that shape their realities. Although the individuals' experiences are essential to the research approach, the individuals themselves are not the focus of inquiry. The institutional ethnographer starts with the personal experiences of the oppressed or "ruled" but proceeds to uncover the institutional power relations that structure and govern those experiences—the social organization of ruling relations. The goal of such inquiry is to uncover forms of oppression that are often overlooked by more traditional types of research.

As Marie Campbell (1998:57) stated:

> Institutional ethnography, like other forms of ethnography, relies on interviewing, observation and documents as data. Institutional ethnography departs from other ethnographic approaches by treating those data not as the topic or object of interest, but as "entry" into the social relations of the setting. The idea is to tap into people's expertise.... The conceptual framing of everyday experiences heard or read about, or observed, constitutes one of the distinctive features of an institutional ethnography, another is its political nature.

Campbell applied this framework in her study of the impact of a new management strategy called the Service Quality Initiative, implemented in a long-term care hospital in Victoria, British Columbia. One major aim of her work was to investigate how this management strategy reorganized the values and practices of the caregivers

institutional ethnography A research technique that uses the personal experiences of individuals (especially women and other members of subordinated groups) to uncover the institutional power relations that structure and govern their experiences.

to take into account fiscal concerns. The entry point of her investigation was the nursing assistants' experiences. Following the institutional ethnography approach, her initial goal was to learn how the setting worked by listening to what these subordinates or "ruled" had to say. Developing an understanding of the social relations from the perspective of the ruled, she then inquired into the effects of specific ruling practices on the nursing assistants—those whose work lives were structured by these practices.

Another key point of Campbell's article concerned methodology and her desire to illustrate the central importance of people's experience in gaining a "trustworthy analysis." In describing her investigation into what was actually going on in the research setting, she stated: "I was not entering it as a naïve observer working in a naturalist mode, nor was I looking for theory to arise out of data, as a grounded theorist might. As an institutional ethnographer, I was informed by prior analysis of the Canadian health care system and its increasingly rationalist stance toward management. I was also informed by a social organization of knowledge approach" (1998:58).

Beginning from the viewpoint of the nursing assistants, she followed the structure of social relations to gain insight into the way they shaped the nurses' thoughts and actions. The trustworthiness of the data, according to Campbell, concerned the extent to which it accounted for their experiences. She, therefore, illuminated how the discourse of management structured the nursing assistants' work lives. The principles of the new initiative—attention to bottom-line budgets, among other things—influenced the organization of social relations and hence the nurses' experiences. She discovered that the emphasis on market concerns came to overshadow the concerns of care in the day-to-day decisions of the healthcare workers.

After using multimethod techniques that included participant observation, recorded in-depth interviews, and focus groups, McGibbon and colleagues (2010) published "Institutional Ethnography of Nurses' Stress." The purpose of their study was to re-examine the various types of stress that nurses experience—as uncovered in previous research—by providing an understanding of the context within which nurses work: the gendered workforce and the type of work they do, which includes care of the body.

In their analysis of the social organization of nurses' stress, their thematic coding produced

> six main forms of nurses' stress, including emotional distress; constancy of presence; burden of responsibility; negotiating hierarchical power; engaging in bodily caring; and being mothers, daughters, aunts, and sisters.
>
> (p. 1357)

The authors stated that the institutional ethnographic approach to examining nurses' stress allowed them to bring to light many core issues in the work life of nurses that the literature had yet to address. For example, they said that

> [b]odily caring, extended time with patients, and aspects of nurses' identities are rarely, if ever, part of the occupational stress discourse, or indeed the VT [vicarious trauma] and moral distress literature. The stress of training physicians, of being the "funnel of all the information about any particular patient," and of taking on the work of other clinicians after the hospital day workers go home, are largely absent in the current discourse of nurses' occupational stress.
>
> (p. 1375)

They noted that recognition of these elements of a nurse's work is highly important to understanding nurses' experiences. As McGibbon and colleagues stated (2010:1356), "Institutional ethnography provides a specific method to link nurses' everyday work with institutional structures that shape practice."

Another illustration of institutional ethnography is taken from Didi Khayatt's (1995) study of the institutionalization of compulsory heterosexuality in schools and its effects on lesbian students. In 1990, Khayatt began her research by interviewing 12 Toronto lesbians, 15 to 24 years of age. Beginning with the young women's viewpoint, she then expanded her inquiry to other students, teachers, guidance counsellors, and administrators.

Khayatt found that the school's administrative practices generated a *compulsory heterosexuality*, which produced a sense of marginality and vulnerability among lesbian students. For example, the school didn't punish harassment and name-calling against gay students. The issue of homosexuality was excluded from the curriculum lest it appear to students as an alternative to heterosexuality.

Khayatt's inquiry began with the women's standpoint: lesbian students. However, instead of emphasizing the subjects' viewpoints, her analysis focused on the power relations that shaped these women's experiences and reality.

PARTICIPATORY ACTION RESEARCH

The role of the researcher in **participatory action research** (PAR) is to serve as a resource to those being studied—typically, disadvantaged groups—as an opportunity for them to act effectively in their own interest. In this approach, the researcher's attempt to provide alternatives to the conventional view of the status and power differences between researchers and subjects is quite clear. The disadvantaged subjects define their problems, define the remedies desired, and take the lead in designing the research that will help them realize their aims.

The approach comes from a critique of classical social science research. From the perspective of PAR, traditional research is seen as an "elitist model" (Whyte et al. 1991) that reduces the "subjects" of research to "objects" of research. Many who advocate this perspective believe the distinction between the researcher and the researched should disappear. They argue that the subjects who will be affected by research should also be responsible for its design.

The approach began in low-income countries but quickly spread to Europe and North America. Implicit in this approach is the belief that research functions not only as a means of knowledge production but also as a "tool for the education and development of consciousness as well as mobilization for action" (Gaventa 1991:121–122). Advocates of participatory action research equate access to information with power and argue that this power has been kept in the hands of the dominant class, sex, ethnicity, or nation. Once people see themselves as researchers, they automatically regain power over knowledge. Therefore, in this approach both researchers and participant subjects contribute to the research project collaboratively. A major goal of the research is to produce results that are beneficial to the participant subjects of the research. The focus of research attention is usually local, specific problems, and the researcher contributes to the development of specific plans to help solve the problems with the knowledge obtained through the cooperative research. Examples of this approach are community power structure research, corporate research, and "right-to-know" movements (Whyte et al. 1991). Here's an example of community power structure research from applied anthropology.

A research project took place at the initiative of the Dene Cultural Institute and the Dogrib community of Lac La Martre, Northwest Territories. The Dogrib is one of several tribal groups within the Dene Nation.The goal of their collaboration was to document Dene traditional justice among the Dogrib in order to assess whether their system of justice could be usefully revived and sustained if the non-Dene justice system that overlays it were removed. Joan Ryan (1995) was asked to assist this Dene group in gaining research funding and coordinating the project. Her objective was to ensure that the Lac La Martre community's interests were being met by the research project. Thus, she adopted a participatory action research approach.

In the course of documenting traditional Dene justice, the research revealed some of the inconsistencies between traditional rules and values and those imposed on the community by the non-Indigenous institutions. The Dene had their own oral tradition of a rigid system of rules that

participatory action research An approach to social research in which the researcher serves as a resource to those being studied, with the goal of increasing their ability to act effectively in their own interest. Counter to the conventional status and power differences between researchers and subjects, those under study are given control to define their problems, define the remedies they desire, and take the lead in designing the research that will help them realize their aims.

guided behaviour, and group harmony was at its core—harmony among group members and of the group with its environment. The non-Dene justice system that was imposed on the Dene people, however, emphasized individual rights, which were secondary to group harmony in Dene tradition. The adversarial, individualistic nature of non-Dene justice ran counter to the acknowledgment of responsibility and restoration of group harmony central to Dene traditional values.

The Elders of the community indicated a lack of desire to adapt to the non-Dene legal system. Their preference was to regain control of their community and institutions. Maintaining a focus on producing results—knowledge and plans of action—that contribute to positive changes in the lives of the participant subjects, Ryan led the investigation toward an exploration of traditional values that might help the community regain "personal and social control." Key to reclaiming these traditional values was to first overcome the widespread alcohol abuse problem the community faced. This recognition led to the recommendation that the community call in a treatment team and hold healing circles as a way to confront and help resolve the problem. Four other major recommendations were made as well, including the formation of a Dogrib justice committee and the establishment of a pilot project to test the effectiveness of rules, both old and new, in dealing with community social problems. The aim of these recommendations was to help the Dogrib people to reclaim responsibility for administering Dogrib justice and to retake control of other key elements in their community in an effort to revitalize their own institutions and cultural systems.

In reporting the research, Ryan discussed many of the problems and challenges the PAR project faced as well as its successes. For example, the community advisory committee unexpectedly hired the Indigenous interviewers without consultation with Ryan, who was the principal investigator (PI), or the project director (PD). There were gender and other issues as well that the PI and PD had to contend with as strangers in the community, causing both of them some stress. Other difficulties included how the project prematurely set off community action. Midway through the project, a major problem that severely destabilized it was the loss of three out of the four Indigenous research team members: one was dismissed due to an assault conviction and two because of alcohol-related absences. Nonetheless, two other Indigenous members were hired to replace them and the research was able to continue.

This project was a combination of an ethnographic description of traditional Dene justice and PAR. The members of the community instigated, and were actively involved in, the research. Ryan served as a resource to the participant subjects and maintained a focus on the practical, political considerations that motivated the research. The field research uncovered the feelings shared by the Dogrib Elders and some of the problems that required resolution. Steps for action were then recommended for how the community and other Dene people might re-establish control.

Although PAR is commonly an approach by researchers who serve as a resource to disadvantaged groups, it is sometimes used to serve those of varied means and advantage. For example, Williams and colleagues (2008:111) conducted research on health issues aimed at ensuring "the value of the output to the stakeholders." Their research concerned the outcomes of interest to all those residing in Saskatoon, Saskatchewan. Thus, their focus was on people spanning socioeconomic statuses from low to high.

Nonetheless, many such studies seek to provide assistance to vulnerable groups and groups with lesser means. For example, Minore and colleagues (2004:360) studied healthcare delivery in three communities, but their "community driven participatory action research project" focused on Indigenous communities in northern Ontario. Another example is the work of Ou Jin Lee and Brotman (2011), which focuses on how vulnerable sexual minority refugees managed their identities to gain refugee status. As the authors stated (p. 243):

> Our strong connection to community groups through our advisory committee facilitated trust building and decision making with the

community. Engaging in a participatory and social justice oriented research project ensured that community members, both refugees and community activists, were assured of the usefulness of project outcomes for social change.

As you can see, the seemingly simple process of observing social action as it occurs has subtle though important variations. Thus, a variety of approaches to puzzle posing and solving in field research have been developed to enrich the observation of social life.

CONDUCTING FIELD RESEARCH

We've so far discussed topics appropriate to field research, common terms and issues, special considerations in doing this kind of research, and several different approaches to field research that direct different types of research efforts.

Throughout the chapter we've presented some examples that illustrate field research in action. It's now time to turn to specific ideas and techniques for conducting field research, starting with how researchers prepare for fieldwork.

PREPARING FOR THE FIELD

Suppose for the moment that you've decided to undertake field research on a campus political organization. Let's assume further that you're not a member of that group, that you do not know a great deal about it, and that you will identify yourself to the participants as a researcher. This section will discuss some of the ways you might prepare yourself before undertaking direct observations.

As is true of all research methods, you would be well advised to begin with a search of the relevant literature, filling in your knowledge of the subject and learning what others have said about it.

In the next phase of your research, you might wish to discuss the student political group with others who have already studied it or with anyone else likely to be familiar with it. In particular, you might find it useful to discuss the group with one or more informants. Perhaps you have a friend who is a member, or you can meet someone who is. This aspect of your preparation is likely to be more effective if your relationship with the informant extends beyond your research role. In dealing with members of the group as informants, you should take care that your initial discussions do not compromise or limit later aspects of your research. Keep in mind that the impression you make on the informant, the role you establish for yourself, may carry over into your later effort. For example, creating the initial impression that you may be an undercover government agent is unlikely to facilitate later observations of the group.

You should also be wary about the information you get from informants. Although they may have more direct, personal knowledge of the subject under study than you do, what they "know" is probably a mixture of fact and point of view. Members of the political group in our example would be unlikely to give you completely unbiased information (as would members of opposing political groups). Before making your first contact with the student group, then, you should already be quite familiar with it, and you should understand its general philosophical context.

There are a variety of ways to establish your initial contact with the people you plan to study. How you do it will depend, in part, on the role you intend to play. Especially if you decide to take on the role of complete participant, you must find a way to develop an identity with the people to be studied. If you wish to study dishwashers in a restaurant, the most direct method would be to get a job as a dishwasher. In the case of the student political group, you might simply join the group.

Many of the social processes appropriate to field research are open enough to make your contact with the people to be studied rather simple and straightforward. If you wish to observe a mass demonstration, just be there. If you wish to observe patterns in jaywalking, hang around busy streets.

Whenever you wish to make more formal contact with the people, identifying yourself as a researcher, you must establish a certain rapport with them. You might contact a participant with whom you feel comfortable and gain that person's assistance. In studying a formal group, you might approach the group's leader. Or you may find that one of your informants can introduce you.

While you'll probably have many options in making your initial contact with the group, realize that your choice can influence your subsequent observations. Suppose, for example, that you're studying a university and begin with high-level administrators. Important consequences might result from this choice. First, your initial impressions of the university are going to be shaped to some degree by the administrators' views, which will be quite different from those of students or faculty. This initial impression may influence the way you observe and interpret events subsequently, particularly if you're unaware of the influence.

Second, if the administrators approve of your research project and encourage students and faculty to cooperate with you, the latter groups will probably look on you as somehow aligned with the administration, which can affect what they say to you. Faculty might be reluctant to tell you about plans to organize through the teamsters' union.

In making a direct, formal contact with the people you want to study, you'll be required to give them some explanation of the purpose of your study. Here again, you face an ethical dilemma. Telling them the complete purpose of your research might eliminate their cooperation altogether or affect their behaviour in important ways. On the other hand, giving only what you believe would be an acceptable explanation may involve outright deception. Your decisions in this and other matters will probably be largely determined by the purpose of your study, the nature of what you're studying, the observations you wish to use, and similar factors—but ethical concerns must be considered as well.

Previous field research offers no fixed rule—methodological or ethical—to follow in this regard. Your appearance as a researcher, regardless of your stated purpose, may result in a warm welcome from people who are flattered that a scientist finds them important enough to study. Or it may result in your being totally ostracized or worse. For example, it likely wouldn't be a good idea to burst into a meeting of an organized crime syndicate and announce that you're writing a term paper on organized crime.

Another important issue to consider when trying to develop an identity with the people you desire to study concerns the statuses or roles they may attribute to you. These may be independent of, or even contrary to, those you attempt to establish. The statuses, roles, and/or resources that are attributed to researchers often play a part in how people react to them and what kinds of information they are willing to share. It is frequently the case that contrasts such as gender, race, and class must be taken into account. Such ascribed roles may limit or assist researchers in establishing identities and connections with those under study. They can affect the experiences and information available to them. Being alert to possible role attributions by those in the field environment can help you sort out the information you are gathering and the interpretations you place on that information. Sometimes field workers are surprised when they learn of particular interpretations that study participants have been making about their identities. Such discoveries can lead to fruitful reconsiderations of observations collected earlier.

In part, field research is a matter of going where the action is and simply watching and listening. You can learn a lot merely by paying attention to what's going on. At the same time, as we've already indicated, field research can involve more active inquiry. Sometimes it's appropriate to ask people questions and record their answers. Your on-the-spot observations of a full-blown riot will lack something if you don't know why people are rioting. Ask somebody.

Because various methodological techniques involve qualitative interviewing, Chapter 11 is devoted to this topic. As you'll see, much of what we discussed in Chapter 8 on interviewing applies to qualitative interviewing; however, the interviewing you'll do in connection with field observation is different enough to demand a separate treatment. Although interviewing is discussed in the next chapter, keep in mind that it is frequently combined with observational techniques in field research.

RECORDING OBSERVATIONS

The greatest advantage of the field research method is the presence of an observing, thinking researcher on the scene of the action. Even digital recorders and cameras cannot capture all the relevant aspects of social processes, although both can be very useful. Thus, in both direct observation and interviewing, it's vital to make full and accurate notes of what goes on. If possible, you should take notes on your observations *as you observe*. When that's not feasible, write down your **field notes** as soon as possible afterward. Figure 10-1 provides in illustrative example of a researcher's field notes.

Your notes should include both your empirical observations and your interpretations of them. In other words, record what you "know" has happened and what you "think" has happened. Be sure to identify these different kinds of notes for what they are. For example, you might note that Person X spoke out in opposition to a proposal made by a group leader (an observation), that you *think* this represents an attempt by Person X to take over leadership of the group (an interpretation), and that you *think* you heard the leader comment to that effect in response to the opposition (a tentative observation).

FIGURE 10-1 Example of Field Notes. An illustration of a working ethnographer's field notes. As she notes, "Complete sentences are rare ... the pages are full of question marks, and square and round parentheses marking off side-comments, reflection or descriptions, and dots marking incomprehension or that time has passed."
Source: Courtesy of Cicilie Fagerlid

Just as you cannot hope to observe everything, neither can you record everything you do observe. Therefore, your observations will represent a sample of all possible observations. Likewise, your notes will represent a sample of your observations. The goal, of course, is to record the most relevant ones.

Some of the most important observations can be anticipated before you begin the study; others will become apparent as your observations progress. Sometimes you can make note taking easier by preparing standardized recording forms in advance. In a study of jaywalking, for example, you might anticipate the characteristics of pedestrians that are most likely to be useful for analysis—age, gender, social class, ethnicity, and so forth—and prepare a form in which observations of these factors can be recorded easily. Or you might develop a symbolic shorthand in advance to speed up recording. For studying audience participation at a mass meeting, you might want to construct a numbered grid representing the different sections of the meeting room; then you could record the location of participants easily, quickly, and accurately.

None of this advance preparation should limit your recording of unanticipated events and aspects of the situation. Quite the contrary: speedy handling of anticipated observations can give you more freedom to observe the unanticipated.

You're already familiar with the process of taking notes, just as you already have at least informal experience with field research in general. Like good field research, however, good note taking requires careful and deliberate attention and involves some specific skills. Some guidelines follow. (You can learn more from Lofland et al. [2006:110–116].)

First, don't trust your memory any more than you have to; it's untrustworthy. To illustrate this point, try this experiment. Recall the last four movies you saw that you really liked. Now name five of the actors or actresses. Who had the

field notes Qualitative evidence in the form of observations, experiences, and interpretations recorded during an ethnographic study.

longest hair? Who was the most likely to start conversations? Who was the most likely to make suggestions that others followed? If you didn't have any trouble answering any of these questions, how *sure* are you of your answers? Would you be willing to bet $100 that a panel of impartial judges watching those same movies would observe what you report having recalled?

Even if you pride yourself on having a photographic memory, it's a good idea to take notes either during the observation or as soon afterward as possible. Be sure to include the place, time, and date in your notes, and as many details about the circumstances and people present as possible. If you take notes during observation, do it unobtrusively, because people are likely to behave differently if they see you taking down everything they say or do.

Second, it's usually a good idea to take notes in stages. In the first stage, you may need to take sketchy notes (words and phrases) in order to keep abreast of what's happening. Then go off by yourself and rewrite your notes in more detail. If you do this soon after the events you've observed, the sketchy notes should allow you to recall most of the details. The longer you delay, the less likely you'll be able to recall things accurately and fully.

We know this method sounds logical, but it takes self-discipline to put it into practice. Careful observation and note taking can be tiring, especially if it involves excitement or tension and if it extends over a long period. If you've just spent eight hours observing and making notes on how people have been coping with a disastrous flood, your first desire afterward will likely be to get some sleep, dry clothes, or a drink. You may need to take some inspiration from newspaper reporters who undergo the same sorts of hardships, and then write their stories to meet their deadlines.

Third, you'll inevitably wonder *how much* you should record. Is it really worth the effort to write out all the details you can recall right after the observation session? The general guideline here is *yes*. Generally, in field research, you can't be really sure of what's important and what's unimportant until you've had a chance to review and analyze a great volume of information, so you should even record things that don't seem important at the outset. They may turn out to be significant after all. Also, the act of recording the details of something "unimportant" may jog your memory of something that is important.

Realize that most of your field notes will not be reflected in your final report on the project. Put more harshly, most of the notes you take will be "wasted." But take heart: even the richest gold ore yields only about 30 grams of gold per metric tonne, meaning that 99.997 percent of the ore is wasted. Yet that 30 grams of gold can be hammered out to cover an area 30 metres square—the equivalent of about 685 book pages. So take a tonne of notes, and plan to select and use only the gold. Like other aspects of field research (and all research for that matter), proficiency comes with practice. The nice thing about field research is you can begin practising now and can continue practising in almost any situation. You don't have to be engaged in an organized research project to practise observation and recording. You might start by volunteering to take the minutes at committee meetings, for example. Or you might sit in a coffee shop window and observe and record particular characteristics of those who pass by. Observing and recording are worthwhile, professional skills that improve with practice.

It may be helpful for you to conceptualize the process of taking notes in the field in terms of stages or types of notes. Some (Bailey 2006; Lofland and Lofland 1995) outline a three-step process involving *mental notes*, gathered while in the field, which then inform *jotted notes*, which are actually written down as brief reminders to help prompt the researcher's memory when they sit down to write more *complete* or *full* field notes.

Berg and Lune (2011) describe four types of notes that are involved in the process of generating full and detailed notes: cryptic jottings, detailed descriptions, analytic notes, and subjective reflections.

1. *Cryptic jottings*: Usually jotted down quickly and inconspicuously in the field; may be shorthand, a drawing, a unique phrase, or memorable quote. These are brief statements or mnemonic aids to prompt recall when making detailed field notes later.
2. *Detailed descriptions*: Written once you've left the field (based on field jottings and memory); include transcripts of

conversations, details of physical features of people, settings, and dynamics of interpersonal interaction. These are ideally undertaken immediately/ASAP after a session in the field and should take more time than is actually spent in the field (approximately a 4:1 ratio).

3. *Analytic notes* (or observer comments): Ideas that emerge as you write up full field notes. These might include possible connections between people, events, patterns/themes, or theoretical speculations that might help explain what is going on in the field. These are bracketed, or kept separate, from actual narrative.
4. *Subjective reflections*: Observations about and reflections on your own reactions and feelings regarding what you see in the field. This personal processing can help deal with stress, and the self-reflexivity can help in evaluating the soundness of other field notes (e.g., were the researchers' observations affected by their own preconceptions or emotional responses?).

SPOTLIGHT ON MIXED METHODS RESEARCH

Mixing Online and Offline Ethnography

Dyke (2013) conducted an ethnographic study that incorporated mixed methods and online and offline sites. She moved between two sites: an online pro-anorexia (pro-ana) community, and a Local Authority–funded eating disorder prevention project located in schools and youth centres in northern England.

Anorexia nervosa is a serious, difficult to treat mental illness with one of the highest mortality rates among psychiatric conditions (Gremillion 2003). Although anorexia is relatively rare (affecting about 1 percent of the population), there has in recent years been a troubling rise in pro-ana websites that portray it as an "aspirational lifestyle choice." Dyke used a "connective ethnographic methodology" in which she followed the movement of the study participants (and anorexia discourse) within and across online and offline spaces. As Dyke (2013:150) explains,

> Rather than conceiving the virtual as outside the scope of "proper" ethnographic interrogation or disruptive to the boundaries of "the field," I attempted to develop ways of engaging with the virtual, and blending it into fieldwork, data collection, field notes and research diary to produce new ways of making the familiar strange and the strange familiar.

Her connective ethnography began at two sites: offline she became involved as a participant observer (attending meetings and workshops and visiting schools and youth centres with project staff) in an eating disorder intervention project; online she began to follow the discussion boards of seven pro-ana websites. She "lurked" the websites, meaning that she was present but did not make contact or misrepresent herself on the sites. (It should be noted that there is some disagreement about the ethicality of lurking). On the seven pro-ana sites she looked for "postings which attracted both a significant amount of comments from various members of the community and had been contributed to over a time period of more than one month" (p. 152). In her field diary, she took note of "connections between people, places, ideas and communities," which helped inform her offline research as well. She also interviewed one participant offline in conjunction with following her activities online. Dyke observed that the pro-ana community was very mobile and moved seamlessly across online and offline modes of meeting and sharing.

She concluded that interventions aimed at reducing the incidence of eating disorders are bound to be less effective if they fail (as the project she observed did) to recognize the important interplay of online and offline activities in young people's lives.

RESEARCH ETHICS IN FIELD RESEARCH

As we've repeatedly said, all forms of social research raise ethical issues. By bringing researchers into direct and often intimate contact with their subjects, field research raises these concerns in a particularly dramatic way. In Chapter 3, we discussed the ethical particularities of a specific field research study, Humphreys's Tearoom Trade study. The following are ethical issues mentioned by John and Lyn Lofland (1995:63) that should be considered when conducting research. Many of these issues are of particular concern to field researchers and warrant serious discussion with supervisors and colleagues when planning to conduct a field research study:

- Is it ethical to talk to people when they do not know you will be recording their words?
- Is it ethical to get information for your own purposes from people you hate?
- Is it ethical to see a severe need for help and not respond to it directly?
- Is it ethical to be in a setting or situation but not commit yourself wholeheartedly to it?
- Is it ethical to develop a calculated stance toward other humans; that is, to be strategic in your relations?
- Is it ethical to take sides or to avoid taking sides in a factionalized situation?
- Is it ethical to "pay" people with trade-offs for access to their lives and minds?
- Is it ethical to "use" people as allies or informants in order to gain entrée to other people or to elusive understandings?

STRENGTHS AND WEAKNESSES OF FIELD RESEARCH

Like all research methods, field research has its strengths and weaknesses. As we've already indicated, field research is especially effective for studying the subtle nuances in attitudes and behaviours and for examining social processes over time. Because of this, the chief strength of this method lies in the depth of understanding that it permits. Although other research methods may be challenged as "superficial," this charge is seldom lodged against field research.

Flexibility is another advantage of field research. As illustrated and discussed earlier, you may modify your field research design at any time. Moreover, you're always prepared to engage in field research, whenever the occasion should arise, whereas you could not as easily initiate a survey or an experiment.

Field research can be relatively inexpensive as well. Other social scientific research methods may require expensive equipment or an expensive research staff, but field research can typically be undertaken by one researcher with a notebook and a pencil. This is not to say that field research is never expensive. The nature of the research project, for example, may require a large number of trained observers. Expensive recording equipment may be needed. Or you may wish to undertake participant observation of interactions in expensive Paris nightclubs.

Field research has a number of weaknesses as well. First, being qualitative rather than quantitative, it's not an appropriate means for arriving at statistical descriptions of a large population. Observing casual political discussions in laundromats, for example, would not yield trustworthy estimates of the future voting behaviour of the total electorate. Such a study would lack representativeness; therefore, the findings would not be generalizable. Nevertheless, the study could provide important insights into how political attitudes are formed.

To assess field research further, let's focus on the issues of validity and reliability. Recall that validity and reliability are both qualities of measurements. Validity concerns whether measurements actually measure what they're supposed to rather than measuring something else. Reliability, on the other hand, is a matter of dependability: If you made the same measurement again and again, would you get the same result? Let's see how field research stacks up in these respects.

Before doing so, however, we should note that the validity and reliability assessment criteria are imported from the traditional, quantitative research model. Since the goal of qualitative research is constructing a narrative that helps us understand the experiences of participants in real-world situations, the primary assessment criterion is **authenticity**. Authentic accounts are those that meaningfully capture the lived experience of participants. For qualitative researchers, traditional considerations of validity and reliability are important to the extent that they contribute to authentic understanding.

VALIDITY

Field research seems to provide more valid measures than survey and experimental measurements, which are often criticized as superficial and not really valid. Let's review a couple of field research examples to see why this is so.

"Being there" is a powerful technique for gaining insights into the rich and complex nature of human affairs. After Lance's wife's diagnosis of pancreatic cancer she spent many hours receiving chemotherapy. During that time, she spoke with other patients undergoing similar treatments about their principal fears. Although dying was feared, it was rarely at the top of the list. Among cancer patients, the following three fears were more salient than dying:

- *Uncontrolled pain*: Physical suffering was often cited as worse than death.
- *Abandonment*: Fighting against cancer is often a long drawn-out process. Patients fear that their friends and family will tire of providing ongoing support.
- *Dependence*: All cancers take a serious toll on the patient. But so do chemotherapy and other treatments. Patients worry about whether the combination of the disease and the responses will rob them of their independence.

These observations are valuable in their own right. In addition, they can provide the basis for further research, both qualitative and quantitative.

Now consider what Joseph Howell had to say about "toughness" as a fundamental ingredient of life on Clay Street, a white, working-class neighbourhood in Washington, D.C.

> Most of the people on Clay Street saw themselves as fighters in both the figurative and literal sense. They considered themselves strong, independent people who would not let themselves be pushed around. For Bobbi, being a fighter meant battling the welfare department and cussing out social workers and doctors upon occasion. It meant spiking Barry's beer with sleeping pills and bashing him over the head with a broom. For Barry it meant telling off his boss and refusing to hang the door, an act that led to his being fired. It meant going through the ritual of a duel with Al.
>
> It meant pushing Bubba around and at times getting rough with Bobbi.
>
> June and Sam had less to fight about, though if pressed they both hinted that they, too, would fight. Being a fighter led Ted into near conflict with Peg's brothers, Les into conflict with Lonnie, Arlene into conflict with Phyllis at the bowling alley, etc.
>
> (1973:292)

Even without having heard the episodes Howell refers to in this passage, you have the distinct impression that Clay Street is a tough place to live in. That "toughness" is conveyed far more powerfully through these field observations than it would be in a set of statistics on the median number of fistfights occurring during a specified period.

Oliffe and colleagues' (2007:229) study concerned beliefs and behaviours on health and illness of men from South Asia who immigrated to Canada. The following description that they reported as part of their findings provides another example of the depth and vividness that field research allows:

> Worship was routinely done at many of the men's homes; however, aside from offering additional opportunities to worship, the temple provided a place to eat, socialize, and do community service (*sewa*). *Sewa*, in particular, was highly valued because it enabled men to demonstrate their humbleness through freely giving their time to help others and making financial contributions to the temple. Doing these "good deeds" was important because they believed that God was

authenticity The criterion for judging qualitative research that concerns itself with whether the constructed narrative meaningfully captures the lived experience of participants.

watching and, therefore, individuals might be rewarded with good karma in their next life. Many activities and interactions observed at the temple indicated strong linkages between spirituality and health.

These examples point to the superior validity of field research, as compared with surveys and experiments. The kinds of comprehensive measurements available to the field researcher tap a depth of meaning in concepts such as common fears of cancer patients and "toughness" (or such as *liberal* and *conservative*) that are generally unavailable to surveys and experiments. Instead of specifying concepts, field researchers commonly give detailed illustrations.

RELIABILITY

Field research has, however, a potential problem with reliability. Suppose you were to characterize your best friend's political orientations based on everything you know about him or her. Your assessment of your friend's politics would appear to have much validity; it's certainly unlikely to be superficial. We couldn't be sure, however, that someone else would characterize your friend's politics the same way you did, even with the same amount of observation.

Although they are in-depth, field research measurements are also often very personal. How someone else judges your friend's political orientation depends very much on his or her own political orientation, just as your judgment depends on your political orientation. Conceivably, then, you could describe your friend as middle of the road, although someone else might believe that he or she had been observing a fire-breathing radical.

As we've suggested earlier, researchers who use qualitative techniques are conscious of this issue and take pains to address it. Individual researchers often sort out their own biases and points of view, and the communal nature of science means that their colleagues will help them in that regard. Nonetheless, it's wise to be wary of purely descriptive measurements in field research, whether it's your own or someone else's. If a researcher reports that the members of a club are somewhat conservative, such a judgment is unavoidably linked to the researcher's own politics. You can be more trusting of *comparative evaluations*: identifying who is more conservative than whom, for example. Even if you and a friend had different political orientations, you would probably agree pretty much in ranking the relative conservatism of the members of a group.

As we've seen, field research is a potentially powerful tool for social scientists, one that provides a useful balance to the strengths and weaknesses of experiments and surveys.

■ MAIN POINTS

- Field research involves the direct observation of social phenomena in their natural settings. Field research is typically qualitative rather than quantitative.
- Field research is particularly appropriate to topics and processes that are not easily quantified, that are best understood in their natural settings, or that change over time. Topics include the study of practices, episodes, encounters, roles, relationships, groups, organizations, settlements, social worlds, and lifestyles or subcultures.
- In field research, observation, data processing, and analysis are interwoven and cyclical processes.
- Field research is typically multimethod, including observation, interviews, and examination of documents. Two terms commonly used by field researchers in describing their research methods are *ethnography* and *participant observation*.
- A case study design is frequently used in qualitative research, although it is used by quantitative researchers as well. It refers to the focus of the study, not to how the data will be gathered. The limitation

of attention to a particular instance of something is the essential characteristic of the case study.

- Among the considerations involved in field research are the various possible roles of the observer and the researcher's relations with subjects. As a field researcher, you must decide whether to observe as an outsider or as a participant, whether to identify yourself as a researcher, and how to negotiate your relationships with subjects.
- Grounded theory, extended case method, institutional ethnography, and participatory action research are examples of different approaches to field research. They communicate variation in researchers' perspectives on what puzzles should be posed and how they should be solved.
- Preparing for the field involves doing background research, determining how to make contact with subjects, and resolving issues of what your relationship to your subjects will be.
- Whenever possible, field observations should be recorded as they're made; otherwise, they should be recorded as soon afterward as possible. Keeping a full and accurate record of what you see and hear in the field is vital.
- Responsible field research involves consideration of ethical issues that arise from the researcher's direct contact with subjects.
- Among the advantages of field research are its flexibility and the depth of understanding it can provide. Many field research studies can also be relatively inexpensive.
- Compared with surveys and experiments, field research measurements generally have more validity but less reliability. However, the governing criterion for assessing field research outcomes is authenticity.

REVIEW QUESTIONS AND EXERCISES

1. Imagine you've been asked to investigate allegations that local automobile dealerships treat men more seriously than women as potential buyers. Describe how you might go about studying this question through direct observation, using field research techniques.
2. Think of some group or activity you participate in or are very familiar with. In two or three paragraphs, describe how an outsider might effectively go about studying that group or activity. What should he or she read, what contacts should be made, and so on? List at least four ethical issues you can imagine this person confronting if the study was conducted.
3. Using the Web, find a research article using the grounded theory method. Summarize the study design and main findings. Do the same for a research article using either the extended case method or institutional ethnography.
4. To better appreciate the strengths and weaknesses of experiments, surveys, and field research, choose a research topic such as crime, worker satisfaction, sexual orientation, or prejudice, and write brief descriptions of studies that could be conducted on that topic using each of these methods. For each description, discuss why the method you chose is the most appropriate for the study you propose.

CONTINUITY PROJECT

REPLICATING SOCIAL CLASS THROUGH SOCIALIZATION

At the micro level, social class rests on the notion that important differences exist in categories of people. The attributes of persons that align them with one social class or another are acquired through socialization. The roots of social class exist in childhood.

Annette Lareau (2011) conducted a wonderful investigation contrasting the socialization styles of middle-class and working-class parents in the United States. Her work vividly illustrates how the social class characteristics of parents are transmitted to their children. Here is a summary of her method:

> Lareau's method is ethnographic. She has studied 12 families in depth, focusing each time on the fourth-grader in the family, a child of about 10 years of age (boy or girl, black or white, middle class or working class/poor). She and her team members (graduate students in social sciences under her supervision) spent a month closely following the daily life of their subjects, at home, in school and participating in activities outside home and school. A team member, Lareau or one of her trained assistants, would visit each child's family for several hours at a time, and once for an overnight, engaging the child and his or her parents in conversation, or silently observing the child interacting with his or her family. (Team members found that, when observing their subjects, their own presence soon went unnoticed.) Team members also talked with the children's teachers and accompanied the children to their extracurricular activities and medical appointments. The schools the children attended were located either in a city or a nearby suburb, reflecting the family's socio-economic circumstances.
>
> (Greene 2013)

Imagine you wanted to replicate Lareau's method to determine if it applies to social class differences in Canada. Outline how you would go about choosing a sample and gaining access to conduct the field research.

© iStockphoto.com/Paula Connelly

QUALITATIVE INTERVIEWING

This chapter discusses some of the guidelines for qualitative interviewing and focuses on three interview-based methods of research: in-depth interview studies, focus group interviews, and oral history.

IN THIS CHAPTER ...

INTRODUCTION

In Chapter 8, we discussed the techniques of survey interviewing. In this chapter, we'll examine a different type of interviewing—one that is less structured and gives the subject of the interview more freedom to direct the flow of conversation. Such interviews provide the researcher with the opportunity to explore topics, particularly unanticipated issues that may arise in the course of an interview. Unlike survey interviews, where standardized questions are asked of each respondent, *qualitative interviews* allow the researcher to pursue issues and topics in greater depth. Qualitative interviews stand alone as a method of gathering data; however, they are frequently used in conjunction with other research methods as well. They are a mainstay of field research used both by participant observers and by researchers who make no pretence of being a part of what is being studied.

Qualitative interview studies are sometimes combined with quantitative techniques like survey research to gain deeper insights into the topic under study.

Like many of the techniques we've already discussed, you'll see that (1) you already engage in qualitative interviews in your daily life, and (2) there are special techniques that move this activity from a casual form of interaction to a powerful scientific tool.

In this chapter, we will first review issues related to qualitative interviewing more generally and offer some guidelines for conducting such interviews. We then turn to three research methods centred on qualitative interviewing: in-depth interview studies, focus group interviews, and oral history. The term *in-depth interview studies* will be used to signify research designs in which qualitative one-on-one interviewing is the primary means of data gathering. The *focus group interview* method occurs when a number of people are brought together in a laboratory-type setting to be interviewed together, as a group. The *oral history* method of qualitative interviewing concerns in-depth interviews that focus on recollections of the past. Although all three qualitative methods rely on interviews, they are distinguished by the fact that in-depth ones are individualized and directed toward the present or recent past, focus groups are conducted with several others present, and oral histories are directed toward recollections of earlier times.

qualitative interview In contrast to a survey interview, a qualitative interview allows the researcher to pursue issues in depth and gives the respondent more freedom to direct the flow of conversation. The researcher typically has a general plan of inquiry but not a standardized set of questions that must be rigidly followed.

QUALITATIVE DEPTH INTERVIEWING: DEFINITIONS AND GUIDELINES

As Patton (1987:108) says:

> Depth interviewing involves asking open-ended questions, listening to and recording the answers, and then following up with additional relevant questions. On the surface this appears to require no more than knowing how to talk and listen. Beneath the surface, however, interviewing becomes an art and science requiring skill, sensitivity, concentration, interpersonal understanding, insight, mental acuity, and discipline.

As we've noted in Chapter 8 on survey research, interviewing has already been discussed. In qualitative interviewing, however, unlike surveys where questionnaires are rigidly structured, the interviews are less structured or are unstructured. Herbert and Irene Rubin (1995:43) make this distinction: "Qualitative interviewing design is flexible, iterative, and continuous, rather than prepared in advance and locked in stone." They further state:

> Design in qualitative interviewing is iterative. That means that each time you repeat the basic process of gathering information, analyzing it, winnowing it, and testing it, you come closer to a clear and convincing model of the phenomenon you are studying.... The continuous nature of qualitative interviewing means that the questioning is redesigned throughout the project.
>
> (Rubin and Rubin 1995:46–47)

A **qualitative interview** is an interaction between an interviewer and a respondent in which the interviewer has a general plan of inquiry but not a rigid set of questions that must be asked in particular words and in a particular order. It is essentially a conversation in which the interviewer establishes a general direction for the conversation and pursues specific topics raised by the respondent. The degree of direction supplied by the interviewer varies from a general set of questions or topics that the researcher wishes to cover in each interview to a very unstructured conversation guided by the interviewer, depending on the researcher and the topic under study. Ideally, the respondent does most of the talking.

The degree of direction provided by the interviewer distinguishes the two principal types of qualitative interviews. The first type, called **unstructured interviews**, has the least direction. Unstructured interviews are opposite to the fully scripted structures used in survey research. In unstructured interviews, the interview begins with a limited number of topics and fluidly probes these through questions and follow-ups guided by a sense of where useful insights might be found. Somewhat more guidance is found in semi-structured interviews. A **semi-structured interview** is organized around general questions and themes declared in advance. Although the inclusion and order of the questions and themes covered varies at the discretion of the interviewer, semi-structured interviews generally explore most of the same topics in roughly similar ways across cases.

Steinar Kvale (1996:3–5) offers two metaphors for interviewing: the interviewer is a "miner" or a "traveller." The first model assumes that the subject has specific information and that the interviewer's job is to dig it out. By contrast, in the second model, the interviewer

> wanders through the landscape and enters into conversations with the people encountered. The traveler explores the many domains of the country, as unknown territory or with maps, roaming freely around the territory.... The interviewer wanders along with the local inhabitants, asks questions that lead the subjects to tell their own stories of their lived world.

Asking questions and noting answers is a natural process, and it seems simple enough to add it to your bag of tricks as a field researcher. Be a little cautious, however. Wording questions is a tricky business. All too often, the way we ask questions subtly biases the answers we get. Sometimes we put our respondent under pressure to look good. Sometimes we ask a question in a particular context so that the most relevant answers are not provided.

Suppose you want to find out why a group of students is rioting and pillaging on campus. You might be tempted to focus your questions on how students feel about the dean's recent ruling that requires students to always carry *Fundamentals of Social Research* with them on campus. (Makes sense to us.) Although you may collect a great deal of information about students' attitudes toward the infamous ruling, they may be rioting for some other reason. Perhaps most are simply joining in for the excitement. It would be better, therefore, to ask them what prompted them to take part in the events that are occurring. Thus, properly done, qualitative interviewing would enable you to find out.

Although you may set out to conduct interviews with a pretty clear idea of what you want to ask, one of the special strengths of qualitative interviewing is its flexibility. The answers evoked by your initial questions should shape your subsequent ones. It doesn't work merely to ask pre-established questions and record the answers. Instead, you need to ask a question, listen carefully to the answer, interpret its meaning for your general inquiry, and frame another question either to dig into the earlier answer or to redirect the person's attention to an area more relevant to your inquiry. In short, you need to be able to listen, think, and talk almost at the same time.

The discussion of probes in Chapter 8 provides a useful guide to getting answers in more depth without biasing later answers. Learn the skills of being a good listener. Be more interested than interesting. Learn to say things like "How is that?"

unstructured interview An open-ended, qualitative interview.

semi-structured interview A qualitative interview organized around a specified set of questions or themes.

"In what ways?" "How do you mean that?" "What would be an example of that?" Learn to look and listen expectantly, and let the person you're interviewing fill in the silence.

At the same time, you can't afford to be a totally passive receiver in the interaction. You should go into your interviews with some general (or specific) questions you want answered and some topics you want addressed. At times you'll have to use the skills of subtly directing the flow of conversation.

We can learn something in this regard from the martial arts. The aikido master never resists an opponent's blow but instead accepts it, joins with it, and then subtly redirects it in a more appropriate direction. Qualitative interviewing requires a similar type of skill. It's best not to try to halt your respondent's line of discussion. Instead, learn to take what he or she has just said and branch that comment back in the direction appropriate to your purposes. Most people love to talk to anyone who's really interested. Stopping their line of conversation tells them you aren't interested; asking them to elaborate in a particular direction tells them you are. Consider the following hypothetical example in which you're interested in why university students chose their majors.

You: What are you majoring in?
Resp: Engineering.
You: I see. How did you come to choose engineering?
Resp: I have an uncle who was voted the best engineer in Alberta in 1981.
You: Gee, that's great.
Resp: Yeah. He was the engineer in charge of developing the new civic centre in Edmonton. It was written up in most of the engineering journals.
You: I see. Did you talk to him about your becoming an engineer?
Resp: Yeah. He said that he got into engineering by accident. He needed a job when he graduated from high school, so he went to work as a labourer on a construction job. He spent eight years working his way up from the bottom, until he decided to go to university and come back nearer the top.
You: So is your main interest civil engineering, like your uncle, or are you more interested in some other branch of engineering?
Resp: Actually, I'm leaning more toward electrical engineering, computers in particular. I started messing around with computers when I was in high school, and my long-term plan is....

Notice how the interview first begins to wander off into a story about the respondent's uncle. The first attempt to focus things back on the student's own choice of major failed—"Did you talk to your uncle ...?" The second attempt, the query about the student's "main interest," succeeded. Now the student is providing the kind of information you're looking for. It's important for you to develop the ability to "control" conversations in this fashion.

Herbert and Irene Rubin offer several ways to control a "guided conversation," such as the following:

> If you can limit the number of main topics, it is easier to maintain a conversational flow from one topic to another. Transitions should be smooth and logical. "We have been talking about mothers, now let's talk about fathers" sounds abrupt. A smoother transition might be "You mentioned your mother did not care how you performed in school—was your father more involved?" The more abrupt the transition, the more it sounds like the interviewer has an agenda that he or she wants to get through, rather than wanting to hear what the interviewee has to say.
>
> (Rubin and Rubin 1995:123)

Because qualitative interviewing is so much like normal conversation, you must keep reminding yourself that you are not having a normal conversation. In normal conversations, each of us wants to come across as an interesting, worthwhile person. If you watch yourself the next time you chat with someone you don't know too well, you'll probably find that much of your attention is spent on thinking up interesting things to say—contributions to the conversation that will make a good impression. Often we don't really hear each other, because we're too busy thinking of what we'll say next. As an interviewer, the desire to appear interesting is counterproductive. What is key is establishing **rapport** (see the How to Do It box "Establishing Rapport"). The interviewer needs to make the other person seem interesting by being interested. This can often be accomplished by listening more than talking. (Do this in ordinary conversations, and people will actually regard you as a great conversationalist.)

Lofland et al. (2006:69–70) suggest that investigators adopt the role of the "socially acceptable incompetent" when interviewing. That is, offer yourself as someone who does not understand the situation you find yourself in, someone who must be helped to grasp even the most basic and obvious aspects of that situation. As they (p. 69) state:

> A naturalistic investigator, almost by definition, is one who does not understand. She or he is "ignorant" and needs to be "taught." This role of watcher and asker of questions is the quintessential *student* role.

You may recall that we stressed the need to review your notes every night when conducting field research—making sense out of what you've observed, getting a clearer feel for the situation you're studying, and finding out what you should pay more attention to in further observations. In this same fashion, you need to review your notes on interviews, or listen to the interviews if you taped them, recording especially effective questions and detecting all those questions you should have asked but didn't. Start asking such questions the next time you interview. In addition, pay attention to the wording you used when asking questions, your responses to what was said, remarks that you let slip by without further probing, statements where you assumed meaning when you should have asked the person what he or she intended to convey by the remark, and times when you let the interview get away from you. Think about ways you might more effectively deal with such issues in your future interviews.

Steinar Kvale (1996:88) details seven stages in a complete interviewing process:

1. *Thematizing*: clarifying the purpose of the interviews and the concepts to be explored
2. *Designing*: laying out the process through which you'll accomplish your purpose, including a consideration of the ethical dimension
3. *Interviewing*: doing the actual interviews
4. *Transcribing*: creating a written text of the interviews
5. *Analyzing*: determining the meaning of gathered materials in relation to the purpose of the study

HOW TO DO IT

Establishing Rapport

A key to successful qualitative interviews is establishing rapport. Rapport can be defined as an open and trusting relationship. How do you establish that?

The first step is to explain the purpose of your research in a nonthreatening way. Communicate that you are there to learn and understand the interviewee. This works best, of course, if you actually have a genuine interest in understanding the people you are interviewing and can communicate that interest to them. This gives them a sense of self-worth, which increases their willingness to be open with you. You also need to be an attentive listener. When you speak it should be to advance your understanding of the interviewee's world and how it makes sense to them. You are not there to argue or to change minds. A little humility helps on this account. You'll be able to hear and understand people better if you don't start with an implicit feeling of superiority.

Be relaxed and act appropriately for the setting. Some people are more formal or informal than others, and you'll do well to take on their general style and be comfortable with it. If you can get them to relax and enjoy the interaction, you'll have achieved the rapport you need.

rapport An open and trusting relationship between researcher and respondent.

6. *Verifying*: checking the reliability and validity of the materials
7. *Reporting*: telling others what you've learned

Interviewing, like many things, improves with practice. Fortunately, it's something you can practise any time you want. Practise on your friends. The following section provides some guidelines.

PREPARING FOR AND CONDUCTING INTERVIEWS

Qualitative interviewing is an art supported by solid preparation and execution. Although personal experience is an invaluable teacher, the experience of others provides useful direction about the qualitative interview process. One key centres on the interview guide.

An **interview guide** is a manual that helps organize the interview process. Interview guides commonly include a list of themes and questions that the interviewer wants to pursue; they also often include probes and other useful tips to which an interviewer can refer. Again, since qualitative interviewing is unscripted, the interview guide is simply a reference that an interviewer can consult as needed.

The questions included in an interview guide can cover whatever the researcher thinks are appropriate. Kvale (1996) presents the following list as potential question types for consideration:

- Introducing questions: open an interview and ask for a respondent's account. Example: Can you tell me about your first encounters with ... ?
- Follow-up, probing, or specifying questions: designed to encourage elaboration on a response. Example: What did you mean when you said ... ?
- Direct questions: typically used near the end of interviews to address topics not yet covered. Example: Did you ever experience ... ?
- Indirect questions: used to get the respondent's views on what others think, feel, or act. Example: How do most of your colleagues react when ... ?
- Structuring questions: used to signal a change of topics. Example: Now I would like to turn our attention to ...
- Interpreting questions: used to confirm the interpretation of a response. Example: If I understand you correctly you are saying ...

Beyond questions, interview guides can also include other useful reminders, such as the use of silence. The strategic use of not saying anything immediately after hearing a response often encourages a fuller elaboration of the reply. In addition, an interview guide can encourage the interviewer to make notes at the conclusion of the interview about their assessments of the setting, how the interview went, and other observations that may help interpret the evidence.

Qualitative interviews are information-rich sources of evidence. Relying on an interviewer's note or memory will not adequately capture the density or depth of the evidence. Interviews need to be recorded. Fortunately, digital technologies have made such recording efficient and effective. Recoding opens up many opportunities. For example, recorded interviews can be transcribed into a written record. **Transcription** should occur as soon as possible after an interview, so that the interviewer still recalls the encounter if questions arise. Full transcription can be an expensive process, so it is common for only the research-relevant parts of the interview to be turned into text. This is called **selective transcription**.

Another option for transcribing recorded interviews is to use a transcription software package such as Express Scribe, Audio Notetaker, Inscribe, or F4/F5 (see Paulus et al. 2014), or voice recognition software (VRS) such as Dragon (Johnson 2011; Perrier and Kirkby 2013). VRS must be trained to the speaker's voice first; then the speaker can listen to a recorded interview with headphones while repeating the participants' words aloud. The VRS then transcribes the user's speech into a word processing document. Dragon does not automatically punctuate sentences, and so the speaker must instruct it

---

interview guide A manual for consultation that helps organize the interview process as needed.

transcription The translation of a recorded interview into written text.

selective transcription Turning only research-relevant parts of a recorded interview into text.

on when and where to add punctuation. VRS can greatly reduce the time and strain involved in transcribing interviews (Perrier and Kirkby 2013). Of course, the transcripts of interviews may accurately record the words, but they will not capture the paralinguistic information such as intonation, facial expression, and so on. This information is integral to understanding the contextual meaning of words, and so the researcher will still need to hear or view the actual interviews in concert with reading the transcribed text. If using VRS, the researcher may make notes while repeating the interviews aloud for the VRS (Perrier and Kirkby, 2013). Transcription software typically provides the ability to hear and/or view the original video or audio recording while reading the transcribed text (Paulus et al. 2014).

IN-DEPTH INTERVIEW STUDIES

When speaking of qualitative interviews, researchers variously refer to them as in-depth interviews, depth interviews, open-ended interviews, unstructured interviews, semi-structured interviews, and even structured "conversations," among other terms. We use the term **in-depth interview study** here to signify the method of using the qualitative interview as the primary means by which the researcher gathers data for his or her study. For example, Mirna Carranza (2007) conducted 32 qualitative in-depth interviews in her study of ways Salvadorian mothers and daughters who settled in Canada attempt to resist racism and prejudice.

In the feminist literature, methodology that allows the researcher to listen to women's voices is prominent. The many forms of qualitative interviewing provide methods that allow such voices to be heard. In a study concerning experiences of mature women students in the United Kingdom, Janet Parr conducted in-depth interviews with 49 mature women students about the barriers they faced when returning to education. Here's what she had to say about why she chose this methodology:

> I was looking more for explanations and processes rather than "numbers of women who...." I realized over the months that if my real interest was in explanations and perceptions, then it was greater depth rather than breadth which was required in the research data. One of the ways of achieving this depth in terms of explanations and perceptions was by listening to, and hearing, what the women themselves had to say. During this period, I was also reading more of the literature on feminist methodology, where the emphasis is on understanding the social and cultural context of events as well as the events themselves.
>
> (Parr 1998:89)

Parr then adopted a grounded theory approach to the analysis of her data (discussed in Chapter 13).

In illustrating interview studies that include some ethnographic component, Reinharz (1992:281) discusses Kaufman's study concerning "newly orthodox Jewish women." Kaufman described how she used "loosely structured interviews"—what she termed "structured conversations"—in order to learn from the women what issues they viewed as significant in their lives. She wanted to gain an understanding of their theology and their family and community relationships. She also spent weeks in each community interacting with its members and engaging in a variety of familial and social activities. She wanted to be able to put in context the experiences that the women she was interviewing were describing to her. Nonetheless, as she said, "[a]lthough this is neither an ethnographic nor participant observation study, I borrowed many of the techniques both kinds of researchers use." Thus, as Reinharz (1992:281) states, "[e]thnographic studies frequently include interviewing components, and interview studies frequently include ethnographic components."

In-depth interviews have been used to study a number of phenomena, including women's experiences and perceptions of menstrual suppression (Repta and Clarke 2013); lesbian, bi, and queer women's experiences of thinking about and trying to become a parent (Luce 2010); how Islamic business ethics affect Muslim women entrepreneurs (Tlaiss 2015); immigrant family

in-depth interview study A research design where qualitative, one-on-one interviewing is the primary means of data gathering.

caregivers' experiences in providing end-of-life care for loved ones (Weerasinghe and Maddalena 2016); and understanding the formation of consumer impressions of corporate social responsibility (Green and Peloza 2014).

While ethnographic or participant observation studies typically involve a small number of people, several times as many could be included in an in-depth interview study for the same or an even lesser investment of time. One trade-off of interview studies versus field observation is that interviews impose a somewhat artificial setting of questions and answers. Nonetheless, the semi-structured to unstructured form, and the length of time invested in each interview, often allows issues and perceptions to emerge that would not emerge in the more structured, briefer interviews used for surveys. The in-depth interview format, however, requires a great deal of cooperation from the subjects of study. Each interview is time consuming and often hard to obtain. Thus small, nonprobability samples are generally used, such as purposive or snowball samples. A potential drawback of this is that such studies may produce idiosyncratic findings. The standardization of questions, the use of probability samples, and the larger sample sizes used in survey interviews make generalizations much more feasible. The in-depth interview, however, provides researchers with the flexibility to pursue issues they may not have anticipated. The exciting potential of confronting serious challenges to your own assumptions when conducting an in-depth interview study must be weighed against the representativeness that large-scale surveys offer.

In-depth interviews are also frequently mixed with other data collection methods. For example, Hodgetts and colleagues (2013) used surveys and in-depth interviews to study parents and professionals' perceptions of family-centred care for children with autism spectrum disorder. Chadwick and Collin (2015) used secondary analysis of Canadian Community Health Survey data and in-depth interviews to study the relationship between social support availability, urban-centre size, and self-perceived mental health of recent immigrants to Canada.

There are also times when the rich data obtained from in-depth interviews are used to help in the design of survey questions. For example, Hecht and Martin (2006) were interested in the characteristics of backpackers who stay in Toronto-area hostels, their service needs, and their service preferences. Before developing a questionnaire that was given to 385 backpackers from 35 countries, they conducted in-depth interviews with 20 backpackers from seven countries. The questionnaire was based on the key requirements of backpackers identified from the interviews.

Let's turn to another qualitative interviewing technique, one in which a number of individuals are interviewed at the same time.

FOCUS GROUPS

Focus groups are often viewed as special forms of interviews because the researcher discusses an issue with a small group of people rather than a single individual. According to David Morgan (1997:2), "The hallmark of focus groups is their explicit use of group interaction to produce data and insights that would be less accessible without the interaction found in a group." The data that result are typically qualitative in nature. Focus groups are a good tool for exploratory research, and social scientists often use them to help them interpret results obtained from quantitative analysis.

This type of qualitative interviewing, which brings people together in one place for discussion and observation, is particularly popular in marketing research. Let's suppose that you've invented a new computer that not only does word processing, spreadsheets, data analysis, and the like, but also contains a fax machine, AM/FM/TV tuner, GPS, MP3, climate change calculator, mini vacuum, microwave oven, denture cleaner, and coffee-maker. To highlight its computing and coffee-making features, you're thinking of calling

focus group An interviewing method in which a number of subjects are brought together to discuss a specific topic or issue. A focus group is typically led by a moderator, who helps facilitate discussion and ensures that no person dominates the conversation, while interfering as little as possible in the discussion.

it "The Compulator." You figure the new computer will sell for about $28,000, and you want to know whether people are likely to buy it. Your prospects might be well served by focus groups.

In a focus group, typically six to ten people are brought together in a room to engage in a discussion, guided by a *moderator*, of some topic—in this case, the acceptability and saleability of the Compulator. The subjects are selected on the basis of relevance to the topic under study. Given the likely cost of the Compulator, your focus group participants would probably be limited to upper-income groups, for example. Other similar considerations might figure into the selection. Focus group participants are not likely to be chosen through rigorous, probability sampling methods. This means that participants do not statistically represent any meaningful population. However, the purpose of the study is to explore rather than to describe or explain in any definitive sense. Nonetheless, typically more than one focus group is convened in a given study, because there is a serious danger that a single group of six to ten people would be too atypical to offer any generalizable insights.

In a similar vein, focus groups are often used to gauge viewer response to movies (testing two different endings, for example), new television shows, and other forms of media entertainment (e.g., How might people respond to a talking dog as a show's host?). They are also used by the news media near election time to gain a sense of voters' preferences for political parties and candidates—especially the undecided voters—and to gather their views on the issues. Political actors and organizations use focus groups to test public response to issues, potential policy positions, and particular political figures (not unlike product marketing).

USING FOCUS GROUPS IN SOCIAL SCIENTIFIC RESEARCH

Focus group interviews have been a widely used method in market research for quite some time. It is more recently, however, that this method has gained wider usage in social scientific research. Sometimes called group interviewing, the technique gained in popularity in the 1980s.

To help illustrate, we will describe Harlton and colleagues' (1998) study using focus groups to determine perspectives on eldercare for the purposes of policymaking and practice. The idea of "partnership" in the care of the elderly has become prominent in Canadian health policy. It stems from the belief that informal care is better and less expensive than formal care. The researchers wanted to know if those involved in eldercare shared this view. They identified seven key stakeholders in eldercare: (1) older adults, (2) family members, (3) neighbours and friends, (4) volunteers, (5) direct service providers, (6) local and provincial policymakers, and (7) federal policymakers. The researchers sought to find out the stakeholders' views on what defines eldercare, the tasks and services that make it up, and who they thought should be responsible for supplying these services. The researchers were also concerned with the stakeholders' views on the criteria that should be used to determine who requires the services.

In order to gather such perspectives, they used the method of focus group interviews. They conducted a focus group with members of each of the seven stakeholder groups using purposive sampling to select participants. One of the bases for selection was experience with eldercare. They noted, "Although members of each group needed to be homogeneous in their structural relationship to eldercare, attempts were made to ensure sufficient variation among participants to allow for contrasting opinions" (1998:283). Yet due to time and funding constraints, and the desire to interview all stakeholder groups, they were only able to hold one focus group per stakeholder category, though they would have preferred to conduct multiple focus groups per category "to allow for saturation of responses."

Given their focus on stakeholder perspectives, the researchers believed the focus group method was particularly suited to this study because it facilitates the gathering of "in-depth, qualitative data about individuals' definitions of problems, opinions and feelings, and meanings associated with various phenomen[a]" (p. 283). The focus group interviews were recorded. Following each session, the researchers met with each other to discuss themes that emerged and other issues that arose from the focus group interviews. They taped these meetings as well.

Using techniques of analysis for developing grounded theory, the researchers were able to identify the main criteria for what constitutes eldercare. The idea of elder independence and choice concerning their care was stressed across groups. A wide range of tasks and services were identified as supporting such independence, yet there were key differences over what these services should entail, some of which stemmed from the group members' relationship to the care and to the elder recipient of care. As Harlton et al. (1998:287) state, "Perhaps the most important finding from this study on stakeholder perspectives is that those with most influence on public policy have a very different interpretation of the new policy paradigm than those whose lives will be most affected by eldercare policy."

In a more recent focus group study, Taylor, Johnston, and Whitehead (2016) put a critical spin on the use of focus groups for market research. The marketing strategy of using countercultural, ethical, or political activist messages and themes to sell products is known critically as "commodifying dissent" or "corporate cooptation" and has been well studied in recent years (e.g., Barkay 2013; Boltanski and Chiapello 2007; Cabrera and Williams 2014; Vogel 2005). Taylor et al. (2016:124) note that most critiques have focused "primarily on the production, rather than reception of such messages." Interested in how people think and feel when they perceive corporations are appropriating their politics for marketing purposes, Taylor et al. (2016) conducted a focus group study to examine how young feminist-identified women felt about the Dove Campaign for Real Beauty. The multimillion dollar Dove marketing campaign is an example of "feminist consumerism," in which corporations deploy feminist messages of empowerment to sell their products to women (Johnston and Taylor 2008).

By way of providing theoretical context for the study they point to Marcuse's (1964) critique of consumer capitalism. Marcuse holds that consumer capitalism promotes the conflation of opposites such as individuality/rebellion and consumer conformity, and in doing so makes it difficult to distinguish the two. For example, by equating individuality with consumer choice (i.e., you are the brands you buy) consumer capitalism deprives the former of its radical or transformative power. Similarly, a number of theorists have observed how corporate marketers have been able to largely disarm and defuse opposition to consumer capitalism by rechanneling protestors' critiques, ideals, and energies into consumer behaviour. Thus, buying a certain brand is made to feel like a political statement or an act of rebellion (e.g., Boltanski and Chiapello 2007; Frank 1997; McGuigan 2009).

Historically, the feminist movement began as political struggle for basic human rights for women such as the right to vote and property rights. It then expanded into seeking equal rights and representation for all women (i.e., intersectionality) in all areas (e.g., family, employment, business, politics, media). Some suggest that recent decades have witnessed the rise of more depoliticized forms of feminism (or "post-feminism") that emphasize notions of personal empowerment, choice, and individualism more than social movements and collective action (McRobbie 2009).

Taylor et al. (2016) sought to elicit participants' opinions on two basic research questions: (1) whether the Dove campaign is compatible with feminism, and (2) whether corporations are potential vehicles for achieving feminist goals.

There were 40 participants in the study comprising six focus groups (four with women in their twenties; two with teens). They recruited participants younger than 30, assuming that individuals from this demographic "grew up in a post-consciousness raising [or post-feminist] era," and hence were less likely "to focus on social questions and issues in a group setting as older cohorts might have" (p. 129). Their focus group questions centred around participants' perceptions about the use of feminist ideals to sell Dove products. First, for the purposes of refreshing their memory, participants watched a ten-minute slide show of the Dove Campaign for Real Beauty advertisements. Although groups were given a focus group guide, they were free to pursue their own stream of conversation. Discussions were tape-recorded and transcribed by the moderator, and transcripts were coded by two of the authors.

The gist of their findings was that, on the first question of the Dove campaign's compatibility with feminism, "participants agreed the Dove Campaign for Real Beauty was not feminist because it preached conformity rather than transgression, and encouraged women to focus on their self-esteem to the neglect of the world around them" (p. 140). On the second question of the suitability of corporations as vehicles for feminist goals, they found that the majority of participants did not think that corporations could or should "do the work" of feminism, because feminism "is intrinsically anti-capitalist, and ... political expression through consumption is not a legitimate strategy for progressive movements" (p. 140).

The authors also argue that contrary to some criticisms of post-feminist individualism, their results "demonstrate how young women were skilled at unpacking power relations, using everyday observations to elaborate their critiques and [identify] the contradictions and trespasses that oppose their visions for the future" (p. 139). Finally, they also suggest that their study underscores the potential of focus groups to help increase our understanding of how individuals engage with corporate social change initiatives and social movement messages in general.

Another example of the use of focus groups is Walsh and colleagues' (2007) research. They interviewed groups of older adults and groups of formal and informal caregivers of such adults in their study of elder abuse in Ontario and Alberta. The study examined "the interconnections among various forms of violence across the lifespan" (p. 491). Other Canadian researchers have used focus groups to study a number of different topics, including the potential link between social casino gaming and online gambling (Kim et al. 2016), the impact of technology on young gay males' dating and sexual relationships (McKie et al. 2015), environmental influences on African migration to Canada (Veronis and McLeman 2014), and HIV stigma in the healthcare system (Wagner et al. 2016).

However, like many modes of gathering data, focus groups are often used in combination with other types of data collection. For example, Aminzadeh and colleagues (2007) used in-depth interviews, focus groups, and tapes of diagnosis disclosure meetings when studying the emotional impact on patients who were recently told about their diagnosis of dementia. More recently, Lee et al. (2017) used focus groups and secondary data analysis with data from the 2008 Canadian Incidence Study of Reported Child Abuse and Neglect to study the experiences of Asian-Canadian (compared to white-Canadian) children and families involved in the child welfare system in Canada.

Focus groups are also a valuable way of testing questions to be used in surveys. For example, the Public Service Employee Survey is conducted every three years by Statistics Canada to get feedback from federal public employees on various aspects of their employment. Statistics Canada uses focus groups to help design and update questions in between surveys. For example,

> The 2017 questionnaire contains 119 questions: 18 new questions, 7 modified questions, and 94 questions repeated from the 2014 survey. To test the content of the 2017 questionnaire, focus group sessions were held in the National Capital Region, Winnipeg and Montréal. Participants were from various departments and agencies, and various occupational groups and levels.
>
> *(Statistics Canada 2018)*

TOPICS APPROPRIATE TO FOCUS GROUP INTERVIEWS

As we've seen from the examples just given, there are several reasons why a researcher may choose focus groups over individual interviews. With multiple people presenting their views, what others have to say often stimulates qualifications and modifications of viewpoints—points that may not be readily elicited in a one-on-one interview. In many situations, the interviewees are likely to talk more candidly to each other. When groups are created on the basis of similar characteristics (such as age, education, occupation) or shared experiences (such as physical attacks by family members or strangers, illness or disease, loss of employment), the discussants may have more access to what each other is thinking and thus spark a more realistic presentation of views.

SPOTLIGHT ON MIXED METHODS RESEARCH

Mixed Methods Online: Combining Quantitative Data with Participant Observation and In-Depth Interviews

Putnam (2000) argued that social capital had been diminishing across the closing decades of the 20th century, as people were increasingly drawn away from engagement in vibrant community life into their own isolated worlds of media consumption. Williams et al. (2006) wondered if this trend was affected by the advent of new interactive and more socially engaging online media spaces like massively multiplayer online (MMO) games. They suggested such effects could occur via increased *bridging social capital*, "the loose connections between relative strangers that lead to diverse networks and information streams" or via increased *bonding social capital*, "which is traditional social, emotional, and substantive support" (p. 339).

To investigate this possibility, they decided to study the social dynamics of players within the MMO game World of Warcraft (WoW). More specifically, they focused "on player behavior, attitudes, and opinions, [to] explore the meanings they make, the social capital they derive, and the networks they form" (p. 339). Their study combined in-depth ethnographic methods with survey-based quantitative data collection, and unfolded in three stages:

1. *Participant observation*: To learn and understand the social context of play, research team members immersed themselves in WoW, playing the game and joining guilds. (Time spent playing by team members ranged between 15 and 1,351 hours over 16 months.)
2. *Quantitative data collection*: They used bot or automated characters that log into the system to collect data on player behaviour around the clock; this allowed them to have an ongoing census of how many players there where, when they were online, and what guilds they belonged to. It also allowed them to map and analyze social networks.
3. *In-depth interviews*: These were conducted with players randomly selected from the sampling frame (generated in stage 2). The interviews were conducted within WoW using direct text chat and guided by 13 base questions, but Williams and colleagues also allowed for spontaneous or off-script exchanges.

Their findings indicate that many players used the game to maintain and reinforce offline relationships, while others used it to meet new people and form new relationships. For most it was a form of affiliation akin to playing on a sports team or hanging out in traditional "third places" (e.g., coffee shops, pubs, clubs, churches) that Putnam holds as integral to vibrant civic life. Thus the authors conclude, although far from a panacea, such socially interactive online third places may be a space "... where such revitalization is possible for some players and in a new way" (p. 357).

In the group interview setting, subjects may challenge each other's statements. This added element may provide a different vantage point on people's perspective. On a practical level, focus groups may be appropriate when there are a large number of people to interview but only a short period of time to do so.

The focus group setting also allows the researcher to examine how people make sense of issues in a collective manner. The process of expressing views in the context of others, potentially meeting challenges, and having ideas or positions sparked or elicited by what others around them say makes the focus group context somewhat more reflective of how opinions and perspectives are articulated and moulded in day-to-day life. Additionally, focus groups are a useful technique when the topic of study concerns psychological issues or deeply embedded attitudes—topics not readily accessed with mere observation. Thus the dynamism of the group forum often brings to light issues that an individual interviewer or participant observer may be unable to access.

CONDUCTING FOCUS GROUPS

There are a number of practical considerations to keep in mind when conducting focus group interviews. As we noted, the group size varies but is typically less than a dozen people. The number of people in a group depends on the topic under study and the success of recruiting people who will show up at the scheduled time. If the topic is complex and requires coverage of a large number of issues, a smaller group is advised. A smaller group is also advisable when an issue is emotionally charged or controversial and thus likely to evoke much discussion.

The number of focus groups varies considerably from one study to another. The best guide is a theoretical one; that is, continue conducting focus groups until the number of new issues arising has diminished to a point where little new information is gathered. In essence, when the moderator is able to anticipate with some degree of accuracy the issues and viewpoints that those in the next group will express—*saturation of responses*—then it is likely that a sufficient number of groups have been conducted. Of course, issues of time and expense play a role in the number of groups conducted, as do the topic of study and the number of factors of concern to the researchers. As a rule of thumb, a range of 10 to 15 groups is rather common in focus group studies. However, if you expect a wide variety of perspectives on a topic, then a larger number of groups would be necessary. For example, if you anticipate that views on your study topic are likely to vary with age, ethnicity, gender, occupation, and other socio-demographic factors, you would likely stratify your groups by such variables. (Recall our discussion of stratified samples in Chapter 6.) When examining a large number of factors, a larger number of focus groups would be needed. Decisions about relevant variables and number of groups also affect decisions about who is selected to participate in the groups. Selection of participants depends on the issue under study and characteristics the researcher anticipates may contribute to variation in views on the topic. Researchers typically select participants for whom the topic is relevant.

A focus group is often led by a trained moderator who helps to facilitate the discussion. The degree of guidance provided by the moderator varies. Some discussions are relatively unguided, while others may have a set of open-ended questions or issues that the researcher desires to have covered over the course of the session. Typically, the goal is to ensure that everyone has an opportunity to speak. The role of the moderator in many focus groups is both to keep the discussion on track and to ensure that no one person dominates the conversation, while interfering as little as possible.

If there is a specified set of questions that the researchers desire to have answered, then the moderator will play a larger role, making sure that each line of questioning is covered in the session. Keep in mind, however, that too much interference may stifle a line of conversation that could prove worthwhile. Allowing the participants some freedom to pursue topics may reveal issues of importance. The setting of the focus group interview is typically one of informality. The participants usually address remarks to each other. As we've noted, in this context, issues and arguments often arise that the researcher in a one-on-one interview would not have thought to address. Practice in guiding group discussions helps in this regard.

If you plan to moderate a focus group yourself, preparation of a guide is advised. You need to introduce the group to the topic and goals of the study. You also need to tell the subjects the basic guidelines for discussion: what to expect in the focus group session and the procedures you will follow. Your introductory remarks should provide you with the opportunity to develop a rapport with the subjects. Allowing the subjects to get to know each other a bit is also useful at the start of the session. For example, you might have them introduce themselves and give a brief statement about their occupation and interests. If a list of questions is to be used to prompt a series of discussions covering certain topics, these should be written down so you can follow them. As in individual interviews, preparing a set of probes in advance may be useful should probes be necessary to keep the conversation moving.

If possible, as in individual interviews, digital audio and/or video recording of the focus group interview is best. When there are several people talking over a period of one to two hours, it's very difficult to recall who said what and in which order. People often talk quickly, interrupt each other, and talk over each other. Who speaks more and whose statements may have the greatest impact on others is something the researcher may want to address. Also, attending to how people express themselves may be as important as the exact words they use. Often the goal of focus group interviews is to examine the dynamic process of people collectively constructing meaning. Digital audio/visual recording of the sessions makes this task much more feasible. However, as one researcher noted when talking about her first experiences with audio recording of focus group interviews, the method is not foolproof. Distinguishing voices can be difficult, especially if someone who was not present in the focus group transcribes the tape. After reviewing the transcript of their initial focus group, the researcher and her colleague realized that it would be necessary to take notes in each focus group session as well as recording it. In their subsequent groups, they noted each person as he or she spoke and the first few words that were said so the transcripts could be corrected for accuracy.

ADVANTAGES AND DISADVANTAGES OF FOCUS GROUPS

Like all methods, focus groups have advantages and disadvantages; they are more appropriate for exploring some kinds of issues than others. The principal advantages of focus groups include the following. First, they are cost-effective. A researcher can gather data from several subjects simultaneously. Moreover, a focus group study can be conducted in fairly short order. Second, they have strong face validity. Hearing real people respond to open-ended questions with their honest opinions has intuitive appeal. Third, focus group methodology is adaptable. The moderator can shape the discussion along fruitful lines of inquiry as participants bring up interesting and important points.

In addition to these advantages, group dynamics that occur in focus groups frequently bring out aspects of the topic that would not have been anticipated by the researcher and would not have emerged from interviews with individuals. In a side conversation, for example, a couple of the participants might start joking about the risk of leaving out one letter from a product's name. This realization might save the manufacturer from great embarrassment later on. The same type of conversation might lead to insights into question wording, policy issues, attitudes, opinions, social problem solutions, or any number of issues of interest to researchers.

While providing many advantages, focus groups contain real drawbacks. The first of these is the moderator effect. The moderator is the leader of the focus group and through shaping of questions, probing, feedback, and development of social connections can have a large influence on what gets expressed. Second, participant selection processes make generalization challenging. In focus groups there are real issues in determining whether the ideas and sentiments expressed are specific to the assembled group or are more characteristic of broadly shared views. Hence, reliability is of concern. A third problem for focus groups concerns groupthink. *Groupthink* refers to a dynamic in which a desire for consensus can lead to overconformity. Within a group, as public consensus emerges it becomes increasingly difficult for those with alternative views to express their opinions.

Despite these challenges, focus group research is a qualitative in-depth interviewing method that allows the researcher to set in motion a free flow of conversation in response to a given question or topic, where issues can emerge and evolve through the dynamics of group interaction. The flexibility of the format also allows the researcher to seek guided responses when such are desired. The focus group interview not only gives researchers the chance to hear people's attitudes, opinions, insights, and so forth; but it also provides them with the opportunity to observe the interactions among the group participants to see how such ideas and issues emerge and unfold. In addition, focus groups are an excellent device for generating questionnaire items for a subsequent survey.

ONLINE INTERVIEWS AND FOCUS GROUPS

Online interviews and online focus groups are becoming increasingly common in social science research. Key dimensions to consider for online interviews and focus groups are whether they are conducted synchronously (people communicating in real time via chat or conference) or asynchronously (people communicating with some time delay, such as via email or online forum), and whether they are text based or audio/video based.

O'Connor and Madge (2017) outline the various pros and cons of online interviews. Some of the advantages of asynchronous online interviews include (1) email interviews may allow efficient access to geographically diverse participants and increase the ability of those with disabilities (e.g., verbal communication impairments) to participate, (2) flexible time limits allow the interviewee to respond at their convenience (may respond immediately or after some time to reflect and compose or redraft their response), and (3) the time-consuming task of transcription is reduced and/or eliminated. The flipside is that these advantages can also pose some problems, such as (1) physical impairments may limit some people's ability to communicate textually via computer, (2) emails are relatively easy to ignore or delete, (3) the ability to edit and redraft responses may inhibit spontaneity and hence the richness of collected data, (4) paralinguistic data (e.g., verbal intonation, facial expression, body language) is lost, and (5) the interviewer cannot ask knowledge questions as the interviewee could look up information before responding.

O'Connor and Madge (2017) note that until recently, most synchronous online interviews were conducted in text via chatroom-like interfaces. Such real-time online interviews limit the ability of respondents to edit and redraft and hence tend to generate more spontaneous answers. In addition to inducing greater spontaneity, real-time online interviews that use webcams and audio/visual applications such as Skype can also allow the interviewer to interact in a more natural conversational manner, and to observe para-linguistic data (although this can be diminished if the visual is limited to a head shot). Other potential drawbacks include that (1) the technical requirements are higher for using webcams and applications such as Skype or teleconferencing software, (2) time delays and reduced image and sound quality may arise if Internet connections are poor or interrupted, (3) building rapport with reserved interviewees may be more difficult than in face-to-face offline interviews, and (4) participants may feel it easier to drop out, since they feel less commitment when at great remove from the interviewer (Deakin and Wakefield 2014).

The proliferation of social networking sites and free instant messaging apps (e.g., WhatsApp, Facebook messenger, Gmail Chat) and webcam-enabled communication apps such as Skype and Facetime, has made it increasingly easy to recruit and interview participants. A number of commercial interviewing software packages are also now available for download onto a smartphone or tablet. O'Connor and Madge (2017) observe that although online interview techniques are entering the mainstream, they are not appropriate for all situations. They conclude that "the production of ever more sophisticated Internet technologies and the rapidity of change in this sector ... will present challenges to the online researcher, demanding that they become ever more contingent, flexible and innovative in adapting these technologies to produce high quality, nuanced online research methodologies."

Various forms of online interviewing have been used to study a range of topics, including internet addiction (Chou 2001), problem gambling (Heiskanen and Egerer 2019), posting self-injury content online (Seko et al. 2015), the dynamics of young men's friendships (Magrath and Scoats 2019), mommy bloggers' representations of motherhood (Orton-Johnson 2017), and the experiences of young adults with cerebral palsy (Ison 2009).

In their overview of online focus groups, Abrams and Gaiser (2017) note several general benefits, such as online groups being less expensive and providing easier (and faster) access to a broader range of participants than traditional face-to-face focus groups. With regard to text-based online focus group facilitation (communication via chat applications, email, or bulletin board/forums) they highlight several specific advantages:

- No transcription is required, since respondents type their own text.
- The likelihood of a participant dominating discussion is reduced. That is, the "silencing" of others by dominant members is less likely, since traditional turn-taking is not necessary and participants may be typing responses at the same time.
- Participants can remain anonymous to the group (which may promote discussion of sensitive topics and reduce social desirability effects).
- Online focus groups can accommodate multiple languages due to the availability of auto-text translators.
- There is a low technological threshold (i.e., lower bandwidth demands, just typing, no specialized applications or Web-browser plug-ins required).

However, there are several caveats to these advantages. For example, although not having to transcribe data is appealing, there are a host of attendant issues related to deciding what data to include and what to edit. Also, off-topic side conversations can happen among participants, and misspellings, grammatical errors, and abbreviations are common, all of which require the moderator to clarify resulting ambiguities. As well, interpretation of meaning can be complicated by intentional misspellings intended to convey tone or nonverbal information, as well as the use of emoticons, emojis, and hashtags. At the same time as anonymity has benefits it also opens up the possibility that some may misrepresent themselves (adopt a false identity), and it is difficult to verify they are truly part of the population of interest.

Another commonly cited shortcoming of text-only focus groups—the lack of verbal and visual interaction—is the main appeal of video-based focus groups. These involve the use of webcams and online video conferencing applications to conduct real-time (synchronous) focus group discussions. In addition to enhancing communication among group participants and between group participants and the moderator, this approach allows access to other nonverbal and paralinguistic information, such as tone of voice, facial expression, and gestures. These could be important for more fully interpreting the meaning of people's communication.

There are a number of possible platforms for conducting online focus groups, including online meeting applications (Skype, Google Hangouts), multi-user virtual environments (Second Life, Meshmoon), online forum tools (ProBorads, Lefora), and specialized focus group software (iTracks, QualBoard). Online focus groups have been used in a number of areas, including advertising (Kelly et al. 2010), healthcare (Stancanelli 2010), and higher education (Galloway 2011). Generally, online focus groups seem to perform similarly to traditional face-to-face focus groups in terms of eliciting information from participants (Stewart and Shamdasani 2017). Given the continued advancements in online group communication applications and virtual reality platforms, online focus groups seem likely to become increasingly common.

ORAL HISTORY

Oral history is a form of historical research that uses in-depth interviewing to gather data. Instead of looking in the archives, the researcher delves into the minds and memories of individuals—learning about their lives, culture, and community. Like in-depth interviewing, it seeks to

oral history A method that uses in-depth interviews as a means of gathering data about the past from individuals' recollections, typically focusing on specific events or periods of time.

gather detailed information on a given topic or about a given individual; however, the focus is historical—it concerns the past.

Peter S. Li (1985:68) summarizes the technique as follows[1]:

> The basic approach of oral history as a research method is straightforward. A researcher speaks to respondents who previously have been exposed to a set of experiences, and asks them to describe the experiences and their feelings about those experiences as they recall them. The information being sought may pertain to an event, a place, a tradition, or a biography. For example, the history of a community, memories of a war, and life stories of individuals are among the many suitable projects of oral history. The objective is to record the recollections of the respondents, which later can be transcribed to written documents. Frequently, the respondents are ordinary people whose verbal accounts represent a folk version of events, as opposed to an official version contained in institutional records.

In the third edition of his book *The Voice of the Past: Oral History*, Paul Thompson (2000:xi) quotes the *New Shorter Oxford English Dictionary* definition of oral history as "tape-recorded historical information drawn from the speaker's personal knowledge; the use or interpretation of this as an academic subject." Thompson notes that historians have used oral history as a primary data-gathering technique for decades. Anthropologists have used oral history in this way as well. Nonetheless, the use of oral history has gained momentum recently in the social sciences. One reason is the growing interest in incorporating the voice of the people into our understanding of past events, particularly the voices of underprivileged members of society.

Oral histories can provide a counter to writings derived from official documents and other works written from the perspective of white, male, dominant members of society. Thompson (2000:vi) believes that

> the richest possibilities for oral history lie within the development of a more socially conscious and democratic history. Of course, a telling case could equally be made, from a conservative position, for the use of oral history in preserving the full richness and value of tradition. The merit of oral history is not that it entails this or that political stance, but that it leads historians to an awareness that their activity is inevitably pursued within a social context and with political implications.

This method has, therefore, become prominent among feminist researchers as a means of allowing women's voices to be heard. It is also advocated as a valuable technique for those studying minority racial and ethnic groups, and it is an advantageous technique in the study of nonliterate populations. For example, anthropologists have long used this method to document societies with limited to no written histories. None of this, of course, precludes the use of oral history in the study of the privileged elite.

Researchers who use the oral history method have used a variety of labels to refer to this technique for gathering data. This creates the potential for confusion. Reinharz found that among feminist researchers "oral history" was used interchangeably with terms such as "case studies, in-depth life history interviews, biographical interviews, life histories, and personal narratives" (1992:129).

While some researchers are trying to convey slight differences with the use of these varied terms, there are clearly overlap and commonalities among these methods. For example, life histories focus on the memories and experiences of a particular—typically elderly—individual's life. Other materials supplement the retrospective information gathered orally. Oral histories may also focus on the lives of individual people, but the method signifies the potential for gathering information that goes beyond their particular life stories.

In oral histories, researchers use in-depth interviews to ask people about past events and to generate information about an individual's personal life, the life of someone else, or any number of topics. In addition to gathering biographical information about a person, social patterns can

1 Peter S. Li, 1985. "The Use of Oral History in Studying Elderly Chinese-Canadians," *Canadian Ethnic Studies*, 17(1), p. 67. Reprinted by permission of Canadian Ethnic Studies.

be abstracted from the stories gathered from a sample of people. Subjects are usually asked to focus on specific events or periods of time such as what it was like living through World War II (WWII) or being a minority female in the 1960s. For example, Li (1985) mentions a study by Marlatt in 1975 of a Japanese-Canadian fishing town. Marlatt used oral histories to describe the process and impact of urban development from the perspective of this racial minority group living near Vancouver.

THE USE OF ORAL HISTORY: SOME ILLUSTRATIONS AND METHODOLOGICAL CONSIDERATIONS

Studs Terkel's account of life during the Great Depression of the 1930s (*Hard Times*, 1970) is a classic illustration of the use of oral history. He interviewed countless people to gain their view of what life entailed during that period. He wrote about the past from the perspective of the people who lived it.

More recently, Li collected detailed life histories of 55 elderly Chinese in Saskatchewan. Writing in 1985, he lamented that "social scientists in general have not paid sufficient attention to oral history as a research method" (p. 67). The goal of his paper was to illustrate the value and use of this method. He detailed how he applied the oral history method to the study of Chinese Canadians and addressed issues of the validity, reliability, and interpretation of the data he collected.

Among the advantages of the oral history method in studying social history, Li noted its potential for helping to fill in the gaps in the knowledge we have gained from official documents and statistical overviews. For instance, the census indicates a major increase in occupations related to the restaurant business among Chinese Canadians from the late 19th century to the 1930s, but these numbers tell us little about why this increase occurred or its effects. Obtaining oral histories, Li was able to gain insights into racism's impact on Chinese Canadians' economic opportunities and how they coped with and understood the racial conflict they experienced.

Li (1985:69) directly addressed "two major methodological issues" of concern when using the oral history method. Are the respondents' stories "reliable or truthful"? Is developing a "valid framework for organizing the case histories" possible? If so, how might the researcher assess the framework's validity? Noting that it's hard to assess the reliability and validity of oral history, he offers several ways to consider these issues. For instance, because selective memory concerning past events and experiences is inevitable on the part of the informant, he suggested the researcher "engage the inevitable." Narrowing the focus of the interview to certain aspects of the informant's past can be helpful in this regard. In his study, for example, they focused on job histories. Helping people with their recollections can also be accomplished by a series of probes and specific questions on a particular topic.

Another issue he addressed is that of subjectivity. The respondent's subjectivity "does not necessarily reduce the reliability of their stories, but rather, it is a part of oral history that enriches it" (1985:71). In examining reliability in the context of oral history, the concept of truth concerns the relationship between the story and what happened in reality. To determine what happened, one often uses other information sources like official reports, records, and news stories. But there are problems with "accuracy" of information in such sources as well. To illustrate this, Li pointed to a number of subjective distortions contained in official reports on Chinese immigration.

How, then, do researchers make sense of inconsistencies between the subjects' stories and official reports? Looking more closely at interpretation in oral history, Li noted that there are a variety of ways to interpret a story's reliability or unreliability by taking into account the different levels of reality when interpreting the data—in short, he was referring to the aspect of the information researchers focus on and the interpretations or conclusions they draw from that information.

When researchers suspect incorrect recall of facts due to inconsistencies between what the informants tell them and information reported in official documents, this might spark a deeper investigation. In the case of the Chinese-Canadian study, upon further investigation the researchers determined that the official records were incorrect, not the informants. The official documents left out cases that were not part of the bureaucratic rules. For example, when those interviewed claimed entrance into Canada between 1923 and 1947, this contradicted the *Chinese Immigration Act* of 1923, which essentially prohibited Chinese immigrants during this period (except for certain classes of Chinese immigrant such as students, diplomats, merchants, and native-born Chinese Canadians returning from schooling in China). One informant, for instance, who reported immigrating in 1936, told how "his father, who was in Canada at the time, bought him a birth certificate with which he could claim to be native-born in Canada" (1985:72). Such stories led them to research practices of illegal immigration and other means by which some Chinese people came to Canada to stay during a period in which the official documents indicated they could not.

Another issue Li raised that speaks to issues of reliability and validity in the use of the oral history method concerns the relationship between what informants believe to be true and what is true in reality. There are times when the distinction is not relevant to the interpretation of the data. For example, a number of the informants were asked to compare the situation of Chinese Canadians pre- and post-WWII. A large number of them felt that things had greatly improved and discrimination had decreased considerably after the war. In this case, whether or not discrimination had decreased considerably is not the point. What's important is their belief. As Li stated (1985:73), "As long as the participants believed that there was no discrimination, their behavior would reflect this belief." Li (1985:73) further stated[2]:

> From the point of view of a researcher, the key question is not so much to find out whether the respondent is stating the facts as they took place, but rather, to sort out the different levels of perception and interpretation which are present in oral history. From the point of view of an interviewer, the task is to assist the respondent to reconstruct the past in the way the respondent sees it.

The issues of reliability and validity in oral history are not always straightforward. Some concerns regarding the information gathered using this method are relevant only in relation to the questions and issues being addressed and the interpretation being offered.

The oral history method is often combined with other modes of gathering data. Kwok Chan studied aging and self-identity among elderly Chinese women in Canada by administering a closed-ended survey and conducting intensive, unstructured interviews with 26 elderly women. The goal of the interviews was "to collect their personal oral histories, with a focus on their histories of work, relationships with spouse, children, grandchildren, and sons- and daughters-in-law, and feelings about living in Chinatown" (1983:38). He also conducted unstructured interviews with community workers from social agencies in Chinatown. In this way, Chan was able to gather a variety of data to probe the social world of elderly Chinese women, gathering evidence that helped to debunk positive and negative myths concerning elderly ethnic minorities in general and elderly Chinese in particular. The oral history component of his study, which focused "on the women's own definition of the situation," enabled him to gain insights into how these women managed their identities and their efforts at maintaining a feeling of self-worth.

Turner and colleagues (1997) used oral histories in conjunction with secondary materials in their study concerning the process of "gendered class struggle." They examined this process by focusing on two groups of landless women in Kenya between 1985 and 1996 who struggled to gain control over their labour in agricultural production. Use of the oral history method helped the researchers gain insights into these women's strategies in the context of the situation they faced. Paying particular attention to relationships, the researchers' goals were "to examine the

2 Peter S. Li, 1985. "The Use of Oral History in Studying Elderly Chinese-Canadians," *Canadian Ethnic Studies*, 17(1), p. 67. Reprinted by permission of Canadian Ethnic Studies.

historical roots of the changing relationships represented in the conflict in question" and to gain insights into "the self-expression of participants with respect to their experiences, conceptions and demands" (pp. 214–215). Oral histories were central to their study because they approached their research from the perspective of "standpoint theories which 'show how to move from including others' lives and thoughts in research and scholarly projects to starting from their lives to ask research questions' (Harding, 1991)" (Turner et al. 1997:215).

The researchers were able to describe how the exploited women farmers fought against agriculture for export. They told how the women gained control over their own labour power by resisting the exploitation and control of their often violent husbands, by going against state policies, and by resisting the demands of private firms (capital) to incorporate them into global markets. The women's struggles have helped to expand sustenance agriculture, which is a more sound and sustainable strategy for them.

The story of the internment of Japanese Canadians during WWII is brought to the fore by Pamela Sugiman (2009), whose study uses oral history interviews of second-generation Japanese Canadians regarding their wartime experiences. At the time of her writing, Sugiman interviewed 75 women and men in her oral history project aimed at shedding light on the historical memories of displaced Japanese Canadians in British Columbia during WWII. Those of Japanese ancestry experienced great discrimination, loss, and unfairness during this period in Canada. She describes her unexpected finding that those narrating their histories reported many positive experiences along with the negative ones. For example, along with their stories of forced relocation, loss of property, loss of privacy, restricted movement, and separation of families came stories of kindnesses that they experienced and for some a perceived belief that their internment likely benefited the third and later generations. Her account of these narratives communicates the message that while they experienced great hardships, many also saw "life as sweet." She provides an interpretation of this duality by looking at both the vulnerabilities that these individuals faced and their need for dignity and self-respect, as well as a need to move on. Her article "points to ways in which the researcher and narrator work toward a 'shared authority' in the presentation and interpretation of these complex memories."

In a more recent example of oral history research, Woolford (2015) analyzed historical documents and oral historical testimony to examine how Indigenous boarding schools were implemented as part of the solution to the "Indian Problem" in Canada and the United States at the end of the 19th century. Indigenous boarding schools were intended to resocialize Indigenous children into European cultural values, attitudes, and identities for the purposes of assimilation, with the ultimate goal being the elimination of "Indigenous communities as obstacles to land acquisition, resource extraction, and nation building."

Woolford looked at four schools—two in Manitoba and two in New Mexico. Describing the mixing of archival and oral history methods in his research, he notes (p. 13):

> Archival documents were useful for capturing policy-based ideas about and institutional applications of the Indian Problem, but they were generally less useful for obtaining glimpses of everyday life within the schools, though some hints about such life could be gleaned from inspector reports, superintendent and principal letters, letters from parents and students, diaries, and other such sources. Still, much of this information is overly formal and did not reveal much more than what those who controlled the schools wanted to show. For this reason, oral histories were important to my study.

Woolford reviewed over 500 oral histories with Indigenous persons in the American southwest as well as numerous oral histories from Indigenous Canadians—sourced primarily from personal statements gathered as part of the Truth and Reconciliation Commission (TRC). Incorporating oral histories into the analyses allowed

Indigenous people's voices to serve as a counter to the dominant official narratives of the schools represented in the (often sanitized) archives. In the process, this drew attention to the destructive character of the schools as assimilative settler colonial institutions.

Another recent oral history project examined the life stories of Canadians displaced by mass violence (High et al. 2014). The oral histories in this collection capture both the individuality and the underlying commonalities that weave through the various stories of survivors whose experiences range across time and place and from political repression to discrimination, dispossession, rape, torture, and mass murder.

AVAILABLE ONLINE DATA

Greater accessibility of oral history sources has contributed to the wider use of this method in recent years. The oral history technique can be expensive and time consuming when the researcher seeks to investigate issues that require interviews with people who live in diverse and faraway places. A number of oral history archives have been available in countries all over the world for quite some time, yet gaining access to the archived data can be costly due to the expense of travelling to another place to make use of the sources. The Internet, however, has now placed a wide range of oral history archives at the researcher's fingertips. The following are examples of some well-designed websites that contain transcribed interviews, audio files, or both.

- Voice/Vision Holocaust Survivor Oral History Archive: http://holocaust.umd.umich.edu/
- Rutgers Oral History Archives of World War II, Korea, Vietnam and Cold War: https://oralhistory.rutgers.edu
- Suffragists Oral History Project: http://bancroft.berkeley.edu/ROHO/projects/suffragist
- Columbia Center for Oral History: http://library.columbia.edu/indiv/ccoh.html
- The British Library Sounds Oral History: http://sounds.bl.uk/Oral-history
- The National Truth and Reconciliation Commission Archives have some publicly available videos from TRC hearings and thousands of private statements that require special permission to access: https://nctr.ca/archives.php
- The Oral History Association website is another good source of information. It is also useful to those who want to build and share resources: http://www.oralhistory.org/resources/

STRENGTHS AND WEAKNESSES OF ORAL HISTORY

The strengths and weaknesses of the oral history method are similar to those of qualitative interviews more generally. The technique is flexible and issues may be pursued in depth, reinforcing the validity of the information obtained. Reliability, however, is relatively weak and difficult to determine. Some argue that relying on people's memories or stories means that the researcher is not necessarily gaining facts. Others argue that it is the memories and perspectives of those who lived the history that are important to understand, and that these are what makes the method a valuable one. As we noted earlier, the issue of reliability in oral history is complex. Problems of reliability often depend on the issue under study and the interpretation being offered.

Generalizability is often a problem when using the oral history method because the individuals interviewed are seldom selected on the basis of probability sampling. For some researchers using this technique, however, generalizability is not at issue—they are documenting a single individual's life story.

Finally, qualitative interviewing is interactive, and as in all forms of interactive research, the researcher has the potential to affect the outcome of the data gathered. This effect is readily apparent in all interviewing methods. Although in-depth interviewing allows the voice of the individual to be heard, what is heard and how it is heard may be coloured by the person to whom the individual is speaking.

MAIN POINTS

- A qualitative interview is an interaction between an interviewer and a respondent. The researcher typically has a general plan of inquiry but not a set of questions that must be rigidly followed. Respondents' answers to initial questions shape a researcher's subsequent questions.
- Qualitative interviews allow the researcher to pursue issues in depth and give respondents more freedom to direct the flow of conversation.
- Effective interviewing involves skills of active listening and the ability to direct conversations unobtrusively.
- Qualitative interviews are often used in combination with other research methods, such as field research; however, they may also be used as the primary means of gathering data.
- The flexibility of in-depth interviews allows respondents to raise novel issues and provides the latitude for researchers to follow these up. Pursuing issues in greater depth reinforces the validity of the information obtained. However, practical considerations usually limit in-depth interview studies to small, nonprobability samples, making generalizations problematic.
- To create a focus group, researchers bring subjects together for an interview and observe their interactions as they explore a specific topic.
- Focus group interviews stimulate viewpoints from respondents that may not be readily elicited in an individual interview. They also allow researchers to examine how people make sense of issues in a collective manner.
- A focus group is led by a moderator who helps to facilitate discussion and ensure that no person dominates the conversation, while interfering as little as possible.
- The best guide to the number of groups to conduct is theoretical; that is, when the moderator is able to anticipate with some accuracy the issues that will be expressed in the next group, enough groups have likely been conducted.
- It is best to both tape focus group interviews and take notes during each session.
- Online focus groups and online interviews are becoming increasingly common data collection methods.
- Oral history is a method that uses in-depth interviews to gather data about the past from individuals' recollections. It typically focuses on specific events or periods of time.
- Oral histories enable researchers to incorporate the voices of the people into the understanding of past events, particularly those of women, members of ethnic minorities, and other underprivileged members of society.
- The use of oral histories allows the researcher to examine issues in depth, which makes the method strong on validity. The issue of reliability in oral history is complex and often depends on the topic under study and the interpretations of data being offered.

REVIEW QUESTIONS AND EXERCISES

1. Conduct a recorded, in-depth interview with a friend concerning his or her future occupational aspirations. Transcribe the interview. Evaluate your interview technique and the questions you asked using the guidelines for the wording of questions discussed in Chapter 8 and the guidelines for qualitative interviewing discussed in this chapter.
2. Let's assume you've been asked to do research to determine the acceptability of a new handheld computer. Plan a focus group session that might yield useful information for this purpose.
3. Use the Web to search for several oral history archives. Design a research question that you could examine using a number of the archived interviews that you have located.
4. Create an interview guide on the subject of binge drinking on campus.

CONTINUITY PROJECT

■ IN-DEPTH INTERVIEWING

As documented in the recent Truth and Reconciliation Commission report (2015) on the experience of Indigenous peoples, race continues to be an important source of inequality in Canadian society.

A recent qualitative study in the United States (Warikoo and de Novais 2015) illustrates that white university students commonly discuss race relations using either a "colour-blind frame" or a "diversity frame." They rarely use a "structural frame" to inform their understanding.

A "colour-blind frame" views society as "post-racial," meaning that race has little social meaning or consequence. A "diversity frame" (multiculturalism) sees race as a "positive cultural identity" among one of multiple perspectives that is beneficial to everyone. A "structural frame" emphasizes that social structures are an important source of racism and racial inequality.

Imagine you were replicating the U.S. study on white students at your university. Using Kvale's framework for constructing an interview guide, what specific interview questions would you use to explore the prevalence of these three interpretive frames among your classmates?

Robert Kneschke/Shutterstock.com

EVALUATION RESEARCH

Now you're going to see one of the most rapidly growing uses of social research: the evaluation of social interventions. You'll come away from this chapter able to judge whether social programs have succeeded or failed.

IN THIS CHAPTER ...

INTRODUCTION

You may not be familiar with *Twende na Wakati* (*Let's Go with the Times*), but it was the most popular radio show in Tanzania. It was a soap opera. The main character, Mkwaju, was a truck driver with some pretty traditional ideas about gender roles and sex. By contrast, Fundi Mitindo, a tailor, and his wife, Mama Waridi, had more modern ideas regarding the roles of men and women, particularly on issues of overpopulation and family planning.

Twende na Wakati was the creation of Population Communications International (PCI) and other organizations working in conjunction with the Tanzanian government in response to two problems facing that country: (1) a population growth rate over twice that of the rest of the world and (2) an AIDS epidemic particularly heavy along the international truck route, where more than a fourth of the truck drivers and over half the commercial sex workers were found to be HIV positive in 1991. The prevalence of contraceptive use was 11 percent (Rogers et al. 1996:5–6).

The purpose of the soap opera was to bring about a change in knowledge, attitudes, and practices relating to contraception and family planning. Rather than instituting a conventional educational campaign, PCI felt it would be more effective to illustrate the message through entertainment.

Between 1993 and 1995, 208 episodes of *Twende na Wakati* were aired, aiming at the 67 percent of Tanzanians who listen to the radio. Eighty-four percent of the radio listeners reported listening to the PCI soap opera, making it the most popular show in the country. Ninety percent of the show's listeners recognized Mkwaju, the sexist truck driver, and only 3 percent regarded him as a positive role model. Over two-thirds identified Mama Waridi, a businesswoman, and her tailor husband as positive role models.

Surveys conducted to measure the impact of the show indicated it had affected knowledge, attitudes, and behaviour. For example, 49 percent of the married women who listened to the show said they now practised family planning, compared with only 19 percent of the nonlisteners.

There were other effects:

> Some 72 percent of the listeners in 1994 said that they adopted an HIV/AIDS prevention behavior because of listening to "Twende na Wakati," and this percentage increased to 82 percent in our 1995 survey. Seventy-seven percent of these individuals adopted monogamy, 16 percent began using condoms, and 6 percent stopped sharing razors and/or needles.
>
> (Rogers et al. 1996:21)

We can judge the effectiveness of the soap opera because of a particular form of social science. *Evaluation research*—sometimes called *program evaluation*—refers to a research purpose rather than a specific research method. This purpose is to evaluate the impact of social interventions such as new teaching methods, innovations in parole, and a wide variety of such programs. Many methods—surveys, experiments, and so on—can be used in evaluation research.

Evaluation research is probably as old as general social research itself. Whenever people have instituted a social reform for a specific purpose, they've paid attention to its actual consequences, even if they haven't always done so in a conscious, deliberate, or sophisticated fashion. In recent years, however, the field of evaluation research has become an increasingly popular and active research specialty, as reflected in textbooks, courses, and projects. Moreover, the growth of evaluation research indicates a more general trend in the social sciences. As a researcher, you'll likely be asked to conduct evaluations.

In part, the growth of evaluation research reflects social scientists' increasing desire to make a difference in the world. At the same time, we can't discount the influence of (1) an increase in government requirements that program evaluations must accompany the implementation of new programs and (2) the availability of research funds to fulfill those requirements. In any event, it seems clear that social scientists will be bringing their skills into the real world more than ever before.

This chapter looks at some of the key elements in this form of social research. After considering the kinds of topics commonly subjected to evaluation, we'll move through some of its main operational aspects: measurement, study design, and execution. As you'll see, formulating questions is as important as answering them. Because it occurs within real life, evaluation research has its own problems, some of which we'll examine. Besides logistical problems, special ethical issues arise from evaluation research generally and from its specific, technical procedures. As you review reports of program evaluations, you should be especially sensitive to these problems.

Evaluation is a form of *applied* research; that is, it's intended to have some real-world effect. It will be useful, therefore, to consider whether and how it's actually applied. As you'll see, the obvious implications of an evaluation research project do not necessarily affect real life. They may become the focus of ideological, rather than scientific, debates. They may simply be denied out of hand for political or other reasons. Perhaps most typically, they are simply ignored and forgotten, left to collect dust in bookcases across the land.

The chapter concludes with a look at a particular resource for large-scale evaluation—*social indicators research.* This type of research is also a rapidly growing specialty. Essentially it involves the creation of aggregated indicators of the "health" of society, similar to the economic indicators that give diagnoses and prognoses of economies.

TOPICS APPROPRIATE TO EVALUATION RESEARCH

Evaluation research is appropriate whenever some social intervention occurs or is planned. A **social intervention** is an action taken within a social context for the purpose of producing some intended result. In its simplest sense, **evaluation research** is a process of determining whether a social intervention has produced the intended result.

Topics appropriate to evaluation research are limitless. When the federal government adopted the *Youth Offenders Act* in Canada in 1984, researchers soon after began to evaluate its impact. Again, following the adoption of the *Youth Criminal Justice Act* in 2003, researchers were quick to begin assessing its effects on the treatment of youth offenders. (See, for example, Tony Doob and Jane Sprott's 2006 evaluation.) Any number of policies and programs are the target of evaluation research. How effective is Vancouver's needle exchange program in reducing the prevalence of HIV? Do school drug use prevention programs actually reduce student drug use? Is the money spent on no-smoking campaigns a worthwhile expenditure? Are programs to limit teen smoking effective? Do community-based sex offender management programs reduce the likelihood of their re-offending? What's the impact of tougher drunk driving policies on morbidity and mortality due to automobile accidents?

There are many variations in the intent of evaluation research. *Needs assessment studies* aim to determine the existence and extent of problems, typically among a segment of the population, such as the elderly. *Cost–benefit studies* determine whether the results of a program can be justified by its expense (both financial and other). *Monitoring studies* provide a steady flow of information about something of interest, such as crime rates or the outbreak of an epidemic.

In general, evaluation assessments are conducted for two purposes, formative and summative. **Formative evaluations** focus on process and how it can be improved. **Summative evaluations** focus on outcomes (product) and whether these meet standards of effectiveness. Your research methods class, for example, could be assessed in both ways. A formative evaluation would focus on teaching and learning activities and how these could be improved. For example, perhaps there should be less individual work and more group work. Or less lecturing and more application exercises. A summative evaluation, by contrast, would

social intervention An action taken in a given social context with the goal of producing an intended outcome.

evaluation research Research undertaken to determine the effect of some social intervention, such as a program aimed at solving a social problem.

formative evaluations Assessments aimed at improving the process of an intervention.

summative evaluations Assessments aimed at evaluating the effectiveness of an intervention in achieving its goals.

focus on whether appropriate levels of student learning occurred, as evidenced, for example, by the distribution of final grades in the class.

Summative evaluation research is often referred to as *program evaluation*: the determination of whether a social intervention is producing the intended result. Here's an example. For over a dozen years, the Canadian military and other agencies were involved in Afghanistan. Beyond conducting combat operations to dislocate insurgent groups like the Taliban, Canadian agencies participated in programs and projects aimed at economic and social development. Canada invested more than 250 million dollars in nation-building projects in Afghanistan. In 2015 a summative evaluation of our investments was released (Foreign Affairs, Trade, and Development Canada 2015). The evaluation was conducted to address the following research question: "To what extent has CIDA [Canadian International Development Agency] contributed to a more secure and democratic Afghanistan, able to deliver key services to Afghans and better provide for its longer-term stability and sustainable development?" The evaluation team used both quantitative and qualitative information, analyzing more than 2,000 documents, doing field work assessments, and conducting over 200 interviews. Here is the researchers' summative conclusion[1]:

> Canada, together with other donors, contributed to important short-term achievements in various sectors, ranging from the construction and rehabilitation of thousands of schools, increased enrolment, especially of girls, improved access to health facilities, construction of community infrastructure, delivery of food to millions of people and support to the Afghanistan Independent Human Rights Commission and women's organizations.

Here's a very different example of evaluation research. In 2003 a controversial program was launched in Vancouver, called *Insite*. Insite is a safe location for persons who inject heroin, cocaine, and morphine to do so in a clean, medically supervised location. The clinic does not supply drugs but does dispense addiction treatment, mental health services, and first-aid services. Hundreds of addicts visit Insite every day. The goal of the programming is "harm reduction," and the site's activities are allowed under a controversial exemption it is granted to the *Controlled Drugs and Substances Act.*

Insite was the first medically supervised drug injection site in North America. Given the huge health, economic, and social challenges drug addiction poses for locations all across the continent, the innovative Insite project has been used for dozens of evaluation studies. Here is a summary of some of the research questions asked and answered by evaluations at Insite (from Urban Health Research Initiative 2015)[2]:

- Is the targeted population of high-risk injection drug users the one that actually uses the location? Yes.
- Which traits or behaviours typify the most common users of the safe-injection site? High-intensity heroin and cocaine injectors who are homeless.
- Does a facility like Insite increase the opportunity to enhance HIV prevention through education and safe equipment? Yes.
- Does a safe-injection site promote the use of drugs? Community drug use patterns were not worsened by the presence of Insite.
- Does a safe-injection site discourage addicts from seeking treatment? No, in fact the site enhances entry into treatment programs.
- Does the presence of a safe-injection site contribute to enhanced drug-related crime in the surrounding neighbourhoods? There was no increase in such crimes.
- Does a site like Insite contribute to lowered amounts of discarded syringes and other drug paraphernalia in the community? Yes.
- Does a safe-injection site contribute to more drug overdoses? No.

---

1 Foreign Affairs, Trade, and Development Canada, *2015 Summative Evaluation of Canada's Afghanistan Development Program 2004–2005—2012–2013—Synthesis Report*, http://www.international.gc.ca/department-ministere/evaluation/2015/dev_eval_afghanistan01.aspx?lang=eng. Accessed July 22, 2015.

2 Urban Health Research Initiative, *2015 Research Summaries*, http://uhri.cfenet.ubc.ca/content/view/72/93/. Reprinted with permission from the Urban Health Research Initiative.

Answering questions like these with the discipline of data is important if public policies are to be guided by empirical evidence rather than ideological positions. Toward this end, evaluation research is necessary.

As we just illustrated, the questions appropriate to evaluation research are of great practical significance: jobs, programs, investments, beliefs, and values are at stake. Let's now examine how these questions are answered—how evaluations are conducted.

FORMULATING THE PROBLEM: MEASUREMENT ISSUES

Several years ago, Earl Babbie headed an institutional research office that conducted research of direct relevance to the operation of the university. Often, his office was asked to evaluate new programs in the curriculum. The following description shows the problem that arose in that context, and it points to one of the key barriers to good evaluation research.

Faculty members would appear at his office to say they'd been told by the university administration to arrange for an evaluation of the new program they had permission to try. This points to a common problem: often the people whose programs are being evaluated aren't thrilled at the prospect. For them, an independent evaluation threatens the survival of the program and perhaps even their jobs.

The main problem we want to introduce, however, has to do with the purpose of the intervention to be evaluated. The question "What is the intended result of the new program?" often produced a rather vague response, such as "Students will get an in-depth and genuine understanding of mathematics, instead of simply memorizing methods of calculations." Fabulous! And how could we measure that "in-depth and genuine understanding"? Often, they reported that the program aimed at producing something that could not be measured by conventional aptitude and achievement tests. No problem there; that's to be expected when we're innovating and being unconventional. What would be an unconventional measure of the intended result? Sometimes this discussion came down to an assertion that the effects of the program would be "unmeasurable."

There's the common rub in evaluation research: measuring the "unmeasurable." Evaluation research is a matter of finding out whether something is there or not there, whether something happened or didn't happen. To conduct evaluation research, we must be able to operationalize, observe, and recognize the presence or absence of what is under study.

Often, desired outcomes are derived from published program documents or agency goals. For example, the researchers assessing the success of Canada's development initiatives in Afghanistan used "internationally agreed principles for evaluations in fragile states." In the case of the safe-injection site Insite, the governing outcome was harm reduction among injection drug users.

While "official" purposes of interventions are often the key to designing an evaluation, this may not always be sufficient. Anna-Marie Madison (1992), for example, warned that programs designed to help disadvantaged minorities do not always reflect what the targets of the aid may need and desire.

> The cultural biases inherent in how middle-class white researchers interpret the experiences of low-income minorities may lead to erroneous assumptions and faulty propositions concerning causal relationships, to invalid social theory, and consequently to invalid program theory. Descriptive theories derived from faulty premises, which have been legitimized in the literature as existing knowledge, may have negative consequences for program participants.
>
> (Madison 1992:38)

In setting up an evaluation, then, researchers must pay careful attention to issues of measurement. Let's take a closer look at the types of measurements that evaluation researchers must deal with.

SPECIFYING OUTCOMES

As we've suggested, a key variable for evaluation researchers to measure is the outcome or what is called the **response variable**. If a social program is intended to accomplish something, we must be able to measure that something. If we want to reduce prejudice, we need to be able to measure prejudice. If we want to increase marital harmony, we need to be able to measure that.

It's essential to achieve agreements on definitions in advance:

> The most difficult situation arises when there is disagreement as to standards. For example, many parties may disagree as to what defines serious drug abuse—is it defined best as 15% or more of students using drugs weekly, 5% or more using hard drugs such as cocaine or PCP monthly, students beginning to use drugs as young as seventh grade, or some combination of the dimensions of rate of use, nature of use, and age of user? ... Applied researchers should, to the degree possible, attempt to achieve consensus from research consumers in advance of the study (e.g., through advisory groups) or at least ensure that their studies are able to produce data relevant to the standards posited by all potentially interested parties.
>
> (Hedrick et al. 1993:27)

In the case of Vancouver's Insite program, the general harm-reduction goal is articulated in the following specific objectives (Dooling and Rachlis 2010):

- Increase access to health and addiction care.
- Reduce overdose fatalities.
- Reduce transmission of blood-borne viral infection.
- Improve public order.

Sometimes the definitions of a problem and a sufficient solution are defined by law or by agency regulations; if so, you must be aware of such specifications and accommodate them. Moreover, whatever the agreed-on definitions, you must also achieve agreement on how the measurements will be made. Because there are different possible methods for estimating the percentage of students "using drugs weekly," for example, you'd have to be sure that all the parties involved understood and accepted the method(s) you've chosen.

In the case of the Tanzanian soap opera, there were several outcome measures. In part, the purpose of the program was to improve knowledge about both family planning and AIDS. Thus, for example, one show debunked the belief that the AIDS virus was spread by mosquitoes and could be avoided by the use of insect repellent. Studies of listeners showed a reduction in that belief (Rogers et al. 1996:21). PCI also wanted to change Tanzanian attitudes toward family size, gender roles, HIV/AIDS, and other related topics; the research indicated that the show had affected these as well. Finally, the program aimed at affecting behaviour. We've already seen that radio listeners reported changing their behaviour with regard to AIDS prevention. They reported a greater use of family planning as well. However, because there's always the possibility of a gap between what people say they do and what they actually do, the researchers sought independent data to confirm their conclusions.

Tanzania's national AIDS-control program had been offering condoms free of charge to citizens. In the areas covered by the soap opera, the number of condoms given out increased sixfold between 1992 and 1994. This far exceeded the increase of 1.4 times in the control area, where broadcasters did not carry the soap opera.

MEASURING EXPERIMENTAL CONTEXTS

Measuring the dependent variables directly involved in the experimental program is only a beginning. As Henry Riecken and Robert Boruch (1974:120–121) pointed out, it's often appropriate and important to measure aspects of the context of an experiment. Though external to the experiment itself, some variables may affect it.

Consider, for example, an evaluation of a program aimed at training unskilled people for employment. The primary outcome measure would be their success at gaining employment after completing the program. You would, of course, observe and calculate the subjects' employment rate, but you should also determine what has happened to the employment/

response variable The outcome measured to determine a program's effectiveness.

unemployment rates of society at large during the evaluation. A general slump in the job market should be taken into account in assessing what might otherwise seem a relatively low employment rate for subjects. Or, if all the experimental subjects get jobs following the program, you should consider whether there has been any general increase in available jobs. Combining complementary measures with proper control group designs should allow you to pinpoint the effects of the program you're evaluating.

SPECIFYING INTERVENTIONS

Besides making measurements relevant to the outcomes of a program, researchers must measure the program intervention—the experimental stimulus. In part, this measurement will be handled by the assignment of subjects to experimental and control groups, if that's the research design. Assigning a person to the experimental group is the same as scoring that person "yes" on the stimulus, and assignment to the control group represents a score of "no." In practice, however, it's seldom that simple.

Let's stick with the job-training example. Some people will participate in the program; others will not. But imagine for a moment what job-training programs are probably like. Some subjects will participate fully; others will miss a lot of sessions or fool around when they are present. So you may need measures of the extent or quality of participation in the program. If the program is effective, you should find that those who participated fully have higher employment rates than do those who participated less.

Other factors may further confound the administration of the experimental stimulus. Suppose we're evaluating a new form of psychotherapy designed to cure gambling addiction. Several therapists administer it to subjects making up an experimental group. We plan to compare the recovery rate of the experimental group with that of a control group, which receives some other therapy or none at all. It may be useful to include the names of the therapists treating specific subjects in the experimental group, because some may be more effective than others. If this turns out to be the case, we must find out why the treatment worked better for some therapists than for others. What we learn will further develop our understanding of the therapy itself.

SPECIFYING THE POPULATION

When evaluating an intervention, it's important to define the population of possible subjects for whom the program is appropriate. Ideally, all or a sample of appropriate subjects will then be assigned to experimental and control groups as warranted by the study design. Defining the population, however, can itself involve specifying measurements. If we're evaluating a new form of psychotherapy, it's probably appropriate for people with mental health problems; but how will "mental health problems" be defined and measured? The job-training program mentioned previously is probably intended for people who are having trouble finding work, but what counts as "having trouble"?

Beyond defining the relevant population, then, the researcher should make fairly precise measurements on the variables considered in the definition. For example, even though the randomization of subjects in the psychotherapy study would ensure an equal distribution of those with mild and severe mental health problems in the experimental and control groups, we'll need to keep track of the relative severity of different subjects' problems in case the therapy turns out to be effective only for those with mild disorders. Similarly, we should measure such demographic variables as *gender, age, race*, and so forth, in case the therapy works only for women, the elderly, or some other group.

NEW VERSUS EXISTING MEASURES

In providing for the measurement of these different kinds of variables, the researcher must continually choose whether to create new measures or to use ones already devised by other researchers. If a study addresses something that's never been measured before, the choice is easy. If it addresses something that others have tried to measure, the researcher will have to evaluate the relative worth of various existing measurement devices in relation to his or her specific research situations and purpose. Recall that this is a general issue in social research that applies well beyond evaluation research. Let's examine briefly the advantages of creating new measures versus using existing ones.

Creating measurements specifically for a study can offer greater relevance and validity than using existing ones. If the psychotherapy we're evaluating aims at a specific aspect of recovery, we can create measures that pinpoint that aspect. We might not be able to find any standardized psychological measures that hit that aspect right on the head. However, creating our own measure will cost us the advantages to be gained from using pre-existing measures. Creating good measures takes time and energy, both of which could be saved by adopting an existing technique. Of greater scientific significance is that measures that have been used frequently by other researchers carry a body of possible comparisons that might be important to our evaluation. If the experimental therapy raises scores by an average of 10 points on a standardized test, we'll be in a position to compare that therapy with others that had been evaluated using the same measure. Finally, measures with a long history of use usually have known degrees of validity and reliability, but newly created measures will require pretesting or will be used with considerable uncertainty.

OPERATIONALIZING SUCCESS/FAILURE

Potentially, one of the most taxing aspects of evaluation research is determining whether the program under review succeeded or failed. The purpose of a foreign language program may be to help students better learn the language, but how much better is enough? The purpose of the conjugal visit program at a prison may be to raise morale, but how high does morale need to be raised to justify the program?

As you may anticipate, there are almost never clear-cut answers to questions like these. This dilemma has surely been the source of what is generally called *cost–benefit analysis*. How much does the program cost in relation to what it returns in benefits? If the benefits outweigh the cost, keep the program going. If the reverse, junk it. That's simple enough, and it seems to apply in straightforward economic situations: if it cost you $20 to produce something and you can sell it for only $18, there's no way you can make up the difference in volume.

Unfortunately, the situations usually faced by evaluation researchers are seldom amenable to straightforward economic accounting. The foreign language program may cost the school district $100 per student, and it may raise students' performances on tests by an average of 15 points. Because the test scores can't be converted into dollars, there's no obvious ground for weighing the costs and benefits.

Sometimes, as a practical matter, the criteria of success and failure can be handled through competition among programs. If a different foreign language program costs only $50 per student and produces an increase of 20 points in test scores, it would undoubtedly be considered more successful than the first program—assuming that test scores were seen as an appropriate measure of the purpose of both programs and the less expensive program had no negative unintended consequences.

Ultimately, the criteria of success and failure are often a matter of agreement. The people responsible for the program may commit themselves in advance to a particular outcome that will be regarded as an indication of success. If that's the case, all you need to do is make absolutely certain that the research design will measure the specified outcome. We mention this obvious requirement simply because researchers sometimes fail to meet it, and there's little or nothing more embarrassing than that.

Thus, researchers must take measurement quite seriously in evaluation research, carefully determining all the variables to be measured and getting appropriate measures for each. As we've implied, however, such decisions are typically not purely scientific ones. Evaluation researchers often must work out their measurement strategy with the people responsible for the program being evaluated. It usually doesn't make sense to determine whether a program achieves Outcome X when its purpose is to achieve Outcome Y. (Realize, however, that evaluation designs sometimes have the purpose of testing for unintended consequences.)

There's a political aspect to these choices, also. Because evaluation research often affects other people's professional interest—their pet program may be halted, or they may be fired or lose professional standing—the results of evaluation research are often argued about.

Let's turn now to some of the evaluation designs commonly used by researchers.

TYPES OF EVALUATION RESEARCH DESIGNS

We noted at the beginning of this chapter that evaluation research is not itself a method but rather one application of social research methods. Therefore, it can involve any of several research designs. In this section, we'll consider three main types of research design appropriate for evaluations: experimental designs, quasi-experimental designs, and qualitative evaluations.

EXPERIMENTAL DESIGNS

Many of the experimental designs discussed in Chapter 7 can be used in evaluation research. To illustrate, let's see how the classical experimental model might be applied to our evaluation of the new psychotherapy treatment for gambling addiction.

We should begin by identifying a population of patients relevant to the therapy. Researchers experimenting with the new therapy might make this identification. Let's say we're dealing with a clinic that already has 100 patients being treated for problem gambling. We might take that group and the clinic's definition of *problem gambling* as a starting point, and we should maintain any existing assessments of the severity of the problem for each specific patient.

For purposes of the evaluation research, however, we would need to develop a more specific measure of problem gambling. Maybe it would involve a questionnaire such as the Problem Gambling Severity Index (PGSI). The more gambling related problems a person reports, the greater their PGSI score and the greater their risk for problem gambling. (See Chapter 5 to review the PGSI.) Alternatively, the outcome measure might be based on the assessments of independent therapists not involved in the therapy who interview the patients later. In any event, we'd need to agree on the measures to be used.

In the simplest design, we would assign the 100 patients randomly to experimental and control groups; the former would receive the new therapy, and the latter would be taken out of therapy altogether during the experiment. (Review Chapter 7 for a refresher on the purpose of control groups and methods of assigning participants to experimental and control groups.) Because ethical practice would probably prevent withdrawing therapy altogether from the control group, however, it's more likely that the control group would continue to receive their conventional therapy.

Having assigned subjects to the experimental and control groups, we would need to agree on the length of the experiment. Perhaps the designers of the new therapy think it ought to be effective within two months, and an agreement could be reached. The duration of the study doesn't need to be rigid, however. One purpose of the experiment and evaluation might be to determine how long it actually takes for the new therapy to be effective. Conceivably, then, an agreement could be struck to measure recovery rates weekly, say, and let the ultimate length of the experiment rest on a continual review of the results.

Let's suppose the new therapy involves participants gambling online with a program that tracks player behaviour and provides personalized feedback via "pop-up" messages (Edgerton et al. 2016). Problem gamblers can get in a flow or zone and lose track of time and/or how much money they have spent. Prompts to help them attend to these cues (i.e., "snap" them out of it) may help reduce problematic gambling. If we wanted to test a new therapeutic intervention based on this reasoning, we might first ask players to pre-set a specific time limit (how much time they will gamble) and a money limit (how much money they will spend). Information about how long players gambled and how much money they spent would be collected as the players gambled online. Then, as they played, pop-up messages would periodically appear to remind them of how close they were to exceeding their pre-set limits. If the treatment is effective, then players' risk of problem gambling (as measured by PGSI scores) should be reduced relative to those control subjects just receiving the conventional treatment.

Having thus designed the intervention, all we have to do is set the study in motion. The observations are made and recorded, and the mass of data is accumulated for analysis. Once the study has run its course, we can determine whether the new treatment had its intended—or perhaps some unintended—consequences. We can tell whether the personalized pop ups were most effective for mild problems or severe ones, whether they worked for young subjects but not older ones, and so forth.

This simple illustration should show you how the standard experimental designs presented in Chapter 7 can be used in evaluation research. But, to be clear, don't think that the randomized classical experimental design is restricted to evaluating small-scale interventions. This approach is just as applicable to assessing large-scale initiatives. The work of professors Banerjee and Duflo (2012) at the MIT Abdul Latif Jameel Poverty Action Lab provides an excellent compendium. For example, randomized control trials demonstrate that, counter to much popular wisdom, providing small, low-interest loans in poor regions of the globe is not that effective in alleviating poverty (Roodman 2012). Nor does distributing low-cost laptops to poor children do much for enhancing academic performance (Keating 2014). However, encouraging challenged regions to hold local elections can improve governance (Christia and Enikolopov 2013). Many—perhaps most—of the evaluations reported in the research literature, however, don't follow such rigorous randomized control trials. Because it's nested in real life, evaluation research often calls for quasi-experimental designs. Let's see what this means.

QUASI-EXPERIMENTAL DESIGNS

Quasi-experiments are distinguished from "true" experiments primarily by the lack of random assignment of subjects to an experimental and a control group. In evaluation research, it's often impossible to achieve such an assignment of subjects. Rather than forgo evaluation altogether, researchers sometimes create designs that give some evaluation of the program in question. This section describes some of these designs.

Time-Series Designs To illustrate the **time-series design**—studies that involve measurements taken over time—we'll begin by asking you to assess the meaning of some hypothetical data. Suppose we come to you with what we claim is an effective technique for getting students to participate in classroom sessions of a course we're teaching. To prove our assertion, we tell you that on Monday, only four students asked questions or made a comment in class; on Wednesday we devoted the class time to an open discussion of a controversial issue raging on campus; and on Friday, when we returned to the subject matter of the course, eight students asked questions or made comments. In other words, we contend, the discussion of a controversial issue on Wednesday has doubled classroom participation. This simple set of data is presented graphically in Figure 12-1.

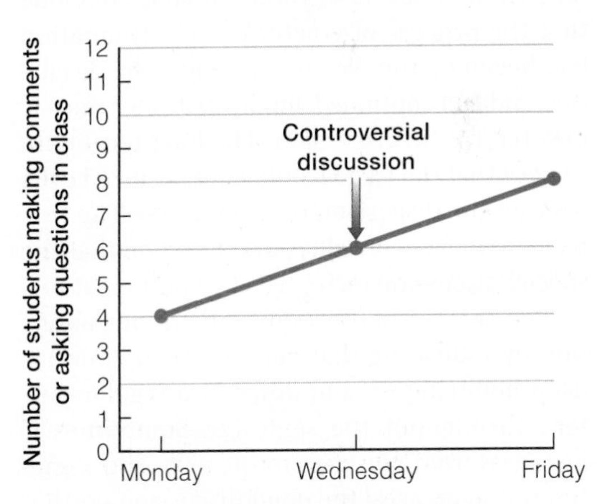

FIGURE 12-1 Two Observations of Class Participation: Before and After an Open Discussion.
Source: © Cengage Learning

quasi-experiments Nonrigorous inquiries somewhat resembling controlled experiments but lacking key elements such as random assignment of subjects to experimental and control groups, pre- and post-testing, and/or any control group.

time-series design A research design that involves measurements made over some period, such as the study of traffic accident rates before and after lowering the speed limit.

Have we persuaded you that the open discussion on Wednesday has had the consequence we say it has? Probably you'd object that our data do not prove the case. Two observations (Monday and Friday) aren't really enough to prove anything. Ideally, we should have had two classes, with students assigned randomly to each. Also, we should have held an open discussion in only one, and then compared the two on Friday. But we don't have two classes with random assignment of students. Instead, we've been keeping a record of class participation throughout the semester for the one class. This record allows you to conduct a time-series evaluation.

Figure 12-2 presents three possible patterns of class participation over time—both before and after the open discussion on Wednesday. Which of these patterns would give you some confidence that the discussion had the impact we contend it had?

If the time-series results looked like the first pattern in Figure 12-2, you'd probably conclude that the process of greater class participation had begun on the Wednesday before the discussion and had continued, unaffected, after the day devoted to the discussion. The long-term data suggest that the trend would have occurred even without the discussion on Wednesday. The first pattern, then, contradicts our assertion that the special discussion increased class participation.

The second pattern contradicts our assertion by indicating that class participation has been bouncing up and down in a regular pattern throughout the semester. Sometimes it increases from one class to the next, and sometimes it decreases; the open discussion on that Wednesday simply came at a time when the level of participation was about to increase. More to the point, we note that class participation decreased again at the class following the alleged post-discussion increase.

Only the third pattern in Figure 12-2 supports our contention that the open discussion mattered. As the figure shows, the level of discussion before that Wednesday had been a steady four students per class. Not only did the level of participation double following the day of discussion, but it also continued to increase further afterward. Although these data do not protect us against the possible influence of some extraneous factor (we might also have mentioned that participation would figure into students' grades), they do exclude the possibility that the increase results from a process of maturation (indicated in the first pattern) or from regular fluctuations (indicated in the second).

nonequivalent control group A control group that is similar to the experimental group but is not created by the random assignment of subjects. This sort of control group can differ greatly from the experimental group with regard to the dependent variable or variables related to it.

Nonequivalent Control Groups The time-series design just described involves only an "experimental" group; it doesn't provide the value that would be gained from having a control group. Sometimes, when researchers can't create experimental and control groups by random assignment from a common pool, they can find an existing "control" group that appears similar to the experimental group. Such a group is called a **nonequivalent control group**. If an innovative foreign language program is being tried in one class in a large high school, for example, you may be able to find another foreign language class in the same school that has a very similar student population: one that has approximately the same composition with regard to grade in school, gender, ethnicity, IQ, and so forth. The second class, then, could provide a point of comparison. (Remember: in a true experiment, the control group is supposed to be equivalent to the experimental group in all respects, except that the control group does not receive the treatment or experimental stimulus; a nonequivalent control group is an approximation of a true control group.) At the end of the semester, both classes could be given the same foreign language test, and you could compare performances.

Here's how two junior high schools were selected for the purposes of evaluating a program aimed at discouraging tobacco, alcohol, and drug use:

> The pairing of the two schools and their assignment to "experimental" and "control" conditions was not random. The local Lung

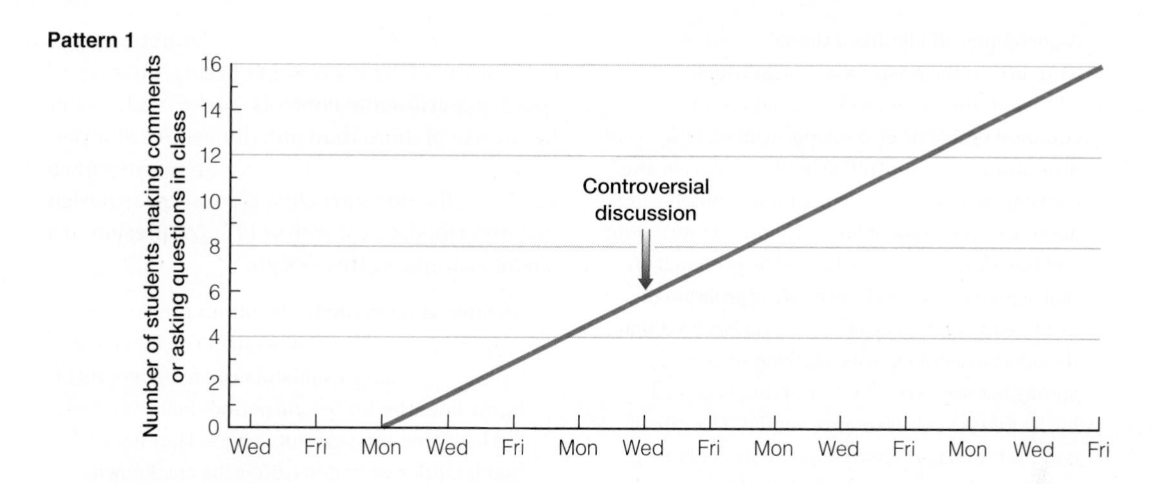

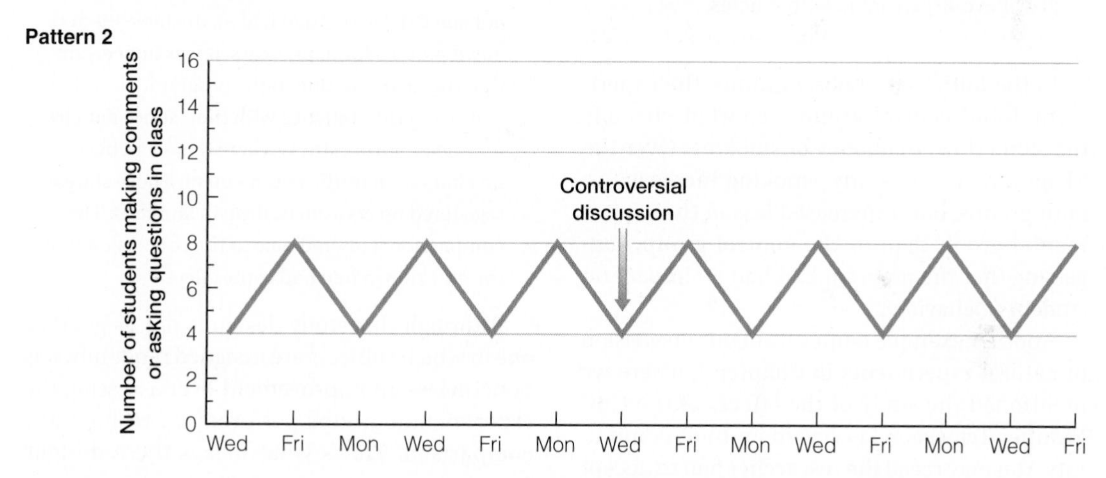

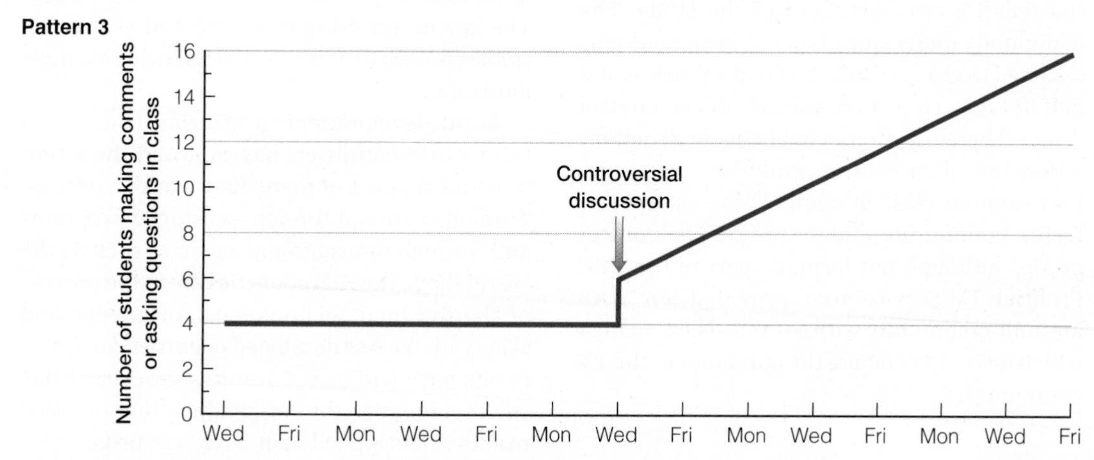

FIGURE 12-2 **Three Patterns of Class Participation in a Longer Historical Period.**
Source: © Cengage Learning

> Association had identified the school where we delivered the program as one in which administrators were seeking a solution to admitted problems of smoking, alcohol, and drug abuse. The "control" school was chosen as a convenient and nearby demographic match where administrators were willing to allow our surveying and breath-testing procedures. The principal of that school considered the existing program of health education to be effective and believed that the onset of smoking was relatively uncommon among his students. The communities served by the two schools were very similar. The rate of parental smoking reported by the students was just above 40 percent in both schools.
>
> (McAlister et al. 1980:720)

In the initial set of observations, the experimental and control groups reported virtually the same (low) frequency of smoking. Over the 21 months of the study, smoking increased in both groups, but it increased less in the experimental group than in the control group, suggesting that the program had had an impact on students' behaviour.

Another example comes from our discussion of natural experiments in Chapter 7, where we mentioned the study of the effects of the CBC Frontier Television Service in an Inuit community. You may recall the researcher had to accept the real-life circumstances of the study. The community under study had not been randomly assigned to groups where half had TV access and half did not. Thus there was no official control group. Therefore, Coldevin (1976) searched for a nonequivalent control group—a community that came as close in composition as possible to the community under study. This "control group," although not formally part of the CBC Frontier TV Service area, provided him with an Inuit community without television against which he could compare the outcomes in the TV community.

multiple time-series designs The use of more than one set of data collected over time (e.g., accident rates over time in several provinces or cities) in order to make comparisons.

Multiple Time-Series Designs Sometimes the evaluation of processes occurring outside of "pure" experimental controls can be made easier by the use of more than one time-series analysis. **Multiple time-series designs** are an improved version of the nonequivalent control group design just described. Carol Weiss (1972:69) presented a useful example of this design:

> An interesting example of multiple time series was the evaluation of the Connecticut crackdown on highway speeding. Evaluators collected reports of traffic fatalities for several periods before and after the new program went into effect. They found that fatalities went down after the crackdown, but since the series had had an unstable up-and-down pattern for many years, it was not certain that the drop was due to the program. They then compared the statistics with time-series data from four neighboring states where there had been no changes in traffic enforcement. Those states registered no equivalent drop in fatalities. The comparison lent credence to the conclusion that the crackdown had had some effect.

Although this study design is not as good as one in which subjects are assigned randomly, it is nonetheless an improvement over assessing the experimental group's performance without any comparison. That's what makes these designs quasi-experiments instead of just fooling around. The key in assessing this aspect of evaluation studies is *comparability*, as the following example illustrates.

Rural development, a growing concern in third-world countries, has captured the attention and support of many first-world countries. Through national foreign assistance programs and through international agencies such as the World Bank, the rich countries are in the process of sharing their technological knowledge and skills with the less developed countries. Such programs have had mixed results, however. Often, such techniques do not produce the intended results when applied in different contexts.

Rajesh Tandon and L. Dave Brown (1981) undertook an experiment in which technological training would be accompanied by instruction in village organization. They believed it was important for poor farmers to learn how to organize and exert collective influence within their villages—getting needed action from government officials, for example. Only then would their new technological skills bear fruit.

Both intervention and evaluation were attached to an ongoing program in which 25 villages had been selected for technological training. Two poor farmers from each village had been trained in new agricultural technologies. Then they had been sent home to share their new knowledge with their village and to organize other farmers into "peer groups" who would assist in spreading that knowledge. Two years later, the authors randomly selected two of the 25 villages (the experimental groups, subsequently called Group A and Group B) to receive special organizational training and randomly selected 11 other villages as controls (they did not receive the organizational training). A careful comparison of demographic characteristics showed the two experimental and 11 control groups to be strikingly similar, suggesting they were sufficiently comparable for the study.

The peer groups from the two experimental villages were brought together for special training in organization building. The participants were given some information about organizing and making demands on the government; they were also given opportunities to act out dramas similar to the situations they faced at home. This training (which the control group villages did not receive) took three days.

The outcome variables considered by the evaluation all had to do with the extent to which members of the peer groups initiated group activities designed to improve their situation. Six types were studied. "Active initiative," for example, was defined as "active effort to influence persons or events affecting group members versus passive response or withdrawal" (Tandon and Brown 1981:180). The data for evaluation came from the journals that the peer group leaders had been keeping since their initial technological training. The researchers read through the journals and counted the number of initiatives taken by members of the peer groups. Two researchers coded the journals independently and compared their work to test the reliability of the coding process.

Figure 12-3 compares the number of active initiatives by members of the two experimental groups with those coming from the control groups. Similar results were found for the other outcome measures.

Notice two things about the graph. First, there's a dramatic difference in the number of initiatives by the two experimental groups as compared with the 11 controls. This seems to confirm the effectiveness of the specialized organizational training program. Second, notice that the number of initiatives also increased among the control groups. The researchers explain this latter pattern as a result of contagion. Because all the villages were near each other, the organizational lessons learned by peer group members in the experimental groups were communicated in part to members of the control villages.

This example illustrates the strengths of multiple time-series designs in situations in which true experiments are inappropriate to the program being evaluated.

QUALITATIVE EVALUATIONS

While we've laid out the steps involved in tightly structured, mostly quantitative evaluation research, evaluations can also be less structured and more qualitative. For example, Pauline Bart and Patricia O'Brien (1985) wanted to evaluate different ways to stop rape, so they undertook in-depth interviews with both rape victims and women who had successfully fended off rape attempts. As a general rule, they found that resistance (e.g., yelling, kicking, running away) was more likely to be successful than to make the situation worse, as women sometimes fear it will.

As an illustration of the focus group method in Chapter 11, we mentioned the qualitative evaluation research conducted by Harlton and colleagues (1998). You may recall that they were interested in evaluating stakeholders' perspectives on the idea of "partnership" in Canadian healthcare policy concerning the elderly. They conducted separate focus group interviews with seven key stakeholder groups identified in eldercare. Their analysis revealed that very different understandings of the new "partnership" policy were held by those stakeholders who had

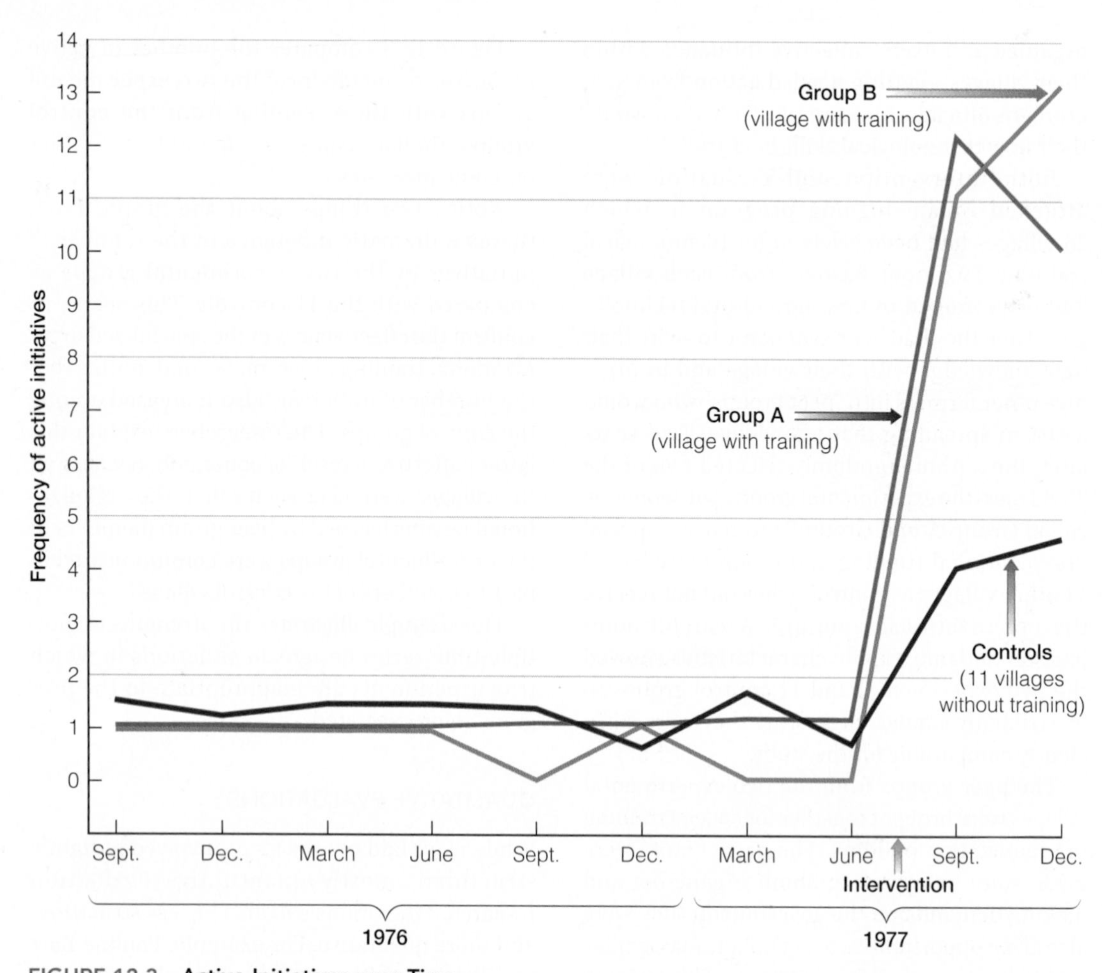

FIGURE 12-3 Active Initiatives over Time.
Source: Rajesh Tandon and L. Dave Brown, "Organization-Building for Rural Development: An Experiment in India," *Journal of Applied Behavior Science* (April–June), p. 182, copyright © 1981 by SAGE Publications. Reprinted by Permissions of SAGE Publications, Inc.

the most influence on eldercare policy and those whose lives would be most affected by the policy.

Focus groups can be used in all kinds of assessments. For example, the Financial Consumer Agency of Canada (FCAC) is responsible for protecting and informing consumers of financial services. Their educational mandate includes developing pamphlets and website materials, with the aim that "the use of plain language makes FCAC's materials and tools easy to use and understand" (FCAC 2015). To test whether their materials were easily understandable, the FCAC used focus groups. Specifically, ten focus groups were conducted in five Canadian cities. The results revealed that, although the results were generally positive, language clarification, organization, and visual layout could be improved in several specific instances.

Sometimes, even structured quantitative evaluations can yield unexpected qualitative results. Paul Steel is a social researcher specializing in the evaluation of programs aimed at pregnant drug users. One program he evaluated involved counselling by public health nurses, who warned pregnant drug users that continued drug use would likely result in underweight babies whose skulls would be an average of 10 percent smaller than normal. In his in-depth interviews with program participants, however, he discovered that the program omitted one important piece of information: that undersized babies were a bad thing. Many of the young women Steel interviewed thought that smaller babies would mean easier deliveries (Personal communication, November 22, 1993).

In many cases, the most effective evaluation research uses mixed methods approaches that combine qualitative and quantitative components. While making statistical comparisons is useful, so is gaining an in-depth understanding of the processes producing the observed results—or preventing the expected results from appearing. The evaluation of the Tanzanian soap opera, presented earlier in this chapter, used several research techniques. We've already mentioned the listener surveys and data obtained from clinics. In addition, the researchers conducted numerous focus groups to probe more deeply into the effect the shows had on listeners. Also, content analyses were done on the soap opera episodes themselves and on the many letters received from listeners. Both quantitative and qualitative analyses were undertaken (Swalehe et al. 1995). Thus, this study demonstrated several of the mixed methods strategies outlined in Chapter 1. Findings from different methods were compared to reinforce conclusions (triangulation), to offset the particular strengths and weaknesses of each method, and to enhance the meaningfulness and completeness of conclusions (complementarity).

THE SOCIAL CONTEXT

Many of the comments in previous sections have hinted at the possibility of problems in the actual execution of evaluation research projects. Of course, all forms of research can run into problems, but evaluation research has a special propensity for it. This section looks at some of the logistical problems and special ethical issues in evaluation research. It concludes with some observations about using evaluation research results.

LOGISTICAL PROBLEMS

In a military context, *logistics* refers to moving supplies around—making sure people have food, guns, and tent pegs when they need them. Here, we use it to refer to getting subjects to do what they're supposed to do, getting research instruments distributed and returned, and other seemingly unchallenging tasks. These tasks are more challenging than you might guess!

Coordinating Service When a team of researchers set out to evaluate a new program aimed at improving coordination of activities among mental health service providers (Forster et al. 1990), they found out just how many problems can occur. The purpose of the research was to evaluate the implementation of a six-month pilot project to help coordinate services among eight agencies in a small city in Western Canada. A previous study of service providers from agencies throughout the city identified problems and concerns related to lack of service coordination that they believed hindered client care. Thus, the pilot project had four specific goals (1990:617)[3]:

1. increased quality and efficiency of direct mental health services to specified clients
2. reduced redundancy in delivery of mental health services to specified clients
3. reduced use of unnecessary mental health services by specified clients
4. increased consumer provider satisfaction with the range and type of services the client is receiving

These goals would be accomplished by, for example, opening up communication among the agencies and increasing joint treatment planning. The expected effect of the project was to reduce the time spent on a specific client's care while improving satisfaction and service.

Service providers from the agencies designed the project. The evaluators were consulted in the design, and the design included the evaluation components. The project was implemented only after all staff were informed about it and instructed on the procedures required for the project. They were asked to participate and

3 Christina L. Forster, Brian Evans, and Ronald J. Fisher, "Evaluation of a Pilot Project in Service Coordination," *Evaluation Review* 14(6), pp. 616–631, copyright © 1990 by SAGE Publications. Reprinted by Permission of SAGE Publications, Inc.

encouraged to give feedback and make suggestions. The committee that oversaw the project consisted of the head administrator from each agency involved. This arrangement might sound promising for evaluation researchers. But, even under these circumstances, the problems of execution in evaluation research can be extensive.

In reality, not all agencies were committed to the project, and it was not properly implemented. Although the researchers had an elaborate and well-planned evaluation design that included baseline questionnaires, service provider daily record sheets, client profile forms, case conference meetings with minutes, case conference questionnaires, and postproject questionnaires, there were problems from the very start.

Fourteen clients were selected in total for both the experimental and control groups, but only seven were chosen in the appropriate time frame. Therefore, not all clients were part of the project for the full six months. This affected the client improvement measures. And, of the 14 chosen, only half were chosen using criteria consistent with the project. For example, some were chosen because they requested to participate and others because they required more help than they were getting. Case conferences weren't properly implemented—regular meetings were not always held, and even when they were held, not all agencies participated.

Commitment to the project was said to be "at least" moderate for five of the eight agencies, which meant that three were not committed. A number of service providers didn't fill out the questionnaires at all, some didn't fill them out completely, and others filled out the wrong questionnaires, contributing to unusable data and a smaller sample size. In addition, the sizes of the treatment and control groups were unequal:

> Fourteen potential clients were identified, but only 8 completed the pretest and 10 the posttest questionnaires. Only 2 of the final 10 respondents were in the control group. Questionnaires were completed by service providers from only six of the eight originally involved agencies.
>
> (1990:623)

With due cautions, the researchers presented results in relation to the pilot project objectives. The authors concluded that the program was neither implemented as intended nor successful. There were "no substantial effects on improving service coordination in any of the five intended areas" (1990:628). Nonetheless, there was much to be learned from the evaluation that might help in the implementation of future service coordination projects.

The special logistical problems of evaluation research grow out of the fact that it occurs within the context of real life. Although evaluation research is modelled after the experiment—which suggests that the researchers have control over what happens—it takes place within frequently uncontrollable daily life. Of course, the participant observer in field research doesn't have control over what's observed either, but that method doesn't strive for control. Given the objectives of evaluation research, lack of control can create real dilemmas for the researcher.

Administrative Control As suggested in the previous example, the logistical details of an evaluation project often fall to program administrators. Let's suppose you're evaluating the effects of a "conjugal visit" program on the morale of marr'ied prisoners. The program allows inmates periodic visits from their spouses during which they can have sexual relations. On the fourth day of the program, a male prisoner dresses up in his wife's clothes and escapes. Although you might be tempted to assume that his morale was greatly improved by escaping, that turn of events would complicate your study design in many ways. Perhaps the warden will terminate the program altogether, and where's your evaluation then? Or, if the warden is brave, he or she may review the files of all those prisoners you selected randomly for the experimental group and veto the "bad risks." There goes the comparability of your experimental and control groups. As an alternative, stricter security measures may be introduced to prevent further escapes, and the security measures may have a dampening effect on morale. So the experimental stimulus has changed in the middle of your research project. Some of the data will reflect the original stimulus; other data will reflect the modification.

Although you'll probably be able to sort it all out, your carefully designed study has become a logistical snakepit.

Or, suppose you've been engaged to evaluate the effect of gender relations lectures on sexual harassment in the military. You've carefully studied the soldiers available to you for study, and you've randomly assigned some to attend the lectures and others to stay away. The rosters have been circulated weeks in advance, and at the appointed day and hour, the lectures begin. Everything seems to be going smoothly until you begin processing the files: the names don't match. Checking around, you discover that military field exercises, KP duty, and a variety of emergencies required some of the experimental subjects to be elsewhere at the time of the lectures. That's bad enough, but then you learn that helpful commanding officers sent others to fill in for the missing soldiers. And whom do you suppose they picked to fill in? Soldiers who didn't have anything else to do or who couldn't be trusted to do anything important. You might learn this bit of information a week or so before the deadline for submitting your final report on the impact of the gender relations lectures.

These are some of the logistical problems confronting evaluation researchers. You need to be familiar with the problems to understand why some research procedures may not measure up to the design of the classical experiment. As you read reports of evaluation research, however, you'll find that—our earlier comments notwithstanding—it is possible to carry out controlled social research in conjunction with real-life experiments.

The accompanying Applying Concepts in Everyday Life box "Testing Soap Operas in Tanzania" describes some of the logistical problems involved in the research discussed at the outset of this chapter.

ETHICAL CONCERNS

Ethics and evaluation are intertwined in many ways. Sometimes the social interventions being evaluated raise ethical issues. Evaluating the impact of mandatory vaccination of schoolchildren will throw the researchers directly into the political, ideological, and ethical debates on parental rights versus public safety. It's not possible to evaluate a sex education program in elementary schools without becoming involved in the heated issues surrounding sex education itself, and the researcher will find it difficult to remain impartial. The evaluation study design will *require* that some children receive sex education—in fact, you may very well be the one who decides which children do. (From a scientific standpoint, you *should* be in charge of selection.) This means that when parents become outraged that their child is being taught about sex, you'll be directly responsible.

Now let's look on the bright side. Maybe the experimental program is of great value to those participating in it. Let's say that the new industrial safety program being evaluated reduces injuries dramatically. But then what about the control group members who were deprived of the program by the research design? The evaluators' actions could be an important part of the reason that a control group subject suffered an injury. Ironically, when a program is effective, it may be ethically dubious to deprive a control group of its benefits.

By its very nature, then, evaluation research is interwoven with real-world issues. We only evaluate programs when it matters whether they make a difference or not, and that means the results of the evaluation matter to people. This brings up another potential problem. Almost always, some people will want the results to turn out a certain way, and other people may want a different result. Often, as in the case of pharmaceutical testing, for example, those paying for the research may want a particular result. Further, the researchers themselves may have personal motives toward a given end. Evaluation researchers, therefore, often find themselves under internal or external pressure to produce a particular finding.

Of course, researchers must not be swayed by either personal desires or sponsors' demands with respect to the design, execution, and analysis of results. This is true in all kinds of social research; however, unethical actions in evaluation research can produce particularly severe consequences. For example, the results of evaluation research

APPLYING CONCEPTS IN EVERYDAY LIFE

Testing Soap Operas in Tanzania

William N. Ryerson
Executive Vice-President, Population Communications International

Twende na Wakati (*Let's Go with the Times*) was broadcast for six years beginning in mid-1993 on Radio Tanzania with support from the United Nations Population Fund. The program was designed to encourage family planning use and AIDS prevention measures.

There were many different elements to the research. One was a nationwide, random-sample survey given prior to the first airing of the soap opera in June 1993 and then annually after that. Many interviewers faced particularly interesting challenges. For example, one interviewer, Fridolan Banzi, had never been in or on water in his life and couldn't swim. He arranged for a small boat to take him through the rough waters of Lake Victoria so he could carry out his interviews at a village that had no access by road. He repeated this nerve-wracking trip each year afterward in order to measure the change in that village.

Another interviewer, Mr. Tende, was invited to participate in a village feast that the villagers held to welcome him and to indicate their enthusiasm about having been selected for the study. They served him barbecued rats. Though they weren't part of his normal diet, he ate them anyway to be polite and to ensure that the research interviews could be carried out in that village.

Still another interviewer, Mrs. Masanja, was working in a village in the Pwani region along the coast of the Indian Ocean when cholera broke out in that village. She wisely chose to abandon the interviews there, which reduced the 1993 sample size by one ward.

The unsung heroes of this research, the Tanzanian interviewers, deserve a great deal of credit for carrying out this important work under difficult circumstances.

may determine whether people are subjected to medical or social remedies. Imagine a medical researcher slanting drug-testing results to suggest that a new drug is more effective than it is or covering up the negative side effects of the drug—with the consequence of more patients being given the drug.

Or imagine an evaluation of a prison rehabilitation program being slanted to make the program seem more effective than it is. Limited resources might be diverted to support the ineffective program and possibly even harm the prisoners subjected to it. That's not the worst example, however.

You may recall that in Chapter 3 we mentioned the Tuskegee Syphilis Study, which began in Alabama in the early 1930s. The program claimed to provide free treatment for syphilis to poor African-American men suffering from the disease. Over the years that followed, several hundred men participated in the program. What they didn't know was that they were not actually receiving any treatment at all; the physicians conducting the study merely wanted to observe the natural progress of the disease. Even after penicillin was found to be an effective cure, the researchers still withheld the treatment. While there is no doubt unanimous agreement today as to the unethical nature of the study, this was not the case at the time. Even when the study began being reported in research publications, the researchers refused to acknowledge they had done anything wrong. When professional complaints were finally lodged with the U.S. Centers for Disease Control in 1965, there was no reply (Jones 1981). This study had a clear absence of informed consent. The subjects were deceived and put at grave risk—the researchers withheld a known and effective treatment.

Research designs that would yield the most scientifically decisive evidence are not always ethical. It is essential to evaluate a research design based on whether the subjects are being treated fairly, whether they are being denied assistance or benefits as a result of the study, and whether they have been clearly informed about the potential risks involved in the research. It is the responsibility of the researcher to ensure that participation is voluntary and that participants may withdraw at any time. In our earlier example of the evaluation of the new psychotherapy treatment for gambling addiction, recall that we said it would likely be unethical to withdraw therapy altogether from the control group. Despite the compromise of ideal design, it would be ethically warranted to allow their conventional therapy to continue. In this same study, it would be our ethical responsibility to honestly inform the subjects of all known risks and the potential for unanticipated consequences. Moreover, it would be unethical to give subjects false hopes of positive treatment outcomes as a way to obtain their voluntary participation.

Issues of responsibility to subjects, informed consent, voluntary participation, and deception are ever-present in evaluation research. Researchers must carefully weigh the risks and benefits to both the human subjects and the larger community.

USE OF RESEARCH RESULTS

One more facts-of-life aspect of evaluation research concerns how evaluations are used. Because the purpose of evaluation research is to determine the success or failure of social interventions, you might think it reasonable that a program would automatically be continued or terminated based on the results of the research.

Reality isn't that simple and reasonable, however. Other factors intrude on the assessment of evaluation research results, sometimes blatantly and sometimes subtly. Research indicating that boot camps are ineffective as a way to control youth crime was becoming prevalent in the literature in the late 20th century. The policy of getting tough with youth and scaring them into good behaviour proved counterproductive. Researchers found that those exposed to the boot camp experience were more likely—not less likely—to reoffend. None of this evidence stopped Premier Mike Harris and his Ontario Conservative government in the 1990s from calling for a get-tough policy on young offenders—more specifically, for putting violent young offenders into boot camps to secure a safer society.

Why are such policies often proposed and at times even implemented? Some argue that it has much to do with politics—it's what the public wants to hear. Promoting such policies can help win elections and voter support, independent of the fact that they may be poorly designed for addressing the issues at hand. There are times, however, when those in charge simply believe, along with others, that the research evidence is wrong. In either case, the research contradicts some deep-seated understanding that is widely held about what *should* work, independent of what the evidence indicates. The research results therefore may be ignored or set aside.

A good example of the neglect of research in the creation of policy can be found in an article by Patricia Erickson (1998). Her abstract nicely summarizes the specific policy her article examines—the creation of a new Canadian drug law:

> After four years, two governments, and three Parliamentary committees, the Controlled Drugs and Substances Act was proclaimed in May 1997. Despite a rich legacy of empirical research pointing drug policy in a new direction, away from aggressive criminalization, the new law reaffirms both the seriously deviant status of illicit drug users and the primacy of the criminal justice model over public health and social justice alternatives.
>
> (1998:263)

Erickson is talking about 25 years of drug policy debate in the Canadian social science research literature—research evidence that was "often presented directly to the policy makers" yet was ultimately rejected.

Less dramatic examples of the failure to follow the implications of evaluation research could be listed endlessly. Undoubtedly every evaluation researcher can point to studies he or she conducted—studies providing clear research results and obvious policy implications—that were ignored.

There are three important reasons why the implications of the evaluation research results are not always put into practice. First, the implications may not always be presented in a way that the nonresearchers can understand. Second, evaluation results sometimes contradict deeply held beliefs as noted above. That's often the case, for example, when it comes to research and evaluation of policies toward crime and punishment. If *everybody knows* that harsh punishment deters criminal behaviour and reduces crime, then it's likely that research results to the contrary will have little immediate impact. By the same token, people thought Copernicus was crazy when he said Earth revolved around the Sun; anybody could tell Earth was standing still. The third barrier to the use of evaluation results is vested interests. Imagine that you've devised a new rehabilitation program that you're convinced will keep ex-convicts from returning to prison, and that people have taken to calling it "the ____ Plan" (fill in your name). How do you think you're going to feel when our evaluation suggests the program doesn't work? You might apologize for misleading people, fold up your tent, and go into another line of work. But more likely, you'd call our research worthless and begin intense lobbying with the appropriate authorities to have your program continue.

By its nature, evaluation research takes place in the midst of real life, affecting it and being affected by it. Here's another example, well known to social researchers.

Rape Reform Legislation For years, many social scientists, advocacy groups, and other observers have noted certain problems with the prosecution of rape cases. The victims of sexual assault were seen as poorly treated when attempting to seek criminal justice. The rate of charges laid was low, and when the offender was brought to trial, all too often, it was felt, the victim ended up suffering almost as much on the witness stand as in the rape itself. Frequently she had to withstand personal attacks about her shady moral character and accusations of encouraging the sex act, attacks aimed at deflecting responsibility from the accused rapist. This negative treatment of sexual assault victims by the criminal justice system and the low level of charges contributed to the high rate of underreporting of such crimes. Criticisms such as these resulted in major changes to the *Criminal Code* of Canada that reformed the rape laws in 1983 (as discussed in Chapter 9).

Julian Roberts and Robert Gebotys (1992:557) tracked the impact of this legislative reform aimed at increasing "the number of reports made to the police" and improving "the processing of cases of sexual aggression by the police and the courts." It was generally expected that the new legislation would encourage women to report acts of sexual aggression while at the same time encouraging a decrease in the number of offences reported as unfounded and an increase in the number of charges laid. (If the investigating officers decide that a crime was not attempted or did not occur, it is reported as unfounded.) To examine these expected outcomes, the researchers used existing statistics from the Canadian Uniform Crime Reports (UCR) and focused on the period from 1979 to 1988.

You may recall from our discussion in Chapter 9 that because the offences of rape and indecent assault were altered significantly in the new Canadian sexual assault law, a comparable valid measure of rape following the legal reform is not directly available in the UCR statistics. Rape and other sexual assaults were incorporated into three levels of seriousness of sexual assault, so there is no direct correspondence of offences pre- and post-reform. Nonetheless, the researchers were able to establish a valid, comparable measure for the pre- and post-reform periods by combining the pre-reform offences of rape and indecent assault and then combining the three levels of sexual assault for the post-reform period, since "the new offences capture all the incidents previously classified as one of the prereform offences." They also analyzed the data on all nonsexual assaults over the same period for the purpose of comparative analysis. In this way they could examine whether there was a change in reporting for assault charges in general or whether change was particular to sexual assaults.

Roberts and Gebotys, therefore, were able to present

> ...national data on the effects of the 1983 reforms on four critical statistics relating to sexual assault: (a) reports made to the police, (b) classification by the police of those reports among the three levels of sexual assault, (c) the founding rate, and (d) the charging rate. These statistics concern the "front-end" of the criminal justice system, and are only part of the story. Rape reform legislation also addresses deep-end issues such as conviction rates and sentencing trends. However, national statistics on conviction rates and sentencing are not published in Canada (see Roberts, 1990a).
> (Roberts and Gebotys 1992:556)

Using time-series analyses to analyze the data, they found that the legislation was successful in meeting one of its goals:

> Ironically, its success has been in attracting more victims into the system, rather than in changing the way that the system functions. The reforms have had no significant effect upon the decision as to whether a particular case is founded and as to whether a charge is laid in the case.
> (Roberts and Gebotys 1992:571)

Finally, since their evaluation study indicated that the reform legislation failed to have an impact on the processing of sexual assault cases by the police, they were able to direct attention to where greater research and intervention is needed. It is the police who determine whether a report is classified as an offence and whether, and at what level, a charge is laid. Their actions have "consequences for all subsequent stages of the criminal justice process" (p. 572). Therefore, attention must be directed to reforming police practices.

This study demonstrates the importance of following up on social interventions to determine whether, in what ways, and to what degree they accomplish their intended results, and where greater research and intervention may be needed to accomplish them.

By now, you've seen various scientific and nonscientific aspects of evaluation research that affect how its results are used. But this "messiness" is balanced by the potential contributions that evaluation research can make toward the betterment of human life.

SOCIAL INDICATORS RESEARCH

We'd like to conclude this chapter with a type of research that combines what you've learned about evaluation research and the analysis of existing data. A rapidly growing field in social research involves the development and monitoring of **social indicators**—aggregated statistics that reflect the social condition of a society or social subgroup. Researchers use social indicators to monitor aspects of social life in much the same way that economists use indexes such as gross national product per capita as an indicator of a nation's economic development.

Suppose we wanted to compare the relative health conditions in different societies. One strategy would be to compare their death rates (number of deaths per 1,000 population). Or, more specifically, we could look at infant mortality: the number of infants who die during their first year of life among every 1,000 births. Depending on the particular aspect of health conditions we were interested in, we could devise any number of other measures: physicians per capita, hospital beds per capita, days of hospitalization per capita, and so forth. Notice that intersocietal comparisons are facilitated by calculating per capita rates (dividing by the size of the population). This general strategy was used in the following example to chart social change in modern societies.

Over the last century, Western societies have changed dramatically. Some research suggests that the core changes in these societies occurred in the decades following 1960. If this is true, have the changes in modern Western societies been quite comparable, with most societies following a typical pattern? Or are modern societies following unique paths of change?

social indicators Measurements that reflect the quality or nature of social life, such as crime rates, infant mortality rates, number of physicians per 100,000 population, and so forth. Social indicators are often monitored to determine the nature of social change in a society.

To investigate this question, a team of Canadian researchers used social indicators to document how Canadian society had changed on 78 indicators between 1960 and 2000. The indicators covered a broad spectrum of social changes, including such topics as lifestyle, social stratification, attitudes and values, labour market conditions, and demography. The results were documented in a book called *Recent Social Trends in Canada, 1960–2000* (Roberts et al. 2005).

Teams of researchers in ten other nations used the same social indicators to document social changes in their societies for the same period. This approach allowed intersociety comparisons in trajectories of change since 1960. Comparison of these national reports allowed the researchers to answer the original question: Modern societies show similar patterns of change, incorporating important cultural variations on the themes (Langlois 1994).

Before we go further, recall from Chapter 9 the problems involved in using existing statistics. They're often unreliable, reflecting their modes of collection, storage, and calculation. With this in mind, we'll look at some of the ways we can use social indicators for evaluation research on a large scale.

THE DEATH PENALTY AND DETERRENCE

In 2010, CBC News reported the results of an EKOS poll in which 40 percent of Canadians supported reintroducing capital punishment (CBC News 2010). In 2007, Gray and colleagues reported that 44 percent of Canadians favoured or somewhat favoured the death penalty for those convicted of murder. People may or may not favour the death penalty, but is it effective?

Does the death penalty deter capital crimes such as murder? This question is hotly debated every time a government considers eliminating or reinstating capital punishment and every time someone is executed in the United States. Those supporting capital punishment often argue that the threat of execution will keep potential murderers from killing people. Opponents of capital punishment often argue that it has no effect in that regard. Social indicators can help shed some light on the question.

Research conducted on the use of the death penalty in the United States, a country where the death penalty exists in some states but not others, provides a good illustration. If capital punishment actually deters people from committing murder, then we should expect to find lower murder rates in those states that have the death penalty than in those that do not. The relevant comparisons in this instance are not only possible, but they've been also compiled and published. William Bailey (1975) compiled data that directly contradict the view that the death penalty deters murderers. In both 1967 and 1968, those states with capital punishment had dramatically *higher* murder rates than those without capital punishment. In 1967, for states without capital punishment, the average rate of first-degree murder was 0.18 per 100,000 population compared to 0.47 murders per 100,000 population for states with capital punishment. In 1968, the respective comparison was 0.21 versus 0.58 first-degree murders per 100,000 population. When looking at second-degree murders in 1967, the rate per 100,000 population in non-capital punishment states was 0.30, but it was 0.92 in capital punishment states. In 1968, the rates respectively were 0.43 compared to 1.03.

Some people criticized the interpretation of Bailey's data, saying that most states had not used the death penalty in recent years, even when they had it on the books. That could explain why it didn't seem to work as a deterrent. Further analysis, however, contradicts this explanation. When Bailey compared those states that hadn't used the death penalty with those that had, he found no real difference in murder rates.

Another counterexplanation is possible, however. It could be the case that the interpretation given Bailey's data was *backward*. Maybe the existence of the death penalty as an option was a consequence of high murder rates: those states with high rates instituted it; those with low rates didn't institute it or repealed it if they had it on the books. It could be the case, then, that instituting the death penalty would bring murder rates down, and repealing it would increase murders and still produce—in a broad aggregate—the murder rates noted above. Not so, however.

Analyses over time do not show an increase in murder rates when a state repeals the death penalty or a decrease in murders when one is instituted. A more recent examination by Bailey and Peterson (1994) confirmed the earlier findings and also indicated that law enforcement officials doubted the deterrent effect. Further, the pattern observed by Bailey in 1967 and 1968 has persisted over time, even when we take into account the substantial increase in the overall murder rate. In 1999, for example, the 38 death penalty states had a combined murder rate of 5.86 per 100,000 and in 2006 it was 5.90, compared with a combined murder rate in 1999 of 3.84 among the 12 states that lack the death penalty and 3.85 in 2006 (U.S. Bureau of the Census 2001:22, 183; 2009:17, 189).

Notice from the preceding discussion that it's possible to use social indicators data for comparison across groups either at one time or across some period of time. Often, doing both sheds the most light on the subject.

At present, work on the use of social indicators is proceeding on two fronts. On the one hand, researchers are developing ever more refined indicators—finding which indicators of a general variable are the most useful in monitoring social life. At the same time, research is being devoted to discovering the relationships among variables within whole societies.

There is special value in evaluation research in general. Throughout human history, we've been tinkering with our social arrangements, seeking better results. Evaluation research provides a way for us to learn more quickly whether a particular tinkering really makes things better.

MAIN POINTS

- Evaluation research is a form of applied research that studies the effects of social interventions.
- A careful formulation of the problem, including relevant measurements and criteria of success or failure, is essential in evaluation research. Key steps in measurement include specifying outcomes—what the intervention is intended to accomplish, measuring experimental contexts, specifying the intervention under study and the target population of the intervention, deciding whether to create new measures or use existing ones, and assessing the intervention's potential cost-effectiveness.
- Evaluation researchers typically use experimental or quasi-experimental designs. Examples of quasi-experimental designs include time-series studies and the use of nonequivalent control groups.
- Evaluation researchers can also use qualitative methods of data collection, and mixed methods research combining quantitative and qualitative approaches is increasingly common in evaluation research.
- Evaluation research entails special logistical and ethical problems because it's embedded in the day-to-day events of real life.
- The implications of evaluation research won't necessarily be put into practice, especially if they conflict with official points of view.
- Social indicators are aggregated descriptions of populations such as societies or social subgroups. They can provide an understanding of broad social processes.

REVIEW QUESTIONS AND EXERCISES

1. Identify at least two deliberate social interventions, such as raising the drinking age to 21. For each, discuss how you would specify the perceived problem and describe the type of research that would evaluate whether the intervention was successful in solving it.
2. Use the Web or the library to locate a report of evaluation research that was conducted to monitor the implementation of a policy or

program for which a federal, provincial, or local government agency is responsible. Write a short summary of the study design and the findings.

3. Suppose a community created a teen clubhouse with a game room, organized sports, and other activities and entertainment in an effort to keep youths off the streets and thus reduce youth crime. Describe how you might go about evaluating the effectiveness of the centre. Indicate whether your design would be experimental, quasi-experimental, or qualitative (or some combination of these).

4. Take a minute to think of the many ways your society has changed during your own lifetime. Specify three social indicators that could be used in monitoring the effects of at least one of those changes on the quality of life in your society.

CONTINUITY PROJECT

■ COUNTING CONSEQUENCES

Sexual inequality has led to a lot of inappropriate conduct both on and off university campuses. A central issue relates to confusion surrounding competing claims of sexual consent. (Think Jian Ghomeshi.)

This discussion is complicated for many reasons. For example, laws are not sufficiently clear and there "is no clear-cut line of decorum for men and women who interact with each other socially or at work" (Hassan 2014). In addition, social context and definitions of the situation complicate the meaning of messages sent and interpretation of what is received.

In California and other states, legislators are trying to clarify matters. New legislation responds to the rising number of sexual assault and rape incidents on university campuses. Rather than using a "no means no" lens to examine the issue, new laws are based on a "yes means yes" perspective. Instead of having to opt out, participants are required to opt in. The California legislation defines consent as "an affirmative, conscious and voluntary agreement to engage in sexual activity" (quoted in Associated Press 2014). This policy rules out silence and lack of resistance as legitimate claims.

Imagine you are retained by the State of California to conduct a formative, qualitative investigation of the new law's implementation and its outcomes on university students. Outline the approach you would take. What indicators would you attend to? Justify how your study could lead to constructive suggestions for improvement in the legislation.

PART 4

ANALYSIS OF DATA

In this part of the book, we'll discuss the analysis of data obtained through social scientific research, and we'll examine the steps that separate observation from the final reporting of findings.

Chapter 13 covers qualitative data analysis. We begin with the search for patterns and themes and proceed to address the role of theory in approaches to analysis. We then cover some common techniques and procedures that are useful aids in bringing order to, and searching for meaning within, a mass of qualitative data. After presenting an example that illustrates this process, we look at the use of computers in managing qualitative data.

Chapter 14 begins by addressing the quantification of data that may have been collected through any of the modes of observation discussed in Part 3. It then turns to an examination of methods of analyzing and presenting the data related to a single variable. Following this, we look at the relationship between two variables and learn how to construct and read simple percentage tables. The chapter ends with an introduction to multivariate analysis.

Chapter 15 pursues multivariate analysis and the logic of causal analysis through an examination of the elaboration model developed by Paul Lazarsfeld. Understanding the logic of the elaboration model in the context of contingency table analysis provides a good foundation for understanding other statistical techniques and the patterns of relationships that such techniques are designed to uncover. The logic of percentage tables and the elaboration model can also be useful when attempting to uncover relationships in qualitative data analysis.

Chapter 16 presents an introduction to some of the more commonly used statistical methods in social science research, including an overview of a more advanced method of multivariate analysis—multiple regression. Rather than merely showing how to compute statistics by these methods (computers can do that), we've attempted to place them in the context of earlier theoretical and logical discussions. Thus you should come away from this chapter knowing when to use various statistical measures as well as how to compute them.

Chapter 17 introduces you to the fundamentals of reading, designing and writing social research. Conducting effective social research requires careful forethought and planning, and such efforts will be fruitless unless the work is communicated effectively to others. So this chapter introduces some special skills involved in reading the research of others as well as designing and writing about your own.

QUALITATIVE DATA ANALYSIS

Bringing order to a mass of observations obtained through participant observation, in-depth interviews, focus groups, archival documents, and other qualitative research techniques is a major goal of qualitative analysis. Discerning patterns and finding the underlying meaning in such observations is aided by a number of procedures and techniques such as coding and memoing. The use of computer programs designed to manage qualitative data can help the researcher in this process.

IN THIS CHAPTER ...

INTRODUCTION

Recall that all research methods aim to link abstract ideas with empirical evidence. One way or another, the goal is to make sense of the empirical patterns that constitute data or evidence. Although the traditional model of social science research focuses on quantitative data analysis techniques, this is not the only approach to making sense of social observations. In recent years, **qualitative analysis**—methods for examining social research data without converting them to a numerical format—is enjoying a resurgence of interest. The data used in qualitative analysis are wide ranging and may include social artifacts, researchers' field notes, audio files, transcribed interviews, and the like. Its utility in helping us understand a broad range of evidence is one thing that makes qualitative analysis so attractive.

Qualitative analysis predates quantitative procedures. Unlike quantitative procedures, which often involve a series of routine steps, qualitative analysis is a more creative craft in its search to understand experience. In this chapter, we begin with the links between research and theory in qualitative analysis. Then we examine some procedures that have proved useful in pursuing the theoretical aims. After considering some simple manual techniques, we'll briefly discuss the use of computer programs in qualitative data analysis.

LINKING THEORY AND ANALYSIS

As indicated in Chapter 10 and elsewhere in this book, qualitative research methods involve a continuing interplay between data collection and theory. Observations are made and patterns are detected. Concepts and propositions are inductively developed to help understand the evidence, which leads to more refined observation. This, in turn, encourages more insightful conceptualization and commentary. In this regard, qualitative analysis uses the image of theory as consisting of "*plausible* relationships proposed among *concepts* and *sets of concepts*" (Strauss and Corbin 1994:278). The stress on "plausible" indicates that theories represent our best understanding of how life operates.

As noted in earlier chapters, qualitative research can be conducted for descriptive or explanatory purposes. For example, Ashley Mears's (2011) qualitative investigation provides an insider's description of what being a fashion model is really like. Diane Vaughan's *The* Challenger *Launch Decision* (1996) provides an ethnography of NASA's culture, which she uses to help explain why the *Challenger* spacecraft exploded. Both of these types of qualitative analysis begin with the search for empirical patterns.

DISCOVERING PATTERNS

Detecting patterns in a set of observations typically begins with a search for similarities and dissimilarities. The similarities researchers seek are those patterns of interaction and events that are generally common to what they're studying. In a study of jaywalking, for example, you might notice common patterns of behaviour, such as the large numbers of participants who check for police officers before darting across the street. Once you become aware of the possibility of a pattern, you should return and check carefully to determine whether the pattern you recognized is indeed widespread. Do all the participants in a religious revival meeting shout "Amen" at the appropriate times? Do all prostitutes dress seductively?

After you notice a commonality, you become more deliberate in observing its frequency and position in the situation you're observing. If something is occurring routinely, you may ask why that should be the case. An explanation may suggest conditions under which you may not observe it, and you may look around for those conditions in order to test your expectations. This leads to attending to differences.

No pattern is universal; every one is contingent on some conditions. Accordingly, researchers are on the watch for deviation from observed patterns. Although most of the participants in a religious revival meeting murmur "Amen" throughout the leader's sermon, you may note a few who don't. Why do they deviate from the

qualitative analysis Methods for examining research evidence without converting it to numerical form.

norm? In what other ways do they differ from the other participants? The researcher might find a range of patterns that leads to a typology of behaviours. This might then lead to the search for potential social characteristics that are associated with these different types.

For example, how do different people handle the problem of standing in a line for tickets at a movie theatre? Some stare into space, some strike up conversations with strangers, some talk to themselves, some keep standing on tiptoes to see if the line is really moving, some keep counting their money, some read, and so forth. In such situations, an important part of your initial task as a researcher is to create a classification of behaviours: an organized list of the variety of types. Having done that, you then seek to discover other characteristics associated with those different types of behaviour. Are the "rich-looking" or "poor-looking" moviegoers more likely to re-count their money? Do men strike up more conversations with strangers than women do? Do old people talk to themselves more than young people do?

John Lofland and colleagues (2006:149–165) suggest six different ways of looking for patterns in a particular research topic. Let's suppose you're interested in analyzing child abuse in a certain neighbourhood. Here are some questions you might ask yourself, in order to make sense out of your data:

1. *Frequencies:* How often does child abuse occur among families in the neighbourhood under study? (Realize that there may be a difference between the frequency and what people are willing to tell you.)
2. *Magnitudes:* What are the levels of abuse? How brutal are they?
3. *Structures:* What are the different types of abuse—physical, mental, sexual? Are they related in any particular manner?
4. *Processes:* Is there any order among the elements of structure? Do abusers begin with mental abuse and move on to physical and sexual abuse, or does the order of elements vary?
5. *Causes:* What are the causes of child abuse? Is it more common in particular social classes or among different religious or ethnic groups? Does it occur more often during good times or bad?
6. *Consequences:* How does child abuse affect the victims, in both the short and the long term? What changes does it cause in the abusers?

For the most part, in examining your data you'll look for patterns appearing across several observations that typically represent different cases under study. This approach is called **cross-case analysis**. There are two basic strategies for cross-case analysis: variable-oriented and case-oriented analysis. **Variable-oriented analysis** is the approach used in the quantitative research model. We will explore this approach in Chapter 14, but as the label indicates this approach focuses analysis on interrelations among variables—with the people observed primarily being the carriers of those variables.

Variable-oriented analysis uses the idea of nomothetic explanation introduced in Chapter 1. In nomothetic explanations, the aim is to achieve a partial, overall explanation using relatively few variables. The political pollster who attempts to explain voting intentions on the basis of two or three key variables is using this approach. No pretence exists that the researcher can predict every individual's behaviour, nor even explain any one person's motivations in full.

By contrast, qualitative analysis relies on idiographic explanation, in which the goal is to understand a particular case fully. In the voting example, we would try to learn everything we could about all the factors that came into play in determining one person's decision on how to vote. This orientation lies at the base of **case-oriented analysis**.

cross-case analysis The use of either a case-oriented or a variable-oriented approach to compare cases in the search for pattern description and explanation.

variable-oriented analysis The examination of a limited set of considerations (variables) across a large number of cases in search of nomothetic explanation.

case-oriented analysis The detailed examination of a limited set of particular cases in search of idiographic explanation.

> In a case-oriented analysis, we would look more closely into a particular case, say, Case 005, who is female, middle-class, has parents with high expectations, and so on. These are, however, "thin" measures. To do a genuine case analysis, we need to look at a full history of Case 005; Nynke van der Molen, whose mother trained as a social worker but is bitter over the fact that she never worked outside the home, and whose father wants Nynke to work in the family florist shop. Chronology is also important: two years ago, Nynke's closest friend decided to go to college, just before Nynke began work in a stable and just before Nynke's mother showed her a scrapbook from social work school. Nynke then decided to enroll in veterinary studies.
>
> (Miles and Huberman 1994:436)

This abbreviated commentary gives a sense of the detail involved in this type of analysis. Of course, an entire analysis would be more extensive and pursue issues in greater depth. When complete, however, a full, idiographic examination does not tell us about people in general. It offers no theory about why people choose to attend college. For this reason, qualitative investigations typically use cross-case analysis—where two or more cases are systematically examined to account for similarities or differences of interest.

GROUNDED THEORY METHOD

The cross-case method just described should sound somewhat familiar. In the discussion of grounded theory in Chapter 10, we saw how qualitative researchers try to establish theories on an inductive basis. This approach begins with observations rather than hypotheses and seeks to discover patterns and develop theories from the ground up, with no preconceptions, although some research may build and elaborate on earlier grounded theories.

Recall that grounded theory was first developed by the sociologists Barney Glaser and Anselm Strauss (1967), in an attempt to come to grips with their clinical research in medical sociology. Since then it has evolved as a method, with the cofounders taking it in slightly different directions. The following discussion will deal with the basic concepts and procedures of the **grounded theory method (GTM)**.

In addition to the fundamental, inductive tenet of building theory from data, GTM employs the **constant comparative method**. As Glaser and Strauss originally described this method, it involved the following four stages (1967:105–113):

1. *Comparing incidents applicable to each category*: As Glaser and Strauss researched the reactions of nurses to the possible death of patients in their care, the researchers found that the nurses were assessing the "social loss" attendant on a patient's death. Once this concept arose in the analysis of one case, they looked for evidence of the same phenomenon in other cases. When they found the concept arising in the cases of several nurses, they compared the different incidents. This process is similar to conceptualization as described in Chapter 5—specifying the nature and dimensions of the many concepts arising from the data.
2. *Integrating categories and their properties*: Here the researcher begins to note relationships among concepts. In the assessment of social loss, for example, Glaser and Strauss found that nurses took special notice of a patient's age, education, and family responsibilities. For these relationships to emerge, however, it was necessary for the researchers to have noticed all these concepts.
3. *Delimiting the theory*: Eventually, as the patterns of relationships among concepts become clearer, the researcher can ignore some of the concepts that were initially noted but are evidently irrelevant to the inquiry. In addition to the number of categories being reduced, the theory itself may become simpler. In the examination of

grounded theory method (GTM) An inductive approach to theory construction using the constant comparative method.

constant comparative method An inductive approach that relies on continuously comparing observations with one another and the evolving inductive theory.

social loss, for example, Glaser and Strauss found that the assessment processes could be generalized beyond nurses and dying patients: They seemed to apply to the ways all staff dealt with all patients (dying or not).

4. *Writing theory*: Finally, the researcher must put his or her findings into words to be shared with others. As you may have already experienced for yourself, the act of communicating your understanding of a topic actually modifies and even improves your own grasp of it. In GTM, the writing stage is regarded as a part of the research process. A later section of this chapter (on memoing) elaborates on this point.

This brief overview gives you an idea of how grounded theory proceeds. The many techniques associated with GTM can be found both in print and on the Web. One of the key publications is Anselm Strauss and Juliet Corbin's *Basics of Qualitative Research* (1998), which elaborates on and extends many of the concepts and techniques found in the original 1967 Glaser and Strauss volume.

GTM is only one analytic approach to qualitative data. In the remainder of this section, we'll look at some other specialized techniques.

SEMIOTICS

Semiotics is commonly defined as the "science of signs" and has to do with symbols and meanings. It's often associated with content analysis, though it can be applied in a variety of research contexts.

Peter Manning and Betsy Cullum-Swan (1994:466) offer some sense of the applicability of semiotics, as follows: "Although semiotics is based on language, language is but one of the many sign systems of varying degrees of unity, applicability, and complexity. Morse code, etiquette, mathematics, music, and even highway signs are examples of semiotic systems."

There is no meaning inherent in any sign, however. Meanings reside in minds. So, a particular sign means something to a particular person. However, the agreements we have about the meanings associated with particular signs make semiotics a *social* science. As Manning and Cullum-Swan point out,

> For example, a lily is an expression linked conventionally to death, Easter, and resurrection as a content. Smoke is linked to cigarettes and to cancer, and Marilyn Monroe to sex. Each of these connections is social and arbitrary, so that many kinds of links exist between expression and content.
>
> (1994:466)

To explore this contention, see if you can link the signs with their meanings in Figure 13-1. We are confident enough that you know all the "correct" associations. The point is this: What do any of these signs have to do with their "meanings"? Draft an email message to a Martian social scientist explaining the logic at work here. (You might want to include some emoticons, like :)—another example of semiotics.)

While there is no doubt a story behind each of the linkages in Figure 13-1, the meanings you and I "know" today are socially constructed. Semiotic analysis involves a search for the meanings intentionally or unintentionally attached to signs.

Consider the sign shown in Figure 13-2, from a hotel lobby. What's being communicated by the rather ambiguous sign? The first sentence seems to be saying that the hotel is up to date with the current move away from tobacco in Canada. Guests who want a smoke-free environment need look no further: This is a healthy place to stay. At the same time, says the second sentence, the hotel would not like to be seen as inhospitable to smokers. There's room for everyone under this

SIGN	MEANING
1. Poinsettia	a. Good luck
2. Horseshoe	b. First prize
3. Blue ribbon	c. Christmas
4. "Say cheese"	d. Acting
5. "Break a leg"	e. Smile for a picture

FIGURE 13-1 Matching Signs and Their Meanings.

semiotics The study of signs and the meanings associated with them.

FIGURE 13-2 **Mixed Signals?**
Source: © Cengage Learning

roof. No one need feel excluded. This sign is more easily understood within a marketing paradigm than one of logic.

The "signs" examined in semiotics, of course, are not limited to this kind of sign. Most are quite different, in fact. **Signs** are any things that are assigned special meanings. They can include such things as logos, animals, people, and consumer products. Sometimes the symbolism is subtle. You can find a classic analysis in Erving Goffman's *Gender Advertisements* (1979). Goffman focused on advertising pictures found in magazines and newspapers. The overt purpose of the ads, of course, was to sell specific products. But what else was communicated? What in particular did the ads say about men and women?

When Goffman analyzed pictures containing both men and women, he was struck by the fact that men were almost always bigger and taller than the women accompanying them. (In many cases, in fact, the picture managed to convey the distinct impression that the women were merely accompanying the men.) Although the most obvious explanation is that men are, on average, heavier and taller than women, Goffman suggested the pattern had a different meaning: that size and placement implied *status*. Those who were larger and taller presumably had higher social standing—more power and authority (1979:28). Goffman suggested the ads communicated that men were more important than women.

In the spirit of Freud's comment that "Sometimes a cigar is just a cigar" (he was a smoker), how would you decide whether the ads simply reflected the biological differences in the average sizes of men and women or whether they sent a message about social status? In part, Goffman's conclusion was based on an analysis of the exceptional cases: those in which the women appeared taller than the men. In these cases, the men were typically of a lower social status—the chef beside the society matron, for example. This confirmed Goffman's main point that size and height indicated social status.

The same conclusion could be drawn from pictures with men of different heights. Those of higher status were taller, whether it was the gentleman speaking to a waiter or the boss guiding the work of his younger assistants. Where actual height was unclear, Goffman noted the placement of heads in the picture. The assistants were crouching down while the boss leaned over them. The servant's head was bowed so it was lower than that of the master.

The latent message conveyed by the ads, then, was that the higher a person's head appeared in the ad, the more important that person was. And in the great majority of ads containing men and women, the former were clearly portrayed as more important. The subliminal message in the ads, whether intended or not, was that men are more powerful and enjoy a higher status than do women.

Goffman examined several differences besides physical size in the portrayal of men and women. As another example, men were typically presented in active roles, women in passive ones. The (male) doctor examined the child while the (female) nurse or mother looked on, often admiringly. A man guided a woman's tennis stroke (all the while keeping his head higher than hers). A man gripped the reins of his galloping horse, while a woman rode behind him with her arms wrapped around his waist. A woman held the football, while a man kicked it. A man took a photo, which contained only women.

sign Any thing that has an assigned special meaning.

Goffman suggested that such pictorial patterns subtly perpetuated a host of gender stereotypes. Even as people spoke publicly about gender equality, these advertising photos established a quiet backdrop of men and women in their "proper roles."

CONVERSATION ANALYSIS

Language is arguably the most important symbolic system humans have. The qualitative study of language is assisted through conversation analysis. **Conversation analysis (CA)** seeks to understand the basic structures of social interaction and social order through the detailed study of everyday talk.

David Silverman (1993:125f), reviewing the work of other CA theorists and researchers, speaks of three fundamental assumptions. First, conversation is a socially structured activity. Like other social structures, it includes established rules of behaviour. For example, we're expected to take turns, with only one person speaking at a time. In telephone conversations, the person answering the call is expected to speak first (as in "Hello"). You can verify the existence of this rule, incidentally, by picking up the phone without speaking.

Second, Silverman points out that conversations must be understood contextually. The same utterance will have totally different meanings in different contexts. For example, notice how the meaning of "Same to you!" varies if preceded by "I don't like your looks" or by "Have a nice day."

Third, CA aims to understand the structure and meaning of conversation through excruciatingly accurate transcripts of conversations. Not only are the exact words recorded, but all the *uhs*, *ers*, bad grammar, and pauses are also noted. Pauses, in fact, are measured to the nearest tenth of a second.

The practical uses of this type of analysis are many. Ann Marie Kinnell and Douglas Maynard (1996), for example, analyzed conversations between staff and clients at an HIV-testing clinic to examine how information about safe sex was communicated. Among other things, they found that the staff tended to provide standard information rather than try to speak directly to a client's specific circumstances. Moreover, they seemed reluctant to give direct advice about safe sex, settling for information alone.

conversation analysis (CA) The search to understand the basic structures of social interaction and social order through the detailed study of everyday talk.

narrative analysis (NA) Strategies for analyzing text (whether talk, document, or other) that focus on how people use stories to make sense of themselves, their experiences, and the world.

NARRATIVE ANALYSIS

> What unites people? Armies? Gold? Flags? ... Stories. There's nothing in the world more powerful than a good story. Nothing can stop it. No enemy can defeat it. And who has a better story than Bran the Broken? The boy who fell from a high tower and lived. He knew he'd never walk again, so he learned to fly. He crossed beyond The Wall, a crippled boy, and became the Three-Eyed Raven. He is our memory, the keeper of all our stories; the wars, weddings, births, massacres, famines, our triumphs, our defeats, our past. Who better to lead us into the future.
>
> Tyrion Lannister[1]

Whether you liked how the hit HBO series *Game of Thrones* ended, or hated it, or were happily oblivious, it was an epic story, whose final plot twist cheekily rested on an appeal to the force of a good story. A key character, Tyrion Lannister, makes this speech to a Council of Lords in the last episode of *Game of Thrones*. After eight seasons and dozens of episodes, tens of millions of viewers (with almost as many hypothesized endings) wanted to know—who would end up being the ruler of the Seven Kingdoms of Westeros? In successfully making the case for another character, Bran Stark, to be king, Tyrion invokes the power and importance of stories to give form and meaning to our lives, our communities and societies. This appreciation of the importance of storytelling to the processes of making sense of our experiences, ourselves, our world, and our social relations with others, is central to the **narrative analysis (NA)** approach to qualitative data analysis.

1 "The Iron Throne," *Game of Thrones*, HBO series.

The importance of storytelling for bringing order and meaning to our lives is what Bruner (1986) termed "narrative modes of knowing." We create interpretations in the form of narratives and these narratives are "the building blocks of the construction of reality and meaning" (Wertz et al. 2011:65). He contrasted narrative knowledge, which is based on rich and multilayered interpretations of meaning that privilege "the particulars of lived experience" (Josselson 2011: 225), with "paradigmatic" knowing, which is rooted in classification and categorization (Bruner 1986). Accordingly, narrative analysis focuses on the detailed stories drawn from participants that reveal how they make sense of their lives. Generally, narrative data is obtained through interviews, but it can also come from written documents. It is important to understand narratives "contextually, as influenced by the circumstances under which they were obtained, with consideration given to the intended audience and the motives the narrator may have had for constructing the narrative in a particular way" (Josselson 2011, p. 225).

Narrative analysis relies in part on other methods, such as discourse analysis and coding, but what perhaps most distinguishes it from other approaches is the emphasis on the whole account, rather than fragments or parts of it. "It is not the parts that are significant in human life, but how the parts are integrated to create a whole—which is meaning ... understanding the whole illuminates the parts, which in turn create the whole" (Josselson 2011, p 226). Other key features of NA are that stories, including self-representation and understanding, are viewed as living and evolving, not fixed. Also, the self is viewed as multiple, as comprised of "different voices in dialogue with one another" (p. 227). Different versions, or aspects, of the self are bidding for air time, rubbing against and playing off one another, threading into the narrative weave.

Although there is no standardized set of steps for conducting NA, there are a number of shared strategies. For the purposes of introducing NA, we will describe four basic operations, as outlined by Josselson (2011, p. 228).[2]

1. We do an overall reading of the interview to get a sense of how the narrative is structured and the general theme or themes. Then, we return to each specific part to develop its meaning, and then consider the more global meanings in light of the deepened meaning of the parts.
2. We do multiple readings to identify different "voices" of the self and to create a view of how these selves are in dialogue with one another.
3. These iterative readings continue until we develop a "good Gestalt"[3] that encompasses contradictions. The different themes make sensible patterns and enter into a coherent unity.
4. The work also enters into conversation with the larger theoretical literature so that the researcher can remain sensitive to nuances of meanings expressed and the different contexts into which the meanings may enter.

In the background to all of this the researcher must practise reflexivity, remaining aware of their own preconceptions, and in the context of the interview, remaining aware of the interview as a social encounter and how this may affect the narrative as a socially constructed text.

To illustrate this approach Josselson conducted a narrative analysis on written and interview texts from a graduate student named "Theresa." The basic subject of the narrative (collected as part of a larger project) was understanding the processes of psychological resilience. Theresa had been an opera singer (in a university program) who lost her singing voice due to throat cancer and subsequently changed paths to become a psychology

2 Republished with permission of Guilford Press, from Ruthellen Josseleson, "Narrative research: Constructing, deconstructing and Reconstructing story," in F. Wertz (Eds), *Five ways of doing qualitative analysis: phenomenological psychology, grounded theory, discourse analysis, narrative research, and intuitive inquiry* (pp. 224–242). © 2011; permission conveyed through Copyright Clearance Center, Inc.

3 *Gestalt* means the general quality or overarching character of something, and that the whole of that thing is greater than the sum of parts that make it up.

graduate student. First Josselson reread the narrative several times looking for general themes and structure. In her repeated readings she noted various passages that seemed to suggest the emergence of two main themes—"coping with loss (the tragic narrative)" and "engendering a new life (the romance narrative)." She paid special attention to Theresa's statements about herself and her descriptions of others in relation to herself. Gradually Josselson grouped these statements into three broad subthemes "emotion and logic," "identity," and "self with others." She then reread the passages within each subtheme category examining their interrelationships, any changes in "voice" that conveyed difference experiences, or orientations of self in relation to the different categories. Then she began to construct an overarching account that incorporated these different subthemes. In doing so she realized that they were interwoven in complex ways that cannot be teased out separately without a loss of understanding, since they contribute to the overarching meaning of the whole narrative and are given meaning in relation to the whole narrative.

In essence, Theresa's story is "a narrative of existential aloneness, of coping with repeated threats of death and loss of function, and of using will and logic to guide her passion to overcome those threats and to live a meaningful life" (p. 238). Interwoven into these two main themes of coping with loss and engendering a new life are subthematic tensions related to her struggle to (1) balance her affective and logical selves, (2) to re-establish a new identity in lieu of her former sense of self (as singer), and (3) to reconcile her desire to be strong and independent while still connected to significant others. "All are intertwined as she makes use of others in the shifting balance between her thinking and feeling selves. Her successful quest for identity represents the triumph of her rational self and is itself shored up by others" (p. 238).

NA has been used to study a wide range of phenomena, including family caregivers' experiences of caring for terminally ill family members at home (Thomas et al. 2018), self-injury behaviour by adolescent girls and young women as portrayed in movies (Bareiss 2017), government policy (Gedalof 2018), notions of sustainability or sustainable development (Frank 2017), and experiences of unemployment and underemployment (Blustein et al. 2013).

DISCOURSE ANALYSIS

Discourse can broadly be defined as "*a particular way of talking about and understanding the world (or an aspect of the world)*" (Jørgensen and Phillips 2002:2). Underlying this idea is that communication is structured by particular patterns of language use that people follow when they enter into particular domains of social life, such as medical discourse or political discourse. In its simplest terms, discourse analysis is the analysis of such patterns. In practice, there are a variety of approaches to, or strands of, discourse analysis. But building on Burr (1995) and Gergen and Pallak (1985), Jørgensen and Phillips (2002) posited that, despite some distinct differences, the bulk of these approaches share several common underlying social constructionist premises.[4]

- *A critical approach to taken-for-granted knowledge:*

  > Our knowledge of the world should not be treated as objective truth. Reality is only accessible to us through categories, so our knowledge and representations of the world are not reflections of the reality "out there," but rather are products of our ways of categorising the world, or, in discursive analytical terms, products of discourse.
  > (Jørgensen and Phillips 2002:5)

- *Historical and cultural specificity*: Our views of, and knowledge about, the world are historically and culturally situated. That is, how we understand the world is specific to, or contingent on, the historical or cultural context from within which we encounter it. "Discourse is a form of social action that plays a part in producing the social world—including knowledge, identities, and social relations—and thereby in maintaining specific social patterns" (Jørgensen and Phillips 2002:5). Thus, the human world is socially and

4 Republished with permission of SAGE Publications Ltd. Books, from *Discourse Analysis as Theory and Method*, © 2002; permission conveyed through Copyright Clearance Center, Inc.

discursively constructed, and does not have an external objective foundation or essence that transcends human action.

- *Recognition of the link between knowledge and social processes*: Our understanding of the world is the product of social processes. "Knowledge is created through social interaction in which we construct common truths and compete about what is true and false" (Jørgensen and Phillips 2002:5).
- *Recognition of the link between knowledge and social action:*

> Within a particular worldview, some forms of action become natural, others unthinkable. Different social understandings of the world lead to different social actions, and therefore the social construction of knowledge and truth has social consequences.
> (Jørgensen and Phillips 2002:5)

In sum, most DA approaches hold that language does not reflect some pre-existing reality. Rather, language is structured or patterned by discourses and thereby maintained and/or transformed by discursive practices; hence, meanings can change from discourse to discourse. Understanding how patterns of discourse are maintained or transformed requires an "analysis of the specific contexts in which language is in action" (Jørgensen and Phillips 2002:10). Furthermore, all DA approaches emphasize, to some degree, the relationships among power, language, knowledge, and being. "Discourses contribute centrally to producing the subjects we are, and the objects we can know something about (including ourselves as subjects)" (Jørgensen and Phillips 2002:12). This view leads to a question fundamental to most DA approaches: "*how is the social world, including its subjects and objects, constituted in discourses?*" (p. 12).

There are no standard set of steps for conducting DA, but generally the discourse analyst gives careful focus to the statements and signs ("texts") used to talk or otherwise communicate about something as well as the context in which the texts are created (social, cultural, political, economic). There are many different forms of text in social life that can be subjected to DA (including spoken and written language, gesture, and visual imagery). Some basic strategies include thematic analysis, deconstruction and asking questions of ("interrogating") the text. O'Connor and Payne (2006:832) list a set of questions that can be asked of a text, with particular focus on governmental or organizational policy[5]:

- Where is it written or published? Is it part of a wider text? (e.g., a series of policies, a newspaper report, or an opinion piece)
- Who wrote or said it? Who has the power to make decisions, and how are they using their power? (For example, a government minister, a manager of a program or department)
- What are their interests? (For example, a political party, a disease-specific advocacy group)
- What is being said in the text, and what is not being said?
- To whom is the text addressed and why? (For example, written for the public or professionals)
- What is the emphasis in the text?
- What is missing that would be expected to be there?
- What is hidden altogether? Are there hidden agendas or biases, hidden issues, or hidden aspects of a bigger issue?
- What sorts of decisions have been made, with what level of authority and influence?
- What is its source and authority? (For example, government or organizational policy, a press release)

Bischoping and Gazso (2016:155–165) describe a number of strategies for analyzing textual data[6] (typically from interview transcripts, but they note that the strategies can apply to other texts as well).

To explore identities and subjectivities (i.e., a person's perceptions and interpretations),

- Explore how discourses shape social interactions and institutions, and vice versa.

5 O'Connor, M., and Payne. Discourse analysis: examining the potential for research in palliative care. *Palliative Medicine* 20(8), pp. 829–834. Copyright © 2006 by SAGE Publications. Reprinted by permission of SAGE.

6 Republished with permission of SAGE Publications Ltd. Books, from *Analyzing talk in the social sciences*, © 2016; permission conveyed through Copyright Clearance Center, Inc.

- Ask how discourses represent or shape social identities and subjectivities, keeping an eye out for contradictions.
- Study the unsaid or implicit discourses underlying understandings of social worlds.

To analyze power and ideology:

- Analyze how some discourses are privileged and others are not—and whose discourses they are.
- Analyze the effects of ideology and the ideological implications of discourses.
- Ask whose or which knowledge is obscured or silenced by dominant discourses.

To analyze time:

- Deconstruct and historically situate keywords (e.g., *addiction, welfare*) in discourses over time.
- Study a discourse's emergence within another discourse (e.g., *Indigenization* within critical anticolonial discourse).

Following Bischoping and Gazso (2016) we differentiate generic/eclectic DA approaches from critical discourse analysis (CDA) and Foucauldian discourse analysis (FDA). The questions and strategies listed above are characteristic of generic/eclectic DA. These analyses are generally concerned with the four constructionist premises described above and the relations between power and language. Or, as Bischoping and Gazso (2016:130) put it, DA is concerned with "... unpacking a web of socially constructed meanings and considering their implications [to help uncover] how social interaction is involved in how discourses are constructed, how they change and what their effects are ... or, more simply, how discourse shapes social relations and vice versa." Generic/eclectic DA approaches may draw from several different theories or conceptual frameworks to understand the construction discourses and their implications. Illustrative examples of these sorts of DA studies include Boyd and Kerr's (2016) examination of police reports on mental health in Vancouver, Funk's (2013) analysis of families' roles and responsibilities in home healthcare, and Pascale's (2008) analysis of common-sense knowledge about race.

CDA and FDA approaches may use some of the same strategies as DA, but adhere more rigorously to a particular theoretical orientation. Although generic/eclectic DA studies may generally take a critical or questioning stance toward power, inequality, and language, they differ from a strict CDA approach in that they typically do not explicitly invoke critical theory. Some researcher may describe their study as informed by CDA, but for current purposes—keeping with Bischoping and Gazso (2016)—we view these as small-*c* critical discourse analysis (cDA) studies to signify that they use a much looser definition of the term. Strictly speaking, CDA is not only inherently political and activist in orientation, but is also typically informed by neo-Marxist and critical theory, such as the Frankfurt School (for a recent treatment, see Ricci 2017). This perspective holds that inequalities in the economic system translate into inequalities in the social and political systems and thus have concrete consequences for people's lives. It also holds that it is "possible and necessary" to adopt "a standpoint from which to assert knowledge, criticize, and prescribe directions for culture and society" with an eye to helping reduce inequality, exploitation, and oppression in society" (Bischoping and Gazso 2016:146). In comparison, FDA rejects the notion that there is one standpoint or truth from which to make claims about what ought to be, and instead invokes a Foucauldian theoretical lens to deconstruct (and thus lay bare) the underlying power-knowledge relations that govern social reality. That is, FDA tends to "describe without prescribing" (Bischoping and Gazso 2016:144). More detailed discussions of CDA and FDA can be found elsewhere (e.g., Fairclough 2001; Van Dijk, 1993; Arribas-Ayllon and Walkerdine 2008; Kendall and Wickham, 1999).

Examples of CDA can be seen in Taylor's (2004) analysis of education policy, Gazso's (2007) work on low income mothers' experiences on social assistance, and Mele and Bello's (2007) analysis of checkpoint encounters between drivers and security personnel in Nigeria. FDA has been widely applied to the analysis of discourse in various sectors of society such as white Australian involvement with Reconciliation, a government-sponsored initiative to address discrimination against Indigenous Australians (Green et al. 2005), nursing knowledge and the nursing profession (Springer and Clinton 2015), and student-athletes' experiences with microaggressions in sport (Lee et al. 2018).

These discussions should give you some sense of the variety of qualitative analysis methods available to researchers. Now let's look at some of the techniques for data processing and data analysis that are commonly used in qualitative research.

QUALITATIVE DATA PROCESSING

Let's begin this section with a warning. The activity we're about to examine is as much art as science. At the very least, there are no cut-and-dried steps that guarantee success.

It's a lot like learning how to paint with watercolours or compose a symphony. You can certainly gain education in such activities; you can even take university courses in both. Each has its own conventions and techniques as well as tips you may find useful as you set out to create art or music. However, instruction can carry you only so far. The final product must come from you. Much the same can be said of qualitative data processing.

At the same time, researchers have developed systematic and rigorous techniques for this type of research. We'll examine some of those here. You can gain a more in-depth view of these techniques from *Constructing Grounded Theory: A Practical Guide through Qualitative Research*, an excellent book by social researcher Kathy Charmaz (2014).

This section presents some ideas on coding qualitative data, writing memos, and mapping concepts graphically. Although far from a how-to manual, these ideas give a useful starting point for finding order in qualitative data.

CODING

Whether you engage in participant observation, in-depth interviewing, collecting biographical narratives, doing content analysis, or some other form of qualitative research, you'll eventually possess a growing mass of data—most typically in the form of textual materials. What do you do next?

The key process in the analysis of qualitative social research data is **coding**—classifying or categorizing individual pieces of data—coupled with some kind of retrieval system. Together, these procedures allow you to retrieve materials you may later be interested in.

Let's say you're chronicling the growth of a social movement. You recall writing up some notes about the details of the movement's earliest beginnings. Now you need that information. If all your notes have been catalogued by topic, retrieving those you need should be straightforward. As a simple format for coding and retrieval, you might have created a set of file folders labelled with various topics, such as "History." Data retrieval in this case means pulling out the History folder and rifling through the notes contained therein until you find what you need.

Coding has another, even more important purpose. As discussed earlier, the aim of data analysis is the discovery of patterns among the data, patterns that point to a theoretical understanding of social life. The coding and relating of concepts is key to this process and requires a more refined system than a set of manila folders. In this section, we'll assume that you'll be doing your coding manually.

Coding Units As you may recall from the earlier discussion of content analysis, for statistical analysis it's important to identify a standardized unit of analysis prior to coding. If you were comparing American and French novels, for example, you might evaluate and code sentences, paragraphs, chapters, or whole books. It would be important, however, to code the same units for each novel analyzed. This uniformity is necessary in a quantitative analysis, as it allows us to report something like "Twenty-three percent of the paragraphs contained metaphors." This is only possible if we've coded the same unit—paragraphs—in each of the novels.

Coding data for a qualitative analysis, however, is quite different. The *concept* is the organizing principle for qualitative coding. Here the

coding Classifying or categorizing individual pieces of data.

units of text appropriate for coding will vary within a given document. Thus, in a study of organizations, "Size" might require only a few words per coding unit, whereas "Mission" might take a few pages. Or, a lengthy description of a heated shareholders' meeting might be coded as "Internal Dissent."

Realize also that a given code category may be applied to textual materials of quite different lengths. For example, some references to the organization's mission may be brief, others lengthy. Although standardization is a key principle in quantitative analysis, this is not the case in qualitative analysis.

Coding as a Physical Act Before continuing with the logic of coding, let's take a moment to see what it actually looks like. Lofland and colleagues offer this description of manual filing:

> Prior to the widespread availability of personal computers beginning in the late 1980s, coding frequently took the specific physical form of filing. The researcher established an expanding set of file folders with code names on the tabs and physically placed either the item of data itself or a note that referenced its location in another file folder. Before photocopying was easily available and cheap, some fieldworkers typed their fieldnotes with carbon paper, wrote codes in the margins of the copies of the notes, and cut them up with scissors. They then placed the resulting slips of paper in corresponding file folders.
>
> (Lofland et al. 2006:203)

As these researchers point out, personal computers have greatly simplified this task. However, the image of slips of paper that contain text and are put in folders representing code categories is useful for understanding the process of coding. In the next section, when we suggest that a textual passage be coded with a certain code, imagine the passage is typed on a slip of paper and placed in a file folder bearing the name of the code. Whenever we assign two codes to a passage, imagine placing duplicate copies of the passage in two different folders representing the two codes.

Creating Codes So, what should your code categories be? Glaser and Strauss (1967:101) allow for the possibility of coding data for to test hypotheses that have been generated by prior theory. In that case, then, the theory would suggest the codes in the form of variables.

In this section, however, we're going to focus on coding used in the inductive approach. In the grounded theory approach, techniques and procedures for coding and processing data are heavily emphasized but qualified. For example, Strauss and Corbin (1998) discuss the coding of data by distinguishing three different stages that help clarify the logic that underlies this analytic process, but they also warn against approaching it as if there are clear and distinct boundaries between them. Nonetheless, they refer generally to the early stage of coding as **open coding**, when the labelling of concepts and categories occurs. As the coding proceeds, specific concepts, categories, and relationships are defined and refined; properties are identified and given categories are examined in depth. This stage is referred to as **axial coding**. **Selective coding** follows, where categories are integrated—relationships among a few particular categories become the focus.

Strauss and Corbin speak of qualitative data analysis as both science and art. As they state, "It is science in the sense of maintaining a certain degree of rigor and by grounding analysis in data. Creativity manifests itself in the ability of researchers to aptly name categories, ask stimulating questions, make comparisons, and extract an innovative, integrated, realistic scheme from masses of unorganized raw data" (1998:13). The researcher can be both scientific and creative in the development of grounded theory as long as procedures of data collection and analysis are followed. Coding procedures are analytic tools to assist the researcher in identifying, developing, and relating concepts both systematically and creatively. Systematic coding is important for

open coding The original conceptualization of the qualitative evidence into meaningful categories.

axial coding The re-examination of open coding in search of conceptual refinements and connections.

selective coding The search for conceptual themes that link the conceptualized evidence into an integrated narrative.

achieving validity and reliability in the analysis of the data.

Although an essential element of this approach to research is the standardization and rigour these procedures lend to the process of data analysis and ultimately theory construction, this rigour is not achieved by lock-step adherence to a rigid set of rules. It is achieved through the deep understanding of the logic that lies behind the coding procedures. The logic of these research procedures is the backbone to grounded theory. The procedures guide the alternating process of data collection and analysis that is central to this approach. Analysis begins at the very outset of interviewing and observation and therefore propels the collection of data.

The researcher becomes intimately connected with her or his data in this process, which raises the issue of "how one can immerse oneself in the data and still maintain a balance between objectivity and sensitivity" (Strauss and Corbin 1998:42). Maintaining such a balance in scientific discovery is the key to making this process work. Strauss and Corbin (1998:42–46) outline numerous techniques that help the researcher guard against bias creeping into analysis while maintaining sensitivity to what the data say. Potential ways of dealing with the problem of objectivity include thinking comparatively, gaining multiple points of view of an event, gathering data on the same phenomenon in various ways, checking out assumptions and hypotheses with respondents on occasion, and periodically stopping to ponder "'What is going on here?' and 'Does what I think I see fit the reality of the data?' The data themselves do not lie." Another technique is to "maintain an attitude of skepticism. All theoretical explanations, categories, hypotheses, and questions about the data arrived at through analysis should be regarded as provisional. These should be validated against data in subsequent interviews or observations." Finally, Strauss and Corbin stress that one's ability to be scientific and objective while also being creative and sensitive to the data requires following the research procedures:

> Although researchers may pick and choose among some of the analytic techniques that we offer, the *procedures of making comparisons, asking questions, and sampling based on evolving theoretical concepts* are essential features of the methodology. They differentiate it from other methods and provide the means for developing theory.... Coding cannot be done haphazardly or at the whim of the analyst. There is a reason for alternating data collection with analysis. Not only does this allow for sampling on the basis of emerging concepts, but it also enables validation of concepts and hypotheses as these are being developed. Those found not to "fit" can then be discarded, revised, or modified during the research process.
>
> (Strauss and Corbin 1998:46)

When reading the literature, it is clear that some researchers make a claim to using a grounded theory approach when they are merely trying to indicate that they have grounded their theory in data. The grounded theory approach is much more than this, as you can see. If you are to engage in grounded theory, reading several books on the topic before you begin is highly recommended.

Let us now consider in more detail the three stages of coding in GTM. We begin with the common process of *open coding.* Strauss and Corbin define it as follows:

> To uncover, name, and develop concepts, we must open up the text and expose the thoughts, ideas, and meanings contained therein. Without the first analytic step, the rest of the analysis and the communication that follows could not occur. Broadly speaking, during open coding, data are broken down into discrete parts, closely examined, and compared for similarities and differences. Events, happenings, objects, and actions/interactions that are found to be conceptually similar in nature or related in meaning are grouped under more abstract concepts termed "categories."
>
> (Strauss and Corbin 1998:102)

Open coding is the logical starting point for GTM qualitative coding. Beginning with some body of text (part of an interview, for example), you read and reread a passage, seeking to identify the key concepts in it. Any particular piece of data may be given several codes, reflecting as many concepts. For example, notice all the concepts contained in this comment by a student interviewee:

> I thought the professor should have given me at least partial credit for the homework I turned in.

Some obvious codes are "Professor," "Homework," and "Grading." The result of open coding is the identification of numerous concepts relevant to the subject under study. The open coding of more and more text will lengthen the list of codes.

As noted previously, in GTM there are two other types of coding in addition to open coding. Axial coding aims at identifying the *core* concepts in the study. Although axial coding uses the results of open coding, more concepts can be identified through continued open coding after the axial coding has begun. Axial coding involves a regrouping of the data, in which the researcher uses the open-code categories and looks for more analytic concepts. For example, the passage just given also carries the concept of "Perceptions of Fairness," which might appear frequently in the student interviews, thereby suggesting that it's an important element in understanding students' concerns. Another axial code reflected in the student comment might be "Power Relationships," because the professor is seen to exercise power over the student.

The last kind of coding, selective coding, seeks to identify *the* central code in the study: the one that all the other codes relate to. Both of the axial codes just mentioned might be restructured as aspects of a more general concept: "Professor–Student Relationships." Of course, in a real data analysis, decisions such as the ones we've been discussing would arise from masses of textual data, not from a single quotation. The basic notion of GTM is that patterns of relationships can be teased out of an extensive, in-depth examination of a large body of observations.

This brief glimpse into a possible analysis gives you some idea of the process by which codes are generated and applied. You should also have begun to see how such coding would allow you to understand better the messages being put forward in a text and to retrieve data appropriately as you need them.

memoing The process of writing memos containing ideas and insights developed during the collection and analysis of qualitative data.

MEMOING

In the grounded theory method, the coding process involves more than simply categorizing chunks of text. As you code data, you should also be using the technique of **memoing**—writing memos or notes to yourself and others involved in the project. Some of what you write during analysis may end up in your final report; much of it will at least stimulate what you write.

In GTM, these memos have a special significance. Strauss and Corbin (1998:217) distinguish three kinds of memos: code notes, theoretical notes, and operational notes.

Code notes identify the code labels and their meanings. This is particularly important because, as in all social science research, most of the terms we use with technical meanings also have meanings in everyday language. It's essential, therefore, to write down a clear account of what you mean by the codes used in your analysis.

Theoretical notes cover a variety of topics: reflections of the dimensions and deeper meanings of concepts, relationships among concepts, theoretical propositions, and so on. All of us occasionally ruminate over the nature of something, try to think it out, to make sense out of it. In qualitative data analysis, it's vital to write down these thoughts, even those you'll later discard as useless. They will vary greatly in length, but you should limit each to a single main thought so that you can sort and organize them all later.

Operational notes deal primarily with methodological issues. Some will draw attention to data-collection circumstances that may be relevant to understanding the data later on. Others will consist of notes directing future data collection.

These memos are written throughout the data-collection and analysis process. Thoughts demanding memos will come to you as you reread notes or transcripts, code chunks of text, or discuss the project with others. It's a good idea to get in the habit of writing out your memos as soon as possible after the thoughts come to you.

APPLYING CONCEPTS IN EVERYDAY LIFE

Pencils and Photos in the Hands of Research Subjects

How would you go about studying the life conditions of Indigenous people of Peru living in the Amazon rainforest? With minimal telecommunications infrastructure and a slow ferry-based postal service in the vast region, a mail or telephone survey wouldn't be the best approach. It might occur to you to conduct in-depth interviews in which you would work from an outline of topics to be covered. Arvind Singhal and Elizabeth Rattine-Flaherty (2006) opted for a very different approach, which put the subjects of study more in control of the research and allowed for important but unexpected discoveries. They derived their inspiration from the work of the renowned Brazilian educator Paulo Freire, who once set out to measure exploitation among street children. Instead of interviewing them, he gave them cameras and asked them to bring back photographs of exploitation. As Singhal and Rattine-Flaherty report:

> One child took a photo of a nail on a wall. It made no sense to adults, but other children were in strong agreement. The ensuing discussions showed that many young boys of that neighborhood worked in the shoe-shine business. Their clients were mainly in the city, not in the barrio where they lived. As their shoe-shine boxes were too heavy for them to carry, these boys, rented a nail on a wall (usually in a shop), where they could hang their boxes for the night. To them, that nail on the wall represented "exploitation." The "nail on the wall" photograph spurred widespread discussions in the Peruvian barrio about other forms of institutionalized exploitation, including ways to overcome them.
>
> (2006:314)[7]

Singhal and Rattine-Flaherty's research involved gauging the quality of life in the Peruvian Amazon and assessing the impact of programs launched by a Peruvian nongovernmental organization (NGO), Minga Peru. To view society through the eyes of children, the researchers set up drawing sessions with coloured pencils. In the spirit of reciprocity, one of the authors sketched pictures of snowmen and jack-o'-lanterns that were a part of her growing up in the U.S. Midwest. In addition to depicting life in their villages and their close relationship with the natural environment, the children's sketches often featured examples of social change being brought about by the NGO's developmental programs.

> These include sketches of chicken coops, fish farms, and agro-forestry projects. These enterprises, all launched by Minga Peru, began in the Peruvian Amazon only in the past few years. For children to sketch these "new" initiatives in their pictures on their own, without prompts, is noteworthy.
>
> (2006:322)[8]

The photographs taken by the adult women were equally revealing. Several drew attention to the patriarchal social structure. As the authors report,

> Several photographs depicted the subservient position of the Amazonian women relative

7 Singhal, A. and Rattine-Flaherty, E. Pencils and Photos as Tools of Communicative Research and Praxis: Analyzing Minga Peru's Quest for Social Justice in the Amazon. *International Communication Gazette* 68(4), pp. 313–330. Copyright © 2006 by SAGE Publications. Reprinted by permission of SAGE Publications, Ltd.

8 Singhal, A. and Rattine-Flaherty, E. Pencils and Photos as Tools of Communicative Research and Praxis: Analyzing Minga Peru's Quest for Social Justice in the Amazon. *International Communication Gazette* 68(4), pp. 313–330. Copyright © 2006 by SAGE Publications. Reprinted by permission of SAGE Publications, Ltd.

(*Continued*)

APPLYING CONCEPTS IN EVERYDAY LIFE (*CONTINUED*)

to men, a situation that Minga Peru seeks to address. For instance, Adela's picture shows a middle-aged Amazonian woman and her husband sitting on their porch and having a conversation. The woman, sporting a forlorn expression, sits with her legs crossed while her husband stares directly into the camera, squatting with his arms and feet spread in an open position. Especially noticeable is the physical distance of about 10 feet [approximately 3 metres] that separates the woman and the man. When Adela was asked why she took the picture and why were the man and woman sitting so far apart, she noted: "The woman is sitting at one side of the house and he is on the other and this was not anything unusual." Upon probing, we learned that Amazonian men determine how close the couple sits. If they are sitting closer, and if the man has his arm around his partner, it is his decision to do so. This authority also applies to initiation of sex: The man determines if and when sex will happen.

(2006:323–324)[9]

9 Singhal, A. and Rattine-Flaherty, E. Pencils and Photos as Tools of Communicative Research and Praxis: Analyzing Minga Peru's Quest for Social Justice in the Amazon. 68(4), pp. 313–330.

This research doesn't just illustrate some unusual data-collection techniques; it also represents the spirit of participatory action research discussed in Chapter 10. With a very different setting and purpose, Pat O'Connor (2006) asked Irish adolescents to write essays about themselves and about Ireland, including drawings, poems, and songs; O'Connor was looking for evidence of the impact of globalization in Ireland. Both studies demonstrate that qualitative field research can involve a lot more than just observing and interviewing.

Morgan and colleagues (2009) used this technique in the examination of a very sensitive topic: chronic vaginal infections among Australian women. In addition to in-depth interviews in which the female interviewers often spoke of their own experiences, the subject-women were asked to draw pictures to illustrate their feelings in relation to the medical condition.

Sources: Singhal and Rattine-Flaherty (2006); O'Connor (2006); Morgan et al. (2009)

Notice that whereas we often think of writing as a linear process, starting at the beginning and moving through to the conclusion, memoing does not follow this pattern. It might be characterized as a process of creating chaos and then finding order within it.

BRINGING ORDER TO DATA: AN ILLUSTRATION

The following example comes from interviews with inmates of Canadian prisons conducted by Benaquisto (2000). It is used to illustrate some of the steps in an analysis of the reasoning and rationales expressed by offenders.

Coding and memoing were integral to the analysis. As Benaquisto read through the interview data, she noted a large number of initial codes and wrote many preliminary memos. For example, one inmate stressed that it was hard for him to live on the outside—it was easier to be inside. Prison was comforting in its own way. Trying to live life independently often made him depressed. He couldn't find work. He was uneducated. There were times when he just couldn't handle being independent—being arrested brought him some relief. Some prison environments made him feel secure. He didn't have to deal with the disappointments and hassles of life. At the time of his criminal act and of the interview, he preferred being inside the prison. He mentioned several times that he got the time he needed. He also said that even if he had been given a longer sentence, he would have accepted it. She coded this inmate as desiring prison.

There was another inmate who indicated at length that life behind bars was neither better nor worse for him. She coded this person as indifferent to being in prison. There were several others who communicated either the desire to be in prison or an indifference to it. And in each of these cases, the inmate expressed that in thinking about the outcome of his actions, he had a high expectation of being caught and he did not care. She eventually grouped together these two types and categorized them as Fatalists. She noted that each inmate had a narrative. Thus, as the coding progressed, one issue that guided her analysis was the recognition of themes that emerged from the stories the inmates told about their actions leading up to the event that landed them in prison. Following the initial coding and search for themes, focused coding in the form of a systematic search for commonalities was undertaken. Eventually, Benaquisto recognized distinctive similarities among certain types. This took her to a higher level of abstraction. She was able to cluster a number of the themes (what she called "dominant motifs") derived from the inmates' narratives, thereby reducing the number of conceptual categories for the purpose of summary. As the analysis progressed, she achieved an even higher level of conceptual abstraction and summary based on further similarities among categories. She referred to this final, further-reduced set as "overarching categories."

As Benaquisto coded, she kept writing memos to organize her thoughts. One idea that emerged was that the means by which many criminal offenders become involved in criminal activity runs counter to the theory of deterrence, which stresses how a person *would* think if they were acting in a calculating and rational way. The data gathered in the interviews with real offenders seemed to contradict many of the findings in support of deterrence theory. These findings had been derived from studies of nonoffenders asked to consider hypothetical situations in which they contemplated engaging in criminal acts. Such studies more often concerned how people believed they would think or behave—thus making deliberate decisions independent of "real-life" contexts. Such studies seem to represent how members of the middle class—taking a moment to fill out a questionnaire—might think or how students in a classroom respond to the hypothetical costs and benefits of engaging in criminal activities. However, crime control policies are not hypothetical or theoretical. Thus, how the actual offenders "think" about crime and its consequences should be understood and incorporated into the development of penal policies.

When the interviews were complete, Benaquisto read through them in a focused and systematic way, noting for each inmate whether or not he "accounted for his actions" when describing the events that led to his ultimate conviction. In each case, she also noted what appeared to be the "dominant rationale" offered by the inmate in his account. The dominant rationale categories developed from the initial code-concepts that had emerged. In determining the dominant rationale, she looked at what the inmate mentioned first and most often—how much he elaborated upon or repeated a given line of reasoning or thought. She also noted secondary and tertiary rationales when they were present. In this process, further themes began to emerge, and she began to notice commonalities among inmate rationales.

She then read through the stories again, once more coding each inmate's story in relation to the dominant rationale he provided for his actions. The patterns were emerging more clearly and becoming more refined. Some of the categories of dominant rationales also had an affinity to each other when examined in light of the idea of rationality and reason—weighing costs and benefits—associated with deterrence theory. This meant that a hierarchical structure of concepts might be useful in organizing and making sense of these data.

From this coding she created a typology or categorization of the rationales the inmates expressed in light of their consideration of the consequences of their actions. The coding of rationale or "criminal reasoning" with respect to deterrence thus emerged from the common central motifs in crime stories offered by the inmates. From the point of view of the observer, the themes (dominant motifs) summarized the motivation or inner mental states that led to the crime. From the subject's perspective, the themes summarized the reasons offered to explain their action. However, it is important to keep in mind that reasons and "reasoned thinking" need not coincide.

Simplifying the analysis and argument for the sake of a brief illustration, there were ultimately 12 dominant motifs or themes that emerged: fed up with life, prison is better, extreme intoxication, situational rage/duress, permanent mental incapacity, prideful neutralizers, politically motivated, thrill seekers, calculators, negligence, drug/alcohol addiction, and thoughtless greedy. Several distinct dominant motifs could be further grouped on the basis of common themes that linked them at a higher level of abstraction. For example, those fed up with life and those who felt prison is better were grouped as Fatalists, as indicated earlier. The motifs of extreme intoxication, situational rage, and permanent mental incapacity were grouped together under Reduced Mental Capacity on the basis that each of them emphasized how they were unable to think about the consequences.

The severe drug addict, the criminally negligent, and the thoughtless greedy were grouped together also. At a higher level of abstraction, the commonality among their stories was how they simply did not think about the consequences despite the fact that they had the ability to do so. Thus they were termed Nonthinkers—or thoughtless criminals.

Finally, two other dominant motifs, the prideful neutralizers and the politically motivated, were grouped as Punishment Neutralizers. These men had in common a sense that consequences would not apply to them, even though their reasoning on why the consequences would not apply to them differed.

With a reduced set of six categories, further grouping was yet possible. Those with Reduced Mental Capacity and the Nonthinkers could be grouped at an even higher level of abstraction, each having in common the self-description that they didn't think about the consequences at all when engaging in their criminal act. They were thus grouped under the category Noncalculators. This category brought together those who couldn't think and those who didn't think. In their self-accounts, each inmate in the Noncalculator category directly emphasized his disconnection from consequence.

The Punishment Neutralizers were grouped with the Thrill Seekers on the basis of their common overestimation of their ability to escape detection or underestimation of the criminal justice actors' abilities. Given the commonality of their miscalculation of the consequences they were likely to face, despite having consciously taken consequences into account, they were categorized as Miscalculators. The Calculators were those who specifically characterized their thoughts and actions in terms of costs and benefits of committing an offence by weighing their gains against their likelihood of being caught and the potential harshness of the punishment they would receive; they remained as a small but distinct category.

The end result was four overarching categories that summarized the variety of dominant motifs and therefore criminal reasoning (or nonreasoning) in light of consequences: Noncalculators, Miscalculators, Fatalists, and Calculators. Benaquisto's findings spoke to the efficacy of deterrence (i.e., the threat of harsher punishment) for such criminal offender types. Focusing on criminal reasoning in light of consequences, these types summarized the mental processing and decision making (or lack of it) that the crime stories revealed. Figure 13-3 briefly summarizes the coding process.

In brief, the threat of harsher penalties was likely to prove ineffective for the vast majority, such as the Fatalists, who preferred or were indifferent to prison, and the Noncalculators—the largest category—comprising those who didn't consider consequences at all prior to their actions. The small percentage of Calculators (13 percent of the sample) was the exception. Comprising primarily higher-level drug dealers,

<table>
<tr><td>Calculators</td><td colspan="2">Fatalists</td><td colspan="6">Noncalculators</td><td colspan="3">Miscalculators</td></tr>
<tr><td></td><td colspan="2"></td><td colspan="3">Reduced Mental Capacity</td><td colspan="3">Non-Thinkers</td><td colspan="2">Punishment Neutralizers</td><td></td></tr>
<tr><td>Calculators</td><td>Fed Up</td><td>Prison Better</td><td>Extreme Intoxication</td><td>Situational Rage</td><td>Mental Incapacity</td><td>Drug Addict</td><td>Criminally Negligent</td><td>Thoughtless Greedy</td><td>Prideful Neutralizers</td><td>Politically Motivated</td><td>Thrill Seekers</td></tr>
</table>

Open coding	Code-concepts were developed from reading various offenders accounts of their crime (reasons and rationales: if and how they thought about/accounted for their actions)
Axial coding	12 dominant themes/motifs emerged regarding the mental processes and decision-making evident in criminals' accounts of their actions
Selective coding	Themes/motifs were further grouped into 2 progressively higher levels of abstraction; concluding with 4 overarching categories that summarized the 12 dominant motifs characterizing criminal non/reasoning in the light of consequences (How do anticipated consequences factor into criminal reasoning?)

FIGURE 13-3 **Coding "Criminal Reasoning".**
Source: Author created

these men discussed how they consciously weighed the benefits of their criminal acts against the likelihood of the costs of punishment and reasoned that the penalty would likely not be severe enough to outweigh the benefits they would gain from their actions. It seems likely that a real threat of harsher punishment might deter such offenders.

One category of Noncalculator, the thoughtless greedy, might be deterred by harsher punishment as well. These men, who were for the most part first-time offenders, indicated that had they thought about the consequences of their actions at the time they engaged in criminal activity, they likely would not have done it—but they hadn't thought about it. Therefore, even for this group harsher punishments would not solve the problem of their lack of thought at the time of the crime. It seemed clear from what they were saying that had they thought in terms of consequences initially, the current level of punishment would have been sufficient to deter their actions.

Thus, the bottom line is that a policy of harsher punishments—enhanced general deterrence—does not look promising as a way to stop criminal behaviour on the part of the vast majority of criminal offenders who are behind bars in Canadian federal correctional facilities.

This example briefly illustrates some of the steps involved in the analysis of qualitative data. What ultimately resulted was a coding of "criminal reasoning" or rationale with respect to deterrence that emerged from common motifs or central themes derived from the narratives (crime stories) offered by the inmates. The coding scheme (a guide that lays out the key concepts, their definitions, and the criteria for identifying each concept) evolved from the themes that first became evident during the interviewing process and were further clarified and systematically pursued in first and second readings of the assembled data.

DEDUCTIVE QUALITATIVE CODING

Sometimes researchers have a qualitative coding scheme that is pre-developed based on previous research or some theoretical or conceptual framework. They then apply this coding scheme deductively to text to identify instances of the concept(s) of interest.

For example, Thomas Scheff and Suzanne Retzinger have theorized that shame is a—perhaps *the*—master emotion, one that underlies many other emotional responses (Scheff and Retzinger 1991). For them, "shame refers to a family of emotions with many variations, from social discomfort and mild embarrassment to intense forms such as humiliation or mortification" (Retzinger 1995:1105). Although some forms of shame, if acknowledged, may be useful (e.g., anticipation of the shame a person might feel may prevent them from behaving poorly toward another), other forms of unacknowledged shame lead to anger and possibly violence. In fact, they argue that unrecognized or unacknowledged shame underlies most acts of aggression at the interpersonal and at the group levels. Or, as Gilligan (1997:110–111) succinctly states, "[t]he emotion of shame is the primary or ultimate cause of all violence.... The different forms of violence, whether toward individuals or entire populations, are motivated (caused) by secret shame."

A wide variety of experiences may illicit feelings of shame:

> Stimulus situations that evoke shame may be either overt or covert, real or imagined. They include messages perceived as disparity in relational experience: Self as the object of disappointment, defeat, rejection or fear of rejection, betrayal, judgmental comparison, loss of face, exposure, rebuff, inattentiveness, unrequited love, disappointment, failure, disrespect, or ridicule.
>
> (Retzinger 1995:1105–1106)

Retzinger (1995) describes a coding scheme for identifying shame and anger in texts (such as verbatim transcripts, novels, historical texts, or other narrative texts). Since Scheff and Retzinger (1991) hypothesize that unacknowledged shame can be quite damaging, identifying and acknowledging it becomes an important task. Their interpretive system (Retzinger 1995) provides categories and hundreds of examples intended to help capture verbal (direct use of words, or indirect references to such), paralinguistic (e.g., intonation, volume, and pitch), and visual indications (e.g., gestures and facial expressions) of shame and anger in texts.

Retzinger (1995:1112) holds that "by identifying shame in interaction, we may be able to make discoveries in many areas of everyday life that would otherwise be impossible. This method lends itself to the exploration of the nature of conflict and reconciliation. It can be used to explore the status quo and social change. By exploring shame, we may be ... able to get a better understanding into the nature of human relationships." The method has been used to analyze transcripts of marital quarrels, novels and plays, popular song lyrics, international political relations, and a case study of Hitler (Retzinger 1995; Scheff 1993; Scheff 2011; Scheff and Retzinger 1991). Recently, Scheff and Mateo (2016) applied the method to a sample of research articles across a number of fields of study. They found a number of indications of the concept shame, but found it was most often identified as a different construct. They contend that this is symptomatic of the deep reluctance to acknowledge the underlying shame that pervades our culture. Indeed, Scheff (2014) argues that acknowledging the central place of shame in human life may hold the key to dealing with some of our most pressing social and political problems.

CONCEPT MAPPING

It should be clear by now that qualitative data analysts spend a lot of time committing thoughts to paper (or to a computer file) and figuring out how they relate to one another. Often, we can think out relationships among concepts even more clearly by putting the concepts in a graphical format, a process called **concept mapping**. Some researchers find it useful to put all their major concepts on a single sheet of paper, whereas others spread their thoughts across several sheets of paper, whiteboards, magnetic boards, computer pages, or other media. Figure 13-4 shows how we might think out some of the concepts of Goffman's examination of gender and advertising.

The use of visual portrayals is often helpful in clarifying the development of concepts and theory in qualitative analysis. For examples of this, see the Applying Concepts in Everyday Life box "Pencils and Photos in the Hands of Research Subjects." Computer programs can be used for concept mapping. They can also be used for qualitative data analysis.

concept mapping The process of putting emerging concepts and their relationships into a graphical format.

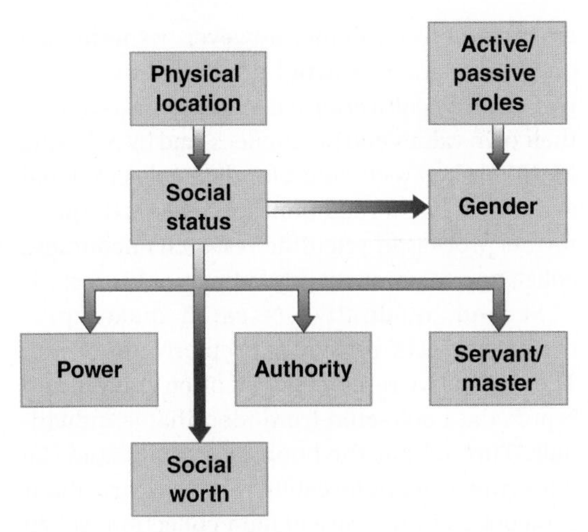

FIGURE 13-4 **An Example of Concept Mapping.**
Source: © Cengage Learning

Having noted the overlap of qualitative and quantitative techniques, it seems fitting now to address an instrument that is primarily associated with quantitative research but that is proving quite valuable for qualitative analysts as well—the personal computer.

COMPUTER PROGRAMS FOR QUALITATIVE DATA

Not so many decades ago, the recording and analysis of qualitative research data was paperbound. Interview transcripts, observational notes, official documents, and the like were all compiled and evaluated by hand. The work of hand-writing documents was eventually streamlined by the advent of typewriters. Copying technologies—first carbon paper, and later photocopying—made it possible to easily reproduce duplicate pages of research information. These printed data could then be cut into slips, with each strip displaying an individual, coded item. This procedure allowed researchers to categorize collected data according to different themes or concepts. One pile of paper slips might contain passages of text referencing one concept, another pile could contain references to another concept, and so forth. And, a given passage might show up in more than one pile. Once this coding and sorting was done, researchers could manually review all the materials within a particular category, allowing them to look for and identify common patterns and important distinctions.

As you can imagine, computers changed all that. Once information has been entered into a computer, copying whole documents or pieces is a trivial matter. Simulating the earlier paperbound method, you can copy an interview comment relevant to, say, discrimination against women, and paste it into another document created to hold anything relevant to that theme. With nothing but the simplest word processor or text editor, you can streamline the coding process in any number of ways. Imagine this paragraph was part of textual materials you were analyzing in a study of technological progress. You could augment this document by adding coding notations such as <computer> <qualitative> <coding>.

You could go through this whole chapter, adding these and other notations wherever appropriate. And once you were finished, you could use a simple search function to review all the materials marked <coding>, for example. You could augment this process by searching the chapter for words such as *code, coding, category, classify*, or other applicable terms.

Such methods may seem like crude tools from the Dark Ages of social research in light of the capabilities of modern qualitative data analysis programs.

QDA PROGRAMS

Today, qualitative data analysis (QDA) programs abound. Where the analyst's problem used to be merely finding any such program, the problem now lies in choosing one of so many. Here are a few commonly used QDA programs, with online sites where you can learn more about them and, in many cases, download demo copies.

- **NVivo:** www.qsrinternational.com
- **Atlas.ti:** www.atlasti.com/index.php
- **Ethno:** www.indiana.edu/~socpsy/ESA/
- **Ethnograph:** www.qualisresearch.com/
- **HyperResearch:** www.researchware.com/
- **HyperTranscribe:** www.researchware.com/products/hypertranscribe.html
- **MAXQDA:** www.maxqda.com/

- **QDA Miner:** https://provalisresearch.com/products/qualitative-data-analysis-software/
- **TAMS:** sourceforge.net/projects/tamsys/
- **Weft:** www.pressure.to/qda/

Another excellent resource is "Choosing a CAQDAS Package" by Christina Silver and Ann Lewins (2014), which can be found at www.surrey.ac.uk/computer-assisted-qualitative-data-analysis/resources/choosing-appropriate-caqdas-package. This working paper will familiarize you with some of the key features in such computer programs and help you choose which one is best suited to your purposes. (See online Appendix 13A for a brief coding example using NVivo.)

ETHICS AND QUALITATIVE DATA ANALYSIS

At least two ethical issues raise special concern in the analysis and reporting of qualitative research. First, because such analysis depends so directly on subjective judgments, there is an obvious risk of seeing what you are looking for or want to find. The risk increases in the case of participatory action research or other projects involving an element of social justice. Researcher bias is hardly an inevitable outcome, however. Experienced qualitative analysts avoid this pitfall in at least two ways: by cultivating a deliberate awareness of their own values and preferences, and by adhering to established techniques for data collection and analysis. And as an additional protection, the peer-review process in scientific research encourages colleagues to point out any failings in this regard.

Second, qualitative research makes protecting subjects' privacy particularly important. The qualitative researcher will often analyze and report data collected from identifiable individuals. Throughout the book, we've indicated the importance of not revealing what we learn about subjects, as in the case of data collection. When writing up the results of your analyses, you'll often need to make concerted efforts to conceal identities. Individuals, organizations, and communities are often given pseudonyms toward this end. Sometimes, you may need to suppress details that would let outsiders figure out the person you're talking about. Thus, it may be appropriate to speak about interviewing "a church leader" rather than "the head deacon." You may also need to suppress or alter age, race, or gender references if that would give away a subject's identity. The key principle is to respect the privacy of those you study.

■ MAIN POINTS

- Qualitative analysis is the nonnumerical examination and interpretation of observations.
- Qualitative analysis involves a continual interplay between theory and analysis. In analyzing qualitative data, we seek to discover patterns such as changes over time or possible causal links between variables.
- Examples of approaches to the discovery and explanation of such patterns are grounded theory method (GTM), semiotics, conversation analysis (CA), narrative analysis, and discourse analysis.
- The processing of qualitative data is as much art as science. Three key tools for preparing data for analysis are coding, memoing, and concept mapping.
- In contrast to the standardized units used in coding for statistical analyses, the units to be coded in qualitative analyses may vary within a document. Although codes may be derived from the theory being explored, more often researchers use open coding, in which codes are suggested by the researchers' examination and questioning of the data.
- Memoing is appropriate at several stages of data processing and it captures code meanings, theoretical ideas, preliminary conclusions, and other thoughts that will be useful during analysis.
- Concept mapping uses diagrams to explore relationships in the data graphically.

- Many computer programs, such as Ethno and QDA Miner, are specifically designed to assist researchers in the analysis of qualitative data.
- The subjective element in qualitative data analysis provides an added challenge to avoiding bias in the interpretation of data.
- Because the qualitative data analyst knows the identity of subjects, taking special steps to protect their privacy is crucial.

REVIEW QUESTIONS AND EXERCISES

1. Review Goffman's examination of gender advertising (1979), and collect and analyze a set of advertising photos you find online or in magazines. What is the relationship between gender and status in the materials you found?
2. Search the Web for a transcription of an interview such as those available in oral history archives. Conduct an open coding of two or three pages of the interview.
3. Imagine that you're conducting a cross-case analysis of revolutionary documents such as the Declaration of Independence (from the United States) and the Declaration of the Rights of Man and of the Citizen (from the French Revolution). What key concepts might you code in the following sentence from the Declaration of Independence?

   When in the Course of human events, it becomes necessary for one people to dissolve the political bands which have connected them with another, and to assume among the Powers of the earth, the separate and equal station to which the Laws of Nature and of Nature's God entitle them, a decent respect to the opinions of mankind requires that they should declare the causes which impel them to the separation.
4. Go to the World Press Review online (www.worldpress.org/) and pick a controversial news topic discussed by several newspapers. See if you can identify characteristics of those newspapers (such as political leaning, region) that might explain the different points of view expressed on the topic.

CONTINUITY PROJECT

EMOTIONAL OUTCOMES OF RANKISM

Thankfully, we are increasingly sensitive to the destructive effects of all kinds of "isms," such as sexism, racism, and ageism. Robert Fuller (2004) applauds this social progress but argues that we are not paying attention to what may be the most important of these "isms": rankism. Rankism refers to the abuses of rank. Rank, of course, is rooted in status inequalities. Statuses come with legitimate rights (privileges). When status occupants extend their claims beyond the legitimate, rankism appears.

Rankism produces unpleasant emotions in those upon whom illegitimate demands are made. But since it is often important for financial, social, political, or other reasons to maintain their status, rankism's victims often keep their emotions secret.

Here is a short list of common emotions and their sources and signs (adapted from Scheff 2011:55)[10]:

Names	Sources	Signs
Grief	Loss	Sadness, crying
Fear	Physical danger	Alarm, shaking, sweating
Anger	Frustration	Intense focus, rapid thoughts and speech
Shame	Disconnection	Feeling unworthy, alone

Visit PostSecret.com, a website where people anonymously post their secrets. Look through the listings and find 10 examples where the relational experience involves rankism (i.e., powerful others making illegitimate demands). Read the postcards and classify the reported emotions. Does rankism produce some kinds of emotions more commonly than others?

10 Adapted from Scheff, T. (2011), Response to Jasper. *Sociological Forum*, 26: 709–710.

conejota/Shutterstock.com

QUANTITATIVE DATA ANALYSIS

In order to conduct quantitative analysis, social data must be converted to numerical form. This chapter will begin with the process of quantifying data and then turn to analysis. Quantitative analysis may be descriptive or explanatory, and it may involve one, two, or several variables. We begin our examination of how quantitative analyses are done with some simple but powerful ways to manipulate data in order to reach research conclusions.

IN THIS CHAPTER ...

INTRODUCTION

This chapter begins by describing methods of converting social science data into a *machine-readable form*—a form that can be read and manipulated by computer programs used in **quantitative analysis**. This process of quantification—converting data to a numerical format—allows data to be recorded on a computer or some other device for storing information that can be read by the computer and then statistically analyzed.

Following our discussion of the techniques by which researchers quantify data, we present the logic and some of the techniques of quantitative data analysis. Researchers analyze data to discover and substantiate patterns and relationships, test our expectations, and draw inferences.

Most social science analysis falls within the general rubric of multivariate analysis, or the examination of several variables simultaneously. The analysis of the simultaneous association among *age*, *education*, and *prejudice* is an example of multivariate analysis. Multivariate analysis is a general term for the analysis of several variables; it does not refer to a specific form of analysis.

The basic logic of multivariate analysis can best be seen through the use of simple tables, called *contingency tables* or *cross-tabulations*. We will first lay the foundation for understanding more complex, multivariate analyses by examining the more fundamental univariate (one variable) and bivariate (two variables) modes of analysis and by focusing on the construction and understanding of bivariate contingency tables. We will then provide a brief introduction to multivariate analyses using three variable contingency tables.

Further discussion of multivariate contingency table analysis is explored in Chapter 15. Other techniques for conducting a multivariate analysis, such as multiple regression, will be covered in Chapter 16. These final three chapters on quantitative data analysis are largely technical, and it is easy to get lost in details. So let's now remind ourselves where these procedures fit into the larger research methods picture.

Research methods are systematic procedures for linking abstract ideas with concrete evidence. The process of constructing such linkages can begin at either the concrete or abstract level. In general, the qualitative research methods tradition begins with concrete observations and uses its tools and techniques to inductively construct a meaningful narrative that makes sense of the observed patterns. By contrast, the quantitative research methods tradition begins with abstract ideas and tests these through the collection of empirical evidence.

The proposition testing in quantitative research, introduced in Chapter 2, follows several steps. First, abstract concepts are translated into variables that act as indicators. This is the operationalization step. Then the variables are translated into instruments (the instrumentation step), which are then applied to measure properties of concrete objects (the measurement step). For example, an abstract concept like "intelligence" gets translated into a variable like "intelligence quotient (IQ)." Operationalization complete. IQ then gets translated into a tool like the Stanford-Binet Intelligence Test. Instrumentation complete. Then the intelligence test is applied to you and you get a score. (Measurement complete.) The scores that result from measurement are numbers.

When this operationalization–instrumentation–measurement process is repeated across many cases and many variables, the result is a large collection of numbers. When organized, this collection of numbers is called a **data set**. All quantitative analysis is the manipulation of numbers in a data set. Quantitative analysis searches for empirical patterns that are interpreted as evidence either supporting or rejecting the abstract ideas that began the research process. Figure 14-1 illustrates what a data set looks like.

The analysis of numerical data can be done by hand, but with large data sets this approach

quantitative analysis The numerical representation and manipulation of observations for the purpose of describing and explaining the phenomena that those observations reflect.

data set A collection of quantitative measurements in which the numbers are organized by variables and cases.

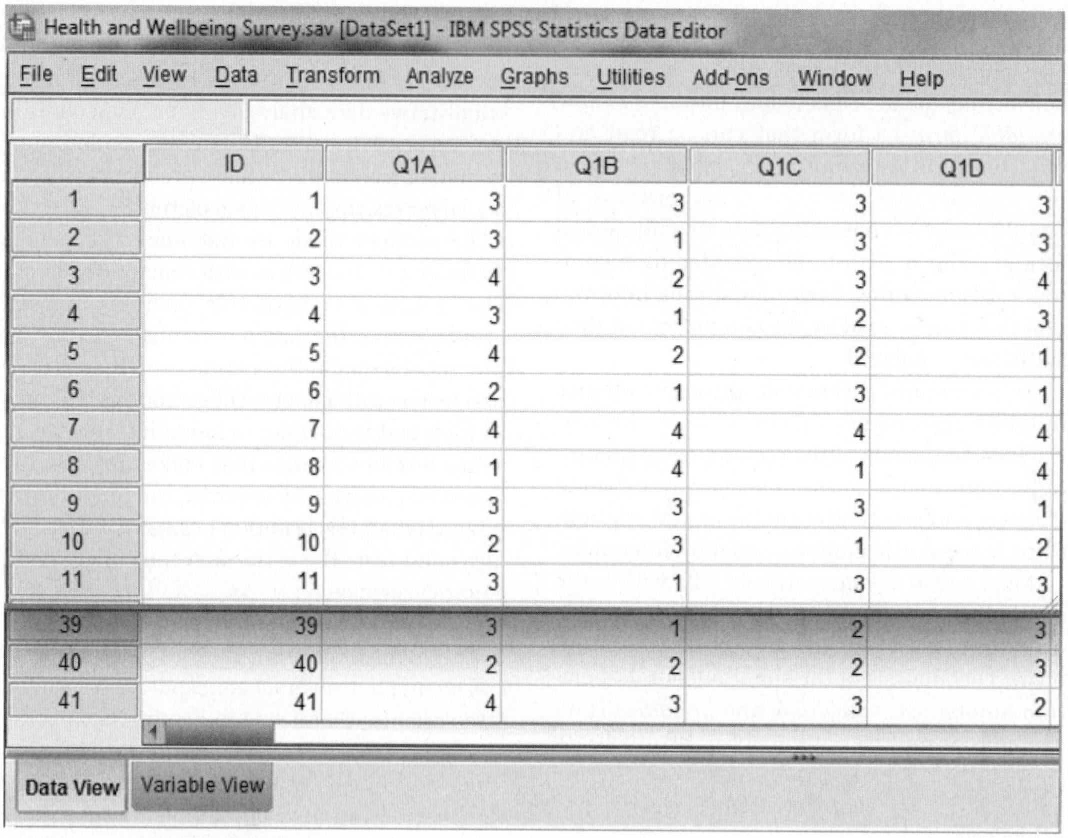

Health and Wellbeing Survey.sav [DataSet1] - IBM SPSS Statistics Data Editor

File Edit View Data Transform Analyze Graphs Utilities Add-ons Window Help

	ID	Q1A	Q1B	Q1C	Q1D
1	1	3	3	3	3
2	2	3	1	3	3
3	3	4	2	3	4
4	4	3	1	2	3
5	5	4	2	2	1
6	6	2	1	3	1
7	7	4	4	4	4
8	8	1	4	1	4
9	9	3	3	3	1
10	10	2	3	1	2
11	11	3	1	3	3
39	39	3	1	2	3
40	40	2	2	2	3
41	41	4	3	3	2

Data View Variable View

FIGURE 14-1 **Sample Data Set**. Part of a data set collected by the author and colleagues on student health and well-being. The rows of the table represent each student from whom data were collected. In the full data set there are over 1,200 rows, representing the 1,200-plus students who completed the survey. The columns represent the variables collected in the survey questionnaire. The first column is the identification number of the survey. The second column includes each student's response to the survey question Q1A; the third column shows their response to question Q1B and so on.
Source: Used with Permission from Microsoft.

is inefficient. Efficient quantitative data analysis comes through the use of computers. So let's begin with a discussion of the basic steps involved in transforming data into machine-readable forms amenable to computer processing and analysis.

QUANTIFYING DATA

Quantitative data analysis is almost always conducted using computer software programs such as SPSS or STATA. For these programs to work their magic, they must be able to read the data you've collected in your research. Therefore, much data must be translated into numeric form by coding, so they may be processed by the computer. If you conducted a survey, for example, some of the information you collected, such as income, weight, or age, is numerical from the start, and may readily be input into the computer without the need for transformation or coding. Other information is easily quantified, such as transforming the values of gender, male and female, into "1" and "2" respectively. Numerical representations can be easily assigned to any number of variables—for instance, *country of origin, province of residence*, or *religious affiliation.*

Some data are a bit more challenging when it comes to numerical transformation. If a survey respondent tells you that he or she thinks the biggest problem facing Charlottetown, Prince Edward Island, today is "the disintegrating ozone layer," you must translate by coding the response. We have discussed coding in connection with content analysis (Chapter 9) and again in connection with qualitative data analysis (Chapter 13). Now we'll look at coding specifically for quantitative analysis. To conduct a quantitative analysis, researchers often must engage in a coding process after the data have been collected. For example, open-ended questionnaire items result in nonnumerical responses, which must be coded before analysis. As with content analysis, the task here is to reduce a wide variety of idiosyncratic items of information to a more limited set of attributes making up a variable. Suppose, for example, that a survey researcher has asked respondents, "What is your occupation?" The responses to such a question would vary considerably. Although it would be possible to assign each reported occupation a separate numerical code, this procedure would not facilitate analysis, which typically depends on several subjects having the same attribute (and assigned numerical code).

The variable *occupation* has many pre-established coding schemes. One such scheme distinguishes professional and managerial occupations, clerical occupations, semiskilled occupations, and so forth. Another scheme distinguishes different sectors of the economy: manufacturing, health, education, commerce, and so forth. Still others combine both. An advantage of using an established coding scheme is the ability to compare your research results with those of other studies. Statistics Canada, for example, has the National Occupational Classification for Statistics (NOC-S) 2011, used in the 2011 National Household Survey, available on its website.

The occupational coding scheme you choose should be appropriate to the theoretical concepts being examined in your study. For some studies, coding all occupations as either white-collar or blue-collar might be sufficient. For others, self-employed and not self-employed might be sufficient. Or a peace researcher might wish to know only whether the occupation depended on the defence establishment or not.

Although the coding scheme should be tailored to meet particular requirements of the analysis, one general guideline should be kept in mind. If the data are coded to maintain a great deal of detail, code categories can always be combined during an analysis that does not require such detail. If the data are coded into relatively few, gross categories, however, there's no way during analysis to recreate the original detail. To keep your options open, it's a good idea to code your data in more detail than you plan to use in the analysis.

DEVELOPING CODE CATEGORIES

There are two basic approaches to the coding process. First, you may begin with a relatively well-developed coding scheme, derived from your research purpose. Thus, as suggested previously, the peace researcher might code occupations based on their relationship to the defence establishment. Or you may want to use an existing coding scheme so that you can compare your findings with those of previous research.

The alternative method is to generate codes from your data, as discussed in Chapter 13. Let's say we've asked students in a self-administered campus survey to say what they believe is the biggest problem facing their university today. Here are a few of the answers they might have written in.

Tuition is too high
Not enough parking spaces
Faculty don't know what they are doing
Advisers are never available
Not enough classes offered
Cockroaches in the dorms
Too many requirements
Cafeteria food is inedible
Books cost too much
Not enough financial aid

Take a minute to review these responses and see whether you can identify some categories represented. Realize that there is no right answer; several coding schemes might be generated from these answers.

Let's start with the first response: "Tuition is too high." What general areas of concern does that response reflect? One obvious possibility is "Financial Concerns." Are there other responses that would fit into that category? Table 14-1 shows which of the questionnaire responses could fit.

TABLE 14-1 Student Responses That Can Be Coded "Financial Concerns"

	Financial Concerns
Tuition is too high	X
Not enough parking spaces	
Faculty don't know what they are doing	
Advisers are never available	
Not enough classes offered	
Cockroaches in the dorms	
Too many requirements	
Cafeteria food is infected	
Books cost too much	X
Not enough financial aid	X

Source: © Cengage Learning

TABLE 14-2 Student Responses That Can Be Coded "Academic" and "Nonacademic"

	Academic	Nonacademic
Tuition is too high		X
Not enough parking spaces		X
Faculty don't know what they are doing	X	
Advisers are never available	X	
Not enough classes offered	X	
Cockroaches in the dorms		X
Too many requirements	X	
Cafeteria food is infected		X
Books cost too much		
Not enough financial aid		X

Source: © Cengage Learning

In more general terms, the first answer can also be seen as reflecting nonacademic concerns. This categorization would be relevant if your research interest included the distinction between academic and nonacademic concerns. If that were the case, the responses might be coded as shown in Table 14-2.

Notice that we didn't code the response "Books cost too much" in Table 14-2, because this concern could be seen as representing both of the categories. Books are part of the academic program, but their cost is not. This signals the need to refine the coding scheme we're developing. Depending on our research purpose, we might be especially interested in identifying any problems that had an academic element; hence we'd code this one "Academic." Just as reasonably, however, we might be more interested in identifying nonacademic problems and would code the response accordingly. Or, as another alternative, we might create a separate category for responses that involved both academic and nonacademic matters.

As yet another alternative, we might want to separate nonacademic concerns into those involving administrative matters and those dealing with campus facilities. Table 14-3 shows how the 10 responses would be coded in that event.

As these few examples illustrate, there are many possible schemes for coding a set of data.

TABLE 14-3 Nonacademic Concerns Coded as "Administrative" or "Facilities"

	Academic	Administrative	Facilities
Tuition is too high		X	
Not enough parking spaces			X
Faculty don't know what they are doing	X		
Advisers are never available	X		
Not enough classes offered	X		
Cockroaches in the dorms			X
Too many requirements	X		
Cafeteria food is infected			X
Books cost too much	X		
Not enough financial aid		X	

Source: © Cengage Learning

Your choices should match your research purposes and reflect the logic that emerges from the data themselves. Often, you'll find yourself modifying the code categories as the coding process proceeds. Whenever you change the list of categories, however, you must review the data already coded to see whether changes are in order.

Like the set of attributes composing a variable, and like the response categories in a closed-ended questionnaire item, code categories should be both exhaustive and mutually exclusive. Every piece of information being coded should fit into one and only one category. Problems arise whenever a given response appears to fit equally into more than one code category or whenever it fits into no category: Both signal a mismatch between your data and your coding scheme.

If you're fortunate enough to have assistance in the coding process, you'll need to train your coders in the definitions of code categories and show them how to use those categories properly. To do so, explain the meaning of the code categories and give several examples of each. To make sure your coders fully understand what you have in mind, code several cases ahead of time. Then ask your coders to code the same cases without knowing how you coded them. Finally, compare your coders' work with your own. Any discrepancies will indicate an imperfect communication of your coding scheme to your coders. Even with perfect agreement between you and your coders, however, it's best to check the coding of at least a portion of the cases throughout the coding process.

If you're not fortunate enough to have assistance in coding, you should still obtain some verification of your own reliability as a coder. Nobody's perfect, especially a researcher hot on the trail of a finding. Let's say you are studying an emerging cult and you have the impression that people who don't have a regular family will be the most likely to regard the new cult as a family substitute. The danger is that whenever you discover a subject who reports no family, you'll unconsciously try to find some evidence in the subject's comments that the cult is a substitute for family. If at all possible, then, get someone else to code some of your cases to see if that person makes the same assignments you made.

CODEBOOK CONSTRUCTION

The end product of the coding process is the conversion of data items into numerical codes. These codes represent attributes making up variables, which in turn are assigned names and locations within a data file. A **codebook** is a document that describes the locations of variables and lists the assignments of codes to the attributes making up those variables.

A codebook serves two essential functions. First, it's the primary guide used in the coding process. Second, it's your guide for locating variables and interpreting codes in your data file during analysis. If you decide to correlate two variables as a part of your analysis of your data, the codebook tells you where to find the variables and what the codes represent.

Figure 14-2 is a partial codebook created from two variables from the General Social Survey. Though there is no one right format for a codebook, this example presents some of the common elements.

Notice first that each variable is identified by an abbreviated variable name: POLVIEWS, ATTEND. We can determine the religious service attendance of respondents, for example, by referencing ATTEND. This example uses the format established by the General Social Survey, which has been carried over into SPSS. Other data sets and/or analysis programs might format variables differently. Some use numerical codes in place of abbreviated names, for example. You must, however, have some identifier that will allow you to locate and use the variable in question.

Next, every codebook should contain the full definition of the variable. In the case of a questionnaire, the definition consists of the exact wording of the questions asked, because, as we've seen, the wording of questions strongly influences the answers returned. In the case of POLVIEWS, you know that respondents were given several political categories and asked to pick the one that best fit them.

---

codebook The document used in data processing and analysis that tells the location of different data items in a data file; typically identifies the locations of data items and the meaning of the codes used to represent different attributes of variables.

POLVIEWS	ATTEND
We hear a lot of talk these days about liberals and conservatives. I'm going to show you a seven-point scale on which the political views that people might hold are arranged from extremely liberal—point 1—to extremely conservative—point 7. Where would you place yourself on this scale? 1. Extremely liberal 2. Liberal 3. Slightly liberal 4. Moderate, middle of the road 5. Slightly conservative 6. Conservative 7. Extremely conservative 8. Don't know 9. No answer	How often do you attend religious services? 0. Never 1. Less than once a year 2. About once or twice a year 3. Several times a year 4. About once a month 5. 2–3 times a month 6. Nearly every week 7. Every week 8. Several times a week 9. Don't know, No answer

FIGURE 14-2 **Partial Codebook.**
Source: © Cengage Learning

The codebook also indicates the attributes comprising each variable. In POLVIEWS, for example, the political categories just mentioned serve as these attributes: "Extremely liberal," "Liberal," "Slightly liberal," and so forth.

Finally, notice that each attribute also has a numeric label. Thus, in POLVIEWS, "Extremely liberal" is code category 1. These numeric codes are used in various manipulations of the data. For example, you might decide to combine categories 1 through 3 (all the "liberal" responses). It's easier to do this with code numbers than with lengthy names.

DATA ENTRY

In order to conduct quantitative analysis, the numerically transformed data must be converted into a machine-readable format, making it possible for computers to read and manipulate the data. This can be accomplished in a variety of ways, depending on the original form of the data and the computer program to be used for analyzing the data. We'll discuss only a few possibilities here.

If your data have been collected by questionnaire, you might do your coding on the questionnaire itself. Then data entry specialists (including you) could enter the data into, say, an SPSS data matrix or into an Excel spreadsheet that could later be imported into SPSS or other data analysis programs.

Social researchers sometimes use optical scan sheets (the familiar sheets used in multiple-choice exams, for example) for data collection. The sheets can be fed into machines that will convert the black marks into data, which can be imported into an analysis program. The use of such sheets works well only with subjects who are comfortable using them, and they are usually limited to closed-ended questions.

Data entry is sometimes accomplished in the process of collecting the data. As we discussed in Chapter 8, for example, in computer-assisted telephone interviewing (CATI) the interviewer inputs responses directly into the computer, where the data are compiled for analysis. With the increased use of online surveys, these may be constructed so that respondents enter their own answers directly into the database. This is even more effortless, since the researcher doesn't require an intervening interviewer or data entry person.

Once data have been fully quantified and entered into the computer, researchers can begin quantitative analysis. Let's look at the three cases mentioned at the start of this chapter: univariate, bivariate, and multivariate analyses.

UNIVARIATE ANALYSIS

Univariate analysis is the examination of the distribution of cases of only one variable. We'll begin with the logic and formats for the analysis of univariate data—the simplest form of quantitative analysis.

DISTRIBUTIONS

The most basic format for presenting univariate data is called a one-way distribution. This is often laid out in a table that records the number of cases observed for each of the attributes of some variable. Let's take an example from Canada's Aboriginal Peoples Survey. Table 14-4 presents the univariate analysis for the variable "self-perceived health status."

Let's examine the table, piece by piece. First, if you look near the bottom of the table, you'll see that the sample being analyzed has a total of 24,803 cases. You'll also see that there are different categories of data defined as "missing." Seventeen Indigenous respondents reported they don't know their health status, while 13 refused to provide an answer, and 698 did not state an answer. In total, the survey was unable to gather self-perceived health status assessment from 728 respondents. So our analysis of self-perceived health status among Indigenous peoples is based on the 24,075 respondents who answered the question.

Go back to the top of the table now. You'll see that 7,543 Indigenous respondents reported they are in "excellent" health. This number in and of itself tells us very little. It does not give us an idea of whether the "average Indigenous" person is in good health or not.

By analogy, if the spokesperson for some company said the company had 20 women executives, is that a lot or a few? The answer would depend on how the number of women executives compares to the total number of executives that firm employs. If there were 40 executives in total, 20 women would represent one-half or 50 percent; but if there were 2,000 executives employed by the company, 20 women would mean that women make up only 1 percent of all executives. So our concern would be the proportion or percentage of women executives in that company—the number of women executives relative to a base.

In the case of Indigenous health status, similarly, we need some basis for assessing the 7,543 respondents who reported that they are in excellent health. First, notice that out of 24,803 respondents, 728 did not give a useable answer. This means there are 24,075 useable (or valid) respondents. We are only interested

univariate analysis The analysis of a single variable, for purposes of description. Frequency distributions, averages, and measures of dispersion would be examples of univariate analysis, as distinguished from bivariate and multivariate analysis.

TABLE 14-4 Self-Perceived Health Status, Aboriginal Peoples Survey, Canada

		Frequency	Percent	Valid Percent	Cumulative Percent
Valid	Excellent	7543	30.4	31.3	31.3
	Very Good	7036	28.4	29.2	60.6
	Good	6212	25.1	25.8	86.4
	Fair	2316	9.3	9.6	96.0
	Poor	963	3.9	4.0	100.0
	Total	24075	97.1	100.0	
Missing	Don't know	17	0.1		
	Refusal	13	0.1		
	Not stated	698	2.8		
	Total	728	2.9		
Total		24803	100.0		

Source: Author analysis of *Aboriginal Peoples Survey 2012*. ODESI Public Use file. August 7, 2015.

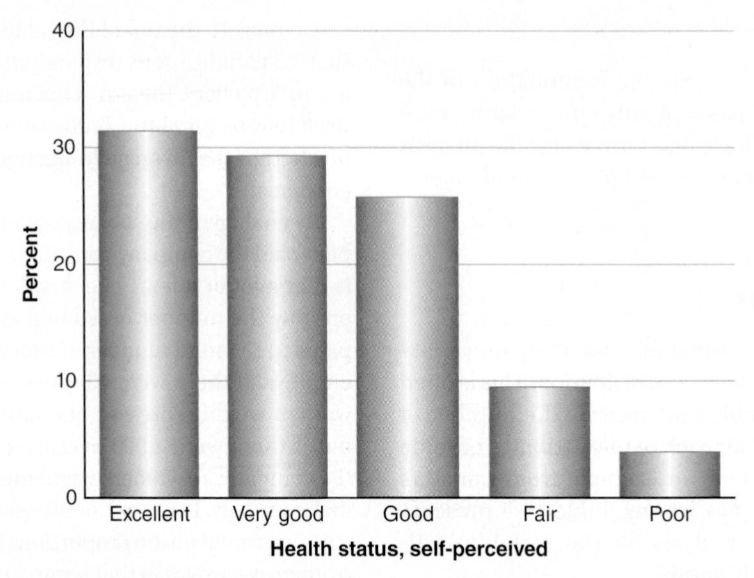

FIGURE 14-3 **Bar Chart, Self-Perceived Health Status, Aboriginal Peoples Survey Canada.**
Source: Author analysis of *Aboriginal Peoples Survey 2012*. ODESI Public Use file. August 7, 2015.

in valid responses. If you were to divide 7,543 by the 24,075 respondents who gave some useable/valid answer, you would get 31.3 percent, which appears in the table as the "valid percent." If we assess the number in this way, we see that 31.3 percent of Indigenous people in Canada rate themselves as being in excellent health. This result is more meaningful, but what does it suggest about the general health of Indigenous people? A further look at Table 14-4 shows that "excellent" is the response category most often chosen. Other widely reported response categories included "very good" (29.2 percent) and "good" (25.8 percent). In total, if you look at the cumulative percent column, 86.4 percent of Indigenous respondents rated their health as good or better. Only 13.6 percent (100% minus 86.4%) rated their health as fair or poor. As you can see, each new comparison gives a more complete picture of the data.

A description of the number of times that the various attributes of a variable are observed in a sample is called a **frequency distribution**. It's sometimes easier to see a frequency distribution in a graph. In Figure 14-3, the vertical scale on the left of the graph indicates the percentages selecting each of the answers displayed along the horizontal axis of the graph. Notice how the valid percentages in Table 14-4 correspond with the heights of the bars in Figure 14-3.

CENTRAL TENDENCY

Beyond simply reporting the overall distribution of values, often referred to as the *marginal frequencies* or just the *marginals*, you may choose to present your data in the form of an **average** or measure of *central tendency*. This is a way of expressing the "typical" value of a variable. For example, your grade point average expresses the "typical" value of all your grades taken together, even though some of them might be As, others Bs, and perhaps even some C grades. One common way in which a GPA is calculated is by

frequency distribution A description of the number of times the various attributes of a variable are observed in a sample. The report that 53 percent of a sample were men and 47 percent were women is a simple example of a frequency distribution.

average An ambiguous term generally suggesting typical or normal—a central tendency. The mean, median, and mode are specific examples of mathematical averages.

converting the letter grades into their numerical representations, and then calculating the arithmetic **mean** by dividing the sum of the values by the total number of cases. The mean is only one way to measure central tendencies or "typical" value. The **mode** (the most frequently occurring attribute) and the **median** (the middle attribute in the *ranked* distribution of observed attributes) are two other options. Here's how the three averages would be calculated from a set of data.

Suppose you're conducting an experiment that involves teenagers as subjects. They range in age from 13 to 19, as indicated in the following table:

Age	Number
13	3
14	4
15	6
16	8
17	4
18	3
19	3

Now that you've seen the actual ages of the 31 subjects, how old would you say they are in general, or on *average*? Let's look at three different ways you might answer that question.

The easiest average to calculate is the *mode*, the most frequent value. As you can see, there were more 16-year-olds (eight of them) than any other age, so the modal age is 16, as indicated in Figure 14-4. Technically, the modal age is the category "16," which may include some people who are closer to 17 than 16 but who haven't yet reached that birthday.

Figure 14-4 also demonstrates the calculation of the *mean*. There are three steps: (1) multiply each age by the number of subjects who have that age, (2) total the results of all those multiplications, and (3) divide that total by the number of subjects.

In the case of age, a special adjustment is needed. As indicated in the discussion of the mode, those who call themselves "13" actually range from exactly 13 years old to those just short of 14. It is reasonable to assume, moreover, that as a group, the 13-year-olds in the country are evenly distributed within that one-year span, making their average age 13.5 years. This is true for each of the age groups. Hence, it is appropriate to add 0.5 year to the final calculation, making the mean age 16.37, as indicated in Figure 14-4.

The *median* represents the "middle" value: half are above it, half below. If we had the precise ages of each subject (e.g., 17 years and 124 days), we'd be able to arrange all 31 subjects in order by age, and the median for the whole group would be the age of the middle subject.

As you can see, however, we don't know precise ages; our data constitute "grouped data" in this regard: for example, three people who are not precisely the same age have been grouped in the category "13 years old."

Figure 14-4 illustrates the logic of calculating a median for grouped data. Because there are 31 subjects altogether, the "middle" subject would be case number 16 if they were arranged by age—15 teenagers would be younger and 15 older. Look at the bottom portion of Figure 14-4, and you'll see that the middle person is one of the eight 16-year-olds. In the enlarged view of that group, we see that case number 16 is the third from the left.

Because we don't know the precise ages of the subjects in this group, the statistical convention here is to assume they're evenly spread along the width of the group. In this instance, the *possible* ages of the subjects go from 16 years and no days to 16 years and 364/365 days. As a practical matter, it's sufficient to call it one year.

If the eight subjects in this group were evenly spread from one limit to the other, they would

mean An average computed by summing the values of several observations and dividing by the number of observations. If you now have a GPA of 4.0 based on 10 courses, and you get an F in this course, your new grade point (mean) average will be 3.6.

mode An average representing the most frequently observed value or attribute. If a sample contains 1,000 Protestants, 275 Catholics, 33 Jews, and 10 Muslims, Protestant is the modal category.

median An average representing the value of the "middle" case in a rank-ordered set of observations. If the ages of five men were 16, 17, 20, 54, and 88, the median would be 20. (The mean would be 39.)

be one-eighth of a year apart from each other—a 0.125-year interval. Look at the illustration and you'll see that if we place the first subject half an interval from the lower limit and add a full interval to the age of each successive subject, the final one is half an interval from the upper limit.

What we've done is calculate, hypothetically, the precise ages of the eight subjects—assuming their ages were spread out evenly. Having done this, we merely note the age of the middle subject from the overall list of subjects (case number 16)—16.31—and that is the median age for the group.

Whenever the total number of subjects is an even number, of course, there is no middle case. To obtain the median, you merely calculate the mean of the two values on either side of the midpoint of the ranked data. For example, suppose there were one more 19-year-old, giving us a total of 32 cases. The midpoint would then fall between case number 16 and case number 17. The median would therefore be calculated as $(16.31 + 16.44)/2 = 16.38$.

As the example in Figure 14-4 illustrates, the three measures of central tendency often produce slightly different values, which is often (but not necessarily) the case. Therefore, which measure of central tendency you choose to report depends on the nature of your data and the goal of your analysis. Whenever means are presented, you should be aware that they are susceptible to extreme values: a few very large or very small numbers. In such circumstances, the different measures of central tendency can produce very different values. It is important, therefore, to be familiar with the distribution of your data when choosing the measure of central tendency to report. For example, if one is attempting to present a relatively accurate picture of the "average" family wealth within a community—in a community where a few families have great wealth—use of the mean, as a measure of central tendency, would likely be misleading. The inequality in the distribution of wealth—the few families with great wealth—would inflate the apparent average. Let's look at a hypothetical example to illustrate. Suppose there were nine families who lived on a block. The families' net worth figures are distributed as follows: $100,000; $100,000; $105,000; $107,000; $109,000; $110,000; $112,000; $114,000; $30,000,000 (the house on the hill). Clearly, reporting the *mean* ($3,428,556) would be a misleading figure of the average wealth of families on this block; a measure such as *median* family wealth ($109,000) would provide a more accurate picture of the "average" family's net worth in this case. Therefore, it is important to carefully choose among the various measures of central tendency. Situations when it is appropriate to use each of the measures of central tendency are covered in greater depth in statistics courses and textbooks.

DISPERSION

Averages offer readers the advantage of reducing the raw data to the most manageable form: a single number (or attribute) can represent all the detailed data collected in regard to the variable. This advantage comes at a cost, of course, because the reader can't reconstruct the original data from an average. Summaries of the **dispersion** of responses—the way values are distributed around some central value, such as the mean—can somewhat alleviate this disadvantage.

The simplest measure of dispersion is the **range**: the distance separating the highest from the lowest value. Thus, besides reporting that our subjects have a mean age of 16.37, we might also indicate that their ages ranged from 13 to 19.

A somewhat more sophisticated measure of dispersion is the **standard deviation**. Essentially, the standard deviation is an index of the

dispersion The distribution of values around some central value, such as an average.

range A simple example of a measure of dispersion, composed of the highest and lowest values of a variable in some set of observations. Thus, we may report that the mean age of a group is 37.9, and the range is from 12 to 89.

standard deviation A measure of dispersion around the mean, calculated so that approximately 68 percent of the cases will lie within plus or minus one standard deviation from the mean, 95 percent will lie within plus or minus two standard deviations, and 99.9 percent will lie within three standard deviations. Thus, for example, if the mean age in a group is 30 and the standard deviation is 10, then 68 percent have ages between 20 and 40. The smaller the standard deviation, the more tightly the values are clustered around the mean; if the standard deviation is high, the values are widely spread out.

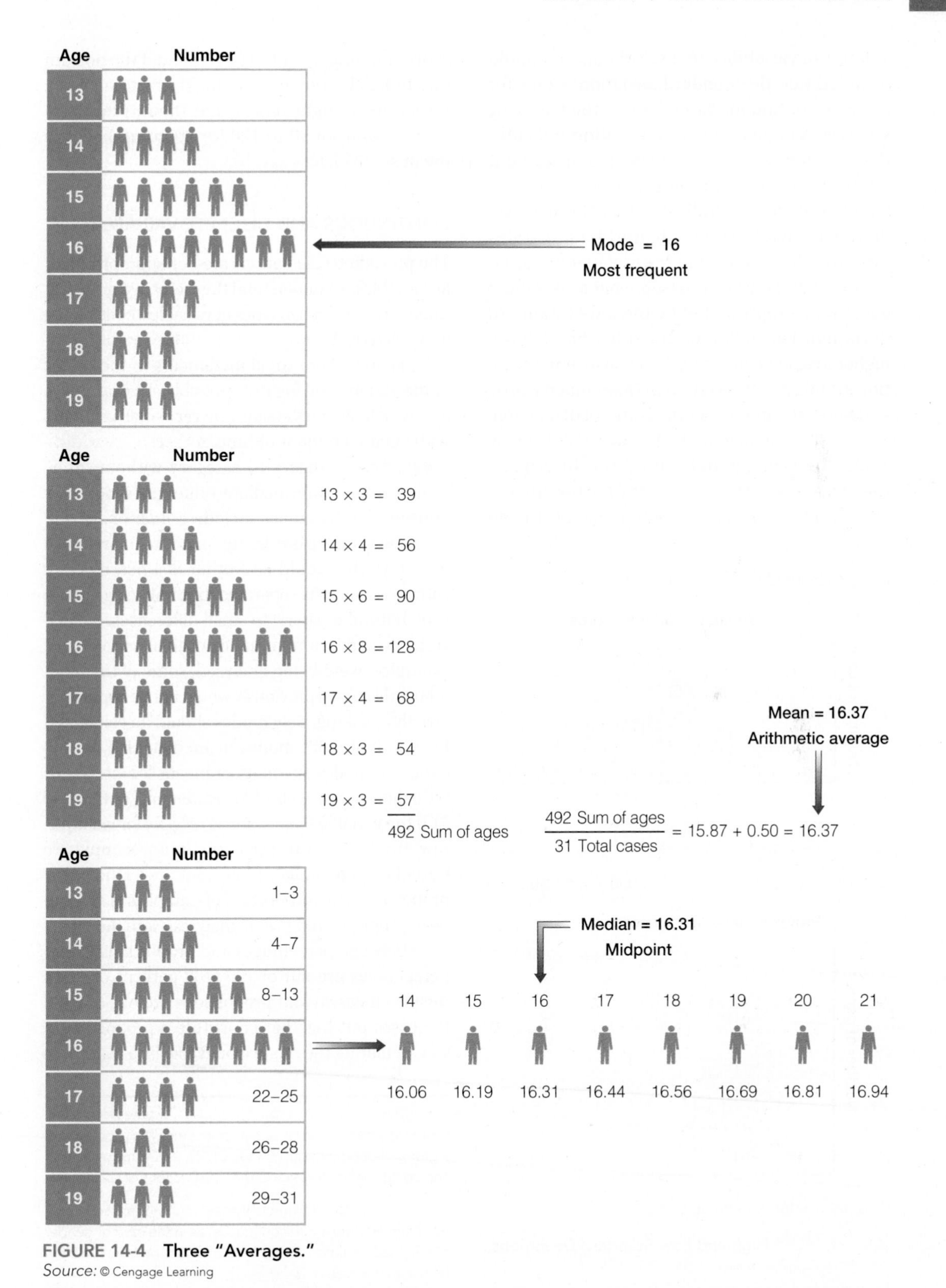

FIGURE 14-4 Three "Averages."
Source: © Cengage Learning

amount of variability in a set of data. It should be noted that the standard deviation is only for use with continuous variables (see the following section). A higher standard deviation indicates that the data are more dispersed or spread out around the central value (e.g., the mean). A lower standard deviation indicates that the data are more bunched together. Figure 14-5 illustrates the basic idea. Notice that the professional golfer not only has a lower mean score but also is more consistent—represented by the lower standard deviation. The duffer, on the other hand, has a higher average and also is less consistent: sometimes doing much better, sometimes much worse.

There are many other measures of dispersion. In reporting intelligence test scores, for example, researchers might determine the interquartile range—the range of scores for the middle 50 percent of subjects. If the top one-fourth had scores ranging from 120 to 150, and if the bottom one-fourth had scores ranging from 60 to 90, the researchers might report that the interquartile range was from 90 to 120 (or 30 points), with a mean score of, let's say, 102.

a. High standard deviation = spread-out values

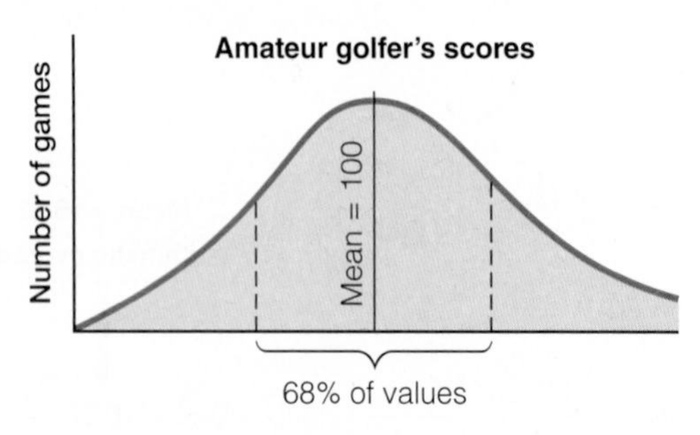

b. Low standard deviation = tightly clustered values

FIGURE 14-5 **High and Low Standard Deviations.**
Source: © Cengage Learning

CONTINUOUS AND DISCRETE VARIABLES

The preceding calculations are not appropriate for all variables. To understand this point, we must distinguish between two types of variables: continuous and discrete. A **continuous variable** (or ratio variable) is one where small increments in the values of the variable are logically possible. An example is age, which changes steadily by very small amounts with each increment of time. A **discrete variable** jumps from category to category without intervening steps—intermediate values are illogical or nonsensical. Examples include *gender* or *marital status*—you go from being single to married in one step. One could add other distinct, discrete categories such as separated, but unlike age, there is no natural meaning to small differences. If a discrete variable—a nominal or ordinal variable, for example—were being analyzed, some of the techniques discussed previously would not be applicable. Strictly speaking, only modes should be calculated for nominal data; modes or medians for ordinal data; and modes, medians, or means for interval or ratio data (see "Levels of Measurement" in Chapter 5). If the variable in question is *religion*, for example, raw numbers (23 respondents in our sample are Catholic), percentages (7 percent are Catholic), or proportions (the proportion of Catholics is .07) can be appropriate and useful analyses. Note the difference between percentages and proportions is that percentages are out of 100 (100 percent of cases means all cases) and proportions are out of 1 (all the cases put together constitute a proportion of 1). Calculating the mode would also be a legitimate

continuous variable A variable whose attributes form a steady progression, such as age or income. Thus, the ages of a group of people might include 21, 22, 23, 24, and so forth, and could even be broken down into fractions of years.

discrete variable A variable whose attributes are separate from one another, or discontinuous, as in the case of gender or religious affiliation. There is no progression from male to female in the case of gender.

step, and reporting it might be helpful when one religion is predominant—for example, if most of the respondents are Protestants. Reports of mean, median, or dispersion summaries, however, would be inappropriate—they would not make sense.

DETAIL VERSUS MANAGEABILITY

In presenting univariate and other data summaries, you'll be constrained by two goals. On the one hand, you should attempt to provide your reader with the fullest degree of detail regarding those data. On the other hand, data summaries should be presented in a manageable form. As these two goals often directly conflict, you'll find yourself continually seeking the best compromise between them. One useful solution is to report a given set of data in more than one form. In the case of *age*, for example, you might report the distribution of ungrouped ages *plus* the mean age and standard deviation.

As you can see from this introductory discussion of univariate analysis, this seemingly simple matter can be rather complex. In any event, the lessons of this section pave the way for consideration of subgroup comparisons and bivariate analyses.

SUBGROUP COMPARISONS

Univariate analyses describe the units of analysis of a study and, if they're a sample drawn from some larger population, allow us to make descriptive inferences about the larger population. Bivariate and multivariate analyses are aimed primarily at explanation. Before turning to explanation, however, we should consider the case of subgroup description.

Often, it's appropriate to describe subsets of cases, subjects, or respondents. Table 14-5, for example, presents the self-perceived health ratings of adult Canadians by whether the respondents did or did not ever work at a job or business. In some situations, the researcher presents subgroup comparisons purely for descriptive purposes. More often, the purpose of subgroup descriptions is comparative. In this case we can ask whether working makes a systematic difference to self-reports of health.

TABLE 14-5 Self-Rated General Health by Whether Ever Worked at a Job or Business (percentages)

	Ever Worked at a Job or Business	
Self-Rated General Health	Yes	No
Excellent	16.9	28.4
Very good	29.0	35.3
Good	25.4	25.4
Fair	16.9	8.4
Poor	11.8	2.5

Source: Author's computations, General Social Survey, Canada, 2013. Cycle 27, Social Identity. August 7, 2015.

Table 14-5 contrasts two subgroups of adult Canadians: those who worked at a job or business, and those who did not. Comparing these two groups on each of the health conditions reveals systematic differences. While 16.9 percent of those who had worked for a job or business reported "excellent" health, 28.4 of those who did not reported excellent health. In terms of "very good" health, the gap was over 6 percent. Almost five times as many job or business workers reported "poor" health. Do these systematic differences between subgroups dampen your enthusiasm for employment?

Before moving on to the logic of bivariate, causal analysis, let's consider another example of subgroup comparisons—one that will let us address some table-formatting issues.

"COLLAPSING" RESPONSE CATEGORIES

"Textbook examples" of tables are often simpler than you'll typically find in published research reports or in your own analyses of data, so this section and the next one address two common problems and suggest solutions.

Let's begin by looking at Table 14-6, which reports the frequency of prayer in selected countries. Part of the World Values Survey, the specific question posed to respondents in these countries was "Apart from weddings and funerals, how often do you pray?" Look at the evidence in Table 14-6 and answer the question: How do these five different nations compare in their frequency of prayer? As you review the table, you may find there are simply

TABLE 14-6 Frequency of Prayer for Selected Countries, 2011–2012 (percentages)

	Country				
Frequency of Prayer	Australia	Germany	Japan	Sweden	United States
Several times a day	9.1	0.0	4.5	3.4	28.3
Once a day	7.6	0.0	15.8	6.9	16.6
Several times a week	11.7	35.2	5.3	8.0	20.2
Only when attending religious services	8.4	0.0	5.3	3.9	4.9
Only on special holy days	1.3	9.1	27.9	3.0	2.1
Once a year	3.1	2.9	9.4	9.3	2.1
Less often than once a year	13.2	16.5	17.7	7.9	7.4
Never, practically never	44.5	34.0	12.8	56.8	16.5
No response	1.1	2.3	1.3	0.8	1.9

Source: Author's computations, World Values Survey, 2010–2014 Wave. August 8, 2015.

so many numbers that it's hard for you to see any meaningful pattern.

Part of the problem with Table 14-6 is that there are so many prayer response categories—ranging from "several times a day" to "never, practically never." This problem is compounded by the fact that several cells in the table contain very small or no responses.

One way to clarify the pattern in results like these is to "collapse" some of the response categories. In this sense, "collapsing" means combining smaller, refined categories in broader ones. To illustrate, Table 14-7 does this by collapsing "several times a day," "once a day," and "several times a week" into a category called "frequently"; collapsing "only when attending religious services," "only on special holy days," and "once a year" into "occasionally"; and collapsing "less often than once a year" and "never, practically never" into "rarely." This revised version of the table makes the patterned differences in prayer among the countries very evident. Prayer practices in the United States are remarkably different from those of the other nations.

HANDLING "DON'T KNOW" RESPONSES

Tables 14-6 and 14-7 illustrate another potential problem in the analysis of survey data. It's usually a good idea to give people the option of saying "don't know" or "no opinion" when asking for their opinions on issues, but what do you do with those answers in analyzing the data?

In the World Values tables on prayer, the "don't know" and "no opinion" responses have been reported as "no response." In these tables a relatively small proportion of respondents in each country are in this category, and not that much difference exists in nonresponse among the countries. Consequently, this category is not obscuring the data pattern very much. But in other analyses, when significant proportions of nonrespondents and/or significant variation occurs among the groups, nonresponse can make data interpretation problematic. So what can we do in that situation?

A common solution is to recalculate the percentages in the table with the "don't knows" or "no responses" excluded. To do this you need to know the total number of respondents in each group. For the data on prayer patterns, the samples included 1,477 Australians, 2,046 Germans, 2,443 Japanese, 1,206 Swedes, and 2,232 Americans. You can use these numbers to recreate the actual number of respondents in each category of the table, and then recalculate percentages with nonresponses excluded. If you do this for Tables 14-6 and 14-7, you will see it makes little difference in this case. However, in other cases the difference can be significant.

Transformations like collapsing categories and excluding nonrespondents affect the appearance of the results. With different versions of the evidence, you may be asking yourself: Which is the *right* one? The answer depends on your purpose in analyzing and interpreting the data. For

TABLE 14-7 Collapsed Version, Frequency of Prayer for Selected Countries, 2011–2012 (percentages)

	Country				
Frequency of Prayer	Australia	Germany	Japan	Sweden	United States
Frequently	28.4	35.2	25.6	18.3	65.1
Occasionally	12.8	12.0	42.6	16.2	9.1
Rarely	57.7	50.5	30.5	64.7	23.9
No Response	1.1	2.3	1.3	0.8	1.9

Source: Author's computations, World Values Survey, 2010–2014 Wave. August 8, 2015.

example, if it is not essential for you to distinguish categories like "several times a day" from "once a day," it makes sense to combine them, because that makes it easier to read the table.

Whether to include or exclude the "don't knows" or "no responses" is harder to decide in the abstract. Take an example like polls before an election. It may be a very important finding that such a large percentage of voters have not made up their minds. On the other hand, it might be more appropriate to exclude the "don't knows" on the assumption that they wouldn't vote or that ultimately they would be likely to divide their votes between the two candidates.

NUMERICAL DESCRIPTIONS IN QUALITATIVE RESEARCH

Although this chapter deals primarily with quantitative research, the discussions are also relevant to qualitative studies. The findings of in-depth, qualitative studies often can be verified by some numerical testing. Thus, for example, when David Silverman wanted to compare the cancer treatments received by patients in private clinics with those in Britain's National Health Service, he primarily chose in-depth analyses of the interactions between doctors and patients:

> My method of analysis was largely qualitative and ... I used extracts of what doctors and patients had said as well as offering a brief ethnography of the setting and of certain behavioural data. In addition, however, I constructed a coding form which enabled me to collate a number of crude measures of doctor and patient interactions.
>
> (Silverman 1993:163)

Not only did the numerical data fine-tune Silverman's impressions based on his qualitative observations, but his in-depth understanding of the situation allowed him to craft an ever-more appropriate quantitative analysis. Listen to the interaction between qualitative and quantitative approaches in this lengthy discussion:

> My overall impression was that private consultations lasted considerably longer than those held in the NHS clinics. When examined, the data indeed did show that the former were almost twice as long as the latter (20 minutes as against 11 minutes) and that the difference was statistically highly significant. However, I recalled that, for special reasons, one of the NHS clinics had abnormally short consultations. I felt a fairer comparison of consultations in the two sectors should exclude this clinic and should only compare consultations taken by a single doctor in both sectors. This subsample of cases revealed that the difference in length between NHS and private consultations was now reduced to an average of under 3 minutes. This was still statistically significant, although the significance was reduced. Finally, however, if I compared only new patients seen by the same doctor, NHS patients got 4 minutes more on the average—34 minutes as against 30 minutes in the private clinic.
>
> (Silverman 1993:163–164)

This example further demonstrates the special power that can be gained from a combination of approaches in social research. The combination of qualitative and quantitative analyses can be especially potent.

BIVARIATE ANALYSIS

In contrast to univariate analysis, subgroup comparisons involve two variables. In this respect subgroup comparisons constitute a kind of **bivariate analysis**—the analysis of two variables simultaneously. The purpose of subgroup comparisons—like univariate analysis—is largely descriptive. Most bivariate analysis in social research adds another element: determining relationships between the variables themselves. Thus, univariate analysis and subgroup comparisons focus on describing the *people* (or other units of analysis) under study, whereas bivariate analysis focuses on the *variables* and their empirical relationships.

Table 14-8 could be regarded as an instance of subgroup comparison. It independently describes the religious service attendance of men and women, as reported in the 2013 General Social Survey conducted by Statistics Canada. It shows, comparatively and descriptively, that the women under study attended religious services more often than the men did. However, the same table, seen as an explanatory bivariate analysis, tells a somewhat different story. It suggests that the variable *gender* has an effect on the variable *religious service attendance*. In other words, we can view the behaviour as a dependent variable that is partially determined by the independent variable, *gender*.

Explanatory bivariate analyses, then, involve the "variable language" introduced in Chapter 1. In a subtle shift of focus, we're no longer talking about men and women as different subgroups but about *gender* as a variable: one that has an influence on other variables. The theoretical interpretation of Table 14-8 might be taken from Charles Glock's Comfort Hypothesis, as discussed in Chapter 2:

1. Women are still treated as second-class citizens in Canadian society.
2. People denied status gratification in the secular society may turn to religion as an alternative source of status.
3. Hence, women should be more religious than men.

The data presented in Table 14-8 confirm this reasoning: 22 percent of the women attend religious services at least weekly, compared with about 17 percent of the men.

Adding the logic of causal relationships among variables has an important implication for the construction and reading of percentage tables. One of the chief bugaboos for new data analysts is deciding on the appropriate "direction of percentaging" for any given table. In Table 14-8, for example, we've divided the group of subjects into two subgroups—men and women—and then described the behaviour of each subgroup. That is the correct method for constructing this table.

Notice, however, that we could—however inappropriately—construct the table differently. We could first divide the subjects into different degrees of religious service attendance and then describe each of those subgroups by the percentage of men and women in them. This method would make no sense as an explanation, however. Table 14-8 suggests that your gender affects your frequency of religious service attendance. Had we used the other method of construction, the table would suggest that your religious service attendance affects whether you are a man or a woman—which makes no sense. Your behaviour cannot determine your gender.

A related problem complicates the lives of new data analysts. How do you read a percentage table? There's a temptation to read Table 14-8 as follows: "Of the women, only 22 percent attended religious services weekly or more, and 78 percent

TABLE 14-8 Religious Service Attendance Reported by Men and Women in 2013 (percentages)

Religious Service Attendance	Gender	
	Men	Women
Weekly or more	17.5	22.1
Less often	82.5	77.9
Total Sample (N)	12,358	14,628

Source: Author's calculations, General Social Survey, 2013 Cycle 27, Social Identity. Statistics Canada. August 8, 2015.

bivariate analysis The analysis of two variables simultaneously to determine the empirical relationship between them. The construction of a simple percentage table or the computation of a simple correlation coefficient are examples of bivariate analyses.

said they attended less often; therefore, being a woman makes you less likely to attend religious services frequently." This is, of course, an incorrect reading of the table. Any conclusion that *gender*—as a variable—has an effect on *religious service attendance* must hinge on a comparison between men and women. Specifically, we compare the 22 percent with the 17 percent and note that *women are more likely than men* to attend religious services weekly or more. The comparison of subgroups, then, is essential in reading an explanatory bivariate table.

In constructing and presenting Table 14-8, we have used a convention called *percentage down*. This term means that you can add the percentages down each column to total 100 percent. You read this form of table across a row. For the row labelled "weekly or more," what percentage of the men attend weekly or more? What percentage of the women attend at least weekly?

Although the direction of percentaging in tables is arbitrary, the common convention is to percentage down. But not all researchers are conventional, so check to make sure that the independent variable is across the top of the table. If the independent variable is on the side of the table, then the table needs to be analyzed by percentaging across. The logic and the conclusion would be the same in either case; only the layout of the table would differ.

In reading a table that someone else has constructed, therefore, you need to find out in which direction it has been percentaged. Usually this will be labelled or be clear from the logic of the variables being analyzed. As a last resort, however, you should add the percentages in each column and each row. If each of the columns totals 100 percent, the table has been percentaged down. If the rows total 100 percent each, it has been percentaged across. The rule, then, is as follows:

1. If the table is percentaged down, read across.
2. If the table is percentaged across, read down.

PERCENTAGING A TABLE

Figure 14-6 reviews the logic by which we create percentage tables from two variables. We've used as variables *gender* and *attitudes toward equality for men and women*.

Here's another example. Suppose we're interested in learning something about newspaper editorial policies were regarding the legalization of marijuana. We undertake a content analysis of editorials on this subject that appeared during a given year in a sample of daily newspapers across Canada, and classify each editorial as favourable, neutral, or unfavourable toward the legalization of marijuana. Perhaps we wish to examine the relationship between editorial policies and the communities in which the newspapers were published, thinking that rural newspapers might have been more conservative in this regard than urban ones. Thus, we classify each newspaper (hence, each editorial) according to the population of the community in which it was published.

Table 14-9 presents some hypothetical data describing the editorial policies of rural and urban newspapers. Note that the unit of analysis in this example is the individual editorial. Table 14-9 tells us that there were 127 editorials about marijuana in our sample of newspapers published in communities with populations under 100,000. (*Note*: This cutting point is chosen for simplicity of illustration and does not mean that *rural* refers to a community of less than 100,000 in any absolute sense.) Of these, 11 percent (14 editorials) were favourable toward legalization of marijuana, 29 percent were neutral, and 60 percent were unfavourable. Of the 438 editorials that appeared in our sample of newspapers published in communities of more than 100,000 residents, 32 percent (140 editorials) were favourable toward legalizing marijuana, 40 percent were neutral, and 28 percent were unfavourable.

When we compare the editorial policies of rural and urban newspapers in our imaginary study, we find, as expected, that rural newspapers were less favourable toward the legalization of marijuana than were urban newspapers. We determine this by noting that a larger percentage (32 percent) of the urban editorials was favourable than the rural ones (11 percent). We might note, as well, that more rural than urban editorials were unfavourable (60 percent compared to 28 percent). Note that this table assumes that the size of a community might affect its newspapers' editorial policies on this issue, rather than that editorial policy might affect the size of communities.

a. Some men and women who either favour (+) gender equality or don't (–) favour it.

b. Separate the men and the women (the independent variable).

c. Within each gender group, separate those who favour equality from those who don't (the dependent variable).

d. Count the numbers in each cell of the table.

e. What percentage of the women favour equality?

f. What percentage of the men favour equality?

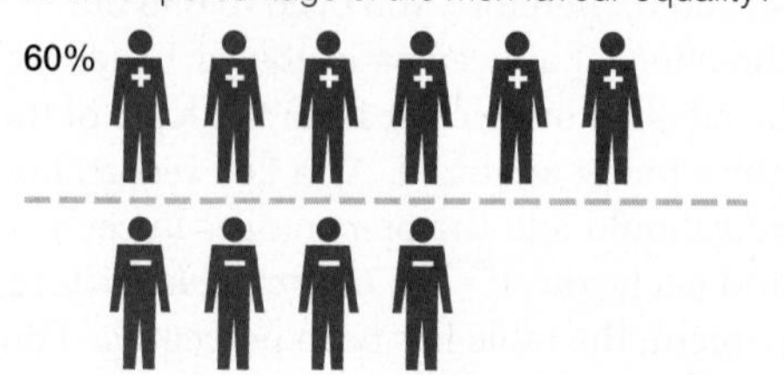

g. Conclusions.

While a majority of both men and women favoured gender equality, women were more likely than men to do so.

Thus, gender appears to be one of the causes of attitudes toward sexual equality.

	Women	Men
Favour equality	80%	60%
Don't favour equality	20	40
Total	**100%**	**100%**

FIGURE 14-6 Percentaging a Table.
Source: © Cengage Learning

TABLE 14-9 Hypothetical Data Regarding Newspaper Editorials on the Legalization of Marijuana

Editorial Policy toward Legalizing Marijuana	Community Size	
	Under 100,000	Over 100,000
Favourable	11%	32%
Neutral	29	40
Unfavourable	60	28
100% =	(127)	(438)

CONSTRUCTING AND READING BIVARIATE TABLES

Let's review the steps involved in the construction of explanatory bivariate tables:

1. The cases are divided into groups according to which attributes of the independent variable they exhibit.
2. Each of these subgroups is then described by attributes of the dependent variable.
3. Finally, the table is read by comparing the independent variable subgroups with one another according to a given attribute of the dependent variable.

Let's repeat the analysis of gender and attitude on gender equality following these steps. For the reasons outlined previously, *gender* is the independent variable; *attitude toward gender equality* constitutes the dependent variable. Thus, we proceed as follows:

1. The cases are divided into men and women.
2. Each gender subgrouping is described on the basis of approval or disapproval of gender equality.
3. Men and women are compared according to the percentages approving of gender equality.

In the example of editorial policies regarding the legalization of marijuana, *size of community* is the independent variable, and a *newspaper's editorial policy* the dependent variable. The table would be constructed as follows:

1. Divide the editorials into subgroups according to the sizes of the communities in which the newspapers were published.
2. Describe each subgroup of editorials using the percentages of favourable, neutral, or unfavourable toward the legalization of marijuana.
3. Compare the two subgroups using the percentages favourable toward the legalization of marijuana.

Bivariate analyses typically have an explanatory causal purpose. These two hypothetical examples have hinted at the nature of causation as social scientists use it. We'll build on this rather simplified approach in Chapter 15 when we cover the elaboration model, where we will look more closely at the complex nature of causation.

Tables such as the ones we've been examining are commonly called **contingency tables**: values of the dependent variable are contingent on (depend on) values of the independent variable. Although contingency tables are common in social science, their format has never been standardized. As a result, you'll find a variety of formats in research literature. As long as a table is easy to read and interpret, there's probably no reason to strive for standardization. However, there are several guidelines that you should follow in presenting most tabular data.

1. A table should have a heading or a title that succinctly describes what is contained in the table.
2. The original content of the variables should be clearly presented—in the table itself if at all possible or in the text with a paraphrase in the table. This information is especially critical when a variable is derived from responses to an attitudinal question, because the meaning of the responses will depend largely on the wording of the question.
3. The attributes of each variable should be clearly indicated. Though complex categories will have to be abbreviated, their meaning should be clear in the table and, of course, the full description should be reported in the text.

contingency table A format for presenting the relationships among variables as percentage distributions.

4. When percentages are reported in the table, the base on which they are computed should be indicated. It's redundant to present all the raw numbers for each category, because these could be reconstructed from the percentages and the bases. Moreover, the presentation of both numbers and percentages can result in a cluttered table that is more difficult to read.
5. If any cases are omitted from the table because of missing data (e.g., "no answer"), their numbers should be indicated in the table.

INTRODUCTION TO MULTIVARIATE ANALYSIS

Our examination of univariate and bivariate modes of analysis has laid the foundation for understanding more complex relationships. Thus we will now focus on the logic of **multivariate analysis**—the analysis of more than two variables simultaneously. We'll begin by discussing the construction and reading of multivariate tables and then turn to the elaboration model in Chapter 15.

CONSTRUCTING AND READING MULTIVARIATE TABLES

The logic of multivariate analysis can be seen as an extension of bivariate analysis. We can construct multivariate tables on the basis of a more complicated subgroup description by following essentially the same steps as outlined for bivariate tables. Instead of one independent variable and one dependent variable, however, we'll have more than one independent variable. Instead of explaining the dependent variable on the basis of a single independent variable, we'll seek an explanation through the use of more than one independent variable.

Let's return to the example of religious service attendance. Suppose we believe that age would also affect such behaviour; Glock's Comfort Hypothesis suggests that older people are more religious than younger people. As the first step in table construction, we would divide the total sample into subgroups based on the attributes of both independent variables simultaneously: younger men, older men, younger women, and older women. Then the several subgroups would be described in terms of the dependent variable, *religious service attendance*, and comparisons would be made. Table 14-10, from an analysis of the 2013 General Social Survey data, is the result.

multivariate analysis The analysis of the simultaneous relationships among several variables. Examining simultaneously the effects of *age*, *gender*, and *social class* on *religiosity* would be an example of multivariate analysis.

TABLE 14-10 Multivariate Relationship: Religious Service Attendance, Gender, and Age (percentages)

How Often Do You Attend Religious Services/Meetings?	Under 40		40 and Older	
	Men	Women	Men	Women
Weekly or more	13.6	15.3	19.2	27.7
Less often	86.4	84.7	80.8	72.3
Total Sample (*N*)	3,845	4,219	8,513	10,409

Source: Author's calculations, General Social Survey, 2013 Cycle 27, Social Identity. Statistics Canada. August 8, 2015.

Table 14-10 has been percentaged down and therefore should be read across. The interpretation of this table warrants several conclusions:

1. Among both men and women, older people attend church more often than younger people do. Among women, 15 percent of those under 40 and 28 percent of those 40 and older attend religious services weekly. Among men, the respective figures are about 13 and 19 percent.
2. Within each age group, women attend more frequently than men do. Among those respondents under 40, 15 percent of the women attend weekly, compared with approximately 14 percent of the men. Among those 40 and over, 28 percent of the women and 19 percent of the men attend weekly.
3. As measured in the table, age appears to have a greater effect on attendance at religious services than does gender.
4. Age and gender have independent effects on attendance at religious services. Within a given attribute of one independent variable, different attributes of the second still affect behaviours.

5. Similarly, the two independent variables have a cumulative effect on behaviours. Older women attend the most often (28 percent), and younger men attend the least frequently (14 percent).

Several of the tables presented in this chapter are somewhat inefficient. When the dependent variable, such as *religious service attendance*, is dichotomous (two attributes), knowing one attribute permits the reader to reconstruct the other easily. Thus, if we know that 15 percent of the women under 40 attend religious services weekly or more, then we know automatically that 85 percent attend less often. So reporting the percentages of women who attend less often is unnecessary. On the basis of this recognition, Table 14-10 could be presented in the alternative format of Table 14-11.

In Table 14-11, the percentages saying they attend religious services weekly or more are reported in the cells representing the intersections of the two independent variables. The numbers presented in parentheses below each percentage represent the number of cases on which the percentages are based. Thus, for example, the reader knows there are 4,219 women under 40 years of age in the sample, and 15.3 percent of them attend religious services weekly or more. We can calculate from this that 646 of those 4,219 women attend weekly or more and that the other 3,573 younger women (or about 85 percent) attend less frequently. This new table is easier to read than the former one, and it doesn't sacrifice any detail.

For another simple example of multivariate analysis, let's examine the issue of gender and income. There has been a long-standing pattern of women in the labour force earning less than men. The most recent Canadian evidence indicates that the gender gap, on average, is about 26 percent (Pay Equity Commission 2014; Beach 2015). Many explanations have been advanced to account for the difference between male and female pay. One explanation is that because of traditional family patterns, women as a group have participated less in the labour force and many began working outside the home only after certain childrearing tasks were completed. Thus, women as a group will probably have less seniority at work than men, and income increases with seniority. The Canadian Survey of Labour and Income Dynamics, however, does not support this. As Table 14-12 shows, women with the same job tenure as men fail to receive comparable earnings.

Table 14-12 indicates, first of all, that job tenure does indeed affect earnings. By reading down the first two columns of the table, it can be seen that among both men and women, those with more years on the job earn more. The table also indicates that women earn less than men regardless of job seniority. This can be seen by comparing average earnings across the rows of the table or by examining the ratio of women-to-men earnings in the third column.

This analysis indicates that the number of years on the job is an important determinant of earnings; it does not provide an adequate explanation for the pattern of women earning

TABLE 14-11 A Simplification of Table 14-10

	Percent Who Attend Religious Services/Meetings Weekly or More	
	Men	Women
Under 40	13.6	15.3
	(3,845)	(4,219)
40 and Older	19.2	27.7
	(8,513)	(10,409)

Source: Author's calculations, General Social Survey, 2013 Cycle 27, Social Identity. Statistics Canada. August 8, 2015.

TABLE 14-12 Gender, Job Tenure, and Annual Earnings (full-year, full-time workers)

	Average Annual Earnings		Women/ Men
Job Tenure	Men	Women	Ratio
Less than 1 year	$33,824	$24,438	72.3%
1 to 5 years	39,395	26,733	67.9
6 to 10 years	43,793	31,303	71.5
11 to 19 years	50,211	35,343	70.4
20+ years	56,984	38,574	67.7

Source: Adapted from Statistics Canada, "Gender, Job Tenure, and Annual earnings (Full-Year, Full Time Workers)," *The Persistent Gap: New Evidence on the Canadian Gender Wage Gap*, Catalogue 11F0019, December 1999. Reproduced and distributed on an "as is" basis with the permission of Statistics Canada.

less than men. In fact, we see that those women with 20 or more years on the job earn on average less ($38,574) than men with one to five years ($39,395).

These data indicate that the difference between men's and women's pay is not a matter of men having more time on the job. But then there are other possible explanations for the difference: education, childcare responsibilities, and so forth. The researcher who calculated the information given in Table 14-12 also examined some of the other variables that might reasonably explain the male/female difference in pay without representing gender discrimination. In addition to the number of years with current employer, the variables the researcher considered included these:

- educational background
- amount of full-year, full-time work experience
- age of youngest family member
- marital status
- part-time status
- region
- union status
- firm size
- duties
- amount of influence in budget and staffing decisions
- type of industry
- type of occupation

Each of these variables listed here might reasonably affect earnings and, if women and men differ in these regards, could help to account for female/male wage differences. When *all* these variables were taken into account, the researcher was able to account for 49 percent of the discrepancy between the wages of men and women. The remaining 51 percent, then, is a function of other "reasonable" variables and/or gender prejudice. This kind of conclusion can be reached only by examining the effects of several variables at the same time—that is, through multivariate analysis.

MAIN POINTS

- The quantification of data, converting data to a numerical form, is necessary when statistical analyses are desired.
- Some data, such as age and income, are intrinsically numerical. Often, quantification involves coding into categories that are then given numerical representations.
- Researchers may use existing coding schemes, such as the occupational classification used by Statistics Canada in the census, or develop their own coding categories. In either case, the coding scheme must be appropriate to the nature and objectives of the study.
- A codebook is the document that describes the identifiers assigned to different variables and the codes assigned to represent different attributes of those variables.
- To conduct quantitative analysis, the numerically transformed data must be converted into a machine-readable format for computer manipulation. Data entry may be accomplished in a variety of ways, including the use of optical scan sheets, direct computer entry from precoded questionnaires, interviewers' direct input into data files of respondents' answers, and respondents entering their own answers directly into a database.
- Univariate analysis is the analysis of a single variable. Because univariate analysis does not involve the relationships between two or more variables, its purpose is descriptive rather than explanatory.
- Data reduction is the process of summarizing the original data to make them more manageable while maintaining as much of

the original detail as possible. Frequency distributions, averages, grouped data, and measures of dispersion are all ways of summarizing data concerning a single variable.

- Subgroup comparisons can be used to describe similarities and differences among subgroups with respect to some variable.
- Bivariate analysis focuses on the relationships between variables rather than comparisons of groups. Bivariate analysis explores the statistical association between the independent variable and the dependent variable. Its purpose is usually explanatory rather than merely descriptive.
- The results of bivariate analyses are often presented in the form of contingency tables, constructed to reveal the effects of the independent variable on the dependent variable.
- Multivariate analysis is a method of analyzing the simultaneous relationships among several variables. It may also be used to understand the relationship between two variables more fully.

REVIEW QUESTIONS AND EXERCISES

1. Create a codebook—with variable and code assignment—for the following questions in a questionnaire:

   a. Did you obtain a high school diploma?

   ☐ Yes → If yes, did you obtain a degree from a higher educational institution?

   ☐ Yes ☐ No

   b. In the spaces provided below, please indicate the three community problems that most concern you by putting a 1 beside the one that most concerns you, a 2 beside your second choice, and a 3 beside your third choice.

   _____ Crime
   _____ Traffic
   _____ Drug abuse
   _____ Pollution
   _____ Prejudice and discrimination
   _____ Recession
   _____ Unemployment
   _____ Housing shortage

2. Write down the first 12 things you see when you walk into your bedroom. Create three different sets of categories that might be used to classify those items.
3. How many ways could you be described in numerical terms? What are some of your intrinsically numerical attributes? Could you express some of your qualitative attributes in quantitative terms?
4. Construct and interpret a contingency table from the following information: 150 women favour raising the minimum wage and 50 oppose it; 100 men favour raising the minimum wage and 300 oppose it.
5. Using the hypothetical data in the following table, construct and interpret tables showing the following:

   a. The bivariate relationship between age and attitude toward abortion.

   b. The bivariate relationship between political orientation and attitude toward abortion.

   c. The multivariate relationship linking age, political orientation, and attitude toward abortion.

Age	Political Orientation	Attitude Toward Abortion	Frequency
Young	Liberal	Favour	90
Young	Liberal	Oppose	10
Young	Conservative	Favour	60
Young	Conservative	Oppose	40
Old	Liberal	Favour	60
Old	Liberal	Oppose	40
Old	Conservative	Favour	20
Old	Conservative	Oppose	80

CONTINUITY PROJECT

DOES AWARENESS OF INEQUALITY MAKE A DIFFERENCE?

Societies with caste systems have inequality built into their social structure. India is a good example. To measure the effects of social inequality on educational performance, Hoff and Pandey (2004) conducted an experiment containing equal numbers (321) of same-age (11–12) and same-sex (boys) participants. The groups differed in caste; half were high caste, half low.

Each group was tasked with solving maze puzzles. First they did so without any public knowledge of each other's caste position (caste unannounced). Before repeating the maze puzzles, each boy was required to confirm his name, village, and caste. This is the "caste announced" situation. The following graph provides a summary of the results under the two experimental conditions (from Wilkinson and Pickett 2009:114).

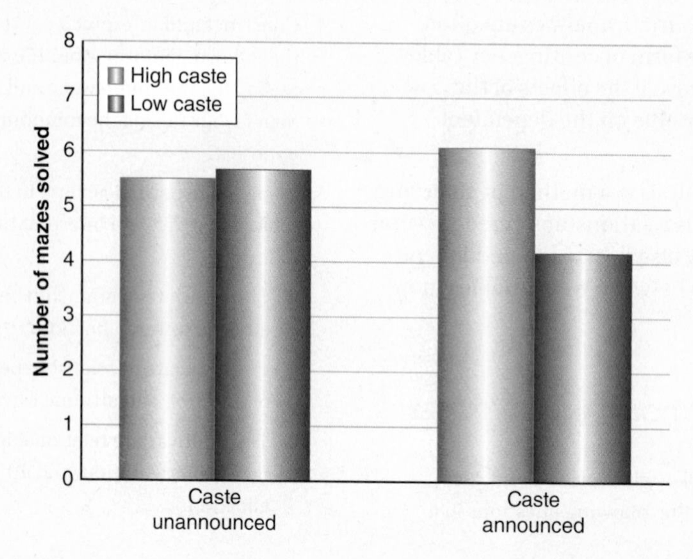

Source: Based on Hoff and Pandey (2004).

1. Look at each pair of bars and provide a description of the dependent variable results. How do low-caste boys perform when others are unaware of their caste?
2. What happens to the performance of the different caste participants when they go from ignorance to awareness of social inequalities?

View Apart/Shutterstock.com

THE LOGIC OF MULTIVARIATE ANALYSIS

The elaboration model is examined to illustrate the fundamental logic of multivariate and causal analysis. Exploring applications of this logic in the form of simple percentage tables provides a foundation for making sense of more complex analytical methods.

IN THIS CHAPTER ...

INTRODUCTION

In this chapter we will delve into multivariate analysis a little more deeply by using the **elaboration model** to illustrate the fundamental logic of multivariate and causal analysis.

This perspective on social scientific analysis is referred to variously as the elaboration model, the interpretation method, the Columbia school, and the Lazarsfeld method. Its many names reflect the fact that it aims at *elaborating* on an empirical relationship among variables in order to *interpret* that relationship in the manner developed by Paul *Lazarsfeld* while he was at *Columbia* University. Thus, the elaboration model is one method for doing multivariate analysis. It is a logical approach to data analysis—a systematic way to analyze cross-sectional data—equally applicable to a number of alternative statistical methods.

Researchers use the elaboration model to understand the relationship between two variables through the simultaneous introduction of additional variables. Though developed primarily through the medium of contingency tables, it may be used with other statistical techniques. Understanding the logic of the elaboration model in the context of contingency table analysis provides a good foundation for understanding other statistical techniques and the types of relationships that are revealed when using them.

We believe that the elaboration model offers the clearest available picture of the logic of causal analysis in social research. This method portrays the logical process of scientific analysis and is particularly accessible when illustrated through the use of contingency tables. Moreover, if you can fully comprehend the use of the elaboration model using contingency tables, you should greatly improve your ability to use and understand more sophisticated techniques.

elaboration model A logical approach to understanding the relationship between two variables through the simultaneous introduction of a third variable, which is usually referred to as a control or test variable. Though developed primarily through the medium of contingency tables by Paul Lazarsfeld, it may be used with other statistical techniques. The various outcomes of an elaboration analysis include replication, specification, explanation, and interpretation.

THE ORIGINS OF THE ELABORATION MODEL

The historical origins of the elaboration model provide a good illustration of how scientific research works in practice. During World War II, Samuel Stouffer organized and headed a special social research branch within the U.S. Army. Of the large number of studies conducted, several examined morale in the military. Morale was deemed important because it seemed to affect combat effectiveness. Stouffer and his research staff sought to uncover some of the variables that affected morale.

In part, the group wanted to confirm empirically some commonly accepted propositions, including the following:

1. Promotions surely affect soldiers' morale, so soldiers serving in units with low promotion rates should have relatively low morale.
2. Given racial segregation and discrimination in the South, African-American soldiers being trained in northern training camps should have higher morale than those being trained in the South.
3. Soldiers with more education should be more likely to resent being drafted into the army as enlisted men than those with less education.

Each of these propositions made sense logically, and common wisdom held each to be true. Stouffer decided to test each empirically. To his surprise, none of the propositions was confirmed.

Stouffer found that soldiers serving in the Military Police (where promotions were the slowest in the army) had fewer complaints about the promotion system than did those serving in the Army Air Corps (where promotions were the fastest in the army). The other propositions fared just as badly. African-American soldiers serving in northern training camps and those serving in southern training camps seemed to differ little if at all in their general morale. And less educated soldiers were more likely to resent being drafted into the army than were those with more education.

Stouffer didn't try to hide the findings or simply run tests of statistical significance and publish the results. He sought an answer to "Why?" He found the answer within the concepts of reference group and relative deprivation. Put simply, Stouffer suggested that soldiers did not evaluate their positions in life according to absolute, objective standards, but rather on the basis of their relative position vis-à-vis others around them. They compared themselves with the people in their reference group, and they felt relative deprivation if they didn't compare favourably in that regard.

Following this logic, Stouffer offered an answer to each of the anomalies in his empirical data. Regarding promotion, he suggested that soldiers judged the fairness of the promotion system based on their own experiences relative to others around them. In the Military Police (MP), where promotions were few and slow, few soldiers knew of a less qualified buddy who had been promoted faster than they had. In the Army Air Corps, however, the rapid promotion rate meant that many soldiers knew of less qualified buddies who had been promoted faster than seemed appropriate. Thus, ironically, the MPs said the promotion system was generally fair, and the air corpsmen said it was not.

A similar analysis seemed to explain the case of the African-American soldiers. Rather than comparing conditions in the North with those in the South, African-American soldiers compared their own status with the status of the African-American civilians around them. In the South, where discrimination was at its worst, they found that being a soldier insulated them somewhat from adverse cultural norms in the surrounding community. Although southern African-American civilians were grossly discriminated against and denied self-esteem, good jobs, and so forth, African-American soldiers had a slightly better status. In the North, however, many of the African-American civilians they encountered held well-paying defence jobs. And with discrimination being less severe, being a soldier did not help one's status in the community.

Finally, the concepts of reference group and relative deprivation seemed to explain the anomaly of highly educated draftees accepting their induction more willingly than did those with less education. Stouffer reasoned as follows (1949–1950:122–27)[1]:

1. A person's friends, on the whole, have about the same educational status as that person does.
2. Draft-age men with less education are more likely to engage in semi-skilled production-line occupations and farming than more educated men.
3. During wartime, many production-line industries and farming are vital to the national interest; workers in those industries and farmers are exempted from the draft.
4. A man with little education is more likely to have friends in draft-exempt occupations than a man with more education.
5. When each compares himself with his friends, a less educated draftee is more likely to feel discriminated against than a draftee with more education.

Stouffer's explanations unlocked the mystery of the three anomalous findings. Because they were not part of a planned study design, however, he lacked empirical data for testing them. Nevertheless, Stouffer's logical exposition provided the basis for the later development of the elaboration model: understanding the relationship between two variables through the controlled introduction of other variables.

Paul Lazarsfeld and his associates at Columbia University formally developed the elaboration model in 1946. In a methodological review of Stouffer's army studies, Lazarsfeld and Patricia Kendall used the logic of the elaboration model to present hypothetical tables that would have proved Stouffer's contention regarding education and acceptance of induction if the empirical data had been available (Kendall and Lazarsfeld 1950).

The central logic of the elaboration model begins with an observed relationship between two variables and the possibility that one variable may be causing the other. In the Stouffer example, the initial two variables were *educational level* and *acceptance of being drafted as fair*. Since the

1 *The American Soldier* by Stouffer, Samuel Andrew. Reproduced with permission of Princeton University Press in the format Book via Copyright Clearance Center.

soldiers' education levels were set before they were drafted (and thus before developing any reaction to being drafted), it would seem that *educational level* was the cause, or independent variable, and *acceptance of induction* was the effect, or dependent variable. As we just saw, however, the observed relationship countered what the researchers had expected.

The elaboration model examines the impact of other variables on the relationship first observed. Sometimes this analysis reveals the mechanisms through which the causal relationship occurs. Other times an elaboration analysis disproves the existence of a causal relationship altogether.

In the present example, the additional variable was whether a soldier's friends were deferred or drafted. In Stouffer's speculative explanation, this variable showed how it was actually logical that soldiers with more education would be more accepting of being drafted, because it was likely that their friends would also have been drafted. Those with the least education were likely to have been in occupations that often brought deferments from the draft, leading those drafted to feel that they had been treated unfairly.

Kendall and Lazarsfeld began with Stouffer's data showing the positive association between education and acceptance of induction—Figure 15-1. In this and the following figures, "should have been deferred" and "should not have been deferred" represent inductees' judgments of their own situation, with the latter group feeling it was fair for them to have been drafted.

Kendall and Lazarsfeld then created some hypothetical tables to represent what the analysis might have looked like had soldiers been asked whether most of their friends had been drafted or deferred. In Figure 15-2, 19 percent of those with high education hypothetically said their friends were deferred, compared with 79 percent of the soldiers with less education. Notice that the numbers of soldiers with high and low education are the same as in Stouffer's real data. In later tables, you see that the numbers who accepted or resented being drafted are kept true to the original data. Only the numbers saying that friends were or were not deferred were made up.

Stouffer's explanation next assumed that soldiers with friends who had been deferred would

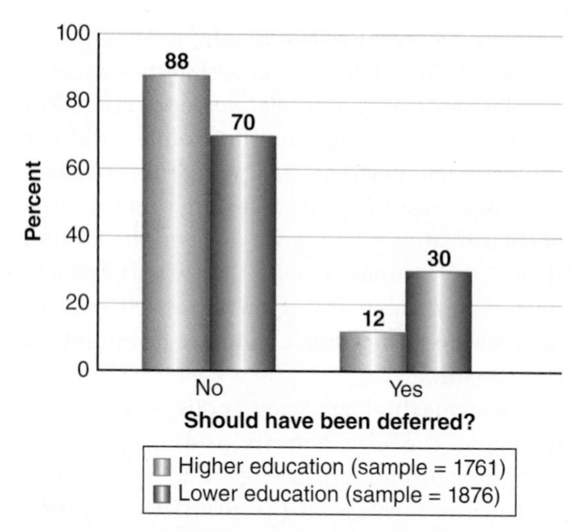

FIGURE 15-1 **Summary of Stouffer's Data on Education and Acceptance of Induction.**
Source: Kendall and Lazarsfeld (1950).

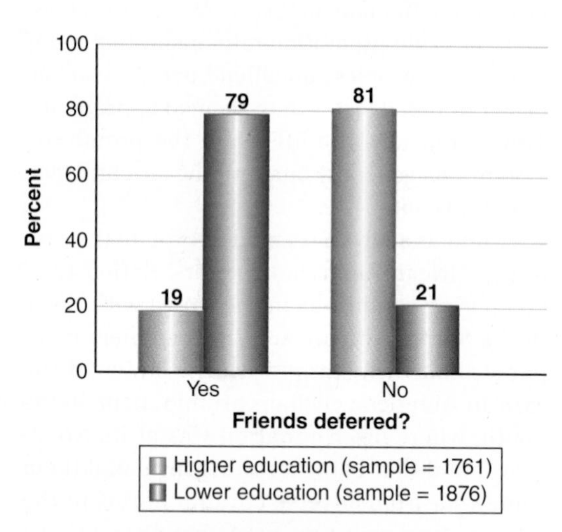

FIGURE 15-2 **Hypothetical Relationship between Education and Deferrment of Friends.**
Source: Kendall and Lazarsfeld (1950).

be more likely to resent their own induction than would those who had no deferred friends. Figure 15-3 presents the hypothetical data that would have supported that assumption.

The hypothetical data in Figures 15-2 and 15-3 would confirm the linkages that Stouffer had specified in his explanation. First, soldiers with low education were more likely to have friends who were deferred than were soldiers with more

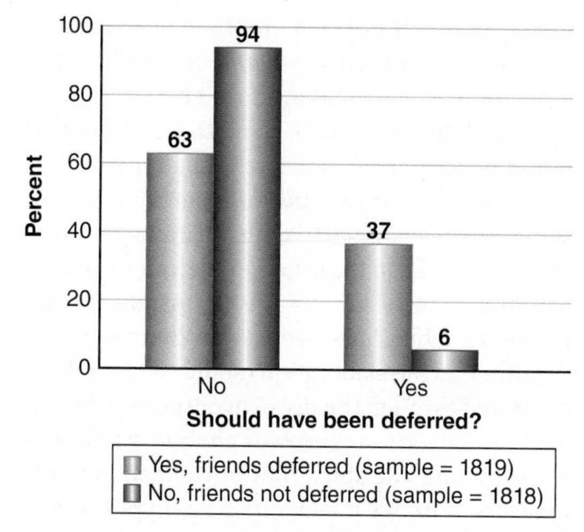

FIGURE 15-3 **Hypothetical Relationship between Deferrment of Friends and Acceptance of One's Own Induction.**
Source: Kendall and Lazarsfeld (1950).

education. Second, having friends who were deferred made a soldier more likely to think he should have been deferred. Stouffer had suggested that these two relationships would clarify the original relationship between *education* and *acceptance of induction.* Kendall and Lazarsfeld created a hypothetical table that would confirm Stouffer's explanation (see Figure 15-4).

Recall that the original finding was that draftees with high education were more likely to accept their induction into the army as fair than were those with less education. In Figure 15-4, however, the graph shows that *level of education* has no effect (i.e. shows no difference between education groups) on the *acceptance of induction* among those who report having friends deferred: 63 percent among both education groups indicate that they accept their induction (i.e., they say they should not have been deferred). Similarly *educational level* has no significant effect on *acceptance of induction* among those who reported having no friends deferred: 94 and 95 percent say they should not have been deferred. Thus, for those whose friends were not deferred, education made little difference to whether they accepted their own induction or not.

Notice that acceptance of induction was lower (only 63%) among those who had friends deferred, regardless of education level. Thus, the hypothetical data in Figure 15-4 would support Stouffer's contention that education affected acceptance of induction only through the medium of having friends deferred. In other words, the apparent effect of education level on attitudes toward deferment was, in part, due to the effect of education level on probability of deferment. Highly educated draftees were less likely to have friends deferred and, by virtue of that fact, were more

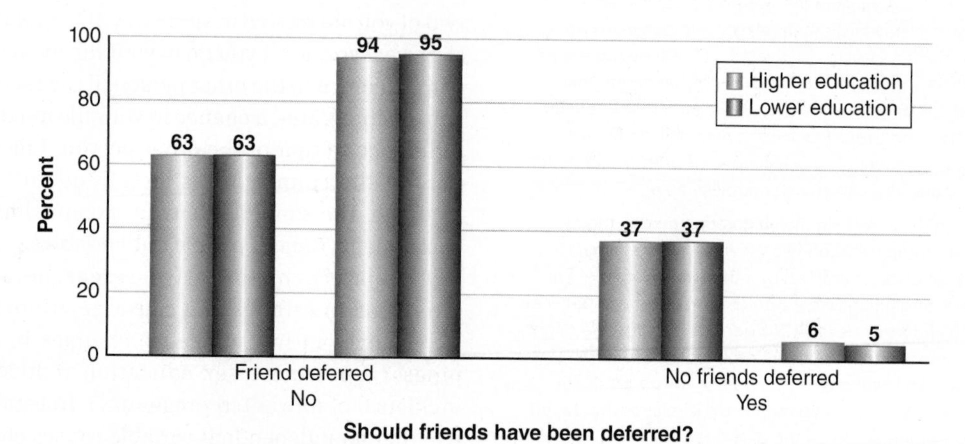

FIGURE 15-4 **Hypothetical Data Relating Education to Acceptance of Induction through the Factor of Having Friends Who Were Deferred.**
Source: Kendall and Lazarsfeld (1950).

likely to accept their own induction as fair. Those with less education were more likely to have friends deferred and, by virtue of that fact, were less likely to accept their own induction.

Recognize that neither Stouffer's explanation nor the hypothetical data denied the reality of the original relationship. As educational level increased, acceptance of one's own induction also increased. The nature of this empirical relationship, however, was interpreted through the introduction of a third variable. The variable, *deferment of friends*, did not deny the original relationship; it merely clarified the mechanism through which the original relationship occurred.

This, then, is the heart of the elaboration model and of multivariate analysis. Having observed an empirical relationship between two variables (such as *level of education* and *acceptance of induction*), we seek to understand the nature of that relationship through the effects produced by introducing other variables (such as *having friends who were deferred*). Mechanically, we accomplish this by first dividing our sample into subsets on the basis of the **test variable**, also called the *control variable*. In our example, having friends who were deferred or not is the test variable, and the sample is divided into those who have deferred friends and those who do not. The relationship between the original two variables (*acceptance of induction* and *level of education*) is then recomputed separately for each of the subsamples. The tables produced in this manner are called the *partial tables*, and the relationships found in the partial tables are called the **partial relationships**, or *partials*. The partial relationships are then compared with the initial relationship discovered in the total sample, often referred to as the **zero-order relationship** to indicate that no test variables have been controlled for.

Although the elaboration model was first demonstrated through the use of hypothetical data, it laid out a logical method for analyzing relationships among variables that have been actually measured. As we'll see, our first, hypothetical example has described only one possible outcome in the elaboration model. There are others.

THE ELABORATION PARADIGM[2]

THE LOGIC

This section presents steps for understanding a multivariate elaboration analysis and determining what relationship exists among the variables. Before we get into details, let's review some fundamental ideas beginning with the notion of "relationship."

In quantitative research, the meaning of *relationship* is the same as in everyday life. Relationships exist when changes in two things are systematically connected. If a change in your life systematically changes someone else's life, the two of you are related in some way. If the relationship weakens, what you do in your life makes less of a difference to the other person. If the relationship disintegrates, a change in your life makes no difference to that of the other person. Life goes on, but the connection is lost. In quantitative research, the same holds true, except that the components are not people but variables.

Ultimately, quantitative researchers are interested in establishing causal relationships. Do changes in income cause changes in happiness? Does more sex education reduce the incidence of unwanted pregnancy? To establish whether an independent variable causes change

test variable A variable that is held constant in an attempt to clarify further the relationship between two other variables. Having discovered a relationship between *education* and *prejudice*, for example, we might hold *gender* constant by examining the relationship between *education* and *prejudice* among men only and then among women only. In this example, *gender* would be the test variable (also called the control variable).

partial relationship In the elaboration model, this is the relationship between two variables when examined in a subset of cases defined by a third (test) variable. For example, beginning with a zero-order relationship between *income* and *attitudes toward gender equality*, we might want to see whether the relationship holds true among both men and women (i.e., controlling for *gender*). The relationship found among men and the relationship found among women would be the partial relationships, also referred to as the *partials*.

zero-order relationship The relationship between two variables when no test variables are being controlled for (i.e., held constant).

2 Parts of this section are a revision of Brym et al. 2016, pp. 52–55.

in a dependent variable, researchers must satisfy three criteria, discussed in Chapter 4. These criteria include association, sequence, and nonspuriousness. Let's review these criteria and illustrate them by examining the question, "Do storks cause babies to appear?"

The first causal criterion requires the researcher to demonstrate that the variables systematically change together. This is the association test, which establishes that the variables are in fact related. In our example, a researcher would have to demonstrate that regions with higher numbers of storks also have higher birth rates. In fact, this is the case in Scandinavia, where regions with fewer storks have lower fertility rates, while those with more storks have higher rates.

The second causal criterion is sequence, showing that the independent variable changes before differences in the dependent variable occur. If the hypothesis is that storks cause babies to appear, a researcher has to demonstrate that the storks arrived prior to the babies (and not vice versa).

The first two causal criteria are straightforward. The third one, nonspuriousness, requires more elaboration. Relationships between people do not exist in isolation, and neither do relationships between independent and dependent variables. Instead, connections between variables and people always exist in a context. In research, a control (test) variable (or several control variables) specifies the context of a relationship. For example, while you may declare your undying love for your date on a Saturday night, the prudent partner will understand that this declaration may be influenced by the context and ask, "What will you say when you're sober on Sunday morning?" Similarly, the relationship between family income and years of schooling a person attains in various countries may depend on whether the national postsecondary system is funded privately or by the state. High-quality state-funded schools will mute the effect of family income on years of education attained. Contexts affect relationships (see Figure 15-5). In our example, the contextual issue is whether other variables are influencing the observed relationship between stork sightings and babies appearing.

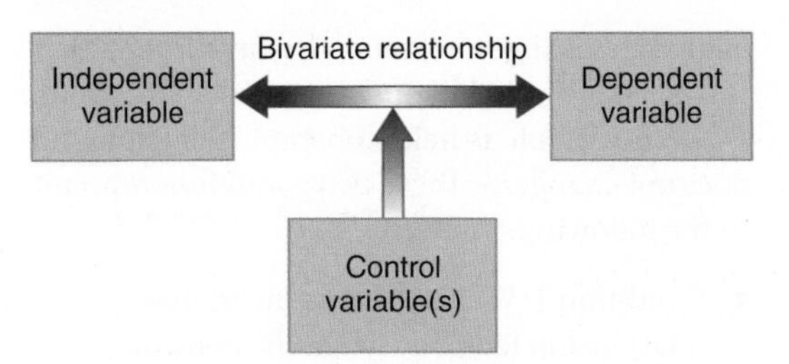

FIGURE 15-5 The Influence of Control Variables. Control variables provide context and may affect bivariate relationships.

The existence of control variables has an important implication for the interpretation of relationships: The appearance of a relationship may not accurately portray its reality. Appearance and reality do not always coincide. Just ask any broken-hearted former sweetheart.

In quantitative research, an important reason for the imperfect alignment between the appearance and the reality of relationships is the operation of control variables. Control variables may affect the nature of any apparent relationship between two variables. Since researchers are interested in identifying real relationships before they are willing to declare that a relationship between two variables is genuine, they must investigate the influences of potentially contaminating control variables. They do this to avoid being fooled by appearances. The application of the elaboration model helps sort out what is occurring among the variables.

The key to understanding the elaboration model is to recognize that variables have their effects by changing. In this respect they are just like people; if you don't do anything (i.e., change), you won't make any difference. When you look at a bivariate relationship, you are determining the connection between the independent and the dependent variable. Multivariate analysis, using the elaboration model, goes a step further and asks: How is the bivariate relationship affected by changes in the third (test) variable?

The key technique in multivariate analysis involves examining the independent–dependent (bivariate) variable relationship under two conditions—first, when the control/test variable is allowed to change and, second, when the control/test variable is held constant (see Figure 15-6). When a variable is held constant it is fixed and does not change. So these two conditions amount to the following:

- Condition 1: What does the bivariate relationship look like when the control variable is operating (i.e., varying)?
- Condition 2: What does the bivariate relationship look like when the control variable is not operating (i.e., held constant)?

When a bivariate relationship is examined under these two conditions, one of two possibilities emerges. The first possibility is that the relationship between the independent and dependent variable *stays the same* under these two conditions. Where this is the case, we can conclude that the third (control) variable is having no effect on the bivariate relationship. A second possibility is that the independent–dependent variable relationship *is different* between the two conditions. In this situation, the control variable is having some kind of effect.

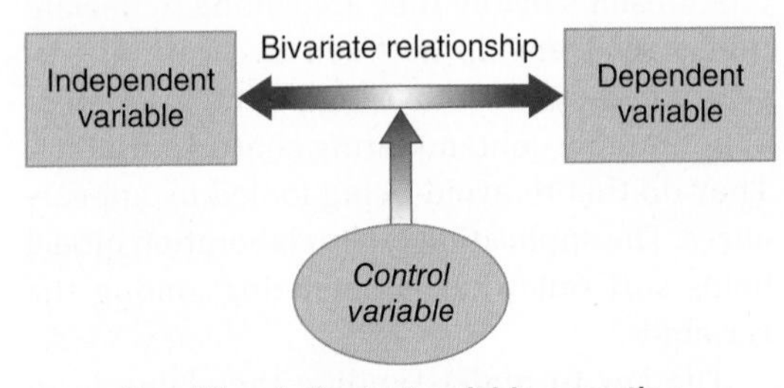

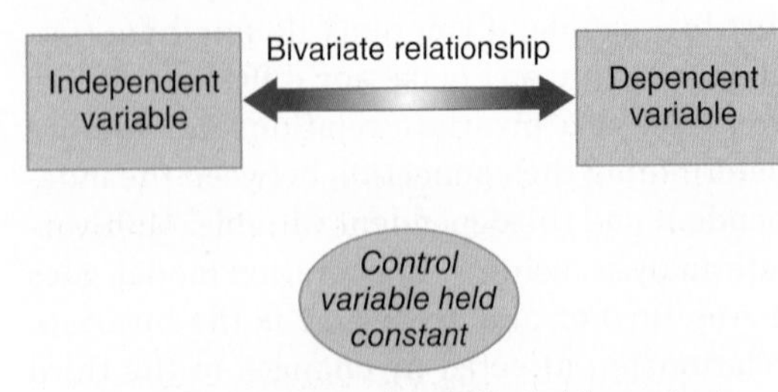

FIGURE 15-6 **Two Conditions in Multivariate Analysis.** When the control variable changes, it may affect the bivariate relationship. When the control variable is constant, it cannot affect the bivariate relationship.

The following analogy should help solidify your understanding of this logic:

> Imagine you are in a romantic relationship; you being person *X*, your partner being person *Y*. You care very much for your partner but are suspicious that some other person (*Z*) might be affecting your relationship. It has crossed your mind that your partner doesn't really love you, as they claim. Instead, you imagine that your partner's declaration of undying love is really just the advice of person *Z*, who is suggesting such a declaration as a way of keeping you in the dark about the true *Y–Z* romance. One way to resolve this concern is to remove person *Z* from the picture. [Let your imagination decide what "remove" means!] If your partner continues to declare their undying love for you even after *Z* has left the scene, then your suspicions about *Z*'s influence were wrong. Alternatively, if *Y*'s behavior toward you changes after *Z*'s removal, something was up.
>
> (Roberts et al. 2015:280)

Here you see the two conditions and their comparison in operation. In Condition 1, *X* and *Y* have some kind of relationship while *Z* is on the scene and operating. In Condition 2, *Z* has ceased operating and the *X–Y* relationship is observed. If these two conditions reveal the same *X–Y* relationship, then *Z* was having no effect. If they are different, *Z* was making a difference.

The results of an elaboration analysis are not as simple as either the control variable is having an effect or it is not. If the test variable is having an effect, the elaboration model can help sort out the type of effect it is having.

THE APPLICATION: FOUR CONVENTIONAL MODELS

Quantitative analysis using the elaboration model presents a number of possibilities. The possibilities are expressed as different kinds of models. Each of the models is interpreted as a different kind of connection among the independent, dependent, and control variables. Next, we describe the standard models, and tell you how to recognize them and what they mean.

To understand these models you need to keep the following points in mind:

- The evidence for Condition 1 (control variable is operating) is found in the original (*zero-order*) bivariate relationship.
- The evidence for Condition 2 (control variable held constant) is found in the *partial* relationship tables.
- There will be as many partial relationships as there are attributes of the control variables. For example, if the control variable is gender, then there will be two partial relationships between the independent and dependent variable—one including only males, the other only females.

The four conventional models are diagrammed in Figure 15-7. Refer to this figure as you read the following descriptions. At the end of each description is an example and question intended to solidify your understanding of the model.

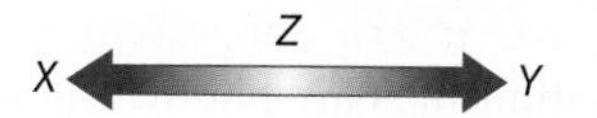

a. Genuine/replication model

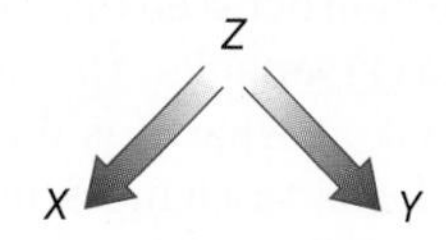

b. Spurious/explanation model

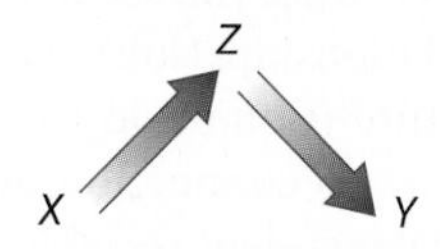

c. Intervening/interpretation model

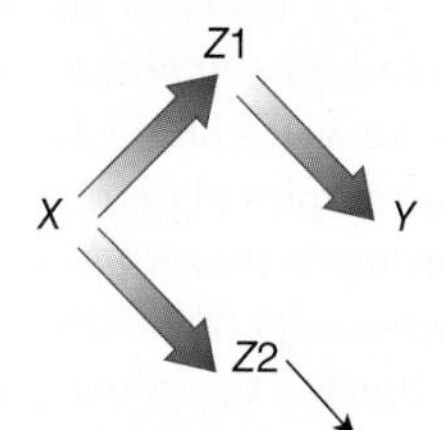

d. Interaction/specification model

FIGURE 15-7 **Standard Models of Elaboration Outcomes.**

Model 1: Genuine Relationship—Replication

When something is genuine, what you see is what you get; appearances match reality. In the language of variables, for genuine relationships the zero-order relationship and the partial relationship display the *same* connection between the independent and dependent variables. For this reason, genuine relationships are also called **replication**, since the original relationship has been replicated under test conditions.

Figure 15-7a diagrams a genuine relationship. Notice that while the independent (*X*) and dependent (*Y*) variables are connected (related), there is no arrow connecting the control (*Z*) variable to the others. This shows that *Z* has no effect. Genuine relationships are what researchers are searching for to demonstrate the third causal criterion, nonspuriousness.

Example and Question:

Independent variable: Time spent studying
Dependent variable: Course grades
Control variable: Peanut butter consumption

To master challenging material takes time and effort. For this reason, a genuine connection exists between the amount of time spent studying and course grades. The amount of peanut butter consumed has nothing to do with this relationship. Whether you consume a lot, a little, or no peanut butter will not affect the studying–grades connection. This result will be displayed in the evidence as follows: A relationship between studying and grades will be evidenced in the zero-order (bivariate) relationship. This same relationship will be found in the partial tables.

Can you think of a control variable that students believe is relevant to the studying–grades relationship but is not? (*Hint:* Think superstition.)

replication A technical term used in connection with the elaboration model to refer to the empirical outcome of the persistence of the observed initial relationship between two variables when a control variable is held constant. This supports the idea that the original, zero-order relationship is genuine.

Model 2: Spurious Relationship—Explanation

Spurious relationships are phony; the way they appear is not what they really are. Figure 15-7b diagrams the spurious model. Notice that there is no direct connection between the independent (*X*) and dependent (*Y*) variables. They are actually unrelated. But look at what *Z* is doing. When *Z* is changing it leads to changes in *X*; it also leads to changes in *Y*. So, if you examine the *X–Y* connection while *Z* is operating, it looks like *X* and *Y* are related. This is what you see in Condition 1, the zero-order relationship. However, if you take *Z* out of the picture (Condition 2), the partial relationships show no connection between the independent and dependent variable.

Spurious relationships are also identified by the label **explanation**, because the control (*Z*) variable's influence helps account for (explain) the appearance of an *X–Y* relationship when none actually exists. The empirical pattern that signals a spurious relationship is this: An *X–Y* relationship is evident in the zero-order (bivariate) relationship (Condition 1) but the *X–Y* relationship is absent in the partials (Condition 2). Look at Figure 15-7b and you can see why this is the case. If you let *Z* operate (Condition 1), it will create changes in *X* and *Y*—so that they appear to be changing together. Now, for Condition 2, cover up *Z* and its effects (the arrows) and you will see no connection between *X* and *Y*.

<u>Example and Question:</u>

Independent variable: Fire trucks in attendance
Dependent variable: Fire damage
Control variable: Severity of fire

If you look at the evidence, you will see a clear pattern. When more fire trucks come to the scene of a fire, there is more fire damage. This might lead people to conclude that, when a fire breaks out, the last thing you should do is call the fire department. After all, you want to minimize fire damage! This apparent connection between fire trucks and fire damage is spurious. The apparent connection is explained by another variable, severity of fire. More severe fires lead to both more fire trucks and more damage.

In Canada, there is a zero-order relationship between ice cream consumption and sexual assault. This may lead you to be wary of being near ice cream shops. What control variable might explain the relationship and ease your fears? (*Hint:* Think seasons.)

Model 3: Intervening Relationship—Interpretation

Look at Figure 15-7c and follow the sequence of arrows. *X* (the independent variable) changes, which leads to a change in *Z* (the control variable), which produces changes in *Y* (the dependent variable). So, with this system operating (Condition 1), would you expect to see a relationship between *X* and *Y*? The answer is yes, because when *X* is changing *Y* is changing. Now take *Z* out of the picture (Condition 2). What happens to the *X–Y* connection? Well, cover up *Z* and its effects in Figure 15-7c and you will observe no connection between *X* and *Y* under Condition 2.

This is what an intervening relationship looks like. The effects of *X* only reach *Y* through a middle (intervening) step (*Z*). Which is why this model is also called **interpretation**. If you (*X*) speak only English and want to be understood by a person (*Y*) who speaks only Russian, you have communication problems. For a relationship between you to exist, you need an interpreter (*Z*) who speaks both English and Russian. When the effects of the interpreter are present (Condition 1), the *X–Y* relationship holds; without the interpreter (Condition 2), the *X–Y* connection is nonexistent.

To be specific, the empirical pattern for an intervening relationship is as follows: A zero-order *X–Y* relationship exists, which disappears in the partial tables. Note that this is the same pattern of evidence as Model 2, spurious relationships. The spurious/explanation model and the intervening/interpretation model are indistinguishable on the basis of empirical evidence. But they are clearly not the same.

---

explanation An elaboration model term describing the situation where a control variable accounts for a spurious connection between the independent and dependent variables.

interpretation An elaboration model term describing the situation where a control variable intervenes between an independent variable and its effects on the dependent variable.

Example and Question:

Independent variable: Family structure of divorce
Dependent variable: Delinquency
Control variable: Supervision

Researchers have observed that children from divorced parents are more likely to become delinquent than are those from non-divorced families. This relationship may be interpreted, however, through the introduction of supervision as a test variable. Among children who are supervised, delinquency rates are not affected by whether or not their parents are divorced. The same is true among those who are not supervised. It is the relationship between divorced parents and the lack of supervision that produced the original relationship.

Can you think of another intervening variable that might influence the relationship between divorced parents and delinquency? (*Hint:* What else is in short supply in some families in which parents are divorced?)

Distinguishing Models 2 and 3 Look at Figures 15-7b and c. They are clearly not the same, but they share the same empirical pattern. So what distinguishes them? Well, look carefully at these two diagrams and you will see they differ in only one way—the direction of the *X*–*Z* arrow. In the spurious model, the arrow goes from *Z* to *X*; in the intervening model it goes from *X* to *Z*. Remember what these arrows signify. They tell you the direction of change. In the spurious model *Z* changes first, which brings about a change in *X*. In the interpretation model *X* changes first, producing a change in *Z*.

This difference between the spurious and intervening models can be stated as a difference in time-ordering or sequence. You will remember that this is the second criterion researchers use to identify causes. So, although spurious and intervening models share the same Condition 1 and Condition 2 empirical patterns, they differ in the sequencing of the variables; specifically, the sequencing of the *X*–*Z* variables. So this is how you distinguish which of these two models is operating.

But where does this time-ordering information come from, since it is not in quantitative data you are analyzing? The general answer is "from some other source." The most common other sources are logic and design. If, for example, the independent variable (*X*) is "child abuse" and the control variable (*Z*) is "adult happiness," then a moment's thought clarifies the sequence. Child abuse occurs long before adult experiences with happiness. In other cases, sequence can be built into a research design. This is most commonly the case in experimental designs where the researchers controls the ordering of events.

However it is done, additional information about the time-ordering of the *X* and *Z* variables is required to distinguish the spurious from intervening models.

Example and Question:

Independent variable: Gender
Dependent variable: Number of traffic accidents
Control variable: Number of kilometres driven

A zero-order relationship exists between gender and traffic accidents. Males have more accidents than females. This relationship, however, disappears when the number of kilometres driven is controlled. Among drivers of few kilometres, men and women have the same number of accidents. Among drivers of many kilometres, men and women also have similar accident profiles.

Do the relationships among these three variables display a spurious or intervening pattern? (*Hint:* Think.)

Model 4: Interaction Relationship—Specification To review, here is the pattern of evidence identifying the first three models.

Model	Zero-Order	Partials
Genuine/ replication	Some relationship	Same as zero-order
Spurious/ explanation	Some relationship	No relationship
Intervening/ interpretation	Some relationship	No relationship

Remember that the evidence you are examining will include one zero-order (bivariate) table and two or more partial tables. The reason for multiple partial tables is that you need one for each attribute of the control variable. This is an important point, since it lets you appreciate the following implications:

- In the genuine model, the zero-order and partial tables are the *same.*
- In the spurious model, the zero-order (some relationship) is *different from the partials* (no relationship), but the *partials are the same* (no relationship).
- In the intervening model, the zero-order (some relationship) is *different from the partials* (no relationship), but the *partials are the same* (no relationship).

This understanding sets the stage for understanding the final convention model, interaction relationships.

Look at Figure 15-7d and you will see it is slightly different from the others. The independent variable (*X*) and dependent variable (*Y*) are conventional, but the control variable (*Z*) appears more than once and includes a number (*Z*1, *Z*2). These numbers indicate different attributes of the control variable. For example, if the control variable is alcohol consumption, then *Z*1 might refer to "few drinks" and *Z*2 "many drinks." With this in mind, let's review Figure 15-7d.

The interaction model begins with changes in the independent variable (*X*). This initial change then connects (interacts) with a *specific attribute* of *Z* (either *Z*1 or *Z*2). Depending on which attribute of *Z* is in play, different consequences for the dependent variable (*Y*) appear. In the diagram, where *X* interacts with *Z*1, then it leads to changes in *Y*. However, where *X* interacts with *Z*2, no connection to *Y* occurs. So the distinguishing pattern in interaction relationships is this:

- In the interaction model, the zero-order (some relationship) is *different from the partials*, but the *partials are different from one another.*

specification An elaboration model term describing the situation where particular attributes of a control variable account for an independent variable's effect on the dependent variable.

In your high school chemistry lab, you observed interaction effects in a scenario like the following. You had a beaker that contained two chemicals (*X* and *Y*). You began, one drop at a time, adding a third chemical (*Z*). Drop 1 produced nothing; so did drops 2, 3, and 4. And then, when Drop 5 was added, suddenly the mixture in the beaker started boiling and steaming and doing all kinds of odd stuff. That's interaction. It was a specific amount of the third variable that produced the relationship between *X* and *Y*.

Interaction relationships are also called **specification** because the analysis specifies which amount of the third variable leads to the effect of *X* on *Y*. You recognize interaction relationships by the following pattern: some relationship in zero-order evidence; a stronger than zero-order pattern in one partial; and little or no relationship in another partial.

Example and Question:

Independent variable: Attending a party
Dependent variable: Having fun
Control variable: Alcohol consumption

Not all parties are fun. It is common that the connection between partying and fun is conditional on a specific amount of alcohol consumption. Just like in your high school chemistry experiment, as drinks are added the party reaches a point where fun explodes on the scene. Can you think of a different control variable that creates a specification relationship between party attendance and fun? (*Hint:* Think partner.)

TWO PRACTICAL CONSIDERATIONS

This review of the replication, explanation, interpretation, and specification models gives you a sense of what patterns you are looking for when trying to interpret the bivariate (zero-order) and partial tables in a multivariate analysis. In conducting this type of quantitative analysis, two practical considerations are important to keep in mind. The first of these points relates to the idea of models.

Models are representations; they are ideal types. The descriptions of the models tell you what a perfect replication, explanation, interpretation, and specification look like. Empirical reality is much messier; it is rarely ideal. Still, the researcher's task is to interpret the evidence as best they can. This, of course, is really no different than what we do in our ordinary lives. Think of your romantic partner. Even though your love is imperfect, you still use the label. The same applies to using multivariate model labels. The practical point is that you should choose the model that most closely approximates the empirical patterns in the zero-order and partial tables.

The second piece of practical advice concerns the selection of control variables. How do you know which test variables need to be included in the analysis? The answer is you should include all (and only) theoretically relevant control variables. If you have good reason for thinking a specific contextual variable might be affecting a relationship, then you should take it into account in the multivariate analysis. If there is no good reason to include it, then leave it out.

To give you a better sense of how the elaboration model is applied in actual research, the final section of this chapter expands the model and provides some data tables.

TABLE 15-1 Example of a Suppressor Variable

I. No Apparent Relationship between Parental Permissiveness and Adolescents' Reports of Psychological Symptoms

	Permissiveness	
Symptoms	High	Low
Many	54%	58%
Few	46	42
	100	100
100% =	(450)	(550)

II. Parental Warmth, Parental Permissiveness, Adolescents' Reports of Psychological Symptoms

	Parental Warmth			
	Warmer		Colder	
	Permissiveness		Permissiveness	
Symptoms	High	Low	High	Low
Many	50%	24%	100%	75%
Few	50	76	0	25
	100	100	100	100
100% =	(419)	(181)	(31)	(369)

Source: Based on constructed data that precisely mirrors the relationships among variables reported by Koeske (1998).

REFINEMENTS TO THE PARADIGM

The preceding sections have presented the primary logic of the elaboration model as developed by Lazarsfeld and his colleagues. Here we look at some logically possible variations, some of which can be found in a book by Morris Rosenberg (1968).

First, the basic paradigm assumes an initial relationship between two variables. It might be useful, however, in a more comprehensive model, to differentiate between positive and negative relationships. Moreover, Rosenberg suggests using the elaboration model even with an original relationship of zero. Gary F. Koeske (1998) explored the apparent absence of a relationship between *permissive parenting* and *adolescents' reports of psychological and somatic symptoms.* The following example presents his evidence in the form of tables.

At the top of Table 15-1, the initial contingency table analysis is reported; there is essentially no observed relationship between *parental permissiveness* and *symptoms.* Fifty-four percent of adolescents who reported relatively permissive parenting styles reported many symptoms, and 58 percent of those reporting less permissive styles claimed many symptoms. However, a different wrinkle is apparent when warmer and colder parenting styles are introduced as a test factor. *Parental warmth* was found to suppress the relationship between *parental permissiveness* and *adolescent symptoms.* Among warmer parents, 50 percent of the adolescents reported many psychological symptoms when parental permissiveness was high, while only 24 percent reported many symptoms when parental permissiveness was low. The difference is 26 percentage points. Among colder parents, 100 percent of the adolescents reported many symptoms when permissiveness was high, but only 75 percent reported many symptoms when permissiveness was low, for a 25 percent difference. Thus, the effect of *permissiveness,* which is not apparent in the original relationship, is substantial (about a 25 percent difference) when *parental warmth* is introduced as a control variable. One can see that warm families produce lower rates of symptoms—within high permissiveness, 50 percent versus 100 percent and within low permissiveness, 24 percent versus 75 percent. Thus, the circumstance that warm families are more likely to also be permissive masks the negative consequences that permissiveness can have. *Parental warmth*, in this case, was a **suppressor variable**, concealing the relationship between *parental permissiveness* and reports of psychological symptoms by adolescents.

Second, the basic paradigm focuses on partials being the same as or weaker than the original relationship but does not provide guidelines for specifying what constitutes a significant difference between the original and the partials. When you use the elaboration model, you'll frequently find yourself making an arbitrary decision about whether a given partial is significantly weaker than the original. This, then, suggests another dimension that could be added to the paradigm.

Third, the limitation of the basic paradigm to partials that are the same as or weaker than the original neglects two other possibilities. A partial relationship might be stronger than the original. Or, on the other hand, a partial relationship might be the reverse of the original—for example, negative where the original was positive.

Rosenberg provides a hypothetical example of the latter possibility by first suggesting that a researcher might find that working-class respondents in his study are more supportive of the civil rights movement in the United States than are middle-class respondents (see Table 15-2). He further suggests that *race* might be a **distorter variable** in this instance, reversing the true relationship between *class* and *attitudes*. Presumably, black respondents would be more supportive of the movement than would whites, but blacks would also be overrepresented among working-class respondents and underrepresented among the middle class. Middle-class black respondents might be more supportive than working-class blacks; however, the same relationship might be found among whites. Holding *race* constant, then, the researcher would conclude that support for the civil rights movement was greater among the middle class than among the working class.

TABLE 15-2 Example of a Distorter Variable (Hypothetical)

I. Working-Class Subjects Appear More Liberal on Civil Rights Than Middle-Class Subjects

Civil Rights Score	Middle Class	Working Class
High	37%	45%
Low	63	55
	100	100
100% =	(120)	(120)

II. Controlling for Race Shows the Middle Class to Be More Liberal Than the Working Class

	Social Class			
	Blacks		Whites	
Civil Rights Score	Middle Class	Working Class	Middle Class	Working Class
High	70%	50%	30%	20%
Low	30	50	70	80
	100	100	100	100
100% =	(20)	(100)	(100)	(20)

Source: *The logic of survey analysis* by ROSENBERG, MORRIS. Reproduced with permission of BASIC BOOKS in the format Republish in a book via Copyright Clearance Center.

All these new dimensions further complicate the notion of specification. If one partial is the same as the original and the other partial is even stronger, how should you react to that situation? You've specified one condition under which the original relationship holds up, but you've also specified another condition under which it holds even more clearly.

Finally, the basic paradigm focuses primarily on dichotomous test variables. In fact, the elaboration model is not so limited—either in theory or in use—but the basic paradigm becomes more

suppressor variable In the elaboration model, a test (control) variable that conceals a true zero-order relationship.

distorter variable A test (control) variable that causes an apparent reversal in the direction of a zero-order relationship (from negative to positive or vice versa).

complicated when the test variable divides the sample into three or more subsamples. And the paradigm becomes more complicated yet when more than one test variable is used simultaneously.

None of this is being said to fault the basic elaboration paradigm. To the contrary, we want to emphasize that the elaboration model is not a simple algorithm—a set of procedures through which to analyze research. Rather, it is primarily a logical device for assisting the researcher in understanding his or her data. A firm understanding of the elaboration model will make a sophisticated analysis easier. However, this model suggests neither which variables should be introduced as controls nor definitive conclusions about the nature of elaboration results. For all these things, you must look to your own ingenuity. Such ingenuity, moreover, will come only through extensive experience. By pointing to oversimplifications in the basic elaboration paradigm, we have sought to bring home the point that the model provides only a logical framework. You'll find sophisticated analyses far more complicated than the examples used to illustrate the basic paradigm.

At the same time, if you fully understand the basic model, you'll understand other techniques such as correlations, regressions, and factor analyses a lot more easily. Chapter 16 places such techniques as partial correlations and partial regressions in the context of the elaboration model.

One final note before we end this chapter. The elaboration paradigm allows researchers to examine various possibilities, helping them to either rule out or provide support for them in turn. Proving hypotheses, however, is not something that researchers can do—there are almost always additional factors that may be considered for examination. Analysis is a continuing process that demands a great deal of ingenuity and perseverance. The image of a researcher carefully laying out hypotheses and then testing them in a ritualistic fashion results only in ritualistic research. The search for understanding and explanation is ongoing. "Scientific proof" is a contradiction in terms. Nothing is ever *proved* scientifically. Hypotheses, explanations, theories, or hunches can all escape a stream of attempts at disproof, but none can be proved in any absolute sense. The acceptance of a hypothesis, then, is really a function of the extent to which it has been tested and not disconfirmed. No hypothesis, therefore, should be considered sound on the basis of one test—whether the hypothesis was generated before or after the observation of empirical data.

MAIN POINTS

- The elaboration model is a method of multivariate analysis appropriate to social research. It's primarily a logical model that can illustrate the basic logic of other multivariate methods.
- A partial relationship (or "partial") is the observed relationship between two variables within a subgroup of cases based on some attribute of the test or control variable.
- A zero-order relationship is the observed relationship between two variables without a third variable being held constant or controlled.
- The basic steps in elaboration are as follows: (1) a relationship is observed to exist between two variables; (2) a third variable is held constant in the sense that the cases under study are subdivided according to the attributes of that third variable; (3) the original two-variable relationship is recomputed within each of the subgroups; and (4) the comparison of the original relationship with the relationships found within each subgroup provides a fuller understanding of the original relationship itself.
- The logical relationships of the variables differ in some models depending on whether

the test variable is antecedent to the other two variables or intervening between them.

- The outcome of an elaboration analysis may be replication (whereby a set of partial relationships is essentially the same as the corresponding zero-order relationship), explanation (whereby a set of partial relationships is reduced essentially to zero when an antecedent variable is held constant), interpretation (whereby a set of partial relationships is reduced essentially to zero when an intervening variable is held constant), or specification (whereby one partial is substantially reduced, ideally to zero, and the other remains about the same as the original relationship or is stronger).
- A suppressor variable conceals the relationship between two other variables; a distorter variable causes an apparent reversal in the relationship between two other variables (from negative to positive or vice versa).

REVIEW QUESTIONS AND EXERCISES

1. Review the Stouffer–Kendall–Lazarsfeld example of education, friends deferred, and attitudes toward being drafted. Suppose they had begun with an association between friends deferred and attitudes toward being drafted, and then they had controlled for education. What conclusion would they have reached?
2. In your own words describe the elaboration logic of (a) replication, (b) interpretation, (c) explanation, and (d) specification.
3. Each description of the four basic multivariate models concluded with an example. Explain why each example is correct by connecting it to the multivariate process of comparing zero-order and partial tables.

CONTINUITY PROJECT

ELABORATING HARM

The report of the Truth and Reconciliation Commission provided many consistent reports of how the residential school experience affected Indigenous people in Canada. The following tables explore the connection between residential school attendance and mental health outcomes. The authors compiled the figures from the data obtained via the Aboriginal Peoples Survey, conducted in 2012 and publicly released in 2015.

1. What variables are included in this analysis? Specifically, identify the independent, dependent, and test variables.
2. What relationship exists in the original bivariate table? Does it confirm or deny the hypothesis that residential school attendance did harm?
3. What relationships exist in the multivariate partial tables? Express these relationships in a simple sentence for each table.
4. Taken together, which multivariate model best approximates the relationship among the variables? What justifies your choice? In a simple statement, how would you express the overall findings of this evidence?

TABLE 1 Self-Reported Mental Health by Residential School Attendance

		Residential School Attendance			
		Participant	Family Member	None	Total
Mental health	Excellent–Good	664 84.4%	4802 89.1%	4879 91.7%	10345 90.0%
	Fair–Poor	123 15.6%	590 10.9%	440 8.3%	1153 10.0%
	Total Count	787 100.0%	5392 100.0%	5319 100.0%	11498 100.0%

TABLE 2 Self-Reported Mental Health by Residential School Attendance, Males

		Residential School Attendance			
		Participant	Family Member	None	Total
Mental health	Excellent–Good	312 87.6%	2057 90.6%	2372 93.0%	4741 91.6%
	Fair–Poor	44 12.4%	213 9.4%	179 7.0%	436 8.4%
	Total Count	356 100.0%	2270 100.0%	2551 100.0%	5177 100.0%

TABLE 3 Self-Reported Mental Health by Residential School Attendance, Females

		Residential School Attendance			
		Participant	Family Member	None	Total
Mental health	Excellent–Good	352 81.7%	2745 87.9%	2507 90.6%	5604 88.7%
	Fair–Poor	79 18.3%	377 12.1%	261 9.4%	717 11.3%
	Total Count	431 100.0%	3122 100.0%	2768 100.0%	6321 100.0%

Source: Freedomz/Shutterstock.com

SOCIAL STATISTICS

In this chapter we will acquaint you with a few simple statistics frequently used in social research. Statistics allow researchers to summarize data, measure associations between variables, and draw inferences from samples to populations—and they are less painful than you may believe.

IN THIS CHAPTER ...

INTRODUCTION

It has been our experience that many students are intimidated by statistics. Sometimes the topic of statistics makes them feel they're ...

A few clowns short of a circus
Dumber than a box of hair
A few feathers short of a duck
All foam, no beer
Missing a few buttons on their remote control
A few beans short of a burrito
About as sharp as a bowling ball
About four cents short of a nickel
Not running on full thrusters[1]

Many people are intimidated by quantitative research because they feel uncomfortable with mathematics and statistics. And indeed, many research reports are filled with unspecified computations. The role of statistics in social research is quite important, but it's equally important that you see this role in its proper perspective.

Empirical research is first and foremost a logical rather than a mathematical operation. Mathematics is merely a convenient and efficient language for accomplishing the logical operations inherent in good data analysis. *Statistics* is the applied branch of mathematics especially appropriate to a variety of research analyses.

In this chapter we'll be looking at two types of statistics: descriptive and inferential. *Descriptive statistics* are a medium for describing data in manageable forms. *Inferential statistics*, on the other hand, assist researchers in drawing conclusions from their observations; typically, this involves drawing conclusions about a population from the study of a sample drawn from it.

DESCRIPTIVE STATISTICS

As we've already suggested, **descriptive statistics** present quantitative descriptions in a manageable form. Sometimes we want to describe single variables, and sometimes we want to describe the associations that connect one variable with another. Let's look at some of the ways to do these things.

1 Thanks to the many contributors to humour lists on the Internet.

DATA REDUCTION

Scientific research often involves collecting large masses of data. Suppose we had surveyed 2,000 people, asking each of them 100 questions—not an unusually large study. We would now have a staggering 200,000 answers! No one could possibly read all those 200,000 answers and reach any meaningful conclusion about them. Therefore, much scientific analysis involves the *reduction* of data from unmanageable details to manageable summaries.

To begin our discussion, let's look briefly at the raw data matrix created by a quantitative research project. Table 16-1 presents a partial data matrix. Notice that each row in the matrix represents a person (or other unit of analysis), each column represents a variable, and each cell represents the coded attribute or value a given person has on a given variable. The first column in Table 16-1 represents a person's gender. Let's say a "1" represents male and "2" represents female. This means that persons 1 and 2 are male, person 3 is female, and so forth.

In the case of age, person 1's "3" might mean 30 to 39 years old, and person 2's "4" might mean 40 to 49. However age has been coded (see Chapter 14), the code numbers shown in Table 16-1 would describe each of the people represented there.

Notice that the data have already been reduced somewhat by the time a data matrix like this one has been created. If age had been coded as suggested previously, the specific answer "33 years old" has already been assigned to the category "30–39." The people responding to our survey may have given us 60 or 70 different ages, but we have now reduced them to six or seven categories.

Chapter 14 discussed some of the ways of further summarizing univariate data: averages such as the mode, median, and mean and measures of dispersion such as the range, the standard

descriptive statistics Statistical computations describing either the characteristics of a sample or the relationship among variables in a sample. Descriptive statistics merely summarize a set of sample observations, whereas inferential statistics move beyond the description of specific observations to make inferences about the larger population from which the sample observations were drawn.

TABLE 16-1 Partial Raw Data Matrix

	Gender	Age	Education	Income	Occupation	Political Affiliation	Political Orientation	Religious Affiliation	Importance of Religion
Person 1	1	3	2	4	1	2	3	0	4
Person 2	1	4	2	4	4	1	1	1	2
Person 3	2	2	5	5	2	2	4	2	3
Person 4	1	5	4	4	3	2	2	2	4
Person 5	2	3	7	8	6	1	1	5	1
Person 6	2	1	3	3	5	3	5	1	1

deviation, and so forth. It's also possible to summarize the associations among variables.

MEASURES OF ASSOCIATION

A data matrix can also represent the association between any two variables, this time produced by the joint frequency distributions of the two variables. Table 16-2 presents such a matrix. It provides all the information needed to determine the nature and extent of the relationship between education and prejudice.

Notice, for example, that 23 people (1) have no education and (2) scored high on prejudice; 77 people (1) had graduate degrees and (2) scored low on prejudice.

Like the raw-data matrix in Table 16-1, this matrix provides more information than can easily be comprehended. A careful study of the table, however, shows that as education increases from "None" to "Graduate Degree," there is a general tendency for prejudice to decrease, but no more than a general impression is possible. For a more precise summary of the data matrix, we need one of several types of descriptive statistics. Selecting the appropriate measure depends initially on the nature of the two variables.

We'll turn now to some of the options available for summarizing the association between two variables. Each measure of association we'll discuss is based on the same model—*proportionate reduction of error* (PRE).

To see how this model works, let's assume that we asked you to guess respondents' attributes on a given variable: for example, whether they answered "yes" or "no" to a given questionnaire item. To assist you, let's first assume you know the overall distribution of responses in the total sample—say, 60 percent said yes and 40 percent said no. You would make the fewest errors in this process if you always guessed the modal (most frequent) response: yes.

Second, let's assume you also know the empirical relationship between the first variable and some other variable—say, *gender*. Now, each time we ask you to guess whether a respondent said yes or no, we'll tell you whether the respondent is a man or a woman. If the two variables are related, you should make fewer errors the second time. It's possible, therefore, to compute the PRE by knowing the relationship between the two variables: The greater the relationship, the greater the reduction of error.

This basic PRE model is modified slightly to take account of different levels of

TABLE 16-2 Hypothetical Raw Data on Education and Prejudice

	Educational Level				
Prejudice	None	Grade School	High School	University	Graduate Degree
High	23	34	156	67	16
Medium	11	21	123	102	23
Low	6	12	95	164	77

measurement—nominal, ordinal, or interval. The following sections will consider each level of measurement and present one measure of association appropriate to each. You should realize that the three measures discussed are only an arbitrary selection from among many appropriate measures.

Nominal Variables If the two variables consist of nominal data (e.g., *gender, religious affiliation, race*), lambda (λ) would be one appropriate measure. (Lambda is a letter in the Greek alphabet corresponding to *l* in our alphabet. Greek letters are used for many concepts in statistics, which perhaps helps account for those who say of statistics, "It's all Greek to me.") Lambda is based on your ability to guess values on one of the variables: the PRE achieved through knowledge of values on the other variable.

Imagine this situation. We tell you that a room contains 100 people and we would like you to guess the gender of each person, one at a time. If half are men and half women, you'll probably be right half the time and wrong half the time. But suppose we tell you each person's occupation before you guess that person's gender.

What gender would you guess if we said the person was a truck driver? Probably you'd be wise to guess "male"; although there are now plenty of women truck drivers, most are men. If we said the next person was a nurse, you'd probably be wisest to guess "female," following the same logic. While you'd still make errors in guessing genders, you'd clearly do better than you would if you didn't know their occupations. The extent to which you did better (the proportionate reduction of error) would be an indicator of the association that exists between gender and occupation.

Here's another simple hypothetical example that illustrates the logic and method of lambda. Table 16-3 presents hypothetical data relating gender to employment status. Overall, we note that 1,100 people are employed and 900 are not employed. If you were to predict whether people were employed, knowing only the overall distribution on that variable, you would always predict "employed," since that would result in fewer errors than always predicting "not employed." Nevertheless, this strategy would result in 900 errors out of 2,000 predictions.

TABLE 16-3 Hypothetical Data Relating Gender to Employment Status

	Men	Women	Total
Employed	900	200	1,100
Unemployed	100	800	900
Total	1,000	1,000	2,000

Let's suppose that you had access to the data in Table 16-3 and that you were told each person's gender before making your prediction of employment status. Your strategy would change in that case. For every man, you might predict "employed," and for every woman, you might predict "not employed." If you did that, you would make 300 errors—the 100 men who were not employed and the 200 employed women—or 600 fewer errors than you would make without knowing the person's gender.

Lambda, then, represents the reduction in errors as a proportion of the errors that would have been made on the basis of the overall distribution. In this hypothetical example, lambda would equal .67; that is, 600 fewer errors divided by the 900 total errors based on employment status alone. In this fashion, lambda measures the statistical association between gender and employment status.

If *gender* and *employment status* were statistically independent, we would find the same distribution of employment status for men and women. In this case, knowing each person's gender would not affect the number of errors made in predicting employment status, and the resulting lambda would be zero. If, on the other hand, all men were employed and none of the women were employed, by knowing gender you would avoid errors in predicting employment status. You would make 900 fewer errors (out of 900), so lambda would be 1.0—representing a perfect statistical association.

Lambda is only one of several measures of association appropriate to the analysis of two nominal variables. You could look at any statistics textbook for a discussion of other appropriate measures.

Ordinal Variables If the variables being related are ordinal (e.g., *social class, religiosity, alienation*), gamma (γ) is one appropriate measure of association. Like lambda, gamma is based on your ability to guess values on one variable by knowing values on another. However, whereas lambda is based on guessing exact values, gamma is based on guessing the ordinal arrangement of values. For any given pair of cases, we guess that their ordinal ranking on one variable will correspond (positively or negatively) to their ordinal ranking on the other.

Let's say we have a group of elementary students. It's reasonable to assume that there is a relationship between their *ages* and their *heights*. We can test this by comparing every pair of students: Sam and Mary, Sam and Fred, Mary and Fred, and so forth. Then we ignore all the pairs in which the students are the same age and/or the same height. We then classify each of the remaining pairs (those who differ in both age and height) into one of two categories: those in which the older child is also the taller ("same" pair) and those in which the older child is the shorter ("opposite" pair). So, if Sam is older and taller than Mary, the Sam–Mary pair is counted as a "same." If Sam is older but shorter than Mary, then that pair is an "opposite." (If they are the same age and/or same height, we ignore them.)

To determine whether *age* and *height* are related to each other, we compare the number of same and opposite pairs. If the same pairs outnumber the opposite pairs, we can conclude that there is a *positive* association between the two variables—as one increases, the other increases. If the opposite pairs outnumber the same pairs, we can conclude that the relationship is *negative*. If there are about as many same as opposite pairs, we can conclude that *age* and *height* are not related to each another; they are *independent* of each other.

Here's a social science example to illustrate the simple calculations involved in gamma. Let's say you suspect that *religiosity* is positively related to *political conservatism*, and if Person A is more religious than Person B, you guess that A is also more conservative than B. Gamma is the proportion of paired comparisons that fit this pattern.

Table 16-4 presents hypothetical data relating *social class* to *prejudice*. The general nature of the relationship between these two variables is that as *social class* increases, *prejudice* decreases. There is a negative association between *social class* and *prejudice*.

TABLE 16-4 Hypothetical Data Relating Social Class to Prejudice

Prejudice	Lower Class	Middle Class	Upper Class
Low	200	400	700
Medium	500	900	400
High	800	300	100

Gamma is computed from two quantities: (1) the number of pairs having the same ranking on the two variables and (2) the number of pairs having the opposite ranking on the two variables. The pairs having the same ranking are computed as follows: The frequency of each cell in the table is multiplied by the sum of all cells appearing below and to the right of it—with all these products being summed. In Table 16-4, the number of pairs with the same ranking would be 200(900 + 300 + 400 + 100) + 500(300 + 100) + 400(400 + 100) + 900(100), or 340,000 + 200,000 + 200,000 + 90,000 = 830,000.

The pairs having the opposite ranking on the two variables are computed as follows: The frequency of each cell in the table is multiplied by the sum of all cells appearing below and to the left of it—with all these products being summed. In Table 16-4, the numbers of pairs with opposite rankings would be 700 (500 + 800 + 900 + 300) + 400(800 + 300) + 400(500 + 800) + 900(800), or 1,750,000 + 440,000 + 520,000 + 720,000 = 3,430,000. Gamma is computed from the numbers of same-ranked pairs and opposite-ranked pairs as follows:

$$gamma = \frac{\text{same} - \text{opposite}}{\text{same} + \text{opposite}}$$

In our example, gamma equals (830,000 – 3,430,000) divided by (830,000 + 3,430,000), or –.61. The negative sign in this answer indicates the negative association suggested by the initial inspection of the table. *Social class* and *prejudice*, in this hypothetical example, are negatively associated with one another. The numerical figure for gamma indicates that 61 percent more of the pairs examined had the opposite ranking than the same ranking.

Note that while values of lambda vary from 0 to 1, values of gamma vary from −1 through 0 to +1, representing the *direction* as well as the magnitude of the association. Because nominal variables have no ordinal structure, it makes no sense to speak of the direction of the relationship. (A negative lambda would indicate that you made more errors in predicting values on one variable while knowing values on the second than you made while you were ignorant of the second, and that's not logically possible.)

Table 16-5 is an example of the use of gamma in social research. To study the extent to which widows sanctified their deceased husbands, Helena Znaniecki Lopata (1981) administered a questionnaire to a probability sample of 301 widows. In part, the questionnaire asked the respondents to characterize their deceased husbands based on the following semantic differentiation scale:

Characteristic								
Positive Extreme								Negative Extreme
Good	1	2	3	4	5	6	7	Bad
Useful	1	2	3	4	5	6	7	Useless
Honest	1	2	3	4	5	6	7	Dishonest
Superior	1	2	3	4	5	6	7	Inferior
Kind	1	2	3	4	5	6	7	Cruel
Friendly	1	2	3	4	5	6	7	Unfriendly
Warm	1	2	3	4	5	6	7	Cold

Respondents were asked to describe their deceased spouses by circling a number for each pair of opposing characteristics. Notice that the series of numbers connecting each pair of characteristics is an ordinal measure.

Next, Lopata wanted to discover the extent to which the several measures were related to each other. Appropriately, she chose gamma as the measure of association. Table 16-5 shows how she presented the results of her investigation.

The format presented in Table 16-5 is called a *correlation matrix*. For each pair of measures, Lopata has calculated the gamma. Good and Useful, for example, are related to each other by a gamma equal to .79. The matrix is a convenient way of presenting the intercorrelations among several variables, and you'll find it frequently in the research literature. In this case, we see that all the variables are quite strongly related to each other, though some pairs are more strongly related than others.

Gamma is only one of several measures of association appropriate to ordinal variables. Again, any introductory statistics textbook will give you a more comprehensive treatment of this subject.

Interval or Ratio Variables If interval or ratio variables (e.g., *age*, *income*, *grade point average*, and so forth) are being associated, one appropriate measure of association is Pearson's product–moment correlation (r). The derivation and computation of this measure of association is complex enough to lie outside the scope of this book, so we'll make only a few general comments here.

TABLE 16-5 Gamma Associations among the Semantic Differentiation Items of the Sanctification Scale

	Useful	Honest	Superior	Kind	Friendly	Warm
Good	.79	.88	.80	.90	.79	.83
Useful		.84	.71	.77	.68	.72
Honest			.83	.89	.79	.82
Superior				.78	.60	.73
Kind					.88	.90
Friendly						.90

Source: Helena Znaniecki Lopata, "Widowhood and Husband Sanctification," *Journal of Marriage and the Family* (May 1981): 442. *Journal of Marriage and the Family* by NATIONAL COUNCIL ON FAMILY RELATIONS. Reproduced with permission of BLACKWELL PUBLISHING, INC. in the format of Book via Copyright Clearance Center.

Like both gamma and lambda, r is based on guessing the value of one variable by knowing the other. For continuous interval or ratio variables, however, it's unlikely that you could predict the precise value of the variable. But on the other hand, predicting only the ordinal arrangement of values on the two variables would not take advantage of the greater amount of information conveyed by an interval or ratio variable. In a sense, r reflects how closely you can guess the value of one variable through your knowledge of the value of the other.

To understand the logic of r, consider the way you might hypothetically guess values that particular cases have on a given variable. With nominal variables, we've seen that you might always guess the modal value. But for interval or ratio data, you would minimize your errors by always guessing the mean value of the variable. Although this practice produces few if any perfect guesses, the extent of your errors will be minimized. Imagine the task of guessing people's incomes and how much better you would do if you knew how many years of education they had as well as the mean incomes for people with 0, 1, 2 (and so forth) years of education.

In the computation of lambda, we noted the number of errors produced by always guessing the modal value. In the case of r, errors are measured in terms of the sum of the squared differences between the actual value and the mean. This sum is called the *total variation.*

To understand this concept, we must expand the scope of our examination. Let's look at the logic of regression analysis and discuss correlation within that context.

REGRESSION ANALYSIS

The general formula for describing the association between two variables is $Y = f(X)$. This formula is read "Y is a function of X," meaning that differences or contrasts in the values of Y accompany or parallel variations in the values of X. In other words, values of Y can be explained in terms of variations in the values of X. Stated more strongly, we might say that X causes Y, so the value of X determines the value of Y. **Regression analysis** is a method of estimating from the data the specific function relating Y to X. There are several forms of regression analysis, depending on the complexity of the relationships being studied. Let's begin with the simplest.

Linear Regression The regression model can be seen most clearly in the case of a **linear regression analysis**, where there is a perfect linear association between two variables. Figure 16-1 is a scattergram presenting in graphic form the values of X and Y as produced by a hypothetical study. It shows that for the four cases in our study, the values of X and Y are identical in each instance. The case with a value of 1 on X also has a value of 1 on Y, and so forth. The relationship between the two variables in this instance is described by the equation $Y = X$; this is called the *regression equation.* Because all four points lie on a straight line, we could superimpose that line over the points; this is the *regression line.*

The linear regression model has important descriptive uses. The regression line offers a graphic picture of the association between X and Y, and the regression equation is an efficient way to summarize that association. The regression

regression analysis A method of data analysis in which the relationships among variables are represented in the form of an equation, called a regression equation.

linear regression analysis A form of statistical analysis that seeks the explanation for the straight line that best describes the relationship between two ratio variables.

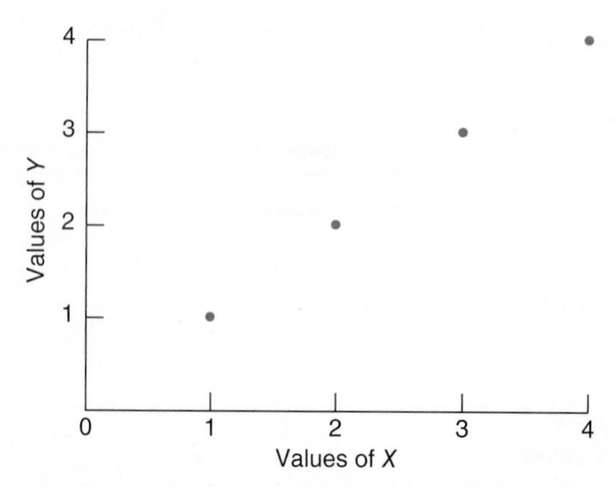

FIGURE 16-1 **Sample Scattergram of Values of X and Y.**

model has inferential value as well. To the extent that the regression equation correctly describes the general association between the two variables, it may be used to predict other sets of values. If, for example, we know that a new case has a value of 3.5 on X, we can predict the value of 3.5 on Y as well.

In practice, of course, studies are seldom limited to four cases, and the associations between variables are seldom as clear as the one presented in Figure 16-1.

A somewhat more realistic example is presented in Figure 16-2, representing a hypothetical relationship between population and crime rate in small- to medium-sized cities. Each dot in the scattergram is a city, and its placement reflects that city's population and its crime rate. As was the case in our previous example, the values of Y (crime rates) generally correspond to those of X (populations); as values of X increase, so do values of Y. However, the association is not nearly as clear as it was for the case in Figure 16-1.

In Figure 16-2 we can't superimpose a straight line that will pass through all the points in the scattergram. But we can draw an approximate line showing the best possible linear representation of the several points. We've drawn that line on the graph.

You may recall from algebra that any straight line on a graph can be represented by an equation of the form $Y = a + bX$, where X and Y are values of the two variables. In this equation, a equals the value of Y when X is 0, and b represents the slope of the line. If we know the values of a and b, we can calculate an estimate of Y for every value of X.

We can now say more formally that regression analysis is a technique for establishing the regression equation representing the geometric line that comes closest to the distribution of points on a graph. This regression equation provides a mathematical *description* of the relationship between the variables, and it allows us to *infer* values of Y when we have values of X. Looking again at Figure 16-2, we could estimate crime rates of cities if we knew their populations.

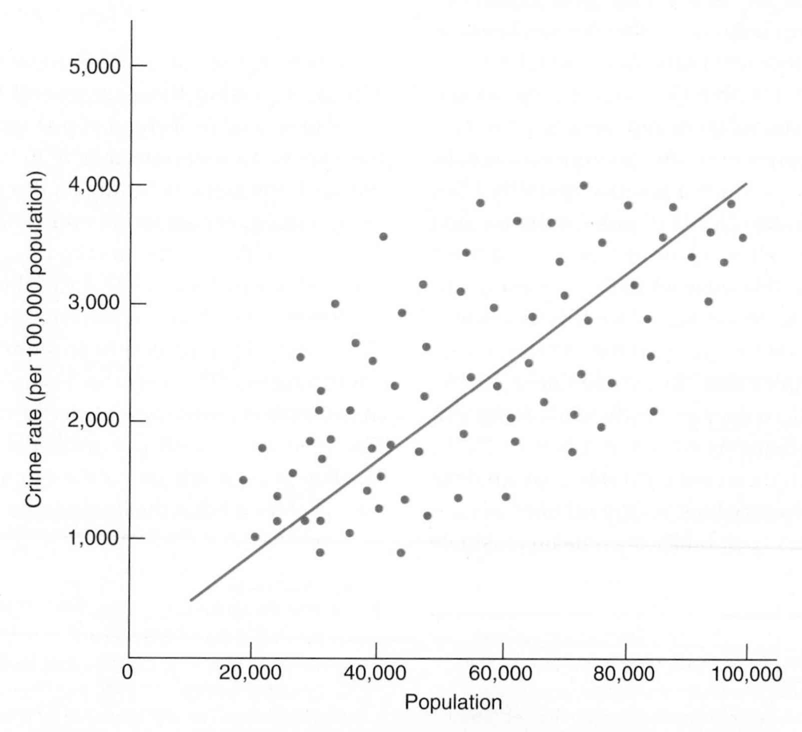

FIGURE 16-2 **A Scattergram of the Values of Two Variables with Regression Line Added (Hypothetical).**

To improve your guessing, you construct a *regression line*, stated in the form of a regression equation that permits the estimation of values on one variable from values on the other. The general format for this equation is $Y = \hat{a} + \hat{b}(X)$, where $\hat{a}$ and $\hat{b}$ are estimated from the data, X is any given value on one variable, and Y is the corresponding estimated value on the other. The values of $\hat{a}$ and $\hat{b}$ are computed to minimize the differences between actual values of Y and the corresponding estimates ($\hat{Y}$) based on the known value of X. The sum of squared differences between actual and estimated values of Y is called the *unexplained variation* because it represents errors that still exist even when estimates are based on known values of X.

The *explained variation* is the difference between the total variation and the unexplained variation. Dividing the explained variation by the total variation produces a measure of the *proportionate reduction of error* corresponding to the similar quantity in the computation of lambda. In the present case, this quantity is the *correlation squared:* r^2. Thus, if r =.7, then r^2 =.49, meaning that about half the variation has been explained. In practice, we compute r rather than r^2, because the product–moment correlation can take either a positive or negative sign, depending on the direction of the relationship between the two variables. (Computing r^2 and taking a square root would always produce a positive quantity.) See any standard statistics textbook for the *method* of computing r, although we anticipate that most readers using this measure will have access to computer programs designed for this function.

Unfortunately, or perhaps fortunately, social life is so complex that the simple linear regression model often does not sufficiently represent the state of affairs. As we saw in Chapter 15, it's possible, using percentage tables, to analyze more than two variables. As the number of variables increases, such tables become increasingly complicated and hard to read. But the regression model offers a useful alternative in such cases.

multiple regression analysis A statistical analysis that provides a way to analyze the simultaneous impact of two or more independent variables on a single dependent variable. The analysis produces an equation that represents the several effects of the multiple independent variables on the dependent variable.

Multiple Regression Very often, social researchers find that a given dependent variable is affected simultaneously by several independent variables. **Multiple regression analysis** provides a means of analyzing such situations. This was the case when Beverly Yerg (1981) set about studying teacher effectiveness in physical education. She stated her expectations in the form of a multiple regression equation[2]:

$$F = b_0 + b_1 I + b_1 X_1 + b_3 X_2 + b_4 X_3 + b_5 X_4 + e,$$

where

F = Final pupil-performance score
I = Initial pupil-performance score
X_1 = Composite of guiding and supporting practice
X_2 = Composite of teacher mastery of content
X_3 = Composite of providing specific, task-related feedback
X_4 = Composite of clear, concise task presentation
b = Regression weight
e = Residual

(Adapted from Yerg 1981:42)

Notice that in place of the single X variable in a linear regression, there are several Xs, and there are also several bs instead of just one. Also, Yerg has chosen to represent a as b_0 in this equation but with the same meaning as discussed previously. Finally, the equation ends with a residual factor (e), which represents the variance in Y that is not accounted for by the X variables analyzed.

Beginning with this equation, Yerg calculated the values of the several bs to show the relative contributions of the several independent variables in determining final student-performance scores. She also calculated the multiple-correlation coefficient as an indicator of the extent to which all six variables predict the final scores. This follows

2 Adapted from Beverly J. Yerg, 1981. "Reflections on the Use of the RTE Model in Physical Education," *Research Quarterly for Exercise and Sport*, March: 42.

the same logic as the simple bivariate correlation discussed earlier, and it is traditionally reported as a capital R. In this case $R = .877$, meaning that 77 percent of the variance ($.877^2 = .77$) in final scores is explained by the six variables acting in concert.

Partial Regression In exploring the elaboration model, we paid special attention to the relationship between two variables when a third test variable was held constant. Thus, we might examine the effect of *education* on *prejudice* with *age* held constant, testing the independent effect of *education.* To do so, we would compute the tabular relationship between *education* and *prejudice* separately for each age group.

Partial regression analysis is based on this same logical model. The equation summarizing the relationship between variables is computed on the basis of the test variables remaining constant. As in the case of the elaboration model, the result may be compared with the uncontrolled relationship between the two variables to clarify further the overall relationship.

Curvilinear Regression Up to now, we have been discussing the association among variables as represented by a straight line. The regression model is even more general than our discussion thus far has implied.

You may already know that curvilinear functions, as well as linear ones, can be represented by equations. For example, the equation $X^2 + Y^2 = 25$ describes a circle with a radius of 5. Raising variables to powers greater than 1 has the effect of producing curves rather than straight lines. And in the real world there is no reason to assume that the relationship among every set of variables will be linear. In some cases, then, **curvilinear regression analysis** can provide a better understanding of empirical relationships than can any linear model.

Recall, however, that a regression line serves two functions. It describes a set of empirical observations, and it provides a *general* model for making inferences about the relationship between two variables in the general population that the observations represent. A very complex equation might produce an erratic line that would indeed pass through every individual point. In this sense, it would perfectly describe the empirical observations. There would be no guarantee, however, that such a line could adequately *predict* new observations or that it in any meaningful way represented the relationship between the two variables in general. Therefore, it would have little or no inferential value.

Earlier in this book, we discussed the need for balancing detail and utility in data reduction. Ultimately, researchers attempt to provide the most faithful, yet also the simplest, representation of their data. This practice also applies to regression analysis. Data should be presented in the simplest fashion (thus, linear regressions are most frequently used) that best describes the actual data. Curvilinear regression analysis adds a new option to the researcher in this regard, but it does not solve the problems altogether. Nothing does that.

Cautions in Regression Analysis The use of regression analysis for statistical inferences is based on the same assumptions made for correlational analysis: simple random sampling, the absence of nonsampling errors, and continuous interval data. Because social scientific research seldom completely satisfies these assumptions, you should use caution in assessing the results in regression analyses.

Also, regression lines—linear or curvilinear—can be useful for *interpolation* (estimating cases lying between those observed), but they are less trustworthy when used for *extrapolation* (estimating cases that lie beyond the range of observations). This limitation on extrapolations is important in two ways. First, you're likely to come across regression equations that seem to make illogical predictions. An equation linking population and crimes, for example, might seem to suggest that small towns with, say, a population of 1,000 should produce 123 crimes

partial regression analysis A form of regression analysis in which the effects of one or more variables are held constant (controlled), similar to the logic of the elaboration model.

curvilinear regression analysis A form of regression analysis that allows relationships among variables to be expressed with curved geometric lines instead of straight ones.

a year. This failure in predictive ability does not disqualify the equation but dramatizes that its applicability is limited to a particular range of population sizes. Second, researchers sometimes overstep this limitation, drawing inferences that lie outside their range of observation, and you'd be right in criticizing them for that.

The preceding sections have introduced you to some of the techniques for measuring associations among variables at different levels of measurement. Matters become slightly more complex when the two variables represent different levels of measurement. Though we aren't going to pursue this issue in this textbook, we offer the Applying Concepts in Everyday Life box "Measures of Association and Levels of Measurement" by Peter Nardi as a useful resource if you ever have to address such situations.

OTHER MULTIVARIATE TECHNIQUES

For the most part, this book has focused on rather rudimentary forms of data manipulation, such as the use of contingency tables and percentages. Multiple regression analysis was briefly discussed. There are many other, more complex multivariate techniques—such as time-series analysis, path analysis, and factor analysis— that you will learn about in future statistics courses. Techniques like time-series analysis, for example, allow you to study long-term trends in a regression format. With various forms of regression analysis you can examine time-series data that represent changes in one or more variables over time. You can test factors that might explain the trend in a variable—say, *crime rates*—to determine if factors such as *population growth* or

APPLYING CONCEPTS IN EVERYDAY LIFE

Measures of Association and Levels of Measurement

Peter Nardi
Pitzer College

Note that this table itself is set up with the dependent variables in the rows and the independent variable in the columns, as tables are commonly organized. Also, notice that the levels of measurement are themselves an ordinal scale.

If you want to use an interval/ratio level variable in a crosstab, you must first recode it into an ordinal-level variable.

		Independent Variable		
		Nominal	Ordinal	Interval/Ratio
Dependent Variable	Nominal	Crosstabs Chi-square Lambda	Crosstabs Chi-square Lambda	
	Ordinal	Crosstabs Chi-square Lambda	Crosstabs Chi-square Lambda Gamma Kendall's tau Sommers' d	
	Interval/Ratio	Means *t*-test ANOVA	Means *t*-test ANOVA	Correlate Pearson *r* Regression (*R*)

economic fluctuations, for instance, account for the trend. This type of analysis could permit forecasting of future crime rates. The more you learn about advanced techniques for data manipulation, the more possibilities are open to you for exploration of your data.

INFERENTIAL STATISTICS

Many, if not most, social scientific research projects involve the examination of data collected from a sample drawn from a larger population. A sample of people may be interviewed in a survey; a sample of divorce records may be coded and analyzed; a sample of websites may be examined through content analysis. Researchers seldom if ever study samples just to describe the samples per se; in most instances, their ultimate purpose is to make assertions about the larger population from which the sample has been selected. Frequently, then, you'll wish to interpret your univariate and multivariate sample findings as the basis for *inferences* about some population.

This section examines **inferential statistics**—the statistical measures used for making inferences about a larger population from findings based on sample observations. Shortly, we'll discuss techniques for univariate data and move to multivariate. But before we do, let's return to the issue of sampling discussed in Chapter 6. We need to understand some features related to the theory and practical uses of probability samples.

PROBABILITY THEORY, SAMPLING DISTRIBUTIONS, AND ESTIMATES OF SAMPLING ERROR

Probability theory is a branch of mathematics that provides the tools researchers need to devise sampling techniques that produce representative samples and to statistically analyze results derived from such samples. More formally, probability theory provides the basis for estimating the parameters of a population. A **parameter** is the summary description of a given variable in a population. The mean income of all families in a city is a parameter; so is the age distribution of the city's population. When researchers generalize from a sample, they're using sample observations to estimate population parameters. A researcher's summary of sample observations is called a **statistic**. Researchers use statistics to estimate parameters.

Probability theory enables them both to make these estimates and to judge how likely the estimates will accurately represent the actual parameters in the population. So, for example, probability theory allows researchers to infer from a sample of 2,000 voters how a population of 15 million voters is likely to vote, and to specify exactly the probable margin of error in the estimates.

Probability theory accomplishes this by way of the concept of **sampling distributions**. A statistic computed from a single sample selected from a population will give an estimate of the population parameter. Other samples would likely yield slightly different statistics and result in slightly different estimates of a population parameter. This variation, even using random selection, is why survey results can be mistaken. For example, in the 2012 Alberta election, pollsters wrongly predicted the Wildrose Party to win (Pona 2012). But such mistakes are unusual. Probability theory tells us about the distribution of parameter estimates that would be produced by a large number of samples.

Let's look at two examples of sampling distributions to see how this works.

The Sampling Distribution of 10 Cases We'll begin with a simple example of a population of only 10 cases.[3] Suppose there are 10 people in a group, and each has a certain amount of money

inferential statistics The body of statistical computations relevant to making inferences from findings based on sample observations to some larger population.

parameter The summary description of a given variable in a population.

statistic A quantitative summary of a set of sample observations.

sampling distribution A distribution of sample statistics of the same variable from repeated random samples of the same size.

3 We thank Hanan Selvin for suggesting this method of introducing probability sampling.

FIGURE 16-3 **A Population of 10 People with $0–$9.** Let's imagine a population of only 10 people with differing amounts of money in their pockets—ranging from $0 to $9.
Source: Currency used with permission of The Bank of Canada.

in his or her pocket. To simplify, let's assume that one person has no money, another has $1, another has $2, and so forth, up to the person with $9. Figure 16-3 presents the population of 10 people.

Our task is to determine the average amount of money in this population: specifically, the mean number of dollars. If you simply add up the money shown in Figure 16-3 you'll find that the total is $45, so the true mean is $4.50. Our purpose in the rest of this exercise is to estimate that mean without actually observing all 10 individuals. We'll do that by selecting random samples from the population and using the means of those samples to estimate the mean of the whole population.

To start, suppose we were to select—at random—a sample of only *one* person from the 10. Our 10 possible samples thus consist of the 10 cases shown in Figure 16-3. The 10 dots shown on the graph in Figure 16-4 represent these 10 samples. Since we're taking samples of only one, they also represent the "means" we would get as estimates of the population. The distribution of the dots on the graph is the sampling distribution. Depending on which person we select, we'll estimate the group's mean as anywhere from $0 to $9. Obviously, it wouldn't be a very good idea to select a sample of only one, since we'll stand a very good chance of missing the true mean of $4.50 by quite a bit.

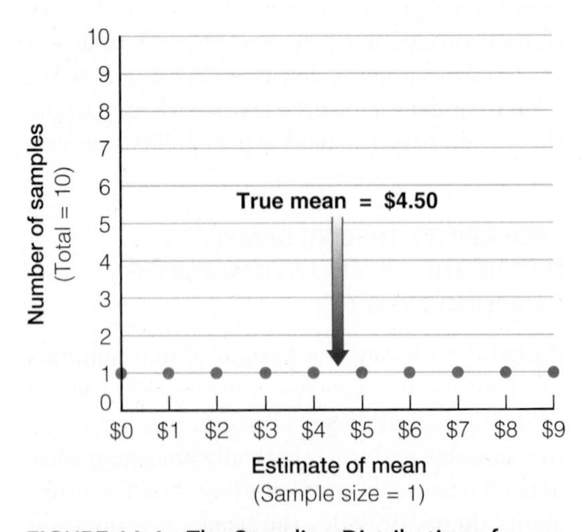

FIGURE 16-4 **The Sampling Distribution of Samples of 1.** In this simple example, the mean amount of money these people have is $4.50 ($45/10). If we picked 10 different samples of 1 person each, our "estimates" of the mean would range all across the board.
Source: © Cengage Learning

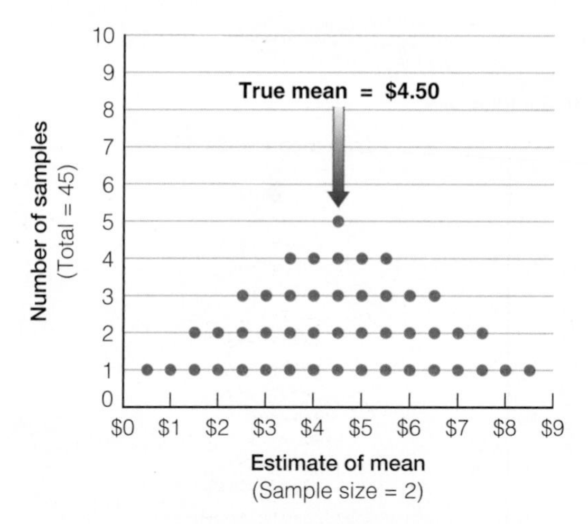

FIGURE 16-5 **The Sampling Distribution of Samples of 2.** After merely increasing our sample size to 2, the possible samples provide somewhat better estimates of the mean. We couldn't get either $0 or $9, and the estimates are beginning to cluster around the true value of the mean: $4.50.
Source: © Cengage Learning

But what if we take samples of two? As Figure 16-5 shows, increasing the sample size improves our estimations. There are now 45 possible samples: [$0 $1], [$0 $2], ... [$7 $8], [$8 $9]. Moreover, some of those samples produce the same means. For example, [$0 $6], [$1 $5], and [$2 $4] all produce means of $3. In Figure 16-5, the three dots shown above the $3 mean represent those three samples.

Moreover, the 45 sample means are not evenly distributed, as they were when the sample size was only one. Rather, they are somewhat clustered around the true value of $4.50. Only two possible samples deviate by as much as $4 from the true value ([$0 $1] and [$8 $9]), whereas five of the samples would give the true estimate of $4.50; another eight samples miss the mark by only 50 cents (plus or minus).

Now suppose we select even larger samples. What do you suppose that will do to our estimates of the mean? Figure 16-6 presents the sampling distributions of samples of 3, 4, 5, and 6. The progression of sampling distributions is clear. Every increase in sample size improves the distribution of estimates of the mean. The limiting case in this example, of course, is to select a sample of 10. There would be only one possible sample (everyone) and it would give us the true mean of $4.50. As we'll see shortly, this principle applies to actual sampling of meaningful populations. The larger the sample selected, the higher the probability of a more accurate estimate of a value of the population from which it is drawn.

Sampling Distributions and Estimates of Sampling Error Let's turn now to a more realistic sampling situation and see how the notion of sampling distribution applies. Assume we want to study the student population of Noname University (NU) to determine approval or disapproval of a student conduct code proposed by the administration. The study population will be that aggregation of, say, 20,000 students contained in a student roster. The elements will be the individual students at NU. We'll select a random sample of, say, 100 students for the purposes of estimating the entire student body. The variable under consideration will be *attitudes toward the code*, a binomial (or dichotomous) variable—that is, a variable composed of two attributes: *approve* and *disapprove*. The logic of probability sampling applies to the examination of other types of variables, such as mean income, but the computations are somewhat more complicated. Consequently, this introduction focuses on binomials.

The horizontal axis of Figure 16-7 presents all *possible* values of the parameter we want to estimate in the population, from 0 percent to 100 percent approval. The midpoint of the axis, 50 percent, represents half the students approving of the code and the other half disapproving.

To choose our sample, we give each student on the student roster a number and select 100 random numbers from a table of random numbers. Then we interview the 100 students whose numbers have been selected and ask for their attitudes toward the student code: whether they approve or disapprove. Suppose this operation gives us 48 students who approve of the code and 52 who disapprove. This summary description of a variable in a sample is called a statistic. We present this statistic by placing a dot on the x-axis at the point representing 48 percent.

Now let's suppose we select another sample of 100 students in exactly the same fashion and

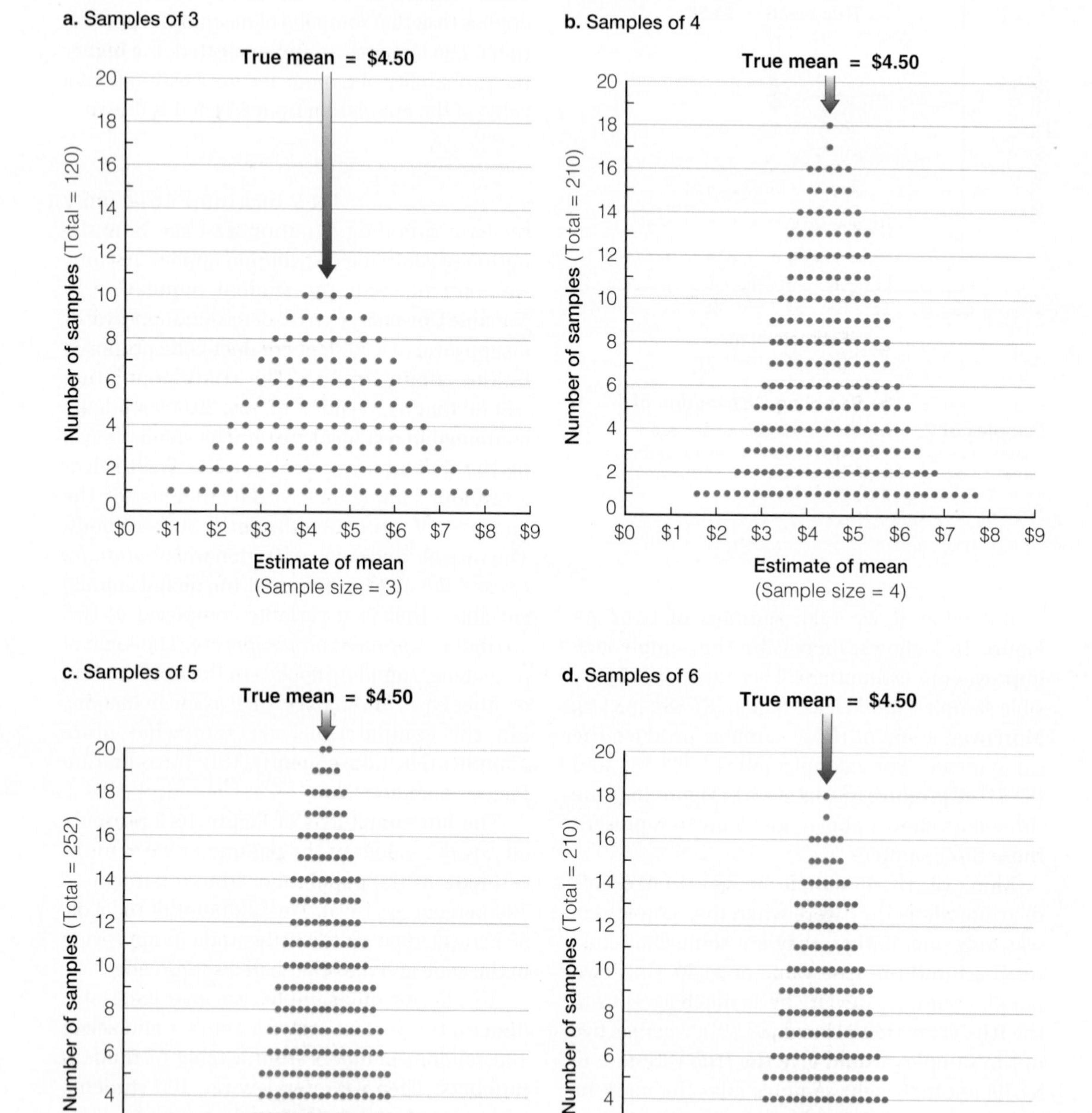

FIGURE 16-6 The Sampling Distribution of Samples of 3, 4, 5, and 6. As we increase the sample size, the possible samples cluster ever-more tightly around the true value of the mean. The chance of extremely inaccurate estimates is reduced at the two ends of the distribution, and the percentage of the samples near the true value keeps increasing.

Source: © Cengage Learning

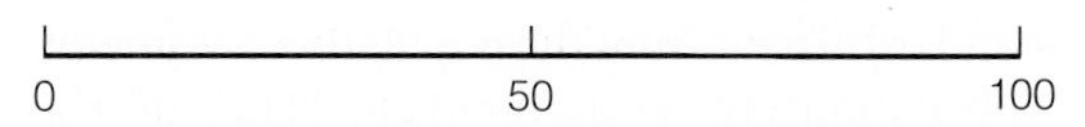

FIGURE 16-7 Range of Possible Sample Study Results. Shifting to a more realistic example, let's assume that we want to sample student attitudes concerning a proposed conduct code. Let's assume that 50 percent of the whole student body approves and 50 percent disapproves—though the researcher doesn't know that.
Source: © Cengage Learning

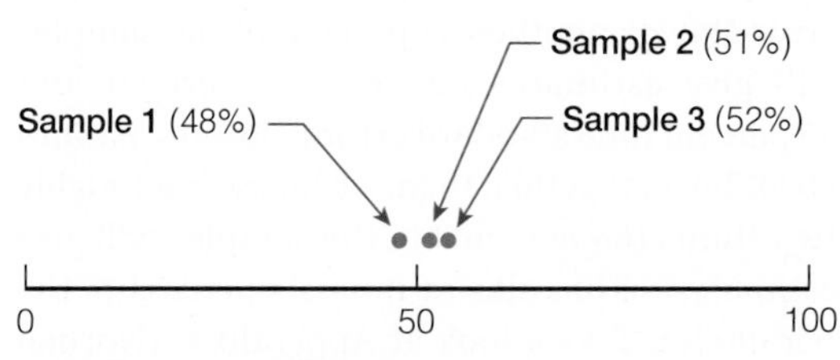

FIGURE 16-8 Results Produced by Three Hypothetical Studies. Assuming a large student body, let's suppose that we selected three different samples, each of substantial size. We would not necessarily expect those samples to perfectly reflect attitudes in the whole student body, but they should come reasonably close.
Source: © Cengage Learning

measure their approval or disapproval of the student code. Perhaps 51 students in the second sample approve of the code. We place another dot in the appropriate place on the *x*-axis. Repeating this process once more, we may discover that 52 students in the third sample approve of the code.

Figure 16-8 presents the three different sample statistics representing the percentages of students in each of the three random samples who approved of the student code. The basic rule of random sampling is that such samples drawn from a population give estimates of the parameter that exists in the total population. Each of the random samples, then, gives us an estimate of the percentage of students in the total student body who approve of the student code. Unhappily, however, we have selected three samples and now have three separate estimates.

To retrieve ourselves from this problem, let's draw more and more samples of 100 students each, question each of the samples concerning their approval or disapproval of the code, and plot the new sample statistics on our summary graph. In drawing many such samples, we discover that some of the new samples provide duplicate estimates, as in the illustration of 10 cases. Figure 16-9 shows the sampling distribution of, say, hundreds of samples. This U-shaped distribution is often referred to as a *normal curve.*

Note that by increasing the number of samples selected and interviewed, we have also increased the range of estimates provided by the sampling operation. In one sense we have increased our dilemma in attempting to guess the parameter in the population. Probability theory, however, provides certain important rules regarding the sampling distribution presented in Figure 16-9.

First, if many independent random samples are selected from a population, the sample statistics provided by those samples will be *distributed around the population parameter* in

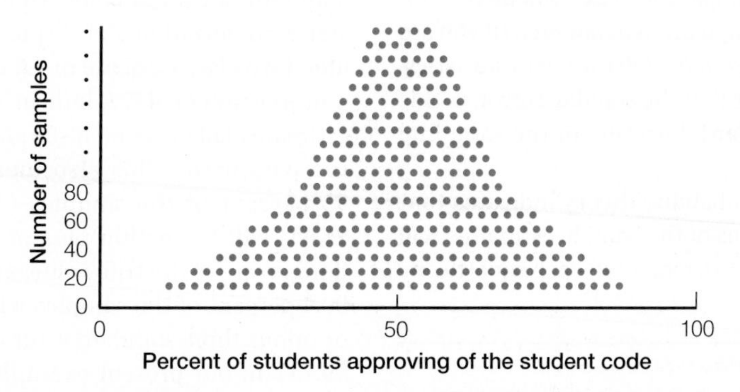

FIGURE 16-9 The Sampling Distribution. If we were to select a large number of good samples, we would expect them to cluster around the true value (50 percent), but given enough such samples, a few would fall far from the mark.
Source: © Cengage Learning

a known way. Thus, although Figure 16-9 shows a wide range of estimates, more of them are in the vicinity of 50 percent than elsewhere in the graph. Probability theory tells us, then, that the true value is in the vicinity of 50 percent.

Second, probability theory gives us a formula for estimating *how closely* the sample statistics are clustered around the true value. In other words, probability theory enables us to estimate the **sampling error**—the degree of error to be expected for a given sample design. This formula contains three factors: the parameter, the sample size, and the *standard error* (a measure of sampling error):

$$s = \sqrt{\frac{P \times Q}{n}}$$

The symbols P and Q in the formula equal the population parameters for the binomial: If 60 percent of the student body approves of the code and 40 percent disapproves, P and Q are 60 percent and 40 percent, respectively, or 0.6 and 0.4. Note that $Q = 1 - P$ and $P = 1 - Q$. The symbol n equals the number of cases in each sample, and s is the standard error.

Let's assume that the actual population parameter is 50 percent approving of the code and 50 percent disapproving. Recall that we've been selecting samples of 100 cases each. When these numbers are put into the formula, we find that the standard error equals 0.05, or 5 percent.

In probability theory, the standard error is a valuable piece of information because it indicates how tightly the sample estimates will be distributed around the population parameter. (If you are familiar with the *standard deviation* in statistics, you may recognize that the standard error, in this case, is the standard deviation of the sampling distribution.)

Specifically, probability theory indicates that certain proportions of the sample estimates will fall within specified increments—each equal to one standard error—from the population parameter. Approximately 34 percent (0.3413) of the sample estimates will fall within one standard error increment above the population parameter, and another 34 percent will fall within one standard error below the parameter. In our example, the standard error increment is 5 percent, so we know that 34 percent of our samples will give estimates of student approval between 50 percent (the parameter) and 55 percent (one standard error above); another 34 percent of the samples will give estimates between 50 percent and 45 percent (one standard error below the parameter). Taken together, then, we know that roughly two-thirds (68 percent) of the samples will give estimates within plus or minus 5 percent of the parameter. Take a look at Appendix C (Normal Curve Areas). The left-hand column (z-scores, or standardized scores) indicates the distance in standard error units from the centre of the distribution (the population parameter). The four-decimal values in the columns to the right indicate the proportion of scores that fall between a particular z-score and the true population value. A z-score of 1.0 indicates a sample estimate that is one standard error away from the population parameter. This z-score has a proportion of .3413, indicating that 34.13% of sample estimates fall between 1 standard error and the population parameter (which always has a standard error of 0). Since the normal curve is symmetrical (the areas below the centre of the distribution are equal to the areas above), this also means that 68.26% of estimates will fall between one standard deviation below (minus one) and one standard deviation above (plus one) the parameter. Likewise, a z-score of 2.0 is associated with a proportion of .4772, indicating that 47.72% of estimates fall between a standard error of 2 and the parameter. This also means that roughly 95 percent of the samples (47.72 + 47.72 = 95.44) will fall within plus or minus two standard errors of the true value, and approximately 99.9 percent of the samples will fall within plus or minus three standard errors (49.87 + 49.87 = 99.74). In our present example, then, we know that only one sample out of 1,000 would give an estimate lower than 35 percent approval or higher than 65 percent.

---

sampling error The difference between a population value and an estimate of that value derived from a sample. Probability theory gives us a formula for estimating sampling error—how closely the sample statistics will tend to cluster around the true values in the population.

The proportion of samples falling within one, two, or three standard errors of the parameter is constant for any random sampling procedure such as the one just described. The size of the standard error in any given case, however, is a function of the population parameter and the sample size. If we return to the formula for a moment, we note that the standard error will increase as a function of an increase in the quantity P times Q. Note further that this quantity reaches its maximum in the situation of an even split in the population. If $P = 0.5$, $PQ = 0.25$; if $P = 0.6$, $PQ = 0.24$; if $P = 0.8$, $PQ = 0.16$; if $P = 0.99$, $PQ = 0.0099$. By extension, if P is either 0.0 or 1.0 (either 0 percent or 100 percent approve of the student code), the standard error will be zero. That is, if everyone in the population has the same attitude (no variation), then every sample will give exactly that estimate.

The standard error is also a function of the sample size—an *inverse* function. As the sample size increases, the standard error decreases. In other words, as the sample size increases, the several samples will be clustered nearer to the true value. Another general guideline is evident in the formula: Because of the square root in the formula, the standard error is reduced by half if the sample size is *quadrupled.* In our present example, samples of 100 produce a standard error of 5 percent; to reduce the standard error to 2.5 percent, we must increase the sample size to 400.

All of this information is provided by established probability theory in reference to the selection of large numbers of random samples. (If you've taken a statistics course, you may know this as the central limit theorem.) If the population parameter is known and many random samples are selected, we can predict how many of the samples will fall within specified intervals from the parameter.

Recognize that this discussion only illustrates the *logic* of probability sampling; it does not describe the way research is actually conducted. Usually, we don't know the parameter: The very reason we conduct a sample survey is to estimate that value. Moreover, we don't actually select large numbers of samples: We select only one sample. Nevertheless, the preceding discussion of probability theory provides the basis for inferences about the typical social research situation. Knowing what it would be like to select thousands of samples allows us to make assumptions about the one sample we do select and study.

Confidence Levels and Confidence Intervals

Although probability theory specifies that 68 percent of that fictitious large number of samples would produce estimates falling within one standard error of the parameter, we can turn the logic around and infer that any single random sample has a 68 percent chance of falling within that range. This observation leads us to the two key components of sampling error estimates, **confidence level** and **confidence interval.** We express the accuracy of our sample statistics in terms of a *level of confidence* that the statistics fall within a specified interval from the parameter. For example, we may say we are confident that in 95 percent of samples, sample statistics (such as 50 percent favour the new student code) are within plus or minus two standard errors of the population parameter. As the confidence interval is expanded for a given statistic, the confidence level increases. For example, we may say we are confident that in 99.9 percent of samples, estimates from samples (i.e., statistics) will fall within plus or minus three standard errors of the true value.

Although we may use confidence intervals to express the ranges of accuracy for the parameter, we've already noted that we seldom know what the parameter actually is. But the formula for estimating sampling error requires that we

confidence level The estimated probability that a population parameter lies within a given *confidence interval*. Given an appropriately constructed confidence interval, such as plus or minus two standard errors around the mean, we may state that in 95 percent of all samples the true population value will be inside the constructed interval.

confidence interval The range of values within which a population parameter is estimated to lie. A survey, for example, may show 40 percent of a sample favouring Candidate A. Although the best estimate of the support existing among all voters would also be 40 percent, we would not expect it to be exactly that. We might, therefore, compute a confidence interval (such as from 35 to 45 percent) within which the actual percentage of the population probably lies. Note that we must specify a *confidence level* in connection with every confidence interval.

specify some value for the parameter. To resolve this problem in the case of the binomial, we substitute our sample estimate for the parameter in the formula; that is, lacking the true value, we substitute the best available guess.

The result of these inferences and estimations is that we can estimate a population parameter and also the expected degree of error on the basis of one sample drawn from a population. Beginning with the question "What percentage of the student body approves of the student code?" you could select a random sample of 100 students and interview them. You might then report that your best estimate is that 50 percent of the student body approves of the code and that the theory of random samples assures us that the range of 40 percent to 60 percent (plus or minus two standard errors) would contain the true value in 95 percent of samples. The range from 40 to 60 percent is the *confidence interval.* (At the 68 percent confidence level, the confidence interval would be 45 to 55 percent.)

The logic of confidence levels and confidence intervals also provides the basis for determining the appropriate sample size for a study. Once you've decided on the degree of sampling error you can tolerate, you'll be able to calculate the number of cases needed in your sample. For example, to achieve an accuracy of plus or minus 5 percent, with confidence of 95 percent, you should select a sample of at least 400. (Appendix D is a convenient guide in this regard.)

This then is the basic logic of probability sampling. Random selection permits the researcher to link findings from a sample to the body of probability theory so as to estimate the accuracy of those findings. All statements of accuracy in sampling must specify both a confidence level and a confidence interval. Here is an example of the language that typically accompanies reports of polling results (Galloway 2015). In this case the poll was conducted prior to the 2015 federal election and probed perceptions of political party support for issues facing Canadian families.

> The hybrid telephone and online random survey of 1,000 Canadians, which was conducted between May 26 and 28, is expected to accurately reflect the opinions of the broader Canadian public within 3.1 percentage points, 19 times out of 20.

Notice that this sentence provides information about the sample size (1,000), data collection period (May 26–28), confidence interval (plus or minus 3.1 percent), and confidence level (19/20 = 95 percent). This type of information is essential so informed readers can evaluate the findings presented. In addition, technically, the reported confidence in the statistics presented is "In theory ... for such samples," or "For samples of this size," and this should somehow be indicated.

When you read statements about polls in the popular media, be warned that such statements are sometimes made when they are not warranted. Be especially wary of survey or poll results that fail to indicate confidence levels and confidence intervals. Without these specifications, the "findings" are of dubious value. Overall, the more information communicated about how the study was conducted, the better able you are to determine whether the claims made are warranted.

Before we conclude this discussion, there are two more cautionary notes. First, the survey uses of probability theory as discussed in this section are, technically, not wholly justified. The theory of sampling distribution makes assumptions that almost never apply in survey conditions. The exact proportion of samples contained within specified increments of standard errors, for example, mathematically assumes an infinitely large population, an infinite number of samples, and sampling with replacement (i.e., every sampling unit selected is then put back so that it could be selected again). Second, the inferential jump from the distribution of several samples to the probable characteristics of one sample has been oversimplified in our discussion.

These cautions are offered to give you perspective on the uses of probability theory in sampling. Social researchers often appear to overestimate the precision of estimates produced by using probability theory. As we'll mention elsewhere in this chapter and throughout the book, variations in sampling techniques and nonsampling factors may further reduce the legitimacy of such estimates. For instance, those selected in a sample who do not participate further detract from the sample's representativeness.

Nevertheless, the calculations discussed in this section can be extremely valuable to you in understanding and evaluating your data. Although the calculations do not provide estimates as precisely as some researchers might assume, they can be quite valid for practical purposes. They are unquestionably more valid than less rigorously derived estimates based on less rigorous sampling methods. Most important, being familiar with the basic *logic* underlying the calculations can help you react sensibly to your own data and to those reported by others.

UNIVARIATE INFERENCES

Chapter 14 dealt with methods of presenting univariate data. Each summary measure was intended as a method of describing the sample studied. Now we'll use such measures to make broader assertions about a population. This section addresses two univariate measures: percentages and means.

If 50 percent of a sample of people say they've had colds during the past year, 50 percent is also our best estimate of the proportion of colds in the total population from which the sample was drawn. (This estimate assumes a simple random sample, of course.) It's rather unlikely, however, that *precisely* 50 percent of the population have had colds during the year. If a rigorous sampling design for random selection has been followed, however, we will be able to estimate the expected range of error when the sample finding is applied to the population.

Chapter 6, on sampling theory, covered the procedures for making such estimates, so we'll only review them here. In the case of a percentage, the quantity

$$\sqrt{\frac{p \times q}{n}}$$

where p is a percentage, q equals $1 - p$, and n is the sample size, is called the *standard error.* As noted in Chapter 6, this quantity is very important in the estimation of sampling error. We may say we are confident that in 68 percent of samples, sample estimates (i.e., statistics) are within plus or minus one standard error of the population value; we may say we are confident that in 95 percent of samples, sample statistics are within plus or minus two standard errors of the population parameter; and we may say we are confident that in 99.9 percent of samples, the estimates will fall within plus or minus three standard errors of the true value in the population.

Any statement of sampling error, then, must contain two essential components: the *confidence level* (e.g., 95 percent) and the *confidence interval* (e.g., plus or minus 2.5 percent). If 50 percent of a sample of 1,600 people say they've had colds during the year, we might say that, in theory for samples of this size, the population figure would be between 47.5 percent and 52.5 percent 19 out of 20 times.

In this example we've moved beyond simply describing the sample into the realm of making inferences about the larger population. In doing so, we must take care in several ways.

First, the sample must be drawn from the population about which inferences are being made. A sample of university students cannot legitimately be the basis for statistical inferences about the general population, but rather only about the population of university students. In addition, if all the students in the sample are from a single university, then inferences can only be made about that university's student population.

Second, the inferential statistics assume simple random sampling, which is virtually never the case in sample surveys. The statistics assume sampling with replacement, which is almost never done—but this is probably not a serious problem. Although systematic sampling is used more frequently than random sampling, it, too, probably presents no serious problem if done correctly. Stratified sampling, because it improves representativeness, clearly presents no problem. Cluster sampling does present a problem, however, as the estimates of sampling error may be too small. Quite clearly, street-corner sampling does not warrant the use of inferential statistics. Finally, this standard error sampling technique also assumes a 100 percent completion rate (i.e., that everyone in the sample completed the survey). This problem increases in seriousness as the completion rate decreases.

Third, inferential statistics are addressed to sampling error only, not **nonsampling error**, such as coding errors or misunderstandings of questions by respondents. Although we might state correctly that between 47.5 and 52.5 percent of the population (95 percent confidence) would *report* having colds during the previous year, we couldn't so confidently guess the percentage who had actually *had* them. Because nonsampling errors are probably larger than sampling errors in a respectable sample design, we need to be especially cautious in generalizing from our sample findings to the population.

TESTS OF STATISTICAL SIGNIFICANCE

There is no scientific answer to the question of whether a given association between two variables is significant, strong, important, interesting, or worth reporting. Perhaps the ultimate test of significance rests with your ability to persuade your audience (present and future) of the association's significance. At the same time, there is a body of inferential statistics to assist you in this regard, called *parametric tests of significance.* As the name suggests, parametric statistics are those that make certain assumptions about the parameters describing the population from which the sample is selected. They allow us to determine the **statistical significance** of associations. *Statistical significance* does not imply importance or significance in any general sense. If refers simply to the likelihood that relationships as large as those observed in a sample could be attributed to sampling error alone.

Although **tests of statistical significance** are widely reported in social scientific literature, the logic underlying them is rather subtle and often misunderstood. Tests of significance are based on the same sampling logic discussed elsewhere in this book. To understand that logic, let's return for a moment to the concept of sampling error in regard to univariate data.

Recall that a sample statistic normally provides the best single estimate of the corresponding population parameter, but the statistic and the parameter seldom correspond precisely. That's why we report the probability that the parameter falls within a certain range (confidence interval). The degree of uncertainty within that range is due to normal sampling error. The corollary of such a statement is, of course, that it is improbable that the parameter would fall outside the specified range *only* as a result of sampling error. Thus, if we estimate that a parameter (99.9 percent confidence) lies between 45 percent and 55 percent, we say by implication that it is extremely improbable that the parameter is actually, say, 90 percent if our *only* error of estimation is due to normal sampling. This is the basic logic behind tests of statistical significance.

THE LOGIC OF STATISTICAL SIGNIFICANCE

We think we can illustrate the logic of *statistical significance* best in a series of diagrams representing the selection of samples from a population. Here are the elements in the logic:

1. assumptions regarding the independence of two variables in the population study
2. assumptions regarding the representativeness of samples selected through conventional probability sampling procedures
3. the observed joint distribution of sample elements in terms of the two variables

Figure 16-10 represents a hypothetical population of 256 people; half are women, half are men. The diagram also indicates whether each person believes women should be equal to men. In the diagram, those favouring equality have open circles; those opposing it have their circles shaded in.

The question we'll be investigating is whether there is any relationship between *gender* and *beliefs about equality* for men and women. More specifically, we'll see if women are more likely to

---

nonsampling error Those imperfections of data quality that are a result of factors other than sampling error. Examples include misunderstandings of questions by respondents, erroneous recordings by interviewers and coders, and data entry errors.

statistical significance A general term referring to the likelihood that relationships observed in a sample could be attributed to sampling error alone.

tests of statistical significance A class of statistical computations that indicate the likelihood that the relationship observed between variables in a sample can be attributed to sampling error only.

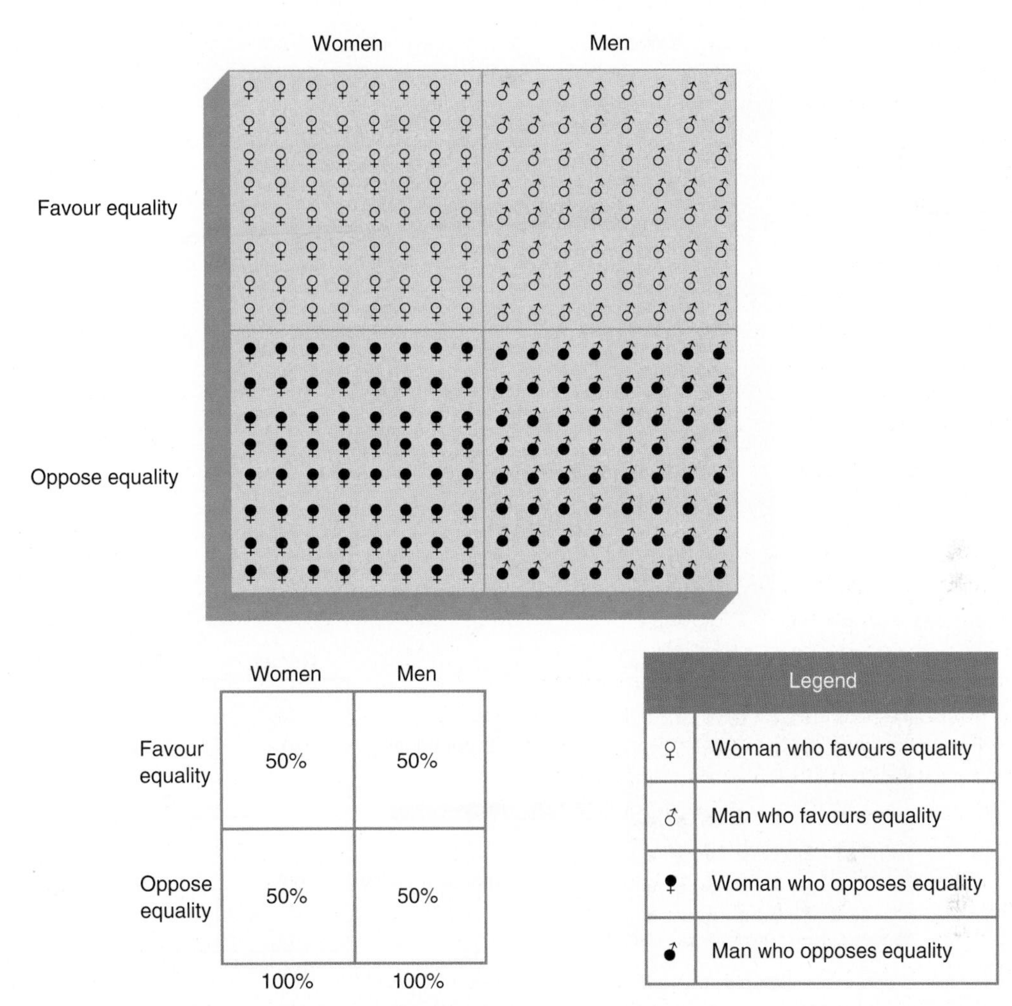

	Women	Men
Favour equality	50%	50%
Oppose equality	50%	50%
	100%	100%

FIGURE 16-10 **A Hypothetical Population of Men and Women Who Either Favour or Oppose Gender Equality.**

favour equality than men are, since women would presumably benefit more from it. Take a moment to look at Figure 16-10 and see what the answer to this question is.

The illustration in the figure indicates there is no relationship between *gender* and *attitudes about equality*. Exactly half of each group favours equality and the other half opposes it. Recall the earlier discussion of proportionate reduction of error. In this instance, knowing a person's gender would not reduce the "errors" we'd make in guessing his or her attitude toward equality. The table at the bottom of Figure 16-10 provides a tabular view of what you can observe in the graphic diagram.

Figure 16-11 represents the selection of a one-fourth sample from the hypothetical population. With regard to the graphic illustration, a "square" selection from the centre of the population provides a representative sample. Notice that our sample contains 16 of each type of person: Half are men and half are women; half of each gender favours equality, and the other half opposes it.

The sample selected in Figure 16-11 would allow us to draw accurate conclusions about the relationship between *gender* and *equality* in the larger population. Following the sampling logic we saw in Chapter 6, we'd note there was no relationship between *gender* and *equality* in the

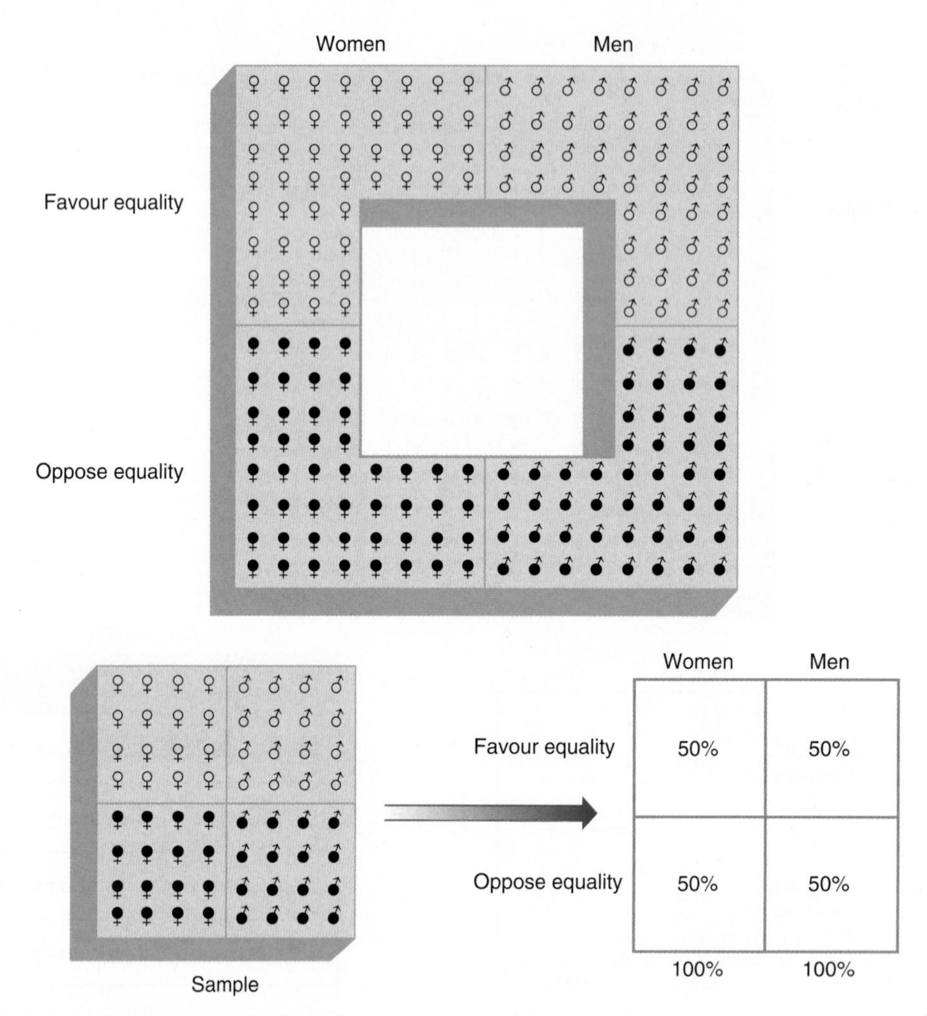

FIGURE 16-11 **A Representative Sample.**

sample. Therefore, we'd conclude there was similarly no relationship in the larger population—since we've presumably selected a sample in accord with the conventional rules of sampling.

Of course, real-life samples are seldom such perfect reflections of the populations from which they're drawn. It would not be unusual for us to have selected, say, one or two extra men who opposed equality and a couple of extra women who favoured it—even if there was no relationship between the two variables in the population. Such minor variations are part and parcel of probability sampling, as we saw in Chapter 6.

Figure 16-12, however, represents a sample that falls far short of the mark in reflecting the larger population. Notice it includes far too many supportive women and opposing men. As the table shows, three-quarters of the women in the sample support equality, but only one-quarter of the men do so. If we had selected this sample from a population in which the two variables were unrelated to each other, we'd be sorely misled by the analysis of our sample.

As you'll recall, it's unlikely that a properly drawn probability sample would ever be as inaccurate as the one shown in Figure 16-12. In fact, if we actually selected a sample that gave us the results this one does, we'd look for a different explanation. Figure 16-13 illustrates the more likely situation.

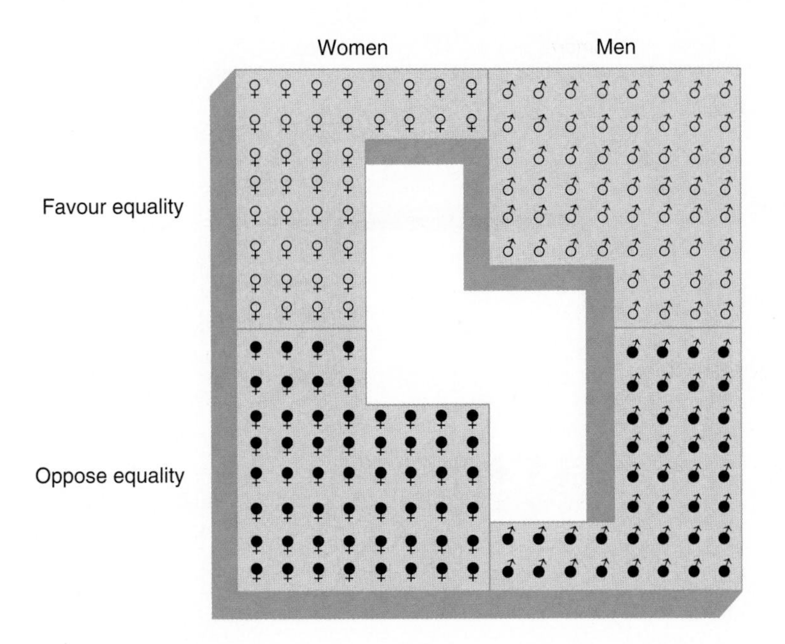

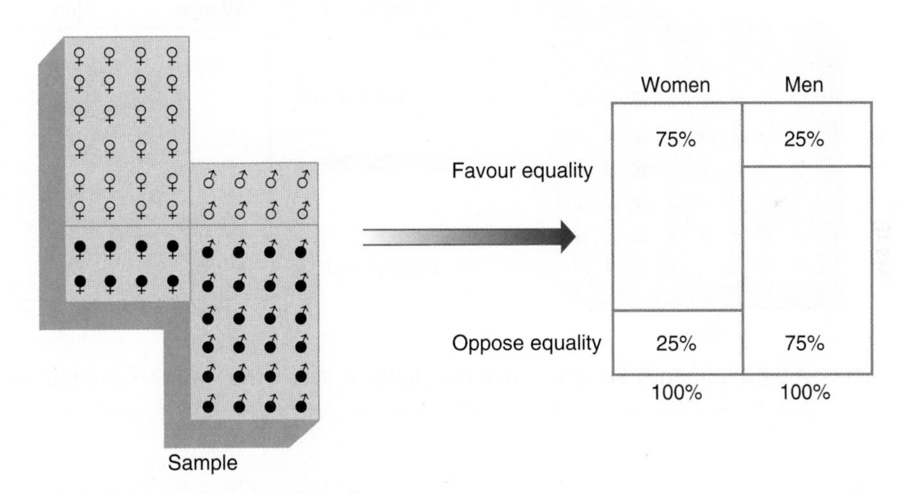

FIGURE 16-12 **An Unrepresentative Sample.**

Notice that the sample selected in Figure 16-13 also shows a strong relationship between *gender* and *equality*. The reason is quite different this time. We've selected a perfectly representative sample, but we see that there is actually a strong relationship between the two variables in the population at large. In this latest figure, women are more likely to support equality than men are—that's the case in the population, and the sample reflects it.

In practice, of course, we never know what's so for the total population; that's why we select samples. Thus, if we selected a sample and found the strong relationship presented in Figures 16-12 and 16-13, we'd need to decide whether that finding accurately reflected the population or was simply a product of sampling error.

The fundamental logic of tests of statistical significance, then, is this: Faced with any discrepancy between the assumed independence

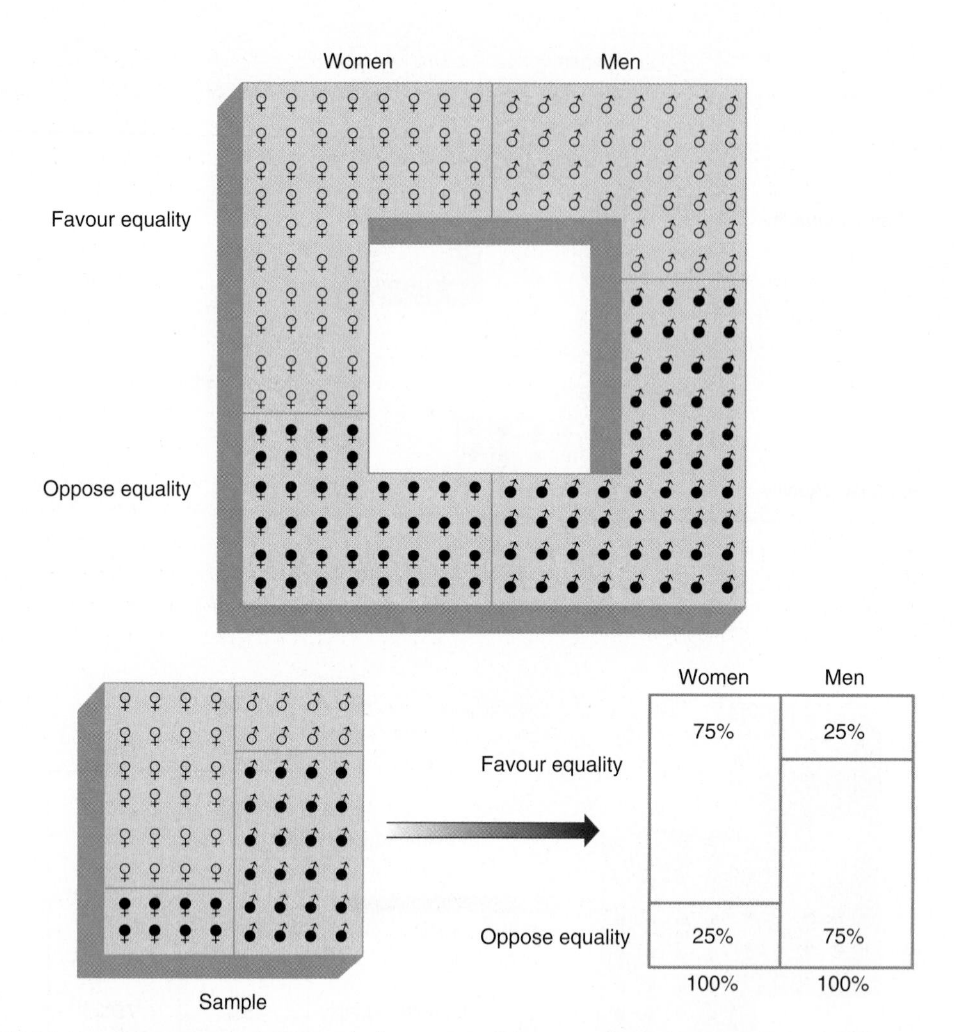

FIGURE 16-13 **A Representative Sample from a Population in Which the Variables Are Related.**

of variables in a population and the observed distribution of sample elements, we may explain that discrepancy in either of two ways: (1) we may attribute it to an unrepresentative sample, or (2) we may reject the assumption of independence. The logic and statistics associated with probability sampling methods offer guidance about the varying probabilities of varying degrees of unrepresentativeness (expressed as sampling error). More simply put, there is a *high* probability of a *small* degree of unrepresentativeness and a *low* probability of a *large* degree of unrepresentativeness.

The *statistical significance* of a relationship observed in a set of sample data, then, is always expressed in terms of probabilities. "Significant at the .05 level ($p \geqslant .05$)" simply means that the probability that a relationship as strong as the observed one can be attributed to sampling error alone is no more than 5 in 100. Put somewhat differently, if two variables are independent of each other in the population, and if 100 probability samples were selected from that population, no more than 5 of those samples would provide a relationship as strong as the one that has been observed.

There is, then, a corollary to confidence intervals in tests of significance, which represents the probability of the measured associations being due *only* to sampling error. This is called the **level of significance**. Like confidence intervals, levels of significance are derived from a logical model in which several samples are drawn from a given population. In the present case, we assume that there is no association between the variables in the population, and then ask what proportion of the samples drawn from such a population would produce associations at least as great as those measured in the empirical data. Three levels of significance are frequently used in research reports: .05, .01, and .001. These mean, respectively, that the chances of obtaining the measured association as a result of sampling error are 5/100, 1/100, and 1/1,000.

Researchers who use tests of significance normally follow one of two patterns. Some specify in advance the level of significance they will regard as sufficient. If any measured association is statistically significant at that level, they will regard it as representing a genuine association between the two variables. In other words, they're willing to discount the possibility of its resulting from sampling error only.

Other researchers prefer to report the specific level of significance for each association, disregarding the conventions of .05, .01, and .001. Rather than reporting that a given association is significant at the .05 level, they might report significance at the .023 level, indicating the chances of its having resulted from sampling error as 23 out of 1,000.

CHI SQUARE

Chi square (χ^2) is a frequently used test of significance in social science. It's based on the **null hypothesis**: the assumption that there is no relationship between the two variables in the total population. Given the observed distribution of values on the two separate variables, we compute the conjoint distribution that would be expected if there were no relationship between the two variables. The result of this operation is a set of *expected frequencies* for all the cells in the contingency table. We then compare this expected distribution with the distribution of cases actually found in the sample data, and we determine the probability that the discovered discrepancy could have resulted from sampling error alone. An example will illustrate this procedure.

Let's assume we're interested in the possible relationship between *church attendance* and *gender* for the members of a particular church. To test this relationship, we select a sample of 100 church members at random. We find our sample is made up of 40 men and 60 women and that 70 percent of our sample report having attended church during the preceding week, whereas the remaining 30 percent say they did not.

If there is no relationship between *gender* and *church attendance*, then 70 percent of the men in the sample should have attended church during the preceding week, and 30 percent should have stayed away. Moreover, women should have attended in the same proportion. Table 16-6 (Part I) shows that based on this model, 28 men and 42 women would have attended church, with 12 men and 18 women not attending.

Part II of Table 16-6 presents the observed attendance for the hypothetical sample of 100 church members. Note that 20 of the men report having attended church during the preceding week and the remaining 20 say they did not. Among the women in the sample, 50 attended church and 10 did not. Comparing the expected and observed frequencies (Parts I and II), we note that somewhat fewer men attended church than expected, whereas somewhat more women than expected attended.

Chi square is computed as follows. For each cell in the tables, the researcher (1) subtracts

level of significance In the context of tests of statistical significance, the degree of likelihood that an observed, empirical relationship could be attributable to sampling error. A relationship is significant at the .05 level if the likelihood of its being only a function of sampling error is no greater than 5 out of 100.

null hypothesis In connection with hypothesis testing and tests of statistical significance, the hypothesis that suggests there is no relationship among the variables under study. You may conclude that the variables are related after having statistically rejected the null hypothesis.

TABLE 16-6 A Hypothetical Illustration of Chi Square

I. Expected Cell Frequencies	Men	Women	Total
Attended church	28	42	70
Did not attend church	12	18	30
Total	40	60	100
II. Observed Cell Frequencies	**Men**	**Women**	**Total**
Attended church	20	50	70
Did not attend church	20	10	30
Total	40	60	100
III. (Observed − Expected)^2 ÷ Expected	**Men**	**Women**	
Attended church	2.29	1.52	$\chi^2 = 12.70$
Did not attend church	5.33	3.56	$p < .001$

the expected frequency for that cell from the observed frequency, (2) squares this quantity, and (3) divides the squared difference by the expected frequency. This procedure is carried out for each cell in the tables, and the several results are added together. (Part III of Table 16-6 presents the cell-by-cell computations.) The final sum is the value of chi square: 12.70 in the example.

This value is the overall discrepancy between the observed conjoint distribution in the sample and the distribution we should have expected if the two variables were unrelated to each other. Of course, the mere discovery of a discrepancy does not prove that the two variables are related, since normal sampling error might produce discrepancies even when there was no relationship in the total population. The magnitude of the value of chi square, however, permits us to estimate the probability of that having happened.

Degrees of Freedom To determine the statistical significance of the observed relationship, we must use a standard set of chi square values. This will require the computation of the *degrees of freedom,* which refers to the possibilities for variation within a statistical model. Suppose we challenge you to find three numbers whose mean is 11. There is an infinite number of solutions to this problem: (11, 11, 11), (10, 11, 12), (−11, 11, 33), and so forth. Now suppose we require that one of the numbers be 7. There would still be an infinite number of possibilities for the other two numbers.

If we told you one number had to be 7 and another 10, there would be only one possible value for the third. If the average of three numbers is 11, their sum must be 33. If two of the numbers total 17, the third must be 16. In this situation, we say there are two degrees of freedom. Two of the numbers could have any values we choose, but once they are specified, the third number is determined.

More generally, whenever we're examining the mean of N values, we can see that the degree of freedom is $N - 1$. Thus, in the case of the mean of 23 values, we could make 22 of them anything we liked, but the 23rd would then be determined.

A similar logic applies to bivariate tables, such as those analyzed by chi square. Consider a table reporting the relationship between two dichotomous variables: *gender* (men/women) and *abortion attitude* (approve/disapprove). Notice that the table provides the marginal frequencies of both variables.

Despite the conveniently round numbers in this hypothetical example, notice there are numerous possibilities for the cell frequencies. For example, it could be the case that all 500 men approve and all 500 women disapprove, or it could be just the reverse. Or there could be 250 cases in each cell, and so forth. Notice that there are numerous other possibilities.

Abortion Attitude	Men	Women	Total
Approve			500
Disapprove			500
Total	500	500	1,000

Now the question is—how many cells could we fill in pretty much as we choose before the remainder are determined by the marginal frequencies? The answer is only one. If we know that 300 men approved, for example, then 200 men would have had to disapprove, and the distribution would need to be just the opposite for the women.

In this instance, then, we say the table has *one degree of freedom.* Now take a few minutes to construct a three-by-three table. Assume you know the marginal frequencies for each variable, and see if you can determine how many degrees of freedom it has.

For chi square, the degrees of freedom are computed as follows: The number of rows in the table of observed frequencies, minus 1, is multiplied by the number of columns, minus 1. This may be written as $(r - 1)(c - 1)$. For a *three-by-three* table, then, there are *four degrees of freedom*: $(3 - 1)(3 - 1) = (2)(2) = 4$.

In the example of gender and church attendance, we have two rows and two columns (discounting the totals), so there is one degree of freedom. Turning to a table of chi square values (see Appendix B), we find that for one degree of freedom and random sampling from a population in which there is no relationship between two variables, 10 percent of the time we should expect a chi square of at least 2.7. Thus, if we selected 100 samples from such a population, we should expect about 10 of those samples to produce chi squares equal to or greater than 2.7. Moreover, we should expect chi square values of at least 6.6 in only 1 percent of the samples and chi square values of 10.8 or more in only a tenth of a percent (.001) of the samples. The higher the chi square value, the less probable it is that the value could be attributed to sampling error alone.

In our example, the computed value of chi square is 12.70. If there were no relationship between *gender* and *church attendance* in the church member population and a large number of samples had been selected and studied, then we would expect a chi square of this magnitude in fewer than 1/10 of 1 percent (.001) of those samples. Thus, the probability of obtaining a chi square of this magnitude is less than .001, if random sampling has been used and there is no relationship in the population. We report this finding by saying the relationship is *statistically significant at the .001 level.* Because it is so improbable that the observed relationship could have resulted from sampling error alone, we're likely to reject the null hypothesis and assume that there is a relationship between the two variables in the population of church members.

Most measures of association can be tested for statistical significance in a similar manner. Standard tables of values permit us to determine whether a given association is statistically significant and at what level. Any standard statistics textbook provides instructions on the use of such tables.

Some Words of Caution Tests of significance provide an objective measure that can be used to estimate the statistical significance of associations between variables. They help us rule out associations that may not represent genuine relationships in the population under study. However, the researcher who uses or reads reports of significance tests should remain wary of several dangers in their interpretation.

First, we've been discussing tests of statistical significance; there are no objective tests of *substantive* significance. Thus, we may be legitimately convinced that a given association is not due to sampling error, but we may be in the position of asserting without fear of contradiction that two variables are only slightly related to each other. Recall that sampling error is an inverse function of sample size—the larger the sample, the smaller the expected error. Thus, a correlation of, say, .1 might very well be significant (at a given level) if discovered in a large sample, whereas the same correlation between the same two variables would not be significant if found in a smaller sample. This makes perfectly good sense given the basic logic of tests of significance: In the larger sample, there is less chance that the correlation could be simply the product of sampling error. In both samples, however, it might represent an essentially zero correlation.

The distinction between statistical and substantive significance is perhaps best illustrated by those cases where there is *absolute certainty* that observed differences cannot be a result of sampling error. This would be the case when we observe an entire population. Suppose we were able to learn the ages of every public official in Canada and also the ages of every public official in Russia. For argument's sake, let's assume further that the average age of Canadian officials was 45 years compared to, say, 46 for the Russian officials. Because we would have the ages of all officials, there would be no question of sampling error. We would know with certainty that the Russian officials are older than their Canadian counterparts. At the same time, we would say that the difference was of no substantive significance. We'd conclude, in fact, that they were essentially the same age.

Second, lest you be misled by this hypothetical example, realize that statistical significance should not be calculated on relationships observed in data collected from whole populations. Remember, tests of statistical significance measure the likelihood of relationships between variables being only a product of sampling error; if there's no sampling, there's no sampling error.

Third, tests of significance are based on the same sampling assumptions we used in computing confidence intervals. To the extent that these assumptions are not met by the actual sampling design, the tests of significance are not strictly legitimate.

Although we have examined statistical significance here in the form of chi square, there are several other measures commonly used by social scientists. Analysis of variance and *t*-tests are two examples you may run across in your studies.

In conclusion, we would like to note that while there are serious problems inherent in too much reliance on tests of statistical significance, at the same time (perhaps paradoxically) we would suggest that tests of significance can be a valuable asset to the researcher—useful tools for understanding data. More generally, we encourage you to use any statistical technique—any measure of association or any test of significance—if it will help you understand your data. Whatever the avenue of discovery, however, empirical data must ultimately be presented in a legitimate manner, and their importance must be argued logically.

MAIN POINTS

- Descriptive statistics are used to summarize data under study. Some descriptive statistics summarize the distribution of attributes on a single variable; others summarize the associations between variables.
- Descriptive statistics summarizing the relationships between variables are called measures of association.
- Many measures of association are based on a proportionate reduction of error (PRE) model. This model is based on a comparison of (1) the number of errors we would make in attempting to guess the attributes of a given variable for each of the cases under study—if we knew nothing but the distribution of attributes on that variable, and (2) the number of errors we would make if we knew the joint distribution overall and were told for each case the attribute of one variable each time we were asked to guess the attribute of the other.
- Measures of association include lambda (λ) (appropriate for the analysis of two nominal variables), gamma (γ) (appropriate for the analysis of two ordinal variables), and Pearson's product–moment correlation (r) (appropriate for the analysis of two interval or ratio variables).
- Regression analysis represents the relationships between variables in the form of equations, which can be used to predict the values of a dependent variable on the basis of values of one or more independent variables.

- Regression equations are computed on the basis of a regression line: that geometric line representing, with the least amount of discrepancy, the actual location of points in a scattergram.
- Types of regression analysis include linear regression analysis, multiple regression analysis, partial regression analysis, and curvilinear regression analysis.
- Inferential statistics are used to estimate the generalizability of findings arrived at through the analysis of a sample to the larger population from which the sample has been selected. Some inferential statistics estimate the single-variable characteristics of the population; others—tests of statistical significance—estimate the relationships between variables in the population.
- Inferences about some characteristic of a population must indicate a confidence interval and a confidence level. Inferences about the generalizability to a population of the associations discovered between variables in a sample involve tests of statistical significance (e.g., chi square). These tests estimate the likelihood that an association as large as the observed one could result from normal sampling error if no such association exists between the variables in the larger population. Computations of confidence levels, confidence intervals, and tests of statistical significance are based on probability theory and assume that conventional probability sampling techniques have been used in the study.
- The level of significance of an observed association is reported in the form of the probability that the association could have been produced merely by sampling error. To say that an association is significant at the .05 level is to say that an association as large as the observed one could not be expected to result from sampling error more than 5 times out of 100.
- Social researchers tend to use a particular set of levels of significance in connection with tests of statistical significance: .05, .01, and .001. This is merely a convention, however.
- Statistical significance must not be confused with substantive significance, the latter meaning that an observed association is strong, important, meaningful, or worth writing home about.
- Tests of statistical significance, strictly speaking, make assumptions about data and methods that are almost never satisfied completely by real social research. Despite this, the tests can serve a useful function in the analysis and interpretation of data.

REVIEW QUESTIONS AND EXERCISES

1. In your own words, explain the logic of proportionate reduction of error (PRE) measures of associations. Next, explain the purpose of regression analyses.
2. In your own words, distinguish between measures of association and tests of statistical significance.
3. Locate a study that reports the statistical significance of its findings. Critique the author's reporting of this on the basis of presentation and clarity.

CONTINUITY PROJECT

LOOKING FOR TRENDS

Richard Wilkinson and Kate Pickett wrote a best-selling volume relating a variety of personal and social outcomes to inequality. Their 2009 book *The Spirit Level: Why More Equal Societies Almost Always Do Better* is worth checking out. Here are two scattergrams from their book.

In these graphs, the "Index of health and social problems" is an aggregate measure (for each society) of the following: life expectancy; math and literacy; infant mortality; homicides;

imprisonment; teenage births; levels of trust; obesity; mental illness; social mobility. In short, it is a very robust measure of inequality.

1. What independent variable is used in each graph? What is the difference between these independent variables?
2. Using the regression line on the scattergram in Figure 1, how would you interpret the relationship? Write out your interpretation in a simple sentence.
3. Draw a regression line on Figure 2 that captures the relationship between the variables. Based on the regression line, how would you interpret the relationship? Write out your interpretation in a simple sentence.
4. If your interpretation of the two figures differs, what conclusion can you draw about the different measures of the independent variable and their relationship to inequality?

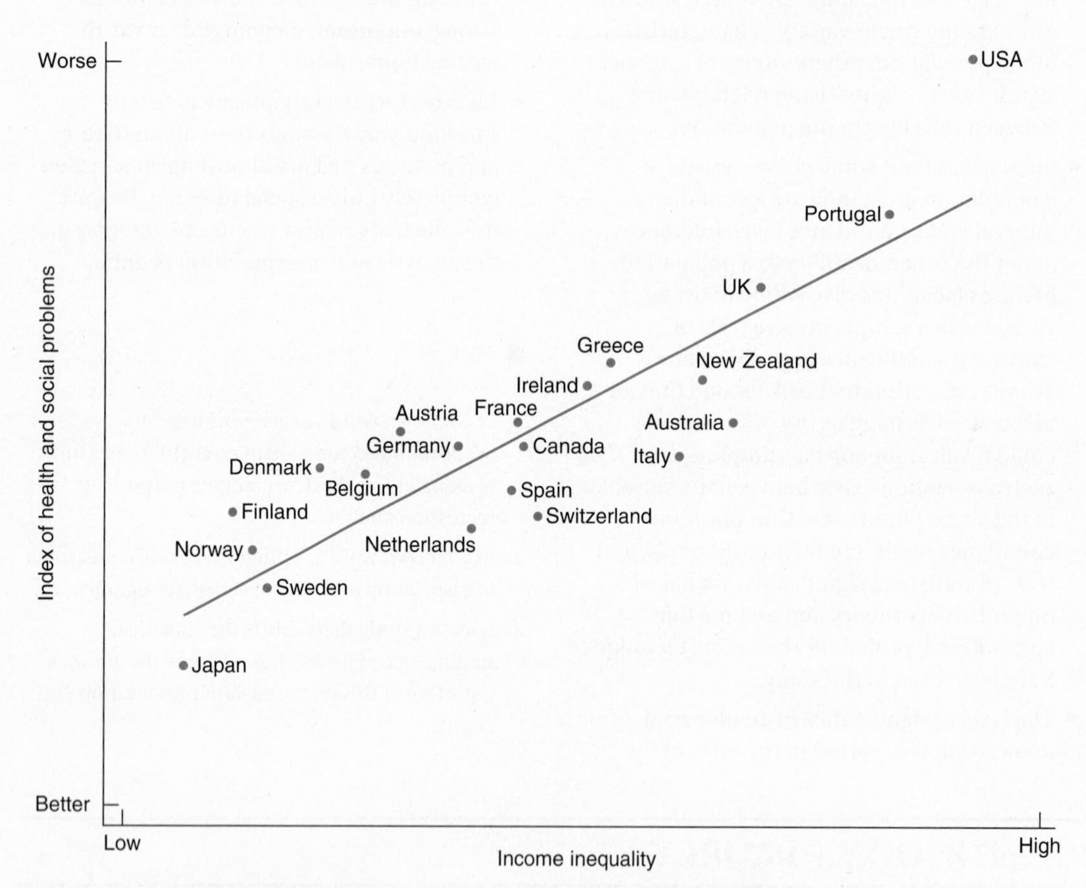

FIGURE 1 Income Inequality within Modern Societies and Its Relationship to Health and Social Problems.

Source: From THE SPIRIT LEVEL: WHY MORE EQUAL SOCIETIES ALMOST ALWAYS DO BETTER by Richard Wilkinson and Kate Pickett (Penguin Books, 2009).

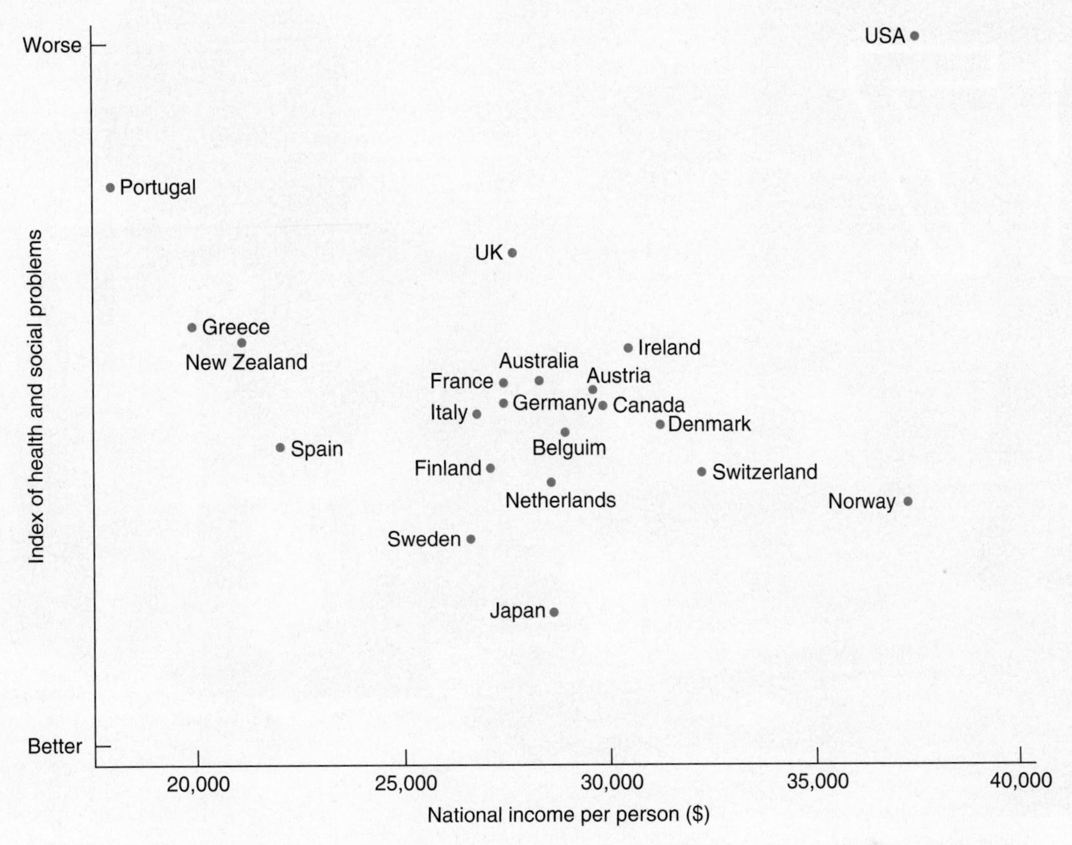

FIGURE 2 **Income Inequality between Modern Societies and Its Relationship to Health and Social Problems.**

Source: From THE SPIRIT LEVEL: WHY MORE EQUAL SOCIETIES ALMOST ALWAYS DO BETTER by Richard Wilkinson and Kate Pickett (Penguin Books, 2009). Copyright © Dr Kate Pickett and Professor Richard Wilkinson, 2009.

Dragon Images/Shutterstock.com

READING, DESIGNING AND WRITING SOCIAL RESEARCH

Social research is useless unless it's communicated effectively to others. Some special skills are involved in reading the research of others and writing about your own. This chapter introduces you to the fundamentals of reading, designing, and writing social research.

IN THIS CHAPTER...

INTRODUCTION

You've now seen a number of methods that are available to social researchers in designing projects. In this chapter, we pull all the parts together by looking at the actual process of designing a research project. Assume you were to undertake a research study. Where would you start? Then where would you go? Although research design occurs at the beginning of a research project, it involves all the steps of the subsequent project. The discussion of research design in this chapter provides both guidance on how to start a research project and a brief review of the relevant topics covered in previous chapters.

As this textbook has shown, sound design is fundamental to sound scientific research. But is also true that meaningful scientific research is inextricably wedded to communication—even if it's not always an easy or comfortable marriage. Scientists—social and other—are not necessarily good at communicating their methods and findings. As a result, it's often hard to read and understand the research of others. You may also find it difficult to write up your own research in ways that communicate your ideas effectively. Thus, in addition to designing social research, this final chapter addresses two related issues: reading and writing social research.

We'll begin with reading social research, and then we'll turn to designing it and writing it. Although we'll offer guidance on all three topics, you'll find that practising each is key. The more you read social science research, the easier it gets, and the same is true of designing and writing it.

READING SOCIAL RESEARCH

"Reading" is not as simple a task as it may seem, especially when it involves social research. First, you need to organize a review of the literature in order to focus on the resources that will help you the most. Then, when you actually sit down to read them, you'll need certain skills for doing so efficiently. Finally, you should know how to find and assess sources on the Internet.

ORGANIZING A REVIEW OF THE LITERATURE

With the exception of some grounded theory methodologists, most social researchers begin the design of a research project with a review of the literature. Most original research is seen as an extension of what has previously been learned about a particular topic. A review of the literature is the way we learn what's already known and not known.

In most cases, you should organize your search of the literature around the key concepts you wish to study; alternatively, you may want to study a certain population: Iraqi War veterans, computer hackers, Catholic priests, LGBTQ athletes, and so forth. In any case, you'll identify a set of terms that represent your core interests.

Your university library will probably have several search routines you can use at the library or online. Let's say you're interested in designing a study of attitudes toward capital punishment. Your library will most likely have some type of reference search program and you might discover, as we did, 8,735 newspaper references and 5,489 periodical references to capital punishment. Narrowing the search, we discovered 249 entries for "public opinion" on capital punishment. Some of the entries were bibliographic citations and some were full-text articles we could read online.

When reading or accessing an article online, you should see if you can download it as a pdf version. This format replicates the document with the original pagination, which will be useful if you wish to quote or cite specific portions of the article.

Sometimes a simple Web search is a useful way to begin. Use a search engine such as Google, Bing, or Yahoo to look for Web resources on "capital punishment" or "death penalty." Be sure to use quotation marks to look for a phrase rather than using two separate words. You might also add "public opinion" to the request to narrow the field of possible resources. In general, online searches tend to turn up huge numbers of entries, most of which will not help you much. You'll need some time to separate the wheat from the chaff. Later in this chapter, we'll give you further guidelines for searching the Web.

No matter how you start the literature-review process, you should always consider a technique akin to snowball sampling, discussed in Chapter 6. Once you identify a particularly useful book or article, note which publications its author cites. Some of these will likely be useful. In fact, you'll probably discover some citations that appear again and again, suggesting that they're core references within the subject matter area you're exploring. This last point is important, because the literature review is not about providing "window dressing" in the form of a few citations. Rather, it's about digging into the body of knowledge that previous researchers have generated—and taking advantage of that knowledge as you design your own inquiry.

Once you've identified some potential resources, you must read them and find anything of value to your project. Here are some guidelines for reading research publications.

JOURNALS VERSUS BOOKS

As you might have guessed, you don't read a social research report the way you'd read a novel. You can, of course, but it's not the most effective approach. Journal articles and books are laid out somewhat differently, so here are some initial guidelines for reading each.

Reading a Journal Article In most journals, each article begins with an **abstract**, or a summary of the article. Read it first. It should tell you the purpose of the research, the methods used, and the major findings.

In a good detective or spy novel, the suspense builds throughout the book and is resolved in some kind of surprise ending. This is not the effect most scholarly writers are going for. Social research is purposely anticlimactic. Rather than stringing the reader along, dragging out the suspense over whether X causes Y, social researchers willingly give away the punch line in the abstract.

abstract A summary of a research article; usually begins the article and states the purpose of the research, the methods used, and the major findings.

research monograph A book-length research report, either published or unpublished. This is distinguished from a textbook, a book of essays, a novel, and so forth.

The abstract serves two main functions. First, it gives you a good idea of whether you'll want to read the rest of the article. If you're reviewing the literature for a paper you're writing, the abstract tells you whether that particular article is relevant. Second, the abstract establishes a framework within which to read the rest of the article. It may raise questions in your mind regarding method or conclusions, thereby creating an agenda to pursue in your reading. (It's not a bad idea to jot those questions down, to be sure you get answers to them.)

After you've read the abstract, you might go directly to the summary and/or conclusions at the end of the article. That will give you a more detailed picture of what the article is all about. (You can also do this with detective and spy novels; it makes reading them a lot faster, but maybe not as much fun.) Jot down any new questions or observations that occur to you.

Next, skim the article, noting the section headings and any tables or graphs. You don't need to study any of these things in your skimming, though it's OK to dally with anything that catches your attention. By the end of this step, you should start feeling familiar with the article. You should be pretty clear on the researcher's conclusions and have a general idea of the methods used in reaching them.

Now, when you carefully read the whole article, you'll have a good idea of where it's heading and how each section fits into the logic of the whole article. Keep taking notes. Mark any passages you think you might like to quote later on.

After carefully reading the article, it's a good idea to skim it quickly one more time. This way you get back in touch with the forest after having focused on the trees.

If you want to fully grasp what you've just read, find someone else to explain it to. If you're doing the reading in connection with a course, you should have no trouble finding someone willing to listen. If you can explain it coherently to someone who has had no prior contact with the subject matter, you'll have an absolute lock on the material.

Reading a Book The approach for reading articles can be adapted to reading a book-length report, sometimes also called a **research monograph**. These longer research reports cover the same basic terrain and structure. Instead of an abstract, the preface and opening chapter of the book should lay out the purpose, method, and main findings of the study. The preface tends to be written more informally and is usually easier to understand than an abstract.

As with an article, it's useful to skim through the book, getting a sense of its organization; its use of tables, graphs, or other visuals; and so forth. You should come away from this step feeling somewhat familiar with the book. And, as we suggested in connection with reading an article, you should take notes as you go along, writing down things you observe and questions that are raised.

As you settle in to read the book more carefully, you should repeat this same process with each chapter. Read the opening paragraphs to get a sense of what's to come, and then skip to the concluding paragraphs for the summary. Skim the chapter to increase your familiarity with it, and then read more deliberately, taking notes as you go.

It's sometimes OK to skip portions of a scholarly book, unlike the way you were taught to read and appreciate literature. This all depends on your purpose for reading it in the first place. Perhaps there are only a few portions of the book that are relevant to your purposes. However, realize that if you're interested in the researcher's findings, you must pay some attention to the methods used (e.g., Who was studied? How? When?) in order to judge the quality of the conclusions offered by the author.

EVALUATION OF RESEARCH REPORTS

In this section, we provide sets of questions you might ask in reading and evaluating a research report. We've organized these questions to parallel some of the preceding chapters in this book, to facilitate your getting more details on a topic if necessary. Although they're hardly exhaustive, we hope these questions will help you grasp the meanings of research reports you read and alert you to potential problems in them.

Theoretical Orientations

- Is there a theoretical aspect to the study, or do no references to theory appear?
- Is the framework adequate, in view of the aim of the study?
- Can you identify the researcher's chief paradigm or theoretical orientation? Authors quoted in the report's review of the literature and elsewhere may offer a clue.
- On the other hand, is the author attempting to refute some paradigm or theory?
- Does the author account for the role given to the theoretical framework during analysis?
- Is a theory or hypothesis being tested?
- In what way has the theoretical orientation shaped the methodology used in the study, such as the data-collection technique and the choice of which data were collected and which were ignored?
- Is the methodology used appropriate for the theoretical issues involved?

Research Design

- What was the purpose of the study: exploration, description, explanation, or a combination?
- Who conducted the research? Who paid for it, if anyone? What motivated the study? If the study's conclusions happen to correspond to the interests of the sponsor or researcher, this doesn't disqualify the conclusions, but you'll want to be especially wary.
- What was the unit of analysis? Was it appropriate for the purpose of the study? Are the conclusions drawn from the research appropriate for the unit of analysis? For example, have the researchers studied cities and ended up with assertions about individuals?
- Is this a cross-sectional or a longitudinal study? Be especially wary of longitudinal assertions being made on the basis of cross-sectional observations.
- If longitudinal data have been collected, have comparable measurements been made at each point in time? In the case of survey data, have the same questions been asked each time? If the report compares, say, crime or poverty rates, are they defined the same way each time? (Definitions of poverty, for example, change frequently.)
- If a panel study has been conducted, how many people dropped out over the course of the study?

Measurement

- What are the names of the concepts under study?
- Has the researcher delineated different dimensions of the concepts? Do the analysis and reporting maintain those distinctions?
- What indicators—either qualitative or quantitative—have been chosen as measures of those dimensions and concepts? Is each indicator a valid measure of what it's intended to measure? What else could the indicator be a measure of? Is it a reliable measure? Has the reliability been tested?
- What is the level of measurement of each variable: nominal, ordinal, interval, or ratio? Is it the appropriate level?
- Have composite measurements (indexes or scales) been used? If so, are they appropriate for the purpose of the study? Have they been constructed correctly?

Sampling

- Was it appropriate to study a sample, or should the entire population have been studied? Remember, it's not always feasible to select a random sample.
- If sampling was called for, were probability sampling methods appropriate, or would a purposive, snowball, or quota sample have been better? Has the appropriate sampling design been used?
- What population does the researcher want to draw conclusions about?
- What is the researcher's purpose? If it's statistical description, then rigorous probability sampling methods are called for.
- If a probability sample has been selected, what sampling frame has been used? Does it appropriately represent the population that interests the researcher? What elements of the population have been omitted from the sampling frame, and what extraneous elements have been included?
- What specific sampling techniques have been employed: simple random sampling, systematic sampling, or cluster sampling? Has the researcher stratified the sampling frame prior to sampling? Have the stratification variables been chosen wisely? That is, are they relevant to the variables under study?
- How large a sample was selected? What percentage of the sample responded? Are there any likely differences between those who responded and those who didn't?
- Even assuming that the respondents are representative of those selected in the sample, what sampling error do you expect from a sample of this size?
- Has the researcher tested for representativeness: comparing the gender distribution of the population and of respondents, for example, or their ages, ethnicity, education, or income?
- Ultimately, do the studied individuals (or other units of analysis) represent the larger population from which they were chosen? That is, do conclusions drawn about the sample tell us anything about meaningful populations or about life in general?
- If probability sampling and statistical representation were not appropriate for the study—in a qualitative study, for example—have subjects and observations been selected in such a way as to provide a broad overview of the phenomenon being examined? Has the researcher paid special attention to deviant or disconfirming cases?

Experiments

- What is the primary dependent variable in the experiment? What effect is the experimenter trying to achieve, for example?
- What is the experimental stimulus?
- What other variables are relevant to the experiment? Have they been measured?
- How has each variable been defined and measured? What potential problems of validity and reliability do these definitions and measurements raise?
- Has a proper control group been used? Have subjects been assigned to the experimental and control groups through random selection or by matching? Has it been done properly? Has the researcher provided any evidence of the initial comparability of experimental and control-group subjects?

- Have there been pretest and posttest measurements of the dependent variable?
- What is the chance of a placebo (or "Hawthorne") effect in the experiment? Has any attention been given to the problem? Does the study use a double-blind design, for example?
- Are there any problems of internal invalidity: history, maturation, testing, instrumentation, statistical regression, selection bias, experimental mortality, or demoralization?
- Are there issues of external invalidity? How has the experimenter ensured that the laboratory findings will apply to life in the real world?

Survey Research

- Does the study stand up to all the relevant questions regarding sampling?
- What questions were asked of respondents? What was the precise wording of the questions? Be wary of researcher reports that provide only paraphrases of the questions.
- If closed-ended questions were asked, were the answer categories provided appropriate, exhaustive, and mutually exclusive?
- If open-ended questions were asked, how have the answers been categorized? Has the researcher guarded against his or her own bias creeping in during the coding of open-ended responses?
- Are all the questions clear and unambiguous? Could respondents have misinterpreted them? If so, could the answers given mean something other than what the researcher has assumed?
- Were the respondents capable of answering the questions asked? If not, they may have answered anyway, but their answers might not mean anything.
- Are any of the questions double-barrelled? Look for conjunctions (such as *and, or*). Are respondents being asked to agree or disagree with two ideas, when they might like to agree with one and disagree with the other?
- Do the questions contain negative terms? If so, respondents may have misunderstood them and answered inappropriately.
- Is there a danger of social desirability in any of the questions? Is any answer so right or so wrong that respondents may have answered on the basis of what people would think of them?
- How would you yourself answer each item? As a general rule, test all questionnaire items by asking yourself how you would answer. Any difficulty you might have in answering might also apply to others. Then, try to assume different points of view (e.g., liberal and conservative, religious and nonreligious) and ask how the questions might sound to someone with each point of view.
- Has the researcher conducted a secondary analysis of previously collected data? If so, determine the quality of the research that produced the data originally. Also, are the data available for analysis appropriate for the current purposes? Do the questions originally asked adequately reflect the variables now being analyzed?

Field Research

- What theoretical paradigm has informed the researcher's approach to the study?
- Has the research set out to test hypotheses or generate theory from the observations? Or is there no concern for theory in the study?
- What are the main concepts in this study? How have they been defined and measured? Do you see any problems of validity?
- How about reliability? Would another researcher, observing the same events, classify things the same way?
- Is there any chance that the classification of observations has been influenced by the way those classifications will affect the research findings and/or the researcher's hypotheses?
- If descriptive conclusions have been drawn—for example, "the group's standards were quite conservative"—what are the implicit standards being used?
- How much can the study's findings be generalized to a broader sector of society? What claims has the researcher made in this regard? What is the basis for such claims?

- If people have been interviewed, how were they selected? Do they represent all appropriate types?
- How much did the researcher participate in the events under study? How might that participation have affected the events themselves?
- Did the researcher reveal his or her identity as a researcher? If so, what influence could that revelation have had on the behaviour of those being observed?
- Does the research indicate any personal feelings—positive or negative—about those being observed? If so, what effect might these feelings have had on the observations that were made and the conclusions that were drawn from them?
- How has the researcher's own cultural identity or background affected the interpretation of what has been observed?

Content Analysis

- What are the key concepts or variables in the analysis? Are they appropriate for the research questions being asked?
- What are the source and form of data being analyzed? Are they appropriate for the research questions being asked?
- Is the time frame of the data being analyzed appropriate for the research questions?
- What is the unit of analysis?
- If a quantitative analysis has been conducted, (1) has an appropriate sample been selected from the data source, and (2) have the appropriate statistical techniques been used?
- If a qualitative analysis has been conducted, (1) has an appropriate range of data been examined, and (2) are the researcher's conclusions logically consistent with the data presented?

Analyzing Existing Statistics

- Who originally collected the data being reanalyzed? Were there any flaws in the data collection methods? What was the original purpose of the data collection? Would that have affected the data that were collected?
- What was the unit of analysis of the data? Is it appropriate for the current research question and the conclusions being drawn? Is there a danger of the ecological fallacy?
- When were the data collected? Are they still appropriate for present concerns?
- What are the variables being analyzed in the present research? Were the definitions used by the original researchers appropriate for present interests?

Comparative and Historical Research

- Is this a descriptive or an explanatory study? Does it involve cross-sectional comparisons or changes over time?
- What is the unit of analysis in this study (e.g., country, social movement)?
- What are the key variables under study? If it is an explanatory analysis, what causal relationships are examined?
- Does the study involve the use of other research techniques, such as existing statistics, content analysis, surveys, or field research? Use the guidelines elsewhere in this section to assess those aspects of the study.
- Is the range of data appropriate for the analysis: for example, the units being compared or the number of observations made for the purpose of characterizing units?
- If historical or other documents are used as a data source, who produced them and for what purposes? What biases might be embedded in them? Diaries kept by members of the gentry, for example, will not reflect the life of peasants of the same time and country.

Evaluation Research

- What is the social intervention being analyzed? How has it been measured? Are there any problems of validity or reliability?
- Have the appropriate people (or other units of analysis) been observed?
- How has "success" been defined? Where would the success be manifested—in individuals, in organizations, in crime rates? Has it been measured appropriately?

- Has the researcher judged the intervention a success or a failure? Is the judgment well founded?
- Who paid for the research, and who actually conducted it? Can you be confident of the researcher's objectivity? Did the sponsor interfere in any way?

Data Analysis

- Did the purpose and design of the study call for a qualitative or a quantitative analysis?
- How have nonstandardized data been coded? This question applies to both qualitative and quantitative analysis. To what extent were the codes (1) based on prior theory or (2) generated by the data?
- Has the researcher undertaken all relevant analyses? Have all appropriate variables been identified and examined? Could the correlation observed between two variables have been caused by an antecedent third variable, making the observed relationship spurious?
- Does a particular research finding really matter? Is an observed difference between subgroups, for example, a large or meaningful one? Are there any implications for action?
- Has the researcher gone beyond the actual findings in drawing conclusions and implications?
- Are there logical flaws in the analysis and interpretation of data?
- Have the empirical observations of the study revealed new patterns of relationships, providing the bases for grounded theories of social life? Has the researcher looked for disconfirming cases that would challenge the new theories?
- Are the statistical techniques used in the analysis of data appropriate for the levels of measurement of the variables involved?
- If tests of statistical significance were used, have they been interpreted correctly? Has statistical significance been confused with substantive significance?

Reporting

- Has the researcher placed this project in the context of previous research on the topic? Does this research add to, modify, replicate, or contradict previous studies?
- In general, has the researcher reported the details of the study design and execution fully? Are there parts of the report that seem particularly vague or incomplete in the reporting of details?
- Has the researcher reported any flaws or shortcomings in the study design or execution? Are there any suggestions for improving research on the topic in the future?
- We hope this section will prove useful to you in reading and understanding social research. The exercises at the end of this chapter will walk you through the reading of two journal articles: one qualitative and one quantitative. As we said earlier, you'll find that your proficiency in reading social research reports will mature with practice.
- Before discussing how to go about creating social research reports for others to read, let's look at how to read and evaluate data from an increasingly popular source of information—the Internet.

USING THE INTERNET WISELY

In the closing decade of the twentieth century, the World Wide Web (WWW) developed into a profoundly valuable tool for social research. As it expands exponentially, the Web is becoming the mind of humanity, the repository of human knowledge, opinions, and beliefs—carrying with it not only intellectual insights but also misconceptions and outright bigotry. Clearly, it will continue to evolve as an increasingly powerful entity. As with gunpowder and television, the power of the technology does not guarantee that it will always be used wisely. We have opted to encourage use of the Web rather than oppose it, but we are mindful of the problems that make many of our colleagues more cautious.

In this section of the chapter, we share websites useful to social researchers and give some general advice on searching the Web. Then we address the major problems inherent in using the Web and suggest ways to avoid them.

Some Useful Websites The website associated with this book has up-to-date links to useful social research websites. We've placed these materials on the Web instead of in an appendix so they can be revised and updated before the next textbook revision. Nevertheless, we want to mention a few key websites here and, more importantly, offer advice on how to search the Web.

Here are just a few generally useful websites that you might like to check out:

- Statistics Canada: www.statcan.gc.ca/start-debut-eng.html
- Statistics Canada videos: www.youtube.com/user/StatisticsCanada/videos
- Finding CANSIM data: www.youtube.com/watch?v=bjd4mKn_lmI&list=PLF8DEED760F1E3898
- Computer Assisted Qualitative Data Analysis Software, University of Surrey, England: www.surrey.ac.uk/computer-assisted-qualitative-data-analysis
- General Social Survey (U.S.): www.norc.org/GSS+Website/
- Qual Page—Resources for Qualitative Research: www.qualitativeresearch.uga.edu/QualPage/
- Social Sciences Virtual Library: www.vlib.org.uk/SocialSciences.htm
- Now, let's assume you need some information that you suspect is somewhere on the Web, but you don't know where to locate it. Here are some ideas to help you become a Web detective.

Searching the Web We won't estimate the number of pages of information on the WWW; its growth curve is so dramatic that any number we might give now would be embarrassingly low by the time you read this. Let's just say there are millions and millions of pages. Similarly, estimating the number of "facts" or pieces of data on the Web would be impossible, but most of the factual questions you might have can be answered on the Web. Finding them involves skill, however.

Let's say you want to know who the fifth prime minister of Canada was. That's easily learned in several ways. The most straightforward would be to open one of the many **search engines** available to you; let's say you use Google, found at www.google.ca. When we searched for *fifth prime minister of Canada* our responses began with those shown in Figure 17-1. (Realize that if you replicate this procedure, you will get somewhat different responses, because the content of the Web is continuously evolving.)

Some responses in the list require you to open the link to find the answer: Sir Mackenzie Bowell. The second response provides the answer directly. In this case, it's not even necessary to follow up on the weblinks, unless we want to know something more about Bowell. Notice that we have the same answer from different websites—each adding to our confidence that we have the right answer.

Here's a more elaborate example. Let's say you want to examine differences in the infant mortality rates of countries around the world. You may already know some websites that are likely to have that information, but let's assume you don't. Go back to Google or another search engine and search for *infant mortality rate.* Figure 17-2 presents the initial results we received.

The third weblink is to the CIA's *World Factbook,* a reference that draws on data from a variety of sources. The fourth references a Conference Board of Canada article on the topic. Realize that Figure 17-2 presents only the first few websites returned by the Google search. Google reported that it had found about 16 million websites that seemed to have the information we were seeking.

If you actually conduct the Web search just reported you will notice that several of the later links are probably more specific than we want—one deals only with Cuba, another gives data only on the United States. Often, an effective Web search requires more than one attempt. In this case, we added the word *world* to the request: *world infant mortality rate.*

Like many other search engines, Google interprets this as a request to find websites that contain the word *world* plus the phrase *infant mortality rate.* (Note that if you put part of your

search engine A computer program designed to locate where specified terms appear on websites throughout the WWW.

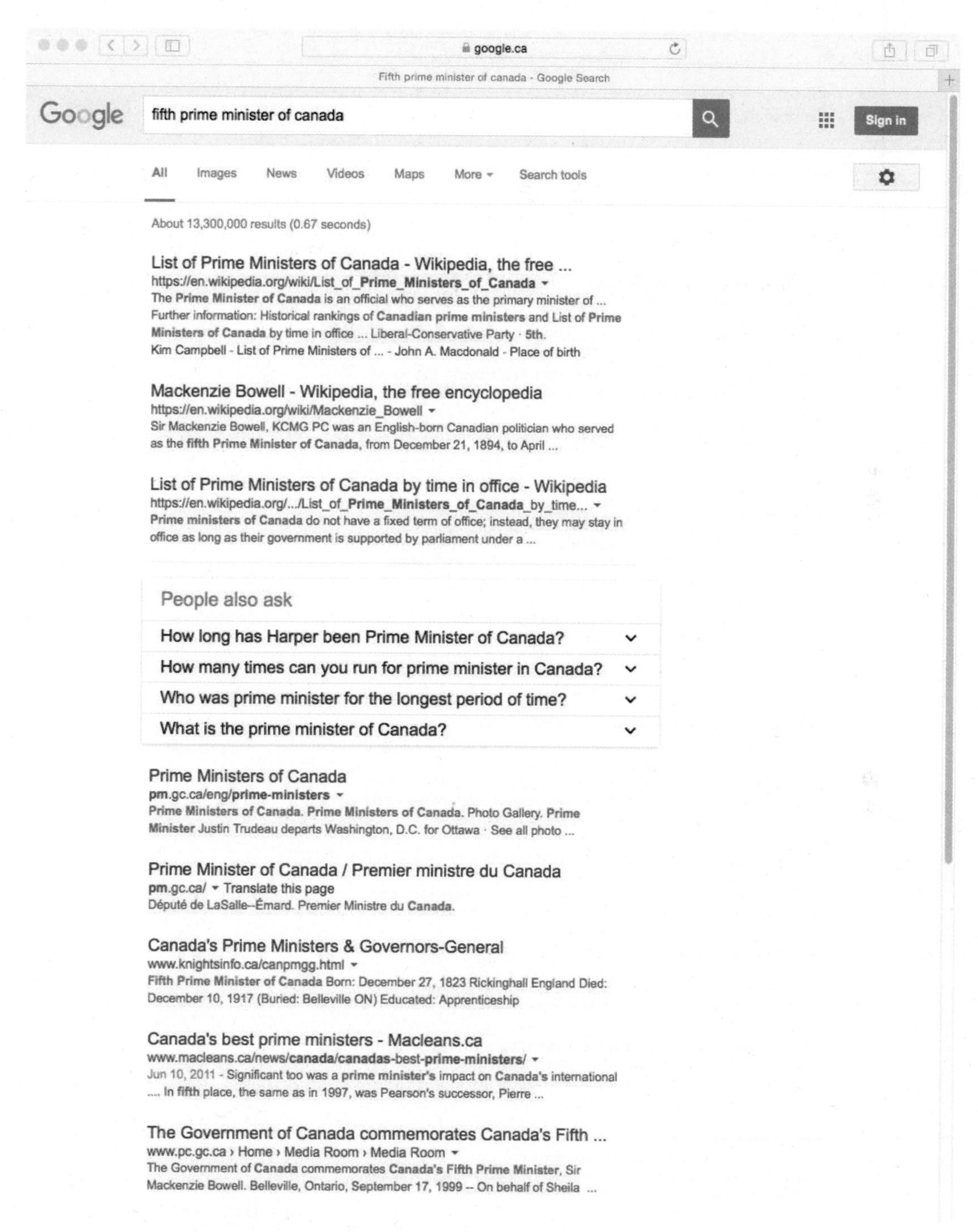

FIGURE 17-1 Finding the Fifth Prime Minister of Canada.
Source: Google and the Google logo are registered trademarks of Google Inc., used with permission.

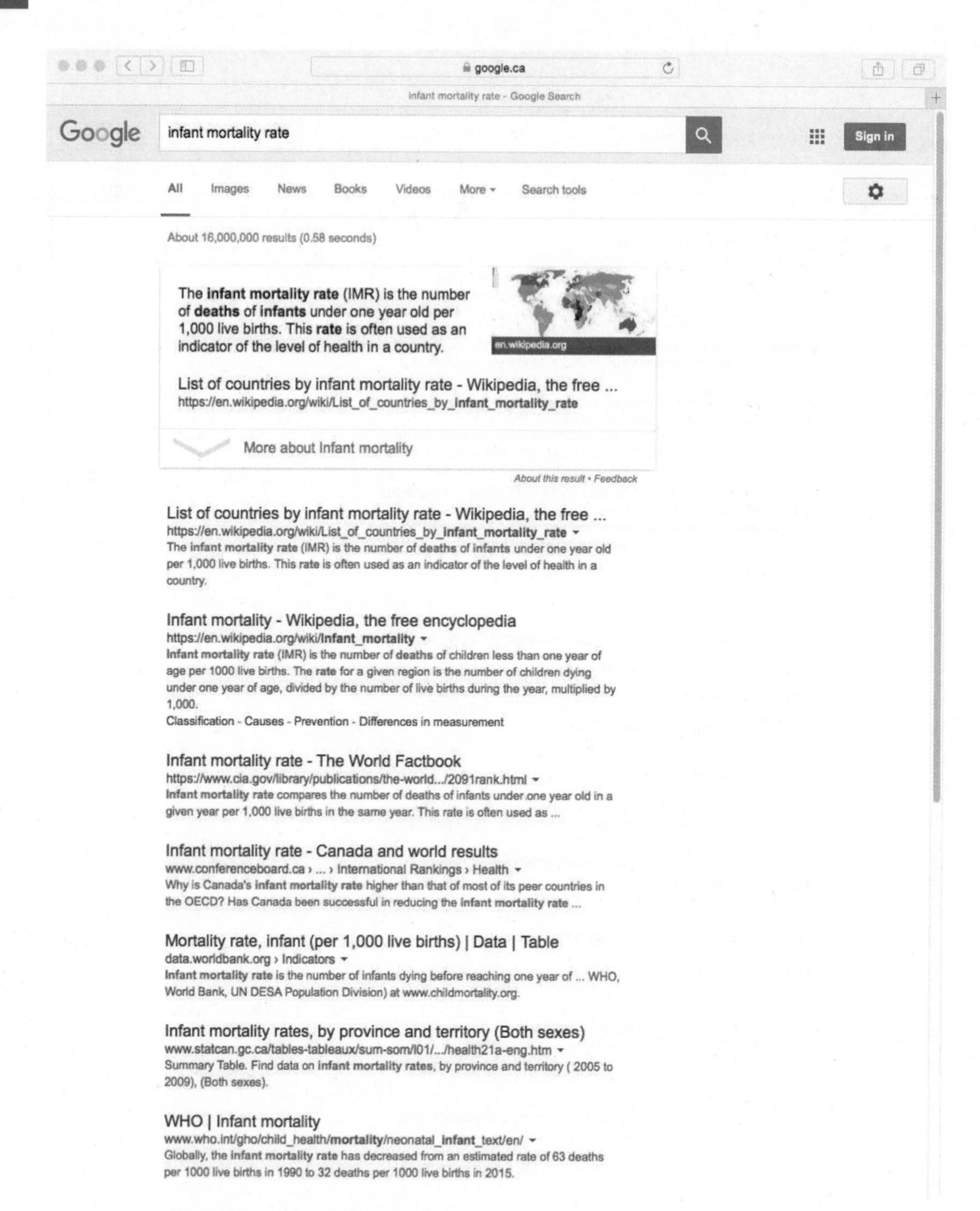

FIGURE 17-2 Search for Infant Mortality Rate.
Source: Google and the Google logo are registered trademarks of Google Inc., used with permission.

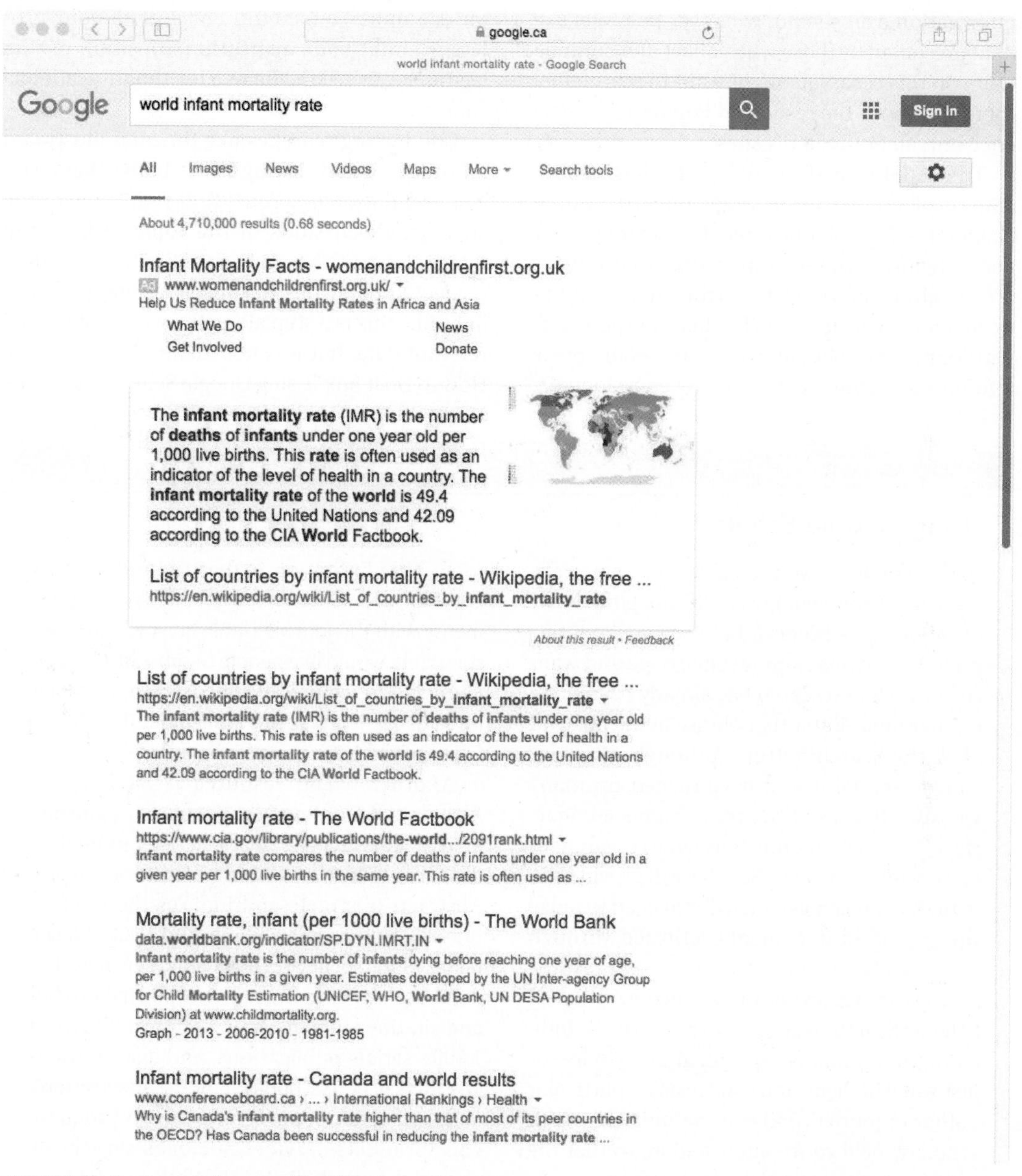

FIGURE 17-3 Search for World Infant Mortality Rate.
Source: Google and the Google logo are registered trademarks of Google Inc., used with permission.

request inside quotation marks, the search engine will look for that exact phrase instead of reporting websites that happen to have all the words.) Figure 17-3 presents this first set of results.

You probably noticed that, like the one in Figure 17-3, our searches returned several results from Wikipedia, a free encyclopedia compiled by the Web community. Although commercial websites and almanacs can be useful sources of information, you should, wherever possible, use data presented by those who collect and compile them. In this case, you might want to search further for links to the respected Population Reference Bureau or to the UN sites.

The rapid growth of Wikipedia has been a source of conversation and concern among academics. No one questions how extensive or user-friendly it is, but some worry that entries are not always accurate and errors may go unnoticed. Rarely, true mischief has been perpetrated, with opposing political candidates maliciously altering each other's entries in the encyclopedia, for example. You should check with your professor about your institution's position on the legitimacy of Wikipedia as a legitimate academic source.

Conducting searches like the ones illustrated on your own and visiting the weblinks that result is a useful exercise. You'll find that some of the sites are discussions of the topic rather than tables of data. Others present a limited set of data ("selected countries"). Thus, compiling a list of links like this is a step along the way to obtaining relevant data, but it is not the final step. See the How to Do It box "Using Google Scholar" for more.

HOW TO DO IT

Using Google Scholar

In searching the Web for research materials, you can narrow your focus with Google Scholar at scholar.google.com/. Let's say you're interested in studying same-sex marriage and want to know what research has already been done on that topic. Enter that phrase in the box and click the Search button. Although a regular Google search would have turned up many websites that used the term "same-sex marriage" but were not much use in a research literature review, Google Scholar will provide you with richer pickings. You will still need to judge the quality of documents returned through your search.

You can also take advantage of the Advanced Scholar Search to specify a set of words, indicating that all must appear in an article—or just some of them. You can specify a particular author or journal, and you can indicate which scholarly field you're interested in, so that the search is limited to articles in that field.

There are some online resources that are especially useful for social science research. Your college library may have a licence for JSTOR, an online repository for hundreds of academic journals. There are over a hundred on sociology alone. If you have access to this service, you can search for specific titles or authors, or you can do a broader search for articles on a particular topic. One limitation is that the most recent issues of journals are not available due to agreements with the journal publishers, who, understandably, would like people to subscribe to their journals. The window of noncoverage is typically three to five years, so anything older than that is freely available for download and use.

Another useful resource is Sociological Abstracts, an online compendium of journal-article abstracts. ProQuest, the publisher, describes their service thusly: "CSA Sociological Abstracts abstracts and indexes the international literature in sociology and related disciplines in the social and behavioral sciences. The database provides abstracts of journal articles and citations to book reviews drawn from over 1,800+ serials publications, and also provides abstracts of books, book chapters, dissertations, and conference papers" (http://www.proquest.com/products-services/socioabs-set-c.html, accessed August 22, 2015). While you will not be able to download the full text of articles, you will be able to locate those most relevant to your research interests, and then set about finding the actual articles in the journals where they were published.

These are only two examples of online resources that may be available at your school library.

Evaluating the Quality of Internet Materials You now know enough about Web searches to begin learning through experience. You'll quickly learn that finding data on the Web is relatively easy. Evaluating what you've found is a bit more difficult, however. We've already alluded to the matter of quality, but there's much more to be said on the topic. In fact, many other people have said many other things about it. What do you suppose is your best source of such advice? If you said, "The Web," you've got it.

Open up a search engine and ask it to find websites having to do with "evaluating websites." (Using alternate spellings can yield more results; for example, you could also enter "evaluating web sites" and get a similar yet different set of entries.) Figure 17-4 gives you some idea of the extent of advice available to you.

As you can tell from the ".edu" in the addresses of most of these sites, this is a topic of concern for colleges and universities. Although each of the various sites approaches the topic differently, the guidance they offer has some elements in common. You would do well to study one or more of the sites in depth. In the meantime, here's an overview of the most common questions and suggestions for evaluating the data presented on websites.

1. *Who or what is the author of the website?* The two biggest risks you face in getting information from the Web are (1) bias and (2) sloppiness. The democratic beauty of the Web is its accessibility to such a large proportion of the population and the lack of censorship. These pluses also present dangers, in that just about anyone can put just about anything on the Web. The first thing you should note, therefore, is who the author of the website is—either an organization or an individual.
2. *Is the site advocating a particular point of view?* Many of the sites on the WWW have been created to support a particular political, religious, nationalistic, social, or other point of view. This fact does not necessarily mean that the data they present are false, though that's sometimes the case. Beyond outright lying, however, you can be relatively sure that the website will present only data supporting its particular point of view. You can usually tell whether a website is reasonably objective or has an axe to grind, and you should be wary of those that go overboard to convince you of something.
3. *Does the website give accurate and complete references?* When data are presented, can you tell where they came from—how they were created? If the website is reporting data collected by someone else, are you given sufficient guidance to locate the original researchers? Or, if the data were compiled by the website authors, do they provide you with sufficiently detailed descriptions of their research methods? If data are presented without such clarifications, you should move on.
4. *Are the data up to date?* Another common problem on the Web is that materials may be posted and forgotten. Hence, you may find data reporting crime rates, chronicles of peace negotiations, and so forth that are out of date. Be sure that the data you obtain are timely for your purposes.
5. *Are the data official?* It's often a good idea to find data at official government research sites, such as the Statistics Canada (www.statcan.gc.ca/), the World Bank (www.worldbank.org/), and the Organisation for Economic Co-operation and Development (OECD) (www.oecd.org/). As we saw in Chapter 9, data presented by official agencies are not necessarily "the truth," but they are grounded in a commitment to objectivity and have checks and balances to support them in achieving that goal.
6. *Is it a university research site?* Like government research agencies, university research centres and institutes are usually safe resources; they are committed to conducting professional research and having checks and balances (such as peer review) to support what they publish. Throughout this book, we've mentioned the General Social Survey (www.statcan.gc.ca/pub/89f0115x/89f0115x2013001-eng.htm), conducted regularly by Statistics Canada. You could use data presented here with

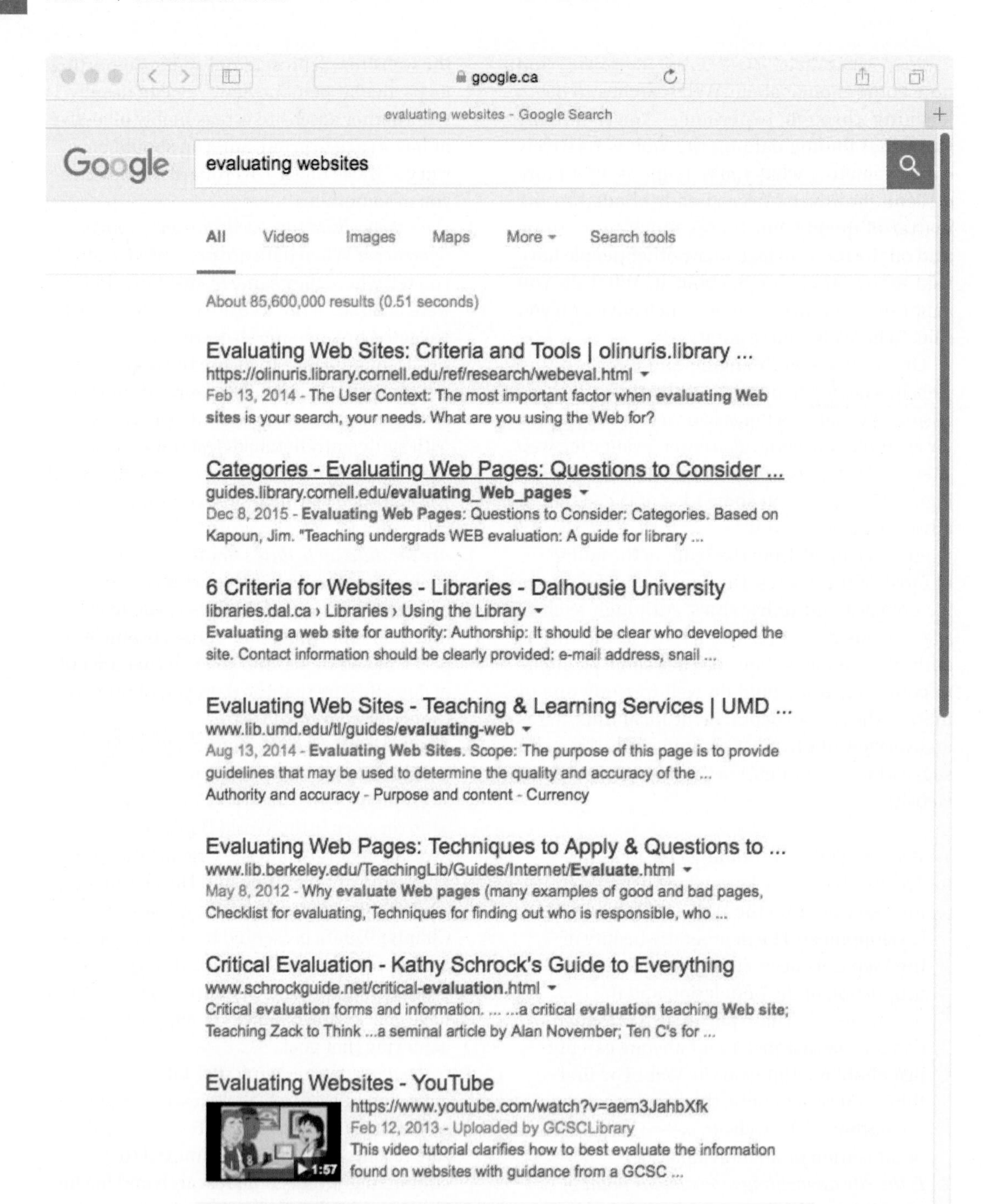

FIGURE 17-4 **Search for Evaluating Websites.**
Source: Google and the Google logo are registered trademarks of Google Inc., used with permission.

confidence: confidence in the legitimacy of the data and confidence that your instructor will not question your use of that resource.

7. *Do the data seem consistent with data from other sites?* Verify (cross-check) data wherever possible. We've already seen that a Web search is likely to turn up more than one possible source of data. Take the time to compare what they present. If several websites present essentially the same data, you can use any of those sources with confidence.

As with so many things, your effective use of the Web will improve with practice. Moreover, the Web itself will be evolving alongside your use of it.

Citing Internet Materials If you use materials from the Web, you must provide a bibliographic citation that allows your reader to locate the original materials—to see them in context. This also protects you from the serious problem of plagiarism, discussed a little later in this chapter.

There are many standardized formats for bibliographic citations, illustrated later in this chapter (see the How to Do It box "Citing Bibliographic Sources"). Web materials, unfortunately, don't fit any of those familiar formats.

Fortunately, each of these organizations—and many, many others—have risen to the challenge of Web citations. If you don't believe us, go to your favourite search engine and look for "Web citations." You'll find plenty of guidance.

Your instructor may prefer a specific format for Web citations. However, here are the elements commonly suggested for inclusion:

- The **URL** or Web address. For example, http://hdr.undp.org/en/content/gender-inequality-index provides data for comparing various countries in terms of the Gender Inequality Index. So, if we tell you that Canada has more gender inequality than Norway but less than the United States, you can go directly to the source of the data we are using to check.
- The date when the site was accessed. Many, like the one just cited, do not change, but many others do. It may be useful for the reader to know when you visited the site in question. Some editing guides say to include this, whereas others say not to. When in doubt, check with your instructor or publisher. It's usually better to have too much information than too little.
- If you're citing textual materials, there may very well be an author and title, as well as publishing information. These should be cited the same way you would cite printed materials, as in the following: Doe, John. 2016. "How I Learned to Love the Web." *Journal of Web Worship* 5 (3): 22–45.
- Sometimes, you'll use the Web to read a published journal article. Such materials may be presented in a print format, with page numbers. If so, cite the appropriate page number. Lacking that, you may be able to cite the section where the materials in question appeared. The goal in all this is to help your reader locate the original Web materials you're using. Although you sometimes cannot give a precise location in an article posted to a website, most browsers allow users to search the site for a specified word or phrase and thus locate the materials being cited.

The fluidity of Web citations is a problem being addressed by the International DOI Foundation (IDF) (the abbreviation stands for Digital Object Identifier). In this system, digital content, such as a journal article, is registered with the IDF and assigned a unique DOI number. The registered content is then locatable via a weblink that persists even if the article has been removed from its original Web location. The DOI number, when available, should be included when citing a source. You can learn more about this valuable citation tool at www.doi.org/.

DESIGNING A SOCIAL RESEARCH PROJECT

Figure 17-5 presents a schematic view of the social science research process. We present this view reluctantly, since it may suggest more of a

URL A Web address, typically beginning with "http://"; stands for "uniform resource locator" or "universal resource locator."

step-by-step order to research than actual practice bears out. Nonetheless, this idealized overview of the process gives a context for the specific details of particular aspects of social research.

At the top of the diagram are interest, idea, and theory, the possible beginning points for a line of research. The letters (A, B, X, Y, and so forth) represent variables or concepts such as prejudice

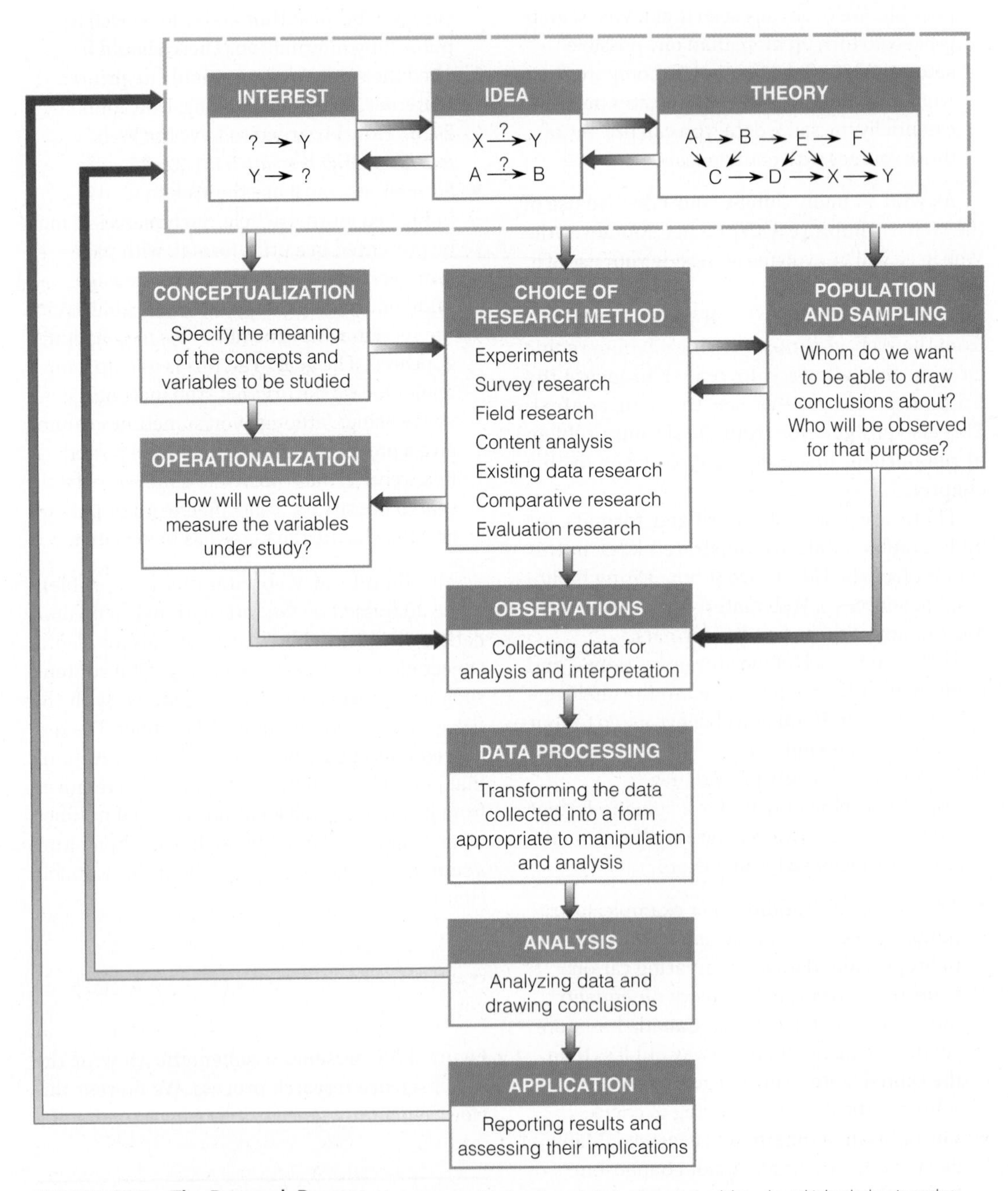

FIGURE 17-5 **The Research Process.** Here are some of the key elements that we've examined throughout this book: the pieces that make up the whole of social research.
Source: © Cengage Learning

or alienation. Thus, you might have a general *interest* in finding out what causes some people to be more prejudiced than others, or you might want to know some of the consequences of alienation. Alternatively, your inquiry might begin with a specific *idea* about the way things are. For example, you might have the idea that working on an assembly line causes alienation. The question marks in the diagram indicate that you aren't sure things are the way you suspect they are. That's why you're conducting the research. Notice that a theory is represented as a set of complex relationships among several concepts.

There is often a movement back and forth across these several possible beginnings—interest, idea, and theory—as the double arrows suggest. An initial interest may lead to the formulation of an idea, which may be fit into a larger theory, and the theory may produce new ideas and create new interests.

Any or all of these three may suggest the need for empirical research. The purpose of such research can be to explore an interest, test a specific idea, or validate a complex theory. Whatever the purpose, the researcher needs to make a variety of decisions, as indicated in the remainder of the diagram.

To make this discussion more concrete, let's take a specific research example. Suppose you're concerned with the issue of abortion and have a special interest in learning why some university students support abortion rights and others oppose them. Going a step further, let's say you've formed the impression that students in the humanities and social sciences seem generally more inclined to support the idea of abortion rights than those in the natural sciences.

A key consideration is what is the basic purpose of your research (see Chapter 4 for a review)? You probably have both descriptive and explanatory interests: What percentage of the student body supports a woman's right to an abortion (description), and what causes some to support it and others to oppose it (explanation)? The units of analysis in this case would be individuals: university students. Let's assume you'd be satisfied to learn something about the way things are now. You might then decide that a cross-sectional study would suit your purposes. Although this would provide you with no direct evidence of processes over time, you might be able to approximate some longitudinal analyses concerning changes in students' attitudes.

GETTING STARTED

When you first begin your project, your interests would likely be exploratory. You might choose among several possible activities in pursuing your interest in student attitudes about abortion rights. At the start, you would want to read something about the issue. If you have a hunch that attitudes are somehow related to a university major, you might want to find out what other researchers may have written about that. In addition, you would probably talk to some people who support abortion rights and some who don't. You might attend meetings of abortion-related groups. All these activities could help prepare you to handle the various decisions of research design we're about to examine.

You must define the purpose of your project before you can design your study. Do you plan to write a paper to satisfy a course or thesis requirement? Is your purpose to gain information that will support you in arguing for or against abortion rights? Do you want to write an article for the campus newspaper or for an academic journal? When reviewing the previous research literature regarding abortion rights, you should note the design decisions other researchers have made, always asking whether the same decisions would satisfy your purpose.

Usually, your purpose for undertaking research can be expressed in the form of a *report*. A later section of this chapter will cover how you organize a research report. We recommend outlining such a report as the first step in the design of your project. Although your final report may look quite different from your initial vision of it, this exercise can help you gauge the appropriateness of different research designs. During this step, clearly describe the kinds of statements you want to make when the research is complete. This will help guide your choices of appropriate research strategies. Here are some examples of such statements: "Students frequently mentioned abortion rights in the context of discussing social issues that concerned them personally." "*X* percent of Forest University students favour a woman's right to choose an abortion." "Engineers are (more/less) likely than sociologists to favour abortion rights."

KEY DESIGN CONSIDERATIONS

Deciding the purpose and desired outcomes of your study is just the beginning. When designing a research project, it will be important to ask many of the same questions of your proposed project that you asked of other research when you read and/or evaluated it. Additionally, there are a number of other important considerations that must be taken into account when designing a social research project.

Conceptualization We often talk pretty casually about social science concepts such as prejudice, alienation, religiosity, and liberalism, but it's necessary to clarify what we mean by these concepts in order to draw meaningful conclusions about them. (See Chapter 5 for a refresher on conceptualization.) For now, let's see what it might involve in our hypothetical example.

If you're going to study how university students feel about abortion and why, the first thing you'll have to specify is what you mean by "the right to an abortion." Support for abortion probably varies according to circumstances, so you'll want to pay attention to the different conditions under which people might approve or disapprove of abortion; for example, when the woman's life is in danger, in the case of rape or incest, or simply as a matter of personal choice.

You'll also need to specify exact meanings for all the other concepts you plan to study. If you want to study the possible effect of a university major on abortion opinions, you'll have to decide whether you want to consider only officially declared majors or include students' intentions as well. What will you do with those who have no major?

In surveys and experiments, such concepts need to be specified in advance. In less tightly structured research, such as open-ended interviews, an important part of the research may involve the discovery of different dimensions, aspects, or nuances of concepts. In this type of research, you may uncover aspects of social life that were not evident at the start of the project.

Choice of Research Method As we discussed in Part 3, each research method has its strengths and weaknesses, and certain concepts are more appropriately studied by some methods than by others. In our study of attitudes toward abortion rights, a survey might be the most appropriate method—either interviewing students or asking them to fill out a questionnaire. Surveys are particularly well suited to the study of public opinion. This is not to say that you couldn't make good use of the other methods presented in Part 3. For example, you might use the method of content analysis to examine blogs or tweets about abortion. Field research would provide an avenue to understanding how people interact with one another regarding the issue of abortion, how they discuss it, and how they change their minds. In Part 3, you were also introduced to other research methods that might be used in studying this topic. Often, the best study design uses more than one research method, taking advantage of their different strengths.

Operational Definitions Once you've specified the concepts to be studied and chosen a research method, the next step is operational definitions—deciding on your variables, instruments, and measurement techniques (Chapter 5). The meaning of concepts in a study is determined in part by how they are measured. One task is deciding how the desired data will be collected—direct observation, review of official documents, a questionnaire, or some other technique.

If you decided to use a survey to study attitudes toward abortion rights, part of operationalization is choosing the wording of questionnaire items. For instance, you might operationalize your main variable by asking respondents whether they would approve of a woman's right to have an abortion under each of the conditions you've conceptualized: in the case of rape or incest, if her life were threatened by the pregnancy, and so on. You'd design the questionnaire such that it asked respondents to express approval or disapproval for each situation. Similarly, you would specify exactly how respondents would indicate their university major and what choices to provide those who have not declared a major.

Ethics Ethical decisions will come into play when making decisions about your choice of topic, concepts, measures, and research methods, as discussed in Chapter 3. The ethical issues of concern to a researcher depend in part on the issue under study and the research method chosen. When using research methods that involve direct interaction between researchers and study participants—such as interviews and surveys—the researcher must consider issues of voluntary participation and consent. In conducting a survey of university students, for example, you would need to obtain their consent to participate and ensure that the students understood they were free to participate or not, as they chose. Statements informing participants about the goals of the study and consent forms would need to be prepared in advance. If any of the students happened to be minors, permission would need to be obtained from parents or legal guardians in order for them to participate.

Research participants also have the right to privacy, the maintenance of dignity, and protection against harm. Researchers must take these issues into account in their choice of methods and measures. Thus, a researcher must balance potential harm and undue inconvenience to participants with his or her desire to obtain the best information possible. In the case of a survey, for example, the questions asked must be thoughtfully considered to avoid topics that might cause undue stress or anxiety for some participants. Designing an efficient study, so that participants are not unduly burdened by long and confusing questionnaires or interviewers who are unprepared for their task, is another consideration.

A researcher must also consider how the confidentiality of the participants will be maintained. For example, a filing system might have to be developed so that respondents' answers could not be connected with respondents' names even if an unauthorized person were to gain access to the data. In designing a study, researchers must continually consider the effect of their choices on the study participants.

Population and Sampling In addition to refining concepts and measurements, you must decide *who* or *what* to study. The *population* for a study is the group (usually of people) about whom we want to draw conclusions. We're almost never able to study all the members of the population that interests us, however, and we can never make every possible observation of them. In every case, then, we select a *sample* from among the data that might be collected and studied. The sampling of information, of course, occurs in everyday life and often produces biased observations. (Recall the discussion of "selective observation" in Chapter 1.) Social researchers are more deliberate in their sampling of what will be observed.

Chapter 6 described methods for selecting samples that adequately reflect the whole population that interests us. Notice in Figure 17-5 that decisions about population and sampling are related to decisions about the research method to be used. Although probability sampling techniques would be relevant to a large-scale survey or a content analysis, a field researcher might need to select only those informants who will yield a balanced picture of the situation under study, and an experimenter might assign subjects to experimental and control groups in a manner that creates comparability.

In your hypothetical study of abortion attitudes, the relevant population would be the student population of your university. As covered in Chapter 6, however, selecting a sample will require you to get more specific than that. Will you include part-time as well as full-time students? Only degree candidates or everyone? International students as well as Canadian citizens? Undergraduates, graduate students, or both? There are many such questions, each of which must be answered in relation to your research purpose. For example, if your purpose is to predict how students would vote in a local referendum on abortion, you might want to limit your population to those eligible and likely to vote.

Observations Having decided what to study, among whom, and by what method, you're now ready to make observations—to collect empirical data. The chapters of Part 3, which described the various research methods, give the different observation techniques appropriate to each.

To conduct a survey on abortion attitudes, you might want to print questionnaires and mail them to a sample selected from the student body. Or you could arrange to have a team of interviewers conduct the survey over the telephone. The relative advantages and disadvantages of these and other possibilities were discussed in Chapter 8.

Data Processing Depending on the research method chosen, you'll have amassed a volume of observations in a form that probably isn't immediately interpretable. If you spend a month observing a street gang firsthand, you'll have enough field notes to fill a book. In a historical study of ethnic diversity at your school, you could amass volumes of official documents, interviews with administrators and others, and so forth. Chapters 13 and 14 described some of the ways social scientific data are processed or transformed for qualitative or quantitative analysis.

In the case of a survey, the "raw" observations are typically in the form of questionnaires with boxes checked, answers written in spaces, and the like. The data-processing phase of a survey typically involves the classification (*coding*) of written-in answers and the transfer of all the information to a computer.

Analysis Once the collected data are in a suitable form, you're ready to interpret them for the purpose of drawing conclusions that reflect the interests, ideas, and theories that initiated the inquiry. Chapters 13 through 16 described a few of the many options available to you in analyzing data. In Figure 17-5, notice that the results of your analyses feed back into your initial interests, ideas, and theories. Often, this feedback represents the beginning of another cycle of inquiry.

In the survey of student attitudes about abortion rights, the analysis phase would pursue both descriptive and explanatory aims. You might begin by calculating the percentages of students who favoured or opposed each of the several different versions of abortion rights. Taken together, these several percentages would provide a good picture of student opinion on the issue.

Moving beyond simple description, you might describe the opinions of different subsets of the student body, like different university majors. If your design included gathering other information about your respondents, you could also look at first-year students versus seniors, undergraduate versus graduate students, men versus women, or any other categories you included. The description of subgroups could then lead you into an explanatory analysis.

Application The final stage of the research process involves the uses made of the research you've conducted and the conclusions you've reached. To start, you'll probably want to communicate your findings so that others will know what you've learned. It may be appropriate to prepare—and even publish—a written report (covered in more detail later in this chapter). Perhaps you'll make oral presentations, such as papers delivered to professional and scientific meetings. Other students would also be interested in hearing what you've learned about them.

You may want to go beyond simply reporting what you've learned to discussing the implications of your findings. Do they say anything about actions that might be taken in support of policy goals? Both the proponents and the opponents of abortion rights would be interested.

Finally, you should consider what your research suggests in regard to further research on your subject. What mistakes should be corrected in future studies? What avenues, opened up slightly in your study, should be pursued further in later investigations?

Research Design in Review As this overview shows, research design involves a set of decisions regarding *what topic* is to be studied in *which population* with *which research methods* for *what purpose*. Although you'll want to consider many ways of studying a subject and use your knowledge of a variety of methods, research design is the process of narrowing your choices and focusing your perspective for the purposes of a particular study. Note that our review of research design has used a traditional, top-down approach. This is not necessary. You could, and researchers do, start anywhere on the flow chart. For example, your study of abortion attitudes could begin with trying to understand why a good friend is wrestling with an abortion choice.

If you're doing a research project for one of your courses, many aspects of research design may be specified for you in advance, including the method (such as an experiment) or the topic (as in a course on the subject of prejudice). The following summary assumes that you're free to choose your topic and research strategy.

In designing a research project, you'll find it useful to begin by assessing three things: your interests, abilities, and available resources.

Each of these considerations will suggest a large number of possible studies.

Simulate the beginning of a somewhat conventional research project: ask yourself what you're interested in understanding. Surely you have several questions about social behaviour and attitudes. Why are some people politically liberal and others politically conservative? Why are some people more religious than others? Why do people join militia groups? Do universities still discriminate against minority faculty members? Why would a person stay in an abusive relationship? Spend some time thinking about the kinds of questions that interest and concern you.

Once you have a few questions you'd be interested in answering for yourself, think about the kind of information needed to answer them. What research units of analysis would provide the most relevant information: university students, young adult men, voters, corporations, cities, or neighbourhoods? This question will probably be inseparable in your thoughts from the question of research topics. Then ask which aspects of the units of analysis would provide the information you need to answer your research question. Keep in mind that you may not be able to study the population or units that would be most appropriate to your research interest using the methods and measures you deem most suitable. If you were interested in issues of child abuse, for example, ethical concerns might bar interviewing 6- to 12-year-olds because of the potential negative impact of raising such topics with victims of abuse.

Once you have some ideas about the kind of information relevant to your purpose, ask yourself how you might go about getting that information. Are the relevant data likely to be already available somewhere (say, in a government publication), or would you have to collect them yourself? If you think you would have to collect the data, how would you go about doing it? Would you need to survey a large number of people or interview a few people in depth? Could you learn what you need to know by attending meetings of certain groups? Could you glean the data you need from books in the library?

As you answer these questions, you'll find yourself well into the process of research design. Keep in mind your own research abilities and the resources available to you. What's the point of designing a perfect study that you can't actually carry out? You may want to try a research method you have not used before so you can learn from it, but take care not to put yourself at too great a disadvantage.

Once you have a general idea of what you want to study and how, carefully review previous research in journals and books to see how other researchers have addressed the topic and what they have learned about it. Your review of the literature may lead you to revise your research design: perhaps you'll decide to use a previous researcher's method or even *replicate* an earlier study. The independent replication of research projects is a standard procedure in the physical sciences, and it's just as important in the social sciences, although social scientists tend to overlook that. Or you might want to go beyond replication and study some aspect of the topic that you feel previous researchers have overlooked.

Here's another approach you might take. Suppose a topic has been studied previously using field research methods. Can you design an experiment that would test the findings those earlier researchers produced? Or can you think of existing statistics that could be used to test their conclusions? Did a mass survey yield results that you'd like to explore in greater detail through some on-the-spot observations and in-depth interviews? As discussed in Chapter 1 (and illustrated with examples throughout the text), the use of several different research methods (MMR) should always be kept in mind as a valuable research strategy. Because each research method has particular strengths and weaknesses, there is always a danger that research findings will reflect, at least in part, the method of inquiry. In the best of all worlds, your own research design should bring more than one research method to bear on the topic.

THE RESEARCH PROPOSAL

Quite often, in the design of a research project, you'll have to lay out the details of your plan for someone else's review and/or approval. In the case of a course project, for example, your instructor might very well want to see a "proposal" before you set off to work. Later in your career, if you wanted to undertake a major project, you might need to obtain funding from a foundation or governmental agency, which would most definitely want a detailed proposal that describes how you would spend their money.

This section concludes with a brief discussion of how you might prepare such a proposal. This will give you one more overview of the whole research process, which the rest of this book details.

Elements of a Research Proposal Although some funding agencies (or your instructor, for that matter) may have specific requirements for the elements or structure of a research proposal, here are some basic elements you should include.

Problem or Objective What exactly do you want to study? Why is it worth studying? Does the proposed study have practical significance? Does it contribute to the construction of social theories, for example?

Literature Review What have others said about this topic? What theories address it and what do they say? What research has been done previously? Are there consistent findings, or do past studies disagree? Are there flaws in the body of existing research that you think you can remedy?

Subjects for Study Who or what will you study in order to collect data? First, identify the subjects in general, theoretical terms. Then, in specific more concrete terms, identify who is available for study and how you'll reach them. Will it be appropriate to select a sample? If so, how will you do that? If there is any possibility that your research will affect those you study, how will you ensure that the research does not harm them?

Observation and Measurement What are the key concepts and indicators in your study? How will you define and measure them? Do your definitions and measurement methods duplicate or differ from those of previous research on this topic? If you have already developed your measurement device (e.g., a questionnaire) or will be using something previously developed by others, it might be appropriate to include a copy in an appendix to your proposal.

Data Collection Methods How will you actually collect the data for your study? Will you conduct an experiment or a survey? Will you undertake field research or will you focus on the reanalysis of statistics already created by others? Perhaps you will use more than one method.

Ethical Approval Once you've decided on your method of data collection, you'll have to determine whether you need to obtain ethical approval of your study. As we discussed in Chapter 3, ethical approval of data collection must be obtained when your research involves human subjects. For instance, if you decided on an experiment or a survey, gaining ethical approval would be necessary. On the other hand, if you chose to analyze existing statistics or gather information from the archives, then gaining ethical approval wouldn't be required.

Analysis Indicate the kind of analysis you plan to conduct. Spell out the purpose and logic of your analysis. Are you interested in precise description? Do you intend to explain why things are the way they are? Do you plan to account for variations in some quality, such as why some students are more liberal than others? What possible explanatory variables will your analysis consider, and how will you know if you've explained variations adequately?

Schedule It's often appropriate to provide a schedule for the various stages of research. Even if you don't do this for the proposal, do it for yourself. Unless you have a timeline for accomplishing the several stages of research and keeping track of how you're doing, you may end up in trouble.

Budget When you ask someone to cover the costs of your research, you need to provide a specific budget. Large, expensive projects include budgetary categories such as personnel, equipment, supplies, telephones, and postage. Even for a project you'll pay for yourself, it's a good idea to spend some time anticipating expenses: office supplies, photocopying, telephone calls, transportation, and so on.

As you can see, if you were interested in conducting a social science research project, it would be a good idea to prepare a research proposal for your own purposes, even if you weren't required to do so by your instructor or a funding agency. If you're going to invest your time and energy in such a project, you should do what you can to ensure a return on that investment.

WRITING SOCIAL RESEARCH

Unless research is properly communicated, all the efforts devoted to the various procedures discussed throughout this book will go for naught. This means, first and foremost, that good social reporting requires good English or French or whatever language you use. Whenever we ask the figures "to speak for themselves," they tend to remain mute. Whenever we use unduly complex terminology or construction, communication suffers.

Our first advice to you is to read and reread (at approximately three-month intervals) an excellent small book by William Strunk Jr. and E. B. White, *The Elements of Style* (2000; see also Birchfield 1998). If you do this faithfully, and if even 10 percent of the contents rub off, you'll stand a good chance of making yourself understood and your findings appreciated.[1]

Next, you need to understand that scientific reporting has several functions. First, your report should communicate a body of specific data and ideas. You should provide those specifics clearly and with sufficient detail to permit an informed evaluation by others. Second, you should view your report as a contribution to the general body of scientific knowledge. While remaining appropriately humble, you should always regard your research report as an addition to what we know about social behaviour. Finally, the report should stimulate and direct further inquiry. See the Applying Concepts in Everyday Life box "Communication Is the Key" for more on the importance of knowing how to read and write well.

SOME BASIC CONSIDERATIONS

Despite these general guidelines, different reports serve different purposes. A report appropriate for one purpose might be wholly inappropriate for another. This section deals with some of the contexts that affect choices in writing.

1 There are many good books on effective writing. Besides Strunk and White, two recommended others include Howard S. Becker. 2007. *Writing for Social Scientists*. Chicago: University of Chicago Press, and Jack R. Hart. 2007. *A Writer's Coach: The Complete Guide to Writing Strategies That Work*. New York: Anchor.

APPLYING CONCEPTS IN EVERYDAY LIFE

Communication Is the Key

No matter what you do with your life—whether in social research or some other worthy pursuit—you're likely to find yourself regularly using the skills discussed in this chapter. When universities ask employers for suggestions on how we can better prepare graduates, the most common response, regardless of professional field, tends to be the same: Teach them to write. Whatever career you choose, you'll benefit greatly from the ability to read a body of literature or a set of data and write coherently about it. Moreover, if you're typical of recent university cohorts, you're likely to have several different careers. The ability to read and write effectively will serve you well in all of them.

Audience Before drafting your report, ask yourself who you hope will read it. Normally, you should make a distinction between scientists and general readers. If the report is written for the former, you can make certain assumptions about their existing knowledge and therefore summarize certain points rather than explain them in detail. Similarly, you can use more technical language than would be appropriate for a general audience.

At the same time, remain aware that any science has its factions and cults. Terms, assumptions, and special techniques familiar to your immediate colleagues might only confuse other scientists. The sociologist of religion writing for a general sociology audience, for example, should explain previous findings in more detail than he or she would if addressing an audience of sociologists of religion.

Form and Length of the Report Our comments here apply to both written and oral reports. Each form, however, affects the nature of the report.

It's useful to think about the variety of reports that might result from a research project. To begin, you may wish to prepare a short *research note* for publication in an academic or technical journal. Such reports are approximately one to five pages long (typed, double-spaced) and should be concise and direct. In a small amount of space, you can't present the state of the field in any detail, so your methodological notes must be abbreviated. Basically, you should tell the reader why you believe your findings justify a brief note, and then tell what those findings are.

Often, researchers must prepare reports for the sponsors of their research. These reports can vary greatly in length. In preparing such a report, you should bear in mind your audience—scientific or lay—and their reasons for sponsoring the project in the first place. It's both bad politics and bad manners to bore the sponsors with research findings that have no interest or value to them. At the same time, it may be useful to summarize how the research has advanced basic scientific knowledge (if it has).

Working papers are another form of research reporting. In a large and complex project especially, you'll find comments on your analysis and the interpretation of your data useful. A working paper constitutes a tentative presentation with an implicit request for comments. Working papers can also vary in length, and they may present all of the research findings of the project or only a portion of them. Because your professional reputation is not at stake in a working paper, feel free to present tentative interpretations that you can't altogether justify—identifying them as such and asking for evaluations.

Many research projects result in papers delivered at professional meetings. These often serve the same purpose as working papers. You can present findings and ideas of possible interest to your colleagues and ask for their comments. Although the length of such professional papers varies, depending on the organization of the meetings, it's best to say too little rather than too much. Although a working paper may ramble somewhat through tentative conclusions, conference participants should not be forced to sit through an oral unveiling of the same. Interested listeners can always ask for more details later, and uninterested ones can gratefully escape.

Probably the most popular research report is the article published in an academic journal. Again, lengths vary, and you should examine the lengths of articles previously published by the journal in question. As a rough guide, however, 25 typed pages is a good length. A subsequent section on the organization of the report is based primarily on the structure of a journal article, so we'll say no more at this point except to indicate that student term papers should follow this model. As a general rule, a term paper that would make a good journal article also makes a good term paper.

A book, of course, represents the most prestigious form of research report. It has the length and detail of a working paper but is more polished. Because publishing research findings as a book lends them greater substance and worth, you have a special obligation to your audience. Although some colleagues may provide comments, possibly leading you to revise your ideas, other readers may be led to accept your findings uncritically.

Aim of the Report Earlier in this book, we considered the different purposes of social research projects. In preparing your report, keep these different purposes in mind.

Some reports focus primarily on the exploration of a topic. As such, their conclusions are tentative and incomplete. If you're writing this sort of report, clearly indicate to your audience the exploratory aim of the study and present the shortcomings of the particular project. An exploratory report points the way to more refined research on the topic.

Most research reports have a descriptive element, describing their subject matter. In yours, carefully distinguish those descriptions that apply only to the sample and those that apply to the population. Give your audience some indication of the probable range of error in any inferential descriptions you make.

Many reports have an explanatory aim: pointing to causal relationships among variables. Depending on your probable audience, carefully delineate the rules of explanation that lie behind your computations and conclusions. Also, as in the case of description, give your readers some guide to the relative certainty of your conclusions.

If your intention is to test a hypothesis based in theory, you should make that hypothesis clear and succinct. Specify what will constitute acceptance or rejection of the hypothesis and how either of those reflects on the theoretical underpinnings.

Finally, some research reports propose action. For example, if you've studied prejudice, you may suggest in your report how prejudice can be reduced on the basis of your research findings. This suggestion may become a knotty problem for you, however, because your values and orientations may have interfered with your proposals. Although it's perfectly legitimate for such proposals to be motivated by personal values, you must ensure that the data actually warrant the specific actions you've proposed. Thus, you should be especially careful to spell out the logic by which you move from empirical data to proposed action.

ORGANIZATION OF THE REPORT

Although the various forms and purposes of reports somewhat affect the way they are organized, knowing a general format for presenting research data can be helpful. The following comments apply most directly to a journal article, but with some modification they apply to most forms of research reports as well. If you prepared a detail research proposal as outlined earlier in this chapter then you may be able to incorporate many of those elements (problem/objectives, literature review, subjects, methods) into your research report.

Purpose and Overview It's always helpful if you begin with a brief statement of the purpose of the study and the main findings of the analysis. In a journal article, as we've seen, this overview sometimes takes the form of an abstract.

Some researchers find this difficult to do. For example, your analysis may have involved considerable detective work, with important findings revealing themselves only as a result of imaginative deduction and data manipulation. You may wish, therefore, to lead the reader through the same exciting process, chronicling the discovery process with a degree of suspense and surprise. To the extent that this form of reporting gives an accurate picture of the research process, it has considerable instructional value. Nevertheless, many readers may not be interested in following your entire research account, and not knowing the purpose and general conclusions in advance may make it difficult for them to understand the significance of the study.

plagiarism Presenting someone else's words or thoughts as though they were your own, constituting intellectual theft.

An old forensic dictum says, "Tell them what you're going to tell them, tell them, and tell them what you told them." You would do well to follow this dictum.

Review of the Literature Next, you must indicate where your report fits into the general body of scientific knowledge. After presenting the general purpose of your study, you should bring the reader up to date on the previous research in the area, pointing to general agreements and disagreements among the previous researchers. Your review of the literature should lay the groundwork for your own study, showing why your research may have value in the larger scheme of things.

In some cases, you may wish to challenge previously accepted ideas. Carefully review the studies that have led to the acceptance of those ideas, and then indicate the factors that have not been previously considered or the logical fallacies present in the previous research.

When you're concerned with resolving a disagreement among previous researchers, you should summarize the research supporting one view, then summarize the research supporting the other, and finally suggest the reasons for the disagreement.

Your review of the literature serves a bibliographic function for readers by indexing the previous research on a given topic. This can be overdone, however, and you should avoid an opening paragraph that runs three pages, mentioning every previous study in the field. The comprehensive bibliographic function can best be served by a reference list at the end of the report, and the review of the literature should focus only on those studies that have direct relevance to the present one.

Avoiding Plagiarism Whenever you're reporting on the work of others, you must be clear about who said what. That is, you must avoid **plagiarism**: the theft of another's words or ideas—whether intentional or accidental—and the presentation of those words and ideas as your own. Because this is a common and sometimes unclear problem for college students, especially in regard to the review of the literature, we'll consider the issue here. Realize, of course, that these concerns apply to everything you write.

The following are the ground rules regarding plagiarism:

- You cannot use another writer's exact words without using quotation marks and giving a complete citation, which indicates the source of the quotation such that your reader could locate the quotation in its original context.
- It's also not acceptable to edit or paraphrase another's words and present the revised version as your own work.
- Finally, it's not even acceptable to present another's ideas as your own—even if you use totally different words to express those ideas.

The following examples should clarify what is or is not acceptable in the use of another's work.

The Original Work

Laws of Growth

> Systems are like babies: once you get one, you have it. They don't go away. On the contrary, they display the most remarkable persistence. They not only persist; they grow. And as they grow, they encroach. The growth potential of systems was explored in a tentative, preliminary way by Parkinson, who concluded that administrative systems maintain an average growth of 5 to 6 percent per annum regardless of the work to be done. Parkinson was right so far as he goes, and we must give him full honors for initiating the serious study of this important topic. But what Parkinson failed to perceive, we now enunciate—the general systems analogue of Parkinson's Law.
>
> The System Itself Tends To Grow At 5 To 6 Percent Per Annum
>
> Again, this Law is but the preliminary to the most general possible formulation, the Big-Bang Theorem of Systems Cosmology.
>
> Systems Tend To Expand To Fill The Known Universe
>
> (Gall 1975:12–14)

Now let's look at some of the acceptable ways you might make use of Gall's work in a term paper.

- *Acceptable*: John Gall, in his work *Systemantics*, draws a humorous parallel between systems and infants: "Systems are like babies: once you get one, you have it. They don't go away. On the contrary, they display the most remarkable persistence. They not only persist; they grow" (Gall 1975).
- *Acceptable*: John Gall warns that systems are like babies. Create a system and it sticks around. Worse yet, Gall notes, systems keep growing larger and larger (Gall 1975).
- *Acceptable*: It has also been suggested that systems have a natural tendency to persist, even grow and encroach (Gall 1975:12).

Note that the last format requires that you give a complete citation in your bibliography or reference list. Complete footnotes or endnotes work as well. See the publication manuals of various organizations such as the ASA or the APA, as well as the *Chicago Manual of Style*, for appropriate citation formats. The How to Do It box "Citing Bibliographic Sources" has some specific examples to get you started.

Here now are some unacceptable uses of the same material, reflecting some common errors.

- *Unacceptable*: In this paper, I want to look at some of the characteristics of the social systems we create in our organizations. First, systems are like babies: once you get one, you have it. They don't go away. On the contrary, they display the most remarkable persistence. They not only persist; they grow. [It's unacceptable to quote someone else's materials directly without using quotation marks and giving a full citation.]
- *Unacceptable*: In this paper, I want to look at some of the characteristics of the social systems we create in our organizations. First, systems are a lot like children: once you get one, it's yours. They don't go away; they persist. They not only persist, in fact: they grow. [It's unacceptable to edit another's work and present it as your own.]
- *Unacceptable*: In this paper, I want to look at some of the characteristics of the social systems we create in our organizations. One thing I've noticed is that once you create a system, it never seems to go away. Just the opposite, in fact: systems have a tendency to grow. You might say systems are a lot like children in that respect. [It's unacceptable to paraphrase someone else's ideas and present them as your own.]

Each of the preceding unacceptable examples is an example of plagiarism and represents a serious offence. Admittedly, there are some grey areas. Some ideas are more or less in the public domain, not "belonging" to any one person. Or you may reach an idea on your own that someone else has already put in writing. If you have a question about a specific situation, discuss it with your instructor in advance.

We've discussed this topic in some detail because, although you must place your research in the context of what others have done and said, the improper use of their materials is a serious offence. Learning to avoid plagiarism is a part of your "coming of age" as a scholar.

HOW TO DO IT

Citing Bibliographic Sources

Your review of the literature and other readings that figure in your paper all need to be cited properly. The good news is that proper citation isn't that hard to do. The bad news is that there are several formats in common use. We'll illustrate a few of the more common formats here, but you should ask your instructor what version you're expected to use. We'll illustrate both a book and an article.

Book Information

Author: C. Wright Mills
Title: *The Power Elite*
City of publication: New York
Publisher: Oxford University Press
Year of publication: 1956

Article Information

Authors: Sharon Sassler and Anna Cunningham
Title: "How Cohabitors View Childbearing"
Journal name: *Sociological Perspectives*
Year of publication: 2008
Month/season of publication: Spring
Volume: 51
Number: 1
Pages: 3–28

With such "raw data" in hand, you can format them by following any of the following bibliographic styles.

ASA Style Guide (American Sociological Association)

Mills, C. Wright. 1956. *The Power Elite*. New York: Oxford University Press.

Sassler, Sharon, and Anna Cunningham. 2008. "How Cohabitors View Child bearing." *Sociological Perspectives* 51:3–28.

MLA Style Guide (Modern Language Association)

Mills, C. Wright. *The Power Elite*. New York: Oxford University Press, 1956. Print.

Sassler, Sharon, and Anna Cunningham. "How Cohabitors View Childbearing." *Sociological Perspectives* 51.1 (2008): 3–28. Print.

APSA Style Guide (American Political Science Association)

Mills, C. Wright. 1956. *The Power Elite*. New York: Oxford University Press.

Sassler, Sharon, and Anna Cunningham. 2008. "How Cohabitors View Childbearing." *Sociological Perspectives* 51 (Spring): 3–28.

APA Style Guide (American Psychological Association)

Mills, C. Wright. (1956). *The power elite*. New York: Oxford University Press.

Sassler, S., & Cunningham, A. (2008). How cohabitors view childbearing. *Sociological Perspectives, 51*(1), 3–28.

Study Design and Execution A research report containing interesting findings and conclusions will frustrate readers if they can't determine the methodological design and execution of the study. The worth of all scientific findings depends heavily on the manner in which the data were collected and analyzed.

In reporting the design and execution of a survey, for example, always include the following: the population, the sampling frame, the sampling method, the sample size, the data collection method, the completion rate, and the methods of data processing and analysis. Comparable details should be given if other methods are used. The experienced researcher can report these details in a rather short space without omitting anything required for the reader's evaluation of the study.

Analysis and Interpretation Having set the study in the perspective of previous research and having described the design and execution of it, you should then present your data. This chapter momentarily will provide further guidelines in this regard. For now, a few general comments are in order.

The presentation of data, the manipulation of those data, and your interpretations should be integrated into a logical whole. It frustrates the reader to discover a collection of seemingly unrelated analyses and findings with a promise that all the loose ends will be tied together later in the report. Every step in the analysis should make sense at the time it is taken. You should present your rationale for a particular analysis, present the data relevant to it, interpret the results, and then indicate where that result leads next.

Summary and Conclusions According to the forensic dictum mentioned earlier, summarizing the research report is essential. Avoid reviewing every specific finding, but review all the significant ones, pointing once more to their general significance.

The report should conclude with a statement of what you've discovered about your subject matter and where future research might be directed. Many journal articles end with the statement "It is clear that much more research is needed." This conclusion is probably always true, but it has little value unless you can offer pertinent suggestions about the nature of that future research. You should review the particular shortcomings of your own study and suggest ways those shortcomings might be avoided.

GUIDELINES FOR REPORTING ANALYSES

The presentation of data analyses should provide a maximum of detail without being cluttered. You can accomplish this best by continually examining your report to see whether it achieves the following aims.

If you're using quantitative data, present them so the reader can recompute them. In the case of percentage tables, for example, the reader should be able to collapse categories and recompute the percentages. Readers should receive sufficient information to permit them to compute percentages in the table in the direction opposite from that of your own presentation.

Describe all aspects of a quantitative analysis in sufficient detail to permit a secondary analyst to replicate the analysis from the same body of data. This means that he or she should be able to create the same indexes and scales, produce the same tables, arrive at the same regression equations, obtain the same factors and factor loadings, and so forth. This will seldom be done, of course, but if the report allows for it, the reader will be far better equipped to evaluate the report than if it does not.

Provide details. If you're doing a qualitative analysis, you must provide enough detail that your reader has a sense of having made the observations with you. Presenting only those data that support your interpretations is not sufficient; you must also share those data that conflict with the way you've made sense of things. Ultimately, you should provide enough information that the reader might reach a different conclusion than you did—though you can hope your interpretation will make the most sense. The reader, in fact, should be in a position to replicate the entire study independently, whether it involves participant observation among heavy-metal fanatics, an experiment regarding jury deliberation, or any other study format. Recall that replicability is an essential norm of science. A single study does not prove a point; only a series of studies can begin to do so. And unless studies can be replicated, there can be no meaningful series of studies.

Integrate supporting materials. We have previously mentioned the importance of integrating data and interpretations in the report. Here is a more specific guideline for doing this. Tables, charts, and figures, if any, should be integrated into the text of the report—appearing near the portion of the text that discusses them. Sometimes students describe their analyses in the body of the report and place all the tables in an appendix. This procedure greatly impedes the reader, however. As a general rule, it is best to (1) describe the purpose for presenting the table, (2) present it, and (3) review and interpret it.

Draw explicit conclusions. Although research is typically conducted for the purpose of drawing general conclusions, you should carefully note the specific basis for such conclusions. Otherwise you may lead your reader into accepting unwarranted conclusions.

Point to any qualifications or conditions warranted in the evaluation of conclusions. Typically, you know best the shortcomings and tentativeness of your conclusions, and you should give the reader the advantage of that knowledge. Failure to do so can misdirect future research and result in a waste of research funds.

As we said at the outset of this discussion, research reports should be written in the best possible literary style. Writing lucidly is easier for some people than for others, and it's always harder than writing poorly. You are again referred to the Strunk and White book. Every researcher would do well to follow this procedure: Write. Read Strunk and White. Revise. Reread Strunk and White. Revise again. This will be a difficult and time-consuming endeavour, but so is science.

A perfectly designed, carefully executed, and brilliantly analyzed study will be altogether worthless unless you can communicate your findings to others. This chapter has attempted to provide some guidelines toward that end. The best guides are logic, clarity, and honesty. Ultimately, there is no substitute for practice.

GOING PUBLIC

Though we have written this chapter with a particular concern for the research projects, you may be called on to undertake in your research methods course, you should realize that graduate and even undergraduate students are increasingly presenting the results of their research as professional papers or published articles.

If you would like to explore these possibilities further, you may find regional and provincial associations to be more open to students than are national associations, although students may present papers to the Canadian Sociological Association, for example. Some associations have special sessions and programs for student participants. You can learn more about these possibilities by visiting the associations' websites to learn of upcoming meetings and the topics for which papers are being solicited.

Typically, you'll submit your paper to someone who has agreed to organize a session with three to five papers on a particular topic. The organizer chooses which of the submissions will be accepted for presentation. Oral presentations at scholarly meetings are typically 15 to 20 minutes long, with the possibility of questions from the audience. Some presenters read a printed paper, others speak from notes, but most now present computer slide shows using programs such as PowerPoint.

To publish an article in a scholarly journal, you would do well to identify a journal that publishes articles on the topic of your research. Again, the journals published by regional or provincial associations may be the most accessible to student authors. Each journal will contain instructions for submitting articles, including instructions for formatting your article. Typically, articles submitted to a journal are circulated among three or so anonymous reviewers, who make comments and recommendations to the journal's editor. This is referred to as the "peer-review" process. Sometimes manuscripts are accepted pretty much as submitted, some are returned for revision and resubmission, and still others are rejected. The whole process from submission to a decision to publish or reject may take a few months, and there will be a further delay before the article is actually published.

The peer-review process is a distinguishing feature in academic publishing. The purpose is to help ensure that the book or article is considered a worthwhile addition to what is known about the topic under study. There is, to be sure, the possibility that peer review may favour established points of view over innovative ones, but the large number of publishing options makes it likely that a friendly journal or publisher might be found. Each would exercise peer judgment as to the scholarly quality of pieces submitted for publication. With the growth of online journals, you will find some that are peer-reviewed and others that are reviewed and judged by the editor in charge.

To meet the costs of publication, a journal will sometimes require that authors pay a small fee on acceptance. Typically, authors receive extra copies of their article—called "reprints"—to give to friends and family and to satisfy requests from professional colleagues.

THE ETHICS OF READING, DESIGNING, AND WRITING SOCIAL RESEARCH

We've already commented on some ethical issues involved in writing research reports. However, there are also some ethical issues at play with respect to reading the research literature. There has always been the risk of reviewing the literature with a special eye toward reports that support a point of view you may be fond of. Although wonderful in most respects, the power of the Internet to provide fast and expansive searches can allow even more "cherry picking" of supportive research literature. This places an ever-greater burden on researchers to exercise professional honesty in representing the history of research findings in a particular area.

Because this chapter concludes the main body of the book, we hope this final section makes clear that research ethics constitute not merely a nice thing to consider as long as it doesn't get in the way. They are, in fact, a fundamental component of social science. Research ethics have not always been recognized in this fashion. When we first began writing this textbook, there was some objection to including this topic. It wasn't so much that researchers objected to the ethical treatment of subjects—ethics simply wasn't considered a proper topic for a book like this one. Attitudes have changed substantially over the years, however. We hope you benefit from understanding the crucial role of ethics in your work as well as in your life.

APPLYING CONCEPTS IN EVERYDAY LIFE

Note the Sources

A vast amount of information is available on the Internet, but it's not all equally trustworthy and usable in scholarly research. This chapter has suggested guidelines for sorting the wheat from the chaff. For example, data provided on government websites or on those of university research centres and institutes, although not perfect, are usually dependable. Clarity regarding how the data were collected is a good sign; so is the clear documentation of any other sources used. Be wary of websites that push a particular point of view or agenda. Their data may be valid and useful, but caution is in order. Never trust websites that are ambiguous about the methods used or about the exact meanings of variables reported on. Finally, look for agreement across several websites, if possible.

In some cases, you may find SourceWatch (www.sourcewatch.org/) a useful tool to help you judge the trustworthiness of Web sources. Sometimes you'll find that a "research team" is actually a public relations firm, or that an individual "expert" always seems to report findings in support of a particular company or industry.

This chapter, and indeed this book, have provided what we hope is a springboard for you to engage in and enjoy the practice of social research. The next time you find yourself pondering the cause of prejudice, observing a political rally, or being just plain curious about the latest trends in television, we trust you'll have the tools to explore your world with a social scientist's eye.

MAIN POINTS

- Sound research design is fundamental to sound science.
- Meaningful scientific research is also inextricably wed to communication.
- Knowing how to read, design, and write social research requires practice.

Reading Social Research

- Social researchers can access many resources, including the library and the Internet, for organizing a review of the literature.
- Reading scholarly literature is different from reading other works, such as novels.
- In reading scholarly literature, you should begin by reading the abstract, skimming the piece, and reading the conclusion to get a good sense of what it is about.
- When you read social science literature, you should form questions and take notes as you're reading.
- The key elements to note in reading a research report include theoretical orientation, research design, measurement methods, sampling (if any), and other considerations specific to the several data collection methods discussed in this book.
- The Internet is a powerful tool for social researchers, but it also carries risks.
- Not everything you read on the Web is necessarily true.
- Original sources of data are preferred over those that take data from elsewhere.
- In evaluating a Web source, you should ask the following:
  - Who or what is the author of the website?
  - Is the site advocating a particular point of view?
  - Does the site give accurate and complete references?
  - Are the data up to date?
- Official data are usually a good source, although they are subject to error.
- The reader of a report should verify (cross-check) data wherever possible.
- Web citations, like other bibliographic references, should be complete enough to allow the reader to locate and review the materials cited. DOI numbers should be included when available.

Designing a Social Research Project

- Research design begins with an initial interest, idea, or theoretical expectation. It proceeds through interrelated steps to narrow the study's focus so that concepts, methods, and procedures are well defined.
- The researcher specifies the meaning of concepts or variables to be studied (conceptualization), chooses a research method or methods, specifies the population to be studied and, when applicable, how it will be sampled, and obtains ethical approval for the study when it's required.
- The researcher operationalizes the concepts to be studied by stating precisely how variables in the study will be measured. Research then proceeds through observation, processing the data, analysis, and application, such as reporting results and assessing their implications.
- Using several different research methods (MMR) to study a topic or test the same finding is a valuable research strategy.

- A research proposal provides a preview of why a study will be undertaken and how it will be conducted. It may be required, but even if it's not, it's a useful device for planning.

Writing Social Research

- Good social research writing begins with good writing, period. Write to communicate rather than to impress.
- Being mindful of one's audience and one's purpose in writing the report is important.
- Plagiarism—presenting someone else's words or thoughts as though they were your own—must be avoided. Whenever using someone else's exact words, you must be sure to use quotation marks or some other indication that you're quoting. In paraphrasing someone else's words or ideas, you must provide a full bibliographic citation of the source.
- The research report should include an account of the study design and execution.
- The analysis of a report should be clear at each step, and its conclusion should be specific but not overly detailed.
- To write good reports, researchers need to provide details, integrate supporting materials, and draw explicit conclusions.
- Increasingly, students are presenting papers at professional meetings and publishing articles in scholarly journals.

The Ethics of Reading, Designing and Writing Social Research

- A review of the literature should not be biased toward a particular point of view.
- Research ethics is a fundamental component of social science, not just a nice afterthought.
- Any original social research project that will require collection of data/information from participants must have ethical approval from an institutional Research Ethics Board.

REVIEW QUESTIONS AND EXERCISES

1. Analyze a quantitative research report: Stanley Lieberson, Susan Dumais, and Shyon Baumann, "The Instability of Androgynous Names: The Symbolic Maintenance of Gender Boundaries," *American Journal of Sociology* 105, no. 5 (March 2000): 1249. Use the following questions as your guide:
   a. What are the theoretical underpinnings of the study?
   b. How are some of the key variables, such as *androgynous*, *racial*, and *gender segregation*, conceptualized and operationalized?
   c. What data are this research based on?
   d. Are there controlling variables?
   e. What is the unit of analysis?
   f. What type of analysis was done?
   g. What did the authors find?
   h. What are the strengths and weaknesses in this study?
2. Analyze a qualitative research report: Dingxin Zhao, "State–Society Relations and the Discourses and Activities of the 1989 Beijing Student Movement," *American Journal of Sociology* 105, no. 6 (May 2000): 1592. Use the following questions as your guide:
   a. What is the author's main research question?
   b. What theoretical frameworks are referred to, and which ones are used?
   c. What methodology is the author using? What type of data collection was chosen? What is the unit of analysis?
   d. Does the author have a hypothesis? If so, what is it?
   e. How does the author conceptualize key terms, such as *state*, *state–society*, and *traditionalism*?
   f. What are the study's findings?
   g. What is the significance of this study? Are you convinced by the author, or do you see weaknesses in the study?

APPENDIXES

A | RANDOM NUMBERS

51426	00609	13501	16557	13914	33401	84598	16256	51886	31407	94431	10793	10437	65142
50202	20368	36181	05719	11720	47252	68129	97583	78197	64506	96094	15565	54451	10894
68568	00811	38612	96130	76686	98080	22397	65709	66476	29072	47294	95575	92207	31912
43803	59549	54997	72125	73689	20448	09636	54932	10780	46568	93704	35864	19104	72771
99389	22930	38246	01741	85862	35913	68450	51989	87203	22966	39965	23689	94496	90819
40012	09599	48287	56312	98800	21764	69339	39265	38708	24879	89908	65194	11479	38897
46202	33334	78502	63224	55138	65208	52970	75762	52422	01538	12774	62448	83373	48356
92106	13420	52252	75044	17710	30572	64791	02170	58265	23490	39625	51822	13088	79273
55478	36951	81131	16564	75192	83624	19837	64199	17127	04287	89202	12485	27127	54445
95888	44841	62382	80884	41749	80051	89305	29619	46255	19437	42118	56365	19354	21687
63752	70740	30727	98221	04142	43663	93794	20051	29352	38160	07908	65877	90653	28600
39706	31586	36108	21662	71438	12980	39471	95774	86372	03985	78977	26533	16177	19726
70394	94351	22457	26801	66505	05939	35468	29290	83141	69893	35443	64588	98379	40997
24328	66613	72883	35679	11468	49960	10713	06650	94072	47238	49989	40700	04282	37164
19300	45923	02358	27187	53193	40040	94551	16006	44819	04925	36322	81318	07767	09898
75264	17274	99313	09819	74081	47019	83766	11652	61463	20523	17156	15633	56306	65756
61801	25803	99036	74158	25691	61586	22711	80610	53411	84833	38944	31905	05475	69018
51217	44878	35559	55558	54991	12802	24869	45978	50192	21129	97197	15798	16251	68202
80240	54443	82312	97509	57848	83730	69741	43918	99146	09401	55696	17022	23857	14574
52058	89814	64024	29716	72872	59060	68771	66883	08409	85650	85535	85659	93365	43147
28459	18054	31177	77817	73215	55952	59266	30908	26528	81941	94064	52738	85015	99236
61246	56005	30027	95365	51401	72313	43067	14424	25467	47268	63945	27477	15643	73537
64100	53865	24106	70497	98741	91230	49381	16109	15636	16555	99646	78224	43983	48557
86649	17968	99209	86506	51521	34845	47716	61783	72090	15828	93790	29199	85979	59513
25994	32188	15125	28244	35374	82169	98415	27443	10709	21036	77242	12126	15384	10038
91142	68443	71595	87285	77954	46246	43484	93725	57598	33343	37333	37216	86209	29308
85900	89177	35463	37290	65502	75996	60430	40129	97891	48432	96420	61864	34334	06783
80799	23668	67958	69297	12726	35953	57968	43241	47098	03344	84356	86620	93556	51283
96429	41318	94091	36041	27081	80307	38085	84416	35484	07293	45607	36954	91408	51122
47970	10032	89346	10458	18396	93085	25303	83518	68633	32246	82215	28022	67577	97594
72469	59185	78412	11529	26258	21622	18997	52703	26386	56264	80550	46328	47601	89508
67758	71528	75788	42499	19816	16366	01923	29047	00929	72309	21973	59609	53886	34762
98899	22430	75503	56128	21692	97528	24181	20498	78282	66143	54062	79651	73197	30479
12783	48846	49102	17462	24321	78119	98103	68108	13053	91442	04370	84795	34596	15559
46012	45951	87514	80718	57246	91049	95869	90799	78772	46759	29270	28549	11024	77259
03802	82683	41036	11652	53416	61231	51368	23180	62110	23975	32641	67415	34552	87859
15233	04412	14981	76133	77223	44150	22899	49528	36601	97438	29735	27053	12035	81149
29038	70437	05264	30181	36015	94583	16736	28591	20148	53382	09045	50572	99809	63712
02961	30256	34194	34334	11052	23123	88313	51754	07802	41996	03053	38116	24801	64168
35986	08834	25394	26990	57065	63223	13898	33035	84740	44562	13701	25133	55081	40397
71900	93567	50485	95879	67273	87232	94444	09030	08914	04127	36022	54394	80624	60780
71636	79416	04009	04816	81154	31183	30180	19287	18649	76657	81725	94613	62678	32329
28010	26202	02931	81693	11016	37412	18796	20687	28658	13534	44323	16054	76065	48823
03870	02084	34849	43767	18860	01671	06733	05498	10132	04989	39545	72690	81462	75170
31477	68171	64406	09515	29907	72703	75049	61420	90245	41068	12575	93035	18373	73411
25614	54466	03882	67569	13505	02072	52211	58587	81052	77367	91151	75498	52612	77712
74941	42963	28344	64694	97337	34082	88194	13248	23073	83715	70668	43871	03296	32279
08517	09792	30412	82657	38555	79673	27647	18285	78424	42930	61875	25523	84968	65998
90480	10239	61101	84024	52762	99826	31814	59060	02842	76857	99268	73679	15476	92050
87847	84094	41958	29071	08573	15421	62826	33761	65766	17441	77041	30304	41012	21646
24391	94530	09143	27232	36091	34644	94255	13645	37154	30047	47498	55516	38359	79844
55283	62245	40637	76395	50206	98347	69760	95167	58415	19706	60279	21390	48122	87803
72589	45685	38527	12482	28532	14584	00017	71969	72628	46885	88039	29798	87566	42624
74982	12483	10512	26011	41648	52838	87777	39674	39136	25753	19433	84394	91015	56247
11886	35640	93381	21030	90738	44326	01786	81989	17993	03289	82912	96744	68234	98726

03777	40789	53138	84902	65517	67119	43016	45594	99378	26264	86455	41026	59843	91783
77434	88814	80202	35045	23861	66976	34547	62509	17306	39141	95877	56427	51271	21327
24031	79905	97125	99910	02012	98644	44131	90151	37559	85274	85888	83933	00595	05395
61411	26229	47339	39764	06203	89006	52147	66580	97816	46291	64695	19294	48456	65158
67605	28722	84993	40213	74203	17588	67884	65144	46757	76731	91814	82825	14921	09640
08399	54673	57424	52049	10022	80280	31618	30265	07223	01091	16857	12886	52200	25183
24661	01155	82608	14475	34709	18864	24666	80520	83407	31450	76563	13025	29970	71077
99946	90982	42196	89827	77686	97350	53420	85961	58836	63948	45483	41791	61909	92707
20479	03337	72012	68631	05734	66688	47879	27971	81284	71171	11497	16424	05229	33760
05878	82649	94108	04121	11154	97428	28550	50033	58366	16488	91552	31099	07497	37391
26765	43188	54789	34860	18404	87493	45808	69413	63670	65165	56961	36021	59176	45006
15069	48616	94053	66582	03240	19418	03006	92491	49077	15557	01484	40976	06847	95247
68642	49316	36286	17395	96578	75722	19864	04578	84155	99469	51186	12091	83697	21341
55787	36896	06645	76602	81478	47159	93149	92944	83403	35955	27043	82757	10447	95157
06646	80150	16643	42758	51005	50512	14497	88500	99547	95014	19788	52496	45661	82747
66780	49368	50975	19424	95851	61634	25554	87257	85018	02944	12394	02527	88003	77793
88208	75978	21467	13547	96535	86968	67281	08110	53381	54810	43583	96063	95300	86188
30356	70518	23955	20891	79713	56715	83046	79108	04521	41114	57848	31624	78945	25332
36986	65744	62601	56588	87171	27663	30679	25292	79814	97617	53606	77353	73868	87559
06312	95954	66193	09065	21998	34974	45725	00429	27951	58058	53538	71743	52870	53884
22033	94983	28160	08825	24088	23067	37465	08067	87338	13078	89357	05941	05270	82129
30452	89567	71981	33583	28892	18855	58394	39515	86250	42349	00832	41061	99545	26312
87612	59785	04514	02606	69365	28933	42218	91714	27058	40027	09691	54653	57232	56866
51590	24073	86172	55704	96959	73360	17055	66148	08078	20372	36932	71432	62588	72328
57163	99264	22454	55588	78458	91353	27547	27991	19627	63115	63099	59856	74653	69930
48780	80362	32025	83247	38147	91095	96062	50857	55831	62380	29003	80076	22990	60988
98912	00813	03183	15462	72115	02817	32788	30368	34305	07644	56157	65898	18561	37797
39402	14014	30652	27732	93899	78595	31964	36084	97566	34682	72458	98496	77969	14661
03842	24891	56006	26115	48801	26504	77741	82048	19748	83084	35668	23498	83585	31927
75596	26192	94550	45662	62572	34149	13402	85687	24250	65416	45033	48814	17003	76631
03591	98982	17722	51727	71369	62706	32211	09130	80850	19401	70052	37468	63436	82305
90888	86243	39999	02703	47268	00308	85152	09997	19070	04917	24351	48171	78505	66626
08573	24734	09760	51974	95354	16357	15969	12817	61896	31250	80066	38064	24088	98685
70629	30816	81429	71243	93048	43257	81387	95825	93165	20492	55200	56831	91286	79550
97402	96506	80817	15478	27808	04941	37273	69213	36638	85812	47422	16816	61468	53373
27250	03388	28225	96621	44165	59379	29178	87172	79478	58092	17710	63104	60684	97932
65971	48407	61392	11205	21776	03233	27068	46038	92918	25029	31686	15337	82092	17198
94424	24776	37573	52605	58251	42114	51162	20341	21685	79477	41030	33130	89819	35592
67035	34237	80576	98987	86458	05605	65635	39528	30420	75826	89077	50686	49972	97172
26583	89285	05050	72244	74086	97706	65120	16301	67917	21787	51785	59042	87324	30893
43684	96716	85263	40147	12867	00177	74088	19076	22915	72550	04976	52557	22961	71430
58977	02675	44573	43331	58957	22473	30080	35672	41973	70946	13049	35109	15024	45136
09507	92785	19629	14846	08127	93307	95036	78313	52446	01067	51465	62061	36698	04085
01738	05229	77024	21950	74783	42771	76450	63057	61615	34045	30701	18141	04768	00347
13403	24248	37469	17695	29452	29346	96446	72124	08531	06716	03668	98751	47708	03926
47813	95237	28518	84809	79497	25096	62922	86883	98553	32668	23650	12537	73446	80052
32411	26508	55034	61179	95124	83411	36322	87567	78589	69819	54656	09644	02350	65753
90886	05927	51880	67581	39310	01761	37345	36425	12883	77970	06829	65588	31084	04563
19712	56193	05978	74167	03347	36293	18145	39273	41897	64083	35547	67152	06188	94961
38191	90572	51923	10301	36802	90114	81194	55254	80329	49383	44090	15160	34222	23886
82520	77570	64671	06575	01907	54598	75591	12631	16676	49430	24133	66462	41574	16974
35050	44842	31469	43533	39343	79219	21618	89864	47156	13642	10654	88072	01650	18002
41269	69507	96835	61976	91903	54412	56619	65650	22130	25349	54952	08277	24992	53833
63840	22761	16566	18174	17073	15678	06395	72369	23714	69974	12838	71230	73589	55864
48616	17356	68349	30107	18604	60016	36241	30883	10979	28281	92015	73791	68528	54736

Source: © Cengage Learning

B | DISTRIBUTION OF CHI SQUARE

	Probability						
df	.99	.98	.95	.90	.80	.70	.50
1	.03157	.03628	.00393	.0158	.0642	.148	.455
2	.0201	.0404	.103	.211	.446	.713	1.386
3	.115	.185	.352	.584	1.005	1.424	2.366
4	.297	.429	.711	1.064	1.649	2.195	3.357
5	.554	.752	1.145	1.610	2.343	3.000	4.351
6	.872	1.134	1.635	2.204	3.070	3.828	5.348
7	1.239	1.564	2.167	2.833	3.822	4.671	6.346
8	1.646	2.032	2.733	3.490	4.594	5.528	7.344
9	2.088	2.532	3.325	4.168	5.380	6.393	8.343
10	2.558	3.059	3.940	4.865	6.179	7.267	9.342
11	3.053	3.609	4.575	5.578	6.989	8.148	10.341
12	3.571	4.178	5.226	6.304	7.807	9.034	11.340
13	4.107	4.765	5.892	7.042	8.634	9.926	12.340
14	4.660	5.368	6.571	7.790	9.467	10.821	13.339
15	5.229	5.985	7.261	8.547	10.307	11.721	14.339
16	5.812	6.614	7.962	9.312	11.152	12.624	15.338
17	6.408	7.255	8.672	10.085	12.002	13.531	16.338
18	7.015	7.906	9.390	10.865	12.857	14.440	17.338
19	7.633	8.567	10.117	11.651	13.716	15.352	18.338
20	8.260	9.237	10.851	12.443	14.578	16.266	19.337
21	8.897	9.915	11.591	13.240	15.445	17.182	20.337
22	9.542	10.600	12.338	14.041	16.314	18.101	21.337
23	10.196	11.293	13.091	14.848	17.187	19.021	22.337
24	10.856	11.992	13.848	15.659	18.062	19.943	23.337
25	11.524	12.697	14.611	16.473	18.940	20.867	24.337
26	12.198	13.409	15.379	17.292	19.820	21.792	25.336
27	12.879	14.125	16.151	18.114	20.703	22.719	26.336
28	13.565	14.847	16.928	18.939	21.588	23.647	27.336
29	14.256	15.574	17.708	19.768	22.475	24.577	28.336
30	14.953	16.306	18.493	20.599	23.364	25.508	29.336

	Probability						
df	.30	.20	.10	.05	.02	.01	.001
1	1.074	1.642	2.706	3.841	5.412	6.635	10.827
2	2.408	3.219	4.605	5.991	7.824	9.210	13.815
3	3.665	4.642	6.251	7.815	9.837	11.341	16.268
4	4.878	85.989	7.779	9.488	11.668	13.277	18.465
5	6.064	7.289	9.236	11.070	13.388	15.086	20.517
6	7.231	8.558	10.645	12.592	15.033	16.812	22.457
7	8.383	9.803	12.017	14.067	16.622	18.475	24.322
8	9.524	11.030	13.362	15.507	18.168	20.090	29.125
9	10.656	12.242	14.684	16.919	19.679	21.666	27.877
10	11.781	13.442	15.987	18.307	21.161	23.209	29.588
11	12.899	14.631	17.275	19.675	22.618	24.725	31.264
12	14.011	15.812	18.549	21.026	24.054	26.217	32.909
13	15.119	16.985	19.812	22.362	25.472	27.688	34.528
14	16.222	18.151	21.064	23.685	26.873	29.141	36.123
15	17.322	19.311	22.307	24.996	28.259	30.578	37.697
16	18.841	20.465	23.542	26.296	29.633	32.000	39.252
17	15.511	21.615	24.769	27.587	30.995	533.409	40.790
18	20.601	22.760	25.989	28.869	32.346	34.805	42.312
19	21.689	23.900	27.204	30.144	33.687	36.191	43.820
20	22.775	25.038	28.412	31.410	35.020	37.566	45.315
21	23.858	26.171	29.615	32.671	36.343	38.932	46.797
22	24.939	27.301	30.813	33.924	37.659	40.289	48.268
23	26.018	28.429	32.007	35.172	38.968	41.638	49.728
24	27.096	29.553	33.196	36.415	40.270	42.980	51.179
25	28.172	30.675	34.382	37.652	41.566	44.314	52.620
26	29.246	31.795	35.563	38.885	42.856	45.642	54.052
27	30.319	32.912	36.741	40.113	44.140	46.963	55.476
28	31.391	34.027	37.916	41.337	45.419	48.278	56.893
29	32.461	35.139	39.087	42.557	46.693	49.588	58.302
30	35.530	36.250	40.256	43.773	47.962	50.892	59.703

Source: From *Statistical Tables for Biological, Agricultural and Medical Research*, 6e, by Ronald A. Fisher and Dr. Frank Yates, Pearson Education Limited.

C | NORMAL CURVE AREAS

z	.00	.01	.02	.03	.04	.05	.06	.07	.08	.09
0.0	.0000	.0040	.0080	.0120	.0160	.0199	.0239	.0279	.0319	.0359
0.1	.0398	.0438	.0478	.0517	.0557	.0596	.0636	.0675	.0714	.0753
0.2	.0793	.0832	.0871	.0910	.0948	.0987	.1026	.1064	.1103	.1141
0.3	.1179	.1217	.1255	.1293	.1331	.1368	.1406	.1443	.1480	.1517
0.4	.1554	.1591	.1628	.1664	.1700	.1736	.1772	.1808	.1844	.1879
0.5	.1915	.1950	.1985	.2019	.2054	.2088	.2123	.2157	.2190	.2224
0.6	.2257	.2291	.2324	.2357	.2389	.2422	.2454	.2486	.2517	.2549
0.7	.2580	.2611	.2642	.2673	.2704	.2734	.2764	.2794	.2823	.2852
0.8	.2881	.2910	.2939	.2967	.2995	.3023	.3051	.3078	.3106	.3133
0.9	.3159	.3186	.3212	.3238	.3264	.3289	.3315	.3340	.3365	.3389
1.0	.3413	.3438	.3461	.3485	.3508	.3531	.3554	.3577	.3599	.3621
1.1	.3643	.3665	.3686	.3708	.3729	.3749	.3770	.3790	.3810	.3830
1.2	.3849	.3869	.3888	.3907	.3925	.3944	.3962	.3980	.3997	.4015
1.3	.4032	.4049	.4066	.4082	.4099	.4115	.4131	.4147	.4162	.4177
1.4	.4192	.4207	.4222	.4236	.4251	.4265	.4279	.4292	.4306	.4319
1.5	.4332	.4345	.4357	.4370	.4382	.4394	.4406	.4418	.4429	.4441
1.6	.4452	.4463	.4474	.4484	.4495	.4505	.4515	.4525	.4535	.4545
1.7	.4554	.4564	.4573	.4582	.4591	.4599	.4608	.4616	.4625	.4633
1.8	.4641	.4649	.4656	.4664	.4671	.4678	.4686	.4693	.4699	.4706
1.9	.4713	.4719	.4726	.4732	.4738	.4744	.4750	.4756	.4761	.4767
2.0	.4772	.4778	.4783	.4788	.4793	.4798	.4803	.4808	.4812	.4817
2.1	.4821	.4826	.4830	.4834	.4838	.4842	.4846	.4850	.4854	.4857
2.2	.4861	.4864	.4868	.4871	.4875	.4878	.4881	.4884	.4887	.4890
2.3	.4893	.4896	.4898	.4901	.4904	.4906	.4909	.4911	.4913	.4916
2.4	.4918	.4920	.4922	.4925	.4927	.4929	.4931	.4932	.4934	.4936
2.5	.4938	.4940	.4941	.4943	.4945	.4946	.4948	.4949	.4951	.4952
2.6	.4953	.4955	.4956	.4957	.4959	.4960	.4961	.4962	.4963	.4964
2.7	.4965	.4966	.4967	.4968	.4969	.4970	.4971	.4972	.4973	.4974
2.8	.4974	.4975	.4976	.4977	.4977	.4978	.4979	.4979	.4980	.4981
2.9	.4981	.4982	.4982	.4983	.4984	.4984	.4985	.4985	.4986	.4986
3.0	.4987	.4987	.4987	.4988	.4988	.4989	.4989	.4989	.4990	.4990

Source: Abridged from Table I of *Statistical Tables and Formulas*, by A. Hald (New York: John Wiley & Sons, Inc., 1952).

D | ESTIMATED SAMPLING ERROR

How to use this table: Find the intersection between the sample size and the approximate percentage distribution of the binomial in the sample. The number appearing at this intersection represents the estimated sampling error, at the 95 percent confidence level, expressed in percentage points (plus or minus).

Example: In the sample of 400 respondents, 60 percent answer yes and 40 percent answer no. The sampling error is estimated at plus or minus 4.9 percentage points. The confidence interval, then, is between 55.1 percent and 64.9 percent. We would estimate (95 percent confidence) that the proportion of the total population who would say yes is somewhere within that interval.

Binomial Percentage Distribution

Sample Size	50/50	60/40	70/30	80/20	90/10
100	0.0	9.8	9.2	8.0	6.0
200	7.1	6.9	6.5	5.7	4.2
300	5.8	5.7	5.3	4.6	3.5
400	5.0	4.9	4.6	4.0	3.5
500	4.5	4.4	4.1	3.6	2.7
600	4.1	4.0	3.7	3.3	2.4
700	3.8	3.7	3.5	3.2	3.0
800	3.5	3.5	3.2	2.8	2.1
900	3.3	3.3	3.1	2.7	2.0
1000	3.2	3.1	2.9	2.5	1.9
1100	3.0	3.0	2.8	2.4	1.8
1200	2.9	2.8	2.6	2.3	1.7
1300	2.8	2.7	2.5	2.2	1.7
1400	2.7	2.6	2.4	2.1	1.6
1500	2.6	2.5	2.4	2.1	1.5
1600	2.5	2.4	2.3	2.0	1.5
1700	2.4	2.4	2.2	1.9	1.5
1800	2.4	2.3	2.2	1.9	1.4
1900	2.3	2.2	2.1	1.8	1.4
2000	2.2	2.2	2.0	1.8	1.3

Source: © Cengage Learning

REFERENCES

Abrahao, B., P. Parigi, A. Gupta, K. Cook, and B. Abrahao. 2017. "Reputation Offsets Trust Judgments Based on Social Biases among Airbnb Users. *Proceedings of the National Academy of Sciences of the United States of America* 114(37): 9848–9853.

Abrams, K., and T. Gaiser. Online Focus Groups. *In* Field N, Lee R, Blank G (eds). 2017. *The Sage Handbook of Online Research Methods.* 2nd ed. pp. 435–450. London: Sage Publications, 2017.

Addona, Vittorio, and Philip A. Yates. 2010. "A Closer Look at the Relative Age Effect in the National Hockey League." *Journal of Quantitative Analysis in Sports* 6(4), Article 9.

Amaturo, Enrica, and Gabriella Punziano. 2017. "Blurry Boundaries: Internet, Big-New Data, and Mixed-Method Approach". In N. Carlo Lauro, Enrica Amaturo, Maria Gabriella Grassia, Biagio Aragona, & Marina Marino, *Data Science and Social Research: Epistemology, Methods, Technology and Applications* (pp. 35–55). Springer.

American Association for Public Opinion Research (AAPOR). 2017. "An Evaluation of the 2016 Election Polls in the United States, Released May 4, 2017." Accessed February 20, 2019 (https://www.aapor.org/Education-Resources/Reports/An-Evaluation-of-2016-Election-Polls-in-the-U-S.aspx).

American Educational Research Association, American Psychological Association, and National Council on Measurement in Education (AERA, APA, and NCME). 2014. *Standards for Educational and Psychological Testing.* Washington, DC: American Educational Research Association.

Aminzadeh, Faranak, Anna Byszewski, Frank J. Molnar, and Marg Eisner. 2007. "Emotional Impact of Dementia Diagnosis: Exploring Persons with Dementia and Caregivers' Perspectives." *Aging & Mental Health* 11:281–290.

Anderson, Ashton, Sharad Goel, Gregory Huber, Neil Malhotra, & Duncan J. Watts. (2014). "Political Ideology and Racial Preferences in Online Dating." *Sociological Science* 1(3), 28–40.

Arribas-Ayllon, M., and V. Walkerdine. 2008. Foucauldian Discourse Analysis. *In* Willig, C., & Stainton-Rogers, W. *The SAGE Handbook of Qualitative Research in Psychology* (pp. 91–108). London: SAGE.

Associated Press. 2012. "Deadliest Shootings around the Globe." *The Huffington Post*, September 19. Retrieved December 30, 2015 (http://www.huffingtonpost.com/2012/07/20/deadliest-mass-shootings_n_1688820.html).

Associated Press. 2014. "California Strengthens College Sexual Consent Laws." *The Star*, September 29. Retrieved August 21, 2015 (http://www.thestar.com/news/world/2014/09/29/california_strengthens_college_sexual_consent_laws.html).

Atkinson, Michael. 2009. "Parkour, Anarcho-Environmentalism, and Poiesis." *Journal of Sport & Social Issues* 33(2):169–194.

Auster, Carol J. 1985. "Manuals for Socialization: Examples from Girl Scout Handbooks 1913–1984." *Qualitative Sociology* 8(4):359–367.

Ayres, I., M. Banaji, and C. Jolls. 2015. "Race Effects on eBay." *RAND Journal of Economics* 46(4), 891–917.

Babbie, Earl. 1970. *Science and Morality in Medicine.* Berkeley: University of California Press.

Backstrom, L., P. Boldi, M. Rosa, J. Ugander, and S. Vigna. 2012. Four Degrees of Separation. In *Proceedings of the 4th Annual ACM Web Science Conference* (pp. 33–42).

Bailey, Carol A. 2006. *A Guide to Field Research.* 2nd ed. Thousand Oaks, CA: Pine Forge Press.

Bailey, William C. 1975. "Murder and Capital Punishment." In Chambliss, W.J. (ed.). *Criminal Law in Action.* New York: Wiley.

Bailey, William C., and Ruth D. Peterson. 1994. "Murder, Capital Punishment, and Deterrence: A Review of the Evidence and an Examination on Police Killings." *Journal of Social Issues* 50:53–74.

Baldassarri, D., and M. Abascal. 2017. "Field Experiments Across the Social Sciences." *Annual Review of Sociology* 43:41–73.

Banerjee, Abhijit, and Esther Duflo. 2012. *Poor Economics: A Radical Rethinking of the Way to Fight Global Poverty.* Public Affairs.

Bapna, Ravi, Jui Ramaprasad, Galit Shmueli, and Akhmed Umyarov. 2016. "One-Way Mirrors in Online Dating: A Randomized Field Experiment." *Management Science* 62(11):3100–3122.

Baram-Tsabari, A., E. Segev, and A. Sharon. 2017. Whats New? The Applications of Data Mining and Big Data in the Social Sciences. In Fielding, N., Lee, R., and Blank, G. (eds.). *The SAGE Handbook of Online Research Methods* (pp. 92–106). London: SAGE.

Bareiss, W. (2017). "Adolescent Daughters and Ritual Abjection: Narrative Analysis of Self-injury in Four US Films." *Journal of Medical Humanities* 38(3):319–337.

Barkay, T. 2013. "When Business and Community Meet: A Case Study of Coca-Cola." *Critical Sociology* 39(2):277–293.

Barnsley, Roger H., and A. H. Thompson. 1988. "Birthdate and Success in Minor Hockey: The Key to the NHL." *Canadian Journal of Behavioural Science* 20(2):167–176.

Baron, Stephen W. 1997. "Canadian Male Street Skinheads: Street Gang or Street Terrorists." *Canadian Review of Sociology and Anthropology* 34:125–154.

Bart, Pauline, and Patricia O'Brien. 1985. *Stopping Rape: Successful Survival Strategies.* New York: Pergamon.

Beach, Mary. 2015. "Gender Pay Gap in Canada More Than Twice Global Average, Study Shows." *The Globe and Mail*, May 5. Retrieved August 8, 2015 (http://www.theglobeandmail.com/news/british-columbia/gender-pay-gap-in-canada-more-than-twice-global-average-study-shows/article24274586/).

Beaumont, Jill. 2011. "Measuring National Well-Being: A Discussion Paper on Domains and Measures." London: Office of National Statistics. Retrieved June 8, 2015 (www.ons.gov.uk/ons/dcp171766_240726.pdf).

Becker, Howard S. 1953. "Becoming a Marijuana User." *American Journal of Sociology* 59:235–242.

Becker, Howard S. 1996. "The Epistemology of Qualitative Research." In *Ethnography and Human Development: Context and Meaning in Social Inquiry*, edited by R. Jessor, A. Colby, and R. Shweer, pp. 53–84. Chicago: University of Chicago Press.

Becker, Howard S. 1998. *Tricks of the Trade: How to Think about Your Research While You're Doing It.* Chicago: University of Chicago Press.

Bellah, Robert N. 1957. *Tokugawa Religion.* Glencoe, IL: Free Press.

Bellah, Robert N. 1967. "Research Chronicle: Tokugawa Religion." Pp. 164–185 in *Sociologists at Work*, edited by Phillip E. Hammond. Garden City, NY: Anchor Books.

Bellah, Robert N. 1970. "Christianity and Symbolic Realism." *Journal for the Scientific Study of Religion* 9:89–96.

Bellah, Robert N. 1974. "Comment on the Limits of Symbolic Realism." *Journal for the Scientific Study of Religion* 13:487–489.

Benaquisto, Lucia. 2000. "Inattention to Sanctions in Criminal Conflict," in Robert Silverman, James Teevan, Vincent Sacco (Eds.), *Crime in Canadian Society.* 6th ed. Toronto: Harcourt Brace and Co.

Benaquisto, Lucia, and Philippe Couton. 2001. "The Liberal Use of Repression: Enhanced Judicial Penetration and the Establishment of the French Third Republic." Paper presented at the American Sociological Association Meetings, Anaheim, CA.

Benton, J. Edwin, and John L. Daly. 1991. "A Question Order Effect in a Local Government Survey." *Public Opinion Quarterly* 55:640–642.

Berg, Bruce L. 2007. *Qualitative Research Methods for the Social Sciences.* 6th ed. Boston: Pearson, Allyn and Bacon.

Berg, Bruce L., and Howard Lune. 2011. *Qualitative Research Methods for the Social Sciences,* 8th ed. Upper Saddle River, NJ: Pearson Education, Inc.

Berger, Peter L., and Thomas Luckmann. 1966. *The Social Construction of Reality: A Treatise in the Sociology of Knowledge.* Garden City, NY: Anchor Books.

Besbris, Max, Jacob William Faber, Peter Rich, and Patrick Sharkey. 2015. "Effect of Neighborhood Stigma on Economic Transactions." *Proceedings of the National Academy of Sciences* 112(16):4994–4998.

Bethlehem, J., and B. Schouten. 2016. Nonresponse Error: Detection and Correction. In Wolf, C., Joye, D., Smith, T. W., & Fu, Y. *The SAGE Handbook of Survey Methodology* (pp. 558–578). London: SAGE.

Beveridge, W. I. B. 1950. *The Art of Scientific Investigation.* New York: Vintage Books.

Bian, Yanjie. 1994. *Work and Inequality in Urban China.* Albany, NY: State University of New York Press.

Bielby, William T., and Denise Bielby. 1999. "Organizational Mediation of Project-Based Labor Markets: Talent Agencies and the Careers of Screenwriters." *American Sociological Review* 64:64–85.

Birchfield, R. W. 1998. *The New Fowler's Modern English Usage.* 3rd ed. New York: Oxford University Press.

Bischoping, Katherine, and Amber Gazso. 2016. *Analyzing Talk in the Social Sciences.* Thousand Oaks, CA: Sage.

Black, Donald. 1970. "Production of Crime Rates." *American Sociological Review* 35 (August):733–748.

Blommaert, L., M. Coenders, and F. van Tubergen. 2014. "Discrimination of Arabic-Named Applicants in the Netherlands: An Internet-Based Field Experiment Examining Different Phases in Online Recruitment Procedures." *Social Forces* 92:957–982.

Blustein, D., S. Kozan, and A. Connors-Kellgren. (2013). Unemployment and Underemployment: A Narrative

Analysis about Loss. *Journal of Vocational Behavior*, 82(3):256–265.

Bolstein, Richard. 1991. "Comparison of the Likelihood to Vote among Preelection Poll—Respondents and Nonrespondents." *Public Opinion Quarterly* 55:648–650.

Boltanski, L., and E. Chiapello. 2007. *The New Spirit of Capitalism*. Brooklyn, NY: Verso Press.

Bottomore, T. B., and Maximilien Rubel, eds. [1843] 1956. *Karl Marx: Selected Writings in Sociology and Social Philosophy*. Translated by T. B. Bottomore. New York: McGraw-Hill.

Boulos, D., P. Yan, D. Schanzer, R.S. Remis, and C. Archibald. 2006. "Estimates of HIV Prevalence and Incidence in Canada, 2005." *Canada Communicable Disease Report 2006* 32(15):165–174.

Boyd, Jade, and Thomas Kerr. 2016. "Policing 'Vancouver's Mental Health Crisis': A Critical Discourse Analysis." *Critical Public Health* 26:418–433.

Bredemeier, Harry C. 1998. *Experience vs. Understanding*. New York: Transaction Publishers.

Bright, Robert, Elaine Coburn, Julie Faye, Derek Gafijczuk, Karen Hollander, Janny Jung, and Helen Syrmbros. 1999. "Mainstream and Marginal Newspaper Coverage of the 1995 Quebec Referendum: An Inquiry into the Functioning of the Canadian Public Sphere." *Canadian Review of Sociology and Anthropology* 36:313–330.

Broadbent Institute. 2014. "The Wealth Gap: Perceptions and Misconceptions in Canada." Retrieved August 19, 2015 (https://www.broadbentinstitute.ca/the_wealth_gap).

Brown, Karen N., and David MacAlister. 2006. "Violence and Threats against Lawyers Practising in Vancouver, Canada." *Canadian Journal of Criminology & Criminal Justice* 48:543–571.

Bruner, J. 1986. *Actual Minds, Possible Worlds*. Cambridge, MA: Harvard University Press.

Brym, Robert, Lance W. Roberts, Lisa Strohschein, and John Lie. 2016. *Sociology: Your Compass for a New World*. Toronto: Nelson.

Brym, Robert, Lance W. Roberts, Lisa Strohschein. 2018. *Sociology: Compass for a New Social World*. Toronto: Nelson.

Bryman, Alan. 2006. "Integrating Quantitative and Qualitative Research: How Is It Done? *Qualitative Research* 6(1):97–113.

Burawoy, M., A. Burton, A. A. Ferguson, K. J. Fox, J. Gamson, N. Gartrell, L. Hurst, C. Kurzman, L. Salzinger, J. Schiffman, and S. Ui, eds. 1991. *Ethnography Unbound: Power and Resistance in the Modern Metropolis*. Berkeley, CA: University of California Press.

Buhrmester, M. D., T. Kwang, and S.D. Gosling. 2011. "Amazon's Mechanical Turk: A New Source of Inexpensive, Yet High-Quality Data?" *Perspectives on Psychological Science* 6:3–5.

Buhrmester, M., S. Talaifar, and S. Gosling. 2018. "An Evaluation of Amazon's Mechanical Turk, Its Rapid Rise, and Its Effective Use." *Perspectives on Psychological Science* 13(2):149–154.

Burr, V. 1995. *An Introduction to Social Constructionism*. London: Sage.

Cabrera, S., and C. Williams. 2014. "Consuming for the Social Good: Marketing, Consumer Citizenship, and the Possibilities of Ethical Consumption." *Critical Sociology* 40(3):349–367.

Campbell, Donald, and Julian Stanley. 1963. *Experimental and Quasi-Experimental Designs for Research*. Chicago: Rand McNally.

Campbell, Marie L. 1998. "Institutional Ethnography and Experience as Data." *Qualitative Sociology* 21:55–73.

Carranza, Mirna E. 2007. "Building Resilience and Resistance against Racism and Discrimination among Salvadorian Female Youth in Canada." *Child & Family Social Work* 12:390–398.

Carroll, Lewis. [1872] 1999. *Through the Looking Glass*. London: Dover Publications.

Carroll, W. 2017. "Canada's Carbon-Capital Elite: A Tangled Web of Corporate Power." *Canadian Journal of Sociology* 42(3):225–260.

CAUT Bulletin. 2014. "Court Upholds Researchers' Right to Protect Confidential Information." 62(2), February. Retrieved April 22, 2015 (https://www.cautbulletin.ca/default.asp?SectionID=0&SectionName=&VolID=376&VolumeName=No%202&VolumeStartDate=February%2018,%202014&EditionID=40&EditionName=Vol%2061&EditionStartDate=January%2023,%202014&ArticleID=0).

CBC News. 2010. "Canadians Split on Pot, Death Penalty: Poll." Retrieved August 31, 2012 (http://www.cbc.ca/news/canada/story/2010/03/18/ekos-poll018.html).

CCJS: Canadian Centre for Justice Statistics. 1999. *The Juristat Reader*. Toronto: Thompson Educational Publishing Inc.

CIHR: Canadian Institutes of Health Research. 2007. CIHR Guidelines for Health Research Involving Aboriginal People. Ottawa.

Centola, Damon. 2010. "The Spread of Behavior in an Online Social Network Experiment." *Science* 329(5996):1194–1197.

Chadwick, K., and P. Collins. 2015. "Examining the Relationship between Social Support Availability, Urban Center Size, and Self-Perceived Mental Health of Recent Immigrants to Canada: A Mixed-Methods Analysis." *Social Science & Medicine* 128: 220–230.

Chamberland, L., G. Émond, D. Julien, J. Otis, and B. Ryan. 2010. L'impact de l'homophobie et de la violence homophobe sur la persévérance et la réussite scholaires . Rapport de Recherche: Québec Ministère de l'Éducation, du Loisir et du Sport (MELS) et le Fonds Québécois de la recherche sur la société et la culture (FQRSC). Retrieved from http://www.fqrsc.gouv.qc.ca/fr/rechercheexpertise/projets/rapports-recherche.php#PRS2006.

Chan, Kwok B. 1983. "Coping with Aging and Managing Self-Identity: The Social World of the Elderly Chinese Women." *Canadian Ethnic Studies* 15:36–50.

Chandler, J., & D. Shapiro. 2016. "Conducting Clinical Research Using Crowdsourced Convenience Samples." *Annual Review of Clinical Psychology* 12:53–81.

Charmaz, Kathy. 2014. *Constructing Grounded Theory: A Practical Guide through Qualitative Research.* 2nd ed. Thousand Oaks, CA: Sage.

Chen, Yan, and Joseph Konstan. 2015. "Online Field Experiments: A Selective Survey of Methods." *Journal of the Economic Science Association* 1(1):29–42.

Choi, H., and H. Varian. 2012. "Predicting the Present with Google Trends." *Economic Record* 88(s1):2–9.

Chou, C. 2001. "Internet Heavy Use and Addiction among Taiwanese College Students: An Online Interview Study." *CyberPsychology & Behavior* 4(5):573–585.

Christia, Fotini, and Ruben Enikolopov. 2013. "Too Much of a Good Thing." *Foreign Policy*, December 18, 2013. Retrieved February 18, 2016 (http://foreignpolicy .com/2013/12/18/too-much-of-a-good-thing/).

Christian, Leah Melani, Don A. Dillman, and Jolene D. Smyth. 2007. "Helping Respondents Get It Right the First Time: The Influence of Words, Symbols, and Graphics in Web Surveys." *Public Opinion Quarterly* 71:113–125.

CIRA. 2014. *Canadian Internet Registration Authority's 2014 Factbook.* Retrieved January 4, 2015 (https://cira.ca/factbook/2014/the-canadian-internet.html).

Clarke, Juanne N., and Michelle M. Everest. 2006. "Cancer in the Mass Print Media: Fear, Uncertainty and the Medical Model." *Social Science & Medicine* 62:2591–600.

Clouston, Sean A. P., and Amélie Quesnel-Vallée. 2012. "The Role of Defamilialization in the Relationship between Partnership and Self-Rated Health: A

Coppock, A., A. Guess, and J. Ternovski. 2016. "When Treatments Are Tweets: A Network Mobilization Experiment over Twitter." *Political Behavior* 38(1):105–128.

Correll, S., S. Benard, and I. Paik. 2007. "Getting a Job: Is There a Motherhood Penalty? 1." *American Journal of Sociology* 112(5):1297–1338.

Cohn, Nate. 2017. "A 2016 Review: Why Key State Polls Were Wrong About Trump." *New York Times.* Retrieved February 20, 2019. (https://www.nytimes.com/2017/05/31/upshot/a-2016-review-why-key-state-polls-were-wrong-about-trump.html).

Coldevin, Gary O. 1976. "Some Effects of Frontier Television in a Canadian Eskimo Community." *Journalism Quarterly* 53:34–39.

Collins, G. C., and Timothy B. Blodgett. 1981. "Sexual Harassment ... Some See It ... Some Won't." *Harvard Business Review* March–April:76–95.

Collins, Randall. 2008. *Violence: A Micro-Sociological Theory.* Princeton: Princeton University Press.

Collins, Randall. 2012. "Mona Lisa Is No Mystery for Micro-Sociology." *The Sociological Eye*, December 27. Retrieved July 7, 2015 (http://sociological-eye.blogspot.com/2012/12/mona-lisa-is-no-mystery-for-micro.html).

Conrad, Clifton F. 1978. "A Grounded Theory of Academic Change." *Sociology of Education* 51:101–112.

Cook, Thomas D., and Donald T. Campbell. 1979. *Quasi-Experimentation: Design and Analysis Issues for Field Settings.* Chicago: Rand McNally.

Couper, Mick P. 2001. "Web Surveys: A Review of Issues and Approaches." *Public Opinion Quarterly* 64(4):464–494.

Couper, Mick P. 2008. *Designing Effective Web Surveys.* New York: Cambridge University Press.

Couper, Mick P., and Peter V. Miller. 2008. "Web Survey Methods: Introduction." *Public Opinion Quarterly* 72(5):831–835.

Creswell, John W., and Vicki I. Plano Clark. 2011. *Designing and Conducting Mixed Methods Research.* 2nd ed. Thousand Oaks, CA: Sage.

Cross-National Comparison of Canada and the United States." *Social Science & Medicine* 75(8):1342–1349.

Currie, S.R., D.C. Hodgins, and D.M. Casey. 2013. "Validity of the Problem Gambling Severity Index Interpretive Categories." *Journal of Gambling Studies* 29:311–327.

D'Ailly, Hsiao. 2004. "The Role of Choice in Children's Learning: A Distinctive Cultural and Gender Difference in Efficacy, Interest, and Effort." *Canadian Journal of Behavioural Science* 36:17–29.

The Daily. 2011. "Canadian Internet Use Survey." May 25. Retrieved September 9, 2012 (http://www.statcan.gc.ca/daily-quotidien/110525/dq110525b-eng.htm).

The Daily. 2014. "Residential Telephone Survey, 2013." June 23. Retrieved April 8, 2019

(https://www150.statcan.gc.ca/n1/daily-quotidien/140623/dq140623a-eng.pdf).

Davis, Fred. 1973. "The Martian and the Convert: Ontological Polarities in Social Research." *Urban Life* 2(3):333–343.

Davis, James A. 1992. "Changeable Weather in a Cooling Climate atop the Liberal Plateau: Conversion and Replacement in Forty-Two General Social Survey Items, 1972–1989." *Public Opinion Quarterly* 56:261–306.

Deakin, H., and K. Wakefield. 2014. "Skype Interviewing: Reflections of Two PhD Researchers." *Qualitative Research* 14(5):603–616.

Dodds, P., R. Muhamad, D. Watts, and P. Dodds. 2003. An Experimental Study of Search in Global Social Networks. *Science* 301(5634):827–829.

Doob, Anthony N., and Jane B. Sprott. 2006. "Punishing Youth Crime in Canada: The Blind Men and the Elephant." *Punishment & Society* 8:223–233.

Dooling, K., and M. Rachlis. 2010. "Vancouver's Supervised Injection Facility Challenges Canada's Drug Laws." *Canadian Medical Association Journal* 182(13):1440–1444.

Doyle, Sir Arthur Conan. [1891] 1892. "A Scandal in Bohemia." First published in *The Strand,* July 1891. Reprinted in *The Original Illustrated Sherlock Holmes.* Secaucus, NJ: Castle, pp. 11–25.

Durkheim, Émile. [1893] 1964. *The Division of Labor in Society.* Translated by George Simpson. New York: Free Press.

Durkheim, Émile. [1897] 1951. *Suicide.* Glencoe, IL: Free Press.

Dyke, Sarah. 2013. "Utilising a Blended Ethnographic Approach to Explore the Online and Offline Lives of Pro-Ana Community Members." *Ethnography and Education* 8(2):146–161.

Edelman, Benjamin, G., Michael Luca and Dan Svirsky. 2016. "Racial Discrimination in the Sharing Economy: Evidence from a Field Experiment." *American Economic Journal: Applied Economics* 9(2):1–22. Harvard Business School NOM Unit Working Paper No. 16-069.

Edgerton, J.D., J. Biegun, and L.W. Roberts. 2016. "Player Behavioral Tracking and Personalized Feedback in Online Gambling: Implications for Prevention and Treatment of Problem Gambling." *Journal of Addiction and Prevention* 4(2):8.

Edgerton, J. D., T. A. Melnyk, and L. W. Roberts. 2014. "Problem Gambling and the Youth-to-Adulthood Transition: Assessing Problem Gambling Severity Trajectories in a Sample of Young Adults." *Journal of Gambling Studies* (online first) DOI:10.1007/s10899-014-9501-2.

Elder-Vass, Dave. 2013. *The Reality of Social Construction.* Cambridge: Cambridge University Press.

Erickson, Patricia. 1998. "Neglected and Rejected: A Case Study of the Impact of Social Research on Canadian Drug Policy." *Canadian Journal of Sociology* 23:263–280.

Evans, Joel R. and Anil Mathur. 2018. "The Value of Online Surveys: A Look Back and a Look Ahead." *Internet Research,* 28(4):854–887, https://doi.org/10.1108/IntR-03-2018-0089.

Fairclough, N. 2001. "Critical Discourse Analysis." In M. McHoul and M. Rapley (eds.). *How to Analyze Talk in Institutional Settings: A Casebook of Methods* (pp. 25–38). London : Continuum Books.

Fedoroff, J. Paul, and Beverley Moran. 1997. "Myths and Misconceptions about Sex Offenders." *The Canadian Journal of Human Sexuality* 6:263–276.

Feldman, Linda, Philippa Holowaty, Linda Shortt, Bart Harvey, Katherine Rannie, and Alykhan Jamal. 1997. "A Comparison of the Demographic, Lifestyle, and Sexual Behaviour Characteristics of Virgin and Non-Virgin Adolescents." *The Canadian Journal of Human Sexuality* 6:197–209.

Ferris, J. and H. Wynne. 2001. *The Canadian Problem Gambling Index: Final Report.* Ottawa, ON: Canadian Centre on Substance Abuse.

Festinger, L., H. W. Reicker, and S. Schachter. 1956. *When Prophecy Fails.* Minneapolis, MN: University of Minnesota Press.

Fikretoglu, Deniz, Alain Brunet, Norbert Schmitz, Stephane Guay, and David Pedlar. 2006. "Posttraumatic Stress Disorder and Treatment Seeking in a Nationally Representative Canadian Military Sample." *Journal of Traumatic Stress* 19:847–858.

Financial Consumer Agency of Canada. 2015. "Focus Groups to Evaluate Consumer Comprehension of FCAC Materials." Retrieved July 22, 2015 (http://www .fcac-acfc.gc.ca/Eng/resources/researchSurveys/Pages/FocusGro-Groupesd.aspx).

Foreign Affairs, Trade, and Development Canada. 2015. "Summative Evaluation of Canada's Afghanistan Development Program 2004–2005 to 2012–2013: Synthesis Report." Retrieved July 22, 2015 (http://www .international.gc.ca/department-ministere/evaluation/2015/dev_eval_afghanistan01.aspx?lang=eng).

Forster, Christina A., Brian Evans, and Ronald J. Fisher. 1990. "Evaluation of a Pilot Project in Service Coordination." *Evaluation Review* 14:616–631.

Foster, I., R. Ghani, R. Jarmin, F. Kreuter, & J. Lane. 2017. *Big Data and Social Science: A Practical Guide to Methods and Ttools.* Boca Raton, FL: CRC Press.

Fox, Katherine J. 1991. "The Politics of Prevention: Ethnographers Combat AIDS among Drug Users." In *Ethnography Unbound: Power and Resistance in the Modern Metropolis*, edited by M. Burawoy, A. Burton, A. A. Ferguson, K. J. Fox. pp. 227–249.

Frank, A. 2017. "What Is the Story with Sustainability? A Narrative Analysis of Diverse and Contested Understandings. *Journal of Environmental Studies and Sciences* 7(2):310–323.

Frank, T. 1997. *The Conquest of Cool: Business Culture, Counterculture, and the Rise of Hip Consumerism.* Chicago, IL: University of Chicago Press.

Fraser Institute. 2015. Income Inequality Measurement Sensitivities. Retrieved August 19, 2015 (http://www.fraserinstitute.org/research-news/display .aspx?id=23121).

Fuller, Robert. 2004. *Somebodies and Nobodies: Overcoming the Abuses of Rank.* New Society Publishers.

Funk, Laura. 2013. "Home Healthcare and Family Responsibility: A Critical Discourse Analysis of Talk and Text. *Healthcare Policy*, 9:86–97.

Gaddis S.M. 2015. "Discrimination in the Credential Society: An Audit Study of Race and College Selectivity in the Labor Market." *Social Forces* 93:1451–1479.

Galarneau, Diane, René Morissette, and Jeannine Usalcas. 2013. "What Has Changed for Young People in Canada?" pp. 1–12 in *Insights on Canadian Society*, Statistics Canada, July. Catalogue number 75-006-X.

Galesic, Mirta, Roger Tourangeau, Mick P. Couper, and Frederick G. Conrad. 2008. "Eye-Tracking Data: New Insights on Response Order Effects and Other Cognitive Shortcuts in Survey Responding." *Public Opinion Quarterly* 72(5):892–913.

Gall, John. 1975. *Systemantics: How Systems Work and Especially How They Fail.* New York: Quadrangle.

Galloway, Gloria. 2015. "NDP the Party Most-Trusted by Canadian Families, Poll Shows." *The Globe and Mail*, June 12. Retrieved June 17, 2015 (http://www.theglobeandmail.com/news/politics/ndp-the-party-most-trusted-by-canadian-families-poll-shows/article24928628/).

Galloway, Kristin L. 2011. "Focus Groups in the Virtual World: Implications for the Future of Evaluation," *Really New Directions in Education: Young Evaluators Perspectives*, S. Mathison, ed., San Francisco, CA: Jossey-Bass and American Evaluation Association (pp. 47–51). New Directions for Evaluation, 131.

Gans, Herbert J. 1962. *Urban Villagers.* New York: Free Press.

Gans, Herbert J. 1967. *The Levittowners.* New York: Random House.

Gartner, Rosemary, and Ross Macmillan. 2000. "Victim–Offender Relationship and Reporting Crimes of Violence against Women." Pp. 128–139 in *Crime in Canadian Society*, 6th ed., edited by Robert Silverman, James Teevan, and Vincent Sacco. Toronto: Harcourt Brace & Co.

Gaudet, Stephanie, Martin Cooke, and Joanna Jacob. 2011. "Working after Childbirth: A Lifecourse Transition Analysis of Canadian Women from the 1970s to the 2000s." *Canadian Review of Sociology* 48(2):153–180.

Gaventa, John. 1991. "Towards a Knowledge Democracy: Viewpoints on Participatory Research in North America." Pp. 121–131 in *Action and Knowledge: Breaking the Monopoly with Participatory Action-Research*, edited by O. Fals-Borda and M. A. Rahman. New York: Apex Press.

Gazso, Amber. 2007. "Balancing Expectations for Employability and Family Responsibilities while on Social Assistance: Low-Income Mothers' Experiences in Three Canadian Provinces." *Family Relations* 56(5):454–466.

Gedalof, I. 2018. *Narratives of Difference in an Age of Austerity.* London: Palgrave Macmillan UK.

Gee, Laura K. 2018. "The More You Know: Information Effects on Job Application Rates in a Large Field Experiment." *Management Science* (advance online) https://doi.org/10.1287/mnsc.2017.2994.

Geertz, C. 1973. "Thick Description." In C. Geertz (ed.), *The Interpretation of Cultures: Selected Essays* (pp. 3–30). New York, NY: Basic Books.

Gelfand, M., J. Raver, L. Nishii, L. Leslie, J. Lun, et al. 2011. "Differences between Tight and Loose Cultures: A 33-Nation Study." *Science*, May 27(33):1100–1104.

Gergen, K., and M. Pallak. 1985. The Social Constructionist Movement in Modern Psychology. *American Psychologist*, 40(3):266–275.

Gilligan, J. 1997. Violence – Reflections on a National Epidemic. New York: Vintage Books.

Gillis, A. R. 1989. "Crime and State Surveillance in Nineteenth-Century France." *American Journal of Sociology* 95:307–341.

Gillis, A. R. 1994. "Literacy and the Civilization of Violence in 19th-Century France." *Sociological Forum* 9:371–401.

Gillis, A. R. 1996. "So Long as They Both Shall Live: Marital Dissolution and the Decline of Domestic Homicide in France, 1852–1909." *American Journal of Sociology* 101:1273–1305.

Gladwell, Malcolm. 2008. *Outliers: The Story of Success.* New York: Little, Brown and Co.

Glaser, Barney, and Anselm Strauss. 1967. *The Discovery of Grounded Theory.* Chicago: Aldine.

Glass, Ira. 2015. "Cops See It Differently: Part 2." *This American Life*, February 13. Retrieved February 20, 2015 (http://www.thisamericanlife.org/radio-archives/episode/548/transcript).

Glock, Charles Y., Benjamin B. Ringer, and Earl R. Babbie. 1967. *To Comfort and to Challenge.* Berkeley, CA: University of California Press.

Goel, Vindu. 2014. "Facebook Tinkers with Users' Emotions in News Feed Experiment, Stirring Outcry." *The New York Times*, June 29. Retrieved June 22, 2015 (http://www.nytimes.com/2014/06/30/technology/facebook-tinkers-with-users-emotions-in-news-feed-experiment-stirring-outcry.html).

Goffman, Erving. 1961. *Asylums: Essays on the Social Situation of Mental Patients and Other Inmates.* Chicago: Aldine.

Goffman, Erving. 1963. *Stigma: Notes on the Management of a Spoiled Identity.* Englewood Cliffs, NJ: Prentice Hall.

Goffman, Erving. 1974. *Frame Analysis.* Cambridge, MA: Harvard University Press.

Goffman, Erving. 1979. *Gender Advertisements.* New York: Harper & Row.

Goldstein, Joseph, and Marc Santora. 2014. "Staten Island Man Died from Chokehold during Arrest, Autopsy Finds." *The New York Times,* August 1. Retrieved February 20, 2015 (http://www.nytimes.com/2014/08/02/nyregion/staten-island-man-died-from-officers-chokehold-autopsy-finds.html).

Gorman, Christine. 2001. "Breast Cancer: A Diagnosis of Deceit." *Time Magazine World,* June 24, 2001. Retrieved August 17, 2012 (http://www.time.com/time/magazine/article/0,9171,164051,00.html).

Goyder, J., and K. Frank. 2007. "A Scale of Occupational Prestige in Canada, Based on NORC Groups." *Canadian Journal of Sociology* 32:63–83.

Granville, Kevin. 2018. "Facebook and Cambridge Analytica: All You Need to Know." *New York Times.* March 19. Retrieved December 10, 2018.

Gray, Emily, Rea Robey, and Daniel Cameron. 2007. "Attitudes to the Death Penalty." Ipsos MORI, International Trend Unit. Retrieved September 10, 2008 (http://www.ipsosmori.com/_assets/internationalsocialtrends/attitudes-to-death-penalty.pdf).

Green, M., C. Sonn, C. Howarth, and D. Hook. 2005. Examining Discourses of Whiteness and the Potential for Reconciliation. *Journal of Community & Applied Social Psychology* 15(6):478–492.

Green, T. and J. Peloza. 2014. "How Do Consumers Infer Corporate Social Responsibility? The Role of Organisation Size." *Journal of Consumer Behaviour* 13(4):282–293.

Greene, J. C., V.J. Caracelli, and W.F. Graham. 1989. "Toward a Conceptual Framework for Mixed-Method Evaluation Designs. *Educational Evaluation and Policy Analysis* 11(3):255–274.

Greene, Robert. 2013. Unequal Childhoods—Book Review. Retrieved August 19, 2015 (http://www.criticalpages.com/2013/unequal-childhoods/).

Grekul, Jana, Harvey Krahn, and Dave Odynak. 2004. "Sterilizing the 'Feeble-Minded': Eugenics in Alberta, Canada, 1929–1972." *Journal of Historical Sociology* 17(4):358–384.

Gremillion, H. 2003. *Feeding Anorexia: Gender and Power at the Treatment Centre.* Durham: Duke University Press.

Grenier, Marc. 1994. "Native Indians in the English-Canadian Press: The Case of the 'Oka Crisis'." *Media, Culture & Society* 16:313–336.

Grimes, William. 2008. "If You Want to Observe 'Em, Join 'Em." *The New York Times,* January 16. Retrieved July 15, 2015 (http://www.nytimes.com/2008/01/16/books/16grimes.html?_r=1&).

Guppy, Neil, and George Gray. 2008. *Successful Surveys: Research Methods and Practice.* 4th ed. Toronto: Nelson.

Hager, Mike. 2015. "Confidentiality Agreement Handcuffs Prominent Assisted-Suicide Researcher." *The Globe and Mail,* January 6. Retrieved April 18, 2015 (http://www.theglobeandmail.com/news/british-columbia/assisted-suicide-researcher-fights-for-subjects-anonymity/article22309317/).

Harlton, Shauna-Vi, Norah Keating, and Janet Fast. 1998. "Defining Eldercare for Policy and Practice: Perspectives Matter." *Family Relations* 47:281–288.

Hartnagel, Timothy F. 1997. "Crime among the Provinces: The Effect of Geographic Mobility." *Canadian Journal of Criminology* 39:387–402.

Hassan, Farzana. 2014. "Men Need Education on Sexual Misconduct." *Toronto Sun,* December 3. Retrieved August 21, 2015 (http://www.torontosun .com/2014/12/04/men-need-education-on-sexual-misconduct).

Hayes, Michael, Ian E. Ross, Mike Gasher, Donald Gutstein, James R. Dunn, and Robert A. Hackett. 2007. "Telling Stories: News Media, Health Literacy and Public Policy in Canada." *Social Science & Medicine* 64:1842–1852.

Hecht, Jo-Anne, and David Martin. 2006. "Backpacking and Hostel-Picking: An Analysis from Canada." *International Journal of Contemporary Hospitality Management* 18:69–77.

Hedrick, Terry E., Leonard Bickman, and Debra J. Rog. 1993. *Applied Research Design: A Practical Guide.* Newbury Park, CA: Sage.

Heiskanen, M., and M. Egerer. 2019. "The Conceptualisation of Problem Gambling in Social Services: Email Interviews with Finnish Social Services Directors." *Nordic Social Work Research*, 9(1):29–41.

Hempel, Carl G. 1952. "Fundamentals of Concept Formation in Empirical Science." *International Encyclopedia of United Science II*, no. 7.

Henry, F., and C. Tator. 2002. *Discourses of Domination: Racial Bias in the Canadian English-Language Press*. Toronto: University of Toronto Press.

Hewson, Claire. 2016. "Ethics Issues in Digital Methods Research." Pp. 206–221 in *Digital Methods for Social Science: An Interdisciplinary Guide to Research Innovation*, edited by Helene Snee, Christine Hine, Yvette Morey, Steven Roberts, and Hayley Watson. New York: Palgrave Macmillan.

Hewson, C., Carl Vogel, & Dianna Laurent. 2016. *Internet Research Methods*. 2nd ed. Thousand Oaks: Sage.

High, S., E. Little, and T. Duong. 2014. *Remembering Mass Violence: Oral History, New Media and Performance*. Toronto: University of Toronto Press.

Highfield, Roger. 2011. "Unshakeable Stereotypes of Science." *New Scientist*, September 13. Retrieved April 6, 2015 (http://www.newscientist.com/article/mg21128290.200-media-presenter-unshakeable-stereotypes-of-science.html#.VSKy0Y4YErI).

Hodgetts, S., D. Nicholas, L. Zwaigenbaum, and D. Mcconnell. 2013. "Parents' and Professionals' Perceptions of Family-centered Care for Children with Autism Spectrum Disorder across Service sectors." *Social Science & Medicine* 96:138–146.

Hoff, Karla, and Priyanka Pandey. 2004. Belief Systems and Durable Inequalities: An Experimental Investigation of Indian Caste. World Bank, Policy Research Working Papers, June. Retrieved August 18, 2015 (http://www.princeton.edu/rpds/seminars/pdfs/hoff_indiancaste.pdf).

Hogan, B. 2017. "Online Social Networks: Concepts for Data Collection and Analysis." In Fielding, N., Lee, R., & Blank, G. (eds.). *The SAGE Handbook of Online Research Methods* (pp. 241–257). London: SAGE.

Holmes, Dawn E. 2017. *Big Data: A Very Short Introduction*. UK: Oxford.

Horton, Alicia. 2013. "Flesh Hook Pulling: Motivations and Meaning-Making from the 'Body Side' of Life." *Deviant Behavior* 34(2):115–134.

Howell, Joseph T. 1973. *Hard Living on Clay Street*. Garden City, NY: Doubleday Anchor.

Howlett, Michael. 1986. "Acts of Commission and Acts of Omission: Legal–Historical Research and the Intentions of Government in a Federal State." *Canadian Journal of Political Science* 19:363–370.

Huey, Laura, and Rose Ricciardelli. 2015. "'This Isn't What I Signed Up For': When Police Officer Role Expectations Conflict with the Realities of General Duty Police Work in Remote Communities." *International Journal of Police Science and Management* 17(3):194–203.

Hughes, Karen D., and Graham S. Lowe. 2000. "Surveying the 'Post-Industrial' Landscape: Information Technologies and Labour Market Polarization in Canada." *The Canadian Review of Sociology and Anthropology* 37:29–53.

Humphreys, Laud. 1970. *Tearoom Trade: Impersonal Sex in Public Places*. Chicago: Aldine.

International Visual Sociology Association (IVSA). 2015. Retrieved July 7, 2015 (http://visualsociology.org/about.html).

Isfeld, Gordon. 2015. "StatsCan Chief Turns to Blog to Dispel Data 'Myths' about National Household Survey." *Financial Post*, June 9. Retrieved June 18, 2015 (http://business.financialpost.com/news/economy/statscan-chief-turns-to-blog-to-dispel-data-myths-about-national-household-survey).

Ison, N. 2009. "Having Their Say: Email Interviews for Research Data Collection with People Who Have Verbal Communication Impairment." *International Journal of Social Research Methodology*, 12(2):161–172.

Janetzko, D. 2017. "Nonreactive Data Collection Online." In Fielding, N., Lee, R., & Blank, G. *The SAGE Handbook of Online Research Methods* (pp. 76–91). London: Sage.

Jasso, Guillermina. 1988. "Principles of Theoretical Analysis." *Sociological Theory* 6:1–20.

Johnson, B.E. 2011. "The Speed and Accuracy of Voice Recognition Software-Assisted Transcription Versus Listen-and-Type Method: A Research Note." *Qualitative Research* 11(1):91–97.

Johnson, R. B., A. J. Onwuegbuzie, and L. A. Turner. (2007). Toward a Definition of Mixed Methods Research. *Journal of Methods Research* 1(2):112–133.

Johnston J. and J. Taylor. 2008. "Feminist Consumerism and Fat Activists: A Comparative Study of Grassroots Activism and the Dove 'Real Beauty' Campaign." *Signs: A Journal of Women in Culture and Society* 33(4):941–966.

Johnston, W.A., Harvey Krahn, and Trevor Harrison. 2006. "Democracy, Political Institutions, and Trust: The Limits of Current Electoral Reform Proposals." *Canadian Journal of Sociology* 31:165–182.

Jones, James H. 1981. *Bad Blood: The Tuskegee Syphilis Experiments*. New York: Free Press.

Jones, Jason B. 2006. "Book Review: *My Freshman Year* by Rebekah Nathan." *Pop Matters*, September 29.

Retrieved July 16, 2015 (http://www.popmatters.com/review/my-freshman-year-by-rebekah-nathan/).

Jones, T. M., P. Van Aelst, and R. Vliegenthart. (2013). "Foreign Nation Visibility in U.S. News Coverage: A Longitudinal Analysis (1950–2006)," *Communication Research* 40(3):417–436.

Jørgensen, M., and L. Phillips. 2002. *Discourse Analysis as Theory and Method*. London: SAGE.

Josselson, Ruthellen. 2011. "Narrative Research: Constructing, Deconstructing and Reconstructing Story," in Wertz, F. et al. (eds), *Five Ways of Doing Qualitative Analysis: Phenomenological Psychology, Grounded Theory, Discourse Analysis, Narrative Research, and Intuitive Inquiry* (pp. 224–242). New York: Guilford.

Kaplowitz, Michael D., Timothy D. Hadlockand, and Ralph Levine. 2004. "A Comparison of Web and Mail Survey Response Rates." *Public Opinion Quarterly* 68(1):94–101.

Kasof, Joseph. 1993. "Sex Bias in the Naming of Stimulus Persons." *Psychological Bulletin* 113(1):140–163.

Kay, Fiona. 1997. "Flight from Law: A Competing Risks Model of Departures from Law Firms." *Law & Society Review* 31:301–335.

Keating, Joshua. 2014. "Random Acts: What Happens When You Approach Global Poverty as a Science Experiment?" *Slate*, March 26. Retrieved February 18, 2016 (http://www.slate.com/articles/business/crosspollination/2014/03/randomized_controlled_trials_do_they_work_for_economic_development.html).

Keller, Reiner. 2011. "The Sociology of Knowledge Approach to Discourse (SKAD)." *Human Studies* 34(1):43–65.

Kelly, L., G. Kerr, and J. Drennan. 2010. "Avoidance of Advertising in Social Networking Sites: The Teenage Perspective," *Journal of Interactive Advertising*, 10(2):16–27.

Kemp, Candace L. 2004. "'Grand' Expectations: The Experiences of Grandparents and Adult Grandchildren." *Canadian Journal of Sociology* 29(4):499–525.

Kendall, G., and G. Wickham. 1999. *Using Foucault's methods*. Thousand Oaks, CA: Sage.

Kendall, Patricia L., and Paul F. Lazarsfeld. 1950. "Problems of Survey Analysis." Pp. 133–196 in *Continuities in Social Research: Studies in the Scope and Method of "The American Soldier,"* edited by Robert K. Merton and Paul F. Lazarsfeld. New York: Free Press.

Kerr, Don, and Joseph H. Michalski. 2007. "Family Structure and Children's Hyperactivity Problems: A Longitudinal Analysis." *Canadian Journal of Sociology* 32(1):85–112.

Khanlou, Nazilla. 2005. "Cultural Identity as Part of Youth's Self-Concept in Multicultural Settings." *eCOMMUNITY: International Journal of Mental Health & Addiction* 3:1–14.

Khayatt, Didi. 1995. "Compulsory Heterosexuality: Schools and Lesbian Students." Pp. 149–163 in *Knowledge, Experience, and Ruling Relations: Studies in the Social Organization of Knowledge*, eds. M. Campbell and A. Manicom. Toronto: University of Toronto Press.

Kiepal, Laura, Peter J. Carrington, and Myrna Dawson. 2012. "Missing Persons and Social Exclusion." *Canadian Journal of Sociology* 37(2):137–168.

Kim, H., M. Wohl, R. Gupta, and J. Derevensky. 2016. "From the Mouths of Social Media Users: A Focus Group Study Exploring the Social Casino Gaming-Online Gambling Link." *Journal of Behavioral Addictions* 5(1):115–121.

Kim, J., J. Kang, S. Kim, T.W. Smith, J. Son, and J. Berktold. 2010. "Comparison between Self-administered Questionnaire and Computer-assisted Self-interview for Supplemental Survey Nonresponse." *Field Methods* 22(1):57–69.

Kinnell, Ann Marie K., and Douglas W. Maynard. 1996. "The Delivery and Receipt of Safer Sex Advice in Pretest Counseling Sessions for HIV and AIDS." *Journal of Contemporary Ethnography* 24:405–437.

Klochikhin, E. and J. Boyd-Graber, 2017. Text Analysis. In Foster, I., Ghani, R., Jarmin, R., Kreuter, F., & Lane, J. *Big Data and Social Science: A Practical Guide to Methods and Tools* (pp. 187–214). Boca Raton, FL: CRC Press.

Koeske, Gary F. 1998. "Suppression in the Study of Parenting and Adolescent Symptoms: Statistical Nuisance and Nonsense, or Scientific Explanation?" *Journal of Social Service Research* 24:111–130.

Kohn, Melvin, and Carmi Schooler. 1983. *Work and Personality: An Inquiry into the Impact of Social Stratification*. Norwood, NJ: Ablex.

Kong, Rebecca. 2000. "Canadian Crime Statistics." Pp. 63–95 in *Crime in Canadian Society*, 6th ed., edited by Robert Silverman, James Teevan, and Vincent Sacco. Toronto: Harcourt Brace & Co.

Koskey, Kristin L. K., Toni A. Sondergeld, Victoria C. Stewart, and Kevin J. Pugh. 2018. "Applying the Mixed Methods Instrument Development and Construct Validation Process: The Transformative Experience Questionnaire." *Journal of Mixed Methods Research* 12(1):95–122.

Kossinets, G. and D.J. Watts. 2006. "Empirical Analysis of an Evolving Social Network," *Science* 311(5757):88–90.

Kramer, Adam, Jamie Guillory, and Jeffrey Hancock. 2014. "Experimental Evidence of Massive-Scale Emotional Contagion through Social Networks." *Science*, June 2, pp. 8788–8790.

Kreuter, Frauke, Stanley Presser, and Roger Tourangeau. 2008. "Social Desirability Bias in CATI, IVR, and Web Surveys: The Effects of Mode and Question Sensitivity." *Public Opinion Quarterly* 72:847–865.

Kubrin, Charis. 2005. "I See Death around the Corner: Nihilism in Rap Music." *Sociological Perspectives* 48(4):433–459.

Kuhn, Thomas. 1970. *The Structure of Scientific Revolutions.* Chicago: University of Chicago Press.

Kvale, Steinar. 1996. *InterViews: An Introduction to Qualitative Research Interviewing.* Thousand Oaks, CA: Sage.

Laflamme, F. & J. Wagner. 2016. "Responsive and Adaptive Designs." In Wolf, C., Joye, D., Smith, T. W., & Fu, Y. *The SAGE Handbook of survey Methodology* (pp. 397–408). London: SAGE.

Lai, Daniel W. L. 2007. "Validation of the Zarit Burden Interview for Chinese Canadian Caregivers." *Social Work Research* 31:45–53.

Lambert, Eric G., David N. Baker, and Kasey A. Tucker. 2006. "Two Americas: Capital Punishment Views among Canadian and U.S. College Students." *International Journal of Criminal Justice Sciences* 1:1–21.

Laminu Mele, M., & Mai Bello, B. 2007. "Coaxing and Coercion in Roadblock Encounters on Nigerian Highways." *Discourse & Society* 18(4):437–452.

Langlois, Simon. 1994. *Convergence or Divergence: Comparing Recent Social Trends in Industrial Societies.* Montreal: McGill-Queen's University Press.

Lareau, Annette. 2011. *Unequal Childhoods: Class, Race, and Family Life.* 2nd ed. Los Angeles: University of California Press.

Lauster N, and A. Easterbrook. 2011. "No Room for New Families? A Field Experiment Measuring Rental Discrimination Against Same-Sex Couples and Single Parents." *Social Problems* 58:389–409.

Lee, B., Fuller-Thomson, E., Fallon, B., Trocmé, N., & Black, T. 2017. "Asian-Canadian Children and Families Involved in the Child Welfare System in Canada: A Mixed Methods Study." *Child Abuse & Neglect*, 70:342–355.

Lee, S., Bernstein, M., Etzel, E., Gearity, B., & Kuklick, C. 2018. "Student-Athletes' Experiences with Racial Microaggressions in Sport: A Foucauldian Discourse Analysis." *The Qualitative Report* 23(5):1016–1042.

Lenton, Rhonda, Michael D. Smith, John Fox, and Norman Morra. 1999. "Sexual Harassment in Public Places: Experiences of Canadian Women." *The Canadian Review of Sociology and Anthropology* 36:517–540.

Leeuw, E. & N. Berzelak. 2016. "Survey Mode or Survey Modes?" In Wolf, C., Joye, D., Smith, T. W., & Fu, Y. *The SAGE Handbook of survey Methodology* (pp. 142–156). London: SAGE.

Lewis, Jacqueline. 1998. "Learning to Strip: The Socialization Experiences of Exotic Dancers." *The Canadian Journal of Human Sexuality* 7:51–66.

Lewis, Kevin, Marco Gonzalez, & Jason Kaufman. 2012. "Social Selection and Peer Influence in an Online Social Network." *Proceedings of the National Academy of Sciences* 109(1):68–72.

Ley, David. 2006. "Explaining Variations in Business Performance among Immigrant Entrepreneurs in Canada." *Journal of Ethnic & Migration Studies* 32:743–764.

Li, Peter S. 1985. "The Use of Oral History in Studying Elderly Chinese-Canadians." *Canadian Ethnic Studies* 17:67–77.

Lim, Leonel. 2014. "Ideology, Rationality and Reproduction in Education: A Critical Discourse Analysis." *Discourse: Studies in the Cultural Politics of Education* 35(1):61–76.

Literary Digest. 1936a. "Landon, 1,293,669: Roosevelt, 972,897." October 31, pp. 5–6.

Literary Digest. 1936b. "What Went Wrong with the Polls?" November 14, pp. 7–8.

Livingstone, Andrew. 2013. "Son Defends Scientist Behind Aboriginal Nutrition Experiments." *Toronto Star*, July 24. Retrieved April 20, 2015 (http://www .thestar.com/news/canada/2013/07/24/son _defends_scientist_behind_aboriginal_nutrition _experiments.html).

Lofland, John, and Lyn H. Lofland. 1995. *Analyzing Social Settings: A Guide to Qualitative Observation and Analysis.* 3rd ed. Belmont, CA: Wadsworth.

Lofland, John, David Snow, Leon Anderson, and Lyn H. Lofland. 2006. *Analyzing Social Settings: A Guide to Qualitative Observation and Analysis.* 4th ed. Belmont, CA: Wadsworth/Thompson.

Luce, J. 2010. *Beyond Expectation Lesbian/Bi/Queer Women and Assisted Conception.* Toronto: University of Toronto Press.

Lynd, Robert S., and Helen M. Lynd. 1929. *Middletown.* New York: Harcourt, Brace.

Lynd, Robert S., and Helen M. Lynd. 1937. *Middletown in Transition.* New York: Harcourt, Brace.

Maclean's. 2000–2001. "We Are Canadian." December 25, 2000/January 1, 2001, Vol. 113, no. 52.

Madison, Anna-Marie. 1992. "Primary Inclusion of Culturally Diverse Minority Program Participants in the Evaluation Process." *New Directions for Program Evaluation* 53:35–43.

Magrath, R., and R. Scoats. 2019. "Young Men's Friendships: Inclusive Masculinities in a Post-University Setting." *Journal of Gender Studies* 28(1):45–56.

Mahoney, James, and Dietrich Rueschemeyer, eds. 2003. *Comparative Historical Analysis in the Social Sciences.* New York: Cambridge University Press.

Manning, Peter K., and Betsy Cullum-Swan. 1994. "Narrative, Content and Semiotic Analysis." Pp. 463–477 in *Handbook of Qualitative Research,* edited by Norman K. Denzin and Yvonna S. Lincoln. Thousand Oaks, CA: Sage.

Marcuse, Herbert. 1964. *One-Dimensional Man.* Boston, MA: Beacon Press.

Marin, A. and B. Wellman. 2014. "Social Network Analysis: An Introduction." In Scott, J., & Carrington, P. J. *The SAGE Handbook of Social Network Analysis* (pp. 11–25). London: SAGE.

Marshall, Catherine, and Gretchen B. Rossman. 1995. *Designing Qualitative Research.* Thousand Oaks, CA: Sage.

Marx, Karl. [1867] 1967. *Capital.* New York: International Publishers.

Marx, Karl. [1880] 1956. *Revue Socialist,* July 5. Reprinted in *Karl Marx: Selected Writings in Sociology and Social Philosophy,* eds. T. B. Bottomore and Maximilien Rubel. New York: McGraw-Hill.

Mazzocchi, Fulvio. 2006. "Western Science and Traditional Knowledge: Despite Their Variations, Different Forms of Knowledge Can Learn from Each Other." *EMBO Reports* 7(5):463–466.

McAlister, Alfred, Cheryl Perry, Joel Killen, Lee Ann Slinkard, and Nathan Maccoby. 1980. "Pilot Study of Smoking, Alcohol, and Drug Abuse Prevention." *American Journal of Public Health* July:719–721.

McGibbon, Elizabeth, Elizabeth Peter, and Ruth Gallop. 2010. "Institutional Ethnography of Nurses' Stress." *Qualitative Health Research* 20(10):1353–1378.

McGuigan, J. 2009. *Cool Capitalism.* London: Pluto Press.

Mckie, R., N. Lachowsky, and R. Milhausen. 2015. "The Positive Impact of Technology on Young Gay Men's Dating and Sexual Relationships in Canada: Results From a Focus Group Study." *Journal of LGBT Youth* 12(1):19–38.

McRobbie A (2009) *The Aftermath of Feminism: Gender, Culture and Social Change.* Los Angeles, CA: Sage.

Mead, Margaret, and Rhoda Métraux. 1957. "Image of the Scientist among High School Students." *Science* 126(3207):384–390.

Mears, Ashley. 2011. *Pricing Beauty: The Making of a Fashion Model.* Berkeley: University of California Press.

Merton, Robert K. 1938. "Social Structure and Anomie." *American Sociological Review* 3:672–682.

Miles, Matthew B., and A. Michael Huberman. 1994. *Qualitative Data Analysis,* 2nd ed. Thousand Oaks, CA: Sage Publications.

Milgram, Stanley. 1967. "The Small World Problem." *Psychology Today* 2:60–67.

Milgram, Stanley. 1969. *Obedience to Authority.* New York: Harper Colophon Books.

Mill, J., Jackson, R., Worthington, C., Archibald, C., Wong, T., Myers, T., ... Mill, J. (2008). HIV testing and care in Canadian Aboriginal youth: a community based mixed methods study. *BMC Infectious Diseases* 8(1):132–132.

Minore, Bruce, Margaret Boone, Mae Katt, Peggy Kinch, and Stephen Birch. 2004. "Addressing the Realties of Health Care in Northern Aboriginal Communities through Participatory Action Research." *Journal of Interprofessional Care* 18:360–368.

Mitchell, Claudia. 2011. *Doing Visual Research.* London: Sage.

Morse, Janice. M. 2003. "Principles of Mixed Methods and Multimethod Research Design." In Abbas Tashakkori and Charles Teddlie (Eds.), *Handbook of Mixed Methods in Social and Behavioral Research* (pp. 189–208). Thousand Oaks, CA: Sage.

Morgan, David L. 1997. *Focus Groups as Qualitative Research.* 2nd ed. Thousand Oaks, CA: Sage Publications.

Morgan, M., F. McInerney, J. Rumbold, and P. Liamputtong. 2009. "Drawing the Experience of Chronic Vaginal Thrush and Complementary and Alternative Medicine." *International Journal of Social Research Methodology* 12(2):127–146.

Mosby, Ian. 2013. "Administering Colonial Science: Nutrition Research and Human Biomedical Experimentation in Aboriginal Communities and Residential Schools, 1942–1952." *Social History* 46(91):145–172.

Mosher, Clayton, and John Hagan. 1994. "Constituting Class and Crime in Upper Canada: The Sentencing of Narcotics Offenders, circa 1908–1953." *Social Forces* 72:613–641.

Moskowitz, Milt. 1981. "The Drugs That Doctors Order." *San Francisco Chronicle,* May 23, p. 33.

Nathan, Rebekah. 2005. *My Freshman Year: What a Professor Learned by Becoming a Student.* Ithaca, NY: Cornell University Press.

Netting, Nancy S. 2006. "Two Lives, One Partner: Indo-Canadian Youth between Love and Arranged Marriages." *Journal of Comparative Family Studies* 37:129–146.

Noh, Samuel, and William R. Avison. 1996. "Asian Immigrants and the Stress Process: A Study of Koreans in Canada." *Journal of Health and Social Behavior* 37:192–206.

O'Connor, H. and C. Madge. 2017. "Online Interviewing." In Fielding, N., Lee, R., & Blank, G. *The SAGE Handbook of Online Research Methods* (pp. 416–434). London: SAGE.

O'Connor, M., and S. Payne. 2006. "Discourse Analysis: Examining the Potential for Research in Palliative Care. *Palliative Medicine* 20(8):829–834.

O'Connor, Pat. 2006. "Globalization, Individualization and Gender in Adolescents' Texts." *International Journal of Social Research Methodology* 9(4):261–277.

Ohm, Paul. 2010. "Broken Promises of Privacy: Responding to the Surprising Failure of Anonymization." *UCLA Law Review* 57:1742–1743.

Oliffe, John L., Suki Grewal, Joan L. Bottorff, Haida Luke, and Harshbir Toor. 2007. "Elderly South Asian Canadian Immigrant Men," *Family & Community Health* 30:224–236.

Ong, David, and Jue Wang. 2015. "Income Attraction: An Online Dating Field Experiment." *Journal of Economic Behavior and Organization* 111:13–22.

Onwuegbuzie, Anthony, J., Rebecca M. Bustamante, and Judith A. Nelson. 2010. "Mixed Research as a Tool for Developing Quantitative Instruments." *Journal of Mixed Methods Research* 4(1):56–78.

Orton-Johnson, K. 2017. "Mummy Blogs and Representations of Motherhood: 'Bad Mummies' and Their Readers." *Social Media + Society* 3(2):1–10.

Osborne. Geraint B. 2006. "Scientific Experimentation on Canadian Inmates, 1955 to 1975." *The Howard Journal* 45:284–306.

Ou Jin Lee, Edward, and Shari Brotman. 2011. "Identity, Refugeeness, Belonging: Experiences of Sexual Minority Refugees in Canada." *Canadian Review of Sociology* 48(3):241–274.

Outhwaite, William. 2006. *The Blackwell Dictionary of Modern Social Thought*, 2nd ed. London: Blackwell.

Padgett, J., and C. Ansell. 1993. "Robust Action and the Rise of the Medici, 1400–1434." *The American Journal of Sociology* 98(6):1259–1319.

Palys, Ted, and John Lowman. 2011. "What's Been Did and What's Been Hid: Reflections on TCPS2." Retrieved February 17, 2012 (http://www.sfu.ca/~palys/PalysLowmanCommentsOnTCPS2-2011.pdf).

Paolacci, G., J. Chandler, and P. G. Ipeirotis. 2010. "Running Experiments on Amazon Mechanical Turk." *Judgment and Decision Making* 5(5): 411–419.

Paperny, Anna Mehler. 2013. "Toronto Ditches National Household Survey for Historical Comparisons." *Global News*, October 16. Retrieved June 18, 2015 (http://globalnews.ca/news/688539/toronto-ditches-national-household-survey/).

Park, Alice. 2012. "Dr. Roger Poisson." *Time Heartland*, January 12. Retrieved August 17, 2012 (http://healthland.time.com/2012/01/13/great-science-frauds/slide/dr-roger-poisson/#dr-roger-poisson).

Parr, Janet. 1998. "Theoretical Voices and Women's Own Voices: The Stories of Mature Women Students." Pp. 87–102 in *Feminist Dilemmas in Qualitative Research: Public Knowledge and Private Lives*, edited by Jane Ribbens and Rosalind Edwards. Thousand Oaks, CA: Sage Publications.

Pascale, C. 2008. Talking About Race: Shifting the Analytical Paradigm. *Qualitative Inquiry* 14(5):723–741.

Pascoe, C. J. 2007. *Dude, You're a Fag: Masculinity and Sexuality in High School*. Berkeley, CA: University of California Press.

Patton, Michael Quinn. 1987. *How to Use Qualitative Methods in Evaluation*. Newbury Park, CA: Sage Publications.

Paulus, T. M., J.N. Lester, and P.G. Dempster. 2014. *Digital Tools for Qualitative Research*. London: SAGE.

Pay Equity Commission. 2014. *The Gender Wage Gap*. Ontario Ministry of Labour. Retrieved August 8, 2015 (http://www.payequity.gov.on.ca/en/about/pubs/genderwage/wagegap.php).

PBS. 2014. "The Mona Lisa Mystery." *Secrets of the Dead*, July 9. Retrieved July 7, 2015 (http://www.pbs.org/wnet/secrets/mona-lisa-mystery-full-episode/1821/).

Peer, E., L. Brandimarte, S. Samat, and A. Acquisti. 2017. "Beyond the Turk: Alternative Platforms for Crowdsourcing Behavioral Research." *Journal of Experimental Social Psychology* 70:153–163.

Perrier, M., J. Kirkby. 2013. "Taming the 'Dragon': Using Voice Recognition Software for Transcription in Disability Research within Sport and Exercise Psychology." *Qualitative Research in Sport, Exercise and Health* 5(1):103–108.

Pew Research Center. 2012. "Assessing the Representativeness of Public Opinion Surveys." Retrieved August 14, 2019 (https://www.people-press.org/2012/05/15/assessing-the-representativeness-of-public-opinion-surveys/).

Pineo, P., J. Porter, and H. McRoberts. 1977. "The 1971 Census and a Socioeconomic Classification of Occupations." *Canadian Review of Sociology and Anthropology* 14:91–102.

Plano Clark, Vicki L. and Nataliya V. Ivankova. 2016. *Mixed Methods Research: A Guide to the Field.* Thousand Oaks, CA: Sage.

Pona, Natalie. 2012. "Alberta Election Upset: The Polls Were Wrong." Canada.com, April 24. Retrieved June 17, 2015 (http://o.canada.com/uncategorized/alberta-election-upset-the-polls-were-wrong).

Ponting, J. Rick. 1988. "Public Opinion on Aboriginal Peoples' Issues in Canada." *Canadian Social Trends* (Winter):9–17.

Popping, R. 2017. "Online Tools for Content Analysis." In Fielding, N., Lee, R., & Blank, G. *The SAGE Handbook of Online Research Methods* (pp. 329–343). London: Sage.

Population Communications International. 1996. *International Dateline* [February]. New York: Population Communications International.

Porter, Stephen R., and Michael E. Whitcomb. 2003. "The Impact of Contact Type on Web Survey Response Rates." *Public Opinion Quarterly* 67(4):579–588.

Powell, Elwin H. 1958. "Occupation, Status, and Suicide: Toward a Redefinition of Anomie." *American Sociological Review* 23:131–139.

Presser, Stanley, and Johnny Blair. 1994. "Survey Pretesting: Do Different Methods Produce Different Results?" Pp. 73–104 in *Sociological Methodology 1994,* ed. Peter Marsden. San Francisco: Jossey-Bass.

Presser, Stanley, Mick P. Couper, Judith T. Lessler, Elizabeth Martin, Jean Martin, Jennifer M. Rothgeb, and Eleanor Singer. 2004. "Methods for Testing and Evaluating Survey Questions." *Public Opinion Quarterly* 68(1):109–130.

Purcell, John, and Kathryn Graham. 2005. "A Typology of Toronto Nightclubs at the Turn of the Millennium." *Contemporary Drug Problems* 32:131–167.

Putnam, R. D. 2000. *Bowling Alone: The Collapse and Revival of American Community.* New York: Simon & Schuster.

QSR International 2011. "NVivo 9: Getting Started." Available online at http://download.qsrinternational.com/Document/NVivo10/NVivo10-Getting-Started-Guide.pdf.

Ragin, Charles C. 1994. *Constructing Social Research.* London: Pine Forge Press.

Rasmussen, K., and H. Thimm. 2015. "Circumventing Nonresponse—Upgrading Traditional Company Survey Data with Unobtrusive Data from Company Websites." *Bulletin de Méthodologie Sociologique* 127(1):85–96.

Redfield, Robert. 1941. *The Folk Culture of Yucatan.* Chicago: University of Chicago Press.

Reimer, Bill (2011) "Social Exclusion through Lack of Access to Social Support in Rural Areas" Pp. 152–160 in *Social Statistics, Poverty and Social Exclusion: perspectives Québécoises, Canadiennes et internationals,* Montréal: Les Presses de l'Université de Montréal.

Reinecke, K., and K. Gajos. 2015. "LabintheWild: Conducting Large-Scale Online Experiments with Uncompensated Samples." *Proceedings of the 18th ACM Conference on Computer Supported Cooperative Work & Social Computing.* Vancouver. pp. 1364–1378.

Reinharz, Shulamit. 1992. *Feminist Methods in Social Research.* New York: Oxford University Press.

Reips, Ulf-Dietrich. 2000. "The Web Experiment Method: Advantages, Disadvantages, and Solutions." Pp. 89–117 in *Psychological Experiments on the Internet,* edited by Michael H. Birnbaum. San Diego, CA: Academic Press.

Renaud, Cheryl A., and E. Sandra Byers. 1999. "Exploring the Frequency, Diversity, and Content of University Students' Positive and Negative Sexual Cognitions." *The Canadian Journal of Human Sexuality* 8:17.

Repta, R., & Clarke, L. 2013. "Am I Going to be Natural or Am I Not?": Canadian Women's Perceptions and Experiences of Menstrual Suppression. *Sex Roles* 68(1):91–106.

Retzinger, S. 1995 "Identifying Shame and Anger in Discourse. *American Behavioral Scientist* 38(8):1104–1113.

Ricci, G. 2017. *The Persistence of Critical Theory.* New Brunswick, U.S.A: Transaction Publishers.

Riecken, Henry W., and Robert F. Boruch. 1974. *Social Experimentation: A Method for Planning and Evaluating Social Intervention.* New York: Academic Press.

Roberts, Julian V., and Robert J. Gebotys. 1992. "Reforming Rape Laws: Effects of Legislative Change in Canada." *Law and Human Behavior* 16:555–573.

Roberts, Lance W., R.A. Clifton, B. Ferguson, K. Kampen, and S. Langlois. 2005. *Recent Social Trends in Canada, 1960–2000.* Montreal: McGill-Queen's University Press.

Roberts, Lance W., Jason Edgerton, Tracey Peter, and Lori Wilkinson. 2015. *Understanding Social Statistics: A Student's Guide to Navigating the Maze.* Toronto: Oxford University Press.

Roethlisberger, F. J., and W. J. Dickson. 1939. *Management and the Worker.* Cambridge, MA: Harvard University Press.

Rogers, Everett M., Peter W. Vaughan, Ramadhan M. A. Swalehe, Nagesh Rao, and Suruchi Sood. 1996. "Effects of an Entertainment-Education Radio Soap Opera on Family Planning and HIV/AIDS Prevention Behavior in Tanzania." Report presented at a technical briefing on the Tanzania Entertainment-Education Project, Rockefeller Foundation, New York, March 27.

Rokeach, Milton. 1964. *The Three Christs of Ypsilanti.* New York: Knopf.

Rollings-Magnusson, Sandra. 2000. "Canada's Most Wanted: Pioneer Women on the Western Prairies." *Canadian Review of Sociology and Anthropology* 37:223–238.

Roodman, David. 2012. "Think Again: Microfinance." *Foreign Policy*, February 1. Retrieved February 18, 2016 (http://foreignpolicy.com/2012/02/01/think-again-microfinance/).

Rose, Gillian. 2012. *Visual Methodologies.* 3rd ed. London: Sage.

Rosenberg, Morris. 1968. *The Logic of Survey Analysis.* New York: Basic Books.

Rosenthal, Robert, and Lenore Jacobson. 1968. *Pygmalion in the Classroom.* New York: Holt, Rinehart & Winston.

Rubin, Herbert J., and Irene S. Rubin. 1995. *Qualitative Interviewing: The Art of Hearing Data.* Thousand Oaks, CA: Sage.

Ruiz, Jorge. 2009. "Sociological Discourse Analysis: Methods and Logic." *Forum: Qualitative Social Research* 10(2). Retrieved July 7, 2015 (http://www.qualitative-research.net/index.php/fqs/article/view/1298/2882#g33).

Ryan, Joan. 1995. *Doing Things the Right Way: Dene Traditional Justice in Lac La Martre, N.W.T.* Calgary: University of Calgary Press and the Arctic Institute of North America.

Sacks, Jeffrey J., W. Mark Krushat, and Jeffrey Newman. 1980. "Reliability of the Health Hazard Appraisal." *American Journal of Public Health* July:730–732.

Saint-Pierre, Yves. 1993. Statistics Canada's Internet Site. Retrieved June 27, 2008 (http://www.statcan.ca/bsolc/english/bsolc?catno=75F0002M1993013).

Salganik, M.J. 2018. *Bit by Bit: Social Research in the Digital Age.* Princeton: Princeton University Press.

Salganik, M., P. Dodds, and D. Watts. 2006. "Experimental Study of Inequality and Unpredictability in an Artificial Cultural Market." *Science* 311:854–856.

Sana, Faria, Tina Weston, and Nicholas J. Cepeda. 2013. "Laptop Multitasking Hinders Classroom Learning for Both Users and Nearby Peers." *Computers & Education* 62:24–31.

Sanders, William B. 1994. *Gangbangs and Drive-bys: Grounded Culture and Juvenile Gang Violence.* New York: Aldine De Gruyter.

Sanscartier, Matthew, D., Jason D. Edgerton, and Lance W. Roberts. 2018. "A Latent Class Analysis of Gambling Activity Patterns in a Canadian University Sample of Emerging Adults: Socio-demographic, Motivational, and Mental Health Correlates." *Journal of Gambling Studies* 34(3):863–880.

Savage, Philip. 2011. "'Sticking to Their Knitting?' A Content Analysis of Gender in Canadian Newspaper Op-Eds." *Journal of Professional Communication* 1(1):169–183.

Schatzman, Leonard, and Anselm L. Strauss. 1973. *Field Research: Strategies for a Natural Sociology.* Englewood Cliffs, NJ: Prentice Hall.

Scheff, T. 1993. "Gender Wars: Emotions in *Much Ado About Nothing.*" *Sociological Perspectives* 36(2): 149–166.

Scheff, Thomas. 2011. *What's Love Got to Do with It? The Emotional World of Pop Songs.* Boulder: Paradigm Publishers.

Scheff, Thomas. 2014. "Ubiquity of Hidden Shame in Modernity." *Cultural Sociology* 8(2):129–141.

Scheff, T. and S. Mateo. 2016. The S-Word is Taboo: Shame is Invisible in Modern Societies. *Journal of General Practice* 4:217.

Scheff, Thomas, and Suzanne Retzinger. 1991. *Emotions and Violence: Shame and Rage in Destructive Conflicts.* Lexington, MA: Lexington Books.

Schuklenk, Udo. 2014. "The Facebook Scandal That Wasn't." *The Philosopher's Eye*, July 21. Retrieved June 22, 2015 (http://thephilosopherseye.com/2014/07/21/facebook-scandal-that-wasnt-udo-schuklenk/).

Scott, John, and Gordon Marshall. 2005. *Oxford Dictionary of Sociology.* Toronto: Oxford University Press.

Seeman, Melvin. 1959. "On the Meaning of Alienation." *American Sociological Review* 24(6):783–791.

Seko, Y., S. Kidd, D. Wiljer, and K. Mckenzie. 2015. "On the Creative Edge: Exploring Motivations for Creating Non-Suicidal Self-Injury Content Online." *Qualitative Health Research* 25(10):1334–1346.

Shaffir, William B., and Robert A. Stebbins, eds. 1991. *Experiencing Fieldwork: An Inside View of Qualitative Research.* Newbury Park, CA: Sage.Sharp, Julia L., C. Mobley, C. Hammond, C. Withington, S. Drew, S. Stringfield and N. Stipanovic. 2012. "A Mixed Methods Sampling Methodology for a Multisite Case Study." *Journal of Mixed Methods Research* 6(1):34–54.

Silver, C., and A. Lewins. 2014. *Using Software in Qualitative Research.* 2nd ed. London: SAGE.

Silverman, David. 1993. *Interpreting Qualitative Data: Methods for Analyzing Talk, Text, and Interaction.* Thousand Oaks, CA: Sage.

Silverman, Robert A., James J. Teevan, and Vincent F. Sacco. 2000. "Introduction." Pp. 1–10 in *Crime in Canadian Society*, 6th ed., edited by Robert Silverman, James Teevan, and Vincent Sacco. Toronto: Harcourt Brace & Co.

Simon, Rita J. 1998. *Abortion: Statutes, Policies, and Public Attitudes the World Over.* Westport, CT: Praeger.

Singel, Ryan. 2009. "Netflix Spilled Your Brokeback Mountain Secret." *Wired.* December 17. Retrieved December 13, 2018.

Singhal, Arvind, and Elizabeth Rattine-Flaherty. 2006. "Pencils and Photos as Tools of Communicative Research and Praxis: Analyzing Minga Peru's Quest for Social Justice in the Amazon." *International Communication Gazette* 68(4):313–330.

Sintonen, Teppo. 1993. "Life Course and Ethnicity: Experiences of Canadian Finns Who Immigrated to Canada in the 1920s." *Canadian Ethnic Studies/Etudes Ethniques au Canada* 25:76–89.

Smith, Andrew E., and G. F. Bishop. 1992. *The Gallup Secret Ballot Experiments: 1944–1988.* Paper presented at the annual conference of the American Association for Public Opinion Research, St. Petersburg, FL, May.

Smith, Dorothy E. 1987. *The Everyday World as Problematic: A Feminist Sociology.* Boston: Northeastern University Press.

Smith, Tom. 2001. "Are Representative Internet Surveys Possible?" Proceedings of Statistics Canada Symposium: *Achieving Data Quality in a Statistical Agency: A Methodological Perspective.*

Social Sciences and Humanities Research Ethics Special Working Committee (SHWC) Report. 2008. "SSHWC Recommendations Regarding Privacy and Confidentiality." Retrieved February 19, 2012 (http://www.pre.ethics.gc.ca/policy-politique/initiatives/docs/SSHWC_PC_Policy_Recommendations_-_January_2008_-_EN.pdf).

Sorokin, Pitirim A. 1937–1940. *Social and Cultural Dynamics,* 4 vols. Englewood Cliffs, NJ: Bedminster Press.

Sosteric, Mike. 1996. "Subjectivity and the Labour Process: A Case Study in the Restaurant Industry." *Work, Employment & Society* 10:297–318.

Sowa, P., B. Pędziński, M. Krzyzak, D. Maślach, S. Wojcik, and A. Szpak. 2015. "The Computer-Assisted Web Interview Method as Used in the National Study of ICT Use in Primary Healthcare in Poland-Reflections on a Case Study." *Studies in Logic, Grammar and Rhetoric* 43(56):137–146.

Springer, R., & M. Clinton. 2015. Doing Foucault: Inquiring into Nursing Knowledge with Foucauldian Discourse Analysis. *Nursing Philosophy* 16(2):87–97.

Srole, Leo. 1956. "Social Integration and Certain Corollaries: An Exploratory Study." *American Sociological Review* 21:709–716.

Stancanelli, Jeanine. 2010. "Conducting an Online Focus Group." *The Qualitative Report* 15(3):761–765.

Stark, Rodney, and Lynne Roberts. 1996. *Contemporary Social Research Methods.* MicroCase Corporation.

Statistics Canada, Toronto Area Survey 1991, an annual survey conducted by the Institute for Social Research at York University. http://www.statcan.gc.ca/edu/power-pouvoir/ch2/questionnaires/5214775-eng.htm. Accessed July 1, 2015.

Statistics Canada. 2001. "2000 General Social Survey, Cycle 14: Access to and Use of Information and Technology." June. Catalogue no. 12M0014GPE.

Statistics Canada. 2011. *Census Dictionary.* Retrieved June 4, 2015 (https://www12.statcan.gc.ca/census-recensement/2011/ref/dict/index-eng.cfm).

Statistics Canada. 2012a. "Average Earnings by Sex and Work Pattern." (http://www.statcan.gc.ca/tables-tableaux/sum-som/l01/cst01/labor01a-eng.htm).

Statistics Canada. 2012b. "Historical Statistics of Canada." (http://www5.statcan.gc.ca/bsolc/olc-cel/olc-cel?lang=eng&catno=11-516-X).

Statistics Canada. 2018. "Public Service Employee Survey (PSES)." (http://www23.statcan.gc.ca/imdb/p2SV.pl?Function=getSurvey&SDDS=4438).

Stewart, David W., and Prem Shamdasani. 2017. "Online Focus Groups." *Journal of Advertising* 46(1):48–60.

Stouffer, Samuel, et al. 1949–1950. *The American Soldier,* 3 vols. Princeton, NJ: Princeton University Press.

Strauss, Anselm, and Juliet Corbin. 1994. "Grounded Theory Methodology: An Overview." Pp. 273–85 in *Handbook of Qualitative Research*, edited by Norman K. Denzin and Yvonna S. Lincoln. Thousand Oaks, CA: Sage.

Strauss, Anselm, and Juliet Corbin. 1998. *Basics of Qualitative Research: Techniques and Procedures for Developing Grounded Theory*, 2nd ed. Thousand Oaks, CA: Sage.

Strunk, William Jr., and E. B. White. 2000. *The Elements of Style,* 4th ed. New York: Longman.

Sue, V. M., and L.A. Ritter. 2012. *Conducting Online Surveys.* Thousand Oaks, CA: SAGE.

Sugiman, Pamela. 2009. "'Life Is Sweet': Vulnerability and Composure in the Wartime Narratives of Japanese Canadians." *Journal of Canadian Studies* 43:186–218.

Swalehe, Ramadhan, Everett M. Rogers, Mark J. Gilboard, Krista Alford, and Rima Montoya. 1995. "A Content Analysis of the Entertainment-Education Radio Soap Opera 'Twende na Wakati' (Let's Go with the Times) in Tanzania." Arusha, Tanzania: Population Family Life and Education Programme (POFLEP), Ministry of Community Development, Women Affairs, and Children, November 15.

Takeuchi, David. 1974. "Grass in Hawaii: A Structural Constraints Approach." M.A. thesis, University of Hawaii.

Tandon, Rajesh, and L. Dave Brown. 1981. "Organization-Building for Rural Development: An Experiment in India." *Journal of Applied Behavioral Science* April–June: 172–189.

Taylor, C. 2011. "Homophobia Creates Hostile World for Canadian Students." News release, University of Winnipeg, May 12. Retrieved May 21, 2015 (http://www.uwinnipeg.ca/index/uw-news-action/story.572/title.homophobia-creates-hostile-world-for-canadian-students).

Taylor, Catherine G., Elizabeth J. Meyer, Tracey Peter, Janice Ristock, Donn Short & Christopher Campbell. 2016. "Gaps between Beliefs, Perceptions, and Practices: The Every Teacher Project on LGBTQ-Inclusive Education in Canadian Schools." *Journal of LGBT Youth* 13(1–2):112–140.

Taylor, C., and T. Peter. 2011a. "Canadian Human Rights Discourse and High School Climate for LGBTQ Students: We Are Not Aliens, We're People and We Have Rights." *Canadian Review of Sociology* (special issue on sexuality, sexual health, and sexual rights) 48(3):631–668.

Taylor, C., and T. Peter. 2011b. *Every class in every school: Final Report on the First National Climate Survey on Homophobia, Biphobia, and Transphobia in Canadian Schools.* Toronto: Egale Canada Human Rights Trust.

Taylor, C., T. Peter, T. Edkins, C. Campbell, and E. Saewyc. 2016. "Final Report of the National Inventory of School District Interventions in Support of LGBTQ Student Wellbeing." Vancouver: Stigma and Resilience Among Vulnerable Youth Centre, School of Nursing, University of British Columbia.

Taylor, J., J. Johnston, and K. Whitehead. 2016. "A Corporation in Feminist Clothing? Young Women Discuss the Dove 'Real Beauty' Campaign." *Critical Sociology* 42(1):123–144.

Taylor, Sandra. 2004. "Researching Educational Policy and Change in 'New Times': Using Critical Discourse Analysis." *Journal of Education Policy* 19(4):433–451.

Teddlie, Charles, and Abbas Tashakkori. (2009). *The Foundations of Mixed Methods Research: Integrating Quantitative and Qualitative Techniques in the Social and Behavioral Sciences.* Thousand Oaks, CA: Sage.

Terkel, Studs. 1970. *Hard Times: An Oral History of the Great Depression.* New York: Pantheon Books.

Thomas, C., Turner, M., Payne, S., Milligan, C., Brearley, S., Seamark, D., … Blake, S. 2018. "Family Carers' Experiences of Coping with the Deaths of Adults in Home Settings: A Narrative Analysis of Carers' Relevant Background Worries. *Palliative Medicine* 32(5):950–959.

Thomas, W. I., and Florian Znaniecki. 1918. *The Polish Peasant in Europe and America.* Chicago: University of Chicago Press.

Thompson, A. H. (Gus). 2012. "Relative Age Studies." Retrieved February 14, 2012 (http://www.socialproblemindex.med.ualberta.ca/relage.htm#Elite).

Thompson, Paul. 2000. *The Voice of the Past: Oral History.* 3rd ed. Oxford, UK: Oxford University Press.

Tindall, D. B. 2002. "Social Networks, Identification and Participation in an Environmental Movement: Low–Medium Cost Activism within the British Columbia Wilderness Preservation Movement." *Canadian Review of Sociology and Anthropology* 39:413–452.

Tindall, D. B. 2014. "A Distinctive Canadian Sociology?" *Canadian Review of Sociology and Anthropology* 51(4):395–401.

Tlaiss, H. 2015. "How Islamic Business Ethics Impact Women Entrepreneurs: Insights from Four Arab Middle Eastern Countries." *Journal of Business Ethics* 129(4):859–877.

Todd, Douglas. 2015. "Controversial Vancouver Assisted Suicide Researcher Yearns to Return to Kwantlen." *Vancouver Sun*, January 5. Retrieved April 18, 2015 (http://www.vancouversun.com/health/Metro+Vancouver+suicide+researcher+yearns+teach+again/10703889/story.html).

Toepoel, V. 2016. *Doing Surveys Online.* Thousand Oaks, CA: SAGE.

Tremblay, Manon. 1998. "Do Female MPs Substantively Represent Women? A Study of Legislative Behaviour in Canada's 35th Parliament." *Canadian Journal of Political Science* 31:435–465.

Tri-Council Policy Statement: Ethical Conduct for Research Involving Humans, Department of Canadian Institutes of Health Research. 2010. http://www.pre.ethics.gc.ca/eng/policy-politique/initiatives/tcps2-eptc2/Default/. Accessed August 6, 2019.

Truth and Reconciliation Commission. 2015. Honouring the Truth, Reconciling for the Future: Summary of the Final Report of the Truth and Reconciliation Commission of Canada. Retrieved August 21, 2015 (http://www.trc.ca/websites/trcinstitution/index.php?p=890).

Tuckel, Peter, and Harry O'Neill. 2002. "The Vanishing Respondent in Telephone Surveys." *Journal of Advertising Research*, September–October:26–48.

Turner, Jonathan. 2010. *Theoretical Principles of Sociology.* New York: Springer.

Turner, Terisa E., Wahu M. Kaara, and Leigh S. Brownhill. 1997. "Social Reconstruction in Rural Africa: A Gendered Class Analysis of Women's Resistance to Export Crop Production in Kenya." *Canadian Journal of Development Studies* 18:213–238.

United Nations. 2007. *Human Development Report 2007/2008.* "Fighting Climate Change: Human Solidarity in a Divided World." United Nations Development Programme (UNDP). Retrieved December 9, 2007 (http://hdr.undp.org/en/reports/global/hdr2007-2008/).

Urban Health Research Initiative. 2015. Research Summaries. Retrieved July 22, 2015 (http://uhri.cfenet.ubc.ca/content/view/72/93/).

U.S. Bureau of the Census. 2001. *Statistical Abstract for the United States.* Washington, DC: U.S. Government Printing Office.

U.S. Bureau of the Census. 2009. *Statistical Abstract for the United States.* Washington, DC: U.S. Government Printing Office.

Van Dijk, T. A. 1993. "Principles of Critical Discourse Analysis." *Discourse and Society* 4(2):249–283.

van de Rijt, Arnout, Soong Moon Kang, Michael Restivo, and Akshay Patil. 2014. "Field Experiments of Success-Breeds-Success Dynamics." *Proceedings of the National Academy of Sciences* 111(19):6934–6939.

Vaughan, Diane. 1996. *The* Challenger *Launch Decision.* Chicago: University of Chicago Press.

Venkatesh, Sudhir. 2008. *Gang Leader for a Day: A Rogue Sociologist Takes to the Streets.* New York: Penguin Press.

Veronis, L., and R. McLeman. 2014. "Environmental Influences on African Migration to Canada: Focus Group Findings from Ottawa-Gatineau." *Population and Environment* 36(2):234–251.

Vogel, D. 2005. *The Market for Virtue: The Potential and Limits of Corporate Social Responsibility*. Arlington, VA: Brookings Institute Press.

Wagner, A., K. Mcshane, T. Hart, and S. Margolese. 2016. "A Focus Group Qualitative Study of HIV Stigma in the Canadian Healthcare System." *The Canadian Journal of Human Sexuality* 25(1):61–71.

Wallace, Walter. 1971. *The Logic of Science in Sociology.* Chicago: Aldine.

Walsh, Christine A., Jenny Ploeg, Lynne Lohfeld, Jaclyn Horne, Harriet MacMillan, and Daniel Lai. 2007. "Violence across the Lifespan: Interconnections among Forms of Abuse as Described by Marginalized Canadian Elders and Their Caregivers." *British Journal of Social Work* 37:491–514.

Warikoo, Natasha K., and Janine de Novais. 2015. "Colour-Blindness and Diversity: Race Frames and Their Consequences for White Undergraduates at Elite US Universities." *Ethnic and Racial Studies* 38(6):860–876.

Warman, Casey, Frances Woolley, and Christopher Worswick. 2006. "The Evolution of Male-Female Wage Differentials in Canadian Universities: 1970–2001." Kingston: Queen's University, Department of Economics, Working Paper No. 1099.

Watts, Duncan. 2012. *Everything Is Obvious: How Common Sense Fails Us.* New York: Crown Business.

Webb, Eugene J., Donald T. Campbell, Richard D. Schwartz, and Lee Sechrest. [1966] 2000. *Unobtrusive Measures* (revised ed.). Thousand Oaks, CA: Sage Publications.

Weber, Max. [1905] 1958. *The Protestant Ethic and the Spirit of Capitalism.* Translated by Talcott Parsons. New York: Scribners.

Weber, Max. [1925] 1946. "Science as a Vocation." Pp. 129–56 in *From Max Weber: Essays in Sociology,* edited and translated by Hans Gerth and C. Wright Mills. New York: Oxford University Press.

Weber, Max. [1934] 1951. *The Religion of China.* Translated by Hans H. Gerth. New York: Free Press.

Weber, Max. [1934] 1952. *Ancient Judaism.* Translated by Hans H. Gerth and Don Martindale. New York: Free Press.

Weber, Max. [1934] 1958. *The Religion of India.* Translated by Hans H. Gerth and Don Martindale. New York: Free Press.

Websdale, Neil. 2010. *Familicidal Hearts: The Emotional Styles of 211 Killers.* Oxford: Oxford University Press.

Weerasinghe, S., and V. Maddalena. 2016. "Negotiation, Mediation and Communication between Cultures: End-of-Life Care for South Asian Immigrants in Canada from the Perspective of Family Caregivers." *Social Work in Public Health* 31(7):665–677.

Weiss, Carol. 1972. *Evaluation Research.* Englewood Cliffs, NJ: Prentice Hall.

Wertz, et al. 2011. "The Establishment of Methodological Traditions." in Wertz, F.J., K. Charmaz, L.M. McMullen, R. Josselson, R. Anderson, and E. McSpadden (Eds), *Five Ways of Doing Qualitative Analysis : Phenomenological Psychology, Grounded Theory, Discourse Analysis, Narrative Research, and Intuitive Inquiry* (pp. 48–74). New York: Guilford.

Whyte, W. F., D. J. Greenwood, and P. Lazes. 1991. "Participatory Action Research: Through Practice to Science in Social Science." Pp. 19–55 in *Participatory*

Action Research, edited by W. F. Whyte. New York: Sage Publications.

Wilkinson, Richard, and Kate Pickett. 2009. *The Spirit Level: Why More Equal Societies Almost Always Do Better*. London: Penguin.

Williams, Allison, Bill Holden, Peter Krebs, Nazeem Muhajarine, Kate Waygood, James Randall, and Cara Spence. 2008. "Knowledge Translation Strategies in a Community–University Partnership: Examining Local Quality of Life (QoL)." *Social Indicators Research* 85:111–125.

Williams, D., Ducheneaut, N., Xiong, X., Zhang, Y., Yee, N., & Nickell, E. 2006. "From Tree House to Barracks: The Social Life of Guilds in World of Warcraft." *Games and Culture* 1:338–361.

Williams, Robert J., and Rachel A. Volberg. 2010. *Best Practices in the Population Assessment of Problem Gambling.* Report prepared for the Ontario Problem Gambling Research Centre. Guelph, Ontario.

Wilson, Camilo. 1999. Private email, September 8.

Wohl, M., H. Kim, M. Salmon, D. Santesso, T. Wildschut, and C. Sedikides. 2018. "Discontinuity-Induced Nostalgia Improves the Odds of a Self-Reported Quit Attempt among People Living with Addiction." *Journal of Experimental Social Psychology* 75:83–94.

Wolf, Daniel R. 1990. *The Rebels: A Brotherhood of Outlaw Bikers.* Toronto: University of Toronto Press.

Wolf, Daniel R. 1991. "High-Risk Methodology: Reflections on Leaving an Outlaw Society." Pp. 211–13 in *Experiencing Fieldwork: An Inside View of Qualitative Research,* edited by William B. Shaffir and Robert A. Stebbins. Newbury Park, CA: Sage.

Wolfsfeld, G., E. Segev, and T. Sheafer. 2013. "The Social Media and the Arab Spring: Politics Comes First," *The International Journal of Press/Politics* 18(2):115–137.

Woolford, A. 2015. *This Benevolent Experiment: Indigenous Boarding Schools, Genocide, and Redress in Canada and the United States.* Winnipeg: University of Manitoba Press.

Wynne, Brian. 1996. "May the Sheep Safely Graze? A Reflexive View of the Expert–Lay Knowledge Divide." In *Risk, Environment and Modernity: Towards a New Ecology,* edited by Scott Lash, Bronislaw Szerszynski, and Brian Wynne. London: Sage.

Yerg, Beverly J. 1981. "Reflections on the Use of the RTE Model in Physical Education." *Research Quarterly for Exercise and Sport* March:38–47.

Yinger, J. Milton, K. Ikeda, F. Laycock, and S.J. Cutler. 1977. *Middle Start: An Experiment in the Educational Enrichment of Young Adolescents.* London: Cambridge University Press.

Young, Kevin, and Laura Craig. 1997. "Beyond White Pride: Identity, Meaning and Contradiction in the Canadian Skinhead Subculture." *Canadian Review of Sociology and Anthropology* 34:175–206.

Young, Nathan, and Eric Dugas. 2011. "Representations of Climate Change in Canadian National Print Media: The Banalization of Global Warming." *Canadian Review of Sociology* 48(1):1–22.

Young, Shelley. 1997. "The Use of Normalization as a Strategy in the Sexual Exploitation of Children by Adult Offenders." *The Canadian Journal of Human Sexuality* 6:285–95.

Zimbardo, Philip. 2007. *The Lucifer Effect: Understanding How Good People Turn Evil.* New York: Random House.

Zimbardo, Philip, and Ken Musen. 1992. *Quiet Rage: The Stanford Prison Experiment.* HarperCollins College Publishers.

Znaniecki Lopata, Helena. 1981. "Widowhood and Husband Sanctification." *Journal of Marriage and the Family* May:442.

GLOSSARY

A

abstract A summary of a research article; usually begins the article and states the purpose of the research, the methods used, and the major findings. (Chapter 17)

abstract experience Imaginary experience occurring in the mind. (Chapter 1)

accuracy The property that refers to the correctness of measurements. (Chapter 5)

aggregate data Evidence gathered about cases that are collections of individuals. (Chapter 4)

agreement reality What we "know" as part and parcel of the culture we share with those around us. (Chapter 1)

analytic induction (1) A process for understanding events that relies on grounding concepts in empirical observation and progressively sharpening them through iteration. (Chapter 4) (2) Searching for general insights by systematically looking for patterns among individual cases. (Chapter 9)

anonymity The guarantee that neither the researchers nor the readers of research can link individuals to their responses. (Chapter 3)

applied research Investigations directed toward insights that allow us to live more efficiently or effectively. (Chapter 1)

artifacts Concrete objects that are expressions of abstract culture. (Chapter 9)

attributes (1) The different scores that comprise a variable. (Chapter 1) (2) A characteristic or quality of some object. (Chapter 5) See *variables.*

authenticity The criterion for judging qualitative research that concerns itself with whether the constructed narrative meaningfully captures the lived experience of participants. (Chapter 10)

average An ambiguous term generally suggesting typical or normal—a central tendency. The mean, median, and mode are specific examples of mathematical averages. (Chapter 14)

axial coding The re-examination of open coding in search of conceptual refinements and connections. (Chapter 13)

axioms Theoretical propositions that are assumed to be true. (Chapter 2)

B

bias A form of systematic error. (Chapter 6)

bivariate analysis The analysis of two variables simultaneously to determine the empirical relationship between them. The construction of a simple percentage table or the computation of a simple correlation coefficient are examples of bivariate analyses. (Chapter 14)

Bogardus social distance scale A measurement technique for determining the willingness of people to participate in social relations—of varying degrees of closeness—with other kinds of people. It's an especially efficient technique in that several discrete answers may be summarized without losing any of the original details of the data. (Web Chapter)

C

case A specific object to which evidence refers. (Chapter 4)

case-oriented analysis The detailed examination of a limited set of particular cases in search of idiographic explanation. (Chapter 13)

case study A focused, detailed investigation of a single instance of some social phenomenon like a town, industry, community, organization, or person. (Chapter 10)

causal reasoning The recognition that future circumstances are rooted in or conditioned by present ones. (Chapter 1)

causes The mechanisms or reasons leading to an outcome. (Chapter 4)

census All the members of a population. (Chapter 6)

closed-ended questions Questions to which the respondent is asked to select an answer from among a list provided by the researcher. These are popular in survey research because they provide a greater uniformity of responses and are more easily processed than open-ended questions. (Chapter 8)

cluster sampling A multistage sampling approach in which natural groups (clusters) are sampled initially, with the members of each selected group being subsampled afterward. For example, you might select a sample of Canadian universities from a directory, get lists of the students at all the selected schools, and then draw samples of students from each. (Chapter 6)

codebook The document used in data processing and analysis that tells the location of different data items in a data file; typically identifies the locations of data items and the meaning of the codes used to represent different attributes of variables. (Chapter 14)

coding (1) The process whereby raw data are transformed into standardized form suitable for machine processing and analysis. (Chapter 9) (2) Classifying or categorizing individual pieces of data. (Chapter 13)

cohort study A study in which some specific subpopulation, or cohort, is studied over time, although data may be collected from different members in each set of observations. (Chapter 4)

computer-assisted personal interviewing (CAPI) A face-to-face interview system in which questions are provided on a computer or tablet device and interview responses are entered into the computer by the interviewer. (Chapter 8)

computer-assisted self-interviewing (CASI) An interview system in which there is no interviewer; instead, the participant reads or listens to questions on a computer or mobile digital device and types their answers directly into the computer or device. (Chapter 8)

computer-assisted telephone interviewing (CATI) A survey research technique in which the telephone interviewer reads the questions from the computer monitor and enters the answers directly into the computer. (Chapter 8)

computer-assisted Web interviewing (CAWI) A form of CASI in which the interviewee reads and fills out the interview questionnaire online (e.g., online questionnaires hosted by platforms like SurveyGizmo or Qualtrics).

concept mapping The process of putting emerging concepts and their relationships into a graphical format. (Chapter 13)

concepts Abstract terms for organizing sensory experience. (Chapter 1)

conceptual definition A statement that indicates the meaning of an abstract term by expressing it in other abstract terms. (Chapter 5)

conceptualization The process by which concepts are formed through the selective organization of sensory experience. (Chapter 5)

concrete experience The empirical experience of sensation, including touch, taste, sight, smell, and hearing. (Chapter 1)

confidence interval The range of values within which a population parameter is estimated to lie. A survey, for example, may show 40 percent of a sample favouring Candidate A. Although the best estimate of the support existing among all voters would also be 40 percent, we would not expect it to be exactly that. We might, therefore, compute a confidence interval (such as from 35 to 45 percent) within which the actual percentage of the population probably lies. Note that we must specify a *confidence level* in connection with every confidence interval. (Chapter 16)

confidence level The estimated probability that a population parameter lies within a given *confidence interval*. Given an appropriately constructed confidence interval, such as plus or minus two standard errors around the mean, we may state that in 95 percent of all samples the true population value will be inside the constructed interval. (Chapter 16)

confidentiality The guarantee that although researchers can link individuals to their responses, they promise not to do so publicly. (Chapter 3)

confirmation bias The tendency to seek out, recall, or interpret information that supports one's existing views. (Chapter 1)

constant comparative method (1) Involves the researching moving back and forth between theory and data; concepts, categories, and hypotheses are constantly checked against, and elaborated in light of, new data/observations. (Chapter 10) (2) An inductive approach that relies on continuously comparing observations with one another and the evolving inductive theory. (Chapter 13)

constants Properties that do not change across objects or over time. (Chapter 1)

construct validity The degree to which a measure relates to other variables as expected within a system of theoretical relationships. (Chapter 5)

content analysis The systematic study and interpretation of cultural products. (Chapter 9)

content validity The degree to which a measure covers the range of meanings included within a concept. (Chapter 5)

contingency question A survey question intended for only some respondents, determined by their responses to some other question. For example, all respondents might be asked whether they belong to the Cosa Nostra, and only those who said yes would be asked how often they go to company meetings and picnics. The latter would be a contingency question. (Chapter 8)

contingency table A format for presenting the relationships among variables as percentage distributions. (Chapter 14)

continuous variable A variable whose attributes form a steady progression, such as age or income. Thus the ages of a group of people might include 21, 22, 23, 24, and so forth, and could even be broken down into fractions of years. (Chapter 14)

control group In experimentation, a group of subjects to whom no experimental stimulus is administered and who should resemble the experimental group in all other respects. The comparison of the control group and the experimental group at the end of the experiment points to the effect of the experimental stimulus. (Chapter 7)

control variable A variable identifying the context for the relationship between independent and dependent variables. (Chapter 4)

conversation analysis (CA) The search to understand the basic structures of social interaction and social order through the detailed study of everyday talk. (Chapter 13)

correlation Empirical evidence that a change in one variable is systematically identified with a change in another (association). (Chapter 4)

criterion-related validity The degree to which a measure relates with some external criterion. For example, the validity of occupational qualifying examinations is shown in their ability to predict future evaluations of the individuals' job performances. Also called predictive validity. (Chapter 5)

cross-case analysis The use of either a case-oriented or a variable-oriented approach to compare cases in the search for pattern description and explanation. (Chapter 13)

cross-sectional study A study based on observations representing a single point in time. Contrasted with a *longitudinal study*. (Chapter 4)

curvilinear regression analysis A form of regression analysis that allows relationships among variables to be expressed with curved geometric lines instead of straight ones. (Chapter 16)

D

data set A collection of quantitative measurements in which the numbers are organized by variables and cases. (Chapter 14)

debriefing Interviewing subjects following their participation in a research project to ensure they are both fully informed and not harmed by their participation. (Chapter 3)

deception When respondents are misled about either the identity of the researcher or the nature of the research. (Chapter 3)

deduction A form of reasoning that moves from the general principles to a specific case. (Chapter 1)

dependent variable A variable whose changes we are interested in explaining. (Chapter 1)

descriptive statistics Statistical computations describing either the characteristics of a sample or the relationship among variables in a sample. Descriptive statistics merely summarize a set of sample observations, whereas inferential statistics move beyond the description of specific observations to make inferences about the larger population from which the sample observations were drawn. (Chapter 16)

deviant case testing Examining outliers (negative cases) in comparison to typical cases to gain a sense of how generalized an insight is. (Chapter 9)

dichotomous variable A variable that has only two attributes; also called a binomial variable. (Chapter 7)

dimension A specifiable aspect or facet of a concept. (Chapter 5)

discourse analysis Qualitative methods for examining texts to explore how meaning, knowledge, and power are created and recreated in everyday experience. (Chapter 9)

discrete variable A variable whose attributes are separate from one another, or discontinuous, as in the case of gender or religious affiliation. There is no progression from male to female in the case of gender. (Chapter 14)

dispersion The distribution of values around some central value, such as an average. (Chapter 14)

distorter variable A test (control) variable that causes an apparent reversal in the direction of a zero-order relationship (from negative to positive or vice versa). (Chapter 15)

double-blind experiment An experimental design in which neither the subjects nor the experimenters know which is the experimental group and which is the control. (Chapter 7)

E

ecological fallacy The reasoning error that occurs when conclusions about individuals are based solely on group observations. (Chapter 4)

elaboration model A logical approach to understanding the relationship between two variables through the simultaneous introduction of a third variable, which is usually referred to as a control or test variable. Though developed primarily through the medium of contingency tables by Paul Lazarsfeld, it may be used with other statistical techniques. The various outcomes of an elaboration analysis include replication, specification, explanation, and interpretation. (Chapter 15)

element The unit of which a population is composed and which is selected in a sample. Distinguished from *units of analysis*, which are used in data analysis. (Chapter 6)

empirical The criterion requiring sensory experience as evidence. (Chapter 1)

empirical deduction The logical process for transforming a theoretical proposition into a research hypothesis. (Chapter 2)

EPSEM (equal probability of selection method) A sample design in which each member of a population has the same chance of being selected into the sample. (Chapter 6)

error Any difference between reported results and true scores. (Chapter 6)

ethnography The term *ethnography* varies somewhat in its use by researchers. It generally refers to a report on social life that focuses on detailed and accurate description rather than explanation. For some it refers also to data collected in the natural setting, while for others it refers to naturalistic observations and holistic understandings of cultures or subcultures. (Chapter 10)

evaluation research Research undertaken to determine the effect of some social intervention, such as a program aimed at solving a social problem. (Chapter 12)

exception fallacy The reasoning error that occurs when conclusions about aggregates are drawn from individual cases. (Chapter 4)

exhaustive A property of a variable ensuring that all objects can be classified. (Chapters 5 and 8)

experiential reality What we "know" from personal experience and discovery. (Chapter 1)

experimental group In experimentation, a group of subjects to whom an experimental stimulus is administered. (Chapter 7)

explanation (1) Accounting for events that have occurred in the past. (Chapter 1) (2) The satisfaction of curiosity by successfully clarifying how or why an event occurred. (Chapter 4) (3) An elaboration model term describing the situation where a control variable accounts for a spurious connection between the independent and dependent variables. (Chapter 15)

extended case method A research technique developed by Michael Burawoy that uses case study observations to discover flaws in and to improve existing social theories. (Chapter 10)

external invalidity Refers to the possibility that conclusions drawn from experimental results may not be generalizable to the "real" world. See also *internal invalidity*. (Chapter 7)

external validation The process of testing the *validity* of a measure, such as an index or scale, by examining its relationship to other, presumed indicators of the same variable. If the index really measures prejudice, for example, it should correlate with other indicators of prejudice. (Web Chapter)

F

face validity That quality of an indicator that makes it seem a reasonable measure of some variable. That the frequency of attendance at religious services is some indication of a person's religiosity seems to make sense without a lot of explanation. It has face validity. (Chapter 5)

falsification The criterion that it is possible for empirical evidence to disconfirm a hypothesis. (Chapter 2)

field experiment The execution of an experimental design in real-world conditions. (Chapter 7)

field notes Qualitative evidence in the form of observations, experiences, and interpretations recorded during an ethnographic study. (Chapter 10)

focus group An interviewing method in which a number of subjects are brought together to discuss a specific topic or issue. A focus group is typically led by a moderator, who helps facilitate discussion and ensures that no person dominates the conversation, while interfering as little as possible in the discussion. (Chapter 11)

formative evaluations Assessments aimed at improving the process of an intervention. (Chapter 12)

frequency distribution A description of the number of times the various attributes of a variable are observed in a sample. The report that 53 percent of a sample were men and 47 percent were women is a simple example of a frequency distribution. (Chapter 14)

G

gambler's fallacy The mistaken belief that random events will "balance out" over time. (Chapter 1)

generalizability (1) The goal of research findings being applicable to as broad a population as possible. (Chapter 3) (2) Refers to how broadly applicable results are to different populations. (Chapter 7)

grounded theory An inductive approach to social research that attempts to derive theory from an analysis of the patterns, themes, and common categories discovered in observational data. This differs from hypothesis testing, in which theory is used to generate hypotheses to be tested through observations. (Chapter 10)

grounded theory method (GTM) An inductive approach to theory construction using the constant comparative method. (Chapter 13)

Guttman scale A type of composite measure used to summarize several discrete observations that combine into a more general variable. (Web Chapter)

H

Hawthorne effect A term coined in reference to a series of productivity studies at the Hawthorne plant of the Western Electric Company in Chicago, Illinois. The researchers discovered that their presence affected the behaviour of the workers being studied. The term now refers to any impact of research on the subject of study. (Chapter 7)

historical and comparative research The examination of societies (or other social units) over time and in comparison with one another. (Chapter 9)

hypothesis A theoretically informed expectation about empirical patterns expressed as a relationship between variables. (Chapter 2)

hypothesis testing Determining whether the expectations specified in a hypothesis are confirmed by concrete, empirical patterns. (Chapter 2)

I

idiographic explanation An accounting that aims to understand or make sense of the multiple causes of a specific event. (Chapter 1)

independent variable A variable believed to produce changes in a dependent variable. (Chapter 1)

in-depth interview study A research design where qualitative, one-on-one interviewing is the primary means of data gathering. (Chapter 11)

index A type of composite measure that combines multiple items that, when aggregated, are intended to represent some more general dimension. (Chapter 5) Contrast with *scale*.

indicator An empirical specification of some abstract concept. (Chapter 5)

individual data Evidence gathered about cases that are specific individuals. (Chapter 4)

induction A form of reasoning that moves from specific cases to the general case. (Chapter 1)

inferential statistics The body of statistical computations relevant to making inferences from findings based on sample observations to some larger population. (Chapter 16)

informant Someone well versed in the social phenomenon that you wish to study and who is willing to tell you what he or she knows. If you were planning participant observation among the members of a religious sect, you would do well to make friends with someone who already knows about them—possibly a member of the sect—who could give you some background information about them. Not to be confused with a *respondent.* (Chapter 6)

informed consent The ethical norm requiring research subjects to base their voluntary participation on a full understanding of the potential risks involved. (Chapter 3)

institutional ethnography A research technique that uses the personal experiences of individuals (especially women and other members of subordinated groups) to uncover the institutional power relations that structure and govern their experiences. (Chapter 10)

internal invalidity Refers to the possibility that the conclusions drawn from experimental results may not accurately reflect what went on in the experiment itself. See also *external invalidity.* (Chapter 7)

interpretation An elaboration model term describing the situation where a control variable intervenes between an independent variable and its effects on the dependent variable. (Chapter 15)

interval measure A level of measurement describing a variable whose attributes are rank-ordered and have equal distances between adjacent attributes. The *Celsius temperature scale* is an example of this, because the distance between 17 and 18 is the same as that between 39 and 40. (Chapter 5)

interview A data-collection encounter in which one person (an interviewer) asks questions of another (a respondent). Interviews may be conducted face-to-face or by telephone. (Chapter 8)

interview guide A manual for consultation that helps organize the interview process as needed. (Chapter 11)

item analysis An assessment of whether each of the items included in a composite measure makes an independent contribution or merely duplicates the contribution of other items in the measure. (Web Chapter)

J

judgmental sampling See purposive sampling.

L

latent content As used in connection with content analysis, the underlying meaning of communications as distinguished from their *manifest content.* (Chapter 9)

level of significance In the context of tests of statistical significance, the degree of likelihood that an observed, empirical relationship could be attributable to sampling error. A relationship is significant at the .05 level if the likelihood of its being only a function of sampling error is no greater than 5 out of 100. (Chapter 16)

Likert scale A type of composite measure developed by Rensis Likert in an attempt to improve the levels of measurement in social research, through the use of standardized response categories in survey questionnaires to determine the relative intensity of different items. Likert items are those using such response categories as strongly agree, agree, disagree, and strongly disagree. Such items may be used in the construction of true Likert scales as well as other types of composite measures. (Web Chapter)

linear regression analysis A form of statistical analysis that seeks the explanation for the straight line that best describes the relationship between two ratio variables. (Chapter 16)

logical The criterion for assessing the validity of arguments. (Chapter 1)

longitudinal study A study design involving the collection of data at different points in time. Contrasted with a *cross-sectional study.* (Chapter 4)

M

macrotheory Theoretical perspectives aimed at understanding the "big picture" of institutions, whole societies, and the interactions among societies. By contrast, see *microtheory.* (Chapter 2)

manifest content In connection with content analysis, the concrete terms contained in a communication, as distinguished from *latent content.* (Chapter 9)

matching In connection with experiments, the procedure whereby pairs of subjects are matched on the basis of their similarities on one or more variables; then one member of the pair is assigned to the experimental group and the other to the control group. (Chapter 7)

mean An average computed by summing the values of several observations and dividing by the number of observations. If you now have a GPA of 4.0 based on 10 courses, and you get an F in this course, your new grade point (mean) average will be 3.6. (Chapter 14)

measurement The process of quantifying observations by assigning numbers to attributes composing a variable. (Chapter 2)

median An average representing the value of the "middle" case in a rank-ordered set of observations. If the ages of five men were 16, 17, 20, 54, and 88, the median would be 20. (The mean would be 39.) (Chapter 14)

memoing The process of writing memos containing ideas and insights developed during the collection and analysis of qualitative data. (Chapter 13)

methodology A set of practices and techniques used to collect, process, and interpret information aimed at enhancing our understanding of reality. (Chapter 1)

microtheory Theoretical perspectives aimed at understanding social life at the intimate level of individuals and their interactions. By contrast, see *macrotheory.* (Chapter 2)

mixed methods research (MMR) Research that combines quantitative and qualitative approaches to increase the breadth and depth of understanding of research problems. (Chapter 1)

mode An average representing the most frequently observed value or attribute. If a sample contains 1,000 Protestants, 275 Catholics, 33 Jews, and 10 Muslims, Protestant is the modal category. (Chapter 14)

multiple regression analysis A statistical analysis that provides a way to analyze the simultaneous impact of two or more independent variables on a single dependent variable. The analysis produces an equation that represents the several effects of the multiple independent variables on the dependent variable. (Chapter 16)

multiple time-series designs The use of more than one set of data collected over time (e.g., accident rates over time in several provinces or cities) in order to make comparisons. (Chapter 12)

multivariate analysis The analysis of the simultaneous relationships among several variables. Examining simultaneously the effects of *age*, *gender*, and *social class* on *religiosity* would be an example of multivariate analysis. (Chapter 14)

mutually exclusive A property of a variable ensuring that every object can be classified into only one attribute. (Chapters 5 and 8)

N

narrative analysis (NA) Strategies for analyzing text (whether talk, document, or other) that focus on how people use stories to make sense of themselves, their experiences, and the world.

natural experiment An experimental approximation in which group assignment and administration of the independent variable are outside the researcher's control (i.e., occur "naturally"). (Chapter 7)

necessary condition A condition that must be present for a specific outcome to occur. (Chapter 4)

nominal measure A variable whose attributes have only the characteristics of being jointly exhaustive and mutually exclusive. In other words, a level of measurement describing a variable that has attributes that are merely different from each other, as distinguished from ordinal, interval, or ratio measures. *Gender* is an example of a nominal measure. (Chapter 5)

nomothetic explanation An accounting that identifies a few common causes of a broad category of events. (Chapter 1)

nonequivalent control group A control group that is similar to the experimental group but is not created by the random assignment of subjects. This sort of control group can differ greatly from the experimental group with regard to the dependent variable or variables related to it. (Chapter 12)

nonprobability sampling Any technique in which samples are selected in some fashion not suggested by probability theory. Examples are *purposive (judgmental)*, *snowball*, and *quota sampling*, as well as *reliance on available subjects*. (Chapter 6)

nonreactive research Methods of studying social behaviour without affecting it. This includes analysis of existing statistics, secondary analysis, content analysis, and historical and comparative research. (Chapter 9)

nonsampling error Those imperfections of data quality that are a result of factors other than sampling error. Examples include misunderstandings of questions by respondents, erroneous recordings by interviewers and coders, and data entry errors. (Chapter 16)

null hypothesis In connection with hypothesis testing and tests of statistical significance, the hypothesis that suggests there is no relationship among the variables under study. You may conclude that the variables are related after having statistically rejected the null hypothesis. (Chapter 16)

O

objectivity A series of observations with high intersubjective reliability. (Chapter 2)

observation An empirical score on an object on a specific variable. (Chapter 2)

open coding The original conceptualization of the qualitative evidence into meaningful categories. (Chapter 13)

open-ended questions Questions to which respondents are asked to provide their own answers. Qualitative in-depth interviewing relies heavily on open-ended questions, but they are sometimes used in other forms of data collection, such as telephone surveys and self-administered questionnaires. (Chapter 8)

operational definition The specific steps ("operations") of measuring abstract concepts at the concrete level. (Chapters 2 and 5)

operationalization The process of translating abstract concepts into variables that indicate the concepts. (Chapter 2)

oral history A method that uses in-depth interviews as a means of gathering data about the past from individuals' recollections, typically focusing on specific events or periods of time. (Chapter 11)

ordinal measure A level of measurement describing a variable with attributes one can rank-order along some dimension. An example would be *socioeconomic status* as composed of the attributes high, medium, low. (Chapter 5)

P

panel attrition The increase in participants' nonresponsiveness over time that reduces the accuracy of longitudinal changes. (Chapter 4)

panel study A type of longitudinal study in which data are collected from the same set of people (the sample or panel) at several points in time. (Chapter 4)

paradigm A theoretical perspective including a set of assumptions about reality that guide research questions. (Chapter 2)

parameter The summary description of a given variable in a population. (Chapter 16)

partial regression analysis A form of regression analysis in which the effects of one or more variables are held constant (controlled), similar to the logic of the elaboration model. (Chapter 16)

partial relationship In the elaboration model, this is the relationship between two variables when examined in a subset of cases defined by a third (test) variable. For example, beginning with a zero-order relationship between *income* and *attitudes toward gender equality*, we might want to see whether the relationship holds true among both men and women (i.e., controlling for *gender*). The relationship found among men and the relationship found among women would be the partial relationships, also referred to as the *partials*. (Chapter 15)

participatory action research An approach to social research in which the researcher serves as a resource to those being studied, with the goal of increasing their ability to act effectively in their own interest. Counter to the conventional status and power differences between researchers and subjects, those under study are given control to define their problems, define the remedies they desire, and take the lead in designing the research that will help them realize their aims. (Chapter 10)

patterns Aggregations of percepts. (Chapter 1)

percepts Components of concrete experience. (Chapter 1)

plagiarism Presenting someone else's words or thoughts as though they were your own, constituting intellectual theft. (Chapter 17)

population The theoretically specified aggregation of the elements in a study. (Chapter 6)

positivism The belief in an objective reality independent of human experience. (Chapter 2)

posttesting The remeasurement of a dependent variable among subjects after they have been exposed to a stimulus representing an independent variable. (Chapter 7)

PPS (probability proportionate to size) A type of multistage *cluster sample* in which clusters are selected, not with equal probabilities (see *EPSEM*), but with probabilities proportionate to their sizes—as measured by the number of units to be subsampled. (Chapter 6)

precision The property that refers to the fineness of measurement distinctions. (Chapter 5)

precoding Embedding numerical translation of questionnaire responses into the instrument. (Chapter 8)

pretesting The measurement of a dependent variable among subjects before they are exposed to a stimulus representing an independent variable. (Chapter 7)

probabilistic reasoning The recognition that effects occur more often, but not always, when specific causes are present. (Chapter 1)

probability sampling The general term for samples selected in accord with probability theory, typically involving some random selection mechanism. Specific types of probability sampling include EPSEM, PPS, simple random sampling, and systematic sampling. (Chapter 6)

probe A technique used in interviewing to solicit a more complete answer to a question. It is a nondirective phrase or question used to encourage a respondent to elaborate on an answer. Examples include "Anything more?" and "How is that?" (Chapter 8)

propositions Statements (ideas) expressing the relationship between concepts. (Chapter 1)

pure research Investigations driven by curiosity and satisfied by understanding something previously unknown. (Chapter 1)

purposive sampling A type of *nonprobability sampling* in which you select the units to be observed on the basis of your own judgment about which ones will be the most useful or representative. Another name for this is *judgmental sampling*. (Chapter 6)

push poll A telephone survey designed to influence respondents' attitudes and opinions for political purposes. (Chapter 8)

Pygmalion effect Differences in study outcomes attributable to the researcher's expectations of participants. (Chapter 7)

Q

qualitative analysis Methods for examining research evidence it converting them to numerical form. (Chapter 13)

qualitative interview In contrast to a survey interview, a qualitative interview allows the researcher to pursue issues in depth and gives the respondent more freedom to direct the flow of conversation. The researcher typically has a general plan of inquiry but not a standardized set of questions that must be rigidly followed. (Chapter 11)

quantitative analysis The numerical representation and manipulation of observations for the purpose of describing and explaining the phenomena that those observations reflect. (Chapter 14)

quasi-experiments Nonrigorous inquiries somewhat resembling controlled experiments but lacking key elements such as random assignment of subjects to experimental and control groups, pre- and post-testing, and/or any control group. (Chapter 12)

question An interrogative sentence that asks for information or clarification. (Chapter 8)

questionnaire A research instrument containing questions and other types of items designed to gather information about specific variables. (Chapter 8)

questionnaire bias A form of systematic error that occurs when properties of questions or statements encourage responses in a particular direction. (Chapter 8)

quota sampling A type of *nonprobability sampling* in which units are selected into the sample on the basis of prespecified characteristics, so that the total sample will have the same distribution of characteristics assumed to exist in the population being studied. (Chapter 6)

R

random assignment The procedure of randomly assigning experimental subjects to experimental and control groups, such that each subject has an equal probability of being in either group. Random assignment increases the likelihood that all known and unknown characteristics (i.e., variables) in the sample will be equally distributed between the experimental and control groups. Not to be confused with probability sampling techniques such as a simple random sample. (Chapter 7)

random-digit dialling (RDD) A telephone number generation system that ensures the equal inclusion of listed and unlisted numbers, as well as cellphones. (Chapter 8)

random error Refers to mistakes that are equally likely to occur. (Chapter 6)

random selection A sampling method in which each element has an equal chance of selection independent of any other event in the selection process. (Chapter 6)

range A simple example of a measure of dispersion, composed of the highest and lowest values of a variable in some set of observations. Thus we may report that the mean age of a group is 37.9, and the range is from 12 to 89. (Chapter 14)

rapport An open and trusting relationship between researcher and respondent. (Chapter 11)

rate of return graph A daily plot of the total (cumulative) number of completed surveys. (Chapter 8)

ratio measure A level of measurement describing a variable whose attributes have all the qualities of nominal, ordinal, and interval measures, and in addition are based on a "true zero" point. *Age* is an example of a ratio measure. (Chapter 5)

rationality The criterion for assessing thinking in terms of its logical consistency. (Chapter 2)

reactivity The change in attitudes and behaviour that may result when people know they are being observed. (Chapter 10)

reasonableness A quality of mind that is open to new ideas and evidence. (Chapter 2)

regression analysis A method of data analysis in which the relationships among variables are represented in the form of an equation, called a regression equation. (Chapter 16)

reification The mistake of treating a conceptual construction as something real. (Chapter 5)

relationship A connection identified by a change in one thing being associated with a systematic change in another. (Chapter 1)

reliability That quality of measurement method that suggests that the same data would have been collected each time in repeated observations of the same phenomenon. In the context of a survey, we would expect that the question "Did you attend religious services last week?" would have higher reliability than the question "About how many times have you attended religious services in your life?" This is not to be confused with *validity*. (Chapter 5)

replication (1) Repetition of a research study in order to either confirm the findings of a previous study or bring them into question. (Chapter 1) (2) A technical term used in connection with the elaboration model to refer to the empirical outcome of the persistence of the observed initial relationship between two variables when a control variable is held constant. This supports the idea that the original, zero-order relationship is genuine. (Chapter 15)

representativeness That quality of a sample of having the same distribution of characteristics as the population from which it was selected. By implication, descriptions and explanations derived from an analysis of the sample may be assumed to represent similar ones in the population. Representativeness is enhanced by *probability sampling* and provides for *generalizability* and the use of *inferential statistics*. (Chapter 6)

research monograph A book-length research report, either published or unpublished. This is distinguished from a textbook, a book of essays, a novel, and so forth. (Chapter 17)

respondent A person who provides data for analysis by responding to a survey questionnaire. (Chapter 8)

response rate The number of people participating in a survey divided by the number selected in the sample, in the form of a percentage; also called the completion rate or, in self-administered surveys, the return rate. (Chapter 8)

response set A form of bias occurring when respondents use a consistent physical pattern to answer questions or statements. (Chapter 8)

response variable The outcome measured to determine a program's effectiveness. (Chapter 12)

S

sample A selection of members from a population. (Chapter 6)

sampling bias Systematic error derived from using nonprobability samples that produces unrepresentative results. (Chapter 6)

sampling distribution A distribution of sample statistics of the same variable from repeated random samples of the same size. (Chapter 16)

sampling error The difference between a population value and an estimate of that value derived from a sample. The more representative the sample, the smaller the sampling error, and the more accurate the sample-derived estimates of population characteristics will be. (Chapter 6 and 16)

sampling frame The list or quasi-list of units that make up a population from which a sample is selected. If the sample is to be representative of the population, it is essential that the sampling frame include all (or nearly all) members of the population. (Chapter 6)

sampling interval The standard distance (k) between elements selected from a population for a sample. (Chapter 6)

sampling ratio The proportion of elements in the population that are selected to be in a sample. (Chapter 6)

sampling unit That element or set of elements considered for selection in some stage of sampling. (Chapter 6)

saturation A sampling principle used in qualitative studies that encourages adding cases until new insights are unlikely. (Chapter 6)

scale A type of composite measure composed of several items that have a logical or empirical structure among them. Examples of scales are Bogardus social distance and the Guttman, Likert, and Thurstone scales. (Chapter 5) Contrast with *index*.

science A body of knowledge about reality as well as a set of systematic methods for generating this knowledge. (Chapter 1)

search engine A computer program designed to locate where specified terms appear on websites throughout the World Wide Web. (Chapter 17)

secondary analysis A form of research in which the data collected and processed by one researcher are reanalyzed—often for a different purpose—by another. This is especially appropriate in the case of survey data. Data archives are repositories or libraries for the storage and distribution of data for secondary analysis. (Chapter 9)

selective coding The search for conceptual themes that link the conceptualized evidence into an integrated narrative. (Chapter 13)

selective transcription Turning only research-relevant parts of a recorded interview into text. (Chapter 11)

semantic differential A questionnaire format in which the respondent is asked to rate something in terms of two, opposite adjectives (e.g., rate textbooks as "boring" or "exciting"), using qualifiers such as "very," "somewhat," "neither," "somewhat," and "very" to bridge the distance between the two opposites. (Web Chapter)

semiotics The study of signs and the meanings associated with them. (Chapter 13)

semi-structured interview A qualitative interview organized around a specified set of questions or themes. (Chapter 11)

sign Any thing that has an assigned special meaning. (Chapter 13)

simple random sampling A type of probability sampling in which the units composing a population are assigned numbers. A set of random numbers is then generated, and the units having those numbers are included in the sample. Although probability theory and the calculations it provides assume this basic sampling method, it's seldom used, for practical reasons. An equivalent alternative is the systematic sample (with a random start). (Chapter 6)

snowball sampling A *nonprobability sampling* method often used in field research in which each person interviewed may be asked to suggest additional people for interviewing. (Chapter 6)

social artifact Any product of human activity. (Chapter 4)

social desirability A form of bias occurring when respondents answer with socially acceptable views rather than their own. (Chapter 8)

social indicators Measurements that reflect the quality or nature of social life, such as crime rates, infant mortality rates, number of physicians per 100,000 population, and so forth. Social indicators are often monitored to determine the nature of social change in a society. (Chapter 12)

social intervention An action taken in a given social context with the goal of producing an intended outcome. (Chapter 12)

specification (1) The process of clarifying the meaning of concepts. (Chapter 5) (2) An explanatory or clarifying comment about handling a difficult or confusing situation that might occur regarding particular questions in an interview. (Chapter 8) (3) An elaboration model term describing the situation where particular attributes of a control variable account for an independent variable's effect on the dependent variable. (Chapter 15)

standard deviation A measure of dispersion around the mean, calculated so that approximately 68 percent of the cases will lie within plus or minus one standard deviation from the mean, 95 percent will lie within plus or minus two standard deviations, and 99.9 percent will lie within three standard deviations. Thus, for example, if the mean age in a group is 30 and the standard deviation is 10, then 68 percent have ages between 20 and 40. The smaller the standard deviation, the more tightly the values are clustered around the mean; if the standard deviation is high, the values are widely spread out. (Chapter 14)

statement A declarative sentence that provides an opinion or observation. (Chapter 8)

statistic A quantitative summary of a set of sample observations. (Chapter 16)

statistical significance A general term referring to the likelihood that relationships observed in a sample could be attributed to sampling error alone. (Chapter 16)

stratification The grouping of the units making up a population into homogeneous groups (or strata) before sampling. This procedure, which may be used in conjunction with simple random, systematic, or cluster sampling, improves the representativeness of a sample, at least with regard to the variables used for stratification. (Chapter 6)

study population That aggregation of elements from which a sample is actually selected. (Chapter 6)

sufficient condition A condition that, when present, produces a specific outcome. (Chapter 4)

summative evaluations Assessments aimed at evaluating the effectiveness of an intervention in achieving its goals. (Chapter 12)

suppressor variable In the elaboration model, a test (control) variable that conceals a true zero-order relationship. (Chapter 15)

systematic sampling A type of probability sampling in which every *k*th unit in a list is selected for inclusion in the sample—for example, every 25th student in the university directory of students. You compute *k* by dividing the size of the population by the desired sample size; *k* is called the *sampling interval.* Within certain constraints, systematic sampling is a functional equivalent of simple random sampling and usually easier to do. Typically, the first unit is selected at random. (Chapter 6)

T

tautology The thinking error that claims to explain something by referring to itself. (Chapter 5)

test variable A variable that is held constant in an attempt to clarify further the relationship between two other variables. Having discovered a relationship between *education* and *prejudice*, for example, we might hold *gender* constant by examining the relationship between *education* and *prejudice* among men only and then among women only. In this example, *gender* would be the test variable (also called the control variable). (Chapter 15)

tests of statistical significance A class of statistical computations that indicate the likelihood that the relationship observed between variables in a sample can be attributed to sampling error only. (Chapter 16)

theoretical sampling The selection of cases based on illustrative, theoretical relevance. (Chapter 10)

theory A set of interrelated propositions providing a logical explanation of empirical regularities (Chapter 1) and used for understanding observed realities (Chapter 2).

Thurstone scale A type of composite measure, constructed in accord with the weights assigned by "judges" to various indicators of some variables. (Web Chapter)

time-series design A research design that involves measurements made over some period, such as the study of traffic accident rates before and after lowering the speed limit. (Chapter 12)

transcription The translation of a recorded interview into written text. (Chapter 11)

trend study A type of longitudinal study in which a given characteristic of some population is monitored over time. (Chapter 4)

U

unit of analysis The object of a study's interest. (Chapter 4)

unit of observation The kinds of objects from which evidence is collected. (Chapter 4)

univariate analysis The analysis of a single variable, for purposes of description. Frequency distributions, averages, and measures of dispersion would be examples of univariate analysis, as distinguished from bivariate and multivariate analysis. (Chapter 14)

unstructured interview An open-ended, qualitative interview. (Chapter 11)

URL A Web address, typically beginning with "http://"; stands for "uniform resource locator" or "universal resource locator." (Chapter 17)

V

validity A term describing a measure that accurately reflects the concept it is intended to measure. For example, your IQ would seem a more valid measure of your intelligence than would the number of hours you spend in the library. Though the ultimate validity of a measure can never be proven, we may agree to its relative validity on the basis of face validity, criterion-related validity, content validity, construct validity, internal validation, and external validation. This must not be confused with *reliability*. (Chapter 5)

values Statements of what is ultimately preferable or desirable. (Chapter 1)

variable-oriented analysis The examination of a limited set of considerations (variables) across a large number of cases in search of nomothetic explanation. (Chapter 13)

variables (1) Properties of objects that can change. (Chapter 1) (2) A property of an object composed of attributes. (Chapter 5)

Verstehen A method that seeks to understand the meaning of actions from the viewpoint of the participants. (Chapter 9)

visual sociology The study of society, culture, and social relationships through the analysis of audio-visual artifacts. (Chapter 9)

voluntary participation The ethical norm requiring that participants be free to choose whether or not to participate in a study. (Chapter 3)

W

weighting A procedure used in connection with sampling whereby units selected with unequal probabilities are assigned weights in such a manner as to make the sample *representative* of the population from which it was selected. When all cases have the same chance of selection, no weighting is necessary. (Chapter 6)

Z

zero-order relationship The relationship between two variables when no test variables are being controlled for (i.e., held constant). (Chapter 15)

INDEX

Note: Page numbers in **boldface** indicate definitions of key terms.

A

B

C

D

E

T

U